Current Issues in IT Education

edited by

Tanya McGill
Murdoch University, Australia

IRM Press
Publisher of innovative scholarly and professional
information technology titles in the cyberage

Hershey • London • Melbourne • Singapore • Beijing

Acquisitions Editor:	Mehdi Khosrow-Pour
Senior Managing Editor:	Jan Travers
Managing Editor:	Amanda Appicello
Copy Editor:	Lori Eby
Typesetter:	Amanda Lutz
Cover Design:	Weston Pritts
Printed at:	Integrated Book Technology

Published in the United States of America by
    IRM Press (an imprint of Idea Group Inc.)
    701 E. Chocolate Avenue, Suite 200
    Hershey PA 17033-1240
    Tel: 717-533-8845
    Fax: 717-533-8661
    E-mail: cust@idea-group.com
    Web site: http://www.irm-press.com

and in the United Kingdom by
    IRM Press
    3 Henrietta Street
    Covent Garden
    London WC2E 8LU
    Tel: 44 20 7240 0856
    Fax: 44 20 7379 3313
    Web site: http://www.eurospan.co.uk

Library of Congress Cataloging-in-Publication Data

McGill, Tanya.
   Current issues in IT education / Tanya McGill.
      p. cm.
Includes bibliographical references and index.
   ISBN 1-931777-53-5 (soft cover) -- ISBN 1-931777-69-1 (ebook)
 1. Information technology--Study and teaching. I. Title.
   T58.5.M38 2003
   004'.071--dc21

                           2002156239

British Cataloguing in Publication Data
A Cataloguing in Publication record for this book is available from the British Library.

Current Issues in IT Education

Table of Contents

SECTION II: INFORMATION TECHNOLOGY LITERACY

SECTION III: INFORMATION TECHNOLOGY IN EDUCATION

Preface

Information technology (IT) is of increasing importance in the world today. Information and communications technologies are pervading all aspects of life at work, school, and home. Businesses depend upon technology, and the growth in IT and the Internet has changed the face of commerce, allowing organizations to provide services that would not otherwise be possible and delivering major productivity gains in many industries. IT has also changed the way we learn, offering vast improvements in flexibility of learning, changing the face not only of distance education but also the way in which courses are delivered on campus and the way in which student research is carried out. Even home life has changed. Many people are now able to work from home because of telecommuting. People use personal organizers and applications such as accounting packages to organize their home life. Technology has also provided new kinds of entertainment and changed forever the way many people communicate on a day-to-day basis.

In order to succeed in our complex world, a wide variety of people require IT education. Students come from different walks of life and are at different stages in their education. They require a vast array of different kinds of IT knowledge and skills. Some wish only to be able to use existing technology effectively; some will become the developers of new information and communications technologies. It is the task of the IT educator to meet this great demand for knowledge and skill across the enormous range of potential participants.

There are many pressures on IT educators. Technology changes rapidly, and educators must keep up; academic institutions face financial pressures that drive increases in class sizes or demands to reduce class contact time; and the wide range of student backgrounds and motivations creates complexities. However, there are also many opportunities to improve teaching and learning by utilizing advances in technology and in the understanding of the learning process. Information accessibility has never been greater, enabling students to study "any time" and "any place." This makes it possible for new groups of students to participate.

This book brings together a number of chapters that address opportunities to improve the teaching and learning of IT in its various forms. The authors are from a wide variety of organizational and cultural backgrounds and are all experts in the fields they discuss. The chapters introduce theoretical developments in IT education, report on successful innovations in teaching and learning, and raise issues that require consideration. The topics covered include IT degree curriculum issues, facilitating the IT literacy of all graduates, and using IT in teaching and learning. The book contains many ideas and suggestions that will be invaluable to all those involved in IT education and the use of IT in education. It is organized into 33 chapters in three sections. The first section relates to IT degree issues, the second section covers issues associated with IT literacy, and the third section is devoted to the use of IT to support teaching and learning. A brief description of each chapter follows.

In Chapter I, entitled, "Belief, Inquiry, Argument and Reflection as Significant Issues in Learning about Information Systems Development Methodologies," by David A. Banks of the University of South Australia (Australia), the development of a Masters-level course on information systems (IS) development methodologies is examined. The course was conceived as taking a "reality as a social construct" view of the world in order to encourage students to challenge assumptions and, hence, enhance their understanding of the subject area. The chapter reflects on problems that were experienced when offering the course and outlines a number of approaches that have been adopted to help students deal with interpretivist approaches to learning.

In Chapter II, entitled, "Making the Case for Case-Based Learning in Computer Information Systems," by Morgan M. Jennings, Charles H. Mawhinney, and Janos Fustos of Metropolitan State College of Denver (Colorado, USA), the results of a study that compared the perceptions of current students about IS careers with those of students in a 1989 study are reported. The authors found that IS students still perceive IS careers as lacking in interaction, and the chapter reports on some programs available in high schools to interest students in IS careers. The chapter also discusses problem-based learning as a means to address perceptions of IS careers.

In Chapter III, entitled, "Introducing Information Systems Students to Research with a Structured Group Project," by Tanya McGill of Murdoch University (Australia), an approach to getting IS research students started is reported. The approach involves beginning research students undertaking a structured group research project in which the instructor is an active participant. This group project provides a gentle, supportive introduction to IS research and benefits students by ensuring that they have participated in a complete research project before they have to assume complete responsibility for their first large individual project.

In Chapter IV, entitled, "Making Way for Java in an Information Technology Masters Program," by Wendy Lucas of Bentley College (Massachusetts, USA), the introduction of Java as a first programming language in an IT Masters program is described. Decisions such as when to introduce object-oriented concepts, which integrated development environment to use, and how to support students with little prior background, are explored.

In Chapter V, entitled, "Analysis of Learner Performance on a Tutoring System for Java," by Henry H. Emurian and Jingli Wang of the University of Maryland Baltimore County (USA) and Ashley G. Durham of the Centers for Medicare & Medicaid Services (Maryland, USA), a teaching methodology based on programmed instruction that provides a series of interactive and cumulative learning experiences to students learning to write a simple Java Applet is presented. This objective is achieved within the context of a Web-based tutoring system.

In Chapter VI, entitled, "Supporting Creativity in Software Development: An Application in IT Education," by Aybüke Aurum, Meliha Handzic, and Adrian Gardiner of The University of New South Wales (Australia), the potential of an individual creativity enhancing technique called SoloBrainstorming to improve the level of creativity of IT students in performing requirements determination is examined. The chapter also offers advice about incorporating creativity enhancing techniques into the IT curriculum.

In Chapter VII, entitled, "Training in Remote Database Server Administration," by Ludwig Slusky and Parviz Partow-Navid of California State University, Los Angeles (California, USA), the establishment of a remote access Unix laboratory to support new server-focused courses in IT degrees is described.

In Chapter VIII, entitled, "Conceiving Architectural Aspects for Quality Software Education through the Constructivist Perspective," by Kam Hou Vat of the University of Macau (Macau), an initiative to incorporate the practice of quality software education into a software engineering curriculum is discussed. This initiative combines action learning with problem-based learning and allows students to acquire collaborative experience in the practice of architected applications development.

In Chapter IX, entitled, "The TCP/IP Game," by Norman Pendegraft of the University of Idaho (USA), a simulation game used to help students understand the operation of TCP/IP is described. In the game, students play various layers of TCP/IP on several machines and collaborate to transmit a message from one application to another.

In Chapter X, entitled, "Framing Leadership Issues for System Developers," by Gayla Jo Slauson and Chad Grabow of Mesa State College (Colorado, USA), a brief introduction to the frame theory of leadership is provided, and how this theory relates to IS is discussed. The authors propose that students in IS degree programs need to be made aware of the leadership potential of the systems through which members of organizations communicate.

In Chapter XI, entitled, "S3: Senior Surf School — A Special Graduate Information Systems Course," by Georg Disterer of the University of Applied Sciences and Arts (Germany), an IS course where students design, organize, and run a training session designed to introduce users (in this case, elderly people) to the Internet is described. In this course, a realistic simulation of the future tasks and responsibilities many graduates will encounter, given the importance of end-user training, is provided.

In Chapter XII, entitled, "How Do IT Students Stay Up to Date with Employers' Skill Requirements?" by Tanya McGill and Michael Dixon of Murdoch University (Australia), a research study that investigated the channels of information that telecommunications management and electronic commerce students use to keep up to date with employers' IT skill requirements is reported. The results suggest that students are diligent in their efforts to keep up to date, and that they favor easily accessible channels of information, such as newspapers and Internet sources. The chapter also discusses the role of instructors in helping students to gain information about skill requirements.

In Chapter XIII, entitled, "Education for a Technology-Based Profession: Softening the Information Systems Curriculum," by Rodney Turner of Victoria University of Technology (Australia) and Glenn Lowry of United Arab Emirates University (UAE), findings from an investigation into the conceptual, academic, and "soft" skills that IT practitioners regard as important in new graduates are reported. Also discussed are IS curriculum reform issues arising from the results and recommendations for addressing barriers to curriculum reform.

In Chapter XIV, entitled, "Tracking Through Information Technology Education," by Erick Slazinski and Susan K. Lisack of Purdue University (Indiana, USA), the trend toward specialization in the IT field is discussed, and the creation of a database track within an IS or IT degree program is described so that students can choose to focus on this specialty area.

In Chapter XV, entitled, "Designing e-Business and e-Commerce Courses to Meet Industry Needs," by Anthony D. Stiller of the University of the Sunshine Coast (Australia), the importance of e-commerce development consultants to small-to-medium enterprises is highlighted, and then the design and development of courses that will better prepare graduates to have a balanced mix of e-business, e-commerce, communication, and leadership skills that will equip them to work as consultants for small-to-medium enterprises is discussed.

In Chapter XVI, entitled, "Adding Reality to Team Projects: E-Business Consulting for Small Business Entities," by Sharon W. Tabor of Boise State University (Idaho, USA), the use of team projects to develop prototype sites for actual businesses is described. In addition to concepts, strategies, and technical skills, students learn transferable consulting skills and improve their teamwork skills.

In Chapter XVII, entitled, "Metacognition in Information Systems Education," by Steve Benson of Edith Cowan University (Australia), the role of metacognitive education in IS teaching is considered, and the introduction of a metacognitive training program to support student learning at an Australian university is described.

In Chapter XVIII, entitled, "Required Software Proficiency in General Education and Business Courses," by Linda Lynam of Central Missouri State University (USA), the implementation of a productivity software proficiency requirement at a Midwestern state university is described. The author found that even students who had received little preparation for self-motivated learning were able to reach the required levels of proficiency.

In Chapter XIX, entitled, "Technology Literacy Issues for Freshmen Education Majors in a Leading Teacher Program," by David D. Carbonara of Duquesne University (Pennsylvania, USA), IT literacy issues in preservice teacher education are discussed, and a leading teacher program that addresses these issues in preparing preservice teachers as technology leaders is described.

In Chapter XX, entitled, "Assessing Computer Literacy: A Comparison of Self-Assessment and Actual Skills," by George Easton and Annette Easton of San Diego State University (California, USA), a study designed to assess university business students' actual computer skills and to measure the difference between students' self-assessment of these skills and an actual assessment of their skills is reported. The authors found that there was a consistent, inflated self-perception of computer literacy. Students were found to be most accurate in self-assessing their Windows capabilities and least accurate with PowerPoint and Excel.

In Chapter XXI, entitled, "Using Modulization Approach to Design Instructional Systems for Computer Literacy Courses," by Kuan C. Chen of Purdue University, Calumet (Indiana, USA), the use of modulization approaches in designing instructional systems are discussed. The chapter also presents a case study of the design of a computer literacy course. This approach to instructional design allows institutions to better serve students with a wide variety of backgrounds.

In Chapter XXII, entitled, "Information Technologies in Educational Organizations: An Innovative Collaborative Course Development, Delivery, and Evaluation," by Pamela Lipe Revercomb and Ruth V. Small of Syracuse University (New York, USA), the collaborative design, development, implementation, and evaluation of an interdisciplinary course about the selection, management, and use of IT for teaching and learning are described. Recommendations are also included for future implementations, including distance delivery.

In Chapter XXIII, entitled, "Developing Graduate Qualities," by Ann Monday and Sandra Barker of the University of South Australia (Australia), a case-study and role-play approach to embedding required graduate qualities in an undergraduate business course is explored. The approach adopted facilitates effective problem solving, working collaboratively, effective communication and lifelong learning, as well as the ability to operate effectively on a body of knowledge. However, the authors note that the approach has a high overhead in terms of staff time.

In Chapter XXIV, entitled, "Real Live Cases in Training Management of Information Resources During the Transition to a Market Economy," by Dimitar Christozov of the American University in Bulgaria (Bulgaria), the use of real live cases based on the experiences of Masters' students in improving the learning outcomes of students taking an information resources management course is discussed. This approach is compared with the use of cases drawn from textbooks. The author concludes that although the use of live cases is demanding, it is beneficial to students.

In Chapter XXV, entitled, "Business Students as End-User Developers: Simulating "Real-Life" Situations through Case Study Approach," by Sandra Barker of the University of South Australia (Australia), the use of case studies to assist business students in understanding the complexities of database development and to facilitate end-user development of databases is explored.

In Chapter XXVI, entitled, "E-Business Education for Everyone: Developing and Implementing Breakthrough Strategies (Or How Can IT Practitioners and Educators Make Computer Morons Surf and Steer on E-Business Space)," by Rumel V. Atienza of De La Salle University (Philippines), the issue of the preparedness of the workforce in the Philippines to face the challenge of e-business is addressed. The chapter investigates strategies that can be implemented to help prepare for e-business and provides a preliminary assessment of their effectiveness.

In Chapter XXVII, entitled, "Information Management in Public Sector Agencies: A Context-Sensitive Conceptual Framework of CIO Competence," by Maurice W. Green of the University of Washington (USA), insight into the problems, challenges, and requisite competencies for public-sector CIOs is provided, and a multidimensional, interdisciplinary conceptual framework of CIO competence is presented. The discussion should be valuable to academicians developing IT management curricula and to practitioners engaged in CIO search and development activities.

In Chapter XXVIII, entitled, "Empirical Study of Students' Perceptions of Online Courses," by Judith C. Simon, Lloyd D. Brooks, and Ronald B. Wilkes of the University of Memphis (Tennessee, USA), a study that determined potential students' perceptions of online programs is described, and these perceptions are then compared with the potential students' perceptions of on-campus programs. The issues that were found to be most important to students in course delivery are discussed, and student beliefs as to whether these issues are more likely to be addressed in online or on-campus course delivery are considered.

In Chapter XXIX, entitled, "Community Informatics — Enabling Emancipatory Learning," by Wal Taylor, John Dekkers, and Stewart Marshall of Central Queensland University (Australia), a philosophical stance and framework for online teaching that emphasizes the importance of placing the student at the center of the learning process is articulated. This approach integrates information and communication technology (ICT) with emerging trends in distance education and lifelong learning, and the authors believe it can help assist local communities in benefiting from a wider interpretation of knowledge available through online distance education.

In Chapter XXX, entitled, "An Examination of ICT Planning Maturity in Schools: A Stage Theory Perspective," by Julie Mackey of Christchurch College of Education (New Zealand) and Annette Mills of the University of Canterbury (New Zealand), ICT planning in schools is examined, and based on case studies conducted in eight primary schools, a four-stage model of the evolution of ICT planning maturity in schools is proposed. The model provides insight into the nature of ICT planning in schools and into the factors that contribute to planning maturity.

In Chapter XXXI, entitled, "On-line Case Discussion: A Methodology," by Henri Isaac of Paris Dauphine University (France), an approach to conducting online case discussion is presented and evaluated. The approach has been trialed in an executive MBA program, and the results of the evaluation are positive.

In Chapter XXXII, entitled, "A Comparison Between the Use of IT in Business and Education: Applications of the Internet to Tertiary Education," by Stephen Burgess and Paul Darbyshire of Victoria University (Australia), the similarities between the use of IT in business and education are discussed, and the categorization of aspects of Web use in education using standard business categories relating to savings and quality is explored. Also reported are the results of a study of academics conducted to survey the perceptions of benefits gained from supplementing teaching with Web-based services.

In Chapter XXXIII, entitled, "Virtual Government: Online-Services within the Public Sector" by Birgit J. Oberer of the University of Klagenfurt (Austria), an overview of electronic government is given. Selected current international electronic government incentives are reviewed, methods for analyzing governmental strategies are introduced, and guidelines for implementing electronic government are presented.

Keeping up to date with issues and developments in IT education is essential for all those who wish to capitalize upon the potential benefits available from IT and to learn from the experience and research of others. The authors of the chapters in this book share their insights into a wide range of topical issues. They address theoretical developments, report on successful experiences with innovations in teaching and learning, and raise issues that require further consideration and research.

This book provides many ideas and suggestions that will be of value to researchers and practitioners. The chapters in which IT degree curriculum issues are discussed will be invaluable to those involved in planning, designing, and teaching a wide range of ICT-related courses and degrees. Those that explore the issues associated with IT literacy for non-IT majors will be useful to those involved in helping to ensure that the broader student population is able to take advantage of the power of IT. Finally, the chapters on the use of IT to support teaching and learning provide practical guidelines for all educators today. Thus, academics, researchers, and practitioners alike, whether specialists in IT or from any other discipline who utilize IT to support their teaching, will all benefit greatly from the ideas and approaches explored in this book in confronting the challenges presented in IT education today.

Tanya McGill
Murdoch University, Australia

Section I:

Information Technology Degree Issues

Chapter I

Belief, Inquiry, Argument and Reflection as Significant Issues in Learning about Information Systems Development Methodologies

David A. Banks
University of South Australia, Australia

ABSTRACT

This chapter examines some of the issues that are driving the development of a master's course designated as "Information Systems Development Methodologies." The course takes a "reality as a social construct" view of the world, the purpose of the approach being to encourage students to challenge assumptions and enhance their abilities to research, reflect, critique, and develop strong arguments to support their understanding of the subject area. An interpretive approach such as this can challenge those students whose experiences of previous educational settings have been more strongly oriented toward rote or positivistic teaching and learning styles. The chapter outlines a number of approaches that have been adopted to help students deal with interpretive approaches to learning and to introduce them to issues of belief, inquiry, argument, and reflection.

INTRODUCTION

Information systems development can broadly be approached from a "hard," or engineering, perspective or from a "soft," human-activity-oriented position. The hard approaches tend to assume a belief that real-world problems can be "formulated as the making of a choice between alternative means of achieving a known end" (Checkland, 1981) and tend to lean toward project-management-based methods, techniques, and tools that have been successfully used to create artifacts such as bridges, computer technology, and spacecraft. These hard approaches have been developed over a number of years and are supported by considerable literature, a body of knowledge, and detailed methods to support practical project management. Although these approaches have proved to be largely successful in the production of a range of artifacts, they appear to have been less successful in the development of management information systems. Studies of the effectiveness of information systems development frequently indicate failure to deliver a viable object in line with time, cost, quality, or usability requirements.

Educators are thus faced with an interesting problem in considering how to teach students about the development of information systems. A hard stance has the potentially attractive feature in that it lends itself to "cookbook" approaches with clearly defined problem, rigid method, and limited range of possible outcomes and provides students with tangible skills. The weakness inherent in such an approach is that it does not take account of the real-world features of technological change accompanied by social, political, financial, legal, and ethical influences and pressures. It can also be argued that such "cookbook" approaches do not appear to work in practice. However, many students appear to be comfortable with the hard end of information systems, that is, with the traditional systems development life cycle (SDLC) or project-management-oriented approaches. In many ways this is to be expected when they have typically previously experienced educational programs that have strong leanings toward employable skills, or they work around cases that have single outcomes and are framed within a relatively static problem situation. Removing the complexities of unexpected change, organizational politics, shifting priorities, multiple worldviews, and so on, offers a simplified view of the world within which can be engineered artifacts that meet a given, and unchanging, specification. This allows the basics mechanics of systems development to be experienced, essentially from a "hard" perspective.

An alternative approach is to use a "soft" orientation to develop a teaching and learning environment that acknowledges and actively explores how the complicating factors that exist in human activity systems align more closely with the real world. The "softer" approaches more strongly take account of the complex and dynamic relationships between the systems, the designers, the users, and the organizational and broader environment. This view differentiates natural or designed systems from human activity systems, the latter being interpreted as the perceptions of human actors who are free to attribute meaning to their perceptions (Checkland, 1981). As the environment, availability of information, business paradigms, and so on, change, so may the interpretation of the system or system requirements by different actors. Not only do the actors need to be considered, but there is also a need to take an holistic view of the organization under consideration, examining perceived relationships and networks of social interaction rather than relying upon formal functions and structures (Espejo & Harnden, 1989). One of the problems with the softer approaches is that even after reading extensive and well-written work describing, for example, Beer's Viable

Systems Model, many students still find the ideas difficult to grasp when they attempt to turn them from theory to practice (Anderton, in Espejo & Harnden, 1989). Iterative approaches with action research foundations seem to many students to be inappropriate in a world where time and cost are crucial factors. Participative design raises questions of who owns and controls the systems, how many people need to be involved in the process, and visions of unmanageable scope and complex ethical issues. Many of the softer approaches appear to offer a somewhat philosophical, "thinking about rather than doing" flavor that is perceived by students as being interesting from an intellectual and academic viewpoint but perhaps of less value in the real world.

Convincing students that thinking about the systems development process in general is as valuable a skill as knowing the steps in a specific systems development approach is not an easy task but is considered by the author to be essential part of the educational process. This approach can be difficult to manage in an educational setting, with increasingly narrow or specialist foci accompanied by course outlines that are specific and increasingly appear to be almost legal contracts, where process and deliverables have to be specified in considerable detail. Students entering the Masters course discussed here typically have been exposed to previous educational experiences that have had a strong positivist leaning, and where single, correct answers are acceptable or even desirable. An interpretive approach that leads to different conclusions being drawn by different thinkers, even though they start from the same set of materials, can pose problems for those students who still feel that a single view of the world should be achievable. Some students are convinced that there is a "right" answer and attempt to extract this from the member of staff, and they sometimes feel that broad responses from staff or presentation of "on the other hand" statements are sometimes a sign of evasiveness or equivocation. There is thus a need to help students appreciate that even if the starting point for exploration of a subject is predicated upon the argument that reality is purely a social construction, it is still possible to offer a considered opinion based upon the application of critical thinking, reflection, and argument. This requires that students examine their own beliefs, knowledge, attitudes, and problem-solving styles and develop skills in presenting persuasive arguments that demonstrate their ability to take a critical and balanced view of the world.

Students sometimes raise the issue that if the process and outcomes of the course are socially constructed around the beliefs of individuals, then surely this means that any idea that they generate in accord with the belief system of the lecturer may be at risk of subjective marking. The response to this question is that the quality of argument presented is the key to obtaining higher marks, and this issue of presentation of credible arguments forms the core theme in the course. If students can be helped to identify and reflect on their own belief systems and biases, carry out rigorous inquiry, and ultimately develop a structured argument for a given position, then there should be no issue of conflict with a personal belief held with the marker. The demonstration of the strength of the argument presented, the depth of the literature used, the recognition of internal personal processes, and critical reflection are the sole bases for the assessment of the outcomes.

The remainder of this chapter outlines a number of strategies that have been used with Masters students studying a subject titled "Information Systems Development Methodologies" (ISDM) in efforts to support the approaches to learning outlined above.

THE COURSE OUTLINE

This is a ten-week course that typically has 20 students and is structured as 10, three-hour sessions that have a mix of activities, including lectures, mini-lectures, seminars, presentations, role playing, and debates. No single systems development methodology, method, tool, or technique is emphasized, the aim of the course is to help students question the need for the several thousand "methodologies" that exist and to develop skills in understanding what criteria may be useful in the selection and application of the available options to specific situations. They are also led to explore their own preferences in the selection and use of development approaches and to reflect on how this may influence the effectiveness of any given approach in practice.

The direction of the course is to introduce students to a range of information systems development methodologies and to encourage them to consider how and under what circumstances the various approaches, or combinations of them, may be usefully applied. The teaching approach adopted assumes a "hard–soft" spectrum with the various methodologies, or their underlying philosophies, placed appropriately along that spectrum, and sets out to explore the relative merits of the approaches for a variety of problem situations. Although the views presented in the lectures ranged broadly across the hard and soft areas, the "soft" were explored in more depth than the "hard," because this was a new perspective for most students. The ontological position of the course could be regarded as being at the nominalist end of the realism/nominalism spectrum, and epistemologically, as leaning toward the interpretive domain (Hirschheim & Klein, 1989).

The early part of the course was used to explore the possible meanings of the term "methodology," working mainly around the views of Avison and Fitzgerald (Avison & Fitzgerald, 1995), who regarded a methodology as more than simply a collection of "procedures techniques, tools and documentation aids," in that it should have a "philosophical" view that distinguishes it from being a method, or recipe. The current levels of "failure" in information systems development were examined, the word "failure" being viewed from the perspectives of the various parties typically involved in the development of human activity systems (Sauer, 1993). A variety of readings were used to encourage students to develop multiple views of the subject area, many of these being critical of method or methodology. These included Floods' "consultant as parasite" and academic as potential dilettante developer (Flood, 1995), and Wastells' "methodology as social defense" (Wastell, 1996). A variety of Web resources were also used to introduce post-modern thinking and to introduce a broader base of development methodologies beyond the set text. Students were required to write short critiques of these materials as part of the assessment requirement and to be prepared to discuss them during the seminar component of the sessions.

Although the major emphasis of this course is upon the higher-level issues relating to development methodologies, there is, in practice, a need to connect these issues with techniques and tools to permit implementation of real-world systems. The final sessions of the course, therefore, introduce a variety of software tools that may be useful to support "softer" approaches to systems development. These tools include cognitive mapping software, repertoire grids, mind maps, electronic meeting systems, and other tools, techniques, and methods that can be used to explore, elicit, and share multiple worldviews. These are offered as tools to help move toward the development of meaningful system specifications that can ultimately be implemented by more formal, "harder," development approaches where appropriate. The overall aim is to produce a balanced, pluralist, or complementarist view rather than suggest that either "hard" or "soft" approaches are the "right" way to develop systems.

THE COURSE IN PRACTICE

Two major problems were experienced by some students in the operation of this course: first, difficulty in understanding the idea of a guiding "philosophy" to underpin methodologies, and second, some difficulty in developing and presenting a critical or balanced view of the wide range of available methodologies.

The symptom of the first problem was typically expressed as a feeling that "philosophy" had little connection to the "real world." Those students involved in information systems projects in their working life were, initially, the most resistant to a theoretical or philosophical analysis of development methodologies. The most commonly used phrase was, "But surely that's just common sense?" Bringing them constantly back to literature describing failed systems kept their scepticism bounded by the unavoidable fact that development failures are commonplace, and that we need to try to understand why this is the case and then consider a variety of possible approaches that may help us at least understand why this high level of failure prevails.

The learning strategy adopted to help students gain some understanding of how a particular "philosophy" would influence a project was achieved through a "role-play" session examining a single, short case study from the viewpoint of a number of key figures. The objective of the exercise was for each student to attempt to express a view of a relatively simple case study through the worldviews of a specified individual drawn from an "A to Z" (or, perhaps more practically, Ackoff to Zuboff) of significant individuals typically represented in the IS and IT quality literature. Each student was allocated a single name to research with the objective of producing a biography (an element of the marked assessment) of their allocated character to try to gain insight through the background, writings, and significant achievements of that individual. In the actual role-play session, each student suggested the views that they felt their individual would have been likely to adopt if confronted with the simple case study. As each student presented "their" credentials and argued the case for their particular approach to be adopted for the common project, it became apparent that they began to appreciate the notion of an underlying worldview. The development project that forms the focus of this exercise is one that the author studied in Adelaide (Banks, 1999) and has the attraction that the actual project manager is invited in after the debate sessions to allow the students to raise any issues that they feel to be significant.

Although the role-play session revealed to the students how individual worldviews would influence the way that a given scenario was approached and the impact upon selection of method and tools, etc., it did not transfer to their written debate work. They still tended to adopt a single view of their chosen topic that was typically based upon their own experience, their previous studies, or a limited range of literature. This second problem area, that of students finding difficulty in developing and presenting a critical or balanced view of the wide range of available methodologies, is addressed by encouraging students to explore belief, inquiry, reflection, and argument. A basic outline of the literature used to explore these issues is presented below.

BELIEVING AND KNOWING

Many students are taught "truths" as part of their education. Challenging a previously held belief, for example, that SDLC may not always be appropriate, can be disturbing for some students unless a sound basis for questioning their previously held beliefs can be offered. Woozley (1967) suggests that to "know" requires that someone must have evidence, must be right about that evidence, and must be right about the relation of the evidence to a conclusion. If a student believes that, for example, business process reengineering (BPR) always leads to business benefits and is a radical "back to a blank sheet of paper," then such a belief needs to be tested. The evidence for their belief needs to be identified and tested, the impact of BPR on organizations needs to be identified and a strong relationship between belief and actuality established. Woozley offered five useful relationships to help explore believing and knowing:

- Being sure and being right, on evidence that is not conclusive
- Being sure and being wrong, on evidence that is not conclusive
- Being unsure and being right, on evidence that is not conclusive
- Being unsure and being wrong, on evidence that is conclusive
- Being sure and being right, on evidence that is conclusive

He argues that only the last case is one on knowing, all the others being belief. For some students, this list offers a useful framework to allow them to test the evidence for their beliefs and to develop a more critical view of evidence that they were previously taught to be "true."

INQUIRY — PROBABILITY OF A PIECE OF EVIDENCE BEING TRUE

When efforts are made to locate and test evidence that may help examine beliefs, the immediate problem that arises is that of the plethora of available evidence, particularly if the Web is used as a source. Evidence may be contradictory, ambiguous, or incomplete, leaving the researcher in a position where they have difficulty deciding on what may be true, what may be commercial or academic "hype," and so on. Locke (1706) offers a number of useful questions to be asked of the identified materials in order to gauge the probability of a given piece of evidence being "true":

- The number [of items presented]
- The integrity of the witness
- The skill of the witness
- The design [purpose] of the author, where it is a testimony cited out of a book
- The consistency of the parts, and the circumstances of the relation
- Contrary testimonies

Other questions to supplement these could include the following:

- When was the material written — what was the prevailing business paradigm?
- Is there a previous source that reveals the precursor to the literature or idea under review?

- What are the personal characteristics of the researcher that may bias the selection of some materials rather than others?

Questions such as these can help students develop a level of probability that the evidence presented is credible. This probability can be stated in their assignment work and so avoid the risk of statements that typically take the form that "it can therefore be categorically stated that…" or "it is obvious that…" and similar statements that weaken many students' work.

A GUIDING FRAMEWORK FOR INQUIRY: TOULMIN

The frameworks previously discussed provide a basis for the gathering and being critical of a variety of evidence that can be used to support debate in a balanced and informed manner. They do not, however, provide a clear structure for the presentation of that evidence, and for that, we can turn to the work of the English philosopher Stephen Toulmin (Toulmin, 1999). Toulmin suggested that our first intellectual obligation is to "abandon the Myth of Stability that played so large a part in the Modern age" and to return to "reasonableness" rather than rationality. He suggested that the future will not be served by the "optimistic daydreams of simple-minded calculators, who ignore the complexities of life, or the pessimistic nightmares of their critics, who find these complexities a source of despair" (Toulmin, 1999). It is the reflective practitioners, in his opinion, steering a middle way between the extremes of abstract theory and personal impulse, who will be able to contribute most to the future. He described a clear structure that helps frame an argument in such a way that a Claim, "C," can be tested by detailing the foundation of the claim (the Data, "D"), and the rules, principles, and inferences that connect the claim to the data (the Warrant, "W"). The items that give the warrant legitimacy (assurances, currency, authority) provide the Backing, "B," and Qualifiers, "Q," are used to indicate the strength of the warrant ("possibly," "probably," for example) with Rebuttals, "R," being used to indicate those conditions that might be capable of defeating the warranted conclusion. The basic "T" shape of the argumentation structure is shown in Figure 1.

Figure 1.

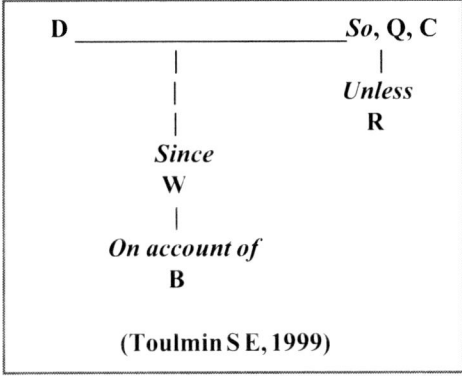

(Toulmin S E, 1999)

This structure has been used to provide a basic framework to guide the students' exploration of arguments relating to development methodologies. The use of individual-written-argument-based exploration of topics and group-based debate sessions should permit students to systematically test ideas expressed in the literature. The use of a qualifier again allows students to express their level of confidence in the argument they are presenting, and the need to consider warrants, backing, and rebuttals provides them with the required balance.

Before the students put the above-structured argument approach into practice, they are exposed to the basic ideas through a lecture structure that is also built on the argument approach and is framed within a broad interpretive ethos. The articulation and overt use of such a structure early in the course should help reduce the danger of students confusing balance and qualification with equivocation, and evenhandedness and exploration with a lack of the lecturer's ability to present the "right" answer. It is also important that the "argument" approach does not become mechanistic, as reflection is seen as an instrumental approach in helping students appreciate the many interpretations that prevail within the IS field. For those students actively involved in the development of IS in practice, it is felt to be important that they be encouraged to reflect on the nature, strengths, and limitations of their currently favored or required practice and to consider the merits or otherwise of alternative strategies or paradigms. For those students not yet in the workplace, it is important that they have a framework that will help them critically evaluate organizational practices and be able to contribute to the strengthening or challenging of those practices, as appropriate. Both groups of students need to carry out this evaluation with a clear awareness of the social and political paradigms that represent their working environments.

REFLECTION

Students are encouraged to constantly test their evidence and thinking through reflective activity. Dewey (1910) considered that reflection arises as a result of a "state of perplexity, hesitation or doubt" and is an act that seeks to bring to light "further facts which serve to corroborate or nullify the suggested belief." This reflective process implies that something is "believed in (or disbelieved in), not on its own direct account, but through something else which stands as witness, evidence, proof, voucher, warrant; that is, as ground of belief." This critical testing of evidence, specifically the search for new evidence to confirm or deny supposition, is the key aspect of reflection, and Dewey considered that it marks the difference between "good and bad thinking." Dewey considered "bad" thinking to be the uncritical acceptance of any suggestion that seems plausible and terminates a state of mental tension. He noted that the most important factor in developing reflective skills is that of acquiring the habit of suspended conclusion and in mastering the various methods of searching for evidence to support or deny a given proposition. The reflective process can be supported in practice by using the kinds of questions and frameworks described earlier. However, there is also a need to help students feel comfortable with such challenging approaches, given that this will necessarily involve direct questioning of the knowledge and beliefs of the learning facilitator. For some students, particularly some overseas students, this is a daunting prospect, and a sensitive and supportive environment needs to be generated.

CONCLUSION

Exploration and comparison of methodologies are undertaken for academic and practical reasons (Avison & Fitzgerald, 1995). Academic study of methodologies should inform future information systems development by providing frameworks that allow categorization of the ever-growing number of methodologies and approaches in such a way that some understanding of their relationships can be obtained. In the "real world," organizations are faced with changing environments and paradigms and by apparent failure in the delivery of systems that can support and adjust to these changes. An understanding of the reasons for the wide range of choices allied with informed selection of appropriate methodologies to meet specific circumstances may help to explain some of the immediate failures and to reduce them in the future.

Helping students to move from a "single right choice" view or from the perception of a methodology as simply a recipe is a difficult process. It typically requires that the learner critically test and perhaps abandon previously held views, acquired through formal education or through workplace experience. To ensure that this process is rigorous but "safe" for the learner requires a clear framework to help them work through the process and a supportive learning environment. The course that forms the focus of this paper has attempted to provide these requirements, but the process is still difficult and a potentially threatening task for some learners and for the learning facilitator. For the learner, it requires exposure to a potentially confusing plethora of methodologies, critical and reflective thinking that may lead to the potential abandonment or adjustment of some existing and deeply embedded views. For the learning facilitator, it means helping to build a learning environment that is confrontational but supportive, broad in scope but clear in direction, and that offers the learner structure but also encourages diversity and risk taking in thinking. The promotion of critical and reflective thinking built around argumentation would appear to be one key element in attaining this goal, and hopefully, the argumentative approach outlined here will, with more development, act as an appropriate framework with which this can be achieved.

The approach described in this chapter is challenging for students who come with a belief that the subject will teach them a number of recognized and formulaic methods that will allow them to build successful information systems. It comes as something of a shock to some of them to engage in a reflective and active questioning approach that challenges previously held beliefs. Such an approach may be inappropriate for undergraduate students, but at the Masters level, it is the author's belief that such challenges are appropriate and necessary in the field of information systems development. Checkland remarked that the prime value embodied in a systems approach is that continuous, never-ending learning is a good thing, suggesting that, "This means that soft systems thinking will not appeal to determinists, dictators or demagogues. It *will* appeal to all those people in any discipline who are knowledgeable enough to know that there is much they do not know, and that learning and re-learning is worth-while" (Checkland, 1999). It is hoped that the approach taken in the course described here will go some way to equipping future systems developers with the attitudes, tools, and skills to engage in a satisfying process of continual reflective learning and relearning and so better understand the complexities of information systems development methodologies.

REFERENCES

Avison, D. E., & Fitzgerald, G. (1995). *Information Systems Development: Methodologies, Techniques and Tools*. London: McGraw-Hill.

Banks, D. A. (1999). Who Needs Methodologies? A Case Study of the Development of a Web-based Information System. In B. Hope & P. Yoong (Eds.), *10th Australasian Conference on Information Systems* (Vol. 1, pp. 42–53). New Zealand: Victoria University of Wellington.

Checkland, P. B. (1981). *Systems Thinking, Systems Practice*. Brisbane: John Wiley.

Checkland, P. B. (1999). *Systems Thinking, Systems Practice*. Chichester, UK: Wiley.

Dewey, J. (1910). *How We Think*. New York: D C Heath and Co.

Espejo, R. & Harnden, R. (1989). *The Viable System Model: Interpretations and Applications of Stafford Beer's VSM*. Chichester, UK: John Wiley.

Flood, R. L. (1995). *Solving Problem Solving: A Potent Force for Effective Management*. Chichester, UK: Wiley.

Hirschheim, R., & Klein, H. K. (1989). Four paradigms of information systems development. *Communications of the ACM, 32,* 10(10).

Locke, J. (1706). *An Essay Concerning Human Understanding*. Abridged by J. W. Yolton (1976), London, UK: J. M. Dent and Sons.

Sauer, C. (1993). *Why Information Systems Fail: A Case Study Approach*. Henley-on-Thames, UK: Alfred Waller.

Toulmin, S. E. (1999). *The Uses of Argument*. Cambridge: Cambridge University Press.

Wastell, D. G. (1996). The fetish of technique: methodology as a social defence. *Information Systems Journal, 6,* 25–40.

Woozley, A. D. (1967). Theory of Knowledge. London, UK: Hutchinson University Library.

Chapter II

Making the Case for Case-Based Learning in Computer Information Systems

Morgan M. Jennings
Metropolitan State College of Denver, USA

Charles H. Mawhinney
Metropolitan State College of Denver, USA

Janos Fustos
Metropolitan State College of Denver, USA

ABSTRACT

In this chapter, we report the results of a study comparing current student's perceptions of computer information systems with student's perceptions of 12 years past. We found that students continue to prefer more interaction than they perceive an IS career to provide. Given this we (1) report on some programs available in high schools to interest students in a CIS career and (2) discuss case or problem-based learning as a means to provide students with the interaction they desire and show them that it is an integral part of a CIS career.

INTRODUCTION

More than a decade ago, Mawhinney, Callaghan and Gale (1989) looked at undergraduate business students' perceptions of the Information Systems (IS) profession and found that their perceptions were inaccurate and narrowly focused. Have such perceptions changed over the intervening years? Have, for example, the World Wide Web and publicity about dot.com companies and millionaires influenced the perception of computer information systems (CIS) careers?

The motivation for the original study was a national decline in IS enrollments in the late 1980s that was adversely affecting staffing in the information systems industry. There is still a need to explore this topic because a decade plus later there is a demonstrated lack of qualified workers. According to the Information Technology Association of America (ITAA) over three-quarters of a million skilled workers are currently needed (Bredin, 2000).

Mawhinney, et al. (1989) believed that the decline in enrollments was due to misperceptions about IS on the part of high school students. The popular understanding was that information systems professionals worked in isolation writing computer programs. This perception is partly true if you look at the majority of the entry-level positions for an IS person.

Another reason for a low number of people entering the field may be that this career opportunity is simply not heavily promoted in high schools. A study out of Australia by von Hellens and Nielson (2001) notes that engineering, mathematics, and science receive more press from high schools than IS. They also report, (a.) "overall perceptions by both male and female students of the IT degree as difficult and demanding" (p. 46) and (b.) perceptions from solely female study participants are that IT people work alone, have little contact with other people and the profession is strongly associated with high math skills. The findings of Mawhinney, et al. (1989) were similar. Both the Mawhinney, et al. and the von Hellens and Nielson studies were conducted in the mid to late 1980s, though the later study has collected data through 2000. Statistical data comparing any differences-over-time were not included in the article so it is not clear if perceptions have changed.

There are high school programs that are encouraging young people to explore information systems careers. For example, Wings 21, a successful program (Greensberg, 2000) located in Omaha, NE, provides long-term exposure to technology and technology careers. This kind of long-term positive exposure to computer technology may be a means to promote accurate information regarding IS jobs as well as alleviate anxiety related to use of technology, particularity computers.

In addition to a lack of understanding related to what an IS worker does in his/her job, the dropout rate within entry-level college IS courses is a problem (Myers, 2001). Many students feel they are computer literate until they enter an IS program. The skills that they possess and the skills needed within an IS degree are likely to be disparate. Rather than a sink or swim attitude on the part of colleges and universities, time spent coaching and encouraging students on relevant computer skills for the IS degree may help them feel confident and able to complete the program (Compeau, 1999). This means more than showing students the benefits of technology or how to use a computer. It may require providing meaningful situations in which to use technology (Venkatesh, 1999).

Using the same questionnaire with minor adaptations for our institution, we revisited the original study by Mawhinney, et al. (1985) and looked at perceptions held by current undergraduate business students. In this chapter we describe the study, the results and report ways in which CIS is being promoted in high schools and discuss the merits of authentic learning environments, particularly problem-based learning.

METHODOLOGY

Hypotheses

The first hypothesis tested was the same as the one tested by Mawhinney, et al. (1985). It compared the current students' perceptions of IS position characteristics against the characteristics of their desired position upon graduation. Stated in null form, the hypothesis tested was:

H_1:   Students perceive no difference between the work style of the typical IS graduate and their own expected starting position's work style.

The second hypothesis tested compared the responses from the current students against the responses from the original study. This two-part hypothesis compares their own expected starting position's work style and compares their perceptions of the work style of IS graduates. Stated in null form, the hypotheses tested were:

H_{2a}:   The two groups of students had the same expectations for the work style of their own starting positions.

H_{2b}:   The two groups of students had the same perceptions of the work style of the typical IS graduate.

Subjects

The subjects were students from fifteen sections of our entry-level computing course. Five hundred and nineteen usable responses were received. Like the original study, our sample came from a course that is taught from a common syllabus and is a combination of hands-on computing labs and hardware, software and personal computing concepts. This course is required of all business majors and is often the first exposure they have to CIS.

Some institutional differences between the two groups of students should be noted. The original study took place in a private college with traditional full-time residential students who were required to take the course as first semester freshmen. The current study took place in a public college with a large portion of non-traditional commuter students. Students have some flexibility concerning when they take the course, though it is the prerequisite for all IS courses.

Instrument and Procedure

We utilized the original questionnaire that appeared in Mawhinney, et al. (1985) with some minor adaptations to our institution. The questionnaire is shown in the Appendix and consisted of 18 items. The first nine items assessed perceptions of the background and work styles of a CIS graduate of the program. Questions 10 - 18 asked the same questions from the perspective of the student's own background and work-style preferences. A five point Likert scale consisting of Strongly Agree, Agree, Undecided, Disagree, and Strongly Disagree was used for the responses. They were converted to a numeric scale for scoring (strongly disagree equaled one and strongly agree equaled five).

Mawhinney, et al. (1985) performed factor analysis and subscale reliability analysis to determine if any subscales existed in the instrument. They concluded that there were no sufficiently interpretable and reliable subscales, and treated the perception measures as separate items. Since we were trying to compare our results to theirs we did not do any subscale investigation and simply used the separate items as they did.

We performed our data collection during the first week of the semester. The questionnaire was distributed in conjunction with an objective computer literacy screening test that we ordinarily perform at that time in this course. The students were not asked to identify themselves when responding to this questionnaire. Mawhinney, et al. (1985) used a somewhat different procedure. The first nine items were included in an initial survey (PRE). Eight months later a follow-up survey using the 18 item questionnaire was mailed to participants who provided their names and addresses.

RESULTS

Table 1 shows the means and standard deviations for the responses regarding Hypothesis 1: First for the IS graduates perceived work style (IS) and then for their own expected starting positions (SELF). The null hypothesis was tested using t-tests for paired comparisons of the corresponding means. For all nine items the average perceptions of the IS graduate's work style were significantly different from the average expectations of the students' own starting positions (one item at $p < .05$ and the other eight items at $p < .001$).

Table 1. Perceptions of MSCD SELF vs. IS graduates work-styles

n = 519			Mean		Standard Deviation			
Item	IS	SELF	t-value	Signif	IS	SELF	f-value	Signif
1	2.83	2.71	2.43	*	0.92	1.03	17.59	***
2	2.79	2.99	-3.67	***	1.02	1.17	18.32	***
3	2.78	2.24	10.94	***	0.93	1.00	0.02	
4	3.58	4.19	-5.81	***	0.88	2.32	0.60	
5	2.83	2.45	7.61	***	0.95	0.98	1.65	
6	2.68	2.12	11.73	***	0.94	0.94	4.13	*
7	3.17	2.63	10.02	***	1.03	1.15	14.07	***
8	3.26	3.49	-4.82	***	0.88	1.01	9.93	**
9	3.33	2.89	8.30	***	0.92	1.15	32.61	***
(2-tailed) * $p \le 0.05$ ** $p \le 0.01$ *** $p \le 0.001$								

Compared with their perceptions of the IS graduates' initial background, the respondents feel they:
- Are weaker at mathematics (Item #1)
- Entered MSCD with a stronger computer background (Item #2)

Compared with their perceptions of the IS graduate's first job, the respondents expect to:
- Spend less time writing computer programs (Item #3)
- Spend more time interacting with other persons (Item #4)
- Spend less time working alone (Item #5)
- Be less involved in designing computer hardware (Item #6)
- Interact less with other computer people (Item #7)
- Receive a higher starting salary (Item #8)
- Be less involved in helping managers select new computer systems (Item #9)

These results are consistent with those of Mawhinney, et al. (1985), except that they did not find significant differences for Items #1 and #2.

The first part of the second hypothesis (Table 2) compared the responses from the current students against the responses from the original study concerning their own background and preferred work style. The analysis was performed using t-tests for indepen-

Table 2. Perceptions of SELF: MSCD vs. Bentley students

Item	MSCD	Bentley	t-value	Signif	MSCD	Bentley	f-value	Signif
			Mean			**Standard Deviation**		
1	2.71	2.59	1.14		1.03	1.04	0.99	
2	2.99	2.52	4.07	***	1.17	1.11	1.11	
3	2.24	1.77	4.76	***	1.00	0.72	1.93	*
4	4.19	4.10	0.41		2.32	0.65	12.69	*
5	2.45	2.21	2.45	*	0.98	0.84	1.37	*
6	2.12	1.67	4.80	***	0.94	0.72	1.69	*
7	2.63	2.21	3.71	***	1.15	0.85	1.83	*
8	3.49	3.41	0.89		1.01	0.90	1.25	
9	2.89	2.58	2.65	**	1.15	0.98	1.38	*
	(2-tailed)		* $p \leq 0.05$		** $p \leq 0.01$		*** $p \leq 0.001$	

dent samples. The values from the current study are shown as "MSCD" and those from the original study as "Bentley." The summary values from the original study were used to perform the analysis. Six of the nine items showed significant differences, some of which were quite strong (one item at p < .05, one item at p < .01, and the other four items at p < .001).

Compared with the self-perceptions of the Bentley students' initial background, the MSCD students felt they:
* Entered College with a stronger computer background (Item #2)

Compared with the self-perceptions of the Bentley students' desired work style, the MSCD students felt they would:
* Spend more time writing computer programs (Item #3)
* Spend more time working alone (Item #5)
* Be more involved in designing computer hardware (Item #6)
* Interact more with other computer people (Item #7)
* Be more involved in helping managers select new computer systems (Item #9)

The second part of the second hypothesis (Table 3) compared the responses from the current students against the responses from the original study concerning the background and work style of IS graduates. The analysis was performed using t-tests for independent samples. The values from the current study are shown as "MSCD" and those from the original

Table 3. Perceptions of IS graduates: MSCD vs. Bentley students

			Mean			Standard Deviation		
Item	MSCD	Bentley	t-value	Signif	MSCD	Bentley	f-value	Signif
1	2.83	2.61	2.18	*	0.92	1.01	0.82	
2	2.79	2.72	0.66		1.02	1.08	0.88	
3	2.78	2.90	-1.34		0.93	0.90	1.07	
4	3.58	3.39	2.05	*	0.88	0.89	0.97	
5	2.83	2.72	1.22		0.95	0.86	1.21	
6	2.68	2.65	0.34		0.94	0.89	1.11	
7	3.17	3.28	-1.12		1.03	0.94	1.20	
8	3.26	3.09	2.00	*	0.88	0.79	1.25	
9	3.33	3.52	-2.07	*	0.92	0.73	1.58	*
(2-tailed) * p ≤ 0.05 ** p ≤ 0.01 *** p ≤ 0.001								

study as "Bentley". The summary values from the original study were used to perform the analysis. Four of the nine items showed significant differences, all at p < .05.

Compared with the Bentley students' perceptions of the initial background of IS graduates, the MSCD students felt they:
- Are stronger at mathematics (Item #1)

Compared with the Bentley students' perceptions of the work style of IS graduates, the MSCD students felt they would:
- Spend more time interacting with other persons (Item #4)
- Receive a higher starting salary (Item #8)
- Be less involved in helping managers select new computer systems (Item #9)

Hypothesis 1 is rejected and it can be concluded that our students do perceive numerous differences between the work style of the typical IS graduate and their own expected starting position's work style. This is consistent with the findings of Mawhinney, et al. (1985), except they did not find significant differences for the first two items. This seems to indicate that, like the students 12 years ago, current students prefer more interaction with other people than they perceive an IS career to provide.

Hypothesis 2_a is also be rejected. The MSCD students clearly have a different background than the Bentley students. It should be expected that students would have a stronger computer background than students of twelve years prior, even though the MSCD students are not traditional students. Some institutional differences between the two groups of students should be noted. The original study took place in a private college with traditional full-time residential students who were required to take the course as first semester freshmen. The current study took place in a public college with a large portion of non-traditional commuter students. Students have some flexibility concerning when they take the course, though it is the prerequisite for all IS courses.

The MSCD students also exhibit differences in their preferred work style – differences that are more in keeping with their perception of the work style of IS graduates. The Mawhinney, et al. (1985) study does not indicate what proportion of their sample was IS majors. However, they do indicate that it took place at a time of rapidly declining IS enrollments. It is quite likely that the MSCD sample had a substantially higher proportion of IS majors (indeed, 24% of our sample indicated they were CIS majors) and that may very well account for this result. Another possibility is that business students in general perceive themselves and jobs as more technically oriented.

Hypothesis 2_b is not so clear-cut. Although four of the nine items were significantly different, five were not, and those that weren't particularly strong differences. We would argue that the perceptions of the two groups of students regarding the background and work style of IS graduates were more alike than different and would not reject this hypothesis.

The similar perceptions are not too surprising if job advertisements influence the perception of information systems work. Between 1970 and 1990 advertisements showed an increase in phrases specifying technical knowledge at the cost of business and systems knowledge (Todd, McKeen, & Gallupe, 1995). This is in contrast to both anecdotal and research evidence that managers often rate the need for 'soft' skills (i.e., problem solving, communication, working in groups) higher than technical skills (Turner & Lowry, 2002;

Shawyunm, 1999). Given this change of focus over time, an extended questionnaire would provide a more in depth picture of student perceptions of information systems.

DISCUSSION

Certainly more research is needed regarding students' perceptions of an IS career. A review of literature found few recent articles focusing on student perceptions or understanding of IS. While we do not have a clear picture of student perceptions, we do have evidence that when students have an opportunity to experience the field of CIS, many find it to their liking. Anecdotal stories regarding the positive effects of partnerships are included in the literature. Companies spend a great deal of money on student programs. GE spends about 1 billion annually on education and training programs with paid college internships being the largest portion (Kolbasuk-McGee & Mateyaschuk, 1999). Kolbasuk-McGee and Mateyaschuk (1999) present an example of a GE success story that turned a math major from a career in actuary work to an IS related full-time job. The intern's reason for her career change was that she had the opportunity to experience information systems work in business and found that she enjoyed it.

In this study we found that compared to the student's in the original study, current student's work style preferences are more in keeping with their perceptions of an IS graduate. While this is positive, there is also indication that more interaction is desired than students perceive an IS career to provide. Given the team or group-based projects approach that are part of a career in this field, promotion of CIS to high school students should include the 'people' aspects along with the technical aspects. In addition, authentic learning environments should be included in CIS curriculum. Authentic learning environments provide students with the interaction they desire and show them that interaction is an integral part of a CIS career. In both cases a combination of accurate and persistent promotion of what IS entails and opportunities to experience realistic use of information systems is important.

High School Programs

Lack of understanding regarding an IS career is not uncommon. As Mawhinney, et al. (1985) and von Hellens and Nielson (2001) found, students' idea of CIS entailed working alone and required a high level of math. Because of this lack of understanding students may be surprised when they start a program or they may decline entering a program because of the scarce or inaccurate knowledge they have regarding such a degree or career. Early intervention at the high school level may help ameliorate the misperception.

There are programs that target high school students. Often it is corporations that are stepping in to train the not-so-future-workers. Cisco is well known for its Networking Academy Program that is open to high school students (Greensberg, 2000). This partnership between business, education and government teach the design, building and maintenance of computer networks. Another partnership program is Generation Yes; a successful nationwide program that partners knowledgeable IT students with teachers. The trained students help the teachers use technology to teach more effectively (Greensberg, 2000).

Kolbasuk-McGee and Mateyaschuk (1999) describe how General Electric, Booz Allen & Hamilton, IBM, and Prudential Insurance Co. of America, Bell Atlantic and KPMG International are working with students and teachers in K-12. The programs that these companies spend millions of dollars on include volunteerism, training, and internships. The purpose of these programs is to increase the use of technology for both teachers and students. The companies know that they are investing in the long term in order to have a technology knowledgeable work force.

Wings 21 located in Omaha, NE, provides long-term exposure to technology and careers (Greensberg, 2000). After completing an introduction to technology course, students have the opportunity to take more advanced courses such as electronic imaging/publishing, computer programming or computer-aided design. Paid internships and contract work with area businesses such as Qwest are also available.

The New Technology High School (NTMS) in Napa, CA, is unique. According to Salpeter (1999), the concept for this award winning school is two-fold: Prepare local students for a technology rich future and draw businesses to the area. Students learn spreadsheets, databases, word processors, and presentation software through real-world projects. In a multimedia design and production class students use appropriate software and learn and related concepts such as ethical issues regarding manipulating emotions and privacy concerns. Additionally, at least one (per semester) advanced computer course is required at the local community college. Students have access to electronic research databases and other Internet sources through the school library.

This kind of a high school environment is enticing because of the real-world collaboration. With authentic learning environments the necessary information technology skills are embedded in the learning process. Also embedded in the learning process are the soft skills that managers say are lacking in employees, such as problem solving, communicating effectively and working in group environments (Lee & Trauth, 1995; Todd et al., 1995).

Making a Case for Cases

Without programs such as Wings 21 or The New Technology High School and even with them, the computer skills that students possess and the skills needed within an IS degree are often disparate (Easton & Easton, 2002; Karsten & Roth, 1998). Other students rightly assume that they will learn the skills that are needed. In either case, students often find themselves failing, which may contribute to the dropout rate within entry-level college IS courses (Myers, 2001). According to a study completed by ITAA (Information Technology Association of America) managers placed four-year colleges and private technical institutions as the best method for acquiring overall "pre-hire" skills. (ITAA, 2000) Colleges may be the best way to learn IT, but we are doing little to help students succeed and to experience a holistic view of CIS. Addressing this problem seems particularly important because of the shortage of qualified workers.

Rather than a sink or swim attitude on the part of colleges and universities, time spent coaching and encouraging students on relevant skills for the IS degree may help them complete the program (Compeau, 1999). As with some of the high school programs, this requires providing meaningful and relevant learning environments in which to use the technology (Venkatesh, 1999) that are similar to actual work-related scenarios (Gallivan, 2000).

Without an accurate picture, it is difficult for students to understand the work style of information system professionals. The content of CIS courses are technically-oriented and many students struggle with the content, usually in isolation. This, however, belies the actual business environment where employees usually work together on projects. Learning should take place in a similar environment. In addition, research suggests that there is a synergistic learning effect within group environments (Savery & Duffy, 1995; Ryan, Bordoloi, & Harrison, 2000). For example, better understanding of a system and development of more accurate mental models was found in a group environment (Gallivan, 2000). An unconstructive aspect of such a learning situation is that negative comments may affect the attitude of group members (Gallivan, 2000). The literature in favor of authentic learning environments outweighs this concern, however.

Authentic Learning Environments

There is a body of research and theory on the importance of providing authentic and relevant learning environments (Gallivan, 2000). This is often within the context of constructivism, an umbrella term that identifies a learning philosophy (Lebow, 1993; Savery & Duffy, 1995; Vanderbilt, 1990). Case or problem-based learning, situated cognition, discovery learning, cooperative learning and anchored instruction are some of the models within a constructivist paradigm. While concepts may vary, overriding principles include active engagement, collaboration and personal relevance. The reasons for learning are embedded within rich, authentic contextually relevant environments (Lebow, 1993).

Case and problem-based learning (PBL) are examples. Neither cases or PBL (Barrows, 1985) are new concepts and there seem to be negligible differences for purposes of this discussion. Originally known as the Harvard Case Method, cases originated in the 60's. The objective of the case method was to enhance judgment and decision-making capability and it is widely used because of its success (Potvin, 2000). Problem-based learning was developed in the mid 50's for medical education (Savery & Duffy, 1995). At many medical schools it has replaced the lecture approach for the first two years of medical science curricula (Savery & Duffy, 1995). Teachers, or facilitators, are mentors and guides who challenge students to problem solve; they model higher order thinking skills (Savery & Duffy, 1995). For discussion purposes we will use these two terms interchangeably.

The interaction between peers provided by such learning environments is a successful means to engage students (Vanderbilt, 1990). It is, however, not often used because of the time commitment and the difficulty in devising 'good' problems. Contextually-rich cases are available in books and online sources, such as Harvard Online. Properly developed holistic learning environments such as PBL are more likely to develop ownership on the part of the students involved (Savery & Duffy, 1995) and may promote what Agarwal & Karahanna (2000) calls cognitive absorption and (Jennings, 2000) calls cognitive aesthetics.

In a PBL environment, over the course of a semester, students work together to devise solutions based on well-articulated problems. The problem is the focus while any use of technology (as is likely to be the case in CIS) is secondary; it is a tool to solve the problem. Focusing on the content and pedagogy rather than on the technology may lead to sustained interest (McKinnon & Nolan, 2000).

Savery and Duffy (1995) subscribe to the following instructional principles for PBL that derive from a constructivist approach:

1. Anchor all learning activities to a larger task or problem
2. Support the learner in developing ownership for the overall problem or task
3. Design an authentic task
4. Design the task and the learning environment to reflect the complexity of the environment they should be able to function in at the end of learning

5. Give the learner ownership of the process used to develop a solution
6. Design the learning environment to support and challenge the learner's thinking
7. Encourage testing ideas against alternative views
8. Provide opportunity for and support reflection on both the content learned and the learning process

As an example, in a problem-based introductory multimedia course students learn about and use the six elements of multimedia (interactivity, audio, video, images, text, animation). The learning is embedded in producing an authentic product, often one that is needed by a local company. The concept is 'sold' to the students in order to elicit their support of the problem. The problem is sufficiently complex in order to challenge a learner, but not so technically advanced that it deters students. While students have a responsibility to learn about and use all of the appropriate technology for the problem, the problem rules the use of the technology. Students alternate using the various technologies as they are needed for the product. The benefits of this approach include: (a.) students concentrate on the relevancy of particular element for the product, (b.) they scaffold each other in learning as the semester progresses and (c.) all students learn the appropriate technology. Help is also available in many different forms including help screens, reference materials, just-in-time tutorials by the instructor and other available sources the students find.

Objectives for a problem include specific content learning. While traditional PBL uses peer and self-evaluation, variations include traditional testing based on the objectives. Traditional testing may help alleviate instructor concerns regarding student's learning and contribution to the group effort.

It is not enough to simply provide a problem. In order for this paradigm to work, students must become a team and team building must be taught. Wells (2002) uses Katzenbach and Smith's definition of teamwork: "A team is a small number of people with complementary skills who are committed to a common purpose, performance goals, and approach for which they hold themselves mutually accountable." Without team building instruction students often perceive group work with disdain: With guidance on team building students are more positive in regard to the experience (Wells, 2002).

Trend Setting

Companies have high expectations for CIS graduates (Shawyunm, 1999). It behooves us as educators to provide the business community with students who have had realistic CIS experience. Authentic learning environments provide this. Working together, faculty within CIS degree programs could construct a curriculum based on authentic learning environments such as case or problem-based learning. Team building concepts could be taught in the ubiquitous entry-level computing course so that students would have the skills to work effectively in groups.

CONCLUSIONS

We repeated a study of undergraduate business majors that was performed in 1989, and compared the perceptions of contemporary students with those previously reported (Mawhinney et al.). We found that current student's perceptions of CIS have not significantly changed: Like students in the original study, current students prefer more interaction than they perceive an IS career to provide.

Promoting the 'soft side' as well as the technical aspects of CIS to high school students may help change perceptions. Additionally, using case or problem-based learning environments in CIS college programs would provide students with real-world skills and an accurate understanding of CIS. With authentic learning environments and team building instruction, the technology and soft skills are embedded in the learning process. By using this learning approach CIS majors experience interesting and varied problems during their student tenure. They enter the work force with immediately usable skills and a realistic understanding of their career of choice.

REFERENCES

Agarwal, R., & Karahanna, E. (2000). Time flies when you're having fun: Cognitive absorption and belief about information technology usage. *MIS Quarterly, 24*(4), 665-694.

Barrows, H. S. (1985). *How to design a problem-based curriculum for the preclinical years.* New York: Springer Publishing.

Bredin, S., Malyan-Smith, J. (2000). *On the fast track*, [Online database]. Wilson Select database [2001, September 23].

Compeau, D. H., C. A. & Huff, S. v23 no2 (June) p 145-58. (1999). Social cognitive theory and individual reactions to computing technology: A longitudinal study. *MIS Quarterly, 23*(2), 145-158.

Easton, G., & Easton, A. (2002, May 19-22). *Assessing Computer Literacy: Are Our Students Getting More Proficient?* Paper presented at the Information Resources Management Association International Conference, Seattle, WA.

Gallivan, M. J. (2000, April 6-8). *Examining workgroup influence on technology usage: A community of practice perspective.* Paper presented at the ACM SIGCPR Conference, Chicago, Il.

Greensberg, R. (2000, October). Filling the gap. *Techniques (Association for Career and Technical Education), 75,* 2-27.

ITAA. (2000). *Executive summary - Bridging the gap: Information technology skills for the new millennium*, [WWW]. Information Technology Association of America. Available: http://www.itaa.org/workforce/studeis/hw00execsumm.htm [2002, April 25].

Jennings, M. M. (2000, April). *What do good designers know that we don't?* Paper presented at the Information Resources Management Association International Conference, Anchorage, AL.

Karsten, R., & Roth, R. (1998). The relationship of computer experience and computer self-efficacy to performance in introductory computer literacy courses. *Journal of Research on Computing in Education, 31*(1), 14-24.

Kolbasuk-McGee, M., & Mateyaschuk, J. (1999, February 15). Educating the masses: Sluga's IT internship with GE. *Information Week, 2002,* 61.

Lebow, D. (1993). Constructivist values for instructional system design: Five principles toward a new mindset. *Educational technology research and development, 41*(3), 4-16.

Lee, D. M. S., & Trauth, E., Douglas. (1995). Critical skills and knowledge requirements of IS professionals: A joint academic/industry investigation. *MIS Quarterly, 19*(3), 313-340.

McKinnon, D. H., & Nolan, C. J. P. (2000). A longitudinal study of student attitudes toward computers: Resolving an attitude decay paradox. *Journal of Research on Computing in Education, 32*(3), 325-335.

Myers, M. E., Beise, C. M. (2001, April 18-21). *Nerd work: Attractors and barriers perceived by students entering the IT field.* Paper presented at the ACM SICCPR Conference, San Diego, CA.

Potvin, J. (December, 2000). *The Case Method,* [WWW]. Bellanet Advisor. Available: http//www.bellanet.org/advisor/index.cfm?Fuseaction=view_article&TheArticle=38 [2002, July 12].

Ryan, S., Bordoloi, B., & Harrison, D. A. (2000). Acquiring conceptual data modeling skills: The effect of cooperative learning and self-efficacy on learning outcomes. *The DATA BASE for Advances in Information Systems, 31*(4), 9-24.

Salpeter, J. (1999). New technology high school : Preparing students for the digital age. *Technology & Learning, 19*(6), 46.

Savery, J. R., & Duffy, T. M. (1995). Problem based learning: An instructional model and it's constructivist framework. *Educational Technology*, 31-37.

Shawyunm, T. (1999). Expectations and influencing factors of IS graduates and education in Thailand: A perspective of the students, academics and business community. *Informing Science, 2*(1), 19-32.

Todd, P. A., McKeen, J. D., & Gallupe, R. B. (1995). The evolution of IS job skills: a content analysis of IS job advertisements from 1970 to 1990. *MIS Quarterly, 19*(1), 1-18.

Turner, R., & Lowry, G. (2002, May 19-22). *Towards a profession of information systems and technology: The relative importance of "hard" and "soft" skills for IT practitioners.* Paper presented at the Information Resourses Management Association International Conference, Seattle, WA.

Vanderbilt, T. c. a. T. G. a. (1990). Anchored instruction and it's relationship to situated cognition. *Educational Researcher*, 2-10.

Venkatesh, V. (1999). Creation of favorable user perceptions: Exploring the role of intrinsic motivation. *MIS Quarterly, 23*(2), 239-260.

von Hellens, L., Nielson, S. (2001, July). Australian women in IT. *Communications of the ACM, 44,* 46-56.

Wells, C. E. (2002). Teaching Teamwork in Information Systems. In E. B. Cohen (Ed.), *Challenges of Information Technology Education in the 21st Century.* Hershey, PA: Idea Group Publishing.

APPENDIX: THE QUESTIONNAIRE

My major is: _____

The following questions deal with your perception of the undergraduate Computer Information Systems program at Metropolitan State College of Denver. Please indicate the strength of your agreement/disagreement with each statement by circling the letter(s) that best describe your feeling about or reaction to each statement.

Legend: Strongly Agree   Agree   Undecided   Disagree   Strongly Disagree

The typical graduate of this program:

1.   Is a whiz at mathematics.   SA   A   U   D   DS
2.   Entered Metro with a strong prior
     background in computers.   SA   A   U   D   DS

During his/her first job after graduation, the typical graduate of this program:

3.   Spends most of his/her working time
     writing computer programs.   SA   A   U   D   DS
4.   Spends most of his/her working time
     interacting with other persons.   SA   A   U   D   DS
5.   Spends most of his/her time working alone.   SA   A   U   D   DS
6.   Designs new computer hardware.   SA   A   U   D   DS
7.   Interacts mostly with other computer people.   SA   A   U   D   DS
8.   Has a starting salary above the average
     Metro graduate.   SA   A   U   D   DS
9.   Helps managers select new computer systems. SA   A   U   D   DS

The following questions deal with your assessment of your own background and job preferences.

I believe that I:

10. Am a whiz at mathematics.   SA   A   U   D   DS
11. Entered Metro with a strong prior
     background in computers.   SA   A   U   D   DS

During my first job after graduation, I expect to:

12. Spend most of my working time writing
     computer programs.   SA   A   U   D   DS
13. Spend most of my working time
     interacting with other persons.   SA   A   U   D   DS
14. Spend most of my time working alone.   SA   A   U   D   DS
15. Design new computer hardware.   SA   A   U   D   DS

16. Interact mostly with other computer people.   SA   A   U   D   DS
17. Have a starting salary above the
    average Metro graduate.   SA   A   U   D   DS
18. Help managers select new computer systems.   SA   A   U   D   DS

Chapter III

Introducing Information Systems Students to Research with a Structured Group Project

Tanya McGill
Murdoch University, Australia

ABSTRACT

This chapter reports on an approach to getting information systems research students started. The approach involves beginning research students undertaking a structured group research project in which the instructor is an active participant. The major purpose of this group project is to provide a gentle, supportive, structured introduction to information systems research. This approach benefits students by ensuring that they have participated in a complete research project before they have to assume complete responsibility for their first large individual project. The chapter discusses the use of this approach at an Australian university. In general, students have participated well, learning from their own experiences and the experiences of others in the group.

INTRODUCTION

Although the majority of information systems students graduate and start work in industry as information technology professionals, a minority reenroll in research degrees. In a number of countries, the initial introduction to information systems research for university students is via an Honors year that includes a substantial research dissertation component (e.g., Australia, the United Kingdom). In Australia, this research component is normally supervised by a single academic or two academics, and usually accounts for at least 50% of the student's grade. The Honors year also commonly contains a number of advanced theory topics and may contain a research methods course. Performance in the Honors year is a major determinant of acceptance into a Ph.D. program.

Starting to undertake information systems research can be a difficult and unsettling time for students (Clarke, 1998). This chapter describes one approach to facilitating the introduction of information systems research students to their research career: a structured group research project with the instructor as an active participant. This approach is intended to be complementary to the traditional means of research training, such as direct guidance by an individual supervisor and formal research methods courses.

BACKGROUND

Various approaches have been proposed as being useful for helping information technology students to acquire the skills and experience they need to undertake successful research. The following section reviews some of these approaches.

Supervision

For many students, their first exposure to the process of undertaking research is when they enroll in a postgraduate research degree, and this may be a relatively solitary experience. Cullen (1994) noted that in a number of countries, a single supervisor or supervisor and associate supervisor is common, and students may not receive much input into their projects from others. For example, in an Australian study he conducted, only 22% of students obtained advice from anyone other than their primary supervisor. He pointed to an inadequacy in this traditional means of supervising postgraduates and recommended that a study be made of other strategies to restructure graduate education. He commented favorably on the American Ph.D. system, which makes greater use of a panel of supervisors and thesis advisers.

In the Honors year, as well as during Ph.D. studies, a student's performance can be dependent upon the input of individual supervisors. However, individual supervisors may not have the time or interest to cover more than is strictly necessary for an individual project, and thus, students may not acquire breadth in their research training. This may particularly be the case when supervising students who are not directly in their area of interest.

Research Methods Courses

Whitten and Bell (1993) acknowledged that many research skills can only be learned under the direction of a supervisor who is expert in the subject matter, but recognized that researchers also need more general research knowledge and skills. Research methods courses can supply breadth in research preparation, allowing students to be exposed to a wider range of research approaches than will be required in their current project, thus preparing them for future research. Whitten and Bell described two courses offered at their institution to train information technology research students. Courses such as these are offered at many universities.[1]

Research methods courses for information systems research students are usually one of two types. They may focus mainly on practical skills such as library research, thesis preparation, and oral presentation skills. Alternatively, they may have a broader focus, introducing students to a range of research methods such as experimentation, survey research, case study research, and action research.

Other Approaches Tried

A number of other approaches to getting information technology research students started have been discussed in the literature. The section below provides a brief overview of them. Ridley (1995) noted the difficulty of starting out in information systems research and discussed the particular difficulty of selecting and focusing information systems research projects. She explored the role of doctoral consortiums in this process and was generally positive about their benefit but suggested that systematic expert review may be of even more benefit.

It has also been suggested that students should be introduced to information technology research at the undergraduate level. Reed, Miller, and Braught (2000) described a comprehensive effort to introduce a research culture throughout an entire undergraduate computer science curriculum.

Cunningham (1995) discussed the difficulty of providing an authentic research experience to undergraduate students and described a successful third-year project (in a databases course) in which information technology students designed, conducted, and wrote up bibliometric experiments. The project was designed to give students experience with the scientific method and to encourage familiarity with the scientific publishing process and with the information technology professional literature. Clarke (1998) also described an approach that used an undergraduate class experiment to teach an empirical approach to designing human computer interaction (HCI). The focus in this approach was on obtaining empirical skills to help specifically in HCI design rather than on undertaking research that is more general.

Borstler and Johansson (1998) described a "conference course," a course designed to introduce undergraduate students to research and improve their written and oral communication skills. The course they described was organized as a "real" conference and open to the public. However, because of time limitations, most of the papers submitted by students were literature review than research papers. Students did not, thus, necessarily gain practice with a range of research skills.

RATIONALE FOR THE STRUCTURED GROUP PROJECT APPROACH

This chapter reports on another approach for getting Honors research students started. It involves Honors students undertaking a structured group research project in which the instructor is an active participant. This project is undertaken as part of a research methods course and is designed to provide concurrent practical illustrations of some of the theoretical concepts being covered in the research methods course.

The major purpose of this group project is to provide a gentle, supportive, structured introduction to information systems research. The introduction is relatively gentle, because the instructor is an active participant in the research project. Students gain the benefit of the instructor's experience, yet are full participants. In his report on the use of class research projects, Clarke (1998) noted that the balance between students and instructor is important. Students should not be expected to execute research perfectly or be seen as research assistants to the instructor.

The approach proposed in this chapter encourages students to discuss and solve problems in groups. This is not possible in their individual Honors projects but is important to facilitate their learning and to prepare them for the fact that much information systems research is done in teams.

Students are encouraged to contribute fully by providing the incentive that if the project is well done, we will try to publish it at a conference. Having a publication record improves a student's chances of admission to a Ph.D. program and improves their chances of obtaining a Ph.D. scholarship.

This approach differs from that of Cunningham (1995), described in the previous section, because the instructor is an active member of the research group. However, it is similar in that the possibility of publication is provided as a performance incentive. It is also similar to that described by Clarke (1998) in that the instructor is an active participant; however, Clarke's projects were not intended to provide a general research grounding, rather, they were to focus on raising awareness of empirical skills in HCI design, so the projects undertaken only involved replication of existing work.

THE PROCESS FOLLOWED

The following section describes the general sequence of stages followed for each project; these are also summarized in Table 1.

Students are first provided with an outline of a possible research area. This is brief (less than two pages in length) and deliberately designed to be general, to allow students some

Table 1. Summary of project stages

1.	The instructor provides students with an outline of a possible research area.
2.	Students undertake a preliminary literature review.
3.	Group negotiation is used to decide the actual research topic and the research questions to be answered.
4.	The research design is planned.
5.	The research project is carried out as a group.
6.	Data analysis is undertaken.
7.	Individual write-ups are done by students.
8.	A joint paper is written by the instructor using the student papers as a starting point.

flexibility in the final project chosen. Two criteria have been used in choosing the suggested research area. First, it should not require too much prior technical knowledge, because the group may contain students with a range of backgrounds and because the time constraints (see Table 2) mean the project must be achievable in three to four months. The second criterion is that the project should be within the instructor's area of expertise, so that good guidance can be provided, problems can be identified early, and the chances of publishing the results can be maximized.

Students then undertake a preliminary literature review prior to finalizing the research topic. This reinforces their information-seeking skills and enables them to make an informed choice of project. It also lays the foundation for making decisions about research design.

In Stages 3 to 7, the instructor participates as a member of the research group. The group next decides on the final research topic and the research questions to be answered. If appropriate to the kinds of research questions, hypotheses are also formulated. While all participants must accept roughly the same set of research questions, there is some scope for individualization and variations on how they are presented. Similarly, there is some scope for variation in hypotheses, so each student can "maintain" their own set.

In the next stage, the research design is planned. As only one project is carried out at a time, all group members must accept the chosen research design. The work is then divided (e.g., two participants may be primarily responsible for questionnaire design, two may

Table 2. Outline of possible submissions that provide opportunities for feedback

1.	Problem formulation — submit end of Week 3
1.1	Problem statement (two pages) — including a brief review of the literature relevant to the problem and an explicit statement of the research question(s) to be answered
1.2	Statement of hypotheses (and model if appropriate), along with reference to any supporting literature
1.3	Annotated bibliography of at least five relevant references
2.	Research design — submit end of Week 6
2.1	Description of the research design
2.2	Explanation of why this design was chosen
3.	Final submission — submit Week 15
3.1	Problem statement
3.2	Brief review of the literature relevant to the problem
3.3	Statement of research question
3.4	Statement of hypotheses (and model if appropriate)
3.5	Description of the research design, including an explanation of why this design was chosen
3.6	Presentation of results
3.7	Discussion of results
3.8	References

organize piloting, etc.) and the project carried out. The projects carried out so far have involved between two to five students as well as the instructor.

Analysis of the data has been primarily overseen by the instructor, as many Australian information systems students have little previous statistical experience. All group members receive a core set of results, plus they may undertake additional individual analysis. The issue of lack of statistical background has been addressed somewhat in the later offerings of the research methods course, with a formal introduction to SPSS and the use of statistics in information systems research. This has led to an improvement in students' ability to actively participate in this stage of the project.

The final stage of the project is the write-up. Students submit an individual report in the format of a conference paper, and students are marked on them individually. At a later stage, the instructor writes up a joint paper using the student papers as a starting point. Those students who are still interested can also be involved in the final write-up and benefit from seeing the importance of making iterative improvements to project write-ups.

The entire project must be carried out within one semester (about 15 weeks). In order to encourage students to start the write-up early, a schedule, such as the example shown in Table 2, is suggested to them. Those who make the suggested submissions receive detailed feedback, which improves the quality of their final paper.

EXAMPLE PROJECTS

This section describes several successful projects as examples of the scale of project that can be used. Most of the projects completed so far have been related to end user computing. While students may not have formally studied end user computing in their undergraduate studies, it is a concept with which they are familiar and which does not require significant prior theoretical knowledge.

The first project was undertaken by the instructor and two Honors students. The research question investigated was:

Do end users experience higher user satisfaction using applications that they have developed themselves than do other end users using the same application?

The research question was addressed by designing an experiment where 40 business student participants used their own and another spreadsheet application created as part of a course they were taking. After using each spreadsheet, they completed a questionnaire that measured end user computing satisfaction. During analysis, the project group compared the satisfaction ratings of applications that were evaluated by their end user developers with ratings of the same application by other end users.

The results of the project were interesting, as end users were found to be significantly more satisfied with applications they had developed themselves. The results of this project were published in the *Proceedings of the 1998 IRMA Conference* (McGill et al., 1998). Both of the students involved in the project felt that they had benefited from it, and while neither continued to undertake a Ph.D., both published the research from their Honors theses in international conferences.

A later project built upon the results of the initial project described above. This project addressed the following research question:

Does the positive relationship between system quality and user satisfaction discussed in the organizational information systems literature hold in the end user development domain?

The system quality of the spreadsheet applications from the initial study was measured following the development of an instrument to do so. The data were then compared with the user satisfaction data from the initial study. The results of the study indicated that although a positive relationship existed between system quality and user satisfaction when the user of the application was not the developer, that relationship was not present when the user was also the developer. The results of this study were published in the *Proceedings of the 11th Australasian Conference on Information Systems* (McGill et al., 2000). Five of the six students involved in this project continued on to enroll in a Ph.D. program.

Both of the projects described above followed the intention of the instructor fairly closely. However, this is not always the case. In one project, the group had difficulty reaching a decision about what they wished to research. The students were uninterested in the tentative topic provided by the instructor, yet found it difficult to settle on another topic. Eventually (after being asked not to leave a meeting until a research question was chosen), they chose the following research question:

What is the relationship between end user developer satisfaction with applications they have developed, and satisfaction with the development tools used to create the applications?

After an instrument had been developed to measure satisfaction with a development tool, the research question was addressed via a survey of 120 business students who had recently used Microsoft Excel© to develop a spreadsheet as part of a major assignment. Satisfaction with a user-developed application was found to be significantly correlated with satisfaction with the tool used to create the application. The role of experience in this relationship was also explored. The results of this study were published in the *Proceedings of the 2001 IRMA Conference* (McGill, van der Heyden, & Hopkins, 2001).

CONCLUSION

This chapter reports on an approach to getting information systems research students started. The approach involves beginning research students undertaking a structured group research project in which the instructor is an active participant. The major purpose of this group project is to provide a gentle, supportive, structured introduction to information systems research. This approach benefits students by ensuring that they have participated in a complete research project before they have to assume complete responsibility for their first large individual project. In general, students have participated well, learning from their own experiences and the experiences of others in the group. While the individual papers produced by students at the end of the project have not been of publishable quality, many of the students have gone on to publish the results of their Honors projects (i.e., their second attempt to write a conference paper), something that occurred rarely prior to students participating in this kind of a project.

ENDNOTES

[1]   For examples, see the following Web sites: http://cisnet.baruch.cuny.edu/phd/U821.htm; http://cisnet.baruch.cuny.edu/phd/U822.htm; http://infosys.massey.ac.nz/papers/pn/157720.html; and http://cis.gsu.edu/~drobey/syl9300_new.htm.

REFERENCES

Borstler, J., & Johansson, O. (1998). The students conference — A tool for the teaching of research, writing, and presentation skills. *Proceedings of ITiCSE '98*, 28–31.

Clarke, M. C. (1998). Teaching the empirical approach to designing human-computer interaction via an experimental group project. *SIGCSE Bulletin, 30*(1), 198–201.

Cullen, D. J., Pearson, M., Saha, L. J., & Spear, R. H. (1994). *Establishing effective PhD supervision*. Canberra: Department of Employment, Education and Training, AGPS.

Cunningham, S. J. (1995). An introduction to research and the CS/IS professional literature for undergraduates. *SIGCSE Bulletin, 27*(4), 5–8.

McGill, T., Payne, C., Bennett, D., Carter, K., Chong, A., Hornby, G., & Lim, L. (2000). System quality, user satisfaction and end user development, *Proceedings of the 11th Australasian Conference on Information Systems*. Brisbane, Australia.

McGill, T. J., Hobbs, V. J., Chan, R., & Khoo, D. (1998). User satisfaction as a measure of success in end user application development: An empirical investigation. In M. Khosrowpour (Ed.), *Proceedings of the 1998 IRMA Conference* (pp. 352–357). Hershey, PA: Idea Group Publishing.

McGill, T. J., van der Heyden, J., & Hopkins, G. (2001). End user development: satisfaction with tools and satisfaction with applications. In *Managing Information in a Global Economy: 2001 IRMA International Conference, Toronto, Canada* (pp. 617–620). Hershey, PA: Idea Group Publishing.

Reed, D., Miller, C., & Braught, G. (2000). Empirical investigation throughout the CS curriculum. *Proceedings of SIGCSE 2000*, 202–206.

Ridley, G. (1995). Focusing information systems postgraduate research projects. *Proceedings of the 6th Australasian Conference on Information Systems. 2*, 807–819.

Whitten, I. H., & Bell, T. C. (1993). Getting research students started: A tale of two courses. *SIGCSE Bulletin, 25*(1), 165–169.

Chapter IV

Making Way for Java in an Information Technology Masters Program

Wendy Lucas
Bentley College, USA

ABSTRACT

The object-oriented programming paradigm has gained popularity in industry and academia, and Java is becoming the language of choice. Yet, it can be a difficult language to learn, with many hurdles for novice programmers. This chapter describes our experiences transitioning to Java as the first programming language in an information technology Masters program. Careful consideration was given to a variety of factors, including when to introduce object-oriented concepts, which integrated development environment to use, and how to support students with minimal prior experience. The impact of these choices on the learning experience is described, and the factors that led to the successful implementation of Java as a first programming language are presented.

INTRODUCTION

Object-oriented technology (OOT) is becoming increasingly prevalent throughout the system development process (Jordan, Smilan, & Wilkinson, 1994). Students must be knowledgeable in OOT in order to adequately prepare for their future careers. The ACM/AIS 2000 model curriculum includes object-oriented concepts within several courses, including analysis and design, software engineering methodologies, databases, and programming (Gorgone & Gray, 2000). The Java™ programming language, which became generally available in 1995, has achieved a high level of adoption in industry and in the classroom. Information systems programs have also begun to integrate OOT in general, and Java in particular, into their course offerings (Lim, 1998).

The Master of Science in Information Technology (MSIT) at Bentley College, introduced in the fall of 2001, is built upon the object-oriented paradigm, with Sun's Java platform providing the technical foundation. Formerly, the first programming course was taught in Microsoft® Visual Basic® 6.0, an object-based language. This paper focuses on the transition to teaching the first programming course in Java.

Many of our students have little or no programming experience. Java can be a difficult language to learn for several reasons, including the complexity of its extensive class libraries; the instability of the Java platform, which is updated on a regular basis, often with significant changes to the language itself; the lack of standard methods for reading keyboard input; and a hard-to-use graphics model (Roberts, 2001). Yet, Java is in many ways less complex than C and C++, to which it bears a strong surface resemblance. This is largely due to the lack of pointers, which is a major stumbling block for students (Mehic & Hasan, 2001). Advantages for students learning Java include automatic garbage collection and the use of String objects rather than the null-terminated arrays of characters found in C/C++. In addition, Java was designed from the start as an object-oriented language and has all of the advantages inherent to this paradigm, including the reusability of objects, flexibility and extensibility from inheritance and polymorphism, and enhanced reliability and modifiability from encapsulation.

Proactive ways were sought to combat the anticipated high level of frustration for novice programmers enrolled in this course. Choices made concerning the course Web site, the student support structure, course content, how to deal with increasingly complex topics, and the frequency and difficulty of programming assignments, were critical to the success of this course.

This chapter describes the choices that were made and presents their effects. The next section describes key issues associated with introducing Java to the curriculum and summarizes related research on this topic. This is followed by a description of the object-oriented programming course introduced at Bentley College in the fall of 2001. Results of a survey given to all the students in this course were presented and compared to results from a similar survey given to students in the predecessor course taught in Visual Basic. Survey results are then discussed, followed by concluding remarks on the successful transition to Java in a first programming course.

BACKGROUND

The Java object-oriented programming language was developed at Sun Microsystems in 1991 for use in consumer electronics devices, such as television sets and VCRs (Lemay

& Perkins, 1996). It therefore needed to be small and portable. While the language has grown in size with each new release, the Java virtual machine (JVM) continues to ensure implementation-independent code that can be run under a variety of operating systems. Coupling this capability with the ability to run Java applets from Web pages was what first attracted interest in the language when it was initially released in 1995. Since that time, Java has developed into a general-purpose language used throughout enterprise-wide distributed applications with multitiered architectures.

While Java has gained acceptance and widespread use in industry, it has also made inroads into academia. It is now taught extensively in intermediate programming courses, but its inclusion in introductory courses has been more problematic due to inherent difficulties in the language. Biddle & Tempero (1997) described the benefits and problems with teaching Java as the first programming course. Among the promises of Java is that it is a simple language to learn, but in fact, this claim cannot be strongly supported. Unlike C/C++, it does not support multiple inheritance, but it allows classes to extend multiple interfaces. This is a similar concept to multiple inheritance and is difficult for beginning programmers to understand. It is true that Java does not permit pointer arithmetic and hides pointers from the user, but beginning programmers must understand the concept of references in order to work with objects and arrays. Thus, novices are presented with implicit pointers early on. While C/C++ programmers must understand memory management (or suffer the consequences), Java provides automatic memory management in the form of a garbage collector. In this respect, Java truly is simpler than C/C++. Other difficulties with using Java include the fact that a large number of methods in the class library throw exceptions that must be caught or passed to a caller, library documentation is often ambiguous, and the encapsulation model is actually more complicated than that of C++. In conclusion, they find that Java is only marginally better than C++ as a language for teaching beginning programmers, but that its popularity, availability, and standard libraries help tilt the balance in its favor.

Given that Java is not really so simple after all, some, such as Mehic & Hasan (2001), chose not to teach this language at the introductory level. An alternative approach aimed at reducing difficulties associated with teaching Java as a first language is to limit student exposure to some of the language's complexities. The "Introduction to Programming" course at Georgia Institute of Technology was taught using Java for the first time in the fall of 1996 (Hong, 1998). Previously, this had been a procedural programming course that used Pascal. Hong pointed out the importance of teaching programming *with* Java, as opposed to teaching programming *in* Java. This is a significant distinction, because it is more important for students to learn the fundamentals of programming, which remain constant, than the ins and outs of a particular language. Hong also identified several problems encountered with teaching programming using Java. One of the most difficult of these is the Java syntax, which makes it possible to combine several complex concepts into one deceptively simple statement. Students were shielded from some of this complexity by starting with skeleton programs in which they filled in the code, using driver programs for the first few assignments so that they could focus on the basic syntax without handling input, and using input routines that caught errors for them. Because Java's Abstract Windowing Toolkit (AWT), which contains classes for creating user interfaces, is difficult to use and Java-specific (as opposed to exposing students to general programming concepts), its use was held off until the end of the quarter. The greatest problem was not with Java itself, or even limited to object-oriented programming, but with teaching students to design good programs. This was tackled by letting the students learn by example and by using a system tentatively called the Educational Software Process (ESP), which teaches industry best practices and has students assess their own processes in order to learn from their mistakes.

Roberts (2001) also pointed out a number of weaknesses in teaching Java at the introductory level, including the size of the language and its libraries, the instability of its platform, the complexity of input operations, the forced use of exception handling for even simple programs, the need for wrapper classes to represent primitive types as objects, and a graphics model that is difficult to teach in introductory courses. To combat these problems, Roberts described the use of the MiniJava environment, which contains a subset of the standard Java release along with simplifying enhancements that make it easier to use. MiniJava has only 17 classes in its standard core, as opposed to over 2600 in version 1.4 of the Java 2 Platform, Standard Edition (J2SE v1.4), does not allow the use of inner classes, limits the variety of control statements, and treats all values, even primitives, as objects. MiniJava also provides a console window that reads and evaluates expressions from the user and prints the result, and an interactive graphical environment. Once students become proficient in the programming concepts, they can then work without these simplifications.

Kölling and Rosenberg (2000) noted that Java development environments are often designed for professional programmers and have a steep learning curve for novice programmers. In addition, most do not take an object-oriented approach, forcing users to deal with files and directories rather than classes, objects, and relationships. The BlueJ Java development environment (available free of charge from http://www.bluej.org/) was specifically designed with teaching in mind (Kölling & Rosenberg, 2000; Sanders, Heeler, & Spradling, 2001). It provides an easy-to-use interface with customizable templates for class skeletons, and lets the user instantiate objects and test methods without having to write a driver program. Kölling and Rosenberg (2001) used the BlueJ system in class during three semesters of an introductory object-oriented programming course. Because it is designed specifically for beginners, students were able to use BlueJ competently after a brief tutorial. The system supports an "objects first" approach, as it works around the need for a main method by letting students interact directly with classes and objects. It also provides visual representations that help students understand the relationship between classes and objects, and supports student experimentation, thereby promoting frequent and early testing of code.

All of the above examples describe the use of Java in introductory programming courses for computer science (CS) students. Little research exists on the use of Java as a first programming language in graduate information systems (IS) or information technology (IT) programs. While we face a number of the same issues that have been described here, there are differences between IT Masters-level students and undergraduate CS majors that affect the delivery of Java in an introductory programming course. For IS and IT students, their first programming course may well be the only one they take. In addition, many of these students have significant work experience and expect to see environments and applications that reflect what they have been exposed to in the workplace. Some of the students may have extensive procedural programming experience, some may have had exposure to object-oriented concepts, and others may never have programmed before. While the lessons learned from introductory CS courses provided valuable guidance, it was necessary to take the differences inherent to graduate IT students into account when designing the course described next.

OBJECT-ORIENTED PROGRAMMING COURSE

The graduate-level object-oriented programming course within the MSIT program of the Computer Information Systems (CIS) Department at Bentley College was taught for the first time in the fall of 2001 to 58 Masters students in three sections. There are no prerequisites, as this is one of three foundation courses that all incoming MSIT students must take. Most of the enrolled students did not have significant prior programming experience. On a scale from one (*novice/beginner*) to seven (*expert*), the average student experience level was 3.14 ± 1.78. Figure 1 shows the distribution of these self-rankings.

Given the generally low level of programming experience, a proactive approach was taken to support students in what for many was their first exposure to programming.

Following are descriptions of choices that were made for enhancing the learning experience without adding to student anxiety about learning to program in Java.

Supporting Materials

An early and critical decision concerned which integrated development environment (IDE) to use in this course. After extensive trials with a number of environments, the Borland® JBuilder IDE was selected due to the strength of its built-in help facilities and its tools for writing, running, and debugging code. While it can be confusing at first, JBuilder is easier to use than most of the professional environments used in industry (Savitch, 2001). Plus, several students expressed interest in working with JBuilder because it was being used in their own work environments.

JBuilder was installed on the computers in all of the technology classrooms and in the student computer labs. Students could also download their own copies from the Web for use on their personal computers, but were encouraged to try JBuilder first in the CIS Department's student lab, where student assistants were available to help them. Students were shown how

Figure 1. Self-ranking of prior programming experience

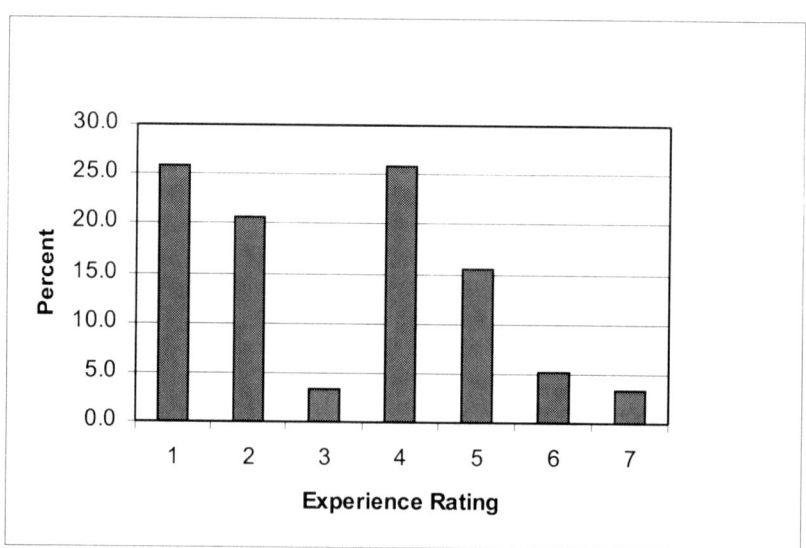

to use the debugger in the classroom, and JBuilder was used in class throughout the term for demonstrating programs as well as writing, compiling, and running new code examples.

A review of several textbooks led to the selection of "Computing with Java: Programs, Objects, and Graphics" by Gittleman (2001). This book was chosen due to its in-depth coverage of critical course concepts, the clarity of its text, and its frequent and easy to follow code examples.

Students were also provided with weekly lecture notes, available from the course Web site (http://cis.bentley.edu/cs603/wlucas/web603). These notes, which were projected during lectures, limited the amount of writing students needed to do. Students could therefore focus on understanding the concepts being discussed and on working through the many programming problems presented during the class.

In addition to lecture notes, the course Web site provided access to all assignments and individualized grades and comments on those assignments, source code for programs written or discussed during the lecture, and links to relevant sites, such as Java's class libraries. The site was created specifically for this course, following the design used successfully in previous courses (Lucas & Frydenberg, 2000).

Course Organization

The course was organized as a weekly two-hour and 15-minute lecture with 10 programming assignments, a midterm exam, and a final exam. Lectures followed the topics covered in the text and in the notes that students printed from the Web site prior to coming to class. These notes included sample code along with related problems to try in class. Some of these problems were worked on individually, while others were tackled by the entire class. In addition, a practice problem was distributed during each lecture for students to work on individually. The instructor would walk around the classroom to see the various approaches being taken and to speak with the students. Then, either the instructor (earlier in the term) or a student (later in the term) would type a completed solution into the classroom computer using JBuilder's editor. Everyone would watch to see if the code compiled and ran correctly. It was often most educational when one of these processes failed and the class would have to determine how to correct the errors. The instructor was also able to comment on the effectiveness and efficiency of the various approaches taken by members of the class.

The primary purpose of the 10 programming assignments given throughout the 15-week course was to reinforce the concepts covered in the lecture and written materials. Assignments were to be completed on an individual basis, with stiff penalties imposed for failure to comply with the stated and posted academic honesty policy. Rather than discussing assignments with others in the class, students were strongly advised to seek the help of lab assistants for questions involving syntax or environmental issues, or the instructor for more complex questions.

The first seven assignments were one week in length and were primarily logic intensive. Short, focused assignments forced the students to stay up to date with the material and to put into practice what they had been learning. For the first assignment, students were required to use Sun's Java™2 SDK software from a DOS shell program along with a text editor of their choice. This exposed the students to the concepts of compilers, byte code, and the JVM. Help facilities within this environment are limited, and compiler and runtime errors are often difficult to interpret. Students were then required to complete the second assignment using JBuilder. Subsequent assignments could be completed using the environment of their choice.

The last three assignments were each two weeks in length and encouraged creativity and investigation of Java's class libraries. Assignments accounted for 30% of each student's grade. Midterm and final exams made up 30 and 35%, respectively, of the class grade, and each were given for a full class period. The remaining 5% of the grade was for class participation.

Course Content

The content of lectures and assignments began at a rudimentary level and increased in complexity throughout the semester. Most of the course focused on server-side applications rather than client-side applets, as the latter require an understanding of a predefined startup sequence of method calls, system-defined and system-passed arguments, and inheritance that is gained as the course progresses. In addition, applets are most typically run from a browser, which will have its own interpreter that may or may not support the latest version of Java. This leads to a high probability for user frustration that is best held off until students are more prepared to cope with it.

The first few weeks of the course focused on basic programming concepts, with students getting minimal exposure to Java's class libraries. Topics covered included data types, operators, and control structures. Following the approach taken in Gittleman (2001), a component from Java's Swing class was used for keyboard input, with detailed explanations of the component and the package containing it held off until later in the course.

Class and object concepts were first introduced using built-in classes (namely, the Math and String classes), as well as arrays, which are defined as objects in Java. User-defined classes came next, followed by the object-oriented concepts of inheritance, polymorphism, encapsulation, and abstract and interface classes. Additional topics included dynamic data structures, exception handling, and file I/O.

Students were first guided through Java's class libraries and then, as the weeks progressed, encouraged to explore the libraries to find classes and methods for use in assignments. In the last few weeks of the course, graphics and event handling were taught using applets.

SURVEY RESULTS

Midway through the first semester of the new MSIT programming course, a total of 58 students from all three sections filled out a survey in which they were asked to rank their prior programming experience (as previously remarked upon), the degree of difficulty of the course, the helpfulness of JBuilder, of the course Web site, and of the textbook, and the amount of time spent on the course each week. A total of 143 students from six preceding semesters of the programming course taught using Visual Basic (VB) had filled out a similar survey. In the following sections, results of the Java survey are presented and contrasted to results from the VB survey whenever possible.

Supporting Materials

The use of JBuilder was only required for the second assignment, yet the majority of students (86%) continued using this IDE for subsequent assignments. The average rating of JBuilder was 5.57 ± 1.25 on a seven-point scale ranging from one (*no value*) to seven (*high value*). Figure 2 shows the distribution.

Figure 2. Student ranking of JBuilder

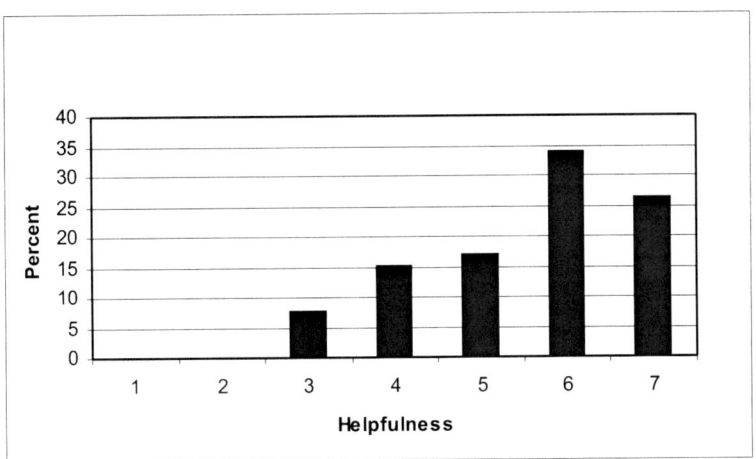

The average rating of the text on the same seven-point scale was 4.59 ± 1.57, and the overall helpfulness of the course Web site was 6.02 ± 0.98. Distributions are shown in Figures 3 and 4, respectively.

Course Content

The average difficulty of the course was rated on a seven-point scale as 4.79 ± 1.14, where *one* represents *not challenging*, and *seven* represents *very demanding*. Figure 5 contrasts the difficulty ratings to those for the prior programming course taught in VB. The average difficulty rating for the VB course was 4.69 ± 1.15. The mean difference between the two groups is not significant.

Figure 3. Student ranking of the textbook

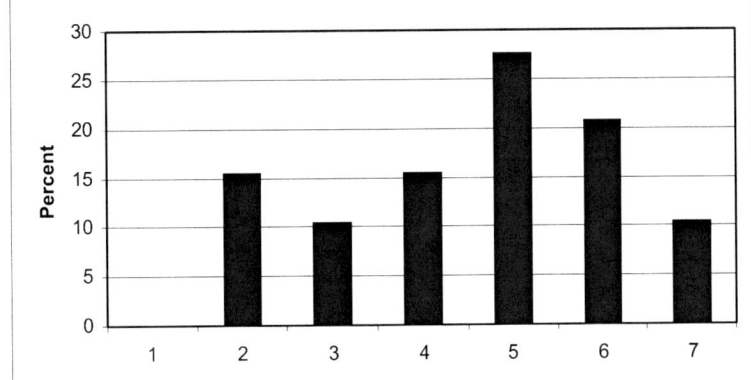

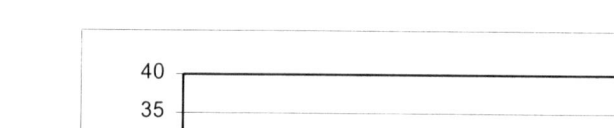

Figure 4. Student ranking of course Web site

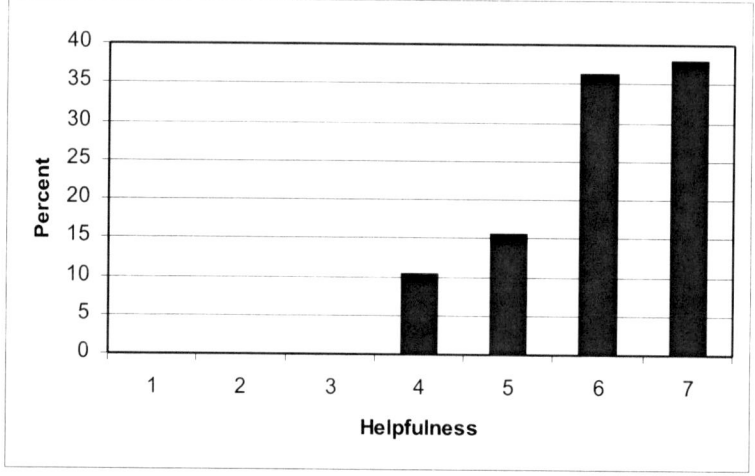

The mean difference in perceived difficulty for students in the Java course with prior programming experience versus those without is significant at the 0.05 level. Figure 6 shows this relationship, where *little* experience refers to those who rated their experience as a one or a two, *somewhat* refers to those in the three to five range, and *very* includes those with a rating of six or seven.

The average number of hours worked per week was 8.24 ± 4.62, while the average for the VB course had been 6.59 ± 4.35. The mean difference between the two is significant at the 0.05 level. There was also a significant difference between means for those students with prior

Figure 5. Comparison of VB course difficulty to Java course difficulty

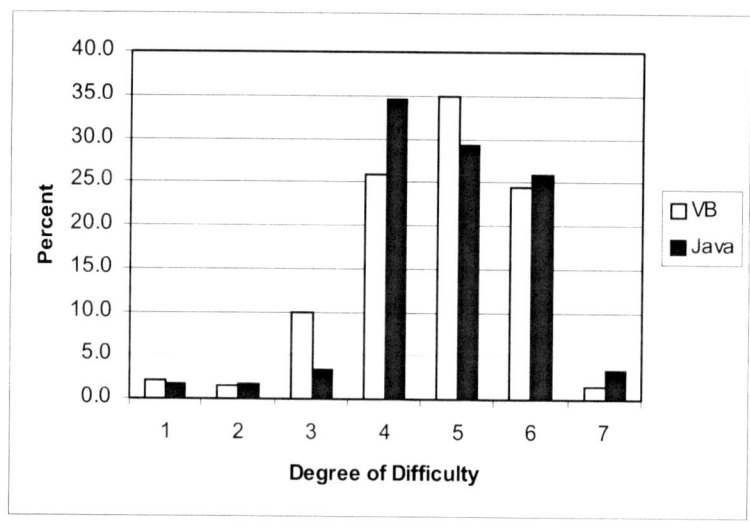

Figure 6. Java course difficulty as a function of prior experience

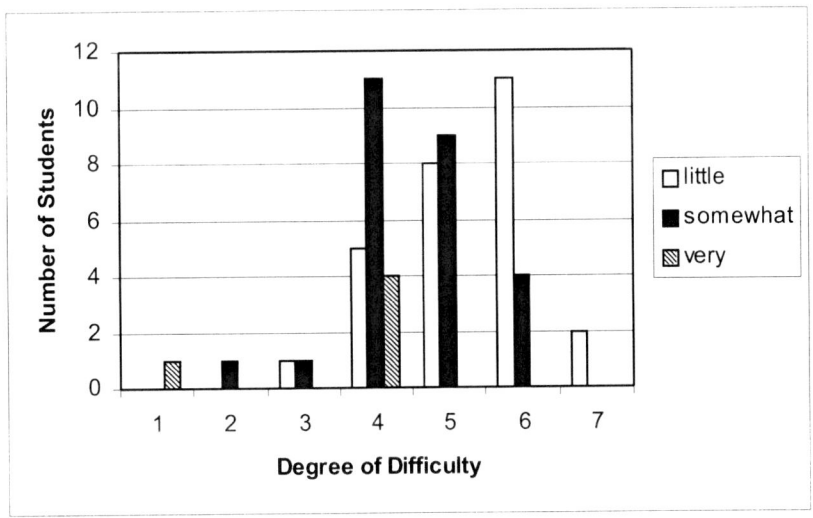

experience versus those without. Figure 7 illustrates these differences, using the same categorizations as in Figure 6.

DISCUSSION

Students were in general pleased with the supporting materials provided for this course. Ratings of JBuilder plus comments from students throughout the term indicated positive feelings about the environment. In addition, many students quickly learned how to use the debugging tools and were observed to make good use of them.

The course Web site was highly valued, and students consistently printed the lecture notes prior to coming to class. While the textbook received a lower average rating with more variation in responses than JBuilder or the Web site, it should be noted that students are not typically enthusiastic about technically oriented textbooks, so that an average of 4.59 out of 7 can be considered a positive result.

Students in the programming course taught with Java did not find the degree of difficulty to be significantly different from those in the course taught with VB. This is supported by the fact that there were not noticeable differences in the number of students seeking help from lab assistants or instructors or in the grades on assignments and exams for these two courses. While students with prior programming experience found the course to be less challenging than those without, it should be noted that the survey was distributed before many of the more advanced object-oriented concepts had been introduced. As the course proceeded, even those students with prior procedural programming experience had difficulty with some of these concepts, based on their performance on assignments and the final exam. This lends support to Mehic and Hasan (2001), who found that prior procedural language experience could actually create an obstacle for students learning object-oriented design.

Figure 7. Hours worked in Java course as a function of prior experience

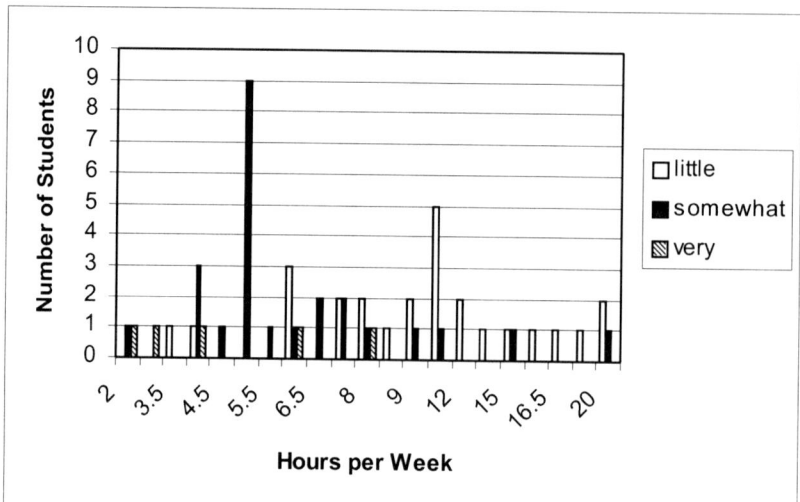

CONCLUSION

There are several factors that led to the successful implementation of this Java course. Students particularly liked the frequent programming assignments, which reinforced their understanding of course material. Earlier assignments covering the fundamentals of programming boosted confidence in their ability to write functioning code. Those successes helped students maintain a positive attitude when the level of complexity increased due to the introduction of more advanced object-oriented concepts. The incremental dependence upon Java's class libraries also helped students learn to navigate the extensive documentation without becoming overwhelmed.

Holding off on introducing applets until after covering object-oriented concepts enhanced the students' ability to understand the code. In addition, they were able to differentiate between logical errors and environmentally caused ones, which would have stymied them earlier in the course. Students enjoyed working with event-driven, visual interfaces, ending the course on an upbeat note.

The support structure for the students definitely had a positive impact on their impression of the course, with lab assistants being a key component from students' and instructors' perspectives. While they were not allowed to give solutions, their help in debugging code and deciphering error messages was greatly valued. JBuilder's debugging environment was also useful for the students, and the IDE as a whole was well received. Finally, access to lecture notes, code, and grades with comments from the course Web site was most appreciated and contributed to the positive view of the course held by most of the students.

One negative aspect to this course from the instructors' perspective was the tremendous amount of grading. For this reason, we are currently working on an automated testing system to which students will be able to submit their assignments. The benefits of frequent programming assignments to reinforce learning cannot be overstated and will therefore continue to be a major component of this course. They, in conjunction with a carefully structured and well thought-out curriculum and a strong support structure, made the transition to an object-oriented programming language in an IT Masters program a success.

REFERENCES

Biddle, R., & Tempero, E. (1997). *Learning Java: Promises and pitfalls.* Paper presented at the 14th Uniforum NZ Conference.

Gittleman, A. (2001). *Computing with Java: Programs, objects, graphics* (2nd ed.). El Granada, CA: Scott/Jones, Inc.

Gorgone, J. T., & Gray, P. (Eds.). (2000). *Model curriculum and guidelines for graduate degree programs in information systems*: Joint ACM/AIS Task Force on Graduate IS Curriculum.

Hong, J. (1998). The use of Java as an introductory programming language. *ACM Crossroads, Summer, 1998.*

Jordan, R., Smilan, R., & Wilkinson, A. (1994). *Streamlining the project cycle with object-oriented requirements.* Paper presented at the Ninth Annual Conference on Object-Oriented Programming Systems, Language, and Applications, Portland, OR.

Kölling, M., & Rosenberg, J. (2000). *Objects first with Java and BlueJ.* Paper presented at the 31st SIGCSE Technical Symposium on Computer Science Education.

Kölling, M., & Rosenberg, J. (2001). *Guidelines for teaching object orientation with Java.* Paper presented at the Sixth Annual Conference on Innovation and Technology in Computer Science Education, Canterbury, United Kingdom.

Lemay, L., & Perkins, C. L. (1996). *Teach yourself Java in 21 days* (1st ed.). Indianapolis, IN: Sams.net.

Lim, B. L. (1998). *Teaching Web development technologies in CS/IS curricula.* Paper presented at the 29th SIGCSE Technical Symposium on Computer Science Education.

Lucas, W. T., & Frydenberg, M. (2000). *Enhanced learning with personalized course pages.* Paper presented at the 11th International Conference of the Information Resources Management Association, Alaska.

Mehic, N., & Hasan, Y. (2001). *Challenges in teaching Java technology.* Paper presented at the Informing Science Conference, Krakow, Poland.

Roberts, E. (2001). *An overview of MiniJava.* Paper presented at the 32nd SIGCSE Technical Symposium on Computer Science Education, Charlotte, NC.

Sanders, D., Heeler, P., & Spradling, C. (2001). Introduction to BlueJ. *The Journal of Computing in Small Colleges, 16*(3).

Savitch, W. (2001). Using JBuilder, *Java: An Introduction to Computer Science and Programming* (2nd ed., p. 1027). New York: Prentice Hall.

Chapter V

Analysis of Learner Performance on a Tutoring System for Java

Henry H. Emurian
University of Maryland–Baltimore County, USA

Jingli Wang
University of Maryland–Baltimore County, USA

Ashley G. Durham[1]
Centers for Medicare & Medicaid Services (CMS), USA

ABSTRACT

This chapter presents a teaching methodology, programmed instruction, that provides a series of interactive and cumulative learning experiences that teach a student how to understand and write a simple Java Applet. Fine-grain performance records of three students' interactions with the tutoring system show the individual patterns of skill acquisition and retention over five successive observational occasions. The tutoring system is also used as the first technical exercise in a course entitled "Graphical User Interface Systems Using Java." Performance and self-reported ratings of programming confidence by 17 graduate students show the benefit of programmed instruction to generate a history of competency and confidence in all students. The positive initial experience prepares and motivates information systems students for the presentation and mastery of advanced programming techniques.

INTRODUCTION

The purpose of this chapter is to demonstrate student learning and retention on components of a Web-based tutoring system that teaches a Java Applet within the framework of a competency model of instructional design: programmed instruction. The objective of the tutoring system is to provide an initial and positive learning experience for information systems students who may lack a background in computer programming. The learning experience is intended to foster a student's tested competency in writing and understanding a simple Java Applet. The teaching objective is accomplished within a learning framework that is intended to generate a history of symbol manipulation and understanding within the context of a tutoring system that offers structured rehearsal to a criterion of mastery. The use of the system is also intended to produce a positive affective experience for the learner. Finally, the tutoring system is designed to be used only as the introductory laboratory in a technically oriented course in which subsequent classes are taught by lecture, supervised laboratory, and collaboration formats.

The instructional model is based upon programmed instruction, which combines teaching, practice, and competency testing within a single conceptual framework, and it assures the achievement of a criterion of mastery at the level of the individual student (e.g., Anger et al., 2001; Holland, 1960; Scriven, 1969; Skinner, 1958). The examples to be presented in this chapter build upon our previous work (Emurian et al., 2000; Emurian & Durham, 2001; Emurian & Durham, in press) that provides a pedagogical context and rationale for the adoption of programmed instruction approaches for technical training in information technology.

BACKGROUND

Computer programming appears in the recommendations for core courses in several curriculum guidelines for the academic discipline of information systems.[2] The activity of constructing and understanding a computer program has been extensively investigated in the literature, and the complexity of current end-user applications suggests the relevance of that research to general issues of approaches to information technology education and software training (Bannert & Reimann, 2000). Early work in this area of research emphasized the conditions that promote a learner's exploratory mastery of logical constructions and flow of control (Papert, 1980). Research perspectives related to classroom teaching and student learning of computer programming were later addressed by Mayer (1988), and the activity of constructing and comprehending a computer program and command sequences continues to be investigated (e.g., Altmann, 2001; Campbell, Brown, & DiBello, 1992; Sohn & Doane, 1997; Soloway, 1985; Van Merrienboar & Paas, 1990). It is the case, perhaps, that the impact of this stream of research has yet to be realized in the classroom, as evidenced by the adoption of new teaching methods by computer programming instructors.

A similar situation may exist with respect to investigations of training for end-user computing applications. For example, some approaches to the development of interface software tools are relevant to suggesting prerequisite competencies for learning an advanced tool (Myers, Hudson, & Pausch, 2000), and learning effective strategies may help users to optimize performance on software tools (Bhavnani & John, 2000). Moreover, the training literature has begun to show appreciation of the potential impact on learning of the trainer's personal style (Compeau, 2002) and the motivation of learners to acquire new skills (Ryan,

1999). However, studies evaluating alternative approaches to training for end-user computing applications typically employ post-training tests to assess the comparative effectiveness of various methods, such as lectures, self-paced manuals, and behavior modeling (Simon et al., 1996) and exploration and instruction (Davis & Bostrom, 1993). Although this literature, together with the computer programming literature, may offer suggestions for structuring the presentation of information and problems to groups of learners, individual differences in such factors as prior experience, motivation, and learning skills must be invoked to account for learning outcomes that differ among the students. Alternatively, a focus on the individual learner interacting with a tutoring system as a generic "teacher" might be anticipated to offer benefits similar to those of a human tutor, where the objective is for the learner to attain a given level of competency at the conclusion of a learning episode (Bloom, 1984).

Although guidelines to structure an entire course in Java have been published (e.g., Stiller & LeBlanc, 2001), it is the content that was emphasized, not the manner in which students should be taught and assessed. In contrast, the present tutoring system design is based upon principles that have yet to be applied and evaluated widely in computer-based instructional systems having practical value in the classroom (cf. Anderson et al., 1995). Rather than focusing on group outcomes as the only unit of analysis, the work reported in this chapter first reveals the process of teaching and learning at the level of the individual student. This is accomplished by analyses of the rate of three learners' correct input, response errors, and help requests on the tutoring system, all portrayed graphically as a function of time in cumulative records. The purpose is to reveal the details of a learner's disciplined study behavior in achieving mastery of the subject Java Applet. Next, we show the application of the tutoring system to a class of students, and we present performance data and ratings of the tutoring experience and self-efficacy.

LEARNING OBJECTIVES

The overall objective of the tutoring system is to teach a learner to construct a stream of up to 36 Java items (i.e., atomic units, elements, items, or symbols) that together constitute a Java computer program that displays a text string in a Netscape© browser window. The approach taken is first to specify the learning objectives, which are as follows:

1.   Understand the meaning of each item of code as evidenced by passing a multiple-choice test that is administered following the display of an explanation of the item.
2.   Enter the item into a key-in field by recall.
3.   Understand the meaning of one to several items that are presented in a row of code, as evidenced by passing a multiple-choice test on each of 10 rows of code.
4.   Enter the row of items into a key-in field by recall.
5.   Enter the entire program into a text window by recall.

The objectives are accomplished by a learner's interactions with the tutor in a series of incremental steps that progress to these objectives by the method of successive approximation (Sulzer-Azaroff & Mayer, 1991). The outcome is the learner's correct production of the program together with tested mastery of the meaning of each of the elements and the interrelationships among those elements and similar mastery when the code is organized into rows. Explanations of the meanings of the items and rows include several general rules of object-oriented programming that are presented in the tutoring system.

Progressive increase in the learner's understanding and recall of the program is similar to the size of a *learn unit* approach suggested by Greer and McDonough (1999). Moreover, Swezey and Llaneras (1997) emphasized the importance of structured practice, which is a feature of the present tutoring system, as a critical factor in models of training. The full instruction set presented to the learner is available for observation within the online tutor, which is freely available for use.[3] Access to the tutoring system will show the source of data presented here, although the interfaces accessible on the Web are subject to updates, as they were for Study 2 in this chapter. The interfaces and operational details for Study 1, however, are fully explained in Emurian et al. (2000).

STUDY 1: INDIVIDUAL PERFORMANCE

The first study emphasized the detailed characterization of knowledge acquisition, testing, and retention in three students.[4] These students used the Web-based programmed instruction tutor to learn to write a Java Applet, which is a computer program than can run in a browser on the World Wide Web. The design of the tutoring system is a synthesis of principles of programmed instruction (Holland, 1960; Skinner, 1958), verbal behavior (Skinner, 1957), verbal learning and memory (Li & Lewandowsky, 1995), the elaboration theory of instruction (Mayer, 1981; Reigeluth & Darwazeh, 1982), practice and retention (Durham & Emurian, 1998), and instructional design (Tennyson & Elmore, 1997). The system bears similarities to those categorized by Federico (1999) as microtreatment approaches to adaptive instructional systems. These principles will be illustrated in the examples presented for Study 1 and Study 2.

Learning and Retention

Task completion and mastery were accomplished by the learner's correct input entered into the text editor emulation interface, which was the final interface in the tutor and the one into which the learner wrote the entire Java program. The performance measurements were taken on five separate occasions, where each of the first four occasions was spaced from five to seven days apart. During Sessions 2 through 5, the learner began each session with the item learning interface. At the conclusion of the fourth session, the learner ran the Applet as discussed below. The Applet was not run until the fourth session so that retention and relearning could be studied under standardized conditions involving only symbol manipulations. The running of the Applet involved discussions with the expert, and these discussions introduced factors that may have differed across the learners and that may be difficult to quantify. As a test of long-term retention, the learner repeated the tutor on a fifth occasion, which occurred at least 3 months after the fourth session. This procedure studied the behavior of three learners with a research version of the tutor, which time stamped each interactive event with the system into a logfile.

We studied the performance of three graduate students who volunteered for participation. These students were paid $10 for the first session and $5 for all other sessions. No student reported previous experience with Java. Two students reported *c* and *c++* experience, and one student reported *COBOL* experience. The age and sex of each student were as follows: S-1 (24, male); S-2 (26, female); S-3 (41, female). The third student, S-3, reported the *COBOL* experience.

Figures 1, 2, and 3 present detailed performance data for all three learners, respectively, across the five successive session occurrences. Each figure is a cumulative record of all interactive events that occurred during performance on the item interfaces and the serial stream interfaces. The day of each session is presented relative to the first session. The figures show that S-3 had the first four occurrences spaced apart seven days, and S-1 and S-2 had some session occurrences that were somewhat less than seven days apart. The performance data did not support learning outcome differences that could be attributable to these small differences in occurrence intervals over Sessions 1 through 4. The figures also show that the fifth session, which involved a fifth exposure to the tutor, occurred approximately three months following the fourth session for all learners.

The primary data of interest are **Item Correct** and **Stream Correct**. These entries refer to the correct input of individual Java items on the item interface and correct input on the serial stream interface, respectively. The serial stream interface required entering up to three successive items of code as a unit. The **Observe Item** dash reflects the selection of a pop-up window displaying the correct item input. The interpretation of these figures and those below would be assisted by the reader's use of the tutoring system.

Figure 1. Detailed performance data for S-1. Enter Correct = correct item input in the key-in field, Java = display the item, Line Correct = up to three items input correctly as a serial stream, and Explain = display an explanation of the item

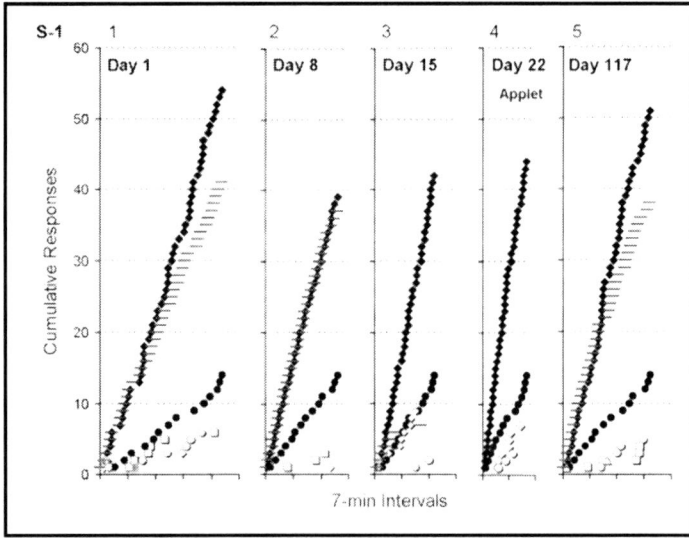

Figure 2. Detailed performance data for S-2

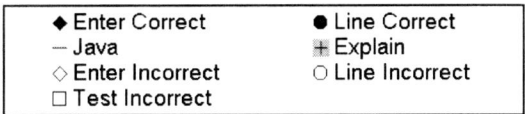

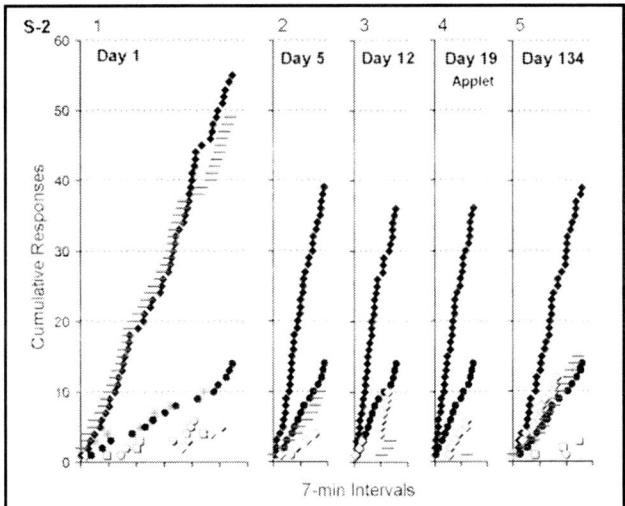

The figures show similarities and differences among the three learners. In general, the frequency of observing a Java item declined over the first four successive sessions for all learners. By the fourth session, only S-2 showed an observation of a Java item. The figures also showed that observing the Java items dropped between Sessions 1 and 2 for S-2 and S-3. In contrast, S-1 showed a continuous stream of such observations during Session 2. The figures also showed an increase in the rate of correct entries for the Java key-in items and serial streams across the first four sessions. By the fourth session, these rates appeared similar for all learners. However, performance was never error free. All learners showed errors even on the fourth session, although errors on the Java key-in item might be attributable to careless typing, which was corrected without additional support. The frequency of correct Java entries that sometimes exceeded 36 was attributable to repetitions of the item interface, when input on the serial stream interface was incorrect. With the exception of the data for S-2 on Day 1, the selection of the explanation (**Explain Item**) of the Java item was rarely observed for any subject. The interpretation of this finding led to the conclusion that the correct choices on the multiple-choice tests were obvious, and this prompted a revision of these tests.

The data in Figures 1 to 3 also show the performance degradation that occurred in Session 5, after the lengthy delay interval. All three learners showed errors on all interfaces, and they also showed selections to observe the Java item. These data indicate the forgetting that occurred after the delay interval, despite the previously documented mastery of the task and the repetitions that were programmed for the learners.

The performance data presented in Figures 1 to 3 also indicated that one instance of completing the tutor presented an incomplete index of the state of the learner's knowledge and competency. All learners showed performance improvement across the first four session occurrences and performance degradation in Session 5. This suggests that performance stability, as evidenced in Session 4, may be a more important index of the readiness to learn new material immediately than one single occasion of correct performance, which was required by the design of the tutoring system on the first and all subsequent session occurrences.

Figure 4 presents performance on the row interface and the text editor emulation interface for all three learners across the five successive session occurrences. Markers are omitted from the figure if all values were zero for a category. The row interface (Row-by-Row Responses) required three iterations, but the multiple-choice test was only presented during the first iteration. These data reveal similarities and differences among the three learners within and across successive sessions. The figure shows that the most pronounced improvement occurred during Session 1 for all learners. With the exception of errors in Session 2 for S-1, errors, hints, and reviews dropped to relatively low values by the third session. By the fourth session, errors and hints were very low for S-1 and S-2, and absent for S-3. However, incorrect test input was observed during Session 4 for S-2 and S-3. In Session 5, S-1 and S-2 showed errors, hint selections, and reviews that were similar in magnitude to the data in Sessions 1 and 2. Only S-3 showed no loss of performance in relationship to Session 4.

On the text editor emulation interface (Text Window Responses), all learners showed accurate input during Session 3 and Session 4, with no errors and no reviews. Incorrect input was observed during the first two sessions, but only S-3 selected a review, which occurred during Session 1. Interestingly, following the review, S-3 made no errors in Sessions 2 to 5. The burst of errors exhibited by S-2 during Session 1 indicated repeated attempts to correct an error, which was accomplished after seven errors. During Session 5, however, S-2 showed another incorrect entry, which was corrected without the selection of a review.

Figure 3. Detailed performance data for S-3

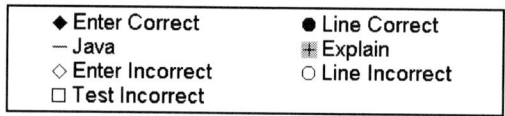

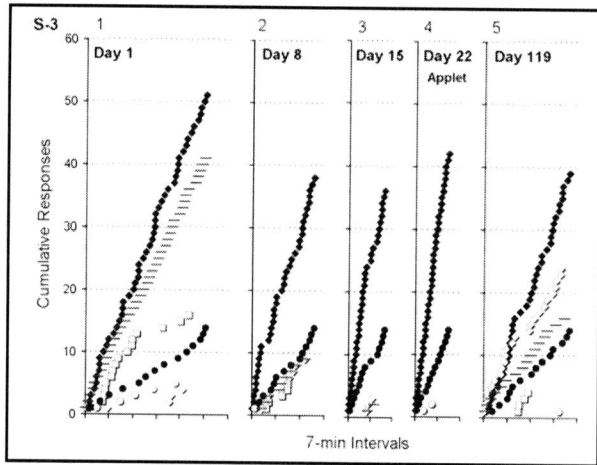

Figure 4. Performance on the row interface (Row-by-Row Responses) and the text editor emulation interface (Text Window Responses) for each learner

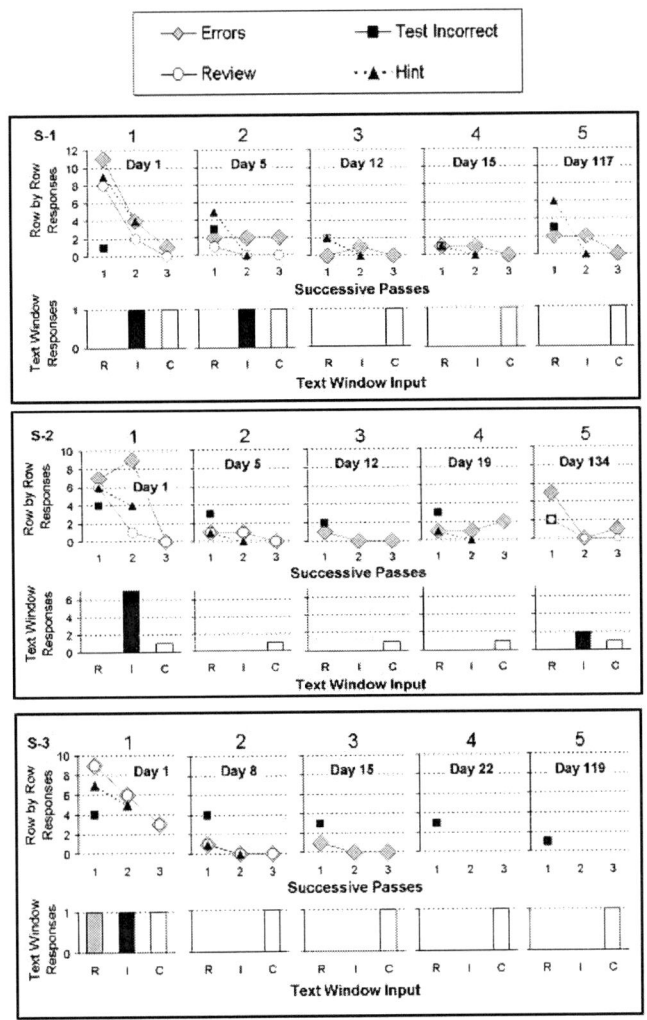

Task Completion

At the conclusion of the fourth session, the learner logged onto his or her Unix account. This part of the learning experience involved an interaction with an *expert*, who was one of the authors. The www tree was explained to the learner, who then typed the program into a file using a text editor that was available on the Unix platform. The compilation of the Java source code into a class file was then explained and demonstrated. Next, the expert explained the writing and use of an HTML file to start the Applet class file. The learner then used the Netscape© browser to access the URL, and the text string "This is my first program." was displayed in the browser window. All learners entered the code correctly into the Unix text editor. These events are similar to those used in the classroom.

Discussion

Three individual learners constructed a Java Applet from recall on five separate occasions, as the final performance requirement in a Web-based tutoring system. All learners showed performance improvement over the first four sessions. The most pronounced improvement was noticed between Session 1 and Session 2, a general outcome that is consistent with practice effects and the power function of learning (Lane, 1987; Wickens & Hollands, 2000, Chapter 7). Furthermore, each learner showed an idiosyncratic acquisition process that culminated in mastery of the Java code. It is the individual acquisition process that is often obscured by relying on group averages to characterize performance. However, the common features of learning, in terms of improvement over successive sessions, were similar to acquisition curves found in many different knowledge domains (Swezey & Llaneras, 1997). And the fact that all learners showed at least some forgetting between successive session occurrences, despite the accurate writing of the Java code at the conclusion of each session, indicated the importance of repetition in achieving a steady-state asymptote in performance on the task. Shute and Gawlick (1995) also demonstrated relearning of a task, after a 2-year delay interval, as an index of initial learning effectiveness. Additionally, the fine-grain data records over successive sessions may lend themselves to interpretation in terms of a power integration diffusion model of performance following breaks in learning (Sikstrom & Jaber, 2002). Finally, the pronounced drop in performance effectiveness that was observed during the fifth session suggested that even a well-practiced skill may suffer degradation if it is not regularly used.

STUDY 2: CLASSROOM PERFORMANCE

The validation of the tutoring system, by studying fine-grain performance with a small sample of learners, provided the occasion for adopting this approach in the classroom. Our subsequent research reported the classroom application of this programmed instruction tutoring system (Emurian & Durham, 2001). The latter research showed that experience with the tutoring system, together with subsequent classroom instruction, produced dependable improvements in students' self-reports of confidence in the use of Java symbols. It was the case, however, that the students' writing of an error-free Java Applet did not always carry over from the tutor to a later assessment occasion. In fact, only two of 12 learners observed in that study were able to write the program correctly immediately after completing the tutor. This outcome was observed despite the fact that one error-free production of the program was required to exit the tutor. Although the tutor presented explanations of the code, together with revised multiple-choice tests of the meaning of individual items of code and rows of code, a more robust transfer of training was anticipated between the tutor experience and subsequent transfer assessments of retention of the program.

Against that background, Study 2 within this chapter intended to show enhancements of student learning and retention of the Java Applet under consideration by using the previous classroom study results as a baseline for comparison. This approach to programmatic improvements follows the experimental design methodology of systematic replication (Sidman, 1960). In this research methodology, enhancements are undertaken to select independent variables under analysis with the objective to potentiate an effect that has practical rather than statistical significance. In the present circumstance, it is the objective of the enhancements to improve all students' constructions of an error-free Java program across four assessment occasions during a semester-long course. This approach also has the benefit of showing the generality of the prior findings, when the tutor is administered to a different group of learners, and of showing the reliability of the previous learning effects observed under a somewhat different, but related, set of conditions. These conditions constitute the enhancements to the tutoring system to be described below.

The program that was investigated in Study 2 was identical to the program presented in our previous classroom work (Emurian & Durham, 2001), with the modification that some atomic units (i.e., items) in the previous study were combined to yield 21 unique atomic units and 32 total atomic units. An atomic unit or item was the smallest Java symbol or group of symbols that was presented for learning and testing. For example, in the previous tutor, the *add* symbol and the (*myLabel*) symbol were separate items, and they were combined to *add*(*myLabel*) in the present version of the tutor. The rationale for that modification was to improve the explanatory text of an item by grouping a method name and its argument into a single item to be learned. Table 1 presents the atomic units as they were organized into 10 rows of code.

TUTORING SYSTEM INTERFACES

The learner progresses through the tutoring system in seven stages: (1) introduction, (2) item familiarity, (3) item identification, (4) item learning, (5) row familiarity, (6) row learning, and (7) program learning.

The Stage 1 introduction presents a general orientation of the tutoring system to the learner. Figure 5 presents three of the windows that are displayed in the introduction. There are no interactive interfaces in the introduction. The first two windows display the Java code and the HTML file, respectively. This is to allow the learner to observe the Java code that will be taught by the tutor. The HTML file is taught in the classroom. The bottom window displays the running Applet to show the learner what he or she will be able to produce after completing the tutor and participating in the subsequent classroom presentation. The latter presentation, administered on the immediately succeeding class period, includes a lecture discussion of the code, while the students enter the program in a Unix text editor. Compilation

Table 1. Units of code in the Applet; each cell is an atomic unit

Row 1	import	java.applet.Applet	;			
Row 2	import	java.awt.Label	;			
Row 3	public	class	MyProgram	extends	Applet	{
Row 4	Label	myLabel	;			
Row 5	public	void	init()	{		
Row 6	myLabel	=	new	Label("This is my first program.")	;	
Row 7	add(myLabel)	;				
Row 8	myLabel	.	setVisible(true)	;		
Row 9	}					
Row 10	}					

Figure 5. Three windows presented during the introduction stage. Top view = an overview of the Java program; middle view = an overview of the HTML file; and bottom view = the program running in a browser

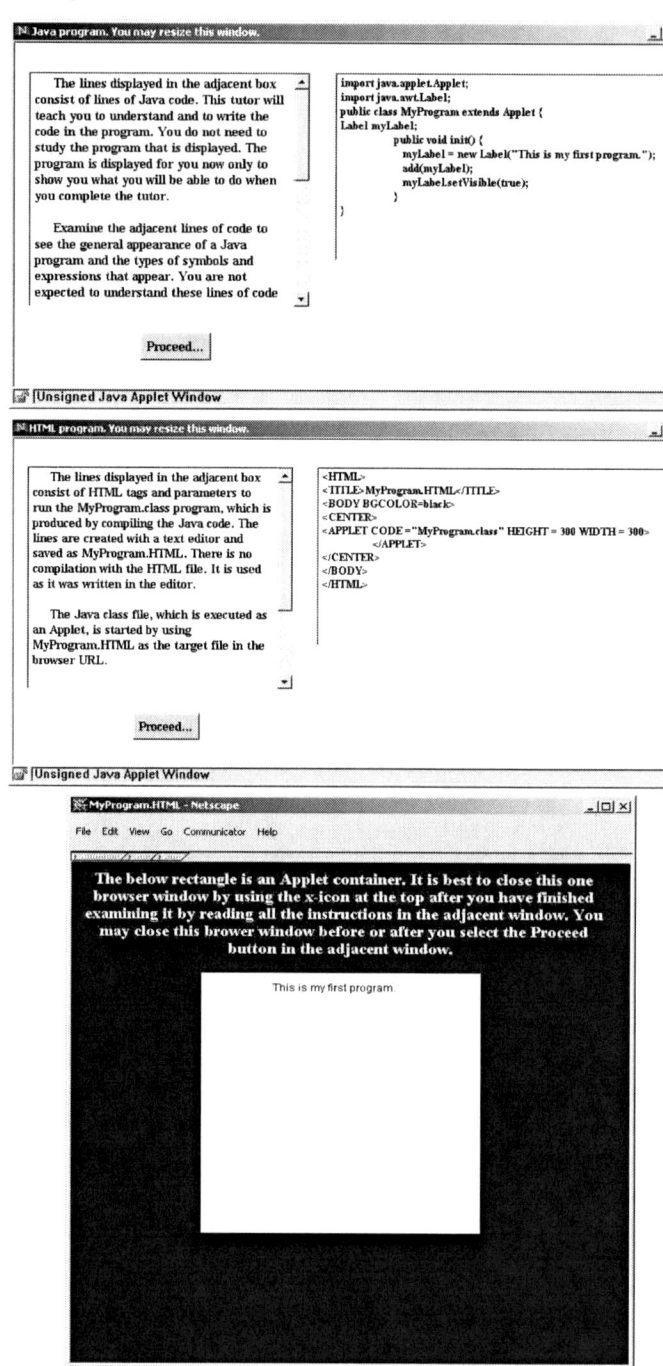

Figure 6. Top view = item familiarity interface showing the extends keyword displayed and entered into the key-in field. This is the first interactive interface in the tutoring system. Bottom view = item identification interface showing the extends keyword displayed for highlighting in the list of items

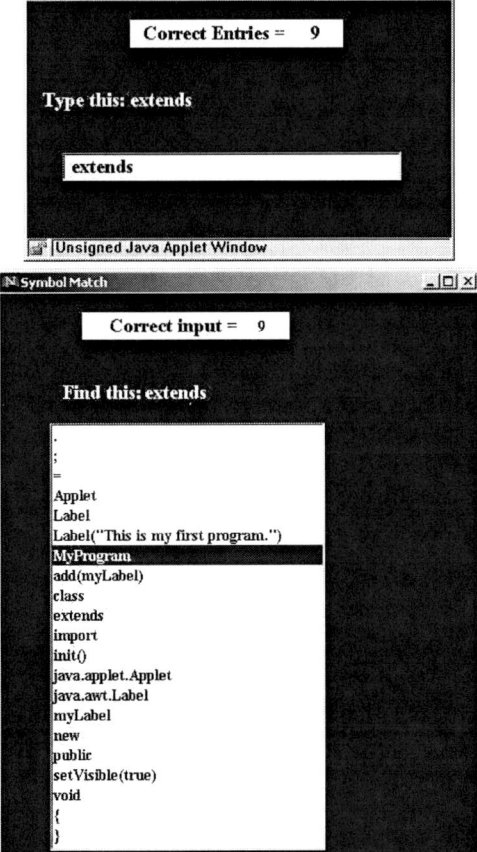

of the MyProgram.java file is explained, and the HTML file is taught. Students then run the Applet on the Web.

The Stage 2 item familiarity and the Stage 3 item identification interfaces are presented next, and these are interactive interfaces, as are all remaining interfaces in the tutoring system. Figure 6 presents these two interfaces as they would appear for the following Java keyword: extends.

Figure 6 (top view) displays the *item familiarity interface*, which is labeled Symbol Familiarity in the title bar. This interface is intended to give new learners the opportunity to rehearse the formal properties of the items prior to learning the meaning of the items. The learner is required to type the displayed item in the key-in field, and this action is repeated until the item is typed correctly. The purpose of this exercise is to help the learner develop a minimal transcription repertoire (Skinner, 1957) to facilitate subsequent learning of the meaning of the items. The order of the items rehearsed is exactly the same as the 32 items in the program, thereby affording the opportunity to acquire initial associative strength between successive items.

Figure 6 (bottom view) displays the *item identification* interface, which is labeled Symbol Match in the title bar. This interface is intended to provide the learner with the opportunity to rehearse discriminating the formal properties of the items in the program. The purpose of this exercise is to help the learner discern differences among the items, and this is a method of discrimination training (Catania, 1998). The learner is required to highlight the displayed item from the list of all items, and this action is required until the item is highlighted correctly. Similar to the *item familiarity* interface, the order of the items rehearsed in the *item identification* interface is the same as the 32 items in the program, thereby affording a second opportunity to acquire initial associative strength between successive items.

The Stage 4 *item interface* is presented next. Figures 7 through 10 present four *item interface* views, which are labeled Learn Java Items in the title bar of each view. Interactive

Figure 7. The item interface with the extends keyword displayed. In the tutor, the color of the item to be learned is blue to distinguish it from the previously learned items. The display of the item is generated by the user's selection of the "Show Java" button at the bottom of the interface. The next available step in the sequence is for the user to select the "Explain it" button, which is enabled, to see a window presenting the explanation of the item. The "Help" button is continuously available, and its selection displays a window explaining the functionality of the interface and buttons

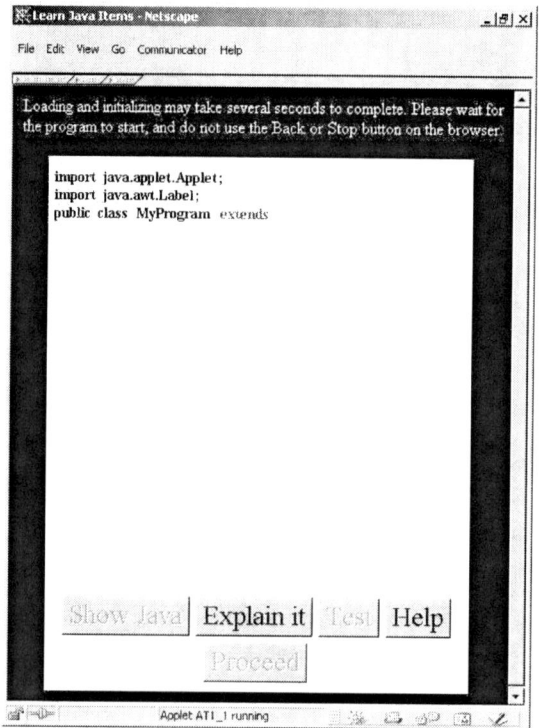

Figure 8. An explanation window for the extends keyword. The "Test" button is now enabled for the user to move to the next step in the sequence

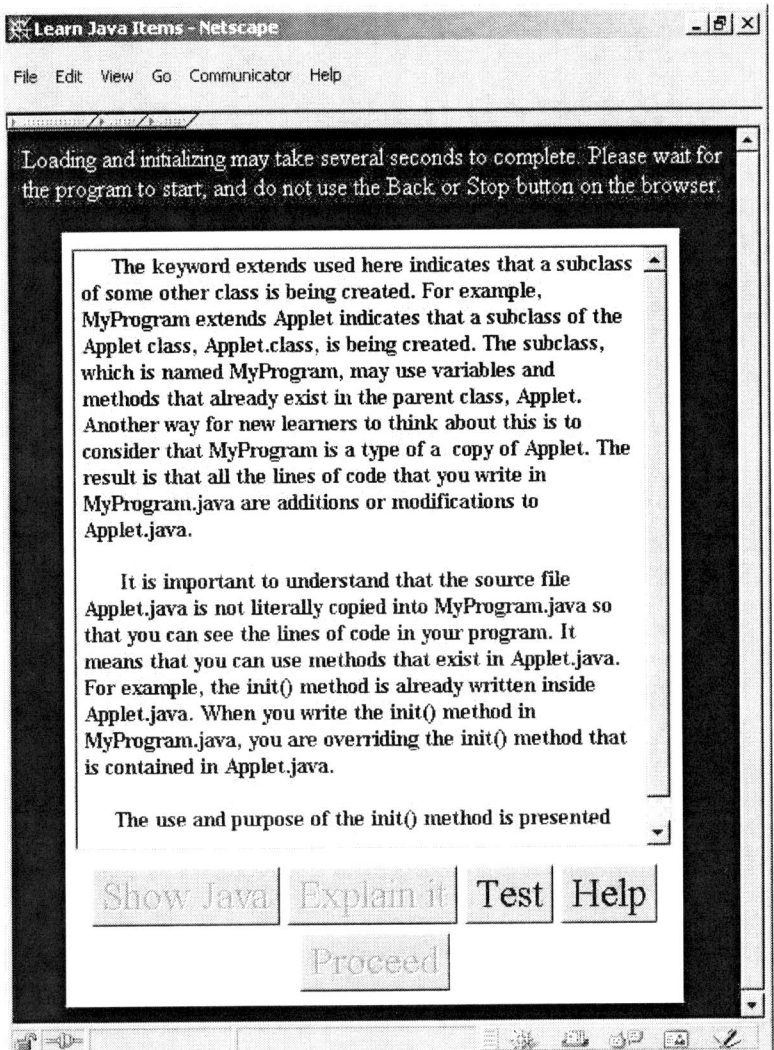

events are sequenced by the learner's use of the buttons at the bottom of the interface that are selectively enabled and disabled to regulate the learner's progress through this interface. First, the learner is shown the Java symbol to enter, which is displayed in Figure 7 for the Java keyword "extends." The color of an item displayed for learning is blue, and that item stands out from the remaining black items. Next are presented an explanation of the item (Figure 8) and a multiple-choice test on the item's meaning (Figure 9). When the learner enters the item correctly in a key-in box (Figure 10), the next item is displayed. Otherwise, the cycle repeats until the item under consideration is learned, which is determined by correctly answering the multiple-choice test followed by correctly typing the item into the key-in field by recall.

Figure 9. A multiple-choice test window for the extends keyword. If the answer is incorrect, the "Explain It" button is enabled, and the sequence repeats. If the answer is correct, the key-in field is presented for the learner to type the item by recall

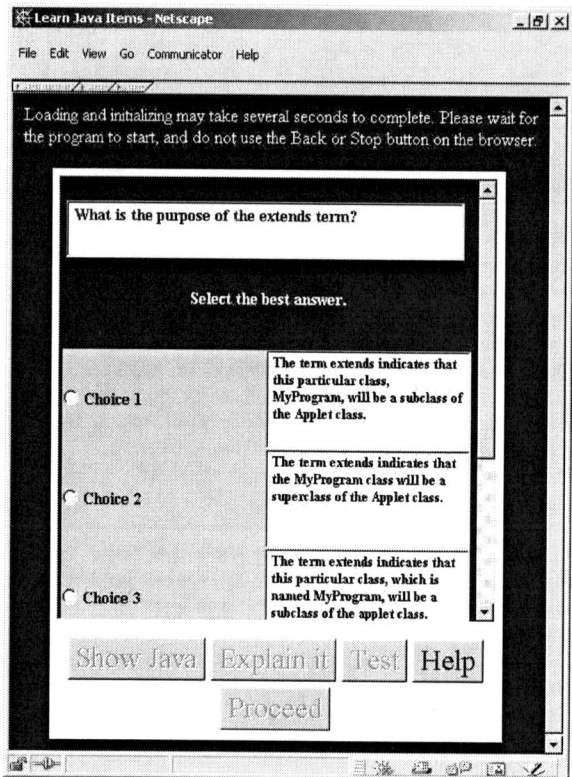

Next are presented the Stage 5 *row familiarity* interface and the Stage 6 *row* interfaces. Figure 11 (top view) presents a view of the *row familiarity* interface, which is labeled Row Symbol Familiarity in the title bar. The *row familiarity* interface is functionally similar to the *item familiarity* interface, except that the input is based on the rows of code rather than on the items of code. Figure 11 (bottom view) presents a view of the row interface with accurate code entered into each of the 10 rows. There are three successive iterations, or passes, through the row interfaces. The first pass is similar to the item interface. The task is for the learner to enter the code accurately in rows by recall. The learner may display the row code and keep attempting to input the row until it is entered correctly. Figure 12 (top view) presents a row explanation window, which displays the meaning of the code in a row. The multiple-choice test, displayed in Figure 12 (bottom view), appears after a row is entered correctly, and the cycle is functionally similar to the item interface. In the second pass through the row interface, there is no multiple-choice test, and there are no explanation windows. The learner, however, can still display the code in a row before trying to enter it or after making an error. Each row of code must be entered correctly by recall before moving to a succeeding row of code. The third pass requires the learner to enter all 10 rows accurately without displaying the code for any row. Whenever the learner selects to display the code in a row, all rows of

Figure 10. The item interface with the extends keyword typed into the key-in field. If the input is correct, the "Show Java" button is enabled for the next item to be learned. If the input is incorrect, the key-in field is cleared, and the "Show Java" button is enabled for the learner to repeat the sequence of steps for that item

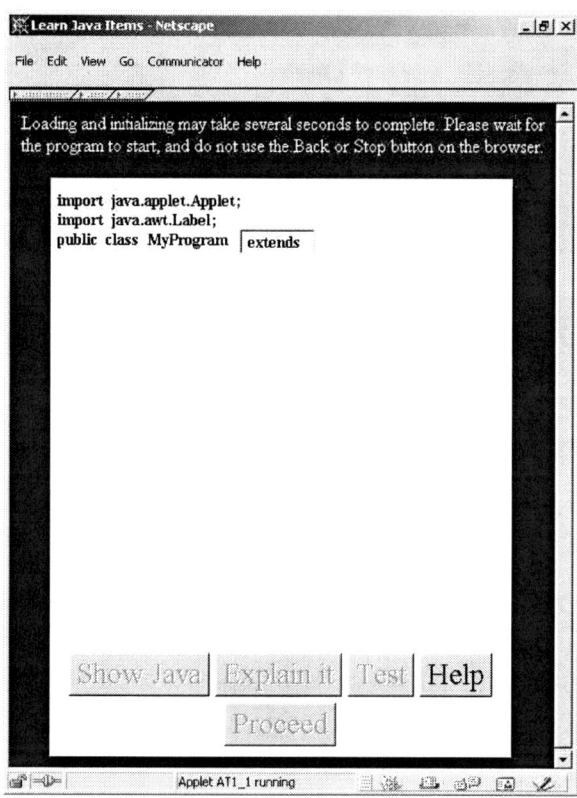

the interface are cleared, and the learner starts to enter the code again from the first row. This continues until all 10 rows are entered correctly without the learner displaying the code for any row. Buttons to control the actions available on the row interface are selectively displayed to the right of each row.

The Stage 7 program interface is presented as the final interactive interface. In this interface, the learner enters the entire program with a relaxed format. The discipline of the previous format requirements is eliminated, and the learner may enter the code in any format. Figure 13 presents a view of the program interface, labeled Text Editor Emulation in the title bar, with correct code in the text window.

If the code is incorrect when submitted for evaluation, the learner may attempt to make corrections and submit the code again. If the learner is unable to find and correct the error, the Review may be selected. This choice sends the learner back to the third pass of the row interface, and the tutor progresses again from that point. When the learner completes the tutor in the classroom, the student exits the tutor and awaits additional instruction in the subsequent class period. Other learners may progress to information that explains how to compile the program, write the HTML file, and run the Applet.

Figure 11. Top view = row familiarity interface with input for the displayed row. Bottom view = row interface with accurate code in all 10 rows for Pass 1. The "Take Test" button is enabled for row 10

Classroom Applications

The tutor was presented as the first exercise in a seven-week graduate course (Summer, 2001) entitled "Graphical User Interface Systems Using Java." The three-hour class met twice each week, and there were 14 class periods in the course. There were 17 graduate students in Information Systems in the class (eight females, median age = 25.5; nine males, median age = 28). Prior to using the tutor, each student completed a questionnaire that presented two rating scales. The first five-point rating scale assessed the student's prior experience with Java, where the scale anchors were **1 = No experience, I am a novice in Java** to **5 = Extensive experience, I am an expert in Java**. The second five-point rating scale assessed the student's confidence in being able to use each of the 21 Java items to write a Java computer program,

Figure 12. Top view = an explanation window for the code in row 7. Bottom view = the multiple-choice test for the code in row 7

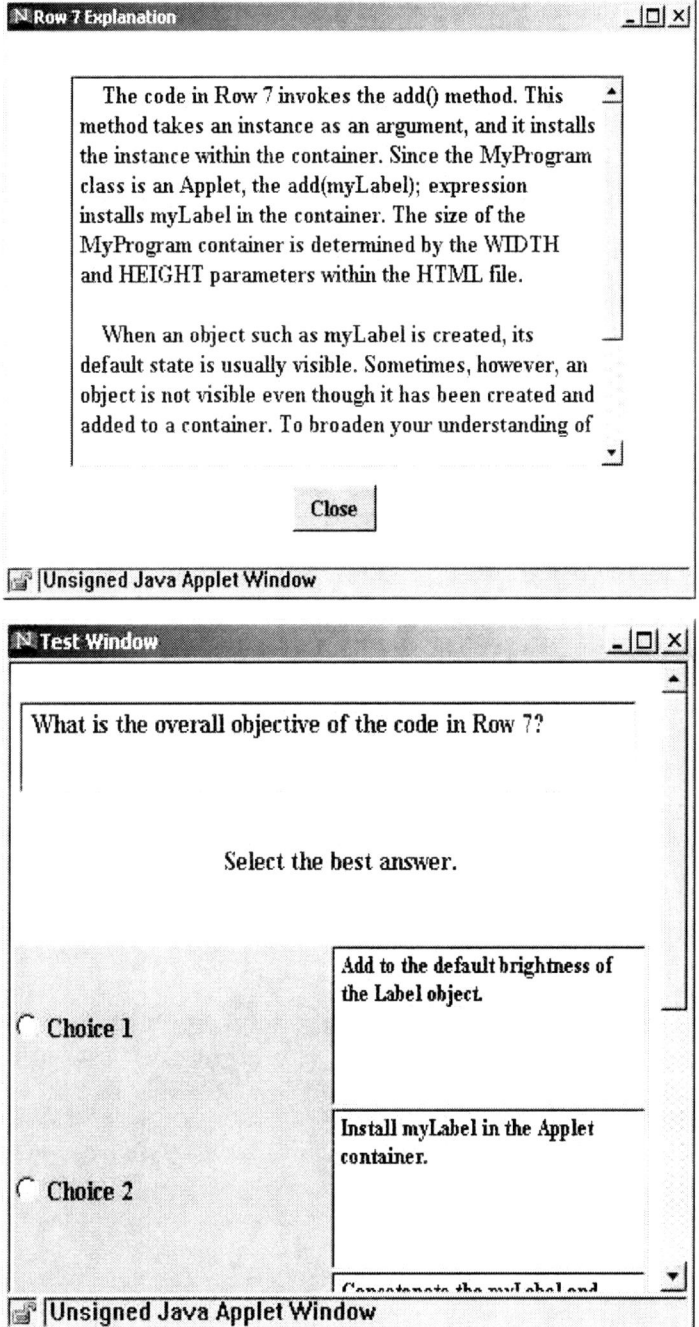

Figure 13. A view of the program interface, labeled "Text Editor Emulation" in the title bar. The previously required format for entering the program is eliminated for this interface, and this is evident in the correct code displayed in the white key-in space. The "Review" button takes the learner back to the third pass in the row interface

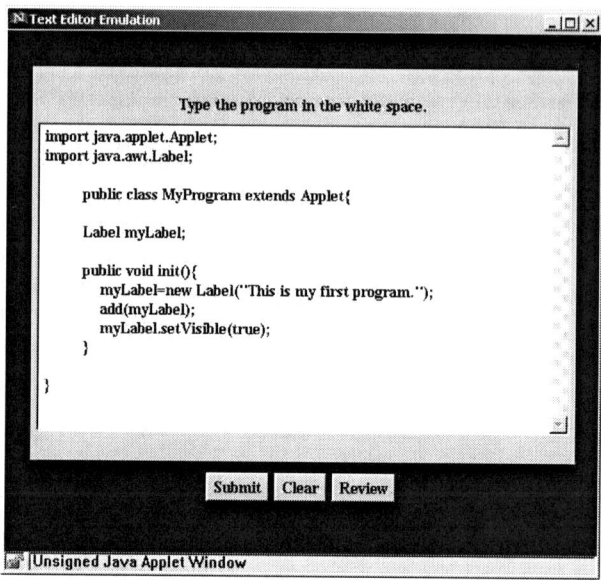

where the scale anchors were **1 = Not at all confident, I do not know how to use the symbol to 5 = Totally confident, I know how to use the symbol**. The student was also asked to write a Java Applet, entered into a WebCT text box that was saved for analysis, to display a text string as a Label object in a browser window. Previous research has also used the learner's construction of a program as an index of training effectiveness in such programming languages as BASIC (e.g., Perkins, Schwartz, & Simmons, 1988).

At the conclusion of the 3 hours that were allotted to the tutoring system or whenever a student finished the tutor prior to that time, a post-tutor questionnaire was administered. This questionnaire repeated the above confidence assessment, and it also included writing the Java Applet into the WebCT text box. A third five-point rating scale assessed the student's overall reaction to the tutor, where the scale anchors were **1 = Totally negative, I did not like the tutor** to **5 = Totally positive, I liked the tutor**. A fourth five-point rating scale assessed the student's opinion of the effectiveness of the tutor in learning Java, where the scale anchors were **1 = Totally negative, The tutor did not help me to learn Java** to **5 = Totally positive, The tutor did help me to learn Java**. A fifth five-point rating scale assessed the student's opinion about the usability of the tutor interfaces, where the scale anchors were **1 = Totally negative, The tutor was difficult to use** to **5 = Totally positive, The tutor was easy to use**. The students were then dismissed from the class, and the tutor continued to be available for those students who were motivated to access the tutor outside of class.

During the immediately succeeding class period, which occurred five days later, the instructor discussed the Applet code with the students using a lecture and discussion format. The students entered the code into a Unix text editor at the time the items were presented and discussed on the board. The WWW directory tree and HTML file were also presented and discussed. The students then compiled the Java code and ran the Applet in a Netscape Communicator© browser by accessing the HTML file as a URL on the Web. To foster a collaborative learning environment, the students were encouraged to help each other and to seek help from the instructor and course assistant as needed. This part of the classroom experience was based upon the Personalized System of Instruction (Keller, 1968), which included interpersonal interactions as a further means of learning and competency testing (Ferster & Perrott, 1968). After all students ran the Applet on the Web, they again completed the confidence ratings and the writing of the Applet code in the WebCT text box. This identical assessment was repeated during the 14th class, the final class of the course.

The enhancement to the version of the tutoring system under consideration also included the addition of a *brief row tutor* interface. This interface was similar to the first pass through the *row* interface in the full tutoring system. Whenever an error was made on any row in the brief row tutor interface, the learner was given the opportunity to view the correct code for that particular row and to enter the code repeatedly until the row code was accurate. There was also a multiple-choice test on each row, and the test was identical to the one given in the full tutoring system. The purpose of this brief row tutor interface was to provide additional rehearsal and overlearning of the Java Applet at different temporal occasions throughout the course. The brief row tutor interface was administered on classes three, seven, and ten of the 14-class course. It was administered at the beginning of these classes, and 30 min were allotted for the learners to complete the brief row tutor. This was sufficient time for all students to complete this interface.

In pursuing this classroom study, at least two constraints were evident. First, we wanted to offer the tutor to students, rather than to research "subjects." Accordingly, the tutor was administered as a class exercise, and the procedure was exempted by the Institutional Review Board, because it dealt with instructional technology. Second, we were bound by the length of the class. This led to a consideration of performance differences that manifested themselves between those students who completed all stages of the tutor and those students who did not. Although students might have been encouraged, if not required, to complete the tutor outside of class, experience suggested that this option would introduce uncontrolled factors into the interpretation of the results.

Results

At the conclusion of the class time allotted for completing the full Java tutor during the first class, 11 students ("Completers") had finished all parts of the tutor, and six students ("Noncompleters") were still working on the row (Stage 6) or program (Stage 7) interface. The data analysis is reported as a between-group comparison between these two groups of students. The rationale for this approach was to investigate potential early indicators that a student would not complete the tutor in the time allotted. This evidence might prove useful in future tutor enhancements that require different degrees of rehearsal or practice in relationship to the knowledge and skill levels of the learners, perhaps detected early in the tutor exercises.

Figure 14 presents box-plots of confidence ratings for both groups across the four assessment occasions. The data are based upon the median confidence rating for each student across the 21 items evaluated. The figure shows graphically that the ratings of confidence, as evidenced by the median and interquartile range values, increased for both groups across all occasions. This is evidenced graphically by the increases in median

Figure 14. Box-plots of confidence ratings for Completers (C) and Noncompleters (N-C) across the four observation occasions

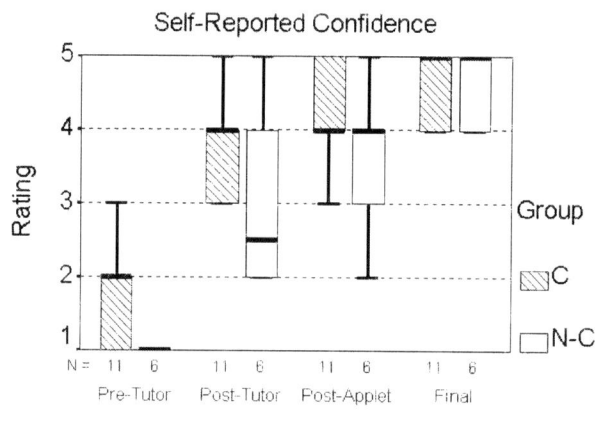

confidence and by shifts in the interquartile range across all occasions. A test of trend, undertaken by comparing the six successive differences between medians with a population of zeros, was significant, $F(1, 10) = 8.57, p < 0.02$. The figure also suggests that the Completers showed greater confidence ratings, in comparison to the Noncompleters, over the first three occasions. The difference between the medians on the Pre-Tutor assessment was significant, Kruskal-Wallis chi-square $= 4.57, p < 0.04$. The difference between the medians on the final assessment was not significant, Kruskal-Wallis chi-square $= 0.22, p > 0.50$. These delimited tests were undertaken, because the sample size is small and because parametric tests may not be appropriate for ordinal data in a factorial split-plot design.

Table 2 presents median ratings for Completers and Noncompleters for previous Java experience, overall impression of the tutor, effectiveness of the tutor in learning Java, and usability of the tutor interfaces. The outcomes were equivalent between the two groups, with the single exception of the range for the effectiveness in learning Java ratings. These ratings show that the students reported minimal Java experience prior to this course. They also show the favorable ratings of the tutor on all other scales.

The tutoring system provided records of errors made on the item familiarity, row, and program interfaces. Figure 15 presents box-plots of errors on the item familiarity interface for

Table 2. Self-reported ratings; median (interquartile range) [range]

Scale	Group	
	Completers	Non-Completers
Experience	1 (1-2)[1-2]	1 (1-2)[1-2]
Overall	5 (4-5)[3-5]	5 (4-5)[3-5]
Learning Java	5 (4-5)[3-5]	5 (4-5)[4-5]
Usability	5 (4-5)[4-5]	5 (4-5)[4-5]

Figure 15. Box-plots of total errors on the item (symbol) familiarity interface for Completers (C) and Noncompleters (N-C)

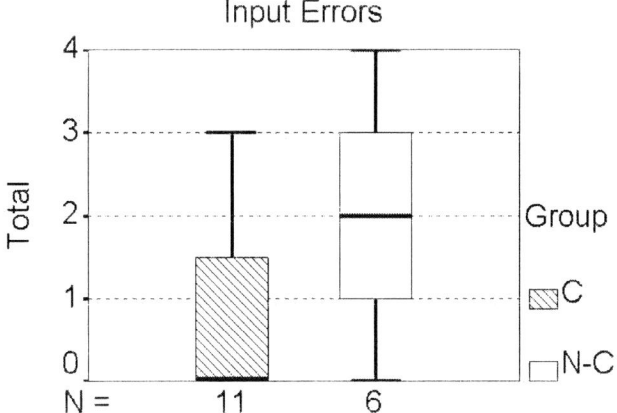

the two groups. The figure graphically shows that the Noncompleters showed greater errors on this first interactive interface, in comparison to the Completers. The difference in mean errors was marginally significant between the Completers (mean = 0.8) and the Noncompleters (mean = 2.0), $F(1,15) = 3.44, p < 0.09$.

Figure 16 (top view) presents the total errors made by each learner across the three successive passes through the row interface. The individual totals are presented to reveal at least some of the learning effects at the level of the individual learner. Also presented are the medians. Because many learners showed identical values across passes, the individual data points are often on top of each other, but the entire group of 13 learners, all of whom completed this interface, is presented. The individual data suggest that most learners dropped in errors across successive passes, but there is graphical evidence that some learners showed an increase, at least between Pass 2 and Pass 3. Many learners show errors in excess of the number of rows, especially on the first pass. This is attributable to a learner's repeated unsuccessful attempts to enter the code on a row. The medians displayed on the figure clearly show the overall decline in errors across successive passes, as evidenced by this measure of central tendency. A test of trend undertaken by comparing the slopes of the regression line for each learner with a population of zeros (Maxwell & Delaney, 2000, p. 597) was significant, $F(1,24) = 19.21, p < 0.001$.

Figure 16 (bottom view) presents the total times that learners selected to see the code in a row across successive passes. The form of the figure is similar to the top view, and the outcome is also similar. Several learners show selections in excess of 10 during the first pass. Similar to errors, the individual data suggest that most learners dropped in selections across successive passes, but there is graphical evidence that some learners showed an increase between Passes 1 and 2 and between Passes 2 and 3. The medians displayed on the figure clearly show the overall decline in selections across successive passes. A test of trend

Figure 16. Top view = total errors for each learner across successive passes through the row interface. The median errors for all passes are also presented. Solid lines are Completers, and broken lines are Noncompleters, who did not complete the program interface. Bottom view = total times that each learner selected to see the code in a row across successive passes. The median times for all passes are also presented

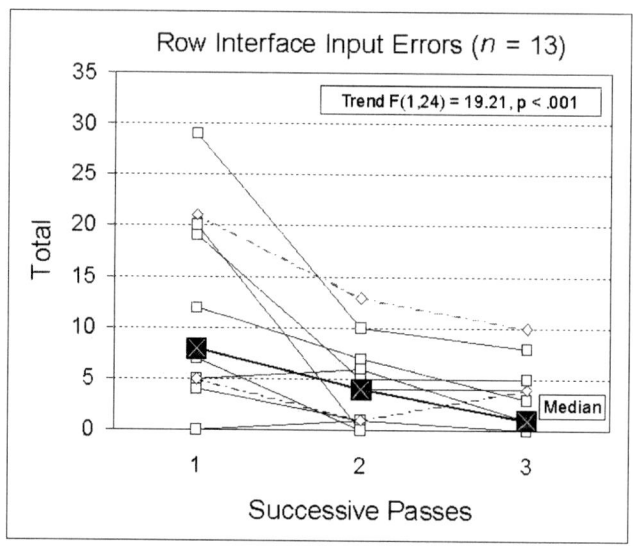

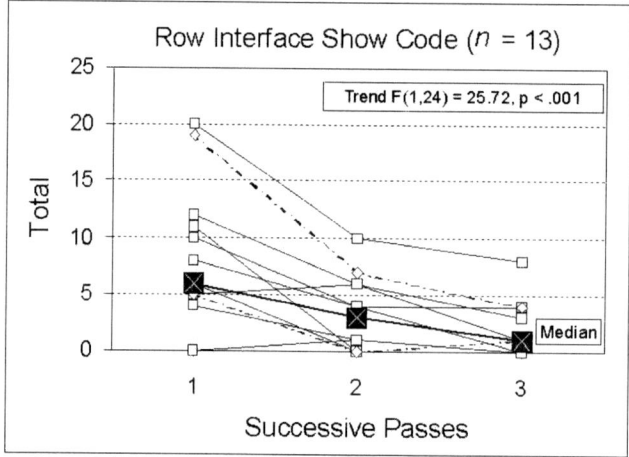

undertaken by comparing the slopes of the regression line for each learner with a population of zeros was significant, $F(1,24)=25.72, p<0.001$.

The correlations between errors and selections for Pass 1, Pass 2, and Pass 3 were as follows, respectively: Pass 1 — $0.92, p<0.01$; Pass 2 — $0.93, p<0.01$; and Pass 3 — $0.77, p<0.01$. In general, learners who made errors required the support of the selections to observe the code in a row. This relationship was strong during Passes 1 and 2, and the correlation was somewhat smaller during Pass 3. The procedure for Pass 3 was more stringent than the other passes, and that may have driven down the number of times that the learner would use the selection to observe the code.

Three of the 11 Completers selected one review on the program interface, and they made no errors. Two other Completers made two errors each on the final program interface, and neither of these learners selected the review option.

Figure 17 presents the total number of correct Java programs that were written into the WebCT questionnaire over the four assessment occasions for both groups. The accuracy of the programs was judged independently by two Java instructors who showed 100% agreement. There was no feedback given for incorrect responses, and there was no opportunity to compile the code to test for compilation errors and to revise the code. The assessment consisted only of the learner's memory in entering a correct serial stream of Java items that would produce a Label object in an Applet container.

In Figure 17, it is shown that no learner wrote a correct program during the Pre-Tutor assessment. Immediately after completing the tutor, which required one accurate construction of the entire program, nine Completers entered the code correctly during the Post-Tutor assessment, and one Noncompleter entered the code correctly. This shows the skill acquisition effects afforded by the succession of tutor interfaces, even when the final program interface was not completed by all students. After receiving classroom instruction, which involved writing and compiling the program and running the Applet, eight Completers and two Noncompleters entered the code correctly during the Post-Applet assessment. At the end of the course, nine Completers and three Noncompleters entered the code correctly during the Final assessment. There were only two instances in which a correct program written by a learner on an early assessment was not written correctly on a later assessment.

Discussion

The present classroom study followed the methodology of systematic replication (Sidman, 1960), and it was intended to extend and clarify the outcomes observed in the prior

Figure 17. Total number of correct Java programs that were written into the transfer assessment questionnaire for Completers (C) and Noncompleters (N-C) across the four observation occasions

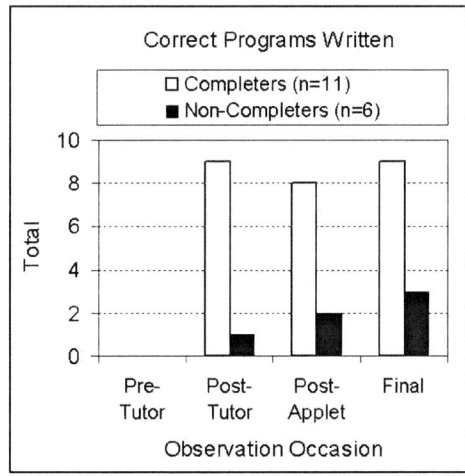

classroom study (Emurian & Durham, 2001). Rather than using a "control group" for comparison, the tutoring system as an "independent variable" was enhanced by adjusting factors that were considered instrumental in potentiating the learning effects, and all prior observations are considered the "control" observations. In the present study, the greatest change in skill and self-reported confidence occurred between the Pre-Tutor and Post-Tutor assessment occasions, at least for the Completers, and this outcome is consistent with the power function of learning (Lane, 1987). This outcome was also observed in the previous study, and the effect was stronger under the present enhancements. The enhancements to the tutoring system interfaces, especially the row interface, led to robust transfer in writing the Java code after use of the tutoring system, and the programmed use of the brief row tutor interface by the students had the effect of maintaining the acquired skill for the Completer group and improving the skill for the Noncompleter group over the duration of the course.

These outcomes showed the reliability of the learning and self-reported effects over a broader population of learners. Because the learners in both studies were similar in terms of self-reported prior experience, demographics, and evaluation of the tutor, the effects observed in the present study were confidently attributable to the tutoring system enhancements rather than to between-group bias. In fact, even following a demonstration of relative effectiveness in a statistical paradigm of decision making, any further observation of the utility of a tutoring system is perforce undertaken with a different learner at a different point in time. It is for this reason that systematic replication is favored as an efficient and demonstrably effective research methodology when a series of programmatic enhancements is intended.

The confidence ratings for Completers and Noncompleters were similar at the conclusion of the course, as were the ratings of satisfaction with the tutor. It was also the case, however, that the behavior of the Noncompleters sometimes differed in important ways from that of the Completers, in terms of confidence ratings and performance. Prior to using the tutor, Noncompleters reported relatively less confidence than Completers, and by the end of the course, only three of the six Noncompleters were able to write the Java Applet correctly during the final transfer assessment. That the group of Noncompleter students came to the course with less readiness for learning Java than did the Completer students was also indicated by the observation that the former group showed more errors on the item familiarity interface. That interface required only copying the Java item into a key-in box, showing the importance of basic symbol transcription and data entry skills that may set the occasion for more advanced learning of the meaning of the Java items. It should not always be assumed, then, that students with similar intellectual abilities and having the prerequisites for a course are equally prepared to master a new knowledge domain, when the instructional technology is not engineered to overcome individual differences. There are fundamental skills that all learners must possess, and programmed instruction provides a series of cumulative experiences that allow adequate preparation for each successive stage in the learning process.

The assessment of writing the code correctly in the tutoring system and on the transfer task was undertaken without benefit of observing compile-time or run-time errors, which are obviously important ingredients of a professional's program development and testing. Nevertheless, the present enhancement to the tutoring system resulted in robust increases in correct serial constructions in contrast to the previous study (Emurian & Durham, 2001), where few learners showed similar transfer of learning between the tutoring system and subsequent assessment occasions. The change in skill observed in the present study was most pronounced between the Pre-Tutor and Post-Tutor occasions, and only a few learners thereafter were not able to produce the serial stream accurately. This improvement in performance was observed in relationship to the enhancements to the tutoring system, which included three presentations of the brief row tutor interface. It should also be noted that the tutoring system was used only for the first technical exercise, and compile-time and run-time error interpretation was taught throughout the remainder of the course. Although the writing of the code in the transfer assessment constituted rote recollection ("regurgitation"), the student's performance on that task was mindful, informed, purposeful, and skilled recollection.

Rather than concluding that the transfer performance failures are always problematic, it may be more reasonable to suggest that even a professional programmer's "baseline" of code construction contains errors that might be readily overcome with the feedback provided by a system during program development. In contrast to such an approach, this study focused on the serial stream of code as it might be mastered in a textual learning paradigm (Li & Lewandowsky, 1995), and it would be informative to compare the present outcome with a baseline of errors exhibited by expert programmers.

CONCLUSION

This chapter presented individual and classroom performance on a Web-based tutoring system for acquiring knowledge of a simple Java Applet. The instructional design of the tutor followed programmed instruction principles, which were supplemented with students' personal interactions with an expert and collaborations with peers. In contrast to passive online tutorials that display information,[5] no matter how skillfully organized and delivered within a hypermedia environment, the present tutoring system required learners to actively construct correct responses during the learning experience. Furthermore, the size of the learned and constructed response was systematically increased, until the final response was the production of the entire Java program. The programmed instruction component was augmented by a discussion with an expert that culminated in the learner's running of the Applet on the World Wide Web. These experiences together characterize many of the features of a Personalized System of Instruction (Keller, 1968).

The outcomes for the three individual learners together with the classroom observations indicate the importance of repetition in acquiring competency in at least the domain of writing an Applet from memory. Learners in the individual and classroom observations completed the full version of the tutor and the brief row tutor or both on four separate occasions that were similarly spaced apart over a four- to five-week interval. All three individual learners showed performance improvement across the first four learning occasions, and for the class of students, nine of the 11 Completers and three of the six Noncompleters wrote the Applet correctly in the final assessment questionnaire that followed one use of the full tutor and three completions of the brief row tutor. Although the dependability and generality of these observations require intersubject and systematic replication (Sidman, 1960), this tactic to gain confidence in the effectiveness of a tutoring system and its enhancements offers an alternative to null hypothesis testing with "control groups" by relying on fine-grain performance records and interbehavioral processes observed over replications.

It is perhaps obvious that high-achieving students will apply effective study tactics to their own behavior management during learning (Schunk, 2000), and there is growing evidence that self-regulated learning styles can be acquired, by appropriate teacher–student interactions, even in grade school (Perry et al., 2002). However, programmed instruction approaches, in which the learning history is controlled, may also benefit novitiate students, in that they provide public conceptualizations of the reinforcement contingencies that account for progressive development of a complex repertoire or at least of a repertoire displaying many new components (Ferster & Perrott, 1968). It is rare, however, that the analysis of programmed instruction has been approached from the perspective of providing an occasion for the investigation of a learner's interactive behavioral history during learning. The individual and classroom observations reported in this chapter, then, analyzed the repeated acquisition of performance on a programmed instruction tutoring system and the application of such a strategy in the classroom. It is our position that programmed instruction approaches are well suited for the design of an instructional system, when the teaching objective is to achieve a student's documented mastery of understanding and writing a simple Java computer program. This experience sets the occasion for a student's advanced learning with traditional formats of instructional delivery.

The classroom self-reported data indicate that the students felt good about themselves after using the tutor. The increase in students' self-reports of confidence in using a set of Java symbols shows the dynamic changes in a learning context. The importance of these contextual changes has been recognized as contributing to the effectiveness of automated instructional systems (Tennyson, 1999). These ratings of confidence are similar to task-specific self-efficacy measures used in other studies of computer-related training (e.g., Potosky, 2002). Importantly, Noncompleters were identified in the present study by relatively lower self-efficacy, in comparison to Completers, prior to using the tutoring system. Moreover, all students gave favorable ratings on the functionality of the interfaces and on the value of the tutor in learning Java. Despite the repetition and enforced learning discipline associated with using the tutor, students are apparently willing to move through a rigorous training experience when the outcome is a desired level of understanding and skill regarding an Applet. An important by-product of acquiring such skill, then, is an enhancement in self-efficacy (Bandura, 1991).

The analysis also suggests the potential benefits of repetition and step-wise learning, reflecting the method of successive approximations (Sulzer-Azaroff & Mayer, 1991), although the decisions about the unit sizes were more artful than scientific. A scientific account of the value of the various tutor components might include comparative evaluations of the effects on learning and retention of many of the steps and requirements that are now embedded in the tutoring system. Parameters such as the number of passes through the row interface or the frequency of repetition in the program interface lend themselves to evaluation. Other programmed instruction studies have reported performance gains when there was a high density of responses required by the learners (Kritch & Bostow, 1998), and the value of deliberate practice has long been recognized as instrumental to the development of expertise (Ericsson & Lehmann, 1996; Ericsson, Krampe, & Tesch-Romer, 1993). Although the importance of rote memorization in science and mathematics has been questioned (Bransford, Brown, & Cocking, 2000), other guidelines continue to recommend repetition and overlearning as effective techniques for mastering many of the essential fundamental details in science and engineering.[6] The ongoing discussions and dynamic interplay between instructivist and constructivist approaches, when applied to tactics in information technology education, will ultimately determine the relative importance and optimal timing for a student's use of each approach to mastering a knowledge domain (Finn & Ravitch, 1996).

The contribution of this analysis is to be understood first in terms of codifying the moment-by-moment actions of study behaviors that are emitted by the individual learner across several study occasions. Within each occasion, the learner reached a criterion of mastery, which was to write a Java program correctly. By reference to these records, teachers may communicate to novice learners the level of intellectual effort ("learning force") that may be required to master this knowledge domain, with or without a tutoring system. This information may assist new learners in structuring their personal study commitment to achieve mastery, when the process of effective studying has been documented and communicated. Too often, perhaps, studies of training effectiveness in groups of learners measure performance, when some learners are still in transition to mastery of the task at hand, and there are few, if any, proven guidelines that inform students exactly how to study and how long it may take to master a particular knowledge domain.

The tutoring system also teaches a simple Java Applet to a class of students whose members may be only marginally interested and skilled in computer programming but may require the latter as a technical tool. The instructional framework combines teaching, practice, and assessment of learning that are directed to the status of the individual student. In this way, the needs of the individual student are met with respect to the pace of learning and the repetition possibly required to attain error-free input during successive stages in the tutor. This approach fosters an initially positive learning experience for students majoring in information systems, and it provides preparatory knowledge and self-efficacy that will facilitate subsequent learning of more advanced programming topics taught with traditional approaches. We witnessed the benefits of the programmed instruction tutoring system to majors in information systems often enough to be convinced of its value to our students.

FUTURE TRENDS

Programmed instruction, used here as a tactic for technology education, is a general instructional methodology that may be applicable to other knowledge domains, where step-wise progression to a competency objective is the intended outcome. Although this chapter focused upon an introductory exercise in Java, there is every reason to believe that this methodology lends itself to adoption in other areas of information technology, especially end-user computing applications. When an instructional technology can facilitate acquisition and practice of fundamental skills under conditions that do not demoralize and disrespect a learner for lacking assumed preparation for study, otherwise reluctant students might find accessible the experiences needed to embark on subsequent advanced study with confidence. The potential applications of programmed instruction are limited only by the ingenuity of the instructional designer who is motivated to offer technology that will provide all learners the opportunity to reach a common state of excellence.

ENDNOTES

[1]   This paper represents the author's views and not those of the Centers for Medicare & Medicaid Services (CMS).

²   http://www.aisnet.org/Curriculum; http://www.irma-international.org/crclm919.html

³   http://nasa1.ifsm.umbc.edu/learnJava/tutorLinks/TutorLinks.html

⁴   Portions of these data were presented at a professional convention (Emurian, Wang, & Durham, 2000).

⁵   http://java.sun.com/docs/books/tutorial/index.html

⁶   http://www.ucc.vt.edu/stdysk/remember.html

REFERENCES

Altmann, E. M. (2001). Near-term memory in programming: A simulation-based analysis. *International Journal of Human-Computer Studies, 54,* 189–210.

Anderson, J. R., Corbett, A. T., Koedinger, K. R., & Pelletier, R. (1995). Cognitive tutors: Lessons learned. *Journal of Learning Science, 4,* 167–207.

Anger, W. K., Rohlman, D. S., Kirkpatrick, J., Reed, R. R., Lundeen, C. A., & Eckerman, D. A. (2001). cTRAIN: A computer-aided training system developed in SuperCard for teaching skills using behavioral education principles. *Behavior Research Methods, Instruments, & Computers, 33,* 277–281.

Bandura, A. (1991). Social theory of self-regulation. *Organizational Behavior and Human Decision Processes, 50,* 248–287.

Bannert, M., & Reimann, P. (2000). Guest editorial: Approaches to the design of software training. *Journal of Computer Assisted Learning, 16,* 281–283.

Bhavnani, S. K., & John, B. E. (2000). The strategic use of complex computer systems. *Human–Computer Interaction, 15,* 107–137.

Bloom, B. S. (1984). The 2 sigma problem: The search for methods of group instruction as effective as one-to-one tutoring. *Educational Researcher, 13,* 4–16.

Bransford, J. D., Brown, A. L., & Cocking, R. R. (2000). *How People Learn: Brain, Mind, Experience, and School (Expanded Edition).* Washington, DC: National Academy Press.

Campbell, K. C., Brown, N. R., & DiBello, L. A. (1992). The programmer's burden: Developing expertise in programming. In R. R. Hoffman (Ed.), *The Psychology of Expertise* (pp. 269–294). New York: Springer-Verlag.

Catania, A. C. (1998). *Learning.* Upper Saddle River, NJ: Prentice-Hall, Inc.

Compeau, D. (2002). The role of trainer behavior in end user software training. *Journal of End User Computing, 14,* 23–32.

Davis, S. I., & Bostrom, R. P. (1993). Training end users: An experimental investigation of the roles of the computer interface and training methods. *Management Information Systems Quarterly, 17,* 61–85.

Durham, A. G., & Emurian, H. H. (1998). Learning and retention with a menu and a command line interface. *Computers in Human Behavior, 14,* 597–620.

Emurian, H. H., & Durham, A. G. (2001). A personalized system of instruction for teaching Java. In M. Khosrowpour (Ed.), *Managing Information Technology in a Global Environment* (pp. 155–160). Hershey, PA: Idea Group Publishing.

Emurian, H. H., & Durham, A. G. (in press). Computer-based tutoring systems: A behavioral approach. In J. A. Jacko & A. Sears (Eds.), *Handbook of Human–Computer Interaction*, Mahwah, NJ: Lawrence Erlbaum & Associates.

Emurian, H. H., Hu, X., Wang, J., & Durham, A. G. (2000). Learning Java: A programmed instruction approach using Applets. *Computers in Human Behavior, 16,* 395–422.

Emurian, H. H., Wang, J., & Durham, A. G. (2000). Repeated Acquisition of Performance on a Java Programmed Instruction Tutor. Presented at the Annual Convention of the American Psychological Association, Washington, DC.

Ericsson, K. A., & Lehmann, A. C. (1996). Expert and exceptional performance: Evidence of maximal adaptation to task constraints. *Annual Review of Psychology, 47,* 273–305.

Ericsson, K. A., Krampe, R. T., & Tesch-Romer, C. (1993). The role of deliberate practice in the acquisition of expert performance. *Psychological Review, 100,* 363–406.

Federico, P. -A. (1999). Hypermedia environments and adaptive instruction. *Computers in Human Behavior, 15,* 653–692.

Ferster, C. B., & Perrott, M. C. (1968). *Behavior Principles.* New York, NY: Appleton-Century-Crofts.

Finn, C. E., & Ravitch, D. (1996). *Education Reform 1995–1996.* Indianapolis, IN: Hudson Institute, Inc.

Greer, R. D., & McDonough, S. H. (1999). Is the learn unit a fundamental measure of pedagogy? *The Behavior Analyst, 22,* 5–16.

Holland, J. G. (1960). Teaching machines: An application of principles from the laboratory. *Journal of the Experimental Analysis of Behavior, 3,* 275–287.

Keller, F. S. (1968). Goodbye teacher... *Journal of Applied Behavior Analysis, 1,* 79–89.

Kritch, K. M., & Bostow, D. E. (1998). Degree of constructed-response interaction in computer-based programmed instruction. *Journal of Applied Behavior Analysis, 31,* 387–398.

Lane, N. E. (1987). *Skill Acquisition Rates and Patterns: Issues and Training Implications.* New York: Springer-Verlag.

Li, S., & Lewandowsky, S. (1995). Forward and backward recall: Different retrieval processes. *Journal of Experimental Psychology: Learning, Memory, and Cognition, 21,* 837–847.

Mayer, R. E. (1981). An evaluation of the elaboration model of instruction. *Journal of Instructional Development, 5,* 23–25.

Mayer, R. E. (1988). *Teaching and Learning Computer Programming: Multiple Research Perspectives.* Hillsdale, NJ: Lawrence Erlbaum Associates.

Maxwell, S. E., & Delaney, H. D. (2000). *Designing Experiments and Analyzing Data.* Mahwah, NJ: Lawrence Erlbaum Associates.

Myers, B., Hudson, S., & Pausch, R. (2000). Past, present and future of user interface software tools. *ACM Transactions on Computer–Human Interaction, 7,* 3–28.

Papert, S. (1980). *Mindstorms: Children, Computers and Powerful Ideas.* New York: Basic Books.

Perkins, D. N., Schwartz, S., & Simmons, R. (1988). Instructional strategies for the problems of novice programmers. In R. E. Mayer, *Teaching and Learning Computer Programming* (pp. 153–178). Hillsdale, NJ: Lawrence Erlbaum Associates.

Perry, N. E., VandeKamp, K. O., Mercer, L. K., & Nordby, C. J. (2002). Investigating teacher–student interactions that foster self-regulated learning. *Educational Psychologist, 37,* 5–15.

Potosky, D. (2002). A field study of computer efficacy beliefs as an outcome of training: The role of computer playfulness, computer knowledge, and performance during training. *Computers in Human Behavior, 18,* 214–255.

Reigeluth, C. M., & Darwexeh, A. N. (1982). The elaboration theory's procedures for designing instruction: A conceptual approach. *Journal of Instructional Development, 5,* 22–32.

Ryan, S. D. (1999). A model for the motivation for IT retraining. *Information Resources Management Journal, 12,* 24–32.

Schunk, D. H. (2000). Self-regulation. In D. H. Schunk, *Learning Theories: An Educational Perspective* (pp. 355–401). Upper Saddle River, NJ: Macmillan Publishing Company.

Scriven, M. (1969). The case for and use of programmed texts. In A. D. Calvin (Ed.) *Programmed Instruction: Bold New Adventure* (pp. 3–36). Bloomington, IN: Indiana University Press.

Shute, V. J, & Gawlick, L. A. (1995). Practice effects on skill acquisition, learning outcome, retention, and sensitivity to relearning. *Human Factors, 37,* 781–803.

Sidman, M. (1960). *Tactics of Scientific Research.* New York: Basic Books.

Sikstrom, S., & Jaber, M. Y. (2002). The power integration diffusion model for production breaks. *Journal of Experimental Psychology: Applied, 8,* 118–126.

Simon, J. S., Grover, V., Teng, J. T. C., & Whitcomb, K. (1996). The relationship of information system training methods and cognitive ability to end-user satisfaction, comprehension, and skill transfer: A longitudinal field study. *Information Systems Research, 7,* 466–490.

Skinner, B. F. (1957). *Verbal Behavior.* New York, NY: Appleton-Century-Crofts.

Skinner, B. F. (1958). Teaching machines, *Science, 128,* 969–977.

Sohn, Y. W., & Doane, S. M. (1997). Cognitive constraints on computer problem-solving skills. *Journal of Experimental Psychology: Applied, 3,* 288–312.

Soloway, E. (1985). From problems to programs via plans: The content and structure of knowledge for introductory LISP programming. *Journal of Educational Computing Research, 1,* 157–172.

Stiller, E., & LeBlanc, C. (2001). Teaching client/server programming in the context of computing curricula 2001. *Journal of Computing in Small Colleges, 16,* 122–133.

Sulzer-Azaroff, B., & Mayer, G. R. (1991). *Behavior Analysis for Lasting Change.* Orlando, FL: Holt, Rinehart and Winston, Inc.

Swezey, R. W., & Llaneras, R. E. (1997). Models in training and instruction. In G. Salvendy (Ed.), *Handbook of Human Factors and Ergonomics* (pp. 514–577). New York, NY: Wiley.

Tennyson, R. D. (1999). Goals for automated instructional systems. *Journal of Structural Learning and Intelligent Systems, 13,* 215–226.

Tennyson, R. D., & Elmore, R. L. (1997). Learning theory foundations for instructional design. In R. D. Tennyson, F. Schott, N. M. Seel, & S. Dijkstra (Eds.), *Instructional Design: International Perspectives* (pp. 55–78). Mahwah, NJ: Lawrence Erlbaum Associates.

Van Merrienboer, J. J. G., & Paas, F. G. W. C. (1990). Automation and schema acquisition in learning elementary computer programming: Implications for the design of practice. *Computers in Human Behavior, 6,* 273–298.

Wickens, C. D., & Hollands. J. G. (2000). Chapter 7: Memory and Training, *Engineering Psychology and Human Performance* (pp. 241–292). Upper Saddle River, NJ: Prentice Hall.

Chapter VI

Supporting Creativity in Software Development: An Application in IT Education

Aybüke Aurum
The University of New South Wales, Australia

Meliha Handzic
The University of New South Wales, Australia

Adrian Gardiner
The University of New South Wales, Australia

ABSTRACT

This chapter examines the potential of the application of an individual creativity-enhancing technique (called SoloBrainstorming, or SBS) to improve the level of creativity of Information Technology (IT) students in performing information system (IS) requirements determination. Requirements determination, in the context of software development, involves gaining an understanding of the underlying issues related to a business problem, and also considering potential solutions. The chapter begins with a definition of creativity, followed by an overview of strategies suggested to enhance creativity. The SBS technique is then introduced, followed by a report of empirical results from its application. Finally, we offer advice for IT education in terms of incorporating creativity-enhancing techniques into the IT course curriculum.

INTRODUCTION

Most business problems have a number of potential solutions, some of which may prove to be more beneficial than others. As many of these solutions may not be at first obvious, or previously imagined, management needs to be highly creative in order to identify the best candidate solutions. However, identification of candidate solutions may depend upon first successfully identifying the underlying issues associated with the business problem. Identification of these issues also requires creativity, as a full understanding of the problem may only emerge through extensive creative discourse (e.g., through Joint Application Development). As contemporary solutions to business problems frequently require the development of computer-based IS, it therefore follows that creativity is important to IS design and development. As Keegan (1998, p. 239) put it: "Today's constraining factor is not the software, not the hardware, not the network. It is human creativity. We still need skilled, imaginative individuals who can research a business opportunity and integrate the technology needed to put the required process in place."

If we accept the argument that the level of creativity applied to a business problem may significantly impact the quality of the resulting IS, it seems reasonable to expect that students studying systems analysis should be well-versed in the importance of creativity within the software development process and also be skilled in applying creativity-enhancing techniques. However, the authors fear that for many university courses in IS, creativity is not emphasized, and students may therefore graduate with only a rudimentary understanding of this important area. In this respect, the authors feel that the IS teaching community can learn from other disciplines that also focus upon the creation of artifacts, such as architecture and engineering. These disciplines have long acknowledged the importance of creativity by encouraging their students to express themselves creatively, and by incorporating creative problem solving and design techniques throughout their curricula.

We therefore argue that IT education and training should more openly acknowledge the role and importance of creativity training and support to the successful development of IS. We believe that training IS and IT professionals in creativity will allow them to be more successful in their future roles as innovative professionals and business people. Moreover, these concerns have motivated the authors to investigate the potential of an individual creativity-enhancing technique to facilitate requirements determination.

BACKGROUND ON CREATIVITY

Defining Creativity

The literature offers diverse conceptual definitions of *creativity.* Tomas (1999), for example, defined creativity in terms of an original idea. Synonyms used by researchers to describe this quality may include uniqueness, surprising, novel, unusualness, innovative, and newness (Thurstone, 1952). A more restricted definition of creativity focuses solely on rare revolutionary and paradigm shifting ideas, while a looser definition includes useful evolutionary contributions that refine and apply existing paradigms (Shneiderman, 2000).

The appropriateness of new ideas is also important in order to distinguish creative ideas from surreal ideas that may be unique but have unlawful or highly unrealistic implications. Synonyms used by researchers to describe this quality may include workable, practical, worthwhile, plausible, relevant, and intelligible. What is seen as appropriateness may change depending upon prior insights, the initial problem definition, and the level of available resources for implementing ideas.

Furthermore, when discussing creativity, it is helpful to distinguish between the four elements of creativity as identified by Mooney (1963):

- The creative environment (place, context, setting, or situation)
- The creative person (levels of individual creativity)
- The creative process (how creativity is undertaken)
- The creative product (all output).

Supporting Creativity

Most findings from past empirical studies indicate that creative performance is highly contingent upon a variety of environmental, cognitive, technological, and other factors. Variables that produced different degrees of creativity include problem importance, common perspectives, familiarity with possible solutions, trust, flexibility of process, external forces, and feedback (Ford & Gioia, 2000). The optimal condition for high creativity involves working alone with no expectation of evaluation (Shalley, 1995). In addition, being given creative examples and informational feedback can also improve creative performance (Shalley & Perry-Smith, 2001).

Consistent with the view that creative thinking can be learned by appropriate stimulation and instruction, many techniques for idea generation have been developed to assist the production of novel ideas. For general reviews, see Van Gundy (1988), who identifies 61 tools for group idea generation; and Higgins (1994), who offers 101 creative problem-solving techniques that can be used to increase the level of corporate innovation. Mind mapping is an example of a method that involves recording the free flow of ideas by drawing a map that iterates your ideas (Tomas, 1999). Moreover, a variety of technologies have been developed that follow specific creative techniques (e.g., Ideafisher, Mindlink, IdeaPro, etc.) to facilitate "out of the box" thinking (Sridhar, 2001).

Many of the available techniques to facilitate creativity are derivatives of *brainstorming*. Brainstorming was originally proposed by Alex Osborn (1957) as a means of generating as many ideas as possible from group work. He claimed that a group can generate twice as many ideas as individuals working alone, provided that the group follows a systematic approach and adopts four rules. Osborn's purpose in suggesting these rules was to overcome social and motivational difficulties that might inhibit the generation of ideas in groups.

The four rules are as follows:

1. No criticism is allowed.
2. Freewheeling is welcome.
3. Quantity is wanted.
4. Combination and improvement are sought.

For a brainstorming session, which can be conducted electronically or verbally, a group is formed, and members of the group are encouraged to think freely and propose ideas. The objective of brainstorming is to encourage associations. The basic assumption is that it is possible to generate many ideas, provided that the individual is exposed to stimuli and has experience, knowledge, the personal flexibility to develop various permutations and combinations, and the capacity to make correct selections. The best ideas are listed, and this forms the basis on which the group develops its solution strategy. This method initially emphasizes the quantity of ideas generated, leaving the assessment of quality to a later stage. This method is used to uncover ideas without being constrained, as the outcome is not permanent. Brainstorming also allows individuals or groups to capture all of their thoughts.

Individual Brainstorming

While most brainstorming-related techniques are designed for group use, individuals can also perform brainstorming. Individual brainstorming may produce a greater number of ideas than group brainstorming, as less time is generally spent on developing ideas in depth (Mullen, Johnson, & Salas, 1991; Stroebe & Diehl, 1994). Development of individual ideas may also be thwarted from the individual running up against problems they cannot solve on their own.

One individual creativity technique is SoloBrainstorming (SBS), originally proposed by one of the authors (Aurum, 1997). This technique uses a form of brainstorming and is especially suited to environments where sentential analysis is appropriate or where information sources are document based (e.g., reports, abstracts, testimonies, interview transcripts, Web publications). The SBS technique (as shown in Figure 1) requires the individual to adhere to a formal protocol (procedure), where a series of documents are examined ("reading" stage), and then edited ("editing" stage). The editing stage consists of the following activities: typing a summary of each document; making lateral comments and links (e.g., making connections between documents; noting ideas as they occur); and nominating issues to be followed up. The ultimate aim in a SBS session is to determine a sufficient set of issues. As applications of the SBS protocol have been computer-based, all issues are automatically available in electronic form for further analysis.

Figure 1. Overview of the SBS technique (adapted from Aurum et al., 2001)

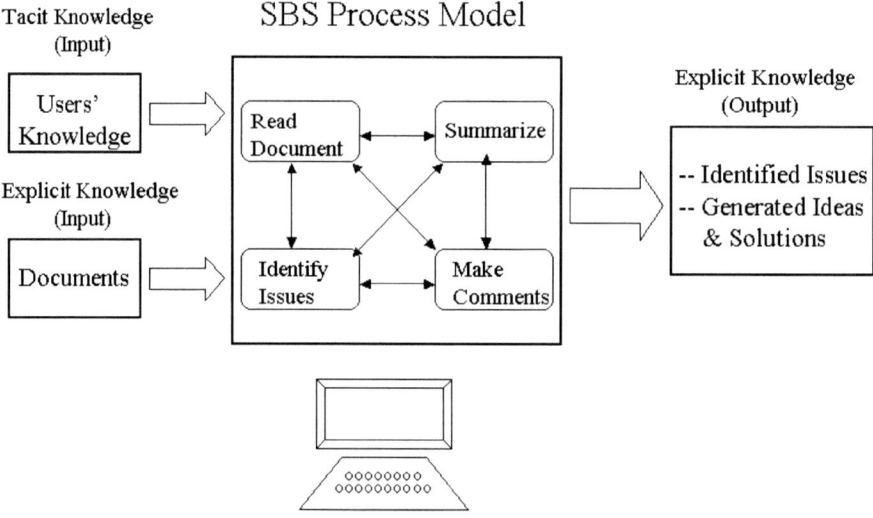

Typically, to measure the level of creativity attributable to application of the protocol, before interacting with the document set, users are asked to list issues they are already aware of. Once the individual has completed to their satisfaction the SBS protocol (i.e., all documents have been examined), the issues that were raised can be analyzed across various dimensions (e.g., originality, workability, and relevance).

Central to the SBS protocol is the encouragement of participants to use their cognitive abilities by asking them to make "lateral comments" (e.g., being instructed to make conceptual connections between issues and between documents). Lateral thinking is a function of knowledge and imagination that may bring out discovery, innovation, imagination, and exploration. It is also an aid to creativity when one needs to have diverse ideas. Lateral thinking is a way of thinking that seeks as many alternative options as possible to the extent of one's adventurousness. In other words, it is a mental activity involving making connections between knowledge and ideas that were previously unrelated. In idea generation sessions, it is important to think expansively and to suspend judgment.

In a SBS session, lateral comments involve input from the participant as well as from different "authors" of the abstracts and views featured within the other documents. The interaction between these two sources of inputs brings forth creativity, acts as a rich source for stimuli that will trigger greater recollection of relevant knowledge (tacit knowledge), and makes it possible for the participant to see relationships between different elements, make analogies, and look at scenery from different points of view. If the participant does not have any "lateral comments," then essentially they are restricted to only the material in abstracts. There is no universally accepted set of lateral-thinking or creative-thinking criteria. Aurum (1997) suggested that the level of "laterality" for any thought for a given problem can only be assessed with respect to the thoughts generated by others for the same problem.

In addition, the value of SBS also lies in it being a "formal" protocol — one that places specific (yet flexible) demands upon participants to adhere to a set of behaviors designed to enhance the level of an individual's creativity. Adherence to the SBS regime will thus encourage a higher level of intrinsic motivation (discipline), application of a systematic and thorough approach to analysis, as well as reflective and lateral thinking.

As a technique to facilitate creativity, the SBS protocol touches upon an important issue in creativity: the link between an individual's level of domain knowledge and their capacity to be creative within that domain. (For example, does being truly creative require a rich mental model of the domain?; or can only experts within a domain truly provide creative insights or solutions?) In a typical SBS session, participants are presented with factual-type information. It can, therefore, be argued that this information may allow participants to learn more about the domain, thereby evolving their mental model of causal connections (e.g., identifying previously unknown variables, parameters, or links; or weakening existing links and associations). Supporting this view is Amabile (1983), who identifies domain knowledge or expertise as the foundation of creative activity. A similar view of the importance of knowledge in creativity is held by Holyoak and Thagard (1995), who regard analogical reasoning (which requires a rich source of potential referents and, therefore, knowledge) as an important potential source of creative thinking. In contrast, Finke et al. (1992) specifically mention the need to suspend one's expertise as a precursor to creativity, and in doing so, reduce the possibility of fixation. Purcell and Gero (1996), commenting about architectural design, explain fixation as people being unable to see new ways of using objects, which could lead to an innovative solution to a problem, because they are blocked or fixated on well-learned uses or properties of the object. It follows that experts would be expected to have more well-learned routines and ways of problem solving than novices, which thus may lead to fixation on more established ways of doing things. In addition, proponents of the view that an individual's level of creativity is an individual trait may argue that any increase in creativity possible from mere provision of a richer level of domain knowledge will be constrained by the individual's intrinsic level of creative ability. Individuals may also need a requisite level of motivation and degree of reflection to integrate new information successfully and overcome the cognitive load (mental demands) required to integrate and preprocess the incoming information in order to be able to leverage this information within a demanding creative task. Overall, the relationship between one's knowledge and level of creativity may be mitigated by a number of factors (e.g., personal level of creativity). Thus, one cannot merely assume that availability of a richer information set (and hence, greater available domain knowledge) will necessarily lead to the level of mental connections and permutations of cognitive structures required to produce creative insights.

INDIVIDUAL BRAINSTORMING FOR REQUIREMENTS DETERMINATION

Aurum et al. (2002) (see, also, Aurum & Martin, 1999, for related findings) reported results of a study investigating whether application of the SBS protocol would deliver a richer set of requirement statements and insights.

Experimental Task

An experiment was conducted in which participants were told to assume the role of a systems analyst (SA), who had been retained by a fictitious organization to write a requirements specification for their main information systems. The fictitious organization was the Cultural Heritage Authority (CHA), with a corporate charter that was to coordinate the marketing of Australia's cultural heritage.

In developing their requirements specification, each participant was required to utilize the software developed for the experiment, which was specifically designed to support application of the SBS protocol. This tool allowed subjects free access to the document set. The type of documents within the document set included fictitious interviews with users and other people holding authoritative positions within CHA and the wider industry and abstracts from published articles addressing heritage or marketing issues. In developing the tool, particular attention was paid to designing the interface. It was important to prevent substantial cognitive resources from being diverted from the task in response to demands from the user-interface. The aim was to produce an interface that would have minimal impact on cognitive load: one that could be learned easily by a novice user and yet was comprehensive enough to satisfy the experienced user.

Subjects and Procedure

A total of 16 subjects participated in the study on a voluntary basis. The participants were drawn from a pool of graduate students enrolled in a System Analysis and Design course at a large Australian university. Each received a monetary incentive of $45 for their participation. The experimental session was conducted in a microcomputer laboratory. On arrival, subjects were seated at individual workstations and worked alone. They received instructions regarding the case study and task requirements. They also had an opportunity for practice prior to commencing the experiment and to ask questions during the experiment. The session lasted 3 hours.

Dependent Measures and Results

Before using the SBS software (and therefore accessing the document set), participants were asked to generate ideas with respect to the anticipated requirements for CHA's information systems. These ideas were then compared with the ideas generated during application of the protocol in order to determine whether the application of the SBS protocol had led to a richer level of requirement specifications. Specifically, this study focused upon whether application of the protocol would result in identification of more *relevant, workable*, and *original* requirements issues (in other words, a subject's creative performance was evaluated in terms of *relevance, originality*, and *workability* of ideas generated before and after interaction with the tool, as assessed by an expert judge). The judge was a software developer with over 30 years of experience. The judge examined students' ideas and evaluated them for relevance, originality, and workability by rating each on a 5-point Likert scale, with 1 as the lowest and 5 as the highest possible score.

In order to understand the effects of the proposed learning tool on subjects' creative performance, we statistically analyzed the changes in the nature of ideas generated "after" the interaction with the tool compared to those "before." The paired t-test was selected as the most suitable method for the analysis (Huck et al., 1974). Results of the analysis are shown graphically in Figure 2.

Overall, the results of the analysis indicated that the tool had a significant positive impact on the originality of ideas generated but had no significant impact on their relevance or workability. As shown in Figure 2, there was a significant increase in the originality of ideas generated by the participants after their interaction with the tool. More specifically, the overall

Figure 2. Mean rating scores for participants' creative performance before and after their interaction with the technology

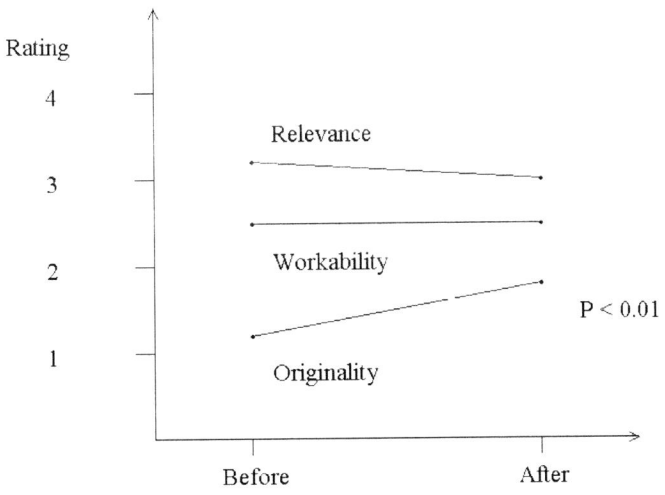

mean score for originality increased significantly from 1.4 before to 1.8 after the interaction ($p < 0.01$). These scores indicated a qualitative change from mostly "very common" (low score) to "slightly novel" (high score) thoughts.

In contrast, the analysis indicated no significant impact of the tool on *relevance* or *workability* of the ideas generated. Figure 2 shows that the mean rating score for relevance decreased slightly after interaction with the tool. However, the change was not statistically significant (3.1 versus 3.0, ns). These scores indicated that similarly "relevant" requirements were addressed by the participants, irrespective of the change in their originality.

Similarly, there was no significant change in the workability of the ideas generated due to tool use. The mean rating score after interaction was not significantly different from that before the interaction with the tool (2.5 versus 2.5, ns). These scores also suggest that "workable" ideas were generated, irrespective of their increased level of originality.

The value of increasing originality of ideas would have been undermined if the ideas were less workable or relevant – however, this was not the case. Therefore, application of the protocol increased the overall quality of the elicited requirements. The results of this study support the idea that thought-assisting applications can be developed, learned, practiced, and used to generate ideas.

Findings

The main findings of the present study indicate that a solo-brainstorming-based learning tool had a positive effect on students' creative performances in a systems requirements specification task. This outcome was evident in the originality aspect of task performance but not in relevance and workability. Users were found to generate significantly more original ideas as the result of their interaction with the tool, while maintaining similar levels of relevance and workability (i.e., increases in originality did not come at the cost of less workable or less relevant ideas).

The results of the current study provide support for the view that creative performance can be enhanced by appropriate stimulation and instruction as suggested by some theorists (Ford & Gioia, 2000; Marakas, 1998). More specifically, the study revealed that significant improvement was achieved in the originality of ideas generated by the participating students due to their interaction with the tool studied here. Participants were found to shift their thoughts from common and well-known concepts to slightly novel ones after participating in the interacting session. The results also agree with our earlier findings of improved quality of creative performance from another similar empirical study conducted in the decision-making context (Aurum et al., 2001). Essentially, the results support the idea that thought-assisting applications can be developed, learned, practiced, and used to generate ideas. Thus, they can enable an individual to think creatively, provided that the principles are clearly understood.

Furthermore, the results of the current study indicate that increased originality did not have an adverse effect on the appropriateness of ideas (e.g., workability, relevance) generated by the participants. The study found that participants tended to continue generating similarly relevant and workable ideas irrespective of the change in their originality. This is an important finding, as it suggests that the tool encouraged innovative rather than simply original thought. According to Shalley and Perry-Smith (2001), translating creative ideas into innovative products requires these ideas to be appropriate. The current study demonstrated the required appropriateness in terms of adequate relevancy and workability of generated ideas. It is possible that the design feature of the proposed tool that provided idea storage and retrieval capabilities helped participants in the final assessment.

The results of our study also indicate that the brainstorming technique underlying our tool is a promising method for stimulating creative thinking and idea generation in a software development task. It has been suggested in the literature (Satzinger et al., 1999) that the idea generation method is one of the most important sources of encouraging creativity. Essentially, the brainstorming session helped students uncover ideas without being constrained, stimulate their own thinking by external influences, and capture their thoughts.

Finally, the results of the study support the proposition that an electronic tool following a specific creativity-enhancing technique can assist the creative process (Sridhar, 2001). One of the main advantages of such a tool is the speed at which ideas can be produced. Furthermore, the ideas can be stored and revisited at a later time. The tool can also provide a variety of stimuli that can enhance creativity. The electronic tool tested in this study provided all of the above, plus a formal protocol that brought a much needed structure to the idea generation process.

Although the overall results of this study are encouraging, there is room for further improvement to originality. The level or originality of ideas achieved due to interaction with the proposed tool was less than desired. One possible reason for the lack of "highly original" thought may be the participants' feeling of pressure from consideration of implementation issues. Alternatively, it can be attributed to the participants' traditional IT education, which places more emphasis on developing their analytical and systems thinking skills rather than creative and innovative thinking skills. Furthermore, the subjects in the study had only one interactive session with the tool, and this might have been insufficient to produce a more substantial shift in their thinking patterns.

Limitations and Future Research

While the current study provides a number of interesting findings, some caution is necessary regarding their generalizability due to a number of limiting factors. The application of laboratory conditions is a major limitation of this study. Furthermore, the conclusions drawn based on the assessments of expert judges may be biased. We also speculate that the performance of users in an interaction session can be affected by their state of mind or previous experience. The emphasis of the present study was on individual students. It would be interesting to examine the effect of the tool on the creative performance of groups. Future research may address some of these limitations.

IMPLICATIONS FOR FUTURE IT EDUCATION

Our findings may have some important implications for IT education. They suggest that creativity can be improved to an extent that higher-quality software designs may be possible. Thus, IT schools need to acknowledge this and include creativity within their courses to prepare students. It is encouraging that some governments and educational institutions are starting to emphasize the significance of promoting creative thinking of the young through education (Sunderland, 2000) and are beginning to implement changes in courses taught in business schools (Sangran, 2001). The results of this study suggest that the type of tool tested here may be a useful teaching tool in a variety of courses involving creative thinking and problem solving. Furthermore, the tool is likely to be most valuable in situations where the problem is unstructured, goals are indistinct, and the outcome of an action cannot always be clearly identified. The tool is rather generic, because it uses a technique that can be applied to a variety of scenarios and can help people process relevant documents while identifying issues. These documents act like a "trigger" to stimulate domain-specific ideas from users.

CONCLUSION

This study proposed and empirically tested a specific learning tool aimed at stimulating creative problem solving of IT students. The tool was designed on the basis of a brainstorming technique. The essence of the tool was to provide users with external stimuli and expose them to a large number of ideas over a short period of time. The tool was tested in the context of an information system requirements specification task. The results of the test indicated that the tool was useful in enhancing creative performance of the users. After interacting with the tool, participants were able to generate more original ideas while maintaining levels of relevance and workability necessary for innovative software designs. Our findings imply that creativity can and should be taught to IT students, and that the learning tool described in this study can potentially be a valuable facilitator of the process.

REFERENCES

Amabile, T. (1983). *The Social Psychology of Creativity*, New York: Springer-Verlag.

Aurum, A. (1997). *Solo brainstorming: Behavioral analysis of decision-makers,* Unpublished Ph.D. thesis, University of New South Wales, Australia.

Aurum, A. (1999). Validation of semantic techniques used in solo brainstorming documents. In H. Jaakkolam, H., Kangassalo, & E, Kawaguchi (Eds.), *Information modelling and knowledge bases X*, 67–79.

Aurum, A., Handzic, M., & Gardiner, A. (2002). Preparing IT professionals for the knowledge economy. *Proceedings of Information Resources Association International Conference*, Seattle, WA.

Aurum, A., Handzic, M., Cross, J., & Van Toorn, C. (2001). Software support for creative problem solving. *Proceedings of the IEEE, International Conference on Advanced Learning Technologies (ICALT'2001)*, Madison, WI, 160–163.

Finke, R. A., Ward, T. B., & Smith, S. M. (1992). *Creative Cognition*, Cambridge, MA: MIT Press.

Ford, C. M., & Gioia, D. A. (2000). Factors influencing creativity in the domain of managerial decision making, *Journal of Management, 26*(4), 705–732.

Higgins, J. M. (1994). *101 Creative Problem Solving Techniques: The Handbook of New Ideas for Business.* Florida: The New Management Publishing Company.

Holyoak, K. J., & Thagard, P. (1995). *Mental Leaps*, Cambridge, MA: MIT Press.

Huck, S. W., Cormier, W. H., & Bounds, W. G. Jr. (1974). *Reading Statistics and Research*, New York: Harper and Row Publishers.

Keegan, D. (1998). The virtual countinghouse: Finance transformed by electronics. In D. Leebart (Ed.), *The Future of Electronic Marketplace,* Cambridge, MA: MIT Press.

Marakas, G. M. (1998). *Decision Support Systems in the Twenty-First Century*, Upper Saddle River, NJ: Prentice Hall.

Mooney, R. L. (1963). A conceptual model for integrating four approaches to the identification of creative talent. In C. W. Taylor & F. Barron (Eds.), *Scientific Creativity: Its Recognition and Development* (pp. 331–340), New York: Wiley.

Mullen, B., Johnson, C., & Salas, E. (1991). Productivity loss in brainstorming groups: A meta-analytic integration. *Basic and Applied Social Psychology, 12,* 3–23.

Osborn, A. (1957). *Applied Imagination: Principles and Procedures of Creative Thinking.* New York: Charles Scribner's Sons.

Purcell, T. A. & Gero, J. S. (1996). Design and other types of fixation. *Design Studies, 17*(4), 363–383.

Sangran, S. (2001). Preparing students to be K-professionals. *Computimes Malaysia,* February 22, 1–2.

Satzinger, J. W., Garfield, J. M., & Nagasundaram, M. (1999). The creative process: The effects of group memory on individual idea generation. *Journal of Management Information Systems, 14*(4), Spring, 143–160.

Shalley, C. E. (1995). Effects of coaction, expected evaluation and goal setting on creativity and productivity. *Academy of Management Journal, 38,* 483–503.

Shalley, C. E., & Perry-Smith, J. E. (2001). Effects of social-psychological factors on creative performance: The role of informational and controlling expected evaluation and modelling experience. *Organizational Behaviour and Human Decision Processes, 84*(1), 1–22.

Shneiderman, B. (2000). Creating creativity: User interfaces for supporting innovation, *ACM Transactions on Computer–Human Interaction, 7*(1), 114–138.

Sridhar, R. (2001). India: Software for breaking mental blocks! *Business Line, India,* February 22, 1–3.

Stroebe, W., & Diehl, M. (1994). Why groups are less effective than their members: On productivity losses in idea-generating groups. In W. Stroebe & M. Hewstone (Eds.) *European Review of Social Psychology,* London: Wiley.

Sunderland, K. (2000). The power of a silly idea. *Charter, 71*(6), July, 49–51.

Thurstone, L. L. (1952). Creative talent, In L. L. Thurstone (Ed.), *Applications of Psychology* (pp. 18–37). New York: Harper and Row.

Tomas, S. (1999). Creative problem solving: An approach to generating ideas, *Hospital Material Management Quarterly, 20*(4), 33–45.

Van Gundy, A. B. (1988). *Techniques for Structured Problem Solving,* 2nd ed. New York: Van Nostrand Reinhold.

Chapter VII

Training in Remote Database Server Administration

Ludwig Slusky
California State University, Los Angeles, USA

Parviz Partow-Navid
California State University, Los Angeles, USA

ABSTRACT

This chapter introduces the development of a Unix Lab at the Department of Information Systems at California State University, Los Angeles. It also describes the lab's impact on our curriculum and the future plans for the inclusion of remote access and wireless technology.

INTRODUCTION

In January 2001, the Department of Information Systems at California State University, Los Angeles, received a $140,000 Workforce Enhancement grant from the State of California for improving instructional facilities. This chapter describes our experience in setting up a Unix Lab, incorporating it in our program, and our future plans for its expansion.

BACKGROUND

A comprehensive university, California State University, Los Angeles (CSLA), offers a broad range of liberal arts and professional programs. The college of Business and Economics is nationally accredited, at graduate and undergraduate levels, by AACSB. The college offers undergraduate programs leading to bachelor's degrees in Business Administration, Computer Information Systems (CIS), and Economics.

Traditionally, the information technology (IT) training and practices for students are based on the client technology of the client-server architecture (Watson, 2001). As the Internet shifts the emphasis from clients to servers and as the clients are more frequently implemented as personal servers, it becomes apparent that there is a need to enlarge the scope of the CIS curriculum by providing more server-focused courses.

Technological support of such server-focused training is fairly complex, as it goes to the core functions of the server operating system administration and to the core of the database server administration. Server-focused knowledge and skills are also at the center of e-business. This leads us to a new (and much in demand) category of *server-focused courses* at CIS department.

MISSION

The Unix Lab, an innovative academic resource for CIS students and faculty, is currently designed to provide server-focused training for Unix/Linux Administrators and Oracle DBAs. It is committed to (Djoudi, 2001):

- Supporting traditional and innovative curriculum content
- Advancing the learning and teaching experience in Unix, Linux, and Oracle in a predictable atmosphere of competence, control, and satisfaction
- Using information-based techniques with promising new capabilities for enhancing quality of IT education for CIS students, such as personal database servers, interactive learning, virtual classrooms, distance learning, and wireless technology

To accomplish this, the CIS Department established academic and business contact with similar labs at other universities and IT businesses from whom the experience, methodological materials, and advisement have been secured. Certificate of knowledge is a current trend in corporate training. The CIS Department is seeking educational and IT resources for the Unix Lab necessary to collaborate with recognized certificate programs such as Sun, Oracle, and Rational Software.

ARCHITECTURE

The Unix Lab (UL) consists of two branches — the *main* walk-in UL branch — Direct Access Unix Lab (DAUL) facility and UL extension — *Remote Access Unix Lab (RAUL)* facility at Academic Technology Support (ATS) department. Both, DAUL and RAUL, are built on Sun servers and Sun workstations (used as microservers) for server-centered and server-critical training, as illustrated in Figure 1.

RAUL is a new solution to the need for the server-focused training such as Oracle DBAs or system administrators on an individual basis: a dedicated microserver is assigned to a

Figure 1. Unix lab architecture

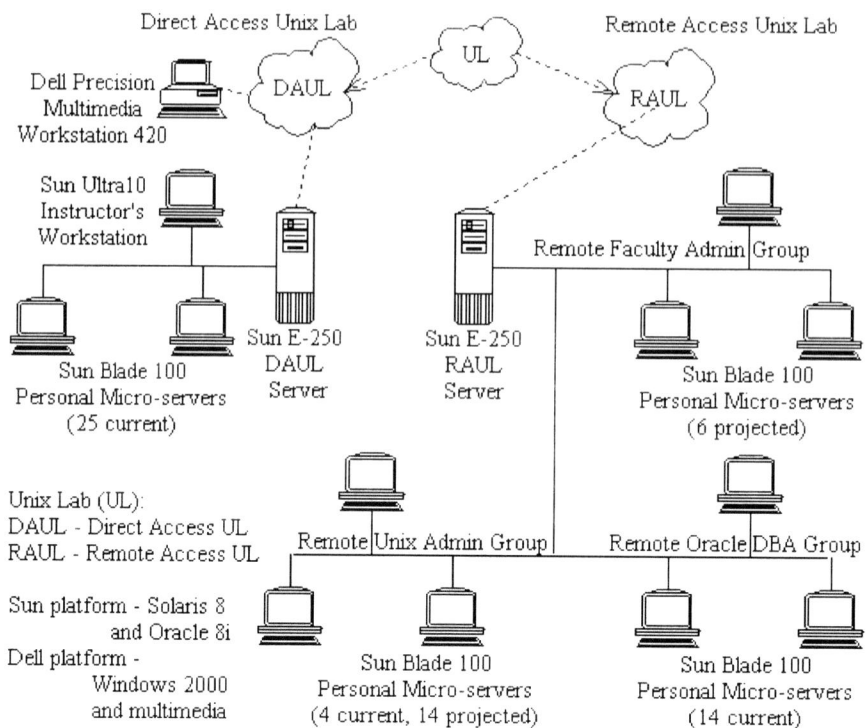

student (or to a team of two students). Furthermore, these RAUL microservers are available to students remotely over the Internet. The department's ability to train students in performing server-critical Oracle DBA or system administrative functions on servers remotely over the Internet is a much in-demand resource for students and is also a valuable asset for the department and the college.

The main classroom facility UL includes:

- First server (Sun Enterprise 250 model) controls access to microservers, supports rebuilding software installation images on microservers, provides share ability for some optional software resources, and supports regular UL operations
- Twenty-five students' microservers are based on Sun Blade 100 workstations for Unix/Linux/Java and Oracle DBA training
- One instructor's microserver is based on Sun Ultra 10 workstation
- One instructor's multimedia workstation (Dell Precision WorkStation 420) supports multimedia interactive and distance-learning development and presentations

The Remote Access extension of the Unix Lab — RAUL — includes a server and three groups of microservers:

- Second server (Sun Enterprise 250 model) supports remote access to RAUL microservers for faculty experimental development, remote products' evaluations and testing, testing students' server-based projects and exercises, etc.

- The Student Oracle DBA group consists of 16 microservers (based on Sun Blade 100 workstations) for Oracle DBA training (located at ATS and accessed remotely)
- The Student Unix Administration group consists of four microservers (based on one Sun Ultra5, one Sun Ultra10, and two Sun Blade 100); there is a plan to expand this group to 14 microservers
- A faculty Administration group will be added over a period of time to support faculty involved in Unix/Oracle distance-learning curriculum development; here, each participating faculty member will use an individual remotely accessed microserver

Distributed architecture of DAUL and RAUL with separate environments for Unix Admin and Oracle DBA supported by different groups and microservers is needed to decouple Unix and Oracle administrative users who do development having full control of microservers. Both servers store the default installation images for DAUL and RAUL microservers and use the Sun's JumpStart utility as a convenient way to rapidly rebuild these images on damaged machines.

CHALLENGES

Critical issues involved in server-focused courses are related to granting students powerful administrative privileges to work on Sun-based servers as Oracle DBAs or Solaris (Sun Unix-like operating system) Administrators:

- Oracle DBA (and Solaris Admin) privileges allow full administration of Oracle (and Solaris) installation, including operations on Oracle structures (databases, data dictionaries) and on files controlled by Solaris. Lack of this knowledge or improper use of it may result in system (server) crashes, shutdowns, data destruction, etc. Thus, mixing Oracle DBA training of one student with Unix Admin training of another student using the same microserver must be avoided.
- RAUL is setup as a training platform to provide technology necessary for building DBA and system administration skills, and at the same time, as a secure environment that limits the impact of personal errors on a microserver to only one or two students assigned to that machine, so other students can continue their work unaffected.
- Training in DBA (and system administration) functions on servers requires a much higher level of support, and entails a much greater risk of maintenance repairs for the support personnel than it is on a client side (in client-server architecture). Therefore, it is critical to have maintenance procedures and students' guides developed, tested, and implemented, for proper and uninterrupted operations with remote servers without sacrificing the quality of self-paced practice for students.
- With security, students are assigned different levels of access security to Sun servers and to Oracle as they gain expertise and progress through the courses. Thus, maintenance of students' access security is a time-consuming responsibility of ATS and the instructor.
- Predictably, limits of network access capacity for off-campus RAUL users became the most complex issue: distance learning shifts networks loads from in-campus to off-campus users. Information Resource Management's plan to expand network infrastructure at CSLA addresses this issue.

ORGANIZATIONAL TASKS

Several tasks and measures have been accomplished for successful implementation of UL with RAUL extension:

- The Lab administration has been set up as follows:
  - Faculty Lab Administrator, a faculty member — responsible for overall planning and administrating of the lab
  - Managing team consisting of two faculty members — responsible for the use of the lab resources
  - ATS specialist — responsible for the hardware and software installation and access privileges control — as the Lab Administrator and the Managing Team gain more experience in lab supervision, they are becoming increasingly involved in sharing with ATS the responsibilities of assigning and managing students' access privileges (direct and remote) in accordance with the university network access policy
- Lab hardware and software are purchased, installed, and implemented in courses; currently, we are in the process of expanding microservers to install Oracle 9i
- The administration of the Unix Lab has adopted and implemented a plan for periodical hands-on training workshops on using the lab resources for faculty and staff
- The following courses have been modified to take advantage of the new lab facilities:
  - Java Programming
  - C++ Programming
  - Database Design
  - Application Programs and Database Connectivity
  - Unix Operating System
- Two courses are added to the curriculum:
  - Linux Operating System
  - Oracle DBA with Solaris

The RAUL has already proved itself as an indispensable resource for distance-learning courses that require a dedicated microserver per each individual or collective user. The scope of RAUL can further be extended in the future to support such server-centered, "server administration" courses as Web Server Administration and Application Server Administration. The following section provides a brief review of available remote administration tools and applications.

Remote Administrative Tools and Applications

Remote access and files transfer are used for a variety of educational and business applications: from traditional business databases to music archives. For example, students of the University of Washington (2002) are provided with Remote Access and File Transfers to the Computer Music Lab based on Linux machines.

UNIGIS (2002) is a worldwide network of educational institutions, which offers distance-learning courses in Geographic Information Systems (GIS). It includes associated universities in 14 countries. Among others, the topics covered in the UNIGIS courses include Spatial Data Modeling, Database Theory, and Data Acquisition and Quality.

Satellite data and image processing for studying oceans is implemented at Stanford University (2002) as a remote Lab for Satellite Remote Sensing of the Oceans. Students can start an X-session to connect and do practices on the UNIX server.

Students at Ohio State University (2002) and Ohio high school students are offered remote access to servers to study and practice Calculus & Mathematica with Remote Calculus Mentors. The automated help is based on "Socratic interactive model": student questions are answered with more questions instead of giving a straight answer. The implementation platform includes UnixWare with Apache HTTP Server.

Keeping grades and online attendance of sessions is an important task of group remote online sessions. Software such as Gradekeeper (2002) can help faculty with course management. An instructor can record the session attendance and the performance scores of a student for the entire course. "Personalization" of supervised remote sessions can be enhanced by allocating specific times for "instant messaging" with students in a course.

The concept of remote access lab can be extended further to remote experiment lab. One example of implementation of this concept is Remote Experiment Lab at Federal University of Santa Catarina (2002). The lab allows students to log remotely and to perform *Remote Experimentation* and interact with the physical world via external devices connected to a remote server. Among the main benefits cited are better uses of university-networked computers, and users (both students and faculty) access to the resources that may not be available otherwise. It is also beneficial in building students' skills of managing, configuring, and troubleshooting computer applications remotely, saving time and expense.

Remote DBA

A new business challenge for database administration is that Database Administrators (DBAs) can no longer specialize in just one database. They frequently need to respond quickly to database problems in multiple distributed databases on various platforms.

Remote DBA for management, monitoring, and mentoring is an innovative and growing component of database administration services. It can be implemented with various technologies: SSH for Access Networks (2002), Web-enabled PCs, and wireless devices.

Remote database administration from a browser-enabled PC is a user-friendly approach for novice users' remote DBA technology. BMJC Software (2002), a leading international software provider, developed SmartDBA Cockpit (also formerly known as Web DBA), a tool that allows DBAs (experienced and novice alike) to manage various databases with a Web browser. Connected from any Web-enabled PC, users of SmartDBA Cockpit can perform user administration functions (roles, privileges, etc.), editing and running DDL scripts for routine database functions, data objects management and performance monitoring, and viewing and editing multimedia-rich data (.gif, .jpg, .mp3, and .avi, etc.). SmartDBA Cockpit is an ideal tool for a novice DBA, allowing tasks normally done by senior staff to be easily performed.

SmartDBA Cockpit also serves as an integrated launch point for other BMC's expert DBA tools for a real-time diagnostic and visualization, intelligent space management, SQL analysis, and tuning. A list of database management systems using Web-only browsers is available on the Internet Product Watch (2002) http://ipw.internet.com/data_management/database_gateways/957540653.html.

Contemporary Technologies Inc. (CTI) (2002) is a pioneer in providing remote Oracle Database Administration for client sites throughout the United States. With a proliferation of small- and medium-sized database servers, such service is a unique and cost-effective alternative to an on-site DBA. DBA training supported with RAUL is targeting the pool of such installations. Remote DBAs provide clients with more project-oriented DBA activities, such as migration, upgrade, validation, design, backup and recovery, and installation. Monitoring focuses on ongoing database management with software agents and problem resolution. Software agents monitor every aspect of database use and notify a Remote DBA of any warnings, alerts, or fatal errors. To differentiate between various levels of required support, CTI uses an assessment scale, at the top of which is CTI's "SmartSource" database administration.

Other examples include the following:

1. Optimum Computing Resources (2002) is a new provider of remote DBA. Among others, the company cites two major reasons for customers to choose remote DBA as opposed to on-site DBA:

    - To reduce the cost of DBA services by avoiding hiring a permanent DBA and paying for the actual time of DBA services (which can widely fluctuate in time)
    - To acquire specific DBA expertise

2. Virtual-DBA (2002), from Xtivia, offers comprehensive remote virtual database management designed to meet the database maintenance and management needs. A remote database needs to be continually monitored and have its system optimization parameters tuned and adjusted for the best possible operation. The cost of having the database down at a critical moment can be devastating for the businesses operating in today's dynamic environments. Details of tuning, optimizing, and maintaining databases often escape the attention of top management.

    Training a resident database expert DBA with a narrow specialization in a particular platform or a database product can be lengthy and costly. Frequently, other business requirements take higher priority over database maintenance and tuning issues. The concept of virtual database management addresses remote monitoring of critical database operational functions and remote monitoring of database system resource utilization.

3. Ntirety (2002) technologies offers a variety of Remote DBA services depending on the level of service required http://www.ntirety.com/services/remoteDBA.html.

4. Burleson (BEI) (2002) Remote DBA provides automated remote Oracle support for database administration tasks in the United States and Mexico. For comparison with a resident DBA, the Gold-level support, offered by BEI Remote DBA service, provides complete Oracle database administration remotely at $1400/month per database instance. The service includes the following:

    - Initial Oracle database configuration, installation, and periodic upgrades
    - Installation of a statistics collection mechanism
    - Monitoring, performance, analysis and tuning
    - Resolving serious database alert log messages

5. Technical experts of Pangea Database Systems (2002), a division of Oxford Global Technologies (OGT), provide remote DBA services for new and existing Oracle Applications.

6. An IT certification training company, Hello Computers (2002), provides free hands-on remote lab access to Sun Solaris Labs and Oracle Labs through the Internet. These labs are clearly defined, and hardware is wired for you to implement them. The applicant requesting access to free hands-on labs completes an application online, specifies the product (Sun Solaris or Oracle), and three four-hour time slots for operations will be allocated to the applicant. A Web site is designated for online conversations. Training is supported with an instructor who leads real-time classes for students accessing the system from their home or office.

7.   SystemGuard (2002) offers a number of remote support services for Oracle databases in the areas of data integrity, resource usage, performance, configuration, and security.

Data Management with SQL Remote Database Access relies on the ISO/IEC RDA SQL standard, which specifies a message format for remote communication of SQL database language statements, query, and update, to a remote database. This specification defines uses of the message fields and other implementation information, such as sequencing and optional features. It shows how SQL statements map to the Remote Database Access (RDA) protocol.

Recognizing that the performance of a database can only be as good as the performance of the server, DBA Zone Inc., a pioneer in database management, initiated remote managed Systems Administration (SA) services for its large and medium client organizations that need ongoing database administration support (http://www.dbazone.com/).

Wireless Mobile DBA

Mobile DBA is a database administrator supporting multiple databases in remote geographical locations of an organization's network. Using a wireless device, mobile DBA can control Enterprise databases from anywhere in the world. Several database-monitoring PDA-based tools are already available to support Mobil DBA functionality.

Various vendors provide technical solutions for wireless learning environments. For example, Wireless Mobile Classroom from HP (http://government.hp.com/solutions_detail.asp?agencyid=136&am=0&solutionid=38) addresses the wireless connectivity requirements for a learning environment without walls, in particular, an environment of wireless handheld devices.

Proactive Technologies, Inc. (2002) is a premier provider of database administration products and services targeting wireless database administration technology. It developed and offers Mobile-DBA software, an Oracle database administration utility loaded onto a wireless handheld device. With Mobile-DBA loaded onto a PocketPC or Palm device, database administrators can provide real-time remote database diagnosis, manage users, sessions, database objects, performance, etc. The Mobile-DBA software package includes server software and thin client. It supports security with VPN, SSL, DESX, and other encryption protocols.

Main DBA functionality supported by Mobile-DBA includes the following:

* Diskspace management — monitoring and managing table space size, adding data files to a table space, managing rollback segments, and placing objects online and offline
* Object management — monitoring database objects and changing storage parameters, managing partitioned tables and indexes, granting and revoking object privileges, etc.
* Session management — performing tasks such as monitoring user connections, viewing session statistics and details, and killing a session
* Security management — managing users, roles, privileges, and profiles
* Performance management — monitoring system resource utilization

The Wireless DBA Kit from The Ultimate Software Consultants (TUSC) (2002) is a turnkey wireless solution for delivering remote UNIX and database server administration over a wireless Internet service provider. It includes two components: Hand-held TUSC Palm

VII DBA and TUSC Cellular DBA. Palm VII DBA supports user-level security for UNIX or new restricted shell log-ins for wireless access. The command menus can be customized with choices for privileged and regular users, and it supports any UNIX command issued from the Palm VII. Common database operations are supported with prebuilt database scripts.

FUTURE WIRELESS SERVICES AND RAUL

Mobile access to data will bring significant changes to distance-learning services. According to Sun Microsystems, "The number of wireless communications devices installed worldwide already exceeds the number of desktop PCs." This proliferation of mobile information technologies is creating new demand for educating IT managers.

For example, the MBA High Technology Program at Arizona State University (http://www.cob.asu.edu/mba/courses/tech_curriculum.cfm) offers Compaq iPAQ Pocket PCs preloaded with course materials to the students of the program. The focus of the program is on a "continuous project in which teams develop a new product from beginning to end" (http://www.cob.asu.edu/mba/asu_mba_tech.cfm). The specific feature of the project is addressing "the issues of cross-team coordination, particularly when the teams are geographically dispersed."

Students of courses based on the Unix Lab use computers extensively and are expected to have access to personal computers off-campus. With wireless access planned for the winter quarter of 2002, the RAUL will offer the complete learning solution for students who will be able to access RAUL resources, with firewall restrictions, from off-campus, and on-campus, using wireless mobile devices such as Pocket PCs and Handheld PCs.

Sun identifies three components in mobile architecture: new services; utility-like quality and availability; and a flexible, future-oriented platform (Sun Microsystems, 2000). Enhanced RAUL server configuration will include Oracle9iAS Wireless and Oracle9i Lite on students' Pocket PCs. Oracle9i Lite provides infrastructure and application services specifically for mobile devices. Oracle9i Lite is an add-on to Oracle9iAS Wireless, providing a simple mobile e-business environment (Oracle, 2001).

Students will communicate with RAUL resources using mobile devices like iPAQ preloaded with Windows CE and Oracle 9i Lite for mobile applications (other databases for iPAQ are also available).

CONCLUSION

Planning and setting up a Unix lab architecture has been progressing through several phases:
- Setting the direct access UL facility (DAUL)
- Setting the remote access UL facility (RAUL)
- Expanding RAUL resources for various functional groups of users (Solaris administrators, DBAs, etc.)
- Expanding RAUL resources to remote and wireless services for on-campus and off-campus users

The first two phases were completed without major setbacks. The third phase is in progress and may never stop, as new categories of functional users continue joining RAUL. The fourth phase of implementation will begin in Winter 2003.

REFERENCES

BMJC Software. (June 2002). http://www.bmc.com/products/proddocview/ 0,,19052_0_0_9030,00.html.

Burleson. (2002). http://www.remote-dba.net/.

Contemporary Technologies Inc. (2002). http://www.oracle-remote-dba.com/remote-dba.htm.

DBA Zone Inc. (2002). http://www.dbazone.com/.

Djoudi, M., & Harous, S. (2001). "Simplifying the Learning Over the Internet," *T.H.E. Journal*, November.

Federal University of Santa Catarina. (2002). http://www.inf.ufsc.br/~jbosco/lexrem2i.htm.

Gradekeeper. (2002, June). http://fmhs.el-tejon.k12.ca.us/technology_proficiency/ gradekeeper/.

Hello Computers. (2002). http://china.hellocomputers.com/other/Free_Labs/free_labs.htm.

Internet Product Watch. (2002, June). http://ipw.internet.com/data_management/ database_gateways/957540653.html.

Ntirety. (2002). http://www.ntirety.com/services/remoteDBA.html.

Ohio State University. (June 2002). http://socrates.math.ohio-state.edu/about/labrem.php3.

Optimum Computing Resources. (2002). http://www.optimumcomputing.com/ remote_dba.shtml.

Oracle Corp. (2001, November). "Oracle9i Lite: The Internet platform for mobile computing." http://technet.oracle.com/products/lite/content.html.

Pangea Database Systems. (2002). http://www.pangeadb.com/about.htm.

Proactive Technologies, Inc. (2002). http://www.mobile-dba.com/supp_faq.html.

SSH Communications Security. (2002, June). http://www.ssh.com.

Stanford University. (2002, June). http://ocean.stanford.edu/GP235/.

Sun Microsystems. (2000, October). "Enabling the wireless net effect: How Sun drives wireless architectures to 3G and beyond," White paper, Revision 11, http:// www.sun.com/sp/supplements/wireless_whitepaper.pdf.

SystemGuard. (2002). http://www.systemguard.com/services/.

The Ultimate Software Consultants (TUSC). (2002). http://www.tusc.com/; http:// www.tusc.com/oracle/remdba/remote_dba.pdf.

UNIGIS. (2002, May). http://www.geocomm.com/links/education/onlinecourse.html.

University of Washington. (2002, July). http://www.dxarts.washington.edu/music/courses/ 401-3/remote.html.

Virtual-DBA. (2002). http://www.virtual-dba.com/.

Watson, R. (2001). "The Trumbull County community network project," *T.H.E. Journal*, May.

Chapter VIII

Conceiving Architectural Aspects for Quality Software Education through the Constructivist Perspective

Kam Hou Vat
University of Macau, Macau

ABSTRACT

This chapter describes the initiative to incorporate the practice of quality software education (QSE) into our undergraduate curriculum concerning the engineering of software. We discuss how the constructivist's method of problem-based learning (PBL) helps develop this QSE practice in our students' daily learning. We also expound the idea of an architectural context to building information systems (IS) solutions, supported by the industry's emerging consensus that architecture provides the kind of thinking and methods we need to develop today's complex systems. Our QSE approach focuses on designing problems, which require the building of a sensible IS architecture characterized by objects of different services. Our QSE approach is outlined in terms of a state-of-the-practice management philosophy called action learning, modified for educational scenarios, so that our students could learn to acquire their collaborative software engineering and management experience in the practice of architected applications development. To conclude, the criteria used to evaluate the working of our learning scenario and the challenge in combining action learning with PBL in innovating different QSE experiences for our students is discussed.

INTRODUCTION

In today's knowledge economy (OECD, 1996), as the possibilities of the information revolution challenge traditional business logic, many an organization has embarked on the journey of electronic transformation (Cook, 1996; Umar, 1997). According to Hammer and Champy (1993), this is the fundamental rethinking and radical redesign of business processes to achieve dramatic organizational improvements. In the past, the order of the day was to reorganize the technology each time a business changed. Yet, the reoriented consensus was to facilitate software solutions that adapted as the business adapted. This support for an increasingly adaptive business is currently achieved through the reuse of business components (Eeles, 2000), which are executable units of code that provide physical black-box encapsulation of related business services, accessed through a consistent, published interface that includes an interaction standard with other components. These business components support a process-based view of the business as it changes. Consequently, it is important to derive the necessary business models, which are traceable back to the originating requirements, in order to provide a secure foundation to develop the component-based information systems (IS) support. Indeed, this is often the backdrop behind which most of our universities' undergraduate programs in Software Engineering and Information Systems have been running. The fact of the matter is, we are often confronted with the situation (Dawson & Newsham, 1997) that most of our graduates today begin their careers lacking an appreciation of real-world conditions (Speed, 1999; Wasserman, 1996; Shaw, 1990). As academics, the haunting question is this: How do we cultivate future graduates who become more prepared to tackle real-world problems in the engineering of software for quality IS solutions, starting from their university education? This chapter serves as an educational response to devise suitable quality software education (QSE) scenarios for our students' active learning experiences. In the following discussion, we first introduce our architectural context for IS education, then provide a briefing on our pedagogy of action learning (Dean, 1998; Dilworth, 1998b; Revans, 1998) substantiated with problem-based learning (PBL) (Albanese & Mitchell, 1993; Engel, 1991; Ryan, 1993; Barrows, 1985). Next, we present some scenarios for enterprise's electronic transformation pivoted by e-business initiatives, followed by our elaboration of some architectural topics of our QSE curriculum. Finally, we discuss our criteria in evaluating the practice of PBL as well as some lessons learned from conducting the QSE.

THE ARCHITECTURAL CONTEXT FOR IS EDUCATION

Our discussion of the architectural context for IS education is centered about several themes: first, to clarify why we need architecture to build IS solution; second, to define what constitutes architecture in the IS context; and third, to provide a high-level introduction to the architectural approach to building IS solutions.

The WHY of Architecture in IS

The key technical issue in developing an information system — be it a conventional IS or a Web IS — is why we need an architecture in IS construction. We could resort to the insight and intuition of a building architect to extrapolate to the IS world and propose a list of requirements to be fulfilled by our architecture in the context of IS solution building. Essentially, the function of a building architect can be summarized as follows (Buffam, 2000; McConnell & Tripp, 1999):

> *The architect creates in his or her mind a concept of the overall form of the building to fit the intended purpose. This same architect creates a tangible set of blueprints that express his or her concept with sufficient clarity and rigor that the building owners can verify that the design satisfies their needs. Also, the architect — before committing to construction — can verify, through inspection, simulation, and calculation, that the building will stand up to its anticipated load, withstand environmental conditions and requirements, and meet regulatory standards. Tellingly, craftsmen can construct a building fulfilling that concept.*

Accordingly, in the IS context, we could provide a number of reasons to support the provision of an architecture. First, we need this architecture to ensure that the IS environment is aligned with the organization's imperatives. Namely, this architecture provides the basis for IS professionals and organizational leaders to ensure that the proposed system is properly aligned with the mission, objectives, and processes of their business. Such an alignment supports typical organizational goals as enhancing the capabilities of existent information systems and taking advantage of new strategic opportunities. Second, we need the architecture to help build an IS environment that can be easily changed and extended, so as to retain its alignment with changing business imperatives in the organization. Third, we need architecture to communicate appropriate views of the solution to, and among, the various stakeholders, so as to ensure that the solution gets built on time and within budget, while fulfilling the intended requirements. Fourth, we need architecture to help keep our IS environment (and its supporting processes) intellectually manageable. We recognize that information systems are complex. The control of complexity, and through it the ability to keep our systems understandable, is the biggest single challenge in the IS construction. One of the most important functions of the architecture is to support a "divide-and-conquer" approach. Other functions include to provide a framework for making and communicating technology choices, to give us freedom of choice of information technology (IT) components through component interoperability and through component portability, and to maximize our efficiency in building and evolving the IT environment through reuse of earlier work. In other words, it is too important for IS/IT professionals to neglect the essence of architecture — the reminder of a whole sequence of organizational and technological concerns.

The WHAT of Architecture in IS

The architectural context of IS solution building could be considered as a set of principles acting on and intimately integrated with, the total process of creating IT solutions. This process is often formulated in several distinct directions, such as the common-component sense, the design sense, the blueprinting sense and the framework sense (Pour, Griss, & Lutz, 2000; Bourque et al., 1999; Repenning et al., 2001; Zachman, 1987):

- The *Common-Component Sense*: This sense is based on the idea of reusability; namely, design is based on leveraging reusable standard components, subassemblies, frameworks, patterns, and idioms. To understand its significance, we can compare a traditional IS design with one guided by architectural principles. Traditional IS design involves such activities as understanding the business domain, abstracting models for this domain, and crafting application components to realize the models. Often, we attempt to excavate reusable components from previously developed systems. In contrast, the architectural way of IS design involves the following: understand the business domain, match the business domain to standardized architectural models, and adapt the components associated with these models to meet domain requirements.

- The *Design Sense*: This sense is based on a number of requirements for architecture to ensure that the IT environment is aligned with business imperatives. First is the mission of designing a solution to meet a client's needs. Second is the conscious imposition of principles and guidelines into the design activity, governing the structure of design. Third is the formulation of standards to be observed in implementing the design. Fourth is the activity dealing with the higher levels of abstraction in design. In this sense, what is important is the discipline we bring to the design process, the principles and guidelines that impose order so as to shape and constrain the design in ways that will ensure its ultimate success. To achieve elegant designs, as opposed to those that are merely adequate, the software architect's challenge is to create systems that are in perfect harmony with their intended purpose. The word "elegance" captures this quality most aptly, because it represents a clear, intuitive mapping between a function and its implementation. Elegance is desirable, because it brings intellectual manageability in the design activity.

- The *Blueprinting Sense*: The blueprinting sense of the word architecture is to produce blueprints that are comprehensible at appropriate levels of abstraction, to fulfill the needs of different stakeholders viewing the system from different angles. In current practice, the blueprinting function is effectively integrated into the modeling activity. We model the business, and we model the information systems that support its business processes. The methods that we use in these modeling activities incorporate the blueprinting function.

- The *Framework Sense*: The framework sense denotes a finished design of some kind. Where architecture in the finished-design sense is helpful, is where we can abstract some more generalized, or completely domain-independent, behavior that can serve as a framework for other solutions. The word architecture used in this sense is supportive of the common-component sense. Namely, by applying architectural principles in our solution building, we tend to produce designs that reuse proven frameworks.

The HOW of Architecture in IS

Following our discussion of a set of requirements that the word "architecture" has to fulfill, and a set of directions commonly attached to this word, we could conceptualize the architectural way to IS solution building as follows:

- *Targeting for client needs*: This is the most important characteristic of the architectural approach; we must design a solution to fit our client's needs.

- *Using validated principles*: The architectural approach conducts design according to vital principles that have been found to be common to successful systems. Examples include a clear separation of concerns between interface and implementation, and construction based on a hierarchy of well-defined layers of abstraction.

- *Reusing components, patterns, and frameworks*: As far as possible, we assemble our systems from available prebuilt components, in commonly understood and well-recognized patterns, structured around familiar frameworks.
- *Achieving elegance in all endeavors*: We strive for the elegant solution, for the simple and obvious. We should adhere to implementation principles covering any topic required to provide the proper guidance in decision making, including those for technology selection and for requirements governing nonfunctional attributes of the system to be built.
- *Adopting formal description for records*: We should use a formal description and recording discipline that represents the requirements for the IS system and its functional and environmental characteristics at various levels of abstraction. All the stakeholders in the system can relate to one or more representations of the system specification to verify that their needs are being fulfilled and that they understand how to advance the realization of the system to the next level of refinement.

All of these ideas are meant to help develop in our students their abilities in handling the software challenges of the Internet age. These include the following (Allen & Frost, 1998; Lethbridge, 2000; Meyer, 2001): support increasingly adaptive businesses, capitalize on the rapid advances in component technology; deal with legacy systems; plan and build for reuse; prepare for quality issues; and retain a pragmatic focus in the face of increasing complexity. Collectively, these challenges represent the drivers of change, worthy enough to secure a place in our discussion of QSE.

THE ACTION LEARNING MODEL OF EMPOWERMENT

To facilitate students' involvement of IS design and construction, and to understand the way organizations learn to improve themselves, we suggest adopting the discipline of action learning (PIQ, 1998) as an empowerment companion in the students' excursion of electronic transformation among enterprises. We interpret action learning (Dean, 1998) as a voluntary, participant-centered, evolutionary process to solve real, systemic, and pending organizational problems in the workplace. Its central mission (Dilworth, 1998b) is to increase the capacity of individual learners and the learning of the organizations they are associated with, to adapt to a rapidly changing environment. Revans (1998), who is widely known as the principal pioneer of action learning, suggested that it is eclectic, cutting across many fields. It emphasizes action, reflection, the need for critical thinking, and a climate of trust and authenticity. In action learning, the learning process is fueled by real problem solving among the participants. Its basic learning model can be characterized as follows:

A number of managers get together at regular intervals to discuss a problem or challenges they are facing in the workplace. The group referred to as the set in action learning literature, usually has a resource person, though the role of this person changes from context to context. After discussing the problem, project, or challenge with the set and the resource person, the managers return to the workplace to take action. After a period of time, the set meets again to discuss progress to date, results achieved, and problems still to be resolved. The managers then return to the workplace to take further action. The two phases of reflection (discussion) and action continue to alternate throughout the life of the learning period.

The Pedagogy of Problem-Based Learning

To translate Revan's description of action learning into terms applicable to the IS students' exploration, we have chosen to substantiate the action-learning context with problem-based learning (PBL) activities (Savery & Duffy, 1995; Albanese & Mitchell, 1993; Engel, 1991; Ryan, 1993) as follows:

1. Students, divided into small groups of three to five members and assigned a facilitator, are encouraged to perceive themselves as managers of their own in terms of time, material resources, and complexity of the problems that can be handled one at a time by the group.
2. Students are made aware that initially they will not possess enough prior information to solve the problem at hand or to clarify the scenario immediately.
3. Students are challenged to construct a solution to an often ill-structured problem chosen according to some concrete, open-ended situations.
4. Students are reminded that they must identify, locate, and use appropriate resources, and ask questions referred to as learning issues on the various aspects of the problem. These learning issues help the IS students realize what knowledge they require, and thus focus their learning efforts and establish a means for integrating the information they acquire.

It is expected that the IS students' groups generally have to iterate through some relevant stages of activities: analysis, research, and reporting, with discussion and feedback from peers and the facilitator at each stage:

- *Analysis*: Throughout this stage, students organize their ideas and prior knowledge related to the problem, and start defining its requirements. This helps them devise a specific statement of the problem. Meanwhile, they are urged to pose learning issues, defining what they know and what they have to know. This helps them assign responsibilities for research, eliciting and activating their existing knowledge as a crucial step in learning new information.

- *Research*: Throughout this stage, students collect necessary information on specific learning issues raised by the group. They may conduct library searches, seek sources on the Internet, collect data, and interview knowledgeable authorities. More importantly, when they come to realize the complexity and texture of the problem, they become their own experts to teach one another in the group; they use their learning to reexamine the problem. In the process, they are constructing knowledge by anchoring their new findings on their existing knowledge base.

- *Reporting*: After a specified period of time, students reconvene and reassess the problem based on their newly acquired knowledge. Once the students feel that the problem task has been successfully completed, they discuss the problem in relation to similar and dissimilar problems in order to form generalizations. Meanwhile, the facilitator's feedback should help students clarify basic information, focus their investigations, and refine their problem-solving strategies, besides addressing whether the original learning issues were resolved and whether the students' understanding of the basic principles, information, and relationships is sufficiently deep and accurate.

The Unifying Formula of Action Learning

A frequent formula (Dilworth, 1998a) that action learning proposes is $L = P + Q + R$, where Learning (L) equals Programmed Instruction (P) plus Questioning (Q) plus Reflecting (R). Here, P represents the knowledge coming through textbooks, lectures, case studies, computer-based instructions, and others. This is an important source of learning but carries with it an embedded caution flag. Namely, P is based in the past. Q means continuously seeking fresh insight into what is not yet known. This Q helps avoid the pitfall of imperfectly constructed past knowledge. By going through the Q step first, we are able to determine whether the information available is relevant and adequate to our needs. It will point to areas that will require the creation of new P. R simply means rethinking, taking apart, putting together, making sense of facts, and attempting to understand the problem. Following the use of this formula, action steps are planned and carried out with constant feedback and reflection as the implementation takes place. In short, what action learning can provide for the IS student-groups is elevated levels of discernment and understanding through interweaving action and reflection.

THE LEARNING SCENARIO FOR QSE

It is understood that collaborative project work (Favela & Pena-Mora, 2001) is recognized as having many educational and social benefits (Wills, 1998), in particular, providing students with opportunities for active involvement with their study. However, teaching, directing, and managing group-based project work is not an easy process. This is because projects are often expensive, demanding considerable supervision and technical resources; and complex, combining design, human communication, human–computer interaction, and technology to satisfy objectives ranging from consolidation of technical skills through provoking insight into organizational practice, teamwork, and professional issues, to inculcating academic discipline and presentation skills. More tellingly, PBL as a process-oriented instructional method helps prepare our students to get started with group project work to initiate their immediate journey as future IS/IT professionals in software development. Our learning scenario for QSE, based on real-world findings, is designed incrementally to arouse students' attention to different areas of concerns in the electronic transformation of today's enterprises.

The Demand of e-Transformation

It is increasingly obvious that e-business (Amor, 2000), conducted in and around the global marketplace, has presently become one of the most important drivers for electronic transformation (e-transformation) of today's enterprises. Yet, it has been commented that the long-term potential of e-business requires prudent contemplation and planning on the part of management. The formulation and implementation of e-business strategies, applications, and services involves many business issues that the traditional IS/IT department could not handle on its own (Kalakota & Whinston, 1996). Instead, the emerging consensus is to develop a cross-functional team composed of technical staff as well as business architects who may not know much about technology but who understand the core business. It is believed that such teams could integrate efforts and streamline cooperation among different functional departments to create business processes that are efficient, effective, and responsive.

The New Trade Model in e-Business

With the emergence of the Web-based e-business, enterprises today need a new model for trade that addresses new requirements in the Internet economy. It is found that the term "dynamic trade" (Leif, 1998) is often used to define an enterprise ability to satisfy current demand with customized response. Dynamic trade is expected to go beyond today's Web efforts, which extend traditional trade with easily available online data, and with customer self-service for simple inquiries like reviewing account history or checking order status. Instead, dynamic trade is meant to enable companies to maximize the lifetime value of a business relationship, through such value-added services as creating product and service bundles based on actual consumer preferences, and using traditional data to react to market changes.

The New Role of IS/IT in e-Business

It has been commented (McCarthy, 1999) that traditional IS/IT departments have largely adopted an inward-looking perspective to cater to only the internal users of an enterprise, but organizations must now work with a new externally focused business model like dynamic trade. This will inevitably present challenges to the internally focused IS/IT, often preoccupied with such goals as cutting costs and reducing risks. As Internet economy develops, the emphasis will shift from dumping product information onto the Web pages to delivering customized services, like buying assistance for consumers or proactive inventory management for business partners. According to Cameron (1999), one of the new roles for IS/IT departments is to become involved in developing new business software that will help companies exploit the promise of dynamic trade by enabling firms to capture information, analyze it, and respond to customers in real time. Meanwhile, IS/IT technology personnel will need more integration specialists, project managers, and business liaisons to ensure that business processes flow smoothly across internal and external boundaries of the enterprise.

The Enabling Technologies Behind e-Business

One of the main enabling technologies behind e-business development is the reuse of software components over some standardized distributed-object middleware (Berstein, 1996), through which such components can be moved around at execution time and deployed in a way that optimizes the technology in order to deliver the most business benefit. These advances in component technology have resulted in the movement toward separation of software applications from the increasingly heterogeneous technology platforms on which the services are deployed (Anderson & Dyson, 2000; Cook, 2000; Braude, 2001). It provides the potential for an application to be physically distributed so that it services the needs of the business and not the technology. We call this the service-based view of software construction, where components provide a method of packaging related services into prefabricated pieces of software from which solutions can be constructed. This service-based approach is also applicable in the area of legacy software, where most development is about enhancing existing systems, providing new front-ends to established back-ends, capitalizing on existing relational technology for data storage, and building interfaces to existing packages. It allows organizations to wrap the existing services into new offerings or products, so as to reuse their investments in existing packages, databases, and legacy systems within the context of component technology.

The Critical Problems Underlying e-Business Development

The overall picture confronting enterprises today could be characterized as this (Cook, 1996, 2000): at the core is the installed base of existing IT systems, which includes the legacy data and business logic. Around the edge are increasingly proactive customers, to which the enterprise must offer an increasing quality of service through existing and new channels. In between, the enterprise is reengineering its business processes, with a focus on knowing its customers better, and offering continuous improvement of its products and services. From an IT perspective, the legacy systems become surrounded by a matrix of go-between componentry providing services to support the changing business, with increased flexibility and reduced development times as compared with legacy systems. This is often a challenge requiring skilled and thorough design, taking into account such attributes as reliability, efficiency, usability, maintainability, testability, portability, and the most essential reusability. Nonetheless, a common reaction to the pressure of immediate business needs is to virtually abandon planning and control in the name of producing fast results (Gartner Group, 1995). Yet, incremental releases that are developed in isolation solely to meet tight deadlines will eventually result in fragmented systems that lack consistency and fail to provide integrated support. Worse still, this presents a problem that grows out of control exponentially with the number of increments delivered.

The Architectural Way to e-Business Solution Building

We believe that a key requirement of an incremental approach to e-business solution building is to base increments on a sound architecture (Boehm & Basili, 2000) that enables components to be plugged in as service providers to the increments. Besides, this should be an architecture for model building (Zachman, 1987), which supports such goals as management of scale and complexity, interoperability, and adaptability. In large organizations with complex business processes, there is a need to manage scale and complexity in software development in such a way that the resulting software structure mirrors business needs as closely as possible (Gartner Group, 1996). This requires the architecture to establish the definitions, rules, and relationships that will form the infrastructure of models from business process to code. More, this architecture should support the idea of software evolution among a mix of legacy systems and databases, off-the-shelf packages, and newer applications.

ARCHITECTURAL MODELING BASICS FOR QSE

To help our PBL students embark on their journey of system development, we selected some recurring architectural modeling concepts for them to learn and practice through trial, error, and mentoring. These concepts are based on fundamental principles (Hartley, Hruschka, & Pirbhai, 2000) that we believe are applicable to IS modeling, regardless of the underlying techniques used.

The Layer-System Concept

We believe each system is a component of one or more larger systems. The larger systems are the context or environment in which the component system must work. Systems comprise, thus, a layered set of subsystems below the layer with which we happen to be dealing and a layered set of supersystems above that layer. This layered structure can be exploited in representing systems and in defining the system development process. Most systems are members of multiple-layered sets. The particular set(s) chosen to represent a system are determined by the viewpoint(s) that are important for the particular system. Also, every system has a set of essential requirements, which meet the needs of the context or environment, and a set of physical requirements, which reflect the architectural and design decisions made to satisfy the essential requirements. To succeed in the development of complex systems, all system artifacts invoked by these principles must be represented separately, but their relationships and interactions must also be represented.

The Modeling Concept

A model is an abstraction highlighting some aspects of real-world systems in order to depict those aspects more clearly. A model has an objective (the question we want it to answer) and a viewpoint—the point of view of one or more stakeholder(s). Abstract models reduce the complexity of the real world to digestible chunks that are simpler to understand. Different types of models answer different types of questions about the system they represent. If we decide to build more than one model of a given system to investigate different aspects, then we should somehow organize these models according to their relationships to one another and to the system. Hence, we often need a framework to accommodate different models.

The Separation of Concerns Concept

Every system has a specification comprising two important parts: system requirements and system architecture. Both of these parts contain models. The "system requirements" model is a technology-independent model of the problem the system is to solve. It represents the "what." The "system architecture" model is a technology-dependent model of the solution to the problem. It represents the "how." Typically, these two models are created for the entire system and for every subsystem down to the lowest level in the system hierarchy. And, it is important to separate the "what" and the "how" for the following reasons: It is often useful to understand a problem independently of any particular solution. Any given problem has many possible solutions. Selection of a particular solution is a trade-off process; we often need to make numerous different trade-offs while keeping the problem statement unchanged. The separation should support the principle of separation of concerns, which means dealing with only one part of the system's complexity at a time. The "requirements" model has to cope with only the essential problems; the "architecture" model has to cope with many constraints imposed by technology and organization. This separation of the "what" and the "how" gives us the flexibility to re-implement the "what" using new technology, but it also gives us the convenience of reusability — not just for software or hardware but for requirements as well. This is particularly important, because requirements are relatively more stable over longer periods of time than technology.

The Major Modeling Relationships for Layer-System

Four types of modeling relationships have been of particular interest, which are distinctly different from one another. They are, respectively, the relationships of aggregation-decomposition, abstracting-detailing, supertype-subtype and controlling-controlled. They all serve distinct and important roles in system development. They can be integrated smoothly, where appropriate, with other models, including object-oriented models. The following provides features of each relationship:

- *Aggregation/decomposition relationship*: Through this relationship, elements in the higher layers actually consist of the elements in the lower layers, or conversely, elements in the lower layers are decompositions of those in the higher layers. This structure is also known as a whole/part structure or a container/content structure: namely, a given layer provides the container for the layer below, which is the content of the layer above. In practice, an aggregate involves more than just collecting sub-elements into a set. The sub-elements must also interface with one another, requiring linkages between them that may not be evident when they are considered separately. When applied to software, we can imagine an architecture module at the highest software layer; major subprograms it contains are modules in the next layer down; sub-subprograms or subroutines form a further layer.

- *Abstraction/detailing relationship*: Through this relationship, the higher layers are simply more abstract expressions of the lower layers, or conversely, the lower layers are more detailed expressions of the higher layers. It is important to notice this. An abstract requirement statement does not contain the more detailed requirements statements that describe it. If we assemble a set of detailed requirements, we merely have a collection of detailed requirements — the abstract and detailed requirements exist independently of each other, with an abstraction/detailing relationship between them.

- *Supertype/subtype relationship*: Through this relationship, an element in the higher layer — the supertype — includes all of the features that are common to its associated elements in the lower layer — its subtypes. These features are attributes that are inherited by the elements on the lower layer. Starting from the lower level, supertypes are formed for sets of elements that share common attributes. Supertype/subtype models are important in object orientation. This relationship is the foundation for inheritance. Moreover, object orientation has taken this relationship and extended it to more complex forms of inheritance than just attribute inheritance: The lower layer may also inherit functions and the behavior of the supertypes. With the supertype/subtype relationship, it is important that the supertype contain all the commonalities of the subtypes. The main use of this relationship is to discover commonalities and to describe them only once, thus reducing redundancy. The structure then allows the lower layers to inherit whatever commonalities have been discovered. We can see that this relationship is a subtype of the abstraction/detailing relationship. A supertype is an abstraction of its subtypes, and the subtypes are detailed instances of the supertype. Other names used for this relationship include generalization/specialization, class hierarchies, inheritance structures, and "is-a" hierarchies.

- *Controlling/controlled relationship*: Through this relationship, the upper layers control elements of the lower layers. Other terms used for this relationship are control hierarchy, or the is-boss-of (is-supervised-by) relationship. Sometimes, we simply say that the higher element uses the lower elements. The higher layer must have knowledge of the lower layer, but the lower layer — that is, the one being used — does not necessarily have to know anything about the boss. In terms of client/server models, the client is the boss that delegates work to the server; the server provides certain services that are performed whenever a client asks for them.

Typically, layered models based on the four types of relationships can be used simultaneously to represent different aspects of a system. For example, the required functional capabilities of a system can be captured by a process model, which is based on the abstraction/detailing relationship. The required behavioral capabilities are captured by a control model, which is based on a controlling/controlled relationship. The information structures in the system are captured in an entity-relationship model based on the supertype/subtype relationship. Also, the physical structure can be captured by the architecture model, which is based on an aggregation/decomposition relationship. In sum, the layered models allow us to represent different views of the system separately, but when done as part of the requirements and architecture models, the links between these views are carefully maintained.

THE COMPONENT-BASED IS ARCHITECTURE AND PROCESS

Our study of component-based development (CBD), based on the Allen and Frost (1998) model, is evolutionary in nature. We aim to harness a service-based method with effective object-oriented modeling to capitalize on the increasing power of the fast-developing component technology. The idea is to provide an overall design philosophy for realizing the vision of service-based reuse of components (Allen & Frost, 1998; Anderson & Dyson, 2000; Cook, 2000). We call this philosophy the *service-based architecture* for CBD, which employs the concept of *service packages* to facilitate a business-oriented modeling process. A service package provides a set of services belonging to a single service category. Each service from a service package is realized by an individual component, which is also a container of different objects. This provides a business-oriented basis for modeling deployment of components using *services packages*, which are implementation packages of objects, providing services through their interfaces. That way, components provide a means of packaging related objects together into prefabricated pieces of software. And, service packages provide a mechanism for grouping those objects into units (in the form of components) that are cohesive to the needs of a particular set of services from which business solutions can be constructed. It is important to notice that the promise of component-based development is that software solutions can be composed from reusable components, in analogous fashion to hardware (Cox, 1986; Eeles, 2000; Repenning et al., 2001). Nevertheless, the service packages must be modeled in a way that makes the resulting components useful building blocks, simple to activate and inexpensive to administer. The level of granularity of a component can vary from large and complex to small and simple. In practice, large components have the greatest potential for reuse but are often not cohesive and may be difficult to assemble into solutions with other components. Small components are usually more cohesive but often need to be coupled with many other components to achieve significant reuse, resulting in excessive intercomponent coupling. Clearly, settling on a good and useful level of granularity is a trade-off between these two extremes.

The term "process" as used in our pedagogic context for architected applications development (AAD), carries the connotation of process models designed to view the real world from the viewpoint of architectural software development. Thus, the process to be described is an abstract description of the software development activities within the service-based architecture (Stapleton, 1997). We are interested in a two-tier process to achieve an AAD methodology: the solution process, and the component process. The former is aimed at development of solutions, typically in terms of user services, to maximize reuse of existing services and provide early user value. The latter is aimed at developing components that provide commonly used business and data services across different departmental systems or for use by third parties. It is important to notice that we often need to use elements of both processes adapted to our specific needs. Typically, the key driver of the solution process is a set of specific requirements to meet the needs of a business process. Various models are produced throughout the process, which evolve in detail as the process unfolds. We continually seek opportunities to extend and refine existing generic models. Such models are often selected on a use-case by use-case basis (Jacobson et al., 1992) for incremental development of user services. On the other hand, the generic business requirements that drive the component process may come from the need to reuse existing legacy assets, and the feedback from solution projects. An important part of the component process is to evolve the models so that they can be specialized and refined by solution builders to form an evolving set of components.

In practice, the use of a process by a software development team should assist project management in numerous tasks. These include identification and partitioning of work, identification of progress achieved, planning of the staff resource profile, planning of the requirement for physical resources, and provision of cost and time scale estimates for the work yet to be performed. From a technical viewpoint, a process should assist in such areas as identification of preconditions required before each activity is started, specification of the products and deliverables required from each activity, techniques that may be used during each activity, and experience gained from earlier work. Clearly, building and refining generic models is an important aspect of CBD, where we want to leverage model reuse more than code reuse. Service packages provide a means of structuring a project in terms of architectural context and allow us to build on and capitalize on the best work of others. A service package can be effectively employed in a component process to contain a generic model, which can be refined and extended to meet the specific needs of a solution process. The model solution space evolves to contain more detail as a project moves through the iterations of the process. Eventually, portions of the model are mature enough to be transformed into code. The tested code represents the model at its most detailed level of abstraction. As for deliverables, they are simply views of a maturing model. Indeed, the service-based process for AAD is an adaptive process that can be tuned and customized to specific organizational needs. Checkpoints can also be built into the process to help evolve it. This includes documenting the lessons learned so that others can avoid making the same mistakes.

TEAM SKILLS DEVELOPMENT FOR MANAGING SOFTWARE REQUIREMENTS

To partially address the requirements challenge in architectural IS solution development, we often suggest some team-based activities (DeMarco, 1982; Jacobson et al., 1992;

Leffingwell & Widrig, 2000; Brown & Dobbie, 1998) to be experienced by our PBL students within their curriculum activities:

- *Analyzing the problem*: This includes a set of skills to understand the problem to be solved before application development begins. It is the process of understanding real-world problems and user needs and proposing solutions to meet those needs. We consider a problem as the difference between things as perceived and things as derived (Gause & Weinberg, 1989). Accordingly, if the user perceives something as a problem, it is a real problem, and it is worthy of addressing. Typical techniques include gaining agreement on the problem definition, understanding the root causes to induce the problem, and identifying the stakeholders and the users, with the former being anyone who could be materially affected by the implementation of the new application.

- *Understanding user needs*: This introduces a variety of techniques to elicit requirements from the system users and the stakeholders. Software teams are rarely given effective requirements specifications for the systems they are going to build. Often, they have to go out and get the information they need to be successful. Typical methods include interviewing and questionnaires, requirements workshop, brainstorming and idea reduction, storyboarding, use cases derivation, role playing, and prototyping. Each represents a proactive means of pushing knowledge of user needs forward and thereby converting fuzzy requirements to those that are better known.

- *Defining the system*: This describes the initial process, by which the team converts an understanding of the problem and the users' needs to the initial definition of a system or application that will address those needs. Our PBL teams should learn that complex systems require comprehensive strategies to organize information for requirements. This information could be expressed in terms of a hierarchy, starting with user needs, transitioning through feature sets, then into the more detailed software requirements. The latter could be expressed in use cases or traditional forms of requirements documents, say, the vision document defining at a high level of abstraction, both the problem space and the solution space.

- *Managing the project scope*: This reminds our teams that they should be aware not to initiate projects with too large a scope to be accomplished. Project scope is presented as a combination of the functionality to be delivered to meet users' needs, the resources available for the project, and the time allowed in which to achieve the implementation. The purpose of scope management is to establish a high-level requirements baseline for the project. The team has to establish the rough level of effort required for each feature of the baseline, including risk estimation on whether implementing it will cause an adverse impact on the schedule. Also, each team has to actively engage its customers in helping solve the scope management problem to ensure the quality and the timeliness of the software outcomes.

THE CRITERIA FOR PBL EVALUATION

Throughout our students' study period, we have borne in mind that our instructional method should be evaluated in part by its ability to explain practice. The following explicit criteria (Greening, 1998; Ryan, 1993; Savery & Duffy, 1995) have been found useful in order to later judge the learning outcome with respect to the process of problem diagnosis, action intervention, and reflective learning:

- *Learning is an active and engaged process*: Instead of being told what to do or how to solve problems, students within a PBL atmosphere are to generate their own learning issues. It is expected that a sense of ownership should be born, leading to greater cognitive engagement. Students are actively engaged in working at tasks situated in an authentic setting, which should lead to greater ability in transfer to other real-world contexts.

- *Learning is a process of knowledge construction*: PBL purports that learners construct their own knowledge. The constructivist epistemology states that the known is internal to the knower and is subjectively constructed based on individual responses to experience. Thus, in order to harness the reality of learning, we need to consider the opportunity to find knowledge for oneself, contrast one's understanding of that knowledge with others' understanding, and refine or restructure knowledge as more relevant experience is gained.

- *Learners function at a metacognitive level*: Constructivist learning focuses on initiative thinking activities rather than working on the "right answer the teacher wants." Students generate their own strategies for problem formulation and possible solutions. The instructor's role is that of a facilitator, a guide, or a coach, probing students' thinking, monitoring their activities, and generally keeping the process moving. Thus, PBL should promote metacognition through encouraging students to reflect upon the problem-solving process. It is believed that reflection on recent experiences is an effective method of learning.

- *Learning involves social negotiation*: We accept the constructivist perspective that knowledge is socially negotiated. The quality or depth of one's understanding can only be determined in a social environment, where we can see if our understanding can accommodate the issues and views of others and to see if there are points of view that we could usefully incorporate into our understanding. A learning community, where ideas are discussed and understanding is enriched, is critical to the development of our students into self-directed work teams of software professionals.

REMARKS FOR CONTINUING CHALLENGE

It is experienced that the conventional approach to education remains the instructivist one, in which knowledge is perceived to flow from experts to novices. This transmissive view of learning is most evident in the emphasis on lectures, in the use of textbooks to prescribe reading, and in the nature of tutorials and assessment methods. It assumes that the process of good teaching is one of simplification of the truth in order to reduce student confusion. Yet, this simplification could deny students the opportunity to apply their learning to dynamic situations, such as quality software development through team-based collaboration. We question the transferability of the instructivist learning and ask how much of that which is assigned to academic learning ever gets applied to actual scenarios, when there is such a rapid surge in knowledge commonly associated with the birth of the "Information Age." This is a transference problem. Actually, the content product of learning is assuming a less important role relative to the process of learning, as the life of information content shortens, and the need for continual learning increases. In designing the learning scenario for QSE to be injected into our project courses for software engineering and information systems, we tried to reorient toward a meaningful direction by reducing the obsession with knowledge reproduction. And, PBL represents one such relief from the constructivist pedagogy (Duffy & Jonassen, 1991). Greening (2000) described it as a vehicle for encouraging student ownership of the learning activities. There is an emphasis on contextualization of the learning scenario, providing a basis for later transference, and learning is accompanied by reflection as an important metacognitive exercise; for example, assessing how a project should be approached by an architectural context. Also, the implementation of PBL is done via group-based work, reflecting the constructivist focus on the value of negotiated meaning (Perkins, 1992). More importantly, it is unconfined by discipline boundaries, encouraging an integrative approach to learning, which is based on requirements of the problem as perceived by the learners.

On the other hand, when technology meets pedagogy, we insist that education of the architectural way to IS solution building should start with the ability to construct different models of interests, including the various business models and IS models. The result includes the design of a suitable IS architecture, denoting the integrated structural design of the system, its elements and their relationships depending on given system requirements. Conversely, this architecture has to represent all relevant aspects of a system, which are defined by models representing different system views. Such models are derived from the goals the system has to fulfill and the constraints imposed by the system's environment. From the standpoint of component-based development, we agree that our students should be given training to construct individual components efficiently. Then, their education should evolve through efficient development of component-based solutions in new domains, efficient adaptation of existing solutions to new problems, and efficient evolution of installed solutions by people with limited technical knowledge. Finally, it will achieve the efficient integration and evolution of sets of solutions. The real challenge is to derive a coherent set of architectural principles that will bring the whole of system development, including technology, methodology, and project management, into a single architecture-centric whole.

REFERENCES

Albanese, M., & Mitchell, S. (1993). Problem-based learning: A review of literature on its outcomes and implementation issues. *Academic Medicine, 68*(1), 52–81.

Allen, P., & Frost, S. (1998). *Component-Based Development for Enterprise Systems: Applying the SELECT Perspective*. Oxford: Cambridge University Press.

Amor, D. (2000). *The E-business (R)evolution*. New York: Prentice Hall.

Anderson, B., & Dyson, P. (2000). Reuse requires architecture. In L. Barroca, J. Hall, & P. Hall (Eds.), *Software Architectures: Advances and Applications* (pp. 87–99). Heidelberg: Springer-Verlag.

Barrows, H. (1985). *How to Design a Problem-Based Curriculum for the Pre-Clinical Years*. New York: Springer.

Berstein, P. (1996). Middleware: A model for distributed system services. *Communications of the ACM, 39*(2), 86–98.

Boehm, B., & Basili, V. R. (2000). Gaining intellectual control of software development. *IEEE Computer*, May, 27–33.

Bourque, P., Dupuis, R., Abran, A., Moore, J. W., & Tripp, L. (1999). The guide to the software engineering body of knowledge. *IEEE Software*, November–December, 35–44.

Braude, E. J. (2001). *Software Engineering: An Object-Oriented Perspective*. New York: John Wiley & Sons.

Brown, J., & Dobbie, G. (1998). Software engineers aren't born in teams: Supporting team processes in software engineering project courses. In *Proceedings of IEEE International Conference on Software Engineering: Education & Practice*, Dunedin, New Zealand, January, 26–29.

Buffam, W. J. (2000). *E-Business and IS Solutions: An Architectural Approach to Business Problems and Opportunities*. Reading, MA: Addison Wesley.

Cameron, B. (1999). Driving IT's externalization. January; www.forrester.com.

Cook, M. A. (1996). *Building Enterprise Information Architectures: Reengineering Information Systems*, New York: Prentice Hall.

Cook, S. (2000). Architectural standards, processes and patterns for enterprise systems. In L. Barroca, J. Hall, & P. Hall (Eds.), *Software Architectures: Advances and Applications* (pp. 179–190). Heidelberg: Springer-Verlag.

Cox, B. (1986). *Object-Oriented Programming: An Evolutionary Approach*. Reading, MA: Addison-Wesley.

Dawson, R., & Newsham, R. (1997). Introducing software engineers to the real world. *IEEE Software*, November, 37–43.

Dean, P. (1998). Editorial — Action learning and performance improvement. *Performance Improvement Quarterly, 11*(1), 3–4.

DeMarco, T. (1982). *Controlling Software Projects*. Englewood Cliffs, NJ: Yourdon Press.

Dilworth, R. L (1998a). Action learning in a nutshell. *Performance Improvement Quarterly, 11*(1), 28–43.

Dilworth, R. L. (1998b). Action learning — Setting the stage. *Performance Improvement Quarterly, 11*(1), 5–8.

Duffy, T. M., & Jonassen, D. H. (1991). Constructivism: New implications for instructional technology. *Educational Technology, 31*(5), 7–12.

Eeles, P. (2000). Business component development. In L. Barroca, J. Hall, & P. Hall (Eds.), *Software Architectures: Advances and Applications* (pp. 27–59). Heidelberg: Springer-Verlag.

Engel, J. (1991). Not just a method but a way of learning. In D. Bould & G. Felletti (Eds.), *The Challenge of Problem-Based Learning* (pp. 21–31). New York: St. Martin's Press.

Favela, J., & Pena-Mora, F. (2001). An experience in collaborative software engineering education. *IEEE Software, 18*(2), March/April, 47–53.

Gartner Group. (1995). Rapid application development, Part 2: Organizing for success. Inside Gartner Group This Week, June 7.

Gartner Group. (1996). Best practices in application development project management, Part 2, SPA-650-1293. ADM Research Note, March 20.

Gause, D., & Weinberg, G. (1989). *Exploring Requirements: Quality before Design*. Dorset House Publishing.

Greening, T. (1998). Scaffolding for success in problem-based learning. *Medical Education Online, 3*(4), 1–15, http://www.utmb.edu/meo/.

Greening, T. (2000). Emerging constructivist forces in computer science education: Shaping a new future? In T. Greening (Ed.), *Computer Science Education in the 21st Century* (pp. 47–80). New York: Springer.

Hammer, M., & Champy, J. (1993). *Reengineering the Corporation: A Manifesto for Business Revolution*. UK: Nicholas Brealey.

Hartley, D., Hruschka, P., & Pirbhai, I. (2000). *Process for System Architecture and Requirements Engineering*. Dorset House Publishing.

Jacobson, I., Christerson, M., Jonsson, P. M., & Overgaard, G. (1992). *Object-Oriented Software Engineering: A Use Case Driven Approach*. Reading, MA: Addison-Wesley.

Kalakota, R., & Whinston, A. B. (1996). *Electronic Commerce: A Manager's Guide* (pp. 1–29). Reading, MA: Addison Wesley.

Leffingwell, D., & Widrig, D. (2000). *Managing Software Requirements: A Unified Approach*. Reading, MA: Addison-Wesley.

Leif, V. (1998). Dynamic trade. May; www.forrester.com.

Lethbridge, T. C. (2000). What knowledge is important to a software professional? *IEEE Internet Computing*, May, 44–50.

McCarthy, J. C. (1999). The social impact of electronic commerce. *IEEE Communications, 37*(9), September, 53–57.

McConnell, S., & Tripp, L. (1999). Professional software engineering: Fact or fiction? *IEEE Software*, November–December, 13–18.

Meyer, B. (2001). Software engineering in the academy. *IEEE Computer*, May, 28–35.

OECD. (1996). The knowledge-based economy. Organization for economic co-operation and development, OCDE/GD(96)102, Paris, France.

Perkins, D. N. (1992). What constructivism demands of the learners? In T. M. Duffy & D. H. Jonassen (Eds.), *Constructivism and the Technology of Instruction: A Conversation* (pp. 161–165). Hillsdale, NJ: Lawrence Erlbaum Associates.

PIQ. (1998). Special issues on action learning, *Performance Improvement Quarterly, 11*(1–2).

Pour, G., Griss, M. L., & Lutz, M. (2000). The push to make software engineering respectable. *IEEE Internet Computing*, May, 35–43.

Repenning, A., Ioannidou, A., Payton, M. et al. (2001). Using components for rapid distributed software development. *IEEE Software, 18*(2), March/April, 38–45.

Revans, R. W. (1998). Sketches in action learning. *Performance Improvement Quarterly, 11*(1), 23–27.

Ryan, G. (1993). Student perceptions about self-directed learning in a professional course implementing problem-based learning. *Studies in Higher Education, 18*, 53–63.

Savery, J. R., & Duffy, T. M. (1995). Problem-based learning: An instructional model and its constructivist framework. *Educational Technology, 35*(5), 31–38.

Shaw, M. (1990). Prospects for an engineering discipline of software. *IEEE Software*, November, 15–24.

Speed, J. R. (1999). What do you mean I can't call myself a software engineer? *IEEE Software*, November–December, 45–50.

Stapleton, J. (1997). *DSDM: Dynamic Systems Development Method — The Method in Practice*. Reading, MA: Addison Wesley.

Umar, A. (1997). *Application (Re)Engineering: Building Web-Based Applications and Dealing with Legacies*. New York: Prentice Hall.

Wasserman, A. I. (1996). Toward a discipline of software engineering. *IEEE Software*, November, 23–31.

Wills, C. E. (1998). Group-based software engineering in an introductory computer science course. In *Proceedings of IEEE International Conference on Software Engineering: Education & Practice*, Dunedin, New Zealand, January 26–29.

Zachman, J. A. (1987). A framework for information systems architecture. *IBM Systems Journal, 26*(3), IBM Publication G321-5298.

Chapter IX

The TCP/IP Game

Norman Pendegraft
University of Idaho, USA

ABSTRACT

This chapter describes a simulation game used to help students understand the operation of TCP/IP. In the game, students play various layers of TCP/IP on several machines and collaborate to transmit a message from one application to another. The game is used in a telecommunications management course taken primarily by MIS majors at the senior level. The game consumes about 1 hour, and anecdotal evidence suggests that it is helpful to the students.

INTRODUCTION

Many IS curricula offer a telecommunications management course. Our course attempts to balance the technical and managerial issues involved in TC management, and because of the large subject matter, time is limited for each topic. The technical topics include TCP/IP and the more general ISO layered model. It has been my experience that many students, exposed only to reading and lectures, do not understand the interaction between the layers, or why each is necessary, or how the whole package works. One possible solution is to have the students build a computer simulation of TCP/IP, however, such an assignment is time consuming and technically demanding. For all its value, it seems a misuse of the limited time available in this course. Another alternative is to create a simulated system and let students experiment with it. For example, Campbell (1996) simulated a computer and let students write assembly language programs to run on the computer. Yet another alternative is to develop a simulation game.

SIMULATION GAMING

Simulation gaming is predicated on the notion that students learn better from experience than from lectures and reading. It also introduces a sense of play into learning, which makes it fun, as it should be. Students are actively involved rather than passive, and the connections between pieces are often easier to see when experienced (Corbeil, 1989; Greenblat, 1988). After many years of experience using various games in class, the author has come to believe strongly in their value as pedagogical vehicles (see, for example, Butterfield & Pendegraft, 1996; Pendegraft & Watson, 1990). Informal student response to these games has been enthusiastic. Here, a simulation game was developed to let the students experience the operation of TCP/IP. The purpose of the simulation was to help the students understand the function of each layer and, in particular, to understand how the layers interact with each other.

TCP/IP

There are many excellent discussions of TCP/IP (for example, Hunt, 1998). This section is not intended to give a detailed or technical description of TCP/IP, but rather to clarify some of the simplifications imbedded in the simulation. In order to keep the simulation manageable, many of the specific functions are excluded from the simulation or are included only notionally: that is, they are dealt with via conversation between the students and the instructor.

TCP/IP is a layered packet switching protocol. Messages are broken into pieces (packets), each of which is sent to the destination independently of the other pieces. Each layer performs a set of functions, which together, result in a reliable communications connection. Each layer adds to the packets its own header containing information needed by the same layer at the receiving end. While each layer may take the packet from the higher layer and break it into smaller pieces, this is only done by the TCP layer in the simulation. Error correction is handled notionally. This simplifies the simulation and allows for focus on more important issues. A brief summary of each TCP layer follows.

Application Layer

The application layer includes processes like email, Web services, and database management systems. A port number identifies each application running on top of TCP/IP. Several well-known port numbers are used in the example.

The Domain Name Service (DNS) is an application layer service that converts domain names like www.whitehouse.gov or ebay.com into their IP addresses. DNS services are outside the scope of this exercise and are notional in the simulation. DNS information is assumed available to IP in the simulation.

TCP Layer

The transport control protocol (TCP) creates and maintains connections between machines. It breaks traffic into pieces called segments, calculates and appends a CRC (cyclical redundancy checksum) to each, and sends them to the next layer, IP. Each packet is addressed to the correct port (application) on the receiving machine. TCP on the receiving machine checks the CRC of each segment and acknowledges those correctly received. Those unacknowledged in time are resent. Error detection and retransmission are handled notionally in the simulation: the instructor stipulates during the exercise whether a packet is transmitted and received correctly, and the system (i.e., the students) responds accordingly.

IP Layer

Packets at the IP (Internet protocol) level are called datagrams. While segments may be broken into multiple datagrams, experience has shown that this introduces too much difficulty, so it is not included in the simulation. IP is primarily responsible for routing datagrams, that is, selecting the route they will take to the recipient. If a packet is destined for the current machine, IP sends it to TCP, otherwise, IP forwards the packet.

Two key ideas for forwarding are the use of the routing table and routing protocol. The routing table contains data about the network and, in particular, about the first hop to each destination. The protocol is the rule that updates the routing table as data about the network is received. Exchange of network data is handled notionally.

Network Access Layer

The NAL is responsible for converting an IP address into a hardware or MAC address. NAL also contains error correction data to ensure that frames are correctly received. Again, error correction is handled notionally.

Physical Layer

The physical layer contains the network interface cards (NICs) and the cables/hubs, etc., connecting machines.

SIMULATION DESIGN

The design of the game is most easily described by referring to the handout materials and then walking through its operation. Figures 1 through 5 illustrate the handout materials. Figure 1 contains a diagram of a hypothetical network. Each is labeled with its IP address and MAC address. Nodes also have DNS names. Two machines were given duplicate names (Martha) to illustrate the importance of root domain names. Each of the machines has one or more network ports connected as shown. On those machines with more than one NIC, all are assumed to have the same MAC address (another simplification).

The routing table (Figure 2) shows for each source the first hop to each possible destination. The format is slightly different from a real routing table: * is used as a wild card in order to simplify the discussion. Each node is assumed to know that the nearest router is its gateway. Figures 3 and 4 include a port map to determine the port used by each application and the name map used by the DNS resolver. Figure 5 shows the message form and the header form. The use of all of these is described below.

OPERATION

The class is asked to separate into groups, each representing a network device. Several students per device enables them to each play a different layer in TCP/IP, passing messages between them, thereby emphasizing the nature of a layer protocol. The devices are "con-

Figure 1. Network layout

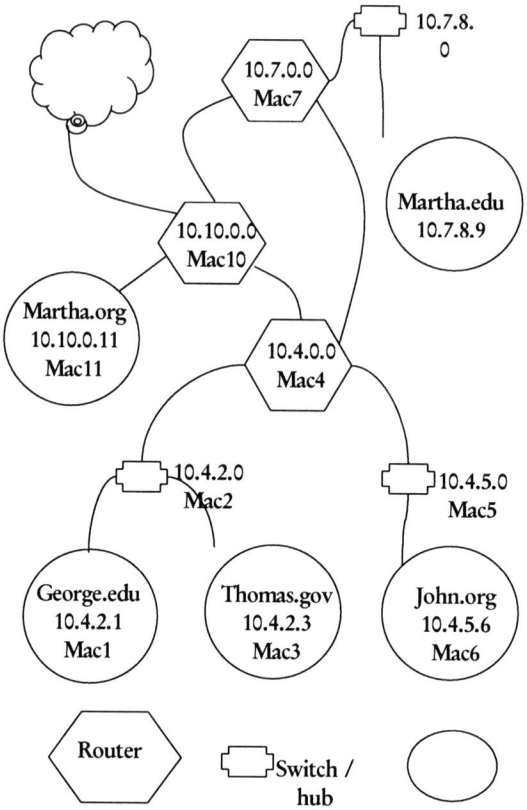

Figure 2. Routing tables

Router IP4	
Destination	Next Hop
10.4.2.*	10.4.2.0
10.4.5.*	10.4.5.0
10.7.*	10.7.0.0
*	10.10.0.0
Router IP7	
Destination	Next Hop
10.4.*	10.4.0.0
10.7.8.*	10.7.8.0
*	10.10.0.0

Figure 3. Application port map

Application	Port
FTP	21
SMTP	25
DHCP	67
HTTP	80
Oracle	1525

Figure 4. Domain name map

Domain Name	IP
George.edu	10.4.2.1
thomas.gov	10.4.2.3
john.org	10.4.5.6
martha.edu	10.7.8.9
martha.org	10.10.0.11

nected" by six to 10 foot long pieces of wire held at each end by the player playing the "NIC." (One player can play two NICs by using one hand for each.)

The operation is summarized in Figures 6 and 7. Column 2 describes the actions of each layer, and Column 3 describes how this is handled in the simulation. [An equals sign (=) indicates that the player follows the instruction in Column 2.] The sending application writes the message on the message form which has only 10 characters per line. TCP then cuts the message into 10 character chunks, adds a sequence number, and appends to each a header. Each of these combinations becomes a packet. TCP adds to each the port number of the sending and receiving applications to the packet and sends it to IP.

IP gets the destination IP address from DNS and appends it along with its own IP address to each packet. IP looks in the routing table and determines the IP address of the first hop. It also calculates a "time to live" and adds it to the packet as well. The packet is sent to NAL.

NAL determines the first hop MAC address and appends it to the packet, which is then sent to the correct NIC. It also calculates a CRC, which is added to the header. The packet is passed to the physical layer.

The physical layer is represented by a six to 10 foot long piece of wire that has been threaded through a hole in an envelope. One end is held by each of the two linked devices. The sending end lifts the wire, and the packet runs down the wire to the next computer. While this may sound silly, it introduces some fun and seems to help actively involve the class in the simulation.

Figure 5. Packet header and data forms

Header

Dest MAC	Send MAC	MAC CRC	To IP	Send IP	Time to live	Dest port	Send Port	TCP CRC	Seq

DATA

1	2	3	4	5	6	7	8	9	10

Figure 6. Operation summary: send

	Determine destination Application Name	notional
	Pass to TCP	=
TCP	Establish Connection (SYN) / End Connection (FIN)	notional
	Break message into segments add sequence #	Tear into 10 character pieces
	Append destination Port#	=
	Append source Port#	=
	Append CRC to each	notional CRC
	Pass to IP	=
IP	Break segment into datagrams	notional
	Add destination IP address to each	=
	Add source IP address to each	=
	Lookup First Hop IP	=
	Determine Output Connection	=
	Add Time to Live	Initial = 10 Each hop -1
	Pass to DLL	=
NAL	Break datagram into frames	notional
	Add destination MAC address	=
	Add source MAC address	=
	Send to Physical	=
Physical	Send to receiving MAC	envelope & wire

At the receiving end, the process is reversed. There are some differences. For example, error checking is performed instead of CRC calculation. IP checks for destination and forwards the packet if necessary. TCP notionally acknowledges each packet.

Example

Figure 8 shows a partially completed header stream for three different messages. This example follows one segment each of the three messages.

The first from george.edu (10.4.2.1) to thomas.gov (10.4.2.3) takes only one jump, because the two devices are on the same network segment. The second, from george.edu to john.org (10.4.5.6) must be routed. The node george does not know where 10.4.5.6 is, so it sends the packet to its gateway, the Router at MAC4 (10.4.0.0). The packet is addressed to IP 10.4.5.6 and MAC4, i.e., to john in care of the router. The router knows where 10.4.5.6 is located, so it can send the packet directly to it.

The third message is from george to martha.edu (10.7.8.9). Again, george does not know where 10.7.8.9 is, so it directs the packet to its gateway (i.e., to IP 10.7.8.9 and MAC4). This time, the router does not know either, so it consults its routing table and finds that the router at 10.7.0.0 is the first hop to 10.7.8.9. The packet is forwarded to 10.7.0.0 (Mac7), which knows where 10.7.8.9 is, and it sends the packet to its destination.

Figure 7. Operation summary: receive

Layer	Receive	Simulation
Physical		envelope & wire
NAL	IF for me continue ELSE discard	=
	Calculate error code IF correct send to IP ELSE request retrans	notional
IP	Read IP address	=
	IF for me keep ELSE store and forward (GO TO SEND)	=
	Pass to TCP	=
TCP	Calculate error code	notional
	Assemble segments	=
	IF correct Send ACK	notional
	Evaluate Destination Port#	=
	Pass to Appl	=
Appl	Read message	=

Figure 8. Partial header data for three messages

From george.edu to thomas.gov

Dest MAC	Send MAC	MAC CRC	Dest IP	Send IP	Time to live	Dest port	Send Port	TCP CRC	Sequence
M3	M1		10.4.2.3	10.4.2.1	10				1

From george.edu to john.org

Dest MAC	Send MAC	MAC CRC	Dest IP	Send IP	Time to live	Dest port	Send Port	TCP CRC	Sequence
M4	M1		10.4.5.6	10.4.2.1	10				1
M6	M4		10.4.5.6	10.4.2.1	9				1

From george.edu to martha.edu

Dest MAC	Send MAC	MAC CRC	Dest IP	Send IP	Time to live	Dest port	Send Port	TCP CRC	Sequence
M4	M1		10.7.8.9	10.4.2.1	10				1
M7	M4		10.7.8.9	10.4.2.1	9				1
M9	M7		10.7.8.9	10.4.2.1	8				1

The instructor can notionally degrade the network by causing a communications line (MAC4-MAC7) to fail or become jammed, thereby forcing traffic to be routed through 10.10.0.0. The class might also be asked to construct the routing table for router 10.10.0.0.

DISCUSSION

The informal anecdotal evidence is, in the author's opinion, strong enough to continue using and improving the simulation. Students have offered a number of unsolicited comments on the simulation, all positive so far. Finally, an additional, somewhat hidden, benefit accrues to the instructor. By designing and running the simulation, the instructor develops a much deeper understanding of the underlying technology; at least that has been my experience.

REFERENCES

Butterfield, J., & Pendegraft, N. (1996). Gaming techniques to improve the team-formation process. *Team Performance Management, 2*(4), 11–20.

Campbell, R. A. (1996). Introducing computer concepts by simulating a simple computer. *SIGCSE Bulletin, 28*(3).

Corbeil, P., Laveault, D., & Saint-Germain, M. (1989). *Games and Simulation Activities, Tools for International Developmental Education*. Quebec: Canadian International Developmental Agency.

Greenblat, C. S. (1988). *Designing Games and Simulations*. Newbury Park, CA: Sage.

Hunt, C. (1998). *TCP/IP Network Administration*. Sebastopol: O'Reilly.

Pendegraft, N., & Watson, W. (1990). Systems analysis, interviewing, and the improv. *Computer Science Education 1*(3).

Chapter X

Framing Leadership Issues for System Developers

Gayla Jo Slauson
Mesa State College, USA

Chad Grabow
Mesa State College, USA

ABSTRACT

This chapter combines the concepts of leadership through "framing," as discussed in books such as "The Art of Framing," published in 1996 and written by Gail Fairhurst and Robert Sarr, with the development of information systems. It provides a brief explanation of the frame theory of leadership and discusses how this theory relates to information systems. The authors propose that students in management information systems degree programs need to be made aware of the leadership potential of the information systems through which members of organizations communicate. Effective use of information systems to lead people in contemporary organizations is so far lacking in curricula, and the authors hope that this chapter may begin to remedy this situation.

INTRODUCTION

Today's systems analysts serve as leaders in ways that they may not realize. By controlling access, form, and distribution of information in organizations, analysts provide frames for people to organize and interpret many organizational issues and events. In their roles as "framers," analysts help to shape the perceptions of people in the organization and help to direct their ways of thinking. Information systems serve as tools for the management of meaning. Managers may give analysts the authority to decide what a set of reports from a system will look like, which interfaces will be used, what data will be collected and maintained in a database, who will be provided with access to the data, how access will be implemented, which information will be protected, how it will be protected, and how well. Perhaps more importantly, systems developers may decide which data will not be collected, disseminated, stored, or secured. Delegating such tasks has far-reaching implications within organizations. Systems analysts and developers need to be cognizant of their leadership roles in modern business. They must realize how their "framing" of information affects decision making and shapes organizational cultures. Information technology education must include this topic for prospective system developers.

Curriculum for MIS (Management Information Systems) or CIS (Computer Information Systems) programs can and should be adapted to include discussions and projects that take students beyond merely a basic understanding of traditional managerial roles and skills. According to Alvin Toffler, the advanced global economy and workplace are incapable of functioning without computer systems (Toffler, 1990). In contemporary organizations with intranets, telecommuters, online reporting mechanisms, virtual hours, instant feedback, and email conversations, systems developers as well as the managers they develop systems for need to understand how to use information systems to communicate and to lead. Students who expect to develop computer systems need to understand what leadership is and how it can be facilitated through the purposeful design and use of information systems.

BACKGROUND

Theories of leadership have not traditionally been joined with the implementation and design of information systems, although the control of information and the control of technology were considered potential sources of power, even before computer systems were commonly used by most organizations (Crozier, 1964). Additionally, most leadership theories stressed the importance of excellent communication skills as characteristic of leaders. Leaders communicate vision (Smith, 1997, p. 114). To the extent that computer information systems have become the primary means of communicating in many organizations, traditional theories of leadership might provide support for those who wish to lead through the use of these systems. However, current authors observe that the leaders of today will need to develop different skills than leaders of the past, including "an ability to develop and convey a shared vision, …comfort and confidence with technology, (and)… competence in systems thinking" (Marquardt & Berger, 2000, p. 1).

Current books on effective management techniques require leaders to manage information as well as people, presumably through the ubiquitous computerized information systems found in most contemporary organizations:

As more companies realize that the key resource of business is not capital, personnel, or facilities but rather knowledge, **information** and ideas, many new ways of viewing the organization begin to emerge.... Organizations are also becoming more and more virtual...linked by information technology....(Technology) enables organizations to... transform....Twenty-first century leaders will need to understand how to restructure, to connect, and to think in a new paradigm (Marquardt & Berger, 2000, pp. 9-10).

However, authors typically offer little to no explanation of what processes would be used to design systems that would specifically assist a leader in leading subordinates (Smith, 1997). Even Gail Fairhurst and Robert Sarr, in their book on how leaders must manage meaning for subordinates through "framing," do not specifically tie information systems into the picture, except in one brief mention of a manager who uses email as a framing tool (Fairhurst & Sarr, 1996, p. 97). Nonetheless, because so many organizations rely increasingly on computer information systems to facilitate communication between managers and subordinates, and "opportunities for framing occur with every communication" (Fairhurst & Sarr, 1996, p. 22), practicality suggests that people who understand how to build, communicate through, and use information systems to assist them with "framing" will lead more effectively than those who do not.

What is framing? People are constantly bombarded with internal and external stimuli. At any given moment in offices around the world, for example, one or more telephones is ringing, people are talking, lights are flashing on or off, machines are humming, computer screens are glowing, posters on the wall are demanding attention, and so forth. Furthermore, the people in those offices may be feeling cold or hot, ill or well, lonely, happy, hungry, or tired. They must decide what to attend to at that moment. And, from an expanding perspective, they must choose what to attend to during any specific hour, day, week, year, and lifetime. They must also determine how to interpret what they experience.

How do people filter out what they should attend to? How do they decide how to interpret things? People decide what to attend to, and how to interpret it, partially by paying attention to leaders, who put frames around issues or events that they consider to be important. As employees decide how to react to significant changes in organizations, they attend to leaders who create frames for them and thereby determine their significance. This framing process affects whether employees notice problems and how they understand and act on them (Entman, 1993). Additionally, "frames exert their power not only through what they highlight, but also through what they leave out" (Fairhurst & Sarr, 1996, p. 4).

How is an information system connected to this framing process? Information flowing through an organization is inevitably framed through the medium used to carry and store it. Imagine someone receiving a notice that he is being fired on a bulletin board. Information is also framed for recipients through its appearance at the point of interface, by who is allowed to access it, by limits placed on its usage, by what it says, and by what it omits. What an opportunity, then, for leaders who can use information systems as tools to frame purposefully. Those people who understand framing as a leadership tool, and who, at the same time, realize the potential of computerized information systems as framing devices, will become the most effective leaders in today's technology-based organizations.

Any communication tool used as extensively as organizational computer systems must be considered as a potential framing mechanism. Email, however, only scratches the surface. Interactive sites on intranets and the Internet provide information for many employees. Reports may be perused online. Some virtual organizations never provide opportunities for managers and subordinates to interact face-to-face in traditional meetings. Communications for employees of those firms occurs exclusively through information systems. Glimpses of the future indicate increasing numbers of global organizations, with increasingly more communications occurring via information technology (Rollier, 2002).

ISSUES

Traditionally, information represented power (Smith, 1997, p. 11). Strategic and tactical managers served as leaders by controlling information that they received by virtue of their positions. They determined how to filter, organize, and disseminate it, and through these decisions, framed the information for subordinates. These managers decided which reports would go to which employees, what these reports would contain, and how they would look. They decided which information to collect and maintain. They communicated why specific information was important. Employees tended to follow the lead of management by attending to information that was presented. Top leaders often hoarded information (Rosen, 1996).

However, in the process of moving from manual to computerized systems, many managers began to depend on the advice of system developers regarding what information could, in fact, be collected or maintained easily using computers. Efforts were made to alter information in ways that computers could easily collect, store, process, and disseminate. Programmers with little to no business background wrote programs to create managerial reports.

Managers were willing to let these changes occur after seeing how effective and efficient the early transaction processing systems were. These computer systems provided them with more up-to-date information than had previously been possible. Managers could see computer systems facilitating managerial functions, such as planning through computerized budgets or controlling through exception reports. They did not necessarily realize that computer systems would drastically alter organizational communications and provide the same up-to-date information provided to them to their subordinates. Furthermore, they did not realize that they were giving to system developers and programmers some of their power.

Certainly, programmers and analysts, during creation of information systems, felt little incentive to maintain status quo wherever information was being hoarded. Managers could not directly control information in the same ways they had controlled it manually. And, perhaps because they did not see how they could control it, some managers quit feeling the need to do so. For example, in *The New Leader: Bringing Creativity and Innovation to the Workplace*, published in 1997, the author stated: "In the past we needed layers of managers to control information. Now computers and information systems minimize the need..." (Smith, 1997, p. 52).

This statement could not be more incorrect. Computers and information systems *cannot* adequately take the place of managerial filtering and framing. Unfortunately, when computer systems are expected to provide filters and frames, and it seems that they often are, the system developers may not even realize it. They have likely not considered that the information systems they are creating should do something more than simply generate numerous facts and figures.

Systems analysts and programmers are not always well prepared to see things from a variety of managerial perspectives. Programmers trained heavily in mathematics and programming languages may lack big-picture organizational vision. They may have little understanding of the strategic vision of top-level management. Consequently, the information provided by systems they create may be limited to quantitative applications. They may focus exclusively on data that is easy to collect, tracking transactions in great detail and overemphasizing numerical analysis. These systems may provide information more suited for operational managers than strategic ones. They may discourage innovative applications designed to help managers lead subordinates.

Managers, on the other hand, are not always sure what computers are capable of accomplishing. They may wait for the technical experts to tell them what a system can or cannot do. They may be reluctant to force development of computer systems to do things in ways that they really would prefer but do not know how to explain. Many of them have not learned how to use the computers particularly well, let alone how to create systems themselves. Some managers have realized the problems that their lack of expertise creates. Ricardo Semler, considered a global leader and the world's "leading maverick" for his demonstrated leadership abilities at Semco, is quoted as saying that computers are "drowning us in (data)" rather than helping us to organize it. He felt that leaders who have limited understanding of technology have been "wrapped around the fingers of computer professionals, who have leveraged their special knowledge into a sort of priesthood" (Marquardt & Berger, 2000, p. 55).

Consequently, as organizations steadily grow more reliant on computer systems to control information flow and presentation, managers may increasingly abdicate their leadership function to system developers. The systems analyst may sometimes become the entity who frames WHAT organizational information will be provided to WHICH employees, as well as HOW and WHERE the information will appear. The system developer may determine what information will be collected and how, who will have access and how they will gain that access, who will have the right to alter the information, and how important the information will be considered for security purposes. Obviously, any well-educated systems analyst will attempt to implement what the decision makers in charge of the project view as the goals and objectives of the system. They will ask questions to determine how the system can best be created to assist the organization in attaining strategic goals. Certainly, the system developer should not make all of the decisions regarding the information collection, usage, and storage of any system. However, if managers take passive roles, systems analysts must fill in the necessary details to create a functioning system within the time limits given.

Communications often take place over and through office information systems. Presentations and calculations, strategic plans, and visions are framed through the software and hardware of management information systems. Systems analysts who create the frames through which the information travels must develop more than technical expertise. To create a system that may be used by leaders to lead, the analysts must be able to lead, and they will likely have little experience with leadership. The ability to lead people differs significantly from technical expertise:

> ...technical expertise does not transform a successful IS professional into an effective leader.... exclusive focus on technical expertise and preoccupation with technological currency interfere with attention to the interpersonal and analytical competencies necessary for effective leadership. (Klenke, 1998)

Systems analysts must understand the big-picture perspective to frame effectively. They must also understand the human side of information technology to understand how to assist managers to use systems to lead. How will the information they are presenting and the way it is presented influence the people who receive it? Rex Mitchell, at CSUN, points out that "Framing requires...a thorough understanding of those we are trying to influence"

(Mitchell, 2000). Framing through the lens of an information system affects the perspectives of the people in the organization. Over time, framing organizational information will significantly affect the organization's culture. How can systems developers be better prepared to handle such an important role?

SOLUTIONS AND RECOMMENDATIONS

Education for prospective systems developers should provide students with leadership theory and leadership opportunities. They need to learn about the effects and potential effects of information technology on people in organizations:

Finally, in today's complex, uncertain, global environment IS/IT leadership requires sophisticated conceptual and analytical skills since concept formation and idea generation play a critical role in the design of IT for competitive advantage. To this date, leadership training, education and development have yet to be incorporated into management information systems (MIS) curricula to prepare today's MIS graduates for their roles as…leaders. I have yet to encounter a graduate program in IS/IT that prepares students to become change agents, motivators,…that teaches them how to craft, articulate, and communicate a vision, and how to build an organizational culture in which IT and leadership are interdependent and mutually reinforcing (Klenke, 1998).

Information system programs often address functional areas, such as accounting or marketing, and students may even build applications to facilitate problem solving in these areas. However, students should understand the leadership potential in computer systems and build applications that help managers lead subordinates. They need to understand what leadership is.

Perhaps the best class in which this understanding should occur is in a course that mixes students who plan to be managers with those who plan to develop information systems. Some 4-year programs in computer information systems, such as the one the authors are involved with at Mesa State College in Grand Junction, Colorado, include a senior-level project-based policies course that might be ideal for this purpose.

Another option might be to bring two or more classes together at particular points during a semester to initiate the development of parallel projects in differing areas. Framing theory might be presented to all of the groups as a whole. Then, for instance, management majors might have a project assigned requiring them to find methods to influence subordinates on a particular issue through framing using computer systems. Computer system majors may have a project in which they are required to create the systems that the management majors have envisioned. They could be required to show how they implemented feedback from the students with other majors.

If such projects are not feasible, framing theory should at least be covered in lecture or readings. Its potential applicability to information systems should be emphasized. This coverage could happen in a sophomore class, such as "Fundamentals of Information Systems"; a junior class, such as "Theories of Information Systems"; or a "Current Topics" course at the senior level.

Among the topics to discuss in whichever course is chosen would be organizational politics as they specifically relate to technology. Robert Thomas, in his 1994 book titled *What Machines Can't Do*, explains that:

> *...it is essential also to ask how technological alternatives are themselves framed, how the worldviews of different organizational actors shape the range of possibilities considered, and, most important, how differences among worldviews influence the outcomes of change.... (Case studies) suggest that the power-process perspective on technological change could both serve as a bridge and inspire much more fundamental change in the way we think about the relationship between technology and organization. (Thomas, 1994, p. 203)*

Naturally, the discussions on how leadership through framing might be implemented on computer systems cannot be limited to computer systems majors. Management majors need to understand this issue equally well. They need to learn how to communicate vision through computer systems:

As we begin to appreciate our role as managers of meaning, we will act on our instincts to seize more framing opportunities (Fairhurst & Sarr, 1996, p. 19).

Managers and systems developers and maintainers need to understand the difference between simply creating direct reports and framing the information. The leader must fit the data into the framework of a larger vision.

In *The Art of Framing*, Fairhurst and Sarr discussed various language tools for framing, such as metaphors, jargon, contrast, and stories. Although these seem to provide useful communication tips for face-to-face conversations, they do not adequately cover what should be discussed regarding framing through information systems.

The book to facilitate this discussion has not yet been written. It would need to examine numerous topics, such as the framing that takes place nonverbally, through choosing to send a message through email rather than speaking with someone in person. It would also make students aware that the content of email messages sent from one person to another in an organization actually matters. It would need to cover interface design in terms of user reaction and consider elements of report design. It would provide examples of leaders who are consciously leading through framing using information systems. It would provide examples of systems created for specific managers to help them lead subordinates. Even without such a book, students should learn about framing.

CONCLUSION

As organizations increasingly rely on computerized information systems as decision-making aides, systems developers and managers must realize the leadership roles they fill through framing information. Only then can the true power of information systems be realized. Curricula should be modified or developed to include course discussion and projects aimed at developing leadership through framing. Effective framing through information systems is a necessary and powerful skill in contemporary organizations.

REFERENCES

Cohen, E. & Tichey, N. (1998). The teaching organization. *Training and Development, 52*(7), 27–33.

Crozier, M. (1964). *The Bureaucratic Phenomenom* (pp. 13–131). Chicago, IL: University of Chicago Press.

Entman, R. M. (1993). Framing: Toward clarification of a paradigm. *Journal of Communications, 43*, 51–58.

Fairhurst, G. & Sarr, R. (1996). *The Art of Framing; Managing the Language of Leadership*, San Francisco, CA: Jossey-Bass Publishers.

Klenke, K. (1998). Developing leadership skills for IS professionals. www.isworld.org/ais.ac.98/proceedings/track31/klenke.pdf.

Marquardt, M. & Berger, N. (2000). *Global Leaders for the 21ˢᵗ Century*. Albany, NY: State University of New York Press.

Mitchell, R. (2000). Framing in communications and leadership. www.csun.edu/~hfmgtool/frameC.htm.

Rollier, B. (2002). Preparing MIS students for a global economy. *Journal of Information Systems Education, 12*(4), 193–199.

Rosen, R. H. (1996). *Leading People*. New York: Viking Penguin Books USA Inc.

Smith, G. P. (1997). *The New Leader: Bringing Creativity and Innovation to the Workplace*. Delray Beach, FL: St. Lucie Press.

Thomas, R. (1994). *What Machines Can't Do: Politics and Technology in the Industrial Enterprise*. University of California Press.

Toffler, A. (1990). *Powershift*. New York: Bantam.

Chapter XI

S3: Senior Surf School – A Special Graduate Information Systems Course

Georg Disterer
University of Applied Sciences and Arts, Hannover, Germany

ABSTRACT

Many elderly people (age of 60+) are keen on getting familiar with the Internet. At the same time, end-user training gets more and more important for IT management. Therefore, we implemented a graduate Information Systems course, where students have to design, organize, manage, and run a training session, where elderly people can see and try using the Internet. The students learned to design a teaching curriculum and teaching materials, to set up and maintain the technical infrastructure, to organize end-user training, and, most importantly, to teach and to train end-users.

INTRODUCTION

Internet Needs of Older People

In the countries of the western hemisphere, we observe a growing elderly population (60+), where many older people are smart and clever enough to focus their attention on management of productive elder years. They are keen to get to know and to use modern tools and techniques, but some circumstances and barriers hinder them in reaching a promising starting point. For example, within the population of the users of the Internet, elderly people

Figure 1. Inhabitants and Internet users by age

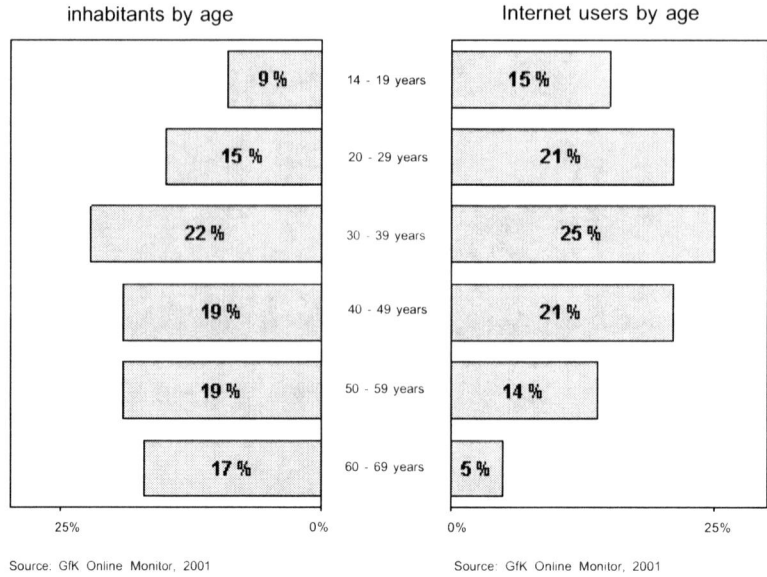

are by far not represented proportionally to their part of all inhabitants. For Germany, the situation is like that shown in Figure 1. Out of 52.5 Mio people in Germany between 14 to 69 years old, 46% (24.2 Mio) have access to the Internet and use it at least sometimes (GfK, 2001). But, only 5% of the older population (60 to 69 years of age) is using the Internet. In other words, while two out of three juniors (14 to 19 years) are using the Internet at least occasionally, only one out of eight older people (60 to 69 years) do so (GfK, 2001).

Various reasons cause these different usage patterns. Some reasons why elderly people are not using the Internet as are younger people are as follows:

- Older people seldom have Internet access at home or at work. Therefore, they are missing possibilities to test and to train in usage of the Internet.
- Older people are often too shy to test newer technologies for the first time.
- Probably, the current generation of older people is the last generation that did not get any experience in using a PC; the following generations use PCs at school and at work.
- Therefore, older people have minor handling skills with PCs and the Internet; this implies that they could not recognize useful and promising ways to use the Internet.
- There may be some language problems, because in Germany, the common language of Data Processing is full of English idioms (e.g., Browser, World Wide Web, Joystick, Display, Windows, Icon, Click, Desktop, Button, Service Provider, Cursor, Download, Homepage, Link, Newsgroup, online, Client, Server, Update) and abbreviations (e.g., PC, WWW, PS/2, MS, USB, VGA, LCD, GB, DVD, ROM, RAM, ISDN, ISP, SMS, BIOS, DFÜ, PDF, SCSI, SSL). But, the language skills of elderly people are probably weaker than the skills of younger people. The lack of understanding of the language will increase their uncertainty with the technology.

End-User Training within IT Management

With modern software architectures such as Enterprise Resource Planning (ERP), more workplaces are integrated into the companies' information technology infrastructure. By networking many workplaces and work flows and vertically and horizontally integrating ERP systems, users' skills in handling the software are critical, because technology networks are more error prone than stand-alone systems.

As the money spent on end-user training adds up to 10 to 20% of implementation costs, it becomes more important to spend that money effectively and efficiently (Olfman/Pitsatorn, 2000). Therefore, end-user training — its design, organization, and management — is an important topic for the future IT manager.

End-user training is also an important point of contact between professionals from the IT department and users from other departments of a company. In addition, end-user training has to cover various aspects: technical aspects of the software, organizational aspects of the situation in which the software should be used, motivational aspects when the implementation of the software will change the way people work, etc. Therefore, the management of end-user training is an important part of managerial skills in IT organizations.

For these reasons, we designed a special graduate Information Systems course, where students of the Department of Business Administration at the University of Applied Sciences Hannover in their (approximately) third year had to train elderly people in how to handle and use the Internet. Older people should have the opportunity to test the Internet — especially the World Wide Web (WWW) and electronic mail (email) — without fear and risk. At the end of the training, they should be able to send and receive emails, handle a standard browser, make a simple search using a search engine, and know basics about PCs and the Internet. In total, the skills of the elderly people in handling and using new media — here, the Internet — should be improved significantly. Barriers, which hinder them in using new media and modern technologies, should be lowered. A systematic performance evaluation was conducted in order to measure how well the older people and trainers (students) reached those goals.

From this point of view, Internet training for older users is a good simulation of some responsibilities graduates will have in their future working environments, when designing and conducting end-user training. The skills and training needs of the trainees are not clear — there are certain barriers in using the application, and there are social and communication problems between trainers and trainees.

Finally, the "S3: Senior Surf School" was conducted by six students at the end of the semester on three afternoons from 3 to 6 p.m. Each of the 33 (older) participants, in groups of eight to nine people, received nine hours of intensive training using the Internet.

COURSE DESIGN

There are various Information Systems courses with different structures and scopes required for our students. One special form of a course is called "project," which means that students in groups of four to 12 people work together on a given task. The volume of their work for a project like this during the semester is calculated as (approximately) 12 hours per week, which adds to approximately 200 hours of work per person. There is no fixed schedule for this work, because the students have to organize all of their work by themselves, with some guidance and support from the lecturer. They can use the (technical) infrastructure of the university but must observe some procedural conditions and rules of the organization.

For the students, two courses of this special form are required. Normally, they participate in these projects in their third or fourth (and last) year. Their participation is graded on a normal scale. The responsible lecturer for a project defines the project task, gives support and guidance, shows adequate tools and techniques, and helps to adjust problems. Often, the lecturer will play the role of a steering committee in a project organization. The project tasks are often defined together, with some cooperation partners from outside the university, who have realistic and practical interests in the results of the project.

In the course documented here, the task was to train users in handling and using a new technology, for instance, elderly people in using the Internet. This is a realistic simulation of future tasks and responsibilities of the graduates when they are heading IT management. We chose the context of "older people" and "Internet," because the technical environment is available at the university and is well known to the students, and the target group is not familiar with the handling and has barriers to use the technology — so it is a realistic context. The training event was named "S3: Senior Surf School." The main tasks of the students were as follows:

- Define detailed goals and rules of "S3: Senior Surf School"; define and maintain target dates and time limits
- Manage the participants (attraction, invitation, registration, etc.)
- Design and develop the structure and program of the surf school
- Design and develop all training materials (teachers guide, handout for participants, etc.)
- Manage resources (rooms, technical equipment, supplies, spare parts, etc.)
- Evaluate: design and manage a performance evaluation system
- Manage the project: manage time and division of labor, report to steering committee, document all activities, etc.
- Conduct the training as teachers

Some organizational prerequisites were set as follows:
- The whole project should be finished within the semester (five months).
- The training of the surf school should take place in rooms and with the technical equipment of the university. Regular courses and other events should not be disturbed. The volume of the Internet training should be 25 to 50 hours.

Detailed Goals of the Surf School

After starting the projects, the students had some intensive discussions with key people of the target group, some older people we know from a division of the biggest labor party in Germany. Before this analysis, together with key people of the target group, it was quite an open question as to which skills elderly people have and which the school can be based on. To conduct end-user training successfully, it is essential to consider the prerequisites the target group brings into the training situation and, furthermore, the training needs of the group.

Finally, some foundations of the surf school were documented as follows:

- The target group is older people (60+) who have no skills or experience in using a PC or using the Internet. They are interested and keen to see and to learn how to handle the Internet. This is the reason why motivation of the end user is not a major topic within this course.
- The content of the training should clearly focus on the Internet services World Wide Web (WWW) and electronic mail (email). Today, these two services build by far the most applications of Internet technology. Rather than giving a detailed introduction "How to use a PC," the content of the training should focus on skills that are absolutely necessary to handle a browser.
- The training should focus on "doing" rather than "showing." The participants should spend most of the time using and handling WWW and email. The trainees should practice using WWW and email as much as possible.
- One direct consequence was that each participant should sit in front of one terminal and that the groups should be rather small (eight to 10 people) in order to give good and intensive support by the trainer.

In detail, the participants should learn the following:

- To recognize structure and diversity of the Internet
- To realize and understand examples using the WWW
- To recognize possible and useful ways of using the WWW
- To handle the WWW in general
- To use search engines, catalogs, metasearch engines, etc.
- To understand electronic mail as an Internet service
- To handle incoming and outgoing emails
- To lower their shyness while testing and using newer technologies
- To start and finish working with a PC, handling a browser
- To use the keyboard and the mouse as input devices
- To know important components of a PC to be able to make buying decisions
- To know the connections between PC and telecommunication networks
- To understand the different roles of Internet Service Provider, Internet Presence Provider, and Internet Content Provider

To support the participants, a detailed handout (booklet) should be prepared and produced to prevent the participants from writing tips and tricks during the training sessions.

Teaching Program of the Surf School

While developing the program, it became clear that some topics have to be taught in rooms with advanced technology; otherwise online banking, animations with flash technology, and three-dimensional graphics would be too slow on medium-sized PCs. For that reason, these topics should be presented in a larger classroom with all participants and the other topics in several smaller PC laboratories, with eight to 10 people in each group. Finally, the program was outlined and scheduled as shown in Table 1, where the gray shaded boxes show topics presented in the plenary room with all participants together, and the nonshaded boxes show topics presented in groups.

Some special features should be outlined. To become acquainted with a PC desktop, participants were shown the user interface, and it was explained. Because many experiences show that beginners have special problems in handling a mouse as an input device, a separate "mouse training" was held: with a special program from the WWW (www.gemeinsamlernen.de), participants had to follow a light point with the cursor. They also had to click on certain boxes, to paint something on the screen, etc.

All participants received an email address and account on the first day, using an Internet Service Provider that gives access to email features immediately after signing in (web.de). With their own email account, the participants could start sending and receiving emails on the first day.

Handout/Booklet

To support the learning progress of the participants, a booklet was prepared that summarized all necessary information and contained all tips and tricks (and Web addresses). Additionally, the booklet gave some basic hints for buying a PC in order to surf the WWW from home and how to get access to the WWW via phone, ISP, etc. The booklet consisted

Table 1.

Time	Day 1	Day 2	Day 3
15:00–15:15	Check in	Three-Dimensional Presentation	Online Banking
15:15–15:30	Welcome, organizational details	Accessing the WWW	Finance
15:30–15:45	Introduction, history, and structure of the Internet	Regional information (2)	Ticketing
15:45–16:00	PC hardware	Travel	Shopping
16:00–16:15	Assigning training groups	Free training session	Free training session
16:15–16:30	Coffee break	Coffee break	Coffee break
16:30–16:45	Handling the mouse	Search engines	Weather
16:45–17:00	PC desktop, browser	Search engines	Information services
17:00–17:15	Electronic mail	Culture	Elderly people
17:15–17:30	Electronic mail	Politics	Health care
17:30–17:45	Regional information (1)	Free training session	Free training session
17:45–18:00	Security issues	Animations with flash	Webcams, discussion, goodbye

of more than 50 pages and contained paragraphs such as history and structure of the Internet, PC hardware/input/output devices/buying hints, operating system, browser, security issues, Internet Service Provider, email provider, access to the WWW, search engines, links, and glossary. The buying hints used the picture of an ordinary advertisement from a newspaper, which listed the important components of a PC and its technical details. With this ad, the components were described and explained in order to support the reader buying a PC.

Organization

There were various organizational tasks on which the students had to concentrate:

* Project management: time management, division of labor, task scheduling, reporting, documentation; especially the cooperation of students, lecturer, administration of university, and key people of the target group had to be coordinated
* Management of participants: attraction and invitation of participants, registration, registration fees
* Preparation and production of teacher's guide and handout (booklet)
* Design and organization of the environment: rooms, technical equipment, supplies, refreshments, etc.
* Composition of training groups

Evaluation

In order to measure systematically how the older people and trainers (students) reached the goals of the "S3: Senior Surf School," a performance evaluation survey was necessary. The survey was designed in order to sample some demographic data of the participants and to get their feedback. A pretest of the questionnaire was conducted, where some older people tested its meaningfulness as well as its clarity, length, and general appearance. Then, the

Figure 2. Cover page and content of handout

▸ Preface

▸ History, structure of the Internet

▸ PCs (hardware, input/output devices, buying hints)

▸ Operating system, browser

▸ Security issues

▸ Access Provider, Email Provider

▸ Search engines

▸ Links

▸ Glossary of terms

questionnaire was handed to the participants before and after attending the school to evaluate training and learning.

Before attending the surf school, the trainees were asked to scale their skills and experiences with the Internet on five-point Likert scales. After the school, we asked the same questions to measure the differences caused by the surf school.

Other questions addressed the barriers, which were assumed to hinder Internet usage by older people, and the detailed goals of the school to lower these barriers. So, the older people were asked anonymously, to what extent they have skills to handle a PC (PC literacy) and to surf in the WWW (Internet literacy). Additionally, they were asked if they see a clear purpose in using the Internet during their daily life, if they had enough opportunity to try the Internet to get acquainted with it, and if they feel that they can handle the Internet without fear. All answers were measured on five-point ordinal scales, where low values stand for low extent of skills, opportunities, etc.

Figure 3 shows the answers the participants of "S3: Senior Surf School" gave before the school started. Obviously, there was room to improve on all dimensions; the main objective of the school was to address all five dimensions and to increase the respective values.

After attending the school, the respondents were asked to answer the same questions again. The answers are summarized in Figure 4, and they show significant improvements in all dimensions. Some of the assumptions concerning the school design were confirmed by the results of the survey. So, the teaching program was, because of the lack of time, not focused on PC literacy but directly on Internet literacy. Corresponding to this, the empirical results that show the improvements along the dimension "Internet literacy" were higher than along the dimension "PC literacy."

Additionally, the participants were asked to judge the school in total, the program, the trainer, and the organization. All grades were outstanding, and Figure 5 shows some results

Figure 3. Skills and opportunities before attending the school (low values ~ low skills, low chances, etc.; n = 27-32)

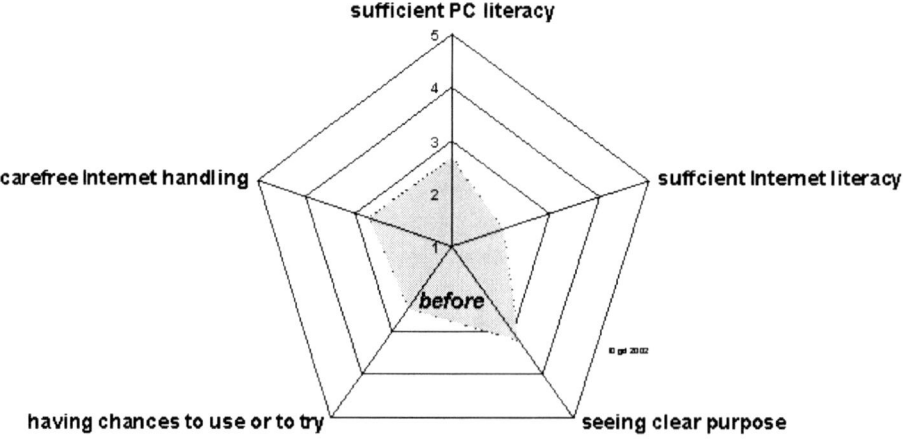

Figure 4. Skills and opportunities before and after attending the school

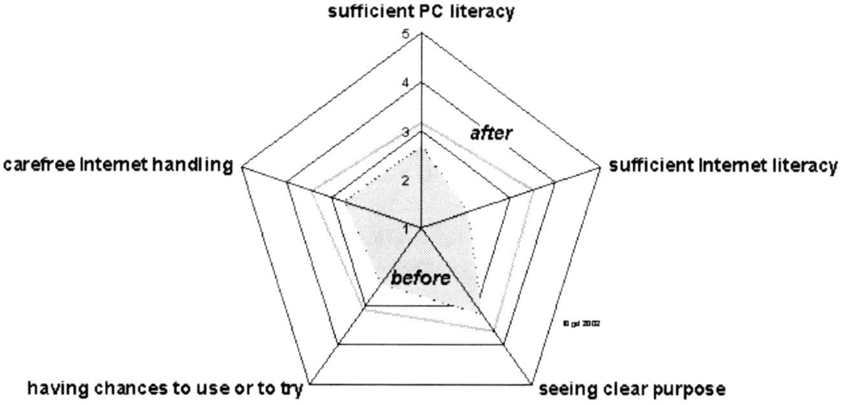

of the survey. Similar excellent ratings were shown by items like "atmosphere," "interesting topics," "organization," and "help and support." In total, 73% of the respondents *completely* agreed with the statement that they will recommend the school. Furthermore, 27% agreed with this statement, no one disagreed or strongly disagreed. A high percentage (97%) of the participants said that their expectations were (at least) met, two out of three said that their expectations were excelled.

CONCLUSION

The project "S3: Senior Surf School" was an assignment for graduate students of Information Systems at the University of Applied Sciences in Hannover. The students had to design, organize, manage, and run a training event, where elderly people could see and try using the Internet. This scenario is a realistic simulation of future tasks and responsibilities for graduates when they are heading IT management, because end-user training becomes more important for IT management.

During the course, the students had to manage various tasks, like recognizing goals and approaches in teaching the Internet, identifying detailed training needs of the target groups, developing training methods and a teaching program, organizing the environment, designing an evaluation performance survey, and finally, conducting the training acting as teachers of the school.

As the discussions with the participants of "S3: Senior Surf School" and the empirical results show, the students were able to improve the level of competence of the older people in handling and using the Internet. Additionally, they received excellent grades on all dimensions and positive feedback referring to items like atmosphere, organization, help, and support. At the end of the school, all participants were happy and would recommend the school to others.

Besides these direct results, the special setting of the "S3: Senior Surf School" provoked some "strange" situations and curious observations:

Figure 5. Overall ratings after attending the school (n = 29 to 30)

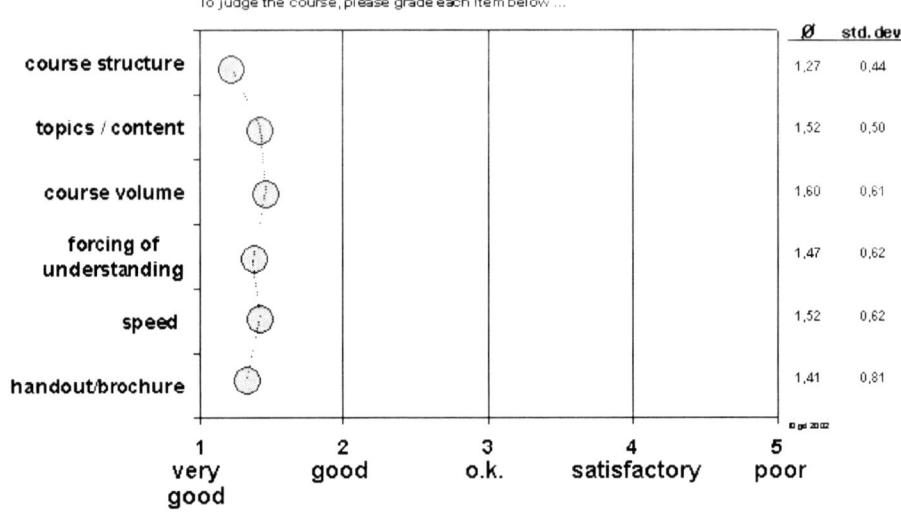

- Young teachers (~ 25) had to train old end users (60+); normally, only within families, there is intensive contact between two generation so far apart, if ever.
- Students not only had to make a concept or suggest some actions, but they also had to implement their suggestions and actually run the school.
- Thoroughly, deep language problems between younger and older people were discovered, because the common languages of the groups differed significantly.
- Students were surprised how eager and enthusiastic the older people were; they seemed to absorb the information the students disseminated.

Some specific lessons learned by the students involved in this project were as follows:
- End-user training needs a considerable amount of preparation. There are some aspects of the course content and some organizational topics that need attention and that will cause substantial work.
- Even with a small group of eight to nine trainees, without a detailed schedule and some discipline of trainers and trainees, a training session will end up "dynamic" but without any learning results. There is no "muddling through" when various trainees ask questions or discuss problems at the same time.
- To teach a group of people for a considerable amount of time is an important experience: to stand before "the crowds," to recognize what the trainees get right and what not, to vary the speed, sensing if the trainees can follow, to talk to people over three hours in free speech.

The success of the school, the experiences, and some of the sociological phenomena made the school an exciting experience for all.

REFERENCES

GfK. (2001). Gesellschaft für Konsumforschung. Online Monitor, Nürnberg.

Olfman, L., & Pitsatorn, P. (2000). End-user training research: Status and models for the future, In: R. W. Zmud (ed.), *Framing the Domains of IT Management* (pp. 129–146). Cincinnati, OH: Pinnaflex.

Chapter XII

How Do IT Students Stay Up to Date with Employers' Skill Requirements?

Tanya McGill
Murdoch University, Australia

Michael Dixon
Murdoch University, Australia

ABSTRACT

The information technology industry is subject to rapid change. There have been concerns expressed in the literature about the ability of information technology professionals to keep up to date with developments, and it is likely that it is even more difficult for students to do so. New graduates require marketable skills in order to gain good employment, but the skills most in demand change regularly. This chapter reports on a project that investigated the channels of information that undergraduate and postgraduate telecommunications management and electronic commerce students use to keep up to date with employers' needs. The role of instructors in this process is also discussed.

INTRODUCTION

Information technology (IT) has been changing rapidly over a long period, and this rate of change is likely to continue or increase (Benamati & Lederer, 2001; Fordham, 2001). This rapid rate of change has produced many opportunities for organizations but has also brought with it many challenges (Lederer & Mendelow, 1990). Among these challenges is the struggle for organizations to obtain personnel with the appropriate knowledge and skills in order to meet the growing demands for IT services (Doke, 1999). This is mirrored by the continual requirement for IT professionals to keep up to date with the skills required by organizations (Benamati & Lederer, 2001; Klobas & McGill, 1993).

Previous research investigated the importance employers place on various skills and perceived deficiencies in these skills (e.g., Doke, 1999; Leitheiser, 1992; Nelson, 1991). While the call for improved communication and social skills has been consistent, the technical skills in demand have varied dramatically over time. Less has been written about students' perception of the importance of various IT skills, though this was addressed in a recent study that compared Australian and American students' perceptions of IT job skills (von Hellens, Van Slyke, & Kittner, 2000).

Given that the skills required by IT professionals change over time, IT professionals need effective methods to keep up to date. The methods used by IT professionals to keep up to date were studied by Klobas and McGill (1993). They identified the existence of a variety of information-gathering strategies and noted that while IT professionals tended to be diligent in their efforts to keep up to date, a majority found it difficult to do so. In a more recent study, Benamati and Lederer (2001) investigated the coping mechanisms adopted by IT professionals and noted that many mechanisms were not successful.

If it is difficult for experienced IT professionals to keep up to date, it is likely that it is even more difficult for IT students to do so. New graduates require marketable skills in order to gain good employment, but the skills most in demand change regularly. Little has been written about how IT students keep informed of employers' requirements or about how they ensure that they can meet these requirements. Yet, this knowledge would be of use to educational institutions aiming to facilitate this process and to potential employers hoping to recruit students with the required skills. This chapter describes a project that investigated the channels of information that undergraduate and postgraduate telecommunications management and electronic commerce students use to keep up to date with employers' needs. The role of instructors in this process was of particular interest, because they are ideally placed to facilitate it.

THE RESEARCH PROJECT

This research was conducted by survey. Participants in the study were students enrolled in several electronic commerce and telecommunications management courses at an Australian university. Students who successfully complete these particular courses can also pursue Cisco certification as the courses make use of the Cisco curriculum. Participants were recruited during class and completed a questionnaire on the spot. It was stressed that the completion of the questionnaire was voluntary and that it formed no part of their assessment in the course.

The questionnaire was designed to be easy to read and understand and to require no more than five minutes to complete (the Appendix at the end of this chapter contains a list of all of the items in the questionnaire). The questionnaire contained three types of items. The first type asked about:

- Age
- Gender
- Amount of previous work experience (both total and IT experience).

The second type of question related to the degree students were undertaking and their perceptions of:

- Whether the skills provided by their degree are those employers require
- The importance of industry certification for their future employment.

The third type of question related to the information that students might use to keep up to date with what skills employers require. Information about IT is available from a variety of sources in a variety of formats, and the term "information channel" can be used to describe the various combinations of sources and formats of information. The questions listed information channels that may be used to keep up to date and asked participants whether they had used each channel within the last 3 months, and also to rate the importance of each channel to them as a means of knowing what skills are in demand. Importance was measured on a five-point Likert-type scale ranging from (1) "Not important" to (5) "Vital." The initial list of channels of information was drawn from Klobas and McGill's (1993) report of the methods used by IT professionals to keep up to date with developments in IT. Several additional channels were included after consultation with industry contacts. The final list of information channels contained the following:

- Newspaper employment pages
- Newspaper IT sections
- University instructors
- Other students
- Work colleagues
- Magazines (e.g., *Packet Magazine*)
- Internet sources (e.g., Cisco, Lucent)
- Books
- Vendor presentations.

The participants in the study were 85 students (57 male, 28 female), with an average age of 26.1. Participants were at undergraduate (41 students or 48%) or postgraduate level (44 students or 52%). The participants had, on average, 4.0 years of work experience of which 1.7 years was in the IT industry. Table 1 summarizes some of the background information about the participants in this study.

RESULTS AND DISCUSSION

Overall, the students appeared to be diligent in their efforts to keep up to date with employers' skill requirements. The average number of channels used by the students during

Table 1. Background information about participants

	Number	Percentage
Gender		
Male	57	67%
Female	28	33%
Degree level		
Undergraduate	41	48%
Postgraduate	44	52%
Work experience* (mean = 4.0 years)		
No	24	28%
Yes	61	72%
IT work experience (mean = 1.7 years)		
No	52	61%
Yes	33	39%

* Work experience includes both IT and non-IT experience

the previous three months was 3.8 (and the most common number used was 5). Thirteen students (15.3%) had not made any attempt to keep up to date during this period, and four (4.7%) had made use of all nine listed channels.

The information channels are ranked by frequency of use in Table 2. The most frequently consulted channels were newspaper employment and IT sections and Internet sources. University instructors had been consulted by about half of the participants during the previous three months. Other students had also been used as a source of information by quite a few students (40%). This high level of use of other students to provide information about employers' skill requirements is understandable, given the easy accessibility of other students (Klobas & McGill, 1993). Work colleagues were ranked seventh overall, but as only around a third of the participants had IT work experience, this means that most of those with prior experience had consulted their colleagues (75% of those with prior IT work experience had consulted their colleagues). The least used channels were books and vendor presentations. It is likely that students were conscious that information about employer skill requirements derived from books was not going to be sufficiently up to date to meet their needs.

Table 3 shows the importance rankings of the individual information channels. The most highly ranked information channel was Internet sources, such as the Cisco and Lucent sites. As well as being frequently used, newspaper IT sections and employment pages were also considered very important (ranked two and three). University instructors were ranked fourth in importance, which was consistent with their frequency of consultation by students. Although other students were consulted by many students, they were not considered an important channel of information (ranked seventh). This suggests that students recognize that although other students are an easily accessible source of information, they are not necessarily an accurate or reliable source. In future research, it would be interesting to determine how well student perceptions match those of employers. Books and vendor presentations were considered of low importance.

Table 2. Information channels ranked by frequency of use

Rank	Information Channel	Number	Percentage
1	Newspaper employment pages	56	65.9
2	Newspaper IT sections	52	61.2
3	Internet sources (e.g., Cisco, Lucent)	47	55.3
4	University instructors	43	50.6
5	Other students	34	40.0
6	IT magazines (e.g., *Packet Magazine*)	29	34.1
7	Work colleagues	24	28.2
8	Books	20	23.5
9	Vendor presentations	17	20.0

In addition to the items about methods used to keep up to date, participants were also asked several questions that addressed whether they believed they were, in fact, obtaining the skills employers required. A majority of participants believed that their degree would provide the skills employers require (67.1% yes, 5.9% no, and 27.1% not sure). This high level of confidence suggests that although only around 50% of students had consulted their instructors about employer skill requirements during the previous 3 months (and instructors were only given a medium ranking of importance), students implicitly accept that instructors know what skills students require. Industry certification was also seen as an important means to ensure that students obtain the necessary skills (mean importance score was 4.18/5 for those students not yet working in the IT industry).

Demographic Differences in Use and Importance

Patterns of use and perceptions of importance were further examined to determine whether gender, level of study, or previous IT work experience had an influence. Differences

Table 3. Information channels ranked by importance

Rank	Information Channel	Mean	Standard Deviation
1	Internet sources (e.g., Cisco, Lucent)	3.55	1.40
2	Newspaper IT sections	3.38	1.44
3	Newspaper employment pages	3.30	1.30
4	University instructors	2.88	1.42
5	IT magazines	2.62	1.43
6	Work colleagues	2.54	1.43
7	Other students	2.41	1.13
8	Books	2.24	1.34
9	Vendor presentations	2.13	1.32

in use were explored using χ^2 tests, and differences in importance were explored using independent sample t-tests. These factors had surprisingly little influence on patterns of use and perceived importance of information channels.

The first demographic factor considered was gender. No significant difference was found between the number of information channels used by male and female students. The only significant gender difference was for the levels of use and perceived importance of Internet sources. Male students used Internet sources more frequently [$\chi^2(1)=6.98, p=0.008$] and perceived them to be more important for keeping up to date with the skill requirements of employers [3.85 versus 2.93, t(80)=-2.96, p=0.004].

The possible impact of previous IT work experience was considered next. No significant difference was found between the number of information channels used by those with and those without previous IT work experience. The only significant difference in usage of information channels was related to consultation with work colleagues and with other students. Those with previous work experience not surprisingly consulted with work colleagues more frequently [$\chi^2(1)=17.97, p<0.001$] and appeared to consider work colleagues a more important channel of information (2.73 versus 2.04, t(80)=-1.98, p=0.051). Presumably, those with previous IT experience would have received better quality information from their work colleagues than would those without IT work experience who would have been receiving information from a pool of people with perhaps limited direct IT experience.

Those without IT work experience consulted other students more frequently [$\chi^2(1)=5.94, p=0.015$], but there was no difference in perceptions of the importance of other students between those with and those without previous IT work experience (2.39 versus 2.48, t(80) = 0.32, p = 0.753). As previously mentioned, this suggests that other students are consulted because of their accessibility rather than their credibility as a source of information. Those with previous IT experience have other accessible sources of more credible information and, hence, do not rely so heavily upon other students.

The differences between undergraduate and postgraduate students were similar to those between those with previous IT work experience and those without. This is consistent with postgraduate students being more likely to have previous IT work experience than are undergraduates (54.5% of postgraduates versus 22% of undergraduates have previous IT work experience). Undergraduate students consulted other students more frequently [$\chi^2(1)=6.69, p=0.010$], but did not value their information more highly [2.63 versus 2.23, t(80)=1.63, p = 0.107]. Postgraduate students also consulted work colleagues more frequently [$\chi^2(1)=4.59, p=0.032$]. However, they did not value their input more highly [2.68 versus 2.37, t(80) =-0.987, p=0.327]. This finding differs from the added importance given to work colleagues by those with previous IT experience, but the means are in the same direction, and the result may reflect the fact that 45.5% of postgraduates do not have previous IT work experience.

CONCLUSION

New graduates require marketable skills in order to gain good employment, but as the IT industry is subject to rapid change, the skills most in demand change regularly. The project reported on in this chapter investigated the means that a sample of IT students used to keep up to date with employers' skill needs.

Overall, the participants appeared to be diligent in their efforts to keep up to date with employers' skill requirements. The average number of channels used by the students during the previous three months was 3.8, and the most common number used was five. The most commonly used channels were newspaper employment and IT sections, and Internet sources. The same three channels were rated most highly in terms of importance, however, the ordering was different, with Internet sources being seen as most important.

Instructors were ranked relatively highly (fourth of nine channels) in terms of frequency of consultation and importance. In addition, the feedback from participants about the match between the skills provided by their degrees and employers' needs suggests an implicit confidence that the knowledge of instructors is up to date. While students have a wide variety of information channels available to them and make use of them, instructors have a major role to play in providing up-to-date information about employers' needs. They need to be highly accessible and to ensure that their knowledge of employers' skill requirements remains current. Instructors should use studies of employers' requirements to assess their course offerings and to help guide their students. They can also use the results of studies such as this one to better understand student information-seeking behavior.

REFERENCES

Benamati, J., & Lederer, A. L. (2001). Coping with rapid changes in IT. *Communications of the ACM, 44*(8), 83–88.

Doke, E. R. (1999). Knowledge and skill requirements for information systems professionals: An exploratory study. *Journal of IS Education, 10*(1), 10–18.

Fordham, D. R. (2001). Forecasting technology trends. *Strategic Finance, 83*(3), 50–54.

Klobas, J. E., & McGill, T. (1993). Computing professionals and information about developments in information technology. *The Australian Computer Journal, 25*(4), 149–158.

Lederer, A. L., & Mendelow, A. L. (1990). The impact of the environment on the management of information systems. *Information Systems Research, 1*(2), 205–222.

Leitheiser, R. (1992). MIS skills for the 1990's: A survey of MIS managers perceptions. *Journal of Management Information Systems, 9*(1), 69–91.

Nelson, R. R. (1991). Educational needs as perceived by IS and end-user personnel: A survey of knowledge and skill requirements. *MIS Quarterly, 15*(4), 503–525.

von Hellens, L., Van Slyke, C., & Kittner, M. (2000). A comparison of Australian and American students' perceptions of IT job skills. *Challenges of Information Technology Management in the 21st Century. 2000 IRMA International Conference* (pp. 915–916).

APPENDIX

1   What level qualification are you currently enrolled in?   o Undergraduate
                                                             o Postgraduate Diploma
                                                             o Masters

2   What is the title of the degree or major(s) you are enrolled in?
    If you are doing a double major please include both.   _____

3   Do you have previous work experience?   o No
                                             o Yes   _____ years

4   Do you have information technology work experience?   o No
                                                           o Yes   _____ years

5   If you **are NOT** currently working in the IT industry:
    a) What do you think your starting salary will be after
    completing your degree? $ _____

    b) How important is industry certification for   Not
    getting your initial job?   Impt.   1 2 3 4 5   Vital

6   If you **are** currently working in the IT industry:
    a) How much do you think you salary will increase
    after you complete your degree?   _____ %

    b) How important is industry certification for   Not
    getting ahead in your current position?   Impt.   1 2 3 4 5   Vital

7   What area of information technology do you
    wish to work in when you graduate?   _____

8   Where do you wish to work when you graduate?
    (name city or country if known)   _____

9   Is degree you are enrolled in: o Too technical?
                                      o Just right?
                                      o Not technical enough?

10 How old are you?   _____ Years

11 What gender are you?   o Female
                           o Male

12 Do you think your degree will provide the skills   o No
    employers require?   o Yes
                         o Not sure

13   What sources of information do you use to keep up to date with what skills employers require? Please indicate whether you have used **each** of the following sources of information in the last 3 months, and rate **each** as to how important it is to you as a source of information about skills that are in demand.

		Used during last 3 months	Not Important				Vital
A	Newspaper employment pages	☐	1	2	3	4	5
B	Newspaper IT sections (e.g., "Tuesdays' Australian")	☐	1	2	3	4	5
C	University instructors	☐	1	2	3	4	5
D	Other students	☐	1	2	3	4	5
E	Work colleagues	☐	1	2	3	4	5
F	Magazines (e.g., *Packet Magazine*)	☐	1	2	3	4	5
G	Internet sources (e.g., Cisco, Lucent)	☐	1	2	3	4	5
H	Books	☐	1	2	3	4	5
I	Vendor presentations	☐	1	2	3	4	5
J	Other _____	☐	1	2	3	4	5

Chapter XIII

Education for a Technology-Based Profession: Softening the Information Systems Curriculum

Rodney Turner
Victoria University of Technology, Australia

Glenn Lowry
United Arab Emirates University, UAE

ABSTRACT

This chapter reports some further findings of an ongoing investigation into conceptual, academic, and "soft" skills that IS/IT practitioners regard as important in new graduates. There has long been agreement that the IS curriculum should be comprised of some combination of technical subjects and nontechnical business subjects, and that graduates also need "soft" business skills. There is far less agreement about what the mix between these should be and how best to prepare students in some areas, notably in the development of "soft" business skills. The research findings reported here present some evidence that traditional "business subjects" such as marketing, economics, or finance do not equate to the business skills that employers of IS graduates are seeking in new hires. The chapter concludes with a discussion of IS curriculum reform issues and strategies for reducing confusion, overcoming tradition and inertia, finding resources, and neutralizing vested interests

INTRODUCTION

How can information systems educators achieve a better fit between the workplace and the university "studyplace"? Discerning and reconciling the aspirations of university students preparing for careers in business information systems with the skills, competencies, personal characteristics, and qualities desired by employers is, at best, the art of finding an acceptable, if not optimal, balance between them.

Students are most concerned with future employability. They classically desire to develop a sufficient base of knowledge and a skills repertoire to secure their first professional position following graduation, to survive in that position, and to feel that their education will also prepare them for advancement in the medium term of five or more years.

Employers, on the other hand, often indicate that they want new graduates who can be immediately productive in their environment, who are teachable, loyal team players who work to deadlines, who possess the ability to make an intelligible presentation, who can write understandable business letters, memoranda, and reports.

Are the aspirations of students and employers fundamentally incompatible? How can IS educators help to find a workable and satisfying balance?

Professional Preparation and Curriculum Design

It is a truism that the preparation of IS professionals must encompass a significant portion of a body of technical skills laid down by various professional bodies (Cheney, Hale, & Kasper, 1990; Gorgone & Gray, 1999; Underwood, 1997). It is also often held that employers desire more well-rounded graduates who possess well-developed business skills in addition to a sound technical repertoire (Trauth, Farwell, & Lee, 1993; Van Slyke, Kittner, & Cheney, 1997).

A persistent research finding that employers want graduates who possess better business skills is often interpreted by academics who typically operate in a business or commerce faculty to mean that more traditional, formal business subjects such as accounting, economics, business finance, and marketing should be taught alongside traditional hard skill subjects, such as systems analysis/design and programming in particular languages. Somehow, the other "soft" areas, such as teamwork, communication skills, ability to accept direction, and others, are "picked up" along the way through an unspecified, osmotic process.

Studies conducted in other practice-oriented business disciplines such as accounting (Stewart, 1997) have indicated that students may not fully appreciate the importance of nontechnical skills sought by prospective employers.

Several writers, including Ang (1992), Ang and Jiwahhasuchin (1998), and Young and Keen (1997) noted the long-term shift from programming and other technical subjects to business analysis and people-oriented skills in IS curricula and in employer requirements expressed in recruiting advertisements over the past two decades. Ashley and Padgett (1997) reported results of a 1996 study of the evaluation of the IS curriculum by IS graduates. The study covered business and nonbusiness courses[1] along with traditional IS courses and compared results with a similar study in 1990 (Beise et al., 1991).

Some of the results appear to go against conventional wisdom. In the nonbusiness area, foreign languages rated quite poorly in both periods. In their business courses, Introduction to Information Systems and Business Communication rated highly, but core business subjects such as Economics, Business Law, Statistics, Quantitative Methods, and even Accounting rated below the average. Predictably, from the IS courses such as Systems

Analysis & Design rated highly, whereas COBOL was becoming less important, and procedural languages such as Pascal, ADA and BASIC were rated lowly but with little change between 1990 and 1996. Lu and Wang (1998–1999) investigated the skills and knowledge needs of IS graduates in Hong Kong. Respondents were mainly middle-level managers, with a smaller proportion of IS professionals. They found communication skills, management issues and project management skills were among the more desired; technical skills sought included programming, systems analysis and design, data communications, and database. They also noted a relative lack of possessed skills in all IS core areas. A number of recommendations were proffered to address the problem, including the adoption of the IS curriculum model with modification to suit local Hong Kong needs.

Athey and Plotnicki (1998) investigated the changing skill requirements in the IS fields. They found that while there was a reduction of demand in some areas such as COBOL, none had completely disappeared, and the levels of demand varied across different parts of the United States. They noticed a strong growth in Internet technologies and client server technologies, suggesting that any IS program lacking these components would be failing the student.

Khalil, Strong et al. (1999) presented a framework of competencies for inclusion in an IS curriculum. They identify a mismatch between the needs of organizations for delivering high-quality information-to-information consumers and what graduating IS professionals are equipped to provide. They suggest substantial curriculum changes in respect to skills in information quality (IQ) necessitating the re-education of educators.

Kuras et al. (1999) reported on problems associated with teaching IS at a school of management in Poland. They mentioned the problems of employing programmers who could produce technologically sound but unsatisfactory for the end-user programs, and mentioned that information systems is not seen as a domain of instruction. They presented recommendations for a new IS curriculum for Poland to address these problems.

Wong (1996) noted the need for IS people who are experts in areas of IT and IS; those who realize the importance of business functions and understand how to fit IT and IS into a business, helping it to gain strategic advantages over its competitors. Westfall (1999–2000) noted that there is a need to address the IT technology-related or hard skills, and interpersonal/management or soft skills in the IT curriculum. He proposed a "learning needs model" to address some of the problems associated with keeping up to date with developments with the rapidly changing field.

The past decades have been characterized by a rapidly and constantly changing business environment. Lee, Truath, & Farwell (1995) argued that technological and sociological developments facilitated by evolving information technology and changing business needs have made it necessary for IS professionals to develop a wider range of nontechnical skills than was previously the case. Similar views have been expressed by many others, including Burn et al. (1995), Cafasso (1996); Lowry et al. (1996), Main (1995), and Morgan et al., (1996). Competition for the best entry positions has been heightened by IS outsourcing (Slaughter & Ang, 1996). Students have become more aware of the need to insure that they develop "career resilience" (Waterman et al., 1994) to prepare themselves to manage their own careers through regular self-evaluation and ongoing, self-initiated training and skills development.

Gupta and Wachter (1998) saw a need for IS students to develop skills and abilities in various areas, including teamwork, creativity, and communication and proposed a capstone course to achieve these aims. Kakabadse and Korac-Kakabadse (2000) highlighted the changing role of the IS/IT professional and identified skills and competencies required for development in the early 21st century.

Identifying the skills sought by employers of new IS graduates is critical for educators in designing curricula and advising students. Van Slyke (1997) found that specific technical skills were less important than basic technical skills and nonacademic skills. In a study across various IS job classifications, Doke and Williams (1999) found that systems development skills and interpersonal skills were common across classifications, but programming skills were more important for entry-level IS positions. Similar results were obtained by Turner and Lowry (1999a) in a pilot study of 102 students and 54 employers of IS graduates. An earlier study by McLean, Tanner, and Smits (1991) found that employers believed that members of staff are motivated primarily by "hygiene factors," such as income, security, and other material components that, in and of themselves, cannot produce job satisfaction, but without which job satisfaction cannot occur (Herzberg, 1968). Wrycza, Usowicz, Gabor, and Verber (1999) found that knowledge and skills needed for work in small businesses is different from that required for larger enterprises. They also found that contemporary firms had a stronger need for IS specialists than they did for computer programmers.

The findings reported in this chapter present a snapshot of some of the evidence that "business subjects," such as those comprising many undergraduate business or commerce courses, do not equate to the business skills that employers of IS graduates are seeking in new hires. The work presented here is part of an ongoing research program that investigates the views of other major stakeholders, including employers, currently enrolled students, and academics (Turner & Lowry, 1999b, 2000, 2001, 2002).

We argue that IS practitioners, employers, and students see little value in some of the more formal business subject areas that often form the core of an IS degree offered in a business or commerce faculty. These stakeholder groups see more value in the development of "soft skills" useful in client interaction. The findings have serious implications for IS educators and IS curriculum design.

Importance of Nontechnical Business Subjects in the Information Systems Curriculum

In a previous study of the content of information system curricula, the authors (Turner & Lowry, 1999b) began to suspect that the "other business skills" desired of new IS graduates were not synonymous with traditional business curriculum subjects. The results of that study indicated that of nine business subjects that are typically included in IS curricula, only three, *Accounting*, *Business Ethics*, and *Management* were judged to be important by students and employers.

Students and employers were asked to indicate what they considered to be the most and least important non-information systems subjects. Their responses are shown in percentages in Table 1. Nine subjects were evaluated by students and employers as "Most Important" in the three columns to the left, and as "Least Important" in the three right-hand columns. For convenience, the superscripted numbers in parenthesis indicate the first, second, and third most and least important subjects, from student and employer perspectives.

There is a surprising level of agreement between students and employers. Assessments of "Most Important" subjects differ only in the rank order, with students viewing "Management" as most important, "Accounting" as second most important, and "Business Ethics" as third. Employers ranked them as "Accounting," "Management," and "Business Ethics."

Table 1. Perceived importance of nontechnical business subjects

Most Important	Student	Employer	Least Important	Student	Employer
Accounting	[2] 13.5	[1] 21.3	Accounting	9.9	1.9
Business finance	6.6	11.6	Business finance	[2] 13.5	6.4
Business ethics	[3] 12.5	[3] 14.8	Business ethics	11.6	7.1
Business law	8.3	4.5	Business law	9.2	[3] 14.1
Business statistics	6.9	9.0	Business statistics	11.2	12.2
Economics	5.6	2.6	Economics	[3] 12.5	[2] 16.0
Foreign language(s)	7.6	3.2	Foreign language(s)	[1] 14.2	[1] 23.1
Management	[1] 24.1	[2] 17.4	Management	3.3	3.2
Marketing	10.9	10.3	Marketing	10.2	9.6

There was somewhat less agreement regarding least important non-information systems subjects, with students rating "Foreign languages" first but rating "Economics" second and choosing "Business law" as third.

These results suggest that employers and students share some degree of agreement regarding the relative importance of non-IS business subjects. The results have interesting implications for tertiary educators. Clearly, students should be advised to include study of Management, Accounting, and Business Ethics in their courses. Unless there is some compelling reason to include further non-IS business subjects, such as fulfilling the requirements for a second major or a dual qualification, study toward acquisition of "soft skills" may be a better choice for students than additional non-IS subjects.

METHODOLOGY OF THE 2001–2002 FOLLOW-UP STUDY

A follow-up study to further explore the "other business skills" aspect of the IS curriculum was conducted in 2001. A multipart questionnaire was devised that solicited views on the importance of formal business subjects and "soft skills" that may be found in the curriculum of many IS degrees. Demographic data including age, gender, and aspects of employment were also gathered.

Web-based survey distribution was used. Mehta and Sivadas (1995) demonstrated that email-based surveys generated response rates comparable to those of postal surveys but significantly faster, at lower cost, and of a higher quality. On the other hand, Tse et al., (1995) in an internal survey of Hong Kong University staff, experienced a much lower return rate for email surveys (6%) compared with conventional mail (27%), that they attribute to the possibility of participant identification with email. Comley (1996) found comparable response rates from the two methods. Comley also indicated that electronic data collection methods are often self-selecting, due to recipients irregularly checking email messages, and consequently, have the potential to introduce bias. He pointed out, however, that although this is a problem for representative samples, it is less of a problem for targeted groups, as in the case of the present research.

The questionnaire was set up using Microsoft FrontPage 2000. Data were captured using Microsoft Access 2000. Electronic surveys have the advantage of being pre-coded and free of ambiguity of response in that only one response per item can be selected. They have the disadvantage that they risk missing those who do not have access to computers and the Web. This was not seen to be a problem for the group being surveyed.

During the first half of 2001, invitations to participate were sent by email to 1008 IS professionals throughout Australia who had attended job fairs in the previous 12 months. Twenty-eight unusable responses were eliminated from the analysis. A total of 136 usable replies were received, and this represented an overall response rate of 13.5% — acceptable for unsolicited surveys of this type but lower than was hoped for. Analysis of the data was carried out using SPSS R10. A similar questionnaire was also sent to 2000 IS decision makers. A total of 137 usable returns were received, along with 241 failed deliveries, giving a 7.8% effective return.

RESULTS

Respondent Client Contact

Respondents were classified into one of two groups, depending on the likely level of "people contact" they normally encounter in their job. This was selected from the principal work function and was classified higher or lower people contact. Table 2 shows the distributions by the respondent's principal work function and their perceived level of people contact in their work.

A review of Table 2 indicates that roles involving higher contact with people account for 56% of the responses, with roles involving lower personal contact with users at 44%. As the Web development role is arguably a role involving higher client contact, the percentage of roles involving lower people contact would decline to only 35%, with those requiring higher contact growing to 64%. Either view is consistent with the view expressed by Ang (1992), that the importance of technology-oriented roles would decline, while roles involving client interaction would grow in importance, a view supported by the data in Table 1.

Respondent Organizational Level

Table 3 shows the position occupied by the IT/IS respondent from the employer group. The job titles represented in Table 3 indicate that the majority of respondents were in a position to appoint or direct the activities of IS staff.

Table 2. Principal work function and level of respondent people contact

	Frequency	Lower People Contact Percentage	Higher People Contact Percentage
Lower People Contact Roles			
Applications programming	34	25.0%	
Web development	12	8.8%	
Systems programming	4	2.9%	
Network administration	10	7.4%	
Higher People Contact Roles			
System support	32		23.5%
Project administration	13		9.6%
IT sales	2		1.5%
IT staff supervision	6		4.4%
Education and training	5		3.7%
Recruiting and staff placement	2		1.5%
Consulting	16		11.8
Total	136	44%	56%

Ranking Academic Subjects

The instrument contained two sections pertaining to academic preparation of graduates. These two sections separately covered the technical areas of an IS business degree and the other academic areas that are not specific to IS. A seven-point Likert scale (1 = irrelevant through to 7 = essential) was used to measure the response for each question. For each group mentioned above, the mean and standard deviation for each question was computed, as shown in Table 4.

Table 4 shows the respondents' views of the importance of academic subjects. The data clearly indicate that core business subjects such as Accounting [3.98 (lower), 4.25 (higher)], Economics [3.38 (lower), 3.83 (higher)], Law [3.62 (lower), 4.42 (higher)], and Statistics [4.00 (lower), 4.32 (higher)] rate rather low in importance among practicing IS professionals. With

Table 3. Organizational level of respondents

Function	Number of Responses	Percent
IT/IS/computing manager	108	78.3
CIO/Chief information officer	9	6.5
IT consultant	5	3.6
IT/IS team leader	4	2.9
Not identified	3	2.2
Manager, recruiting and personnel	2	1.4
Project manager	2	1.4
Personnel consultant	2	1.4
Recruitment officer	2	1.4
Company secretary/finance manager	1	0.7
Total	138	100

a score of four being the midrange and representing a neutral response, these "core" business subjects are seen as less important by practitioners in the discipline of IS.

Management [5.43 (lower), 5.63 (higher)], Ethics [4.85 (lower), 5.24 (higher)] and Organizational Behavior [4.68 (lower), 5.08 (higher)] rate closer to five or higher, indicating these are somewhat more important, especially Management, which rates in the fairly important to very important range. In all cases, respondents in higher people contact roles rated these areas as more important than did those in positions that involve lower people contact.

Overall, these results are unexpected given the popular claims that IS graduates need more understanding about business. Communications and Report Writing, often regarded more as a "soft" skill rather than an academic discipline in its own right, was rated the most important [5.82 (lower), 6.18 (higher)] of the academic areas, supporting many anecdotal reports that employers value and seek these skills. It should also be noted that a subject entitled "Communications & Report Writing" has been included in some business degree programs in the past.

Of the academic disciplines covered in the survey, only three were significantly different at the 0.05% level. These included Project Management, Business or Commercial Law, and Foreign Languages. Not surprisingly, the "higher people contact" group rated these areas as significantly more important than the other group.

*Table 4. Comparative importance of academic subjects (*n = 136*)*

Subject	Low (l) Mean (σ)	High (h) Mean (σ)	
Communications and report writing	5.82 (1.27)	6.18 (0.81)	
Analysis and design	5.82 (1.16)	5.91 (1.05)	
Database design	5.65 (1.27)	5.47 (1.24)	
Business applications	5.62 (1.04)	5.68 (1.17)	
Client server applications	5.60 (0.99)	5.72 (0.86)	
Use operating systems	5.52 (1.03)	5.66 (1.15)	
Apply OOPs	5.45 (1.03)	5.12 (1.39)	
Management	5.43 (1.11)	5.63 (0.96)	
Knowledge of PC apps	5.40 (1.21)	5.46 (1.24)	
E-commerce/E-business development	5.23 (1.44)	5.41 (1.04)	
Project management	5.10 (1.07)	5.70 (1.17)	*
Web design/development	5.05 (1.71)	4.88 (1.39)	
LAN and data communications	5.02 (1.27)	5.38 (1.25)	
Large system experience	4.92 (1.23)	5.28 (1.15)	
Apply 3GLs	4.87 (1.31)	4.57 (1.47)	
Business ethics	4.85 (1.68)	5.24 (1.48)	
Data mining/data warehousing	4.78 (1.38)	4.74 (1.35)	
Organizational behavior	4.68 (1.42)	5.08 (1.38)	
Mathematical modeling	4.38 (1.40)	4.14 (1.48)	
CASE applications	4.38 (1.11)	4.61 (1.47)	
ERP implementations and operations	4.32 (1.31)	4.61 (1.45)	
Knowledge base/expert systems	4.25 (1.48)	4.67 (1.35)	
Operations research	4.22 (1.15)	4.34 (1.35)	
Marketing	4.18 (1.64)	4.47 (1.41)	
Business finance	4.10 (1.50)	4.46 (1.48)	
Business statistics	4.00 (1.43)	4.32 (1.38)	
International business	3.98 (1.66)	4.43 (1.51)	
Accounting	3.98 (1.51)	4.25 (1.58)	
Psychology	3.63 (1.73)	3.75 (1.79)	
Business or commercial law	3.62 (1.54)	4.42 (1.48)	*
Economics	3.38 (1.50)	3.83 (1.48)	
Foreign languages	2.78 (1.83)	3.45 (1.68)	*
n =	60	76	
*Significantly different at 0.05% level			

Even for respondents in low client contact roles, only 13 roles achieved a rating of 5.0 or more, with 19 roles rated at between 4.92 and 2.78 on the seven-point Likert scale. Respondents in high client contact roles rated 15 roles above 5.0, with 17 roles failing to achieve a rating above 4.88.

Some of the subjects that failed to achieve a rating of 5.0 included technical areas such as Large System Experience, Data Mining/Data Warehousing, Applying 3GLs, CASE Applications, ERP Implementations & Operations, and Knowledge Base/Expert Systems. Clearly, the respondents were not seeking additional technical knowledge but valued the soft skills of Communications and Report Writing (5.82) highest of those considered.

The results of subjecting the data to the Kruskall-Wallis procedure are shown in Table 5. In this nonparametric test, variables achieving a score of less than 0.05 are significant.

The data were subjected to the Kurskall-Wallis procedure. The ability to apply OOPs, CASE applications, database design, e-commerce and e-business development, large system experience, the ability to apply 3-GLs, LAN and Data Communications, and Web design and development, all achieved significance. To some extent, the authors believe that the data reflect the particular concerns of the pool of respondents, and that caution should be used in generalizing the findings in curriculum decisions. For example, although large systems

Table 5. IS/IT/CS subjects comparison: Kruskall-Wallis procedure results

Subject	df	Asymp. Sig.
Apply OOPs	1	0.00
CASE applications	1	0.00
Database design	1	0.00
E-commerce/e-business development	1	0.00
Large system experience	1	0.00
Apply 3GLs	1	0.00
LAN and data comms	1	0.02
Web design/development	1	0.03
Client server applications	1	0.06
Project management	1	0.08
Analysis and design	1	0.13
Knowledge base/expert systems	1	0.14
Use operating systems	1	0.21
Business applications	1	0.22
Data mining/data warehousing	1	0.42
ERP implementations and operations	1	0.57
Knowledge of PC apps	1	0.73

experience and the ability to apply 3GLs achieved significance, other research confirms the declining importance of these subjects (Ang, 1992; Ang & Jiwahhasuchin, 1998; Young & Keen, 1997).

Ranking Soft Skills

A third section in the survey solicited rankings of the importance of a range of so-called "soft skills." The results are presented in Table 6. Comparisons between the "higher" and "lower" people contact groups were made. In all cases, Mann-Whitney U tests were used to establish any statistical differences between the two classifications. Table 6 shows that "soft" skills in the main are rated substantially higher than "hard" academic skills. Although the higher people contact grouping tended to rate these soft skills above the rating by the lower people contact grouping, only one variable (Problem Definition Skills) was rated significantly higher by the more client-oriented respondents. Only one "soft" skill, "Able to prepare multimedia presentations," was rated lower than 5.0 by both groups. *ALL* other "soft" skills were rated at 5.0 or higher by *both* groups.

Table 6. Comparative importance of soft skills (n = 136)

Skills	Lower Mean (σ)	Higher Mean (σ)	
Problem-solving skills	6.38 (0.56)	6.49 (0.58)	*
Work as a team	6.47 (0.70)	6.57 (0.62)	
Meet deadlines	6.37 (0.66)	6.34 (0.70)	
Quickly acquire new skills	6.32 (0.62)	6.41 (0.66)	
Work under pressure	6.42 (0.74)	6.42 (0.80)	
Independently acquire new skills	6.32 (0.72)	6.38 (0.71)	
Manage time	6.23 (0.79)	6.20 (1.06)	
Handle concurrent tasks	6.15 (0.73)	6.17 (0.87)	
Be able to interact with people of different backgrounds	6.05 (0.72)	6.20 (0.73)	
Possess problem definition skills	6.03 (0.71)	6.30 (0.75)	
Be able to work with people from different disciplines	6.03 (0.71)	6.05 (0.76)	
Work independently	6.30 (1.03)	6.25 (0.87)	
Possess written communication skills	6.10 (0.86)	6.25 (0.83)	
Have a client-focused service ethic	6.07 (0.92)	6.24 (1.06)	
Be willing to undergo ongoing professional development	6.03 (0.94)	6.29 (0.85)	
Think creatively	5.93 (0.99)	6.20 (0.80)	
Place organizational objectives first	5.72 (0.87)	5.74 (1.01)	
Accept direction	5.87 (1.03)	6.16 (0.73)	
Have business analysis skills	5.63 (0.86)	5.62 (1.15)	
Possess oral presentation skills	5.70 (0.93)	5.86 (1.17)	
Have information-seeking skills	5.68 (1.02)	5.95 (0.91)	
Have leadership potential	5.08 (1.09)	5.25 (1.07)	
Possess a good sense of humor	5.00 (1.30)	5.26 (1.39)	
Be able to prepare multimedia presentations	4.52 (1.44)	4.89 (1.05)	
n =	60	76	
*Significantly different at 0.05% level.			

Table 7. Comparative ratings of hard skills by IS practitioners and employers

Skills	IS/IT Professionals		IS/IT Employers	
	Mean	σ	Mean	σ
Communications and report writing	6.02	1.05	6.09	0.81
Analysis and design	5.87	1.09	5.63	1.26
Client server applications	5.67	0.92	5.37	1.15
Business applications	5.65	1.11	5.76	1.20
Use operating systems	5.60	1.10	5.39	1.27
Database design	5.55	1.25	5.12	1.16
Management	5.54	1.03	5.20	1.10
Knowledge of PC apps	5.43	1.22	5.41	1.37
Project management	5.43	1.16	5.60	1.24
E-commerce/e-business development	5.33	1.23	4.78	1.38
Apply OOPs	5.26	1.25	4.61	1.51
LAN and Data comms	5.22	1.27	5.55	1.22
Large system experience	5.12	1.19	4.54	1.53
Business ethics	5.07	1.57	5.23	1.52
Web design/development	4.96	1.54	4.67	1.15
Organizational behavior	4.90	1.41	4.92	1.34
Data mining/data warehousing	4.76	1.36	4.66	1.36
Apply 3GLs	4.70	1.41	4.15	1.58
CASE applications	4.51	1.32	3.80	1.42
Knowledge base/expert systems	4.49	1.42	4.20	1.37
ERP implementations and operations	4.48	1.39	4.33	1.61
Marketing	4.35	1.52	4.39	1.34
Business finance	4.30	1.50	4.54	1.47
Operations research	4.29	1.26	4.32	1.26
Mathematical modeling	4.25	1.44	3.97	1.49
International business	4.24	1.59	3.69	1.56
Business statistics	4.18	1.40	4.33	1.38
Accounting	4.13	1.55	4.68	1.38
Business or commercial law	4.07	1.55	4.12	1.45
Psychology	3.70	1.76	3.85	1.46
Economics	3.63	1.50	3.68	1.47
Foreign languages	3.15	1.78	3.04	1.46
	136		138	

All but one "soft" skill achieved a mean rating exceeding five for both groupings. Seventeen (out of 24) of the "soft" skills were rated in excess of six by the "higher people contact" group of practitioners. Fifteen of the "lower people contact" group rated these higher than six. Closer inspection of Table 4 and Table 7 reveals that the highest rated IS area, Analysis and Design, rated below all but seven of the soft skills in Table 7.

Teamwork, problem-solving skills, ability to work under pressure, and ability to quickly acquire new skills independently, are each rated quite high, close to essential, by IS practitioners, irrespective of the level of people contact their work activity involves. Only one soft skill, ability to prepare multimedia presentations, rated relatively low, and it could be argued that this is not a true soft IS skill.

Comparison between IT/IS Professionals and IT/IS Employers

Table 7 shows the mean and standard deviations of ratings by IS/IT professionals and IS/IT employees for "hard" skills and business subjects.

Of the 14 subjects and skills that achieved a mean rating of 5.0 or more, the highest rating by practitioners and employers was achieved by Communications and Report Writing, a soft skill. Eleven technical subjects and two "other business subjects" management and business ethics, achieved mean ratings of 5.0 or more. The value placed on these two subjects is consistent with earlier findings by the authors shown in Table 1.

A remaining pool of traditional business subjects, including marketing, business finance, operations research, mathematical modeling, international business, business statistics, accounting, and business or commercial law, failed to achieve a mean rating exceeding 4.35. Three other subjects, psychology, economics, and foreign languages, ranked quite low, none achieving even a neutral rating of 4.0 by either group. The low ratings achieved by these subjects by practitioner and employer groups suggest that the IS curriculum would be improved by their replacement by other, more relevant subjects that help students develop their "business skills."

The data regarding non-IS business subjects were subjected to the Kurskall-Wallis procedure. Only three subjects, accounting, management, and international business, achieved significance. Accounting and management emerged as two of three most highly ranked nontechnical subjects in the earlier study by the authors (Turner & Lowry, 1999b), international business was not included in the 1999 study and was added as a result of insights gained from that work. While business ethics was identified in the 1999 study as one of three most highly ranked nontechnical business subjects, it was ranked a bit lower in the later study.

Table 9 shows the mean and standard deviations of ratings by IS/IT Professionals and IS/IT employees for "soft" business skills.

Table 9 shows a marked similarity between practitioners and employers in their ratings of the importance of "soft" business skills. Once again, consistent with Table 6, only the ability to prepare multimedia presentations failed to achieve a mean rating of 5.0. All other soft business skills were highly rated by IS practitioners and employers.

These included time management, oral presentation skills, good sense of humor, willingness to undergo professional development, ability to prepare multimedia presentations, ability to quickly acquire new skills, ability to meet deadlines, the ability to work under pressure, and well-developed written communication skills. It is interesting to note the position of the ability to prepare multimedia presentations in Table 10, as it was the only soft skill to fail to receive a rating of 5.0 or more from IS practitioners and employers.

DISCUSSION

Information technology is central to the work of computer scientists and information systems professionals. Computer scientists are more oriented toward the technology, while information systems professionals are more oriented toward the users of technology. The model curricula of relevant professional bodies such as the Association for Computing Machinery (2001), the Association of Information Technology Professionals (Davis, 1997), and the Australian Computer Society (Underwood, 1997) have noted and acknowledged the different roles performed by information professionals.

Table 8. Non-IS subjects comparison: Kruskall-Wallis procedure results

Subject	df	Asymp. Sig.
Accounting	1	0.00
International business	1	0.01
Management	1	0.01
Business finance	1	0.09
Mathematical modeling	1	0.12
Business statistics	1	0.24
Business ethics	1	0.41
Foreign languages	1	0.68
Psychology	1	0.74
Economics	1	0.78
Marketing	1	0.78
Operations research	1	0.79
Organizational behavior	1	0.84
Business or commercial law	1	0.92
Communications and report writing	1	0.92

There has long been agreement that the IS curriculum should be comprised of some combination of technical subjects and nontechnical business subjects, and that graduates also need soft business skills. There is far less agreement about what the mix between these should be and how best to prepare students in some areas, notably in the development of soft business skills.

Overall, the data indicate that IS/IT practitioners perceive soft skills as very important, while hard skills, especially some of the more traditional core business subjects such as accounting or economics, are rated lower, perhaps expecting a satisfactory level of technical skill as a given. The data were obtained from a wide representation of professionals across the spectrum of functional areas that require different types and levels of hard and soft skills.

While we agree with the general view that soft skills have become increasingly important, we argue that the traditional business subjects are *not* the business skills primarily sought in studies of the IS marketplace. Does the study of traditional business subjects such as marketing, business law, or economics directly help students to develop a repertoire of soft business skills? The findings suggest that in reality, it is not more core business subjects that are needed, but an appreciation of business processes and activities that are not always covered in IS degree programs is needed.

Some Issues

Some formidable barriers exist to substantive revision of IS curricula to emphasize acquisition and development of soft business skills. These include:

Table 9. Comparison of importance placed on soft skills by IS/IT professionals and employers

Skills	IS/IT Professionals		IS/IT Employers	
	Mean	σ	Mean	σ
Work as a team	6.52	0.66	6.39	0.81
Possess problem-solving skills	6.44	0.57	6.37	0.68
Work under pressure	6.42	0.78	6.27	0.75
Quickly acquire new skills	6.37	0.64	6.15	0.73
Independently acquire new skills	6.35	0.72	6.23	0.71
Meet deadlines	6.35	0.68	6.13	0.81
Work independently	6.27	0.94	6.22	0.65
Manage time	6.21	0.95	5.98	0.84
Possess problem definition skills	6.18	0.74	6.14	0.74
Be willing to undergo ongoing professional development	6.18	0.89	5.93	0.89
Possess written communication skills	6.18	0.85	6.04	0.76
Have a client-focused service ethic	6.16	1.00	6.09	0.94
Handle concurrent tasks	6.16	0.81	6.08	0.81
Interact with people of different backgrounds	6.13	0.73	6.03	0.85
Think creatively	6.08	0.89	6.09	0.71
Work with people from different disciplines	6.04	0.74	6.10	0.82
Accept direction	6.03	0.89	5.98	0.84
Have information seeking skills	5.83	0.96	5.82	0.93
Possess oral presentation skills	5.79	1.07	5.56	0.88
Place organizational objectives first	5.73	0.95	5.74	0.97
Possess business analysis skills	5.63	1.03	5.51	1.04
Have leadership potential	5.18	1.08	4.99	0.94
Have a good sense of humor	5.15	1.35	5.58	1.14
Be able to prepare multimedia presentations	4.73	1.25	4.32	1.38
n =	136		138	

- *Confusion*: Research results that call for more "business skills" have handily and traditionally been interpreted as meaning exposure of students to additional, formal business subjects. While an IS student may gain knowledge and skill in marketing, economic analysis, or international business in that way, our findings suggest that it is the "soft" skills, rather than formal academic skill, that are wanted by IS/IT practitioners and employers.
- *Tradition and inertia*: It is easy to offer traditional business subjects, as they are already being taught. In many institutions, the existing IS academic staff would have to acquire the additional academic background and skills needed to introduce a substantive soft skills emphasis into the IS curriculum. In most instances, there is unlikely to be sufficient time or interest in doing so.
- *Resources*: If a substantial portion of an undergraduate degree program was shifted from traditional business subjects to the acquisition and development of soft skills, who would develop, teach, and assess the new soft skills curriculum component?

Table 10. Soft skills comparison: Kruskall-Wallis procedure results

Skills	df	Asymp. Sig.
Manage time	1	0.00
Possess oral presentation skills	1	0.01
Have a good sense of humor	1	0.01
Be willing to undergo ongoing professional development	1	0.01
Be able to prepare multimedia presentations	1	0.01
Quickly acquire new skills	1	0.01
Meet deadlines	1	0.03
Work under pressure	1	0.05
Possess written communication skills	1	0.05
Have leadership potential	1	0.07
Work independently	1	0.10
Independently acquire new skills	1	0.11
Work as a team	1	0.20
Possess business analysis skills	1	0.33
Be able to work with people from different disciplines	1	0.35
Have a client-focused service ethic	1	0.36
Handle concurrent tasks	1	0.36
Accept direction	1	0.43
Be able to interact with people of different backgrounds	1	0.43
Possess problem-solving skills	1	0.54
Possess problem definition skills	1	0.56
Think creatively	1	0.65
Have information seeking skills	1	0.71
Place organizational objectives first	1	0.80

- *Vested interest*: Some academic institutions supplement the enrollment in less relevant or popular subjects through inclusion of those subjects in a popular curriculum such as Information Systems. In many institutions, economic incentives exist for students to be enrolled in subjects within a single administrative unit, such as a business or IT faculty.

Some Recommendations

There are, of course, no easy solutions to resolve the issues raised. In increasing order of difficulty, some of the barriers to meaningful reform and evolution of the IS curriculum might be surmounted over time and with sufficient dedication.

- *To reduce confusion*: Local course advisory and professional bodies can provide invaluable insight into the mix of technical and nontechnical formal courses and soft skills appropriate for a given institution's service area. Focus groups and local replication of available studies should provide targeted, timely, and authoritative guidance for ongoing curriculum evolution.

- *Overcoming tradition and inertia*: To some extent, prospective students have taken matters into their own hands by opting in larger numbers to bypass traditional university courses in favor of industry-sponsored/sanctioned entry gateways, such as those offered by Microsoft, Oracle, SAP, and others. It is possible that students electing the nonacademic alternative see more value in industry-focused training than in academic education that they see as irrelevant to their career aspirations. A large number of traditional business subjects were rated low in importance by IS practitioners and employers in the tables above. Tertiary educators will need to reconsider the value of these traditional business subjects and will have to extend themselves to develop and deliver revitalized curricula that squarely address the expressed desire for soft skills that have been identified in a number of studies. Have another look at Tables 4 (Comparative Importance of Academic Subjects) and 7 (Comparative Ratings of Hard Skills by IS Practitioners and Employers). Note the position of the majority of traditional business subjects in ratings of importance by IS practitioners and employers. What would your course advisory body or a local study of your service area suggest?

- *Finding resources*: Always a problem, resources are easier to obtain from a body of satisfied clients, such as the firms who employ our graduates. If we are seen to consult with, listen to, and serve the interests of those firms, they will follow their self-interest by becoming industry partners, rich sources of guidance in curriculum planning and development, work experience for students, consultancies for academics, equipment, money, and political weight in our own institution. We must learn to master what we teach about building client ownership to insure system acceptance and success.

- *Neutralizing vested interests*: Senior university managers may oppose substantive IS curriculum reform such as that discussed in this chapter for a number of reasons, including loss of revenue if students enroll in soft skill courses provided by another administrative unit. It is up to IS educators to develop strategies to address the turf issues that preoccupy some administrators. Building effective partnerships with the appropriate industries in our service area can provide a powerful voice to speak on our behalf to senior management. Accrediting bodies can also help in this way.

Toward a Technology-Based Profession

While study after study has called for soft skills acquisition and development by IS students, some IS programs have a clearer and better-developed vision than others of what those skills are and how they may be introduced and cultivated. The growing emphasis on soft skills in IS education is an indication that what began as a fundamentally technology-oriented discipline is evolving into a technology-based profession. We can watch someone else claim that knowledge and the opportunities that it provides or we can embrace it ourselves, hoping that there is still time.

ENDNOTE

1   In this context, what Ashley & Padgett (1997) and others, e.g., Little et al. (1999, pp. 106–112), writing from the US perspective, refer to as a *course* is known as a *subject* in Australia. A course in Australia is a sequence of studies leading to a qualification such as a bachelor's degree.

REFERENCES

Ang, A. Y. (1992). Australian information systems curricula: A comparison between the views of universities and TAFE colleges. *Information Systems as Organisational Processes: Proceedings of Third Australasian Conference on Information Systems, 5–8 October 1992* (pp. 747–758). Wollongong, New South Wales, Australia: Department of Business Systems, University of Wollongong.

Ang, A. Y., & Jiwahhasuchin, S. (1998). Information systems education in Thailand: A comparison between the views of professionals and academics. *Journal of Global Information Management, 6*(4), 34–42.

Ashley, N. W., & Padgett, T. C. (1997). Information systems graduates: Evaluation of their IS curricula. http://www.westga.edu/~bquest/1998/infosys.html.

Association for Computing Machinery. (2001). Model curricula for computing. *ACM.* http://www.acm.org/education/curricula.html.

Athey, S. & Plotnicki, J. (1998). The evaluation of job opportunities for IT professionals. *Journal of Computer Information Systems.* (Spring), 71–88.

Beise, C. M. et al. (1991). What information systems graduates are really doing: An update. *Computer Personnel, 13*(2) (July), 4–11.

Burn, J. M., Ng Tye, E. M. W., & Ma, L. C. K. (1995). Paradigm shift — Cultural implications for development of IS professionals. *Journal of Global Information Management, 3*(2) (Spring), 18–28.

Cafasso, R. (1996). Selling your soft side helps IT. *Computerworld, 18*(35), 60–61.

Cheney, P., Hale, D., & Kasper, G. (1990). Knowledge, skills and abilities of information systems professionals: Past, present and future. *Information Management, 9*(4), 237–247.

Comley, P. (1996). The use of the Internet as a data collection method. Retrieved May 21, 2001 from the World Wide Web: http://www.sga.co.uk/esomar.html.

Davis, G. et al. (1997). *IS'97 Model Curricula and Guidelines for Undergraduate Degree Programs in Information Systems,* Association of Information Technology Professionals.

Doke, E. R., & Williams, S. R. (1999). Knowledge and skill requirements for information systems professionals: An exploratory study. *Journal of IS Education, 10*(1) (Spring), 10–18.

Gorgone, J. T., & Gray, P. (1999). Graduate IS curriculum for the 21st century. *32nd Hawaii International Conference on Systems Science: Proceedings.* http://computer.org/proceedings/hicss/0001/00011/0001toc.htm.

Gupta, J. N. D., & Wachter, R. M. (1998). A capstone course in the information systems curriculum. *International Journal of Information Management, 18*(6), 427–441.

Herzberg, F. (1968). One more time: How do you motivate employees. *Harvard Business Review, 46*(1), 53–62.

Kakabadse, A., & Korac-Kakabadse, N. (2000). Future role of IS/IT professionals. *Journal of Management Development, 19*(2), 97–154.

Khalil, O. E. M. et al. (1999). Teaching information quality in Information Systems education." *Informing Science, 2*(3), 53–59.

Kuras, M. et al. (1999). Changing IS curriculum and methods of instruction. ITiCSE 99, Cracow, Poland, ACM.

Lee, D. M., Truath, E. M., & Farwell, D. (1995). Critical skills and knowledge requirements of IS professionals: A joint academic/industry investigation. *MIS Quarterly, 19*(3), 313–340.

Little, J. C. et al. (1999). Integrating professionalism and workplace issues into the computing and information technology curriculum. *ITiCSE '99 Working Group Reports, 33*(4), 106–112.

Lowry, G. R. et al., (1996), Organisational characteristics, cultural qualities and excellence in leading Australian-owned information technology firms. *1996 Information Systems Conference of New Zealand* (pp. 72–84). Palmerston North, New Zealand: IEEE Computer Society Press, Los Alamitos, CA.

Lu, M. T., & Wang, P. (1998–1999). Knowledge and skills of IS graduates: A Hong Kong perspective. *Journal of Computer Information Systems,* (Winter), 40–46.

Main, R. (1995). Telstra Winnows the best and brightest graduates. *Computerworld, 18*(12), 36.

McLean, E. R., Tanner, J. R., & Smits, S. J. (1991). Self-perceptions and job preferences of entry-level information systems professionals: Implications for career development (pp. 3–13). Paper presented at the Special Interest Group on Computer Personnel Research Annual Conference, Athens, GA.

Mehta, R. & Sivadas, E. (1995). Comparing response rates and response content in mail vs. email surveys. *Journal of the Market Research Society, 37*(4), 429–439.

Morgan, G. W. et al. (1998). Development staff characteristics and service stability in leading Australian-owned information technology firms. *1998 International Conference on Software Engineering: Education and Practice* (pp. 96–103). Dunedin, New Zealand: IEEE Computer Society Press, Los Alamitos, CA.

Padgett, T. et al. (1991). Job preparation of IS graduates: Are they ready for the real world? *Journal of Systems Management, 42*(8), 17.

Slaughter, S., & Ang, S. (1996). Employment outsourcing in information systems. *Communications of the ACM, 39*(7), 47–54.

Stewart, G. (1997). The perceptions of professional practice by IT students. *Eighth Australasian Conference on Information Systems, Adelaide, South Australia, Australian Computer Society & ACIS Executive*, 739–744.

Trauth, E., Farwell, D., & Lee, D. (1993). The IS expectation gap: Industry expectations versus academic preparation. *MIS Quarterly, 17*(3) (September), 293–307.

Turner, R., & Lowry, G. (1999a). The compleat graduate: What students think employers want and what employers say they want in new graduates. *Preparing for the Global Economy of the New Millennium. Proceedings of Pan-Pacific Conference XVI* (pp. 272–274). Fiji: Pan-Pacific Business Association.

Turner, R., & Lowry, G. (1999b). Reconciling the needs of new information systems graduates and their employers in small, developed countries. *South African Computer Journal, 24*(November), 136–145.

Turner, R., & Lowry, G. (2000). Motivating and recruiting intending IS professionals: A study of what attracts IS students to prospective employment. *South African Computer Journal, 25*(November), 132–137.

Turner, R., & Lowry, G. (2001). The third dimension of the IS curriculum: The importance of soft skills for IT practitioners (pp. 683–688). Paper presented at the ACIS 2001, Coffs Harbour, NSW, Australia.

Turner, R., & Lowry, G. (2002). The relative importance of "hard" & "soft"' skills for IT practitioners. *Issues and Trends of Information Technology Management in Contemporary Organizations: 2002 Information Resources Management Association International Conference.* Seattle, WA: May 19–22, 2002.

Underwood, A. (1997). *The ACS core body of knowledge for information technology professionals.* Retrieved July 21, 2001 from the World Wide Web: http://www.acs.org.au/national/pospaper/bokpt1.htm.

Van Slyke, C., Kittner, M., & Cheney, P. (1997). Skill requirements for entry-level IS graduates: A preliminary report from industry. Retrieved April 26, 2000 from the World Wide Web: http://groucho.bsn.usf.edu/~vanslyke/isecon_1.htm.

Waterman, R. H. et al. (1994). Toward a career resilient workforce. *Harvard Business Review, 69* (July–August), 87–95.

Westfall, R. D. (1999–2000). Meta-skills in information systems education." *Journal of Computer Information Systems.* (Winter): 69–74.

Wong, E. Y. W. (1996). The education and training of future information systems professionals. *Education + Training, 38*(1), 37–43.

Wrycza, S., Usowicz, T. W., Gabor, A., and Verber, B. (1999). The challenges and directions of MIS curriculum development in respect of transformation of business requirements. Cracow, Poland: ITiCSE '99. pp. 177–178.

Young, J., & Keen, C. (1997). The emergence importance of broader skills and personal attributes in the recruitment of Australian IS professionals. *Eighth Australasian Conference on Information Systems* (pp. 682–692). Adelaide, South Australia: Australian Computer Society & ACIS Executive.

Chapter XIV

Tracking Through Information Technology Education

Erick D. Slazinski
Purdue University, USA

Susan K. Lisack
Purdue University, USA

ABSTRACT

With a projected 2.26 million additional jobs to fill in various computer fields by the year 2010, there are and will continue to be ample job opportunities in the computer industry. However, the computer field is far too broad for one individual to be an expert in the entire field. Therefore, it may be more useful for students to have the opportunity to concentrate their studies in a specific interest area within a broader information technology degree. This chapter discusses the creation of a database track within an Information Technology (IT) or Computer Information Systems (CIS) degree program so that undergraduate students can choose to focus on this specialty area in their junior and senior years.

INTRODUCTION

IT educators throughout the United States have paid attention to the IT industry. To address the need for IT graduates with specialized skills, many of the leading universities have created an IT program that allows the students to specialize or focus their studies. This chapter will discuss some findings on the state of IT programs and their offerings and examine in-depth one university's database specialization track.

BACKGROUND

The Bureau of Labor Statistics reported 2.9 million computer-related jobs in 2000, with an expected 4.89 million computer jobs by the year 2010. Considering new jobs as well as replacements, over 2.26 million additional people will be needed to fill these jobs (Hecker, 2001, p. 9).

WHERE ARE THE SPECIALIZED IT PROGRAMS?

Starting with an attendance list from the Conference for IT Curriculum (CITC) II, we explored the published curriculum from those institutes. In attendance at the conference were IT educators from around the United States who had an interest in IT curriculum issues. An IT curriculum is focused on the application of technologies to solve problems. To differentiate, a traditional computer science curriculum is focused on algorithm design.

If we look at Table 1, we see that out of the 28 programs represented, 50% (14) had some specialization available for students. Of the 14 programs that offered specializations, 45% (six) of those offered at least a database specialization.

ANATOMY OF A DATABASE TRACK

With the Bureau's computer workforce projections, it is not surprising that computer-related degree programs are in high demand. After many years of accepting all qualified students who applied, our IT program has been forced in recent years to turn away some highly qualified candidates, because our classes are full. In Fall 2001, there were 664 students majoring in our program, whereas in earlier years, we had stabilized at around 400 students.

For many years, we have offered a general IT degree program that provides students with a broad background in systems analysis and design, application development and programming, computer networking, and database modeling and programming. Students had a few computer electives that they could use to develop one or more areas of interest. The curriculum was regularly evaluated and updated to respond to current industry needs and trends.

As the program grew, so did interest in specializations within the department. In 1997, our department created a Telecommunications and Networking specialization within the IT degree. Students could choose between a general IT degree and the telecommunications option. With the success of the telecommunications option, it was natural to expand the specialization options into the remaining areas of faculty expertise — application develop-

Table 1. Programs and specializations

Name	Specialization	Database Specialization
Ball State	No	
Bentley	No	
Brigham-Young University (BYU)	No	
BYU-Hawaii	No	
BYU-Idaho	No	
Capella	Yes	No
Drexel	Yes	Yes
Florida State University	Yes	No
Georgia Southern	No	
George Mason University	Yes	No
Hawaii at Manoa	No	
Houston	No	
Indiana University	Yes	No
Indiana University Purdue University at Indianapolis	Yes	No
Macon State	Yes	Yes
New Jersey Institute of Technology	Yes	No
Northern Alabama	Yes	No
Pace University	No	
Pennsylvania College of Technology	Yes	No
Purdue University	Yes	Yes
Purdue University – Calumet	Yes	Yes
Rochester Institute of Technology	Yes	Yes
Southern Alabama	Yes	Yes
State University of New York (SUNY) Morrisville	No	
Towson University	No	
University of Baltimore	No	
University of Cincinnati-Clermont	No	
USCS	No	

ment, systems analysis and design, and database management. We felt these areas fit the requirements of our customers in industry who hire our students.

Students also had an interest in these areas, as indicated by our fourth year elective course enrollments (18–25 students). In the Spring 2001 senior-level data warehousing elective, all 18 students indicated an intention to get a database job, while in the Fall 2001 semester, 20 out of 26 students in the DBA course planned to get a job in the database area.

Need for a Database Track

The same data from the Bureau of Labor Statistics (Hecker, 2001, p. 9) indicated there were 106,000 jobs for database administrators (DBAs) in 2000, with a projected 176,000 openings to fill by the year 2010. In addition to DBAs, there are also database professionals who specialize in database architecture and database programming.

Topics within the Database Track

There are various job titles given to database activities in the workplace, such as these listed on the ITWORKS-OHIO Web site: Data Analyst, Database Administrator, Database Analyst, Database Developer, and Database Specialist. Many others exist in the marketplace. However, based on the author's opinion, when the job descriptions are examined, one can find that there are really three, interrelated roles. Figure 1 illustrates these roles using the structure of a house as an example. The DBA (as the foundation) keeps a database available, secure, and healthy. Without the DBA, the rest of the database team could not function. The database developer (as the framing of the house) encodes the business logic in the database. Additionally, the developer often develops the interface layer between the system software and the database engine. Last, the database architect (as the roof of the house) is often a senior staff member. Typical duties include determining the amount of business logic to be encoded in the database, developing the database design (including distribution of data, data flows, etc.), and often overseeing the implementation of the database. Like the components of a house, all three roles are codependant and necessary. In addition to the specific duties, each member must maintain several lines of communication within the development team and organization.

The database administrator must often work with the system/network administrators when it comes to purchasing hardware, determining network traffic and bandwidth requirements, coordinating the use of backup devices, etc. They often work with the database architects in providing recommendations for physical implementation issues. The database developer must interact with the database architect since they are implementing the design from the architect, and with the system developers to ensure that the developers have access to the data they need, while maintaining the integrity of the database. The database architect must work with the software architect. Together they determine how to partition the business logic of the system. The database architect works with the DBA in determining the best physical implementation of the supporting database. And, the architect often coordinates the activities of the database developers.

Figure 1. Database roles

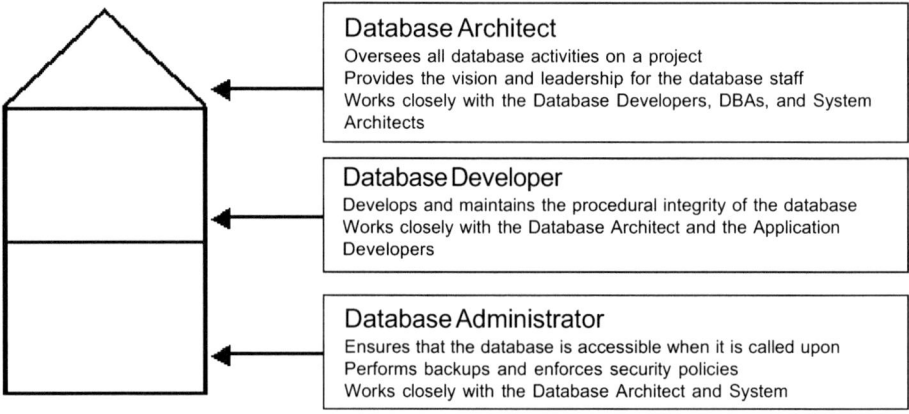

Based on these responsibilities and communication channels, we designed the database track to produce students prepared for these multifaceted jobs. During the first two years of our program, all students gain a broad overview of the Information Technology field, taking introductory courses in programming, Internet technologies, architectures, telecommunications, database, and systems analysis and design:

- *Introduction to Application Development*: Introduction to system development using MS Access
- *Introduction to Computer Programming*: Application development using Visual Basic
- *Internet Foundations and Technologies*: Web page development using XHTML
- *Information Technology Architectures*: Exploration of the history, architecture, and development of the Internet and the World Wide Web
- *Systems Software and Networking*: Introduction to data communications and network operating systems
- *Programming for the Internet*: Internet application development using scripting languages
- *Database Fundamentals*: Normalization, SQL, and application interfaces to databases
- *Systems Analysis and Design Methods*: Introduction to information systems development

Courses in the Database Track

Students specializing in the database area must complete an additional 25 credit hours of technical courses focused on getting the database student prepared for one of the three roles described above. First, we will follow the progression of the database courses in our program and then show how they, in combination with other courses, prepare our students for future jobs.

Figure 2 shows the progression of database courses for a database-track student. A brief description of these database courses follows:

- *Introduction to Application Development (all students)*: This course introduces the development of information systems through the use of a database. Topics include business information systems, system and application development, database management systems, problem solving, logic, data types, and programming using database technology. Given a database design and application requirements, students design, construct, and test a personal computer information system.
- *Database Fundamentals (all students)*: In this course, relational database concepts, including data design, modeling and normalization, are discussed. Students use SQL to query, define, populate, and test a database. This course expands on previous courses by accessing databases from programs and the Web and discusses practical issues that database developers must handle.
- *Database Development*: In this course, some of the programmatic extensions to SQL supported by leading Relational Database Management Systems (RDBMS) vendors are explored. Topics include stored procedure and trigger design and implementation, query optimization to enhance performance, and data transformation to enhance interoperability of data.

- *Database Design and Implementation*: In this course, advanced design techniques and physical issues relating to enterprise-wide databases are covered. Topics include advanced normalization, data distribution, distributed database design and replication, storage estimation and allocation, usage analysis, partitioning of very large tables, metadata analysis, data conversion, and load techniques.
- *Database Administration (elective)*: Explored in this course are the tools and techniques for managing an organization's database technology. Topics include database architecture, database technology installation, database creation and maintenance, RDBMS operations and troubleshooting, and database performance tuning.
- *Data Warehousing (elective)*: In this course, students study the design and implementation of data warehouses (including data marts and operational data stores) using current database technologies. Topics include data modeling for warehouses, data warehousing infrastructure and tool selection, data exploration, data synthesis and reduction, organizational metadata, and data warehouse administration.

Advanced Topics in Database Technology (elective): In this course, contemporary issues in the database arena are explored. These issues may be related to new or breakthrough concepts, technologies, or techniques.

Figure 2. Database courses

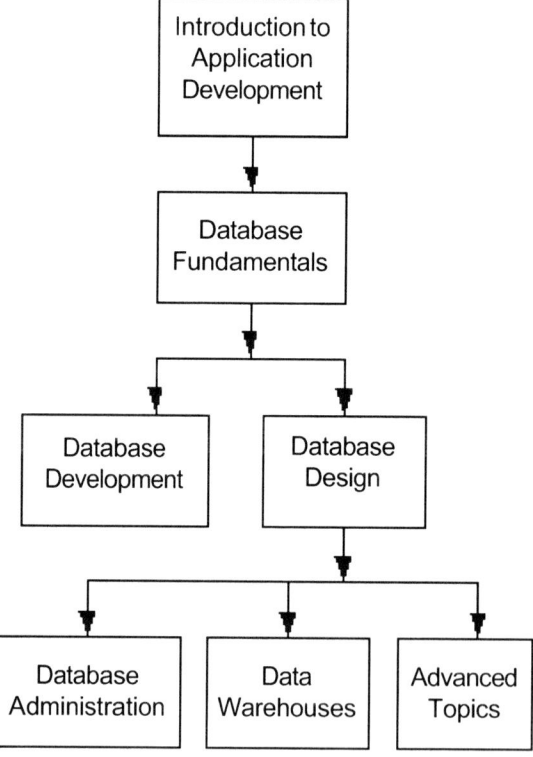

Rounding Out the Students

Because database development has a significant analysis and design component, students are required to take a Systems Requirements Discovery and Modeling course, offered by our systems analysis group. Because many database personnel are often relegated to a distinct group with a project with management requirements, a Project Management course is also required. To support further specialization into the database architect, database programmer, and database architect roles, we provide two separate selective areas: database management selectives and database technology selectives. The students must choose a minimum of 6 credit hours (two courses) in each of the selective areas. The database management selectives are the elective courses listed with the database course flow in Figure 2 — database administration, data warehousing and advanced topics in database management, as well as any graduate-level database course offered during the student's senior year. The database technology selectives provide additional areas of exploration on topics that piqued the students' interest in their first two years. The students are allowed to choose any two courses from the following:

- *Object-Oriented Programming*: Use of object-oriented programming languages (Java) in the development of modern, business applications
- *Advanced Design Techniques*: Advanced study of system design methods and techniques used by systems analysts to develop information systems
- *Software Development Methodologies*: Methodologies and practices commonly used in contemporary software development projects
- *Enterprise Application Development*: Component development and reuse, distributed object technologies, multi-tier applications
- *Senior Software Development Project*: Integrates the software development technologies and techniques taught in prior courses
- *E-Commerce*: Presents components of e-commerce
- *Automatic Identification and Data Capture*: Presents real-time data feeds
- Any other database management selective course(s) not already taken

Looking at the three roles that were defined previously (database administrator, database architect, and database developer) and the selective lists above, we could come up with suitable combinations of courses for each role. An undecided student could even define a general database combination. Please note there are many possible combinations; the combinations shown are merely illustrative.

Database Administrator

- *Database Management Selectives*: Database administration and data warehousing
- *Database Technology Selectives*: E-commerce and automatic identification and data capture

This combination of courses not only prepares the database administrator hopeful technically, but also exposes the student to other facets that they will have to communicate with, namely, software developers and production teams.

Database Architect

- *Database Management Selectives*: Advanced topics in database management and data warehousing
- *Database Technology Selectives*: Advanced design techniques and enterprise application development

This combination of courses not only prepares the database architect hopeful technically, but also exposes the student to other facets that they will have to communicate with, namely, system analysts and software developers.

Database Developer

- *Database Management Selectives*: Database administration and data warehousing
- *Database Technology Selectives*: Object-oriented programming and enterprise application development

This combination of courses not only prepares the database developer hopeful technically, but also exposes the student to other facets that they will have to communicate with, namely, software developers.

General Database

- *Database Management Selectives*: Database administration and data warehousing
- *Database Technology Selectives*: Advanced topics in database management and a graduate-level database course.

Though this combination does not target one specific database role, this student is the best versed in database technologies, allowing the student to take on any role that is available.

FACILITIES

The department has been successful in maintaining up-to-date software and hardware due to generous grants and donations from several companies and by taking advantage of educational programs offered by many companies. Students have access to multiple database servers. Dual-screen monitors in one lab facilitate courses in database programming and administration. Students can readily view their code, data, data model, and results simultaneously.

VMware is a newly acquired tool that promises many benefits, particularly in the database administration course, where students can administer their database inside a virtual computer. This course requires that each student have administrative rights, which our networking personnel are reluctant to give to students. This obstacle is removed with the use of VMware, because having administrative rights in the virtual machine does not transfer onto the school's network.

FACULTY

The mission of our department is to provide the highest quality of information systems and information technology education to prepare practitioners for careers in the application of information systems and technology. Our faculty members are hired on the basis of their industrial experience as well as their academic credentials. Faculty members are not required to hold a doctorate degree; however, a Masters degree plus three to five years of industrial experience is typically expected of all members of faculty. Presently, there are 2.5 faculty members and an Instructional Specialist (lecturer) supporting the database courses. They have spent time on projects and achieved various certifications and recognitions. Their experience covers the majority of topical areas in the database industry, from developing and deploying applications ranging from personal databases through large-scale, n-tier distributed systems and multi-terabyte data warehouses.

INDUSTRIAL ADVISORY BOARD

Currently, the department has two Industrial Advisory Boards, one for the general IT degree and one for the telecommunications specialization. The advisory boards are composed of leading information professionals from well-known companies with large IT or networking departments. These are also the employers of many of our graduates. The chosen representatives are in positions in which they are monitoring the marketplace and helping to make decisions about future directions for their companies. This puts them in a unique position to help guide us on the employee skills they will need in the future. Their suggestions are always carefully considered and often incorporated into new courses and curricula. The goal is for each board to meet on a regular basis at one- to two-year intervals to provide this valuable feedback. The advisory board for the general IT degree met in the past year to review and critique the proposed tracks. They were quite supportive of this new curriculum and were anxious to recruit our graduates. In fact, they challenged us to implement the new curriculum in less than the typical four-year window of a new curriculum.

MODEL CURRICULA

The IEEE and the ACM created a joint task force to update the 1991 curriculum recommendations. The most recent report, available at the ACM Web site, identified Information Management (IM) as a knowledge area within their Computing Curricula 2001. The IM area of knowledge includes 14 components. Three are considered core, and 11 are viewed as electives. The courses in our database track provide significant coverage of the IM areas identified. Additionally, we provide the Database Administration course that is beyond the model. Table 2 shows the mapping from the IM components to our DB-track courses.

FUTURE TRENDS

For our university, the new curriculum implementing the track concept started in Fall 2001. In Spring 2003, the current freshmen will be required to select their track of interest. At that time, we will begin monitoring the demand for this track.

Table 2. Comparison of model curricula to database track courses

IM Knowledge Areas	DB Track
IM1: Information Models and Systems (core)	In first-year course
IM2: Database Systems (core)	In first-year course
IM3: Data Modeling (core)	Second year: Database Fundamentals Third year: Database Design
IM4: Relational Databases (elective)	Second year: Database Fundamentals Third year: Database Design
IM5: Database Query Languages (elective)	Second year: Database Fundamentals (not OO queries)
IM6: Relational Databases Design (elective)	Second year: Database Fundamentals Third year: Database Design
IM7: Transaction Processing (elective)	Second year: Database Fundamentals Third year: Database Development
IM8: Distributed Databases (elective)	Third year: Database Design Fourth year: Data Warehousing
IM9: Physical Database Design (elective)	Third year: Database Design
IM10: Data Mining (elective)	Fourth year: Data Warehousing
IM11: Information Storage and Retrieval (elective)	Fourth year: Data Warehousing (partial)
IM12: Hypertext and Hypermedia (elective)	Candidate for fourth-year Adv. Topics
IM13 Multimedia Information and Systems (elective)	Candidate for fourth-year Adv. Topics
IM14: Digital Libraries (elective)	Candidate for fourth-year Adv. Topics

Additionally, it will be interesting to watch the other programs evolve. Items of interest include seeing if the programs that currently do not offer tracks start offering tracks and, for those programs with tracks, seeing which tracks endure.

CONCLUSION

In this chapter, we have seen that the IT industry is becoming an industry of specialists. Indeed, the IT field is too broad to be comprised of only generalists. In response to this need, IT educators have started offering specializations. We then investigated, in detail, the creation of a specialization in database management.

REFERENCES

Ball State University — Business Education and Office Administration. Retrieved July 13, 2002, from http://www.bsu.edu/web/catalog/undergraduate/programs/Programs02/beoa02_cb.html.

Bentley College — CIS Courses. Retrieved July 13, 2002, from http://cis.bentley.edu/cspages/ courses/courses.asp.

Brigham Young University — Electrical and Computer Engineering. Retrieved July 13, 2002, from http://ar.byu.edu/catalog/undergrad_cat/2001/departments/Electrical&Comp.html.

Brigham Young University–Hawaii — Information Systems. Retrieved July 13, 2002, from http://soc.byuh.edu/is/course.htm.

Brigham Young University–Idaho — Department of Information Systems. Retrieved July 13, 2002, from http://www.byui.edu/Catalog/2002-2003/_jim2.asp?departmentID=1888#680.

Capella University — School of Technology — BS in Information Technology. Retrieved July 13, 2002, from http://www.capella.edu/aspscripts/schools/technology/bs_general.asp.

Computer and Information Systems Technology — Purdue University. Retrieved July 13, 2002, from http://www.tech.purdue.edu/cpt/.

Drexel University — College of Information Science and Technology. Retrieved July 13, 2002, from http://www.cis.drexel.edu/undergrad/bsis/required_2000+_3.asp#dms.

Florida State University — School of Information Studies — Course Descriptions: Undergraduate. Retrieved July 13, 2002, from http://www.lis.fsu.edu/Prospects/Under/ssd23_BS_course_desc.cfm.

George Mason University — Bachelor of Science in Information Technology: Degree Requirements. Retrieved July 13, 2002, from http://ite.gmu.edu/bsit/degree.htm.

Georgia Southern Department of Computer Science. Retrieved July 13, 2002, from http://jharris.mat.gasou.edu/CSProgram/CSWebPage.html.

Hecker, D. (2001, November). Monthly labor review. *Occupational employment projections to 2010*. Retrieved January 6, 2002, from http://www.bls.gov/opub/mlr/2001/11/art4full.pdf.

Indiana University — Bachelor of Science in Informatics: Degree Requirements. Retrieved July 13, 2002, from http://www.informatics.indiana.edu/academics/bs_degree_requirements.asp.

Information Systems and Computer Programming — Purdue University Calumet. Retrieved July 13, 2002, from http://205.215.123.36/.

Information Technology — Bachelor of Science Courses/Concentration — Rochester Institute of Technology. Retrieved July 13, 2002, from http://www.it.rit.edu/degreeprog/bs/courses/concentration.html.

Joint Computer Society of IEEE and Association for Computing Machinery. (2001, August 1). *Computing curricula 2001 — Steelman draft (August 1, 2001)*. Retrieved January 6, 2002, from http://www.acm.org/sigcse/cc2001/steelman/.

Macon State College — I.T. Bachelor's Program. Retrieved July 13, 2002, from http://www.maconstate.edu/it/it-bachelors.asp.

New Jersey Institute of Technology — IT Concentrations. Retrieved July 13, 2002, from http://www.it.njit.edu/concentrations.htm.

Occupational Area Definitions for Information Systems and Support. Retrieved July 11, 2002, from http://www.itworks-ohio.org/ISSdefinit.htm.

Pace University — School of Computer Science and Information Systems. Retrieved July 13, 2002, from http://www.pace.edu.

Pennsylvania College of Technology — Computer Information Systems — Information and Data Processing. Retrieved July 13, 2002, from http://www.pct.edu/degrprog/pd.shtml.

SUNY–Morrisville — Course Curriculum. Retrieved July 13, 2002, from http://www.cosc.morrisville.edu/syllabus.php.

Towson University — Computer and Information Sciences. Retrieved July 13, 2002, from http://pages.towson.edu/webster/cosc/department.html.

University of Baltimore — Specialization in Computer Information Systems. Retrieved July 13, 2002, from http://business.ubalt.edu/DegreePrograms/ungrad_prog/special.html#CIS.

University of Cincinnati Undergraduate Programs. Retrieved July 13, 2002, from http://www.uc.edu/programs/viewprog.asp?progid=687.

University of Hawaii at Manoa — Academics: Degree Programs: Undergraduate: Bachelor of Science. Retrieved July 13, 2002, from http://www.ics.hawaii.edu/academic/degree_programs/undergrad/bs.html.

University of Houston — College of Technology — ITEC Degree Plans. Retrieved July 13, 2002, from http://www.uh.edu/academics/catalog/tec/itec_degree.html#info.

University of Northern Alabama — Computer Information Systems. Retrieved July 13, 2002, from http://www2.una.edu/collbusiness/.

University of South Carolina–Spartanburg — Major in Computer Science Computer Information Systems Concentration. Retrieved July 13, 2002, from http://www.uscs.edu/%7Ejspencer/MCS%20Webpage/CSCISBA.html.

University of Southern Alabama — School of Computer and Information Sciences. Retrieved July 13, 2002, from http://www.southalabama.edu/bulletin/cis.htm.

Chapter XV

Designing e-Business and e-Commerce Courses to Meet Industry Needs

Anthony D. Stiller
University of the Sunshine Coast, Australia

ABSTRACT

This chapter is designed to assist undergraduate program developers in designing and developing courses that will better prepare graduates to have a balanced mix of e-business, e-commerce, communication, and leadership skills that will equip them for roles as consultants for small-to-medium enterprises. Because small-to-medium enterprises do not have a vast budget or knowledge of e-commerce development, they are more likely to contract a consultant within their local community rather than contract a larger consulting firm that is more likely to have a number of staff members with a variety of specialist skills. This being the case, undergraduate courses must equip our professionals with skills sets that focus on e-business strategic planning as well as the e-commerce technology skills that will enable them to design, develop, and implement e-business strategies that meet the needs of small-to-medium enterprises by understanding the environments in which they operate.

INTRODUCTION

Accountability of universities to deliver courses and programs that are relevant for today's society is placing pressure upon educators to find a balance between the philosophical argument for the benefits of a university education and the fiscal constraints for funding a public higher education sector. While government agencies remain the major funding source for universities, course and program content will continue to be subjected to calls by legislative bodies and industry groups to be relevant and have outcomes that enable the graduate to "hit the ground running" with employability skills that match the position description. With employers selecting graduates on their employability qualities, attributes, capabilities, and employability skills, a major concern for course developers must be on what makes this university's course or program immediately recognized and accepted by industry, because there are a large number of universities that offer programs with the same or a similar name.

Three reports by the Australian government — "Backing Australia's Ability" (2001), "Knowledge and Innovation" (1999), and "Investing for Growth" (1997) —have set the framework for a set of desirable skills a knowledge worker in the information age will require to effectively compete within the knowledge economy.

In a project commissioned by the Australian Department of Education, Science, and Training (the major funding source for Australian universities), titled "Employability Skills for the Future" (DEST, 2002), the focus was placed on developing "clear definitions of what Australian industry and leading business enterprises mean by 'employability' skills and the consistency or otherwise between the various terms similarly used" (p. 2). The Australian Vice-Chancellors Committee (AVCC), together with other public-funded training agencies, are required to respond to the outcomes of this report by identifying "implications for policy development and programs…(and) strategies and timelines for implementation of the framework" (p. 58) for "preparing graduates with appropriate skills and attributes" (p. 25).

Future courses and programs developed in Australian universities will have to be developed to enable the graduate to operate "effectively with and upon a body of knowledge of sufficient depth to begin professional practice," (p. 25) so that the transition from university to workplace will not be difficult and so that graduates' expectations will not be unrealistic.

Within the context of the information age, a method for integrating employability skills into courses and programs in electronic commerce and electronic business has been set out in this chapter as a way of assisting course and program developers to better prepare graduates to "hit the road running" with the level of confidence that will enhance their prospects of a successful career.

BACKGROUND

Although there are many and varied definitions for electronic commerce, Lawrence and Lawrence (2000) use the definition "buying and selling of information, products and services via computer networks today and in the future, using any one of the myriad of networks that make up the Internet." Katakota and Whinston (1996) define e-commerce as "a modern business methodology that addresses the needs of organizations, merchants, and consumers to cut costs while improving the quality of goods and services and increasing the speed of service delivery," or as Fellenstein and Wood (2000) define, "the use of online facilities for doing business…Internet, intranets, extranets, private networks, and other networking facility that enables buyers to communicate with sellers (or supplier)…set of buying and selling activities of goods and services that make up a business transaction."

While many writers use the term e-commerce and e-business interchangeably (Schneider & Perry, 2000), many of the courses offered by universities use the terms e-commerce and e-business without making any real distinction, leaving one to wonder why the two terms exist. Fellenstein and Perry et al. use the term e-business in the broader sense, by associating a "Design Quality model [that] helps enterprises establish business environments that provide new e-business values, environments that are secure, well protected, well designed, available 24 hours a day, 7 days a week (on 24x7) the entire year." This model introduces a new element into the field of electronic commerce by introducing the concept of a metrics as a way of measuring the business environment for its success in terms of "usability, scalability, interoperability, and maintainability" by going one stage further than simply designing, developing, and implementing an e-commerce solution with the latest development tools and programming language scripts. Adding to the problem and confusion for the consultant is the fact that there are many SMEs who do not even have a basic business and marketing plan. Sussis (2000), an e-commerce consultant, stated that, "as businesses move into significant e-businesses, good planning strategies, design and implementation becomes more and more essential."

This means that consultants, normally working by themselves with an SME, need skills that go further than simply acquiring broad concepts of e-commerce technologies by integrating them into the total business environment. The integration of e-commerce technologies with an e-business strategy delivers to the SME the predicted outcomes they have identified and written into the e-business strategic plan. In most cases, consultants have to first work with the SME to develop their business plan before attempting to develop an integrated e-business solution that builds on existing strategies. This requires a strong business focus that includes marketing, budgeting, and planning. Care should be taken to ensure the emphasis is not simply placed on developing a Web presence that is visually appealing, using all the latest techniques at the expense of developing the e-business strategy that complements the business and marketing plan. "The adoption of online technologies does not replace business processes (such as ordering, supply and delivery), but has the potential to change the way these processes are performed and improve a firm's profit margin" (DISC, 1998).

The level of success can be determined by how well the e-business analyst can "leverage the organization's existing core operational business systems, as well as meet the new business-critical operational requirements for reliability, scalability, flexibility and 24x7x365 availability in a highly volatile, electronic marketplace" (Agarwal, 2001). This means that there are many more elements that come into effect other than the selection and use of technology and the design of a well-structured Web site, but include business courses in strategic issues in the digital economy, leadership, local and international marketing, user interface design, database modeling, e-commerce technologies, local and global regulatory systems, supply chain management, security issues when doing business online, business law and ethics, finance and economics, as well as the traditional courses in e-commerce technologies, front-end and back-end application integration, security, and Web design.

THE AUSTRALIAN PERSPECTIVE

At the Australian Bureau of Statistics (ABS), various reports on business activity in Australia were produced, and of the estimated 1,107,000 private-sector businesses operating during the 1998–1999 year, 1,055,300 were classified as small businesses employing 3.1 million people, or approximately 50.2% of the total workforce (ABS, 2000). In the Yellow Pages Small Business Index (2000), a small business is identified as one that has "up to 19 full-time employees including the proprietor if he or she is part of the workforce [and] medium-sized business employing between 20 and 200 full-time persons." In addition to this definition, those at the Australian Bureau of Statistics (ABS) identified another category of business operators within this sector, the "Very Small Business (VSB) who employ fewer than five employees" (ABS, 2000).

Approximately 25% of small businesses and 56% of medium businesses surveyed in the "Survey of Computer Technology and E-Commerce in Australian Small and Medium Business" (NOIE, 2000) reported having a homepage. Using the Internet for e-commerce sales accounts for only 0.4%, and only 6% of Australian businesses at all levels are classified as Internet commerce active at the end of June 2000. What is more startling in these sets of figures is that only 2% of businesses generate 50% or more of their sales over the Internet (ABS, 2000). It is unfortunate that the ABS figures do not provide a greater breakdown of Internet active SMEs by industry sector, as we would have a greater understanding of the e-business potential for our graduates. Then, we would focus on course content that can deliver specific objectives to increase awareness of the benefits of Internet technology adoption rather than developing generalized course outcomes. An analysis of the stated objectives from a sample of course outlines from the 30 Undergraduate and Postgraduate Electronic Commerce/ Electronic Business courses located on the Australian Vice-Chancellors' Committee Member Universities (http://www.mis.deakin.edu.au/elsieEC/au_U.htm), identifies that existing courses and programs have been designed to provide a broad knowledge of commerce- and business-related topics, together with in-depth knowledge needed to acquire expertise in electronic commerce systems.

While course outlines detailed specific technologies for online transaction processing, the supply chain; Web page design, development, and implementation; programming languages; text formatting and script writing; data communications; analysis; metrics; and other techniques for conducting business-to-business (B2B) and business-to-customer (B2C) commerce, there is little emphasis placed on providing course content that integrates business principles and practices with specific e-commerce skills expertise for the graduate who will be developing the e-business strategy with the SME.

In the final report, "SME Electronic Commerce Study," by PricewaterhouseCoopers (1999) for the Asian Pacific Economic Cooperation (APEC), on the adoption of electronic commerce, reasons are listed for not adopting Internet technologies provided by the 21 member nation economies, and these include the following:

- Low use of electronic commerce by customers and suppliers
- Concerns about security aspects of electronic commerce
- Concerns about legal and liability issues
- High costs of computer and networking technologies
- Limited knowledge of e-business models and technologies

- Unconvinced of the benefits of electronic commerce for the company
- Quality of telecommunications services inadequate for e-commerce

The reasons offered by SMEs in Australia for not engaging in e-commerce, outlined in the Small Business Index (2000), identify similar reasons for not engaging in e commerce:

- A concern that the use of the Internet for e-commerce could lead to uncontrolled growth
- Satisfaction with current business arrangements
- Uncertainty about the quality and availability of products, and about delivery and supply arrangements
- Fear of alienating intermediaries
- Concern about not having enough understanding of technology to be able to manage and direct the adoption of e-commerce, and about how these skills would be assessed
- Time and expense
- A belief that the business products or services did not lend themselves to the Internet

To overcome these concerns for not adopting e-commerce by SMEs, locally and globally, university graduates in e-commerce and e-business courses must possess the knowledge and skills of e-business analysts who will take on leadership roles, empowering SMEs to take on higher degrees or responsibilities for the development of the e-business strategic plan, so they have ownership over the project, raise awareness, and develop self-confidence, leading to a successful implementation. The Australian Computer Society's (ACS) "Careers In Information Technology" handbook (1998) defined the duties of a business analyst as "providing more detailed project objectives, system requirements, business process analysis and cost–benefit analysis." The ACS defined the personal qualities of the Internet and e-commerce business analyst as being the following:

- A business outcome approach
- An ability to conceptualize and think creatively, and a capacity to articulate visions
- Good oral and written communications skills
- Interpersonal skills to evoke commitment from the client
- Sound administrative skills and good analytical and reporting abilities
- Effective time management and personal organization skills
- An understanding of user needs

STRUCTURED METHODOLOGY

Most lecturers in electronic commerce programs have an Information Systems background and, therefore, would be aware of the "top-down model" used by business analysts as a logical approach for determining the technology specifications that support the business needs and requirements, as described by Goldman, Rawles, and Marga (1999). The emphasis in this model is in the business layer (Figure 1), where the focus is on the analysis of the business objectives as the starting point, and should also be the starting place for e-commerce adoption and diffusion.

Figure 1. Structured methodology

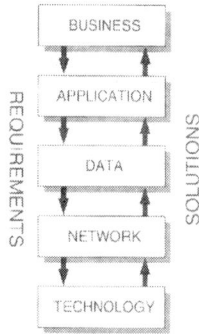

The first layer is to state the business-level objectives. This determines all other levels, finally resulting in the use of appropriate technologies to meet business needs:

- Strategic business planning

- Business process reengineering

- Identification of major business functions

- Identification of business processes

- Identification of business opportunities

For the e-business analyst, this will be the most challenging aspect of their consultancy, as the SME has to focus on the what, how, where, and why of their business.

Using this model for analyzing business needs when developing the e-business strategy, the e-commerce professional will need to develop skills in what Davenport and Short (1990) and Sawy (2001) called the "Business Process Redesign" or "Business Process Reengineering" (BPR). BPR is the analysis and design (redesign) of workflow and processes within and between organizations as information technology is used for doing business. Enterprises moving from a "bricks-n-mortar" to a "bricks-n-click" operation use BPR principles and methodologies to make changes in the traditional way of carrying out transactions. They move to the virtual environment, using real-time access with Internet technologies and Web interfaces that should result in greater efficiencies. Figure 2 shows how the principles of BRP are used in the process of transforming a conventional business into an e-business and the interactions that take place.

STRUCTURE OF AN E-BUSINESS PROGRAM

There is a tendency by designers of e-commerce and e-business courses to concentrate on skills development and knowledge acquisition related to Internet technologies by focusing on Web programming and front-end and back-end applications. While these are important, these topics and courses should be supplemented with business oriented courses, so the graduate has total exposure to the business environment in which the strategy is to be implemented, making their role of integration and implementation much easier and increasing the probability of success.

An analysis of the data obtained from online recruiters advertising for graduates in the categories of e-business, e-commerce, e-commerce architecture consultants, Web developers, business analysts, and Web consultants revealed skills that not only focus on specific industry callings and information skills but also require the successful applicant to be able to deliver solutions that have tangible business benefits. The skills set mixture that gives a consultant the ability to analyze a business need and design a solution to match customers expectations on time and within budget includes:

- Good Web design and development principles
- Exposure to Microsoft CMS and .NET environments
- Knowledge of SQL database
- Knowledge of Microsoft Visual Studio
- Strong management skills
- Strong business focus
- Strong communications skills
- Analytical and problem solving skills
- Knowledge of client business issues
- Ability to develop technology solutions
- Knowledge of Web tools and software
- Knowledge of Java, JavaScript, CGI, and ASP
- Knowledge of HTML/DHTML/XML/UML
- Project management skills
- Strategic thinking skills
- Technical skills

Topics and courses that should be considered when looking to develop this skills set include those discussed below.

Strategic Issues in the Digital Economy

An understanding of the concepts of electronic commerce facilitated by the Internet, World Wide Web, and related technologies is necessary. The topics to be covered include:

Figure 2. Factors that interact with business process changes

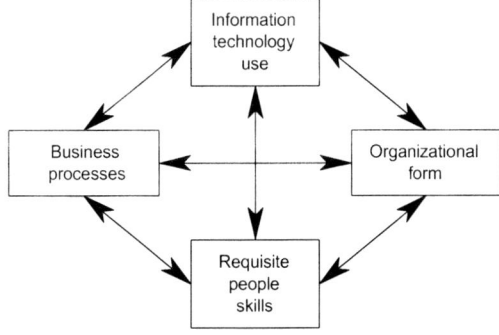

an understanding of e-commerce; an understanding of B2B, B2C, and business-to-government (B2G) commerce; and an ability to develop their own business model that meets their requirements, so they remain in control of the process. The successful graduate will possess the specific skills in information analysis, requirements determination, detailed logical design, physical design, implementation planning, and development of business strategies for using e-commerce within an organization.

Managing through Leadership in the E-Environment

A working knowledge of the principles of electronic commerce from the business perspective is necessary. The origin and growth of e-commerce and the differences and similarities between e-commerce/e-business and traditional commerce are important. Specific skills the graduate should possess include project management (PERT, Gantt), the e-procurement cycle, SLAs, RFP, project contract structures, communications and negotiating skills, collaborative team participation in decision making, and critical thinking and reasoning so that creative solutions can be developed and discussed as possible implementation models.

Fundamentals of Local and International Marketing

These topics provide the basis for understanding the complexities of marketing the organization's goods and services using Internet technologies. An awareness of international marketing, with its focus on reviewing the important strategic advantages that flow to firms that learn how to compete globally, and an ability to present an integrated global marketing strategy are necessary. Graduates must have the skills to analyze situations that marketing managers encounter, locally and globally, in promoting growth and recognizing opportunities that exist in new and existing markets. These topics emphasize the importance of business owners being able to apply marketing principles "outside the box," identifying marketing forces and their competitors, and analyzing data and strategizing to make opportunities within the local and global markets. Topics include marketing management, buyer behavior, product policy, pricing, distribution, advertising and promotion, and competitive strategy.

User Interface Design for the Web

Users of the Web are becoming sophisticated and are demanding more and more, but they become frustrated with delays in downloading pages, accessing and completing online forms, or downloading files. While commercial packages have reduced the burden on user interface designers, they are still required to possess skills in mark-up languages, particularly in cleaning code of unwanted clutter. Topics would include HTML authoring; an overview of VRML, XML, SGML, PERL, and CGI; page composition tools; server technology and server-side processing; active server pages: ActiveX, JavaScript, and applet usage; browser technology; engineering a quality Web site; solving usability issues; site and server management.

Key elements associated with effective Web design that need to be incorporated into the course are related to its stickiness and the probability in fostering customer loyalty. Factors that affect this include the business name, contact information, ease of navigation, use of graphics, company logo, current and up-to-date information, colors, use of multimedia plug-ins, forms, frames, uncluttered design, and the ability to update information without the need of the SME to have highly developed Internet design and development skills or to call upon the Web designer to make simple changes to product descriptions and prices.

Database Modeling

The decision on Web hosting will have a major influence on the level of skills required by the graduate in the design or modification of the database management system (DBMS). While vendors provide DBMS solution software, there may be a requirement to modify such systems so legacy software can be fully integrated at the back end. Specific skills include the provision and integrity of data access, validation processes, authorized manipulation of data, and functionality of the online form between the front-end and the back-end.

E-Commerce Technologies

With the release of new technologies on a regular basis, being able to advise business owners on the suitability of particular technologies for their e-business environment takes on a level of importance that takes it past the hype stage. For e-commerce to be integrated into the business model, advising the SME on the appropriate communications technology and infrastructure must be supported with measurable outcomes that have a cost–benefit component. For this to be accomplished, graduates must have a working knowledge of Internet protocols; intranets, extranets, virtual private networks and intelligent agents or bots; Web server architecture, hardware, software and tools; mobile communications and telephony; distributed systems technologies; sockets; multimedia technology overview; security issues, including firewalls, encryption and authentication; and international standards, emergent and future.

Local and Global Regulatory Systems

The impact of buying and selling across the Internet has impacted upon the legal and regulatory policy environment of e-commerce. Legal concepts on jurisdiction when marketing in cyberspace raise as many questions as answers for SMEs developing their e-business strategy for working without borders. The graduate could find themselves in a position, when designing the Web site that promotes goods and services over the Internet, that may contravene laws and regulations in import and export of certain goods and services. Specific issues that need to be addressed include intellectual property, trademarks, digital copyright, advertising, consumer protection, and taxation responsibilities. While the graduate will need to understand the concepts and implications of commercial transactions, enforcing electronic agreements, performing financial services, securities regulation, antitrust, criminal law, and international laws and ethics, they should also be in a position to advise the SME when to seek professional legal advice before implementing their business strategy to minimize litigation.

Supply Chain Management

No two businesses operate in the same way, each has a unique set of characteristics in sourcing raw materials and shipping finished inventory. To maximize the return on investment, the interrelationship of obtaining materials, working on and storing them internally, delivering them to their final destination in the face of uncertainty, and changing prices with varying demands places the graduate in a unique position in developing a supply chain meeting these sets of circumstances. Specific skills that will be acquired will include the ability to develop a strategy for the flow of information, inventory and reorder policies, order fulfillment, order tracking, receiving payment, negotiating prices, dealing with peak and slack demands, and the ability to respond to market forces that are normally outside of the SMEs control.

Security Issues when Doing Business Online

Regardless of the effectiveness of the e-commerce/e-business strategy, unless the Web site is accessible 24 hours a day, every day of the year, the exposure to the global market has been compromised. While not trying to turn the analyst into an Internet security specialist, the graduate must be able to suggest security methods that will provide overall security of the client's system to make it less vulnerable from denial of service attacks, viruses, hackers, crackers, and intrusions by unauthorized users that can effectively destroy the integrity of the database. Topics will include methods for evaluating security risks, security practices that are cost effective, third party agreements, and an education program for all staff members, as security is the responsibility of all employees. A workplace education program designed by the consultant will include an awareness of the role of firewall protection, the use and secrecy of passwords, virus scanning software, security audits, and the serious consequences for noncompliance to an organization's security and control policy.

Business Law and Ethics

Principles of business law and ethics have different meanings and applications in different states, territories, and countries, as the governments around the world come to terms with the changing nature of Internet commerce. With the development of a raft of laws and regulations, graduates will need to be able to work through these and develop strategies that will assist the organization in its development of an e-business strategy that will identify key concepts that may affect the way in which the business is offering their service across the Internet.

Key strategic knowledge and skills will include the protection of the consumer, privacy of data, digital copyright, taxation of goods and services, and contractual law to support contracts entered into, where digital agreements are replacing paper-based physical contracts.

Finance and Economics

One of the key success factors for an online business operation is a sound and viable business financial plan that shows clearly how the business concepts and ideas can be turned into financial gain. Tracking e-business success involves the integration of financial software that will provide the business owner with an up-to-date method of collecting data on income and expenditure, cash flow, financial assumptions, and break-even points based on changing market forces and currency exchange, where international transactions are involved.

The graduate will require financial, economic, and technical skills in developing and integrating financial software packages that enable online transactions to take place using third party payment methods. Many of the financial and economics issues are closely related to legal and global regulatory systems.

DESIRED OUTCOMES

The lists of courses above are not exhaustive, but they provide a balanced mixture of business, application, data handling, networking, and Internet technology skills that will equip the e-business analyst with the analytical skills to develop creative solutions that are not only compliant with consumer laws and regulations specific to the county in which they will providing goods and services but also provide creative solutions that will attract online consumers with the element of stickiness that can be measured in business benefits.

The approach suggested in this chapter is based on integrating industry requirements for employability skills and projections for the future online B2B and B2C business needs, with those proposed by lecturing staff members at the university, who may be influenced by their past experiences and skills mix. While this may cause some concern within the academic discipline, the focus must be on the graduates and their ability to contribute to society with minimal retraining and further skills acquisition on leaving the university to be able to enter the workforce. If this means staff development for lecturers, recruitment of new lecturers, contracting specialist teaching staff, or providing internships with industry partners, the challenge should be grasped and new creative ways found to make our courses and programs relevant, transferable, and adaptable to change.

AUSTRALIAN GOVERNMENT PERSPECTIVE

Recognizing that universities hold a special place within the education sector in promoting and stimulating learning and discussion, one must also recognize that upon graduating, students want skills and personal qualities that will lead toward employment within their chosen field. While examples of advertising campaigns by some universities that include statements like "training for the real world," "our graduates have the highest employment rate of any other university," the survey of courses and programs do not always match the attributes and qualities outlined in the report on employability skills for the future.

CONCLUSION

While the courses and programs suggested in this chapter match the skills set required for an e-business consultant within the Australian context, it is not suggested that they can be easily transferred to other environments. Course developers will need to carry out their own analysis of skills set requirements, prepare a matrix of desired outcomes, and develop the courses and programs to suit.

The online community becomes more sophisticated in accessing and using the Internet for B2B, B2C, C2C, and B2G commerce, and federal government policies are aimed at encouraging more online business activity. So, the skill sets for the e business analyst working with the SME require a balanced mix of e-business analysis and e-commerce technical skills combined with leadership skills aimed at empowering the SME to take on a higher degree of responsibility for the development of their e-business strategic plan, implementation, and update. Because SMEs have limited time and limited budgets, they are more likely to engage a local consultant, one they can trust and with which they can build a relationship, who has the skill sets to analyze, design, develop, implement, and test an e-business strategy. To equip the graduate, specific courses, subjects, and programs need to be developed that enable the e-business analyst, programmer, or developer to acquire these skills, so they can provide the level of service that will encourage a higher level of adoption, diffusion, and acceptance by the SME.

REFERENCES

Agarwal, B. (2001). Defining the e-business model: A Tanning Technology White Paper," at www.tanning.com.

Australian Bureau of Statistics. (2000). 1321.0 Small business in Australia, 1999.

Australian Bureau of Statistics. (2000). 8127.0 Characteristics of small business 1999.

Australian Bureau of Statistics. (2000). 8129.0 Business use of information technology.

Australian Computer Society. (1998). Careers in information technology. http://www.itcareers.acs. org.au/.

Consumer Affairs Department. (2000). Best practice model and tools for business. Canprint, Australia, at http://www.ecommerce.treasury.gov.au/.

Davenport & Short. (1990, Summer). The new industrial engineering: Information technology and business process redesign. *Sloan Management Review*, pp. 11–27.

Department of the Treasury. (1999). Building consumer confidence in electronic commerce: A best practice model for business. Australia: Aussie Print. http://www.treasury.gov.au/ecommerce.

DCITA. (1998). Taking the plunge. Commonwealth of Australia, at www.dcita.gov.au.

DCITA. (1999). Australia's e-commerce report card, Commonwealth of Australia, at http://www.dcita.gov.au.

DCITA. (1999). E-commerce beyond 2000, Commonwealth of Australia, at www.dcita.gov.au.

DEST. (2002). Employability skills for the future, Commonwealth of Australia.

DISC. (1998). Getting business online. Australia: Green Advertising.

DIST. (1998). Getting business online, Commonwealth of Australia, at http://www.noie.gov.au/publications/noie/sme/gbo.pdf.

Fellenstein & Wood. (2000). *E-commerce, Global E-business, and E-societies*, Englewood Cliffs, NJ: Prentice Hall.

IBM. (1999). E-commerce roadmap, successful strategies for e-commerce, at http://www.ibm.com.

Kalakota & Robinson. (1999). 'e-Business: Roadmap for Success, Reading, MA: Addison-Wesley Longman.

National Best Practices Newsletter. (1997). Issue 11. Australian National Training Authority, at http://www.kdc.com.au/bp_issues/bp11.htm.

NOIE. (1999). E-commerce beyond 2000. Small Business Index. Australia: Commonwealth Department of Communications Information Technology and the Arts.

NOIE. (2000). Survey of computer technology and e-commerce in Australian and medium business. Australia: Telstra Corporation Limited.

Sawy, O. (2001). Redesigning Enterprise processes for e-Business, New York: McGraw-Hill.

Schneider & Perry. (2000). Electronic commerce. Canada: Course Technology.

Schneider & Perry. (2001). Electronic commerce, Second Annual Edition. Canada: Course Technology.

Schulman, J. (2000). E-business dimension model: Transformation dimension. GartnerGroup.

Stiller, A. (2001), Through an integrated business/e-commerce procedural framework, SMEs will survive and prosper in the new digital economy. *Proceedings from the IRMA 2001 Conference*, Toronto, Canada.

Sussis, D. (2000). A useful e-roadmap. e-consultant, at http://commerce.internet.com/e-consultant/print/0,,9571_363881,00.html.

Chapter XVI

Adding Reality to Team Projects: E-Business Consulting for Small Business Entities

Sharon W. Tabor
Boise State University, USA

ABSTRACT

While hiring companies consistently emphasize the importance of communication and team skills for new IT graduates, students consistently emphasize their dislike for academic team projects. In an effort to make the team project a more interesting and valuable experience, an upper-division e-commerce course at Boise State University includes the development of prototype sites for actual businesses. In addition to concepts, strategies, and technical tools, students learn transferable consulting skills and improve necessary team skills. These skills groups are applied to real-world business problems, resulting in successful team experiences for the students and expanded horizons for the participating businesses. Part of the success is attributable to well-defined expectations, team-building exercises, and a structured client engagement process that serves the needs of the businesses as well as the student teams.

INTRODUCTION

Teaching electronic commerce in an IS curriculum is a challenge, primarily due to the cross-functional nature of the topic. While few would disagree that e-commerce requires a great deal of technology to make it happen, many functions within the organization impact an e-commerce project. When the author developed her first upper-division e-commerce course in 1998, she found few textbooks or teaching materials and none that balanced business and technical aspects of the topic. Since that time, the quantity of e-commerce textbooks has exploded, yet most authors still emphasize either business or technology issues and vary extensively in theory versus applicable knowledge.

An additional challenge revealed by e-commerce research shows an increasing tendency for strategy and projects to be initiated outside the Information Technology (IT) organization, a trend we have seen with other technical innovations as well (Swanson, 1994). IT professionals must be aware of the potential for this phenomenon and understand the cross-functional implications. At the same time, many organizations claiming success in e-commerce, emphasize the importance of getting IT involved early in the strategy building process, before a functional business model is developed. In fact, formation of a new breed of IT professional that is business savvy as well as technically competent seems to be a critical factor for e-commerce success (Tabor & Wojtkowski, 2001). This trend supports what academics have been hearing from business advisory boards across the country — that general business knowledge, communication, and team skills are as important as the technology students learn in their degree programs.

To address this interesting challenge, the author searched the academic literature and also drew upon a 20-year business background in management and technical consulting roles. The goal was to find an approach that would improve team skills and the team experience, while better preparing IS students to contribute in our increasingly electronic business environment. After an initial try at small group projects of the teams' own choosing, and a virtual company project that had each class conceptualize a company scenario, working with live companies seemed to be an optimal solution. This method allows students to rapidly apply new skills to business problems, while still in learning mode in the classroom. In addition to being a more successful project effort, students contribute to the local business community by developing e-commerce models and prototype Web sites that help small organizations expand their horizons and explore the potential of e-commerce. This chapter outlines the issues and challenges of teaching e-commerce as a realistic collaborative project effort with the local small business community.

SMES AND E-COMMERCE

Primarily antidotal evidence tells us that small to medium enterprises (SMEs) are adopting e-commerce rather slowly. They typically have limited financial resources, rarely have the technical skills on staff to go very far toward building their own Web presence, and often do not have a clue as to whether or not their business would benefit from the electronic medium. If they think of e-commerce in relation to their business at all, it is often after seeing a competitor take the plunge, or in the hopes of dramatically increasing sales (Auger & Gallaugher, 1997; Lederer, 1997). Other benefits an e-commerce model can offer organizations, such as transaction cost reduction, marketing, information retrieval, or strategic networking (Wigand, 1997), rarely come into their thought processes.

Many of those small- to medium-sized enterprises that have ventured forth, however, have found success and are showing profits. This segment of the new economy, labeled the "mini-dots" by *Business Week* (Weintraub, 2001), is predicted to grow to $120 billion by the end of 2002 (Weintraub, 2001). In addition to expected business-to-consumer (B2C) models, SMEs are benefiting from participation in business-to-business (B2B) exchanges, where they share technical infrastructure and sell products and services to each other, often doing business with other SMEs they would never have known about (Ince, 2000). A survey of 453 small businesses conducted in the summer of 2000 indicated that only 17% were currently doing business online, but one-third expected to go online during the next year (Roberts & Pepe, 2000). If that statistic is transferred to the 10 million small businesses in the United States alone, 1.3 million more business will enter the world of e-commerce. While a slowdown in the U.S. economy is undoubtedly impacting these numbers, businesses getting off to the right start with e-commerce may still find success and assist in the economic recovery. Federal government sources, including the National Institute of Standards and Technology's Manufacturing Extension Partnership (MEP) and local Small Business Administration offices, are trying to aid in these efforts (Korchak & Rodman, 2001).

With our own small sample of pilot companies in Boise, Idaho, we see great enthusiasm for expanding electronically but little understanding of the requirements to proceed. Most prospective SME candidates assume they will accept orders online but know little about transaction processing or the security requirements to do so. Most begin the project with a minimal level of technology infrastructure, and often, the owner has the most computer skills. Our consultative prototype project attempts to educate our participant companies to the potential of e-commerce for their individual situation. The project does the following:

1. Gives participating companies a nonthreatening introduction to Web and commerce technology
2. Summarizes what the companies need to know to implement an e-commerce site
3. Provides the companies a choice of prototypes to support their business strategy with a complementary e-commerce model
4. Helps students learn to apply their knowledge and practice communication and team skills

Whether the prototypes evolve into full e-commerce efforts, of course, is up to the business owners, but the first year's efforts proved successful for those companies that went forward with their prototypes and newly defined e-commerce business models.

TEAM PROJECT ISSUES

Why do students not like team projects? The biggest response to that question from the author's experience seems to be the time commitment. Those students who get to know others with similar schedules and work ethics during their academic program typically report better team experiences. Other researchers explored various techniques for team projects, including assigned teams (Fellers, 1996); junior teams with senior team advisors (Nance, 1998); and self-selected, guided teams (Van Slyke et al., 1999). Most of these authors mentioned the problems in expecting students to be natural participants in the team process without any type of teamwork training.

Several educators expanded the concept of student teamwork into group-guided cooperative learning. Fellers (1996) experimented with teams who studied together, completed group assignments, and in several cases, received group grades, with each team member receiving the lowest scoring member's test grade. In general, he found students to be more receptive to the idea of group learning than in sharing a common grade. Nance (1998) deployed a cross-class collaboration effort with students in an advanced class assigned to mentor students in an entry-level class. He found that while his senior students should have had the background and knowledge to assist junior students, some were not prepared to give advice or act in a leadership role. Regardless, he found that over 80% of the participating students felt the collaborative project was "useful, helped develop collaborative skills, and brought together ideas and input that otherwise would not have occurred" (Nance, 1998, p. 148).

The Van Slyke et al. (1999) study specifically targeted teamwork training and used a multi-group quantitative study comparing classes taught with and without teams to attempt to measure attitudes. Pre and post surveys regarding the team experience indicated that factors such as in-class teamwork exercises improved the students' perceptions of success but not their attitude toward working in teams. The latter attitude was impacted by common complaints of scheduling problems, social loafing (non-contributors), and interpersonal conflicts (Van Slyke et al., 1999).

E-COMMERCE CLASS DEVELOPMENT

Starting out as a new professor with a new e-commerce course in 1998, the author chose the best alternative among the business-oriented e-commerce texts and used a practitioner handbook for the technical aspect of the class. Book selection and course content continue to evolve each year, but textbook authors still tend to lean toward either business issues or technical tools. The tools change every year also, with each change in venue an adventure in preparation time for the instructor. The first year's team projects began in a typical mode of letting students form their own teams and choose their own project concept within some general parameters. Some teams chose research-oriented projects, while others dove into the technology, and a few brave teams tried to build Web sites for family, friends, or local nonprofit organizations.

The second year, however, the author raised the bar in suggesting that the class as a whole develop a virtual business concept, then split into three primary teams to address Web commerce, intranet, and extranet functions for the company. While both sections rose to the occasion and turned out innovative concepts, students bitterly complained about having to get together across teams as well as within their own groups to accomplish their tasks. The downfall of this concept was the increased requirement for intergroup communication and time delays waiting for content or group decisions from others. Students did not want to hear that this would be the reality many of them would face in the real world business environment.

In the fall of 2000, a student approached the author wanting to develop an e-commerce application for the company for which he worked as IT manager. This organization needed a closed, extranet application to provide communication, scheduling, specification changes, and an overall closer electronic relationship with its contractor customers. With this interesting possibility and a few phone calls, three additional businesses were found that were interested in working with the class. Each class section formed six teams, delivering three prototypes for each of the two business participants.

Principals of each organization visited the class early in the semester to present an overview of their business plan, information about their products or services, their initial goals in looking at e-commerce, and a pledge to be available by email and our class message board. At the end of the semester, each business owner returned for the prototype presentations and was presented with a copy of each final report and a CD-ROM with full code for the prototype Web sites. Each of the businesses was delighted with the outcomes, and each adopted one primary prototype, often incorporating ideas from others in their final product. One company hired their favorite prototype team to complete the implementation through a local hosting company; one year later, they are pleased with the resulting increase in sales and national exposure.

Lessons Learned

In spite of the successful prototypes developed for our live companies, the process was not as smooth as the author had hoped. While all the students must complete the prerequisite core courses of marketing, accounting, networking, and various technical courses to give them an adequate development background for the e-commerce elective, their work experience varies widely. On the average, they did not have an easy time communicating with their client companies and felt unsure of making suggestions other than what they were directly told. A skeleton milestone plan was available for teams to use to develop their prototype and the ultimate project documentation. Few teams made any additions or modifications to the milestone shell and, consequently, had some trouble putting together all the appropriate components for the Web site and the business plan. While a team contract was used to encourage an equal division of labor, on most teams, a single person developed the majority of the site, and few students tried to learn tools they did not already know.

What was wrong with this approach? It certainly was typical of the kind of projects many of the students would be involved with when they entered the workforce. The students with the least work experience lacked the analytical skills to look at the big picture — in this case, how e-commerce could benefit the business, and how to communicate with a nontechnical client to get the information they needed for a successful prototype. Additionally, project requirements indicated they should discuss other issues in their final reports, such as security, hosting requirements, and additional Web site functionality that the clients would need to understand to go forward. All of these topics were addressed over the course of the semester in lecture and supplemental readings. Some teams did this well, and others did not. While many students indicated in a follow-up survey that they learned more and had a more successful project experience than in other classes, they clearly felt frustrated about aspects of the project that did not go well or communication problems with their SME companies.

Structured Expectations and Process Improvement in 2001

In the fall of 2001, we had major obstacles to overcome in bringing a sense of normalcy to the classroom after the terrorist attacks in the United States. Our students are typically older than average (approximately 26), but many had never experienced a major crisis in their adult lives. Not only did better structure in the classroom assist in getting the semester on track, but new in-class topics and project processes were put in place to ensure that each student was better prepared to work on a team and begin the consulting project.

New Processes

In an effort to address each of the weaknesses and feedback from the prior year's projects, the following processes were added to the team project plan:

1.   The classes voted whether or not to work with live businesses, thereby achieving concept buy-in. Students made suggestions for business participants, but the author carefully screened these options to insure they would provide an appropriate e-commerce project experience and that business owners would have the time to communicate with teams.

2.   The five-part project milestone plan and Team Contract (included in the Appendix) were more tightly structured to include task elements that would fulfill the basic project requirements, while allowing flexibility in how the tasks were accomplished and with the team's choice of technology. It is considered a contract between the team members to encourage equal participation. Each milestone section included task items that, when developed, would become a part of the final project report. Milestone task items are reviewed in class prior to each deadline to improve understanding, and teams were allowed to revise prior milestones after the fact to make up missed points. As part of each milestone submission, members committed to the next set of tasks, responsibilities, and output for that section of their team contract.

3.   Hands-on labs in class and technical homework assignments addressed the basic technical tools available to the teams to complete their prototypes, including JavaScript, ColdFusion, and CGI. Refresher material was linked to the class Web site to cover Web technology the students should have had in other classes. In this manner, every student was exposed to enough technology in the classroom to ensure they had the basic skills for e-commerce development.

4.   A primarily technical textbook was chosen that included basic e-business issues that could be easily supplemented with available materials from the Web and print media. Supplemental materials included business benefits of implementing e-commerce business models, alternative e-business drivers, elements of Web design, analyses of business Web sites, and secure transaction technology.

5.   Team-building and role-playing exercises were conducted in class to help develop rapport among the team, as well as basic consulting skills to prepare team members for working with their client companies. One such exercise was a puzzle that had to be completed without any verbal communication. Each person had their own piece to contribute but had to do so with some kind of logical process. Communication processes were discussed, and sample templates were developed as a group to aid in the client interviewing and interaction process, providing a structured and professional client engagement process.

6.   Information about the SME population was shared to ensure that teams had reasonable expectations about small businesses and their resources. Students were continually amazed that in a few short weeks, they had much more understanding about e-commerce than did their client companies. Communication problems and client perceptions of e-commerce and the required technology were discussed at various times during the semester to share the different team experiences.

Figure 1 summarizes the consulting project process. It stresses the importance of the relationship between conceptual skills developed in incoming prerequisite courses and in the e-commerce course, along with technical, communication, and team skills developed in class. All support the engagement process to produce a successful consulting relationship with the client companies.

Figure 1. E-Biz team process model

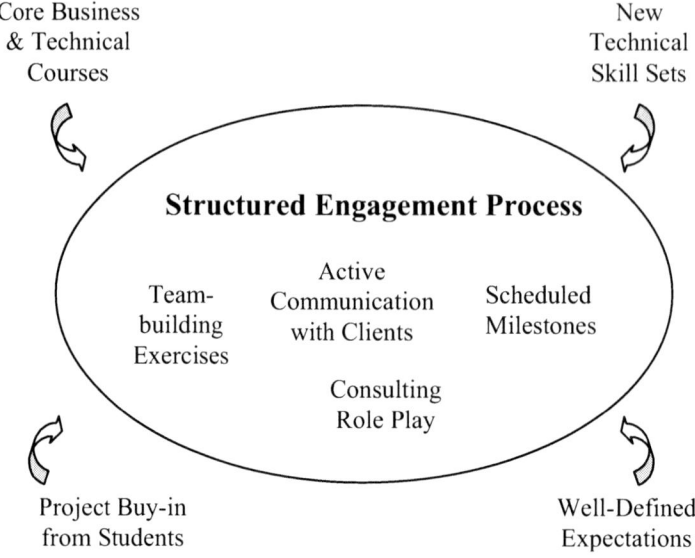

PROJECT OUTCOMES AND CONCLUSIONS

The actual prototype projects and the responses of the client companies to them have been very good. Students are able to understand and implement basic e-commerce business models, and show a high degree of interest in learning and applying Web technologies. Beyond that tangible outcome, however, student learning and attitudes toward team projects were of interest in the ongoing development of this class.

Data Gathering Methodology

To statistically gauge the effect of process changes, a simple pre and post project anonymous survey was conducted for the Fall 2000 and 2001 classes. Of the 47 students who took the class in 2000, results were mixed about past projects, but expectations were positive going into the project on the potential for learning with live companies. Representative questions on expectations and outcomes are shown in Table 1.

Section 1 is the day class and consists of more traditional students. They typically reflect lower expectations going into the project and lower perceived learning outcomes than the evening section, consisting of more working students. This could be a reflection of additional maturity in the evening section as well as more actual work and team experience. Participation was judged to be more equal for this project than on others students had experienced in their major, although obviously not to the level the instructor would have liked.

Outcomes for the Fall 2001 semester with 58 students are shown in Table 2 but reflect few changes that can declare the new processes successful. The students' state of mind given the difficulties on the economic and world fronts could certainly have impacted their entire

Table 1. Pre and post survey means on selected questions, Fall 2000

Pre-project:	S.001	S.002	Combined
On previous teams, all members contributed equally	2.5	2.16	2.3
My expectation for learning for this project is high	3.8	4.04	3.94
Post-project:			
On this team, all members contributed equally	2.88	3.78	3.4
The learning value for this project was high	3.29	4.22	3.82

educational experience for the semester. It was a difficult semester to stay focused for faculty and students alike. Perhaps another year of process tweaking will be needed to determine the actual strength of this learning method.

Students who added optional comments to their surveys often indicated that the projects are too much work, and that the team project concept is not the same as working with coworkers in a real job situation, where they receive a salary for performing their duties. They fail to understand that not all employees are motivated by money, and that team efforts still reflect personality and commitment issues. Perhaps better questions would include whether they learned new skills and if they have a better understanding of the business and technical issues of e-commerce development.

Teaching the E-Commerce Consulting Class

Teaching a structured project class such as this one requires an additional time commitment from the professor for preparation and availability. Planning and up-front preparation is important, as well as the choice of participating businesses and active involvement to insure that businesses and students benefit. This year, for example, a sole-proprietorship artist was one of the organizations selected; almost daily emails with this client added workload for the professor as well as the teams.

Table 2. Pre and post survey means on selected questions, Fall 2001

Pre-project:	S.001	S.002	Combined
On previous teams, all members contributed equally	2.2	2.4	2.6
My expectation for learning for this project is high	4.1	3.9	4.0
Post-project:			
On this team, all members contributed equally	3.6	3.1	3.4
The learning value for this project was high	3.6	3.7	3.6

This first collaborative experience should go as smoothly as possible to help students build confidence, but we also need to communicate that difficult clients are a reality, inside or outside the organization. Students who pursue consulting careers or choose to work within private or government organizations will find their share of difficult clients. It is necessary to guide a class through these unknowns, and hopefully, the learning outcomes will far outweigh the effort, for the professor and the student population. Although the survey numbers do not necessarily reflect it, verbal comments from students at the end of the course are that they liked the course and learned from the project experience. Better yet, occasional notes from graduates reflected that they really learned useful concepts and tools in the class and ranked it as one of their best.

Further research needs to be conducted in the area of team processes and how to teach them in an academic environment. A follow-up survey after students enter the workforce might tell a better story about the value of team projects, and which type proved the most beneficial to workforce success. Ideally, a coordinated effort among business core courses can enhance our individual successes. While we probably cannot address the complete soft skill needs of our students, we can strive for a higher level of achievement and a smoother transition for them into their new careers.

REFERENCES

Auger, P., & Gallaugher, J. M. (1997). Factors affecting the adoption of an Internet-based sales presence for small businesses. *The Information Society, Special Issue: Theory and Practice of Electronic Commerce, 13*, 1 (January–March), 55–74.

Fellers, J. (1996). Teaching teamwork: Exploring the use of cooperative learning teams in information systems education. *Data Base, 27*, 2, 44–59.

Ince, J. F. (2000, November). There's no business like small business. *Upside, 12*, 11, 166–167+.

Korchak, R., & Rodman, R. (2001, Winter). eBusiness adoption among U.S. small manufacturers and the role of manufacturing. *Economic Development Review, 17*, 3, 20–25.

Lederer, A., Mirchandani, D., & Sims, K. (1997). The link between information strategy and electronic commerce. *Journal of Organizational Computing and Electronic Commerce, 7*, 1, 17–34.

Nance, W. D. (1998). Experiences with an innovative approach for improving information systems students' teamwork and project management capabilities. *Proceedings of the ACM SIG MCPR Conference* (pp. 145–151). March 26–28.

Roberts, J., & Pepe, M. (2000). Consulting the wizard on SMB opportunities. Retrieved August 21, 2000, from www.crn.com.

Stevens, M., & Campion, M. (1994). The knowledge, skill, and ability requirements for teamwork: Implications for human resource management. *Journal of Management, 20*, 2, 503–530.

Swanson, E.B. (1994). Information systems innovation among organizations. *Management Science, 40*, 9, 1069–1092.

Tabor, S., & Wojtkowski, W. (2001). Creating a successful Web presence by a leading manufacturer of memory products: A case study. *Proceedings of ISD 2001*, London, September.

Van Slyke, C., Trimmer, K., & Kittner, M. (1999). Teaching teamwork in information systems courses. *Journal of Information Systems Education, 10,* 3&4, 36–46.

Weintraub, A. (2001). The mini-dots. *Business Week,* Issue: 3724, Industrial/technology Edition, March, EB44-EB48.

Wigand, R. (1997). Electronic commerce: Definition, theory, and context. *The Information Society, Special Issue: Theory and Practice of Electronic Commerce, 13,* 1 (January-March), 1–16.

APPENDIX –
PROJECT MILESTONES AND TEAM CONTRACT

Instructions to Students: This team contract represents a living document that breaks your project into logical units and identifies responsibility for individual tasks, building toward the final prototyping report. Do a thorough job of discussing each task item due in each milestone. The final report will be compiled from these sections, with appropriate updates plus the addition of an executive summary and table of contents.

Use the following task tables as a guide, adding or modifying tasks as needed. The goal of the milestone format is to gradually build your final report along with the prototype, adding structure to both processes. You will assign responsibility in each PM for tasks due in the next PM. You may use project management software rather than the table format if you prefer.

PM1 Deliverable: Team Formation & Availability Table — Due: 9/25

Team Name _____

Contract for _____(description and function)_____

Indicate a team leader for contact and coordination purposes.

Member Name   **Phone**   **Email Address**
1.
2.
3.
4.

Availability Table (indicate by number when people have time to meet).

	Sun	Mon	Tues	Wed	Thur	Fri	Sat
1100			2	2	2	2	
1200			1,2	2	1,2	1,2	
1300		1,3	1,2,3				
1400		1	4	4	4		
1500		1,2	4	4	4		
1600							
1700							
1800			3	3	3		

Project Tasks: Schedule meeting times and responsibilities to accomplish the following tasks for the next milestone. A written discussion of these topics is due at that time. Add other tasks as needed to fit your project parameters.

Tasks	Task Manager(s)	Due Date	Initials
Client overview and business problem			
Web site reviews and analyses			
Targeted e-commerce strategy			
Expected user group and profile			
Task list/project plan/ Gantt chart Project assumptions			
Coordinate documentation for PM2 (due 10/25)			

Signature Section:

"My signature below indicates I understand what is required of me. I accept full responsibility for those deliverables or tasks I have initialed."

Team Members:

_____   _____
typed name (date)   typed name (date)

_____   _____
typed name (date)   typed name (date)

PM2 Deliverable: Project Plan & Web Site Map — Due: 10/25

Your PM2 deliverable includes each item in the PM1 task list in discussion form with an appropriate report section heading. For example, item #1, Web Site Reviews & Analyses, includes a discussion of any Web presence your client company may currently have, analyses of competitive sites that have similar products or services, or sites that the client or team members particularly like in terms of layout, design, or function. Indicate how any strong points or weaknesses in these sites will be addressed in your prototype.

Project Tasks: Assign the following tasks for submission with PM3.

Tasks	Task Manager(s)	Due Date	Initials
Project scope and content			
Page layout and design criteria			
Navigation plan with site map			
Printed sample of Web design and page layout			
Development tool options build and plan			
Coordinate documentation for PM3 (due 11/20)			

A write-up on these tasks is due for the next PM.
Add other tasks as needed to fit your project parameters.

PM3 Deliverable: Plan Update with Site Map and Function Document — Due: 11/20

Compile all former summary sections into well-flowing, properly written business report sections, updating the plan and technology choice as needed. To this material, you will add a table of contents, an executive summary that summarizes the client's goals and business problem, and section tabs. Write for your client, not for your professor, particularly in describing your technology choices, options, and future enhancements. For PM4, *please submit two copies (one notebook only) which will not be returned to you*. Include a CD-ROM copy of your report and prototype for the client. One hard-copy report is for your client and will be included in a common binder with other team output. The second copy is for the professor. Include your set of team evaluations for your peers in a sealed envelope. Add other tasks as needed to fit your project parameters.

Project Tasks: Assign the following tasks for report submission next milestone.

Tasks	Task Manager(s)	Due Date	Initials
Executive summary and table of contents			

Web site function
document

Usability test

Security, privacy,
trust issues

Hosting and ongoing
maintenance requirements

Future functionality —
proposal to implement
if your team so desires;
estimated time and costs

Sealed peer ratings

Coordinate documentation
for final report (due 12/4)

PM4 Deliverable: Final Project Report — Due: 12/4

Project Tasks: Submit your prototype report copies and assign the following tasks for the presentation milestone.

Tasks	Task Manager(s)	Due Date	Initials
Plan presentation			
Client and strategy overview			
Development methods			
Site demonstration			

PM5 Deliverable: Prototype Presentation

Use your final team time to complete your prototype and prepare your 30-minute presentation demo. Plan on a brief overview of your project goals and strategy chosen, your development tools and methods, and your final demo. All team members should participate.

Section II:

Information Technology Literacy

Chapter XVII

Metacognition in Information Systems Education

Steve Benson
Edith Cowan University, Australia

ABSTRACT

My interest in producing this chapter arises from the fact that I am mildly afflicted with Asperger's syndrome and have some medium-term memory degradation. The level of introspection that I have had to develop onto my own mental processes in order to function has been useful to me in my role as an academic, because I can understand many of the learning problems that students face. Conversations at international conferences and email interactions suggested that my personal insights would be useful to other academics. Here, I present data from a six-semester period that suggest that it would be beneficial to change Information Systems curricula to incorporate metacognitive education. I also describe the changes that I have made to my own teaching methods and the elements of a metacognitive teaching program.

INTRODUCTION

Educators would state that learning processes are most effective when they are tailored to the cognitive style of the student. There are many instruments for assessing the cognitive style of students. Some of these, such as Myers-Briggs, address personality as a factor (Dewar & Whittington, 2000), while others such as Sternberg-Wagner (Benson & Standing, 2001a) focus on processing styles. However, the more sophisticated the instruments are, the more unwieldy they are in practice. No lecturer can afford the time and effort to present the curriculum from several perspectives, and it would be a logistical nightmare to divide the class into smaller parts. Consequently, many lecturers do not take cognitive style into account in their teaching practice. This last statement gives no indication of the stresses that many Australian academics face as they seek to achieve more with fewer resources. Increases in class sizes and decreases in government funding have occurred, while the number of academics has remained relatively stable. The introduction of performance management, quality controls, and the need to raise revenue combine with the aforementioned problems to add to the general levels of stress in the profession. Accordingly, most academics compromise when it comes to educational practice and aim to produce something that is acceptable rather than excellent.

TEACHING STYLES IN AUSTRALIAN UNIVERSITIES

One of the discussion topics being considered at the Australian Universities reform working party is whether Australian academics should have a teaching qualification. A teaching qualification has been a prerequisite for many academic appointments made in the last 10 years. Most Australian universities provide in-service courses for lecturers, and these include theories of learning and teaching. However, many academics are "time served" in that they have many years of teaching experience but no formal or accredited training. The evaluations carried out in most universities and faculties do little to measure the effectiveness of teaching and become instead measurements of lecturer and subject popularity. Many academics were appointed on the basis of research and publication, and good researchers do not necessarily make good teachers.

A distinction needs to be made between pedagogy and teaching style. The latter depends on a number of personal factors and is often idiosyncratic, because personality plays a major part in curriculum delivery. In an effort to examine the factors that influenced teaching style most, I interviewed 20 academics. While the interviews were informal, I found that the greatest influence on teaching style had nothing to do with teacher training or education. Instead, academics developed teaching styles and approaches based on their own experiences at college and university, basing their teaching practice on academic role models they had found personally appealing, while avoiding practices and styles used by lecturers they had found boring, ineffectual, or inept. All interviewees had some awareness of personality types and cognitive styles, but only two used this in their own teaching. It would seem that the remaining members were teaching to classes they imagined to be predominantly like themselves. The potential for teaching and cognitive style mismatch between staff and students is quite obvious. In addition, I found myself asking whether the mindset of Australian Information Systems Academics was suited to the present conditions.

THE INFORMATION SYSTEMS ACADEMIC MINDSET

By the early 1970s, Information Systems was beginning to appear in the curriculum of major American universities. As an emerging discipline, it was neither pure science nor social science, and its paradigms and infrastructure were ill-defined (Benson & Standing, 2002;

Weber, 1997). In a monistic view of science, the boundaries of the discipline are usually clear, there is a paradigm (system of working) and infrastructure (journals, committees, etc.) that provide coherence (Banville & Landry, 1989). While the research and publication areas of the emerging discipline of Information Systems owed much to the social sciences, its practice relied heavily on scientific, mathematic, and engineering disciplines. Software was closely associated with the underlying hardware — detailed knowledge of the underlying architecture and operation was essential if efficient programs were to be written. As business began to use computers to process and filter huge quantities of data, the demand for systems and their developers increased exponentially. The impact on computer technology in engineering and manufacturing had reduced the number of skilled people required. Many of these people migrated into Information Systems, bringing with them a mindset that was grounded in logical thinking, rigor, and mathematical notation. While the skills required by Information Systems (IS) graduates have been a frequently studied topic (Latham, 2000; Snoke & Underwood, 1999; Standing & Standing, 1999) (of which the debate usually centers on the relative importance of technical skills, interpersonal and communication skills, and the depth of business knowledge and skills), little has been written about the skills required by information systems lecturers.

As near as it may be established, the average age of an Australian Information Systems academic is 53 years. An informal analysis of the backgrounds and qualifications of Australian Information Systems academics shows that the overwhelming majority has qualifications in other disciplines and has migrated to Information Systems in later life, many from computer science. Information Systems curricula show a heavy dependency on the thinking of the 1980s and early 1990s. The traditional systems life cycle view, derived from engineering disciplines, is no longer appropriate for many Information Systems projects. In particular, Web commerce development projects require much shorter timelines and ability to respond to rapidly changing requirements than older projects. Newer systems also require different skills and thinking styles, and it is hard to see where these are being engendered in university curricula.

Lecturers are unlikely to change their mindset and are insufficiently resourced to customize the curriculum at a micro-level. The only practicable approach is to give students the resources they need to customize the curriculum to suit their own cognitive styles.

DEVISING AN INITIAL METACOGNITIVE PROGRAM FOR STUDENTS

To be effective, any metacognitive program would have to consist of three parts:
1.   A self-diagnostic tool
2.   Education in thinking styles, memory, and adapting strategies
3.   Continuing access to suitable resources as metacognitive awareness increases

It should be noticed that diagnosis is the first phase. Consultations with psychologists suggested that students might incorrectly self-label if education preceded diagnosis, and this would lead to inappropriate metacognitive strategies. Obviously, any diagnostic tools would have to be as simple as possible while retaining usefulness. Taking these components in turn, discussion follows.

DIAGNOSIS

Myers-Briggs Type Indicators were rejected as being too complex and potentially unreliable, a view shared by many practicing psychologists. Similarly, schemes that incorporated personality types with cognitive styles were rejected, because their outcomes were too diverse to be useful to individual students at an early stage of metacognitive development. Harrison and Bramson (1999) identified five main modes of thinking. These modes are typified by the philosophers Hegel, Kant, Singer, Liebniz and Locke. The Hegelian and Kantian modes are substantive/value-oriented thinking and knowing styles as distinct from the analyst/realist style represented by the Liebnizian and Lockeian modes. Harrison and Bramson (1999) noted that approximately 50% of people prefer to think in a single style, and that 35% are able to use two related styles. This confirms the view expressed by Benson and Standing (2001) and Stenning, Cox, and Oberlander (1995) that the underlying preferred thinking styles are relatively immutable, but a minority of people (approximately 12%) may prefer several modes equally. While Harrison and Bramson's (1999) framework is useful, the need to incorporate a history of contemporary thinkers and schools of thought into the program was an acceptable overhead. Reverting to work carried out by Ornstein (1997), a simpler classification scheme of left- and right-brain thinking was adopted (this has been discussed in Benson & Standing, 2001a). This division uses the terms left and right as cognitive styles, neurologically speaking, functions may be distributed in either or both hemispheres of the brain (McCrone, 1999; Kelly et al., 1998). Ornstein's divisions give the following:

- Left-brain cognition — sequential analysis: systemic, logical interpretation of information; interpretation and production of symbolic information: language mathematics abstraction and reasoning; memory stored in a language format

- Right-brain cognition — holistic functioning: processing provides a "holistic" picture of environment; visual special skills; coordination of holistic activities such as dancing and gymnastics; memory is stored in auditory, visual, and spatial modalities

In individuals, a small difference in right- and left-brain ability is usually sufficient to guarantee 100% selection for the preferred mode. Work by Benson and Standing (2001a) showed a right-brain bias in IS students.

EDUCATION

A minimalist program was devised in order to fit into the existing curriculum without compromising content or standards. A total of three hours was allocated, a 40-minute introduction and four 20-minute mini-presentations. Because the object was to improve student outcomes, the program focused on knowledge and techniques that would be immediately useful to students. This resulted in the following composition:

1. Basic personality types (introvert, extrovert, judger, perceiver, and control/emote responses) — This allowed students to make a swift assessment of themselves in terms of their broad behavioral patterns, attitude toward deadlines, and motivation. This also enabled them to make a similar assessment of their lecturers. Simple motivational strategies were offered, and the importance of leisure and enjoyment to learning were explained and emphasized.

2. Basic left- and right-brain cognitive styles, auditory, visual, and kinesthetic learning — This provided an introduction to the nature of knowledge and Constructivism.

3. An introduction to memory and its relationship to learning styles, the primacy-recency effect, and its relationship to note taking and revision practices; the conscious and subconscious divide and make use of associative memory and mind mapping for recall — This provided an introduction to problem-solving states and the IPRAM model (a simple conceptual framework for establishing one's intellectual maturity with respect to a particular knowledge domain), developed by Benson and Standing (2001b).

Because greater exposure to metacognitive resources and increasing self-critical awareness would allow more motivated students to add to their metacognitive tool set, URLs were posted onto the unit Web site, and these links gave students access to Web based resources for learning, metacognition, and memory techniques, e.g., www.brain.com, www.intelegen.com, etc. A relevant bibliography was made available.

A small amount of time was devoted to explaining the factors that exert significant influence on student outcomes. Of these, student expectations (locus of control) and staff expectations are the most significant. As a consequence, students were encouraged to develop confidence in their own abilities.

CHANGES TO TEACHING PRACTICE

Although lecturers do not have time to present the curriculum from multiple perspectives, I have found that it is feasible to present material from left- and right-brain perspectives. It has been seen that abstract thinkers (left-brain) perform better than concrete thinkers (right-brain) under certain conditions. This is most notable when the subjects have no prior experience of the subject area. Left-brain thinkers are able to theorize and so make more rapid initial progress (Benson & Standing, 2001). By contrast, right-brain thinkers cope less well with abstraction and require examples and experience to ground their knowledge. Taking the example of teaching normalization in a database course, left-brain thinkers are able to accept a highly theoretical and abstract presentation of the concepts using set theory and are able to apply their knowledge reasonably quickly. Presenting material from both perspectives was the only concession made to learning styles. However, right- and left-brain thinkers require practice and repetition for retention. Simply changing one's position in a lecture theater when beginning a new topic is helpful to kinesthetic learners who associate learning with location.

Regular reinforcement of the metacognitive training program concepts was given during the course. This took the form of brief examples of study practices and suggested activities. In particular, students were referred to social constructivism (vonGlaserfeld, 1993; Ernest, 1995) and were encouraged to discuss their assignments with other students. In order to accommodate students who had a low social-need strength, assessments were constructed so they could be completed on an individual or group basis. A clear statement of objectives was given for each lecture. This statement was revisited at the end of each lecture to confirm that the objectives had been met. The number of objectives was restricted to seven or fewer to correspond with Miller's (1956) thinking. In earlier lectures, students were given suggested strategies to help them remember the subject matter. Subsequently, students were encouraged to develop and use their own methods. However, in each lecture, I presented the objectives in the form of a list and a mind map.

Modifications were made to the timing of subject matter delivery in order to maximize the primacy-recency effect. Students require breaks, and the longest time to lecture should proceed without interruption is approximately 45 to 50 minutes. It is inadvisable to focus on a single task for extended periods, because neurochemical depletion reduces learning productivity. An attention span of seven to eight minutes was assumed, and suitable activities and diversions were introduced on their expiry. Extensive use was made of humor and drama triggers. Forward and backward referencing were used, and where possible, the subject matter was grounded in familiar real-world examples. The most obvious implication is that the most important topics should be introduced in the first session and revisited in the final session. The more mundane topics are ideal for the second session.

Students were given extensive advice on the mechanisms of memory, in particular, how to move items from short- to long-term memory and how to organize information for easier recall. Much of this revolves around good note-taking skills and repetition, but few students had any awareness of how much repetition is required and the timescales involved.

A 50-minute examination preparation session was given at the end of the course. This focused on technique rather than content, in particular, the task of relating question selection, ordering, and answering to learning styles.

Although this seems an extensive alteration to teaching style and practice, the total work involved was less than 16 hours for a 42-hour, single-credit course. The extra work was incorporated into the annual update of the course and has since provided a useful framework for the development of other courses.

EVALUATION

Table 1 shows student perceptions of the course for three semesters before and after the introduction of new teaching practices. The figures are drawn from the same single-credit course, and each enrollment had a minimum of 55 students.

Table 2 shows time series data on marks distributions for the same unit over a three-year period. While the minimum mark has remained relatively constant, the average mark has increased, and the percentage of students performing well has increased, only the attrition rate has decreased.

DISCUSSION

Demonstrating a direct causal link between changes to teaching practices and providing training in metacognition with changes to student outcomes is not possible in the absence of a strictly controlled experiment. Possible objections might include the following:
1.   The lecturer might have made the course, assessments, and examinations simpler in order to increase the number of students receiving good passing grades.
2.   The students are aware that they are part of an uncontrolled experiment.
3.   The improvements could be explained by increases in the quality of the student intake.

Taking these in turn, Item 1 may be countered by the fact that the examinations have been peer reviewed for consistency in style and level of difficulty. Samples of examination scripts and assignments have been similarly peer reviewed.

Table 1. Differences in student opinions of lecturer before and after the introduction of metacognitive education and changes to teaching practice

Criterion	Before new practices n=165	After new practices n=194
Good teaching rating	66.0%	76.6%
Overall lecturer rating	58.8%	84%
Helped to motivate the student	66%	75%
Helped to develop analytical skills in the subject	65%	66%
Helped to develop general problem solving skills	50%	76%
Lecturer understood student learning problems and worked to overcome them	60%	86.6%
Lecturer was extremely good at explaining things	63%	100%

Note: Items 1 and 2 are based upon the entire evaluation instrument with student assessment factored in. The remaining items relate to specific questions within the instrument. Some changes were made to the wording of the instrument in the second semester of the new practices in relation to Items 5 and 6. While the wording was broadly equivalent, I needed to eliminate bias and so took a sample of 16 students and asked them the same questions in the same words and obtained similar results.

Despite being unable to counter Item 2 absolutely, it is argued that the exercise been beneficial. On balance of probability, it is apparent that the changes introduced are in accordance with good educational strategy. Changes to subject matter have been minor, and the assessment methods have been subject to control and scrutiny. The improvement in student outcomes began when the changes were effected and has continued. The overall sample sizes are statistically significant, and the use of the tracking facility in WebCT has enabled me to see that students who have availed themselves of the metacognitive resources provided have tended to perform better in assessment and examination.

With regard to Item 3, the same course and practices were carried out over an eight-trimester period at a private college, whether or not materials were subject to additional scrutiny and control. Here, the survey of student perceptions was not carried out; however, the changes to student outcomes closely paralleled those described above.

Given the time-scale over which the data span, I had the opportunity to track some students' performances in other subject areas. I found some who sustained an improved level of performance in all their subsequent study. I noted that most showed improved performance in Information Systems related units only, not in all their subsequent study (in non-IS study, their averages were significantly lower). Although further investigation is required, I would suggest that this finding tends to confirm the view of Perkins and Solomon (1989) that

Table 2. Student outcomes before and after the introduction of metacognitive education and changes to teaching practice

Criterion	Before New Teaching Practices, Averaged Over Three Semesters ($n = 184$)	After New Teaching Practices, Averaged Over Three Semesters, $n = 207$
Average grade	59.0%	68.0%
Standard deviation	12.0%	19.7%
% students scoring >80%	6.58%	20.8%
% students scoring 70-80%	19.4%	28.2%
Maximum mark	76.6%	93.3%
Minimum mark	40.1%	41.0%
Average attrition rate	12.3%	7.0%

Note: Some filtering was undertaken to remove students who withdrew from or failed for nonacademic reasons. This may introduce a small element of subjectivity into the assessment of the attrition rate.

metacognitive/strategy straining needs to be grounded in the subject area with specific and semi-specific strategies being taught, rather than generic skills, if recidivism is to be prevented. Although it was not possible to go back over the six-semester period and break down the results by age, I noticed that some of the mature students were already using metacognitive techniques of their own devising or choosing, though actual awareness of that fact varied from subconscious to fully conscious. My belief is that younger students benefit more than mature students from metacognitive training, but I accept that further work is required to prove this to a satisfactory level.

CONCLUSIONS

At this stage, I am unable to offer an absolute level of proof that my metacognitive training program and changes to my teaching practice are responsible for the significant improvement in student outcomes described above. However, I would argue on the balance of probability that it is so. Should my hypothesis be vindicated, there are obvious implications for Information Systems curricula and Information Systems lecturers. An informal survey of 30 online information systems curricula of U.S. universities failed to reveal any that addressed metacognition and thinking styles. While this is insufficiently rigorous to draw firm conclusions, I would argue that it is indicative of the general state of affairs. Of the model curricula I reviewed, only the ISCC (Lidtke et al., 1999) model made explicit reference to teaching approaches.

In order to develop a fully convincing case, it will be necessary to carry out a controlled experiment with a larger sample. Campus reorganizations at my university will provide such an opportunity in late 2002. It is anticipated that the data obtained from this experiment will provide the basis for long-term, longitudinal study. It is hypothesized that students will continue to develop metacognitive awareness and skills, resulting in a profile of continued improvement in terms of outcomes. (It is also suggested that such students would perform significantly better in employment than their metacognitive unaware counterparts.)

Even in the absence of such an experiment, I am sufficiently convinced of the value of the exercise to seek to continue with the new work practices. Over the period that the metacognitive training and changes to teaching practice and delivery have been in place, I have seen a substantial improvement in student outcomes for a marginal investment in time and effort.

REFERENCES

Banville, C., & Landry, M. (1989). Can the field of MIS be disciplined? *Communications of the ACM, 32*, 1, 48–60.

Benson, S., & Standing, C. (2001a). Are information systems students in their right minds? *Proceedings of the 2001 Information Resources Management Association International Conference*, Toronto, Canada, May.

Benson, S., & Standing, C. (2001b), Effective knowledge management: Knowledge, thinking and the personal-corporate knowledge nexus problem. *Information Systems Frontiers, 3*, 2, 227–238.

Benson, S., & Standing, C. (2002). *Information Systems, A Business Approach* (Chap. 1). New York: John Wiley & Sons.

Dewar, T., & Whittington, D. (2000). Online learners and their learning strategies, *Journal of Educational Computing Research, 22*, 4, 385–403.

Ernest, P. (1995). *The One And The Many: Constructivism In Education* (pp. 459–486). Hillsdale, NJ: Lawrence Erlbaum.

Harrison, A. F., & Bramson, R. M. (1982). *The Art of Thinking*, New Jersey, Berkeley.

Intelegen Inc. (2000). Online brain portal. Retrieved from the World Wide Web: http://www.intelegen.com/.

Kelley, W. M. et al. (1998). Hemispheric specialization in human dorsal frontal cortex and medial temporal lobe for verbal and nonverbal memory encoding. *Neuron, 20*, 927–936, May 22, 1998.

Latham, A. (2000). Information systems graduates: The challenge for course designers. *Proceedings of the European Conference on Information Systems*, Vienna, pp. 1432–1438.

Lee, D. M., Trauth, E. M., & Farwell, D. (1995). Critical skills and knowledge requirements of IS professionals: A joint academic/industry investigation. *MIS Quarterly, 19*, 3, 313–340.

Lidtke, D. K. et al. (eds.) (1999). An information systems-centric curriculum '99 program guidelines for educating the next generation of information systems specialists, in collaboration with industry. Retrieved from the World Wide Web: http://www.iscc.unomaha.edu/.

McCrone, J. (1999). Left brain, right brain. *New Scientist*, 3 July 1999.

Miller, G. A. (1956). The magical number seven, plus or minus two. *Psychological Review, 63*, 81–87. Also online at http://www.well.com/user/smalin/miller.html.

Ornstein, R. (1997). The right mind — making sense of hemispheres.

Perkins, D. N., & Solomon, G. (1989). Are cognitive skills context bound? *Educational Researcher, 18*, 1, 16–25.

Snoke, R., & Underwood, A. (1999). Generic attributes of IS graduates: An Australian IS academic study. *Proceedings of the Tenth Australian Conference on Information Systems (ACIS)* (pp. 817–824), Wellington, New Zealand.

Standing, C., & Standing, S. (1999). The role of politics in IS career progression. *Systems Research and Behavioural Science, 16*, 519–531.

Stenning, K., Cox, R., & Oberlander, J. (1995). Contrasting the cognitive effects of graphical and sentential logic teaching: Reasoning, representation and individual differences. *Language and Cognitive Processes, 10*, 3, 333–345.

VonGlaserfeld, E. (1993). Questions and answers about radical constructivism. In Tobin (ed.), *The Practice Of Constructivism In Science Education* (pp. 23–28). Hillside, NJ: Lawrence Erlbaum.

Weber, R. (1997). *Ontological Foundations of Information Systems* (pp. 54–67). Australia: Coopers & Lybrand.

Chapter XVIII

Required Software Proficiency in General Education and Business Courses

Linda Lynam
Central Missouri State University, USA

ABSTRACT

Approximately 1,100 students in a general education computer course at a Midwestern state university with a technology focus were required to demonstrate competency in Microsoft Word®, Excel®, and PowerPoint® during the Fall 2001 and Spring 2002 semesters. The entrance requirement at the university requires a minimum of an ACT score of 20 or in the upper two-thirds of their high school graduating class. Many students are in the 20 to 23 range of ACT scores. A large portion of the students lack high school experience in independent study and individual responsibility. Results of the project indicate that students with little experience in self-responsibility can achieve at the university level when required.

LITERATURE SEARCH

While a literature search found many instances of computer testing used in intelligence testing, ability assessment in reading, writing, mathematics, and languages, no references were found concerning mandatory productivity software assessment.

BACKGROUND

Three full-time faculty members teach most of the general education computer literacy courses in the College of Business and Economics have had a long-term goal of requiring all students to demonstrate a basic proficiency in the major business software applications: word processing, spreadsheet, and presentation software. These instructors have long known that students think they know more about the computer than they really do. Professors in other courses assume students know basic computer use, and employers expect graduates to possess basic computer skills.

A pilot project was performed in 1999 with a small group of approximately 35 students in the College of Applied Science and Technology. Software assessment tests were created specifically for this purpose and were individually graded. Students self-evaluated their skill levels before taking the exams. The results indicated that students generally overestimated their knowledge of the various software programs.

The result of this small study encouraged the campus director of assessment, the director of educational development, and the computer information systems faculty to talk to the university administration about implementing an institutional requirement that all students graduating from the university must show a basic proficiency in the most common business software programs. The most logical time to test the students is as they enter the university. If they have the necessary skill level, the requirement would be satisfied. If they do not, they immediately are aware of deficiencies and can enroll in remedial courses to prepare for retaking proficiency exams. The most common reason given not to implement a software proficiency requirement was the logistical problem of adding more activities to the freshman/new student orientation. The current program is a one-day on-campus visit the summer before the student first attends the university. Software testing would add approximately 90 minutes to the schedule. Another reason given is that not all students are majoring in computers. To counter this objection, it was pointed out that most employers expect college graduates to know basic computer skills, enough to write a report, keep a budget, and make a simple presentation. The third objection is that it would not be fair to allow one department to get all the credit hours that would be generated as a result of the necessary remedial classes that would be taken.

IMPLEMENTATION

Because the instructors of the general education computer course believed the students needed the software skills now and not when the political battles were settled, a software proficiency requirement was implemented in all sections of the general education course. The course is not only taken by all majors on campus but also is required of all business majors. In the Fall 2001 semester, approximately 600 students enrolled in the course were required to achieve at least 80% on each of the exams in Microsoft Excel, PowerPoint, and Word. When a minimum of 80% was achieved, a pass was recorded for that exam. No points were awarded for the proficiency exams. Students who did not master the three exams could not receive a grade higher than a D in the course, even if grades for other course work were higher than a D. The proficiency exams were only a portion of the course. Regular class periods included lecture and videos over computer hardware, online research, and Internet use. Course work included three multiple-choice exams over lectures, several homework exercises to apply lecture material, and a software project applying class material incorporating into Word, PowerPoint, and Excel.

Basic software skills were required. For example, in all programs, students had to know how to open a file, save a file, insert graphics, change fonts, etc. Additional Word skills were setting margins, headers, footers, and page numbers. Excel required the ability to enter formulas and create a simple graph. PowerPoint requirements included automating bullet entry, changing backgrounds, and making slide transitions.

To automate testing, give immediate feedback, and allow full use of the software programs, including help files, Software Assessment Manager (SAM), a product of Course Technology/Thomson Learning, was used. Students had many chances to take the exams: eight class periods were reserved for testing, every Friday afternoon, and the final exam time. The same exams were given every time. To ensure the correct student was taking the exam, every student had to check into the testing session with a photo ID and was required to show the proctor their passing score.

Remediation was keyed to another Course Technology/Thomson Learning product: Course CBT, a CD-based computer-based training tool. The SAM program created a study guide for each exam. Students could look at the study guide, see exactly what they missed, and see where on the Course CBT the skill was covered.

Students were not given in-class instruction in the software. In fact, the class is taught in a large lecture hall with only one computer for the instructor. At no time were the students in a lab setting with the instructor to learn the software. However, the students were required to complete a project using all the software programs. In the first semester, two class days were used to demonstrate the project and skills required for it.

STUDENT DEMOGRAPHICS

Our students have ACT scores in the 20 to 23 ranges. In high school, many of the students were not required to be responsible. Many are accustomed to having class time to do all homework, to having leniency on due dates, and to having opportunities for extra credit. Our students had little experience in being responsible for learning required material on their own.

Students were surveyed as to their previous software training. Eleven percent of students indicated they had no software training, 56% had taken a high school class, 8% had taken a college class, and 67% were self-taught. The numbers do not add up to 100% due to more than one method selected.

METHODOLOGY

Results were gathered by student surveys. The first survey was completed at mid-semester after the students had two weeks of in-class opportunities (eight class days) to take the proficiency exams. The first round of testing was completed immediately after class rosters were finalized in the third week of the semester. The second round was completed at the semester midpoint. Students had the opportunity to take the exams on Friday afternoons; however, by mid-semester, few students had taken advantage of the Friday afternoon testing.

The Blackboard program was used for the mid-semester survey. Blackboard includes a survey function in the program, making it easy to create and take a survey, but it does not provide a way to get the data out of the program for manipulation. Only the numbers of students taking the survey and summary percentages by section are shown, with no provision to obtain the data in a raw form to use. The Blackboard administrators at the university were unable to determine how to extract the data. Excel was used to attempt to determine the totals overall, but the method was imprecise and clumsy.

A second survey was completed at the end of the semester. Students were asked not to complete the survey until they had completed the course, that is, either passed all three exams or taken advantage of every opportunity to take the exams. The second survey was also Web-based, but Access was used to collect the data, which made the data more accurate and easier to manipulate.

Students received points for completing both surveys. The Blackboard program reported which students had taken the survey, but did not allow survey responses to be matched to student names. The last question of the second survey required students to go to the Blackboard program to indicate they had completed the survey. Again, responses were not tied to student names.

FIRST SEMESTER RESULTS

The overall results of the proficiency testing were much better than anticipated. At the end of the first semester, 81% of students had passed all three exams, 11% had passed two exams, 5% had passed one exam, and 3% had passed no exams. It is important to remember that all three exams had to be passed to get better than a D in the course. Of the students who did not pass all three exams, 2% of the 600 students would have received a grade higher than D had they passed the exams; the remainder of the 19% who did not pass all three would have received a D or F in the course, even if they had passed all three exams.

More important than merely passing exams is the ability to apply the skills in other situations. Students were asked on the second survey if they felt prepared to use Word, Excel, and PowerPoint to complete assignments in other classes. Of the responding students, 92% indicated that they felt they knew enough to use the software.

During the semester, students frequently complained that no points were assigned to the proficiency exams. However, when asked at the end of the semester, 76% advocated keeping the pass/fail scoring, and only 14% recommended assigning a point value to the exams.

The methods of studying for the exams were disappointing. When asked how they studied, the students responded: 60% already knew the skills, and 40% used trial and error on the exams. However, in another question, they were asked if they used the Course CBT to study, and 54% indicated they had used it at least once. Based on the number of times most students took the exams, trial and error was probably the most common method.

The Friday afternoon testing sessions, held in a 30-station lab, were not heavily used until the end of the semester. Until mid-semester, the greatest number attending was 10. Several weeks, no students came to the session. Until mid-semester, the graduate assistant proctor was also available to provide tutoring on the software during the sessions. Only one person took advantage of tutoring. Toward the end of the semester, attendance greatly increased at the Friday sessions. In the last three weeks, lines could be seen at the sessions, with a minimum of 50 students per week taking exams, and many others being turned away.

No time limit was enforced on Friday tests. If a student got on a computer at the beginning of the session, they were not forced to leave after a specific period, even if there was a line.

By the week of finals, most students had passed the exams. A maximum of 10 to 15 students per section took exams during the final week. Sixty students were enrolled in each section. Several students did not take the proficiency exams in the final week, because they had determined they would not get better than a D in the course based on other course work.

A majority, 84%, of the students indicated that they felt proud when they had successfully completed an exam.

SECOND SEMESTER RESULTS

Based on students' comments on the end-of-semester survey, more class days were allotted to software demonstration. A comprehensive project was assigned again during the second semester, and four class days were used to demonstrate all components of the project. Because more time was available, all competency software skills were also demonstrated. Many students chose not to attend the demonstration class days, but those who were interested in learning all the skills were able to see all skills demonstrated.

At the end of the first semester, the three instructors reviewed the skills that were included in the exams and decided to make the exams more comprehensive. All three exams were modified to include more skills, and the time allotted for each exam was also increased. Out of the 500 students enrolled in the spring semester, only two students received a D in the course, because they had not passed all three exams. All other students who earned a course work grade of at least a C passed all three exams. The higher success rate can be related to the maturity level of the students. By the second semester, the freshman students made the adjustment from high school to the university and now understood the need for personal responsibility. The second reason for better success can be attributed to more class time devoted to demonstrating software skills. Also during the second semester, all instructors had to be away from the class for at least 1 day due to travel, and a graduate assistant proctored the hands-on exams while they were away, thus increasing the opportunities for student testing.

No survey was done at the end of the second semester due to university restructuring. The course will be transferred to a different college within the university, and different faculty will be responsible for the course.

CONCLUSION

Students who were not prepared in high school to be self-motivated learners were able to accomplish the goal of achieving at least 80% on each of three software proficiency exams. Students learned the skills, maybe not using the method expected, but the end result was successful completion of the exams. The proficiency requirement will stay in the general education computer course.

Chapter XIX

Technology Literacy Issues for Freshmen Education Majors in a Leading Teacher Program

David D. Carbonara
Duquesne University, USA

ABSTRACT

In this chapter, the literacy issues of a preservice leading teacher education program are discussed. The leading teacher program is constructed on the foundation of the three major themes of leadership, diversity, and technology. The technology theme ensures that the preservice teacher is cognizant of information literacy issues and instructional technology principles and practices. The student is well-prepared to become a leading teacher in the nation's schools, where he or she is entrusted to prepare a citizenry that will communicate and collaborate to solve complex problems in the new millennium.

INTRODUCTION

This chapter will explore the features of a leading teacher program that has foundations in the national and international standards for instructional technology. It will discuss a strong commitment from the department chair, the dean of the school of education, and upper administration to provide the equipment, support, and expectations to transform the school into a home of the nation's leading teachers (Handbook, 2001). The preservice teacher enters the program with technology skills to communicate and complete assignments. They quickly acquire and increase the skills in information technology so that they can obtain sufficient data, synthesize that data into useful information, and create interactive visual presentations and exciting virtual tours (Tomei, 2001). Finally, the leading teacher must be aware of the rapid advancements and changes in technology and how those changes affect the learning process. The teacher must know how to adapt to the changes and to infuse the new technology into the curriculum of the future.

BACKGROUND

The federal government recognized the need to bridge the digital divide to ensure that all students have the opportunity to advance themselves and the U.S. economy. The nation and the nation's businesses need individuals who can acquire data and transform that data into meaningful information. The citizens of this land need to communicate and collaborate with their peers without regard to time and space limitations. To accomplish these goals and anticipate future needs, the workers of tomorrow need to practice the technology skills of today. These workers, university students and military personnel of tomorrow, will come from the current bank of students in the K–12 space. With a high attrition rate for teachers, it appears logical to concentrate on the students in teacher training institutions and inspire them to fulfill the role of guide, facilitator, and leading teacher of our nation's children. Teacher training institutions need to set the expectation that preservice teachers will possess an expert level of instructional technology skills to gather data and synthesize information, to create insightful interactive visual presentations, and to construct meaningful virtual tours of the vast resources of the Internet. This chapter will explore these concepts as they relate to an existing leading teacher program.

MAIN THRUST OF THE CHAPTER

In this chapter, the preparation of preservice teachers as technology leaders will be discussed. While a tremendous amount of money was expended on equipment to bridge the "digital divide," a smaller amount was used to train existing teachers. Given the attrition rate of teachers, a closer examination of the preservice teacher arena is warranted. The teacher preparation institutions have an opportunity to proclaim an admirable program based on standards, post-high school needs, and organizational support. A few of these topics will be examined in this chapter in order to better understand the process of preparing leading teachers that are facilitators and guides in the learning process. Also, the distinction is made between information technology, technology literacy, and instructional technology.

The preparation of preservice teachers as technology leaders will be discussed. The expectation is that students graduate from high school technologically literate to enter post-secondary education, the military, or the private corporate sector. To accomplish this goal, K–12 teachers must be technologically literate to help prepare the students. The current group of K–12 teachers must operate at this level, and new preservice teachers must be trained to operate at this level also. The Commonwealth of Pennsylvania alone dedicated approximately $50 million to staff development from 1996 to 2000 (Edwards, 2001). This effort provided the funding to raise the information technology skills of existing faculty. However, recent attrition rates suggest that current teachers are leaving the field more quickly than they are being replaced (State of the Fund, 1999; State of the Fund, 2001).

Thus, the concern should be directed to the thousands of teachers currently in preservice (undergraduate) programs. These programs must train teachers who are not only literate in information technology but also are leading teachers in instructional technology.

Information technology may be thought of as the practice of accessing and acquiring data, text, and graphic phrases and files. This technology is concerned with the tools known as electronic card catalogs, search engines such as www.google.com or www.altavista.com, meta-search engines such as www.metacrawler.com, and electronic databases, such as ERIC and Proquest.

Instructional technology combines the fields of educational psychology, distance education, and computer technology to form a growing and cohesive body of knowledge that is based on learning theories, best practices, and innovative procedures that help the teacher be a guide or a facilitator of learning.

A number of professional organizations and articles devote their efforts not only to raising the awareness of technology literacy but also for measures to prepare our citizenry for the explosion of information and instructional technology in our global society. The U.S. Department of Education published "Getting America's Students Ready for the 21st Century: Meeting the Technology Literacy Challenge" (Riley, 1996). This guide references the digital divide and calls for action to bridge the gap between the "haves and have-nots" (Riley, 1996, p. 44). It advocates for the achievement of four goals (Riley, 1996, p. 11):

1. All teachers in the nation will have the training and support they need to help students learn using computers and the information superhighway.
2. All teachers and students will have modern, multimedia computers in their classrooms.
3. Every classroom will be connected to the information superhighway.
4. Effective software and on-line learning resources will be an integral part of every school's environment.

Goal 1 discusses the support that is necessary to achieve a technologically literate society. The federal government supports this endeavor by committing over $2.25 billion per year. The support must also occur at the teacher preparation stage. Topp (1995) listed three major areas to build a program in which teachers use the technology: an adequate and accessible equipment store of technology, the proper amount and kind of training, and the expectations to give technology importance in the profession. He further stated that this importance is dependent on the support of those in charge. At Duquesne University, the Instruction and Leadership department chair and the dean of the School of Education support and encourage the use of technology. The use of technology is given the status of a theme in the Leading Teacher Program, along with the concepts of diversity and leadership. Goal 3 from the Riley report (1995) has, to date, cost over $8 billion (Erate, 2001). This initiative was funded by the Universal Service Fund (Erate) and was funded by the Telecommunication Acts of 1994 and 1996. Essentially, telecommunication providers bill every user of telephones (local and long distance), data circuits, and cable television a small percent of their monthly bill to raise the $2.25 billion needed annually.

However, while the hardware was ordered from various manufacturers and installed locally, a smaller proportion of the funds were committed to staff development and teacher preparation programs. The desire to produce a technology-literate workforce continues to be a concern to all involved in the global community. Black (1995, p. 7) stated that "students (need) to be better prepared for workplace challenges requiring a strong technology background." Black further discussed the skills needed by a technology-literate workforce (Black, 1995, p. 21). It is noted that minimal technology skills reside in the areas of word-processing skills, database entry and manipulation, spreadsheet entry and manipulation, desktop publishing, graphic development and manipulation, and audiovisual recording and manipulation (Black, 1995, p. 21). Roman (2001) recently commented on the reasons why businesses like technology education. He stated that the global business community needs workers that are more broad thinking. The current and future worker community needs to think multi-dimensionally. Problems are not clear-cut and do not require unidimensional solutions. Workers need to work in a team and pool their thought processes together to solve the dilemmas and problems that face society. Teamwork is the key to future work environments. The technological tools help to provide a framework for that teamwork. Electronic mail and asynchronous chat sessions provide information to be shared between team members on a variable time schedule. Synchronous chat sessions provide for real-time exchange of ideas without regard to geographical location. Technology education is practicing these new communication procedures and is experimenting with audio and video on-demand environments. As video servers become more popular, one will be able to record an event and have an audience easily play it on-demand from any location on earth. Discoveries in space could be recorded and viewed by students at a later date. The educational implications break down time and space limitations for communication and the collaboration of ideas and solutions in today's and tomorrow's learning and working communities.

These technological tools are meaningless unless the users of tomorrow, the students of today, are properly trained to use them. The students of today are working with today's teachers. The current teaching staff must receive immediate and extensive training in instructional technology. The future teachers must also receive this education if they are to take their place as leading teachers in the classrooms of tomorrow. They must cultivate the critical-thinking skills of their students, as they are challenged (McCoy, 2001).

So, the call to action to prepare our students for success in a global community was presented to all professionals. The immediate response was to install network backbone equipment and enable Internet service providers to connect classrooms and schools to the Internet. Servers, routers, and firewalls were added to thousands of schools. Staff development programs were implemented to provide some support to faculty. Sessions in word processing, graphical presentations, and harvesting images from the Web were conducted. However, the vast numbers of retiring faculty are creating gaps in the numbers of technologically experienced teachers in our nation's school systems. It is imperative that teacher preparation programs incorporate the proper and best practices of instructional technology.

Instruction in the use of technology for preservice teachers needs to begin in the first semester of the freshman year. Teachers are needed to prepare students for the technologically rich 21st century (Black, 1995, p. 15), and those teachers need to be skilled in using technology to teach (Tomei, 2001, p. 4).

Black (1995, p. 7) surveyed corporations to determine the skills needed by a technology literate workforce. She found that America seeks novice workers that possess the skills necessary to create, edit, and print word-processed documents. They must also be capable of reliably entering data into a database and querying that database. Regarding the use of spreadsheets, she found a need to be skilled in entering, editing, and printing spreadsheets and to be able to create and print a graph from spreadsheet data. One must be able to import and manipulate graphics from the Internet and to obtain them from CD-ROM, DVD, and other yet-to-be-named electronic files. Additionally, the workforce should be able to create documents using desktop publishing facilities. Workers need to be able to functionally operate multimedia equipment such as, but not limited to: VCRs, video cameras, and audio recorders. At this point, one can envision a workforce that goes beyond basic word-processing tasks. Skill sets to manipulate databases and publishing and presentation software explode into a multi-varied set of experiences. No longer can workers be content to perform small tasks using technology. They must be able to use somewhat sophisticated software just to become entry-level workers.

The report also discussed the capability of creativity and thinking "out of the box." Cooper (1999, p. 2) advanced the topic of problem-solving and critical-thinking skills. If one reflects on the database querying skills and presentation skills mentioned above, one can come to the conclusion that sophisticated citizenry is sought not only to use data but also to convert it into useful information. The worker of the 21st century must analyze, synthesize, and evaluate knowledge (Cooper, 1999, p. 3) Thus, the student of the 21st century, whether in K–12 schools, or in the corporate world, must not only become proficient in the sophisticated use of technology but also be able to use those skills to create new strategies, products, and services.

The next logical step is to ensure that the nation's teachers are prepared to lead the infusion of technology into the curriculum. This infusion not only provides instruction on how to use these skills, but also inculcates a new paradigm for learning and leading in our students, so that the skills are second nature. They must then use, instruct, and infuse those skills and concepts into the curriculum of their students.

The process begins in the freshman year. A simple survey of basic skills was administered to the incoming class of education majors as part of a class on educational technology. Ninety-two percent of those surveyed knew to use Microsoft Word® to create a research paper and to use email to send information to a friend. However, only 53% knew the difference between a search engine and a Web portal. Further, only 10% were aware of ftp as a utility to download files.

The following table indicates a proficiency in the capabilities of word processing and electronic mail. This level of awareness is probably due to resourcefulness to learn these skills at home (Robinson, 2001, p. 10). Students must prepare papers and assignments in a professional manner using the specified tools (Clark, 2000, p. 179). Some of this profession-alism is taught at the high school level, because the students entered the university with these skills. For example, they needed to prepare word-processed documents. Thus, they acquired the skills to perform in this manner before matriculating. The skill set to operate electronic mail was learned for similar, necessary reasons. Email is probably used in conjunction with Internet use, chat rooms, and one's friends living away from home. Email skills are sharpened so that communication takes place between friends and family.

These students have the ability to quickly take their place as leaders of our world — a world that is rapidly changing. They must receive the necessary training to allow them to be change agents for their students. The citizenry must possess a solid foundation of concepts, the capability to acquire more data as it is generated, to evaluate and synthesize the data into information, and to communicate that information with the rest of society to uniquely solve existing problems and create wonderfully new inventions and innovations of tomorrow. It is increasingly evident that there is a "need for technological literacy in an

Table 1. Number and percent correct of selected survey questions asked of freshmen education majors, September 2001

Question Description	Total Number	Correct	Percent Correct
RAM	94	38	40.40%
Word Processing	94	89	92.71%
QWERTY Keyboard	94	32	34.00%
FTP	94	10	10.42%
Search Engines	94	51	53.10%
Apple Mouse	94	61	63.50%
Email	94	89	92.71%

increasingly global society" (Black, 1995, p. 14 from Boston, Chan, & Mukai, 1991). The Leading Teacher Program goes beyond mere literacy issues. It helps to provide a nurturing environment that allows preservice teachers to grow into the leaders of tomorrow.

The Leading Teacher Program at Duquesne University was created to provide general counsel to assist preservice teachers in achieving success as educational leaders using problem-solving and critical-thinking skills and specific counsel as instructional technology leaders. The skills are not only to be literate in their field of education but also to infuse technology into their practice so that a rich, meaningful, and lifelong learning experience is shared by faculty and students. This process begins in the freshman year of college. The newly matriculated freshmen are enrolled in Instructional Technology I and II. These courses provide a solid foundation in information literacy and instructional technology theory and practices. The students and faculty use a variety of computer labs in the School of Education, in the library, in the living-learning centers, and in other open labs on campus. The students and faculty are able to learn and to work in a comfortable environment. Johnson (1993) found that providing a comfortable environment and many opportunities to use the technology also increased the likelihood that the technology would be used.

Duquesne University's Leading Teacher program provides experiences for faculty and students to be engaged in the process of constructing knowledge (Leading Teacher Program Handbook, 2001, p. 5). Further, "success of society's quest for higher standards of learning is likely to be dependent on...teacher learning" (Leading Teacher Program Handbook, 2001, p. 5, from Darling-Hammonds, 1996). Program and practice are based on the three themes of leadership, diversity, and technology (Leading Teacher Program Handbook, 2001, p. 7). The program also addresses the five domains that define a leading teacher. A leading teacher must be a learning theorist, a curriculum designer, an expert in school context, a master practitioner, and an instructional leader. Students matriculating from this program experience 4 years of leadership growth to enhance and expand the problem-solving and critical-thinking skills of their own K–12 students. The operative idea is that the preservice teachers construct their experiences in the problem-solving arena, using critical-thinking skills to guide them to proficiently use technology tools to assist in the gathering, assimilation, accommodation, and presentation of information. The expectation is set for the students to model these higher-order skill sets in their professional growth and development (Wojnar, 2001, pp. 242–243). It is hoped that they, in turn, will model and expect their students to operate in a problem-solving mode using critical-thinking skills and instructional technology pedagogy.

The School of Education employs the International Society for Technology in Education Standards for teachers and students to guide the program's development and growth (International Society for Technology in Education, 2001). The six major goals of the ISTE standards are the foundation of the curriculum developed for the program. Students receive a solid foundation in basic computer technology operations and concepts, as well as a total infusion of the social, ethical, and human issues of the use of technology. The students are able to construct lessons using common productivity tools and to electronically communicate with their peers, professors, and friends synchronously and asynchronously. The first week immerses the beginning leading teacher in the research process by extensively using information literacy tools and databases to service all library patrons as well as to perform meaningful searches from the many Internet-based databases. Finally, the students are presented with many problem-solving and decision-making scenarios to discuss with their team members in a collaborative environment. The collaboration continues throughout the undergraduate experience into the master's program and also into the doctoral program in Instructional Technology. The program advocates information literacy for all, as McCade (2001) also proposed in his article. In a similar fashion, Easton and Easton (2002) reported at the 2002 International Resource Management Association conference in Seattle, Washington, that a program in the College of Business Administration at San Diego State University, California, addresses the topics of teaching students the fundamentals of information technology and teaching students various business-oriented software applications. Additionally, the School of Education's Instructional Technology program is authorized by the Pennsylvania Department of Education to award the Instructional Technology Certificate. In order to acquire the certificate, the candidate must exhibit the competencies of a leading instructional technologist. The program ensures that all graduates are operationally competent in the basic technology skills of word processing, spreadsheet, database, and graphic presentation. It progresses to skill sets in pedagogy, instructional technology management, and ethical and moral uses of technology to help students learn. It culminates the experience by providing opportunities for the students to practice the infusion of technology into the curriculum (Tomei, 2001, unpublished class notes). Students construct integrated thematic units that use office productivity tools in the context of providing instruction for the students. They will use word-processing tools to create handouts and study guides as well as presentation software to create engaging and interactive electronic slide shows for classroom discussion and individual student use. Virtual tours will be created that take advantage of free Web page creation tools to provide students with a highly interactive journey into a topic of interest. The students have opportunities to construct rich experiences using technology tools to enhance learning. This construction process permits the growth of knowledge from within each student. This growth enhances problem-solving and critical-thinking skills. These skills grow and mature over the 4 years of undergraduate education at Duquesne University.

It must be noted that the expectation for professional growth and development is communicated to the students on the first day of their freshman experience. The Instructional Technology program begins with an assurance that all students will practice the skills of basic office productivity tools. The second semester begins the infusion process of technology into the curriculum. The students experience it in all of their education classes and receive opportunities to use instructional technology tools to construct lessons. It must be noted that the expectation level and practice of technology infused into the curriculum begins in the freshman year. This practice grants each student ample opportunity to grow to their maximum potential. It also ensures that the preservice teacher is ready and skilled to become a leading teacher to the nation's students. Willis (2001) called for a change in the teacher preparation program. Teachers must transform from the givers of knowledge to the teacher/learner as a facilitator or a guide. The education students at Duquesne University will be empowered with the knowledge and skills to provide quality education as content specialists, curriculum designers, and leading teachers to America's students, so they can be better prepared to become a competent and expert workforce and citizenry. This workforce will be poised to lead the global community.

FUTURE TRENDS

The future hopefully holds an opportunity for preservice teachers to break the mold of the past. The role of a guide and a facilitator is a noble one. Preservice teachers need to receive their instruction in the same facilitative role as they are expected to model to their students. The faculty at preservice institutions needs to infuse the technology into the curriculum so that increased levels of communication and collaboration are commonplace. Department chairs and school deans need to continue the excellent level of support that some universities already receive. Preservice teachers need the opportunity to practice the infused technology and to eventually change the landscape to create a different picture of the use of that technology. After all, the technology will rapidly change over the next 40 years. Each practicing teacher must not only be able to adapt to any new changes, but hopefully, as leading teachers, they will champion the change. They should not change just for the sake of change but to be leading teachers of change, because it helps learners synthesize new information, collaborate with their peers, and communicate in a more efficient way.

CONCLUSION

In this chapter, the features of a leading teacher program that has foundations in the national and international standards for instructional technology were explored. A strong commitment from the department chair, the dean of the school of education, and upper administration provided the equipment, support, and expectations to transform the school into a home of the nation's leading teachers. The preservice teacher enters the program with technology skills to communicate and complete assignments and quickly acquires and increases the skill set in information technology so that he or she can obtain sufficient data, synthesize that data into useful information, create interactive visual presentations, and create exciting virtual tours (Tomei, 2001). Finally, the leading teacher must be aware of the rapid advancements and changes in technology and how those changes affect the learning process. The teacher must know how to adapt to the changes and to infuse the new technology into the curriculum of the future.

REFERENCES

Black, M. (1995). Technology integration into secondary experiential/internship education professional development curriculum. Unpublished manuscript, Nova Southeastern University, FL.

Boston, J., Chan, A., & Mukai, G. (1991, January/February). Classroom technology and its global connections. *Media and Methods, 18*, 48–49, 54.

Clark, K. D. (Winter, 2000). Urban middle school teachers' use of instructional technology. *Journal of Research on Computing in Education, 33*, 2, 178–195.

Cohen, M. and Brunner, C. (2000). Integrating technology into teacher education: A review of Bank Street's project EXPERT. *ERIC Clearinghouse on Teaching and Teacher Education*, Washington, DC. Retrieved September 12, 2001 from: http://www.ericsp.org/pages/digests/BankStreet.htm.

Cooper, P. A. & Hirtle, J. S. (1999, March). A constructivist approach to technology literacy for preservice teachers. Unpublished manuscript, Sam Houston State University, TX.

Dugger, W. E. Jr. (2002, March). Standard for technological literacy. *Tech Directions, 61*, 8, 27–31.

Easton, G. & Easton, A. (2002). Assessing computer literacy: Are our students getting more proficient? *Issues and Trends of Information Technology Management in Contemporary Organizations*. In *Proceedings of the 2002 International Resource Management Association Conference* (pp. 952–953). Hershey, PA: Idea Group Publishing.

Erate. (2001). Universal Service Administration. Retrieved September 2, 2001 from http://www.universalservicie.org.

Ertmer, P. A., Gopalakrishnan, S., & Ross, E. M. (Summer, 2001). Technology-using teachers. *Journal of Research on Computing in Education. 33*, 5. Retrieved September 21, 2001 from the World Wide Web: http://www.iste.org/jrte/33/5/ertmer.html.

Fortier, J. D. et al. (1998). Wisconsin's model academic standards. Wisconsin Department of Public Instruction.

International Society for Technology in Education. (2001). Retrieved August 1, 2001 from the World Wide Web: http://www.iste.org.

Johnson, D. G. (1998, December 15). Effectively integrating the World Wide Web and computer software technology into diverse classrooms. Unpublished manuscript, Wright State University, Ohio.

Johnson, R. T. (1993). Context for research on technology and teacher education. *Approaches to Research on Teacher Education and Technology*. Charlottesville, VA: Society for Technology and Teacher Education.

Leading Teacher Program Handbook. (2001). Pittsburgh, PA: Duquesne University.

Link-to-Learn. (2001). Retrieved September 2, 2001 from the World Wide Web: http://www.l2l.org.

McCade, J. M. (2001, October). Technology education and computer literacy. *The Technology Teacher, 61*, 2, 9–13. Retrieved from Proquest on July 13, 2002.

McCoy, R. W. (2001, Fall). Computer competencies for the 21st century information systems educator. *Information Technology, Learning, and Performance Journal, 19*, 2, 21–35.

National Council for the Accreditation of Teacher Education. (2001). Retrieved September 2, 2001 from the World Wide Web: http://www.ncate.org.

Newberry, P. B. (2001, September). Technology education in the U.S.: A status report. *The Technology Teacher. 61*, 1, 8–12. Retrieved from Proquest on July 13, 2002.

Project goals: Reshaping access to electronic communication. (2001). Retrieved from the World Wide Web: http://www.technology.pitt.edu/projects/kiosks/01goals.html.

Riley, R. W. (1996, June). Getting America's students ready for the 21st century: Meeting the technology literacy challenge. *A report to the Nation on technology and education.* Department of Education, Washington, DC.

Robinson, L. H. & Thoms, K. J. (2001, Fall). A longitudinal study of college student computer knowledge. *Journal of Computer Information Systems, 9–12.*

Roman, H. T. (2001, October). Why the business world likes technology education. *The Technology Teacher, 61,* 2, 29–30. Retrieved July 13, 2002 from Proquest.

Sandham, J. L. (2001, May 10). Across the nation. *Education Week, 20,* 35, 67–104.

Stanford, B. (2001, November) National educational technology standards for students. *The Science Teacher, 68,* 8, 86–88. Retrieved March 14, 2002 from Proquest.

State of the Fund. (1999). The Public School Employees' Retirement System of Pennsylvania. Retrieved September 15, 2001 from the World Wide Web: http://www.psers.state.pa.us/publications/newsletters/updates/sof99.htm.

State of the Fund. (2001). The Public School Employees' Retirement System of Pennsylvania. Retrieved September 15, 2001 from the World Wide Web: http://www.psers.state.pa.us/publications/newsletters/updates/sof01.htm.

Teale, W. H. (2002, April). The CTELL project: New ways technology can help educate tomorrow's reading teachers. *The Reading Teacher, 55,* 7, 654–659. Retrieved from Proquest on July 13, 2002.

Tomei, L. A. (2001). *Teaching Digitally: A Guide for Integrating Technology into the Classroom.* Norwood, MA: Christopher-Gordon Publishers, Inc.

Tomei, L. A. (2001). Unpublished class notes. Pittsburgh, PA: Duquesne University.

Topp, N. W., Mortenson, R., & Grandgenett, N. (1995). Building a technology-using faculty to facilitate technology-using teachers. *Journal of Computing in Teacher Education, 11,* 3, 11–14. Retrieved from Proquest on July 13, 2002.

Vannatta, R. A. & Beyerback, B. (2000, Winter). Facilitating a constructivist vision of technology integration among education faculty and preservice teachers. *Journal of Research on Computing in Education, 33,* 2, 132–148.

Willis, E. M. (2001, September). Technology in secondary teacher education. *T.H.E. Journal, 29,* 2, 54–59. Retrieved from Proquest on July 13, 2002.

Wojnar, L. C. (2001). *Distance Learning Course Design: A Comprehensive Program of Instruction for Online Educators.* Boston, MA: McGraw-Hill Publishing, Inc.

Wright, M. D. (2002, March). ITEA president's message: Technology education and ITEA in the future. *The Technology Teacher, 61,* 33–36. Retrieved from Proquest on July 13, 2002.

Chapter XX

Assessing Computer Literacy: A Comparison of Self-Assessment and Actual Skills

George Easton
San Diego State University, USA

Annette Easton
San Diego State University, USA

ABSTRACT

The ubiquity of the Internet in our daily lives and the pervasiveness of computer technology in K–12 education today suggest that incoming college students should be better prepared to use computer technology than their predecessors. This chapter presents the results of a study to determine the incoming computing skills levels of business students. The study also measured the difference between the students' self-assessment of these computer skills and an actual assessment of their computer skills. In discovering what level of computer literacy our students actually have, and pinpointing areas where students lack proficiency, we can look to develop curriculum to address the weaknesses. Our goal would be to look at developing a curriculum model that provides flexibility in tailoring content to accommodate the evolving literacy of students, ultimately providing a richer educational experience for our students.

INTRODUCTION

With the increasing prevalence of computers and computer usage throughout society, one might hypothesize that there would be an increase in overall computer literacy among business students. Trends in education show that students are being exposed to, and using, business application software at relatively early ages. Students in primary school, for example, are using PowerPoint® to make class presentations and are using word processing to generate and edit their homework. Middle school students create worksheets and charts in Excel®. The most pervasive early exposure computer experiences seem to be coming from the Internet.

Given their exposure and experience with computers at a relatively early age, many students arrive at college feeling sufficiently computer literate. Olsen (2000) reported that in Fall 2000, colleges saw at least half of their freshmen arrive with their own computers. Olsen (2000) also noted that these students are proficient at using Windows®, word-processing software, the Internet, and electronic mail. However, she also reported that students had a lower proficiency with spreadsheets, databases, and presentation software. Interestingly, although students feel sufficiently computer literate, what many faculty members discover is that most students' self-perceptions of their computer competency, at least currently, do not match the skill sets often expected in their college study program or the skills sets expected in the business world.

Most business schools provide computer literacy skills via their "Principles of Information Systems" or "Introduction to Computers" class. This class usually serves two main purposes: to teach students fundamentals of information technology, i.e., computer concepts; and to teach students various business-oriented software applications. This course is typically offered at the freshman/sophomore level and is usually required of all business majors.

This chapter reports on a study designed to assess university business students' actual computer skills and to measure the difference between the students' self-assessment of these computer skills and an actual assessment of their computer skills. The measure of actual computer competency is thought to be particularly valuable as a tool to help business schools and MIS departments make informed information systems curriculum decisions and to provide a mechanism for tracking the evolving computer skills of beginning business students. Comparisons between self-perceptions and actual skills will be helpful in determining strategies for educating and motivating students whose self-perceptions are higher than their actual skills.

BACKGROUND

Over time, the definition of computer literacy has evolved from simply a basic understanding of terminology, to understanding how to write computer programs, to understanding how to use specific computer applications. Certainly, defining a specific level of computer literacy is dependent on the specific context of the situation in which it is applied. Van Vliet, Kletke, and Chakraborty (1994) conducted a study to determine if self-appraisal tests are a valid predictor of computer literacy. They defined computer literacy as "the ability to use microcomputers confidently for obtaining needed information, solving specific problems, and performing data-processing tasks. This includes a fundamental understanding of the operation of microcomputers in general, as well as the use of several types of applications software packages." What they reported was that self-appraisal tests were more lenient indicators of a person's computer proficiency than were objective tests. In addition, they concluded that self-leniency decreased as computer expertise increased.

Our primary research goal was exploratory: we wanted to focus on assessing computer literacy to determine an appropriate level and the optimum content of an information technology education program for a typical business student. Rockart and Flannery (1983) and Mackay and Elam (1992) demonstrated that training is more likely to be effective when differentiated among different levels of user types. Most professors have taught classes that have students with a broad range of skills. These wide proficiency levels make it difficult, if not impossible, to effectively reach all of the students. Experienced students are bored with the introductory-level material, while novice students are overwhelmed with the more advanced content. In the end, most are not satisfied with the resulting experience. If we can understand what levels of proficiency exist within our classes, we may increase the opportunity to deliver the most appropriate educational experience.

Further impetus for this study can be found in reviewing the guidelines set forth by the Association to Advance Collegiate Schools of Business (AACSB), the accrediting body for Schools of Business. AACSB (1991) stated the importance of having students understand and apply concepts of management information systems, including computer applications. Accreditation standards mandate that Colleges of Business assess not only how and where these skills are addressed across the curriculum but also the effectiveness of the curriculum. Evaluating curriculum design and student learning can help business schools make progress on addressing AACSB accreditation. Born and Cummings (1994) suggested that assessment of student's computer experience, attitudes, and skills should allow for feedback to faculty in designing curriculum. Further, they proposed a model in which schools would assess students at several points in their school career to more fully determine the effectiveness of the entire curriculum. This is important in demonstrating that technology skills are being learned at various points in the curriculum.

Given the specific purposes of this study, we broadened Van Vliet, Kletke, and Chakraborty's (1994) definition of computer literacy to include a basic understanding of information technology concepts. The revised definition of computer literacy reads: The ability to use microcomputers confidently for obtaining needed information, solving specific problems, and performing data-processing tasks. This includes a fundamental understanding of *information technology concepts*, the operation of microcomputers in general, as well as the use of several types of applications software packages. We have operationalized this new definition of computer literacy in the self-assessment and objective assessment tests devised for this study.

RESEARCH DESIGN

The research was designed to help us understand the level of students' proficiency within the introductory computer class and how students' self-perceptions of their computer skills match their actual computer proficiency. The actual results from the objective-appraisal scores are being used to inform us of the true levels of computer literacy. Additionally, we investigated the specific results related to the different areas of competency studied. This information provides detailed measures of literacy related to specific competency skills.

Approximately 600 students in the Principles of Information Systems course, our introductory computer course required of all undergraduate business students, participated in this study as a required assignment. During the first two weeks of the semester, the participants completed two phases of the research study. Phase I, conducted outside of the research facility, was actually a two-part exercise. The first part involved a Web-based questionnaire that was used to gather basic demographic data from each participant. Additionally, the questionnaire asked the students for a *general* self-assessment of their proficiency (expert, advanced, average, some skill, or beginner) regarding computer concepts, email, WWW, word processing, spreadsheets, database packages, and presentation packages. The second part of Phase I, also a Web-based questionnaire, asked the students to provide a *detailed* self-assessment of their technology proficiency. The self-assessment asked the students to rate their ability using a five-point scale (not at all, not very well, sometimes, most of the time, all of the time) for 29 computer concept questions, 10 Windows Operating System questions, 19 Excel questions, 11 Access questions, and nine PowerPoint questions. The questions were chosen to cover basic skills we would expect the students to achieve in our traditional introductory computer course. A representative sample of the Phase I, Part 2 questions is shown below.

- **Operating and File Management Tasks** (10 questions in total):
  - I am able to display the contents of the computer's hard drive.
- **Access** (11 questions in total):
  - I am able to delete records from a table.
- **Excel** (19 questions in total):
  - I am able to edit a formula to use absolute references.
- **PowerPoint** (9 questions in total):
  - I am able to apply a transition to a slide show.
- **Computer Concepts** (29 multiple choice questions in total):
  - I am able to identify the differences between application software and system software.
  - I am able to explain phases of the Systems Development Life Cycle.

The five areas we chose for more detailed self-assessment in Phase I, Part 2 were based on the design of our current course. We did not ask any detailed questions about word processing in Phase I, Part 2 because of the ubiquity of the application in education today. We imagine that word processing would be one application in which students would self-assess their ability at a relatively high level.

Phase II, conducted in a university research lab, was an actual assessment of the skills that were described in Phase I, Part 2. A Web-based, multiple choice exam was used to assess the students' actual knowledge regarding the computer concepts material. This objective test included an "I don't know" choice for each question in an attempt to avoid having the students guess the answer. SimNet XPert, McGraw-Hill's assessment software for Microsoft Office XP, was used to assess their Windows, Excel, Access, and PowerPoint skills. The assessment software tasks, as well as the concepts questions, mapped directly to the self-assessment questions asked in Phase I, Part 2 of the study. For example, the students had an Access activity to perform that asked them to delete records from a table.

Test administrators used a common script and were trained on the testing procedures to avoid biasing the student answers. Students had a maximum of 90 minutes to complete

Phase II of the study. SimNet realistically simulates the Microsoft Office XP environment and allowed us the ability to track each student's progress through this phase of the study. Each skills area (spreadsheets, etc.) was set up as a separate testing unit. Students were not given any feedback regarding individual test answers or their overall success with the exercise. Students worked at their own speed. When they completed one testing unit, they were free to start the next unit. Both phases of the study were regarded as one of the regular course assignments, which provided ample incentive for student participation.

RESULTS
Student Profiles and Technology Background

Of the 600+ students who began the study, 492 sufficiently completed all of the exercises, so their responses could be included in the analysis. Of this group, 250 (50.8%) were female, and 242 (49.2%) were male. The average age of the participants was 20.2 years; the range of ages was 18 to 48 years. Of the students, 69.9% were freshmen and sophomores. Of the students, 27.9% were from a major other than business. This is somewhat surprising, as

Table 1. Demographics

	count	%
Year in School		
Freshman	161	32.7%
Sophomore	183	37.2%
Junior	114	23.2%
Senior	30	6.1%
Grad Student	4	0.8%
Total	492	100.0%
Ethnicity		
Other	51	10.4%
Asian	69	14.0%
White	288	58.5%
Pacific Islander	17	3.5%
Hispanic	58	11.8%
African American	9	1.8%
Total	492	100.0%
Major/Intended Major		
Accounting	43	8.7%
Finance	51	10.4%
Information & Decision Systems	49	10.0%
International Business	44	8.9%
Management	84	17.1%
Marketing	84	17.1%
Other-business	0	0.0%
Other	111	22.6%
Public Administration	26	5.3%
Total	492	100.0%

the focus of the course is designed primarily as a prebusiness course. Table 1 presents a detailed breakdown of the demographic data.

The students were asked several questions that provided a technology profile of the students enrolled in our introductory computer course: 91.5% of the students owned a computer; 92.1% of the students reported a version of Windows as their primary operating system; and 52.7% of the students reported being on the Internet five or more hours per week. Further, not counting time spent on the Internet, 41.1% of the students reported working on the computer five or more hours per week. Many students, 64.7%, had high-speed access to the Internet (cable modem, DSL, or high-speed access in the dorm via the campus network). Table 2 shows some of the detailed technology demographics.

Table 2. Technology demographics

	Count	%
Internet Access		
Cable Modem	138	28.0%
Dialup	146	29.7%
Do not know	9	1.8%
DSL	44	8.9%
Not Applicable	2	0.4%
Other	5	1.0%
SDSU	137	27.8%
Work	11	2.2%
Total	492	100.0%
Hours/week on Internet		
None	6	1.2%
1-2	95	19.3%
2-4	132	26.8%
5-8	110	22.4%
8-12	75	15.2%
12-16	26	5.3%
16-20	20	4.1%
20-25	11	2.2%
>25	17	3.5%
Total	492	100.0%
Hours/week on Computer (not Internet)		
none	21	4.3%
1-2	127	25.8%
2-4	142	28.9%
5-8	75	15.2%
8-12	50	10.2%
12-16	24	4.9%
16-20	19	3.9%
20-25	12	2.4%
>25	22	4.5%
Total	492	100.0%

Self-Assessment Results

The results of Phase I, Part 2, the self-assessment survey, are shown in Tables 3 through 7. Of all of the software programs evaluated, students considered the Windows operating system as that which they best knew. Only 1.6% of the students rated their Windows skills as none (Not at all) or very little (Not very well). There was a noticeable drop between their confidence with Windows and all other software applications used in the study. Excel was the next software program that the students felt they had the most ability using. Only 39.6% of the students indicated they had no (Not at all) or very little (Not very well) confidence using Excel. Approximately half of the students (49.6%) rated their PowerPoint capabilities as "Not at all" or "Not very well." And, 51.7% of the students rated their computer concepts ability as "Not at all" or "Not very well." Access was the product they felt they knew least, with 63.2% selecting the options "Not at all" or "Not very well" when asked to assess their relational database capabilities.

Table 3. Self-assessment score — Computer Concepts

Concepts		Pre-Test Self-assessment		
Score		Rating	count	%
Average	2.1	All of the time	19	3.9%
Standard Deviation	0.9	Most of the time	57	11.6%
Minimum	1.0	Sometimes	162	32.9%
Maximum	5.0	Not very well	234	47.6%
		Not at all	20	4.1%
		Total	492	100.0%

Table 4. Self-assessment score — Excel

Excel		Pre-Test Self-assessment		
Score		Rating	count	%
Average	2.6	All of the time	86	17.5%
Standard Deviation	1.3	Most of the time	92	18.7%
Minimum	1.0	Sometimes	119	24.2%
Maximum	5.0	Not very well	128	26.0%
		Not at all	67	13.6%
		Total	492	100.0%

Table 5. Self-assessment score — Access

Access		Pre-Test Self-assessment		
Score		Rating	count	%
Average	1.9	All of the time	29	5.9%
Standard Deviation	1.1	Most of the time	54	11.0%
Minimum	1.0	Sometimes	98	19.9%
Maximum	5.0	Not very well	138	28.0%
		Not at all	173	35.2%
		Total	492	100.0%

Table 6. Self-assessment score — PowerPoint

PowerPoint		Pre-Test Self-assessment		
Score		Rating	count	%
Average	2.6	All of the time	128	26.0%
Standard Deviation	1.5	Most of the time	54	11.0%
Minimum	1.0	Sometimes	66	13.4%
Maximum	5.0	Not very well	100	20.3%
		Not at all	144	29.3%
		Total	492	100.0%

Table 7. Self-assessment score — Windows

Windows		Pre-Test Self-assessment		
Score		Rating	count	%
Average	4.3	All of the time	347	70.5%
Standard Deviation	0.8	Most of the time	109	22.2%
Minimum	1.3	Sometimes	28	5.7%
Maximum	5.0	Not very well	8	1.6%
		Not at all	0	0.0%
		Total	492	100.0%

Actual Computer Skills Results

The results of Phase II of the study, the Actual Skills Assessment, are shown in Tables 8 through 12. Each participant was evaluated using a commercial assessment tool, McGraw-Hill's SimNet XPert, for their actual ability using Excel, Access, PowerPoint, and Windows. The students' computer concepts competencies were assessed using a representative sample of multiple-choice questions used in the college's introductory computer course. The following ratings were assigned to each student based on the percentage of correct answers they received for each of the five areas: Beginner (0 to 30%), Some Skill (>30 to 65%), Intermediate (>65 to 80%), Advanced (>80 to 90%), Expert (>90%). These ranges were based on the nature of the specific skills assessed.

The results of the students' test of computer concepts were surprisingly low with 95.3% of all students testing at the "Beginner" and "Some Skill" levels. This ran contrary to our belief that students entering the business school today are fairly knowledgeable regarding computer concepts. Interestingly, only 51.7% of the students rated their self-assessment of their computer concepts skills at no (Not at all) or little (Not very well) knowledge in this area, indicating that 43.6% of the students rated themselves more skilled than they actually demonstrated on the exam.

The results of the actual test of the students' Excel skills yielded 84.9% at the "Beginner" or the "Some Skill" categories. In their self-assessment of Excel skills, only 39.6% of the students estimated their Excel skills to be at the lowest levels (Not at all or Not very well) relative to the Excel tasks they were later asked to perform on the actual skills test. Again, there was a large gap between the students' perceptions of their skills and the students' demonstrated actual skills.

The results of the actual test of the students' Access skills yielded 82.1% at the "Beginner" or the "Some Skill" categories. In their self-assessment of Access skills, 63.2% of the students estimated their Access skills to be at the lowest levels (Not at all or Not very well) relative to the Access tasks they later attempted on the actual skills test. While still lower than their actual skill results, the students' perception of their Access database skills shows movement in the direction of an accurate prediction.

Table 8. Actual skills score — Computer Concepts

Concepts		Pre-Test Actual Skills		
Score		Rating	count	%
Average	39.1%	Expert	0	0.0%
Standard Deviation	13.7%	Advanced	0	0.0%
Minimum	6.9%	Intermediate	23	4.7%
Maximum	79.3%	Some Skill	347	70.5%
		Beginner	122	24.8%
		Count	492	100.0%

Table 9. Actual skills score — Excel

Excel		Pre-Test Actual Skills		
Score		**Rating**	**Count**	**%**
Average	47.5%	Expert	2	0.4%
Standard Deviation	16.7%	Advanced	8	1.6%
Minimum	5.3%	Intermediate	64	13.0%
Maximum	94.7%	Some Skill	353	71.7%
		Beginner	65	13.2%
		Count	492	100.0%

Table 10. Actual skills score — Access

Access		Pre-Test Actual Skills		
Score		**Rating**	**Count**	**%**
Average	47.3%	Expert	7	1.4%
Standard Deviation	20.5%	Advanced	28	5.7%
Minimum	0.0%	Intermediate	53	10.8%
Maximum	100.0%	Some Skill	292	59.3%
		Beginner	112	22.8%
		Count	492	100.0%

Table 11. Actual skills score — PowerPoint

PowerPoint		Pre-Test Actual Skills		
Score		**Rating**	**Count**	**%**
Average	43.9%	Expert	3	0.6%
Standard Deviation	22.2%	Advanced	19	3.9%
Minimum	0.0%	Intermediate	85	17.3%
Maximum	100.0%	Some Skill	264	53.7%
		Beginner	121	24.6%
		Count	492	100.0%

Table 12. Actual skills score — Windows

Windows		Pre-Test Actual Skills		
Score		Rating	Count	%
Average	88.8%	Expert	338	68.7%
Standard Deviation	12.3%	Advanced	91	18.5%
Minimum	30.0%	Intermediate	37	7.5%
Maximum	100.0%	Some Skill	26	5.3%
		Beginner	0	0.0%
		Count	492	100.0%

The results of the actual test of the students' PowerPoint skills yielded 78.3% of the students at the "Beginner" or "Some Skill" categories. In their self-assessment of PowerPoint skills, 49.6% of the students estimated their PowerPoint skills to be at the lowest levels (Not at all or Not very well) relative to the PowerPoint tasks they later attempted on the actual skills test.

The skill area in which the participants tested highest was the operating systems area, specifically the Windows operating system. Only 5.3% tested at the "Some Skill" level, with no students testing at the "Beginner" level. This compares favorably to the students' self-assessment of their operating system skills, where only 1.6% said they had no (Not at all) or little (Not very well) operating system skills. This result suggests that an operating system topic in the introductory computer course may soon become a relatively small skills component of the course.

Self-Assessment Compared to Actual Skills

The preceding section represented an *aggregate* analysis of the students' self-assessed computer skills and their actual computer skills. We thought it would also be interesting to look at individual student's self-assessment compared to their actual assessment for each of the five areas to determine how accurate they were in assessing their actual skill level. Tables 13 through 17 below reflect the results for each of the five skill areas (concepts, spreadsheets, etc.) that compare each student's self-assessed ability for completing the topic tasks (All of the time, Most of the time, Sometimes, Not very well, Not at all) to a five-point rating of their actual skill (Expert, Advanced, Intermediate, Some Skill, and Beginner). In terms of mapping the self-assessment rating to the actual skills rating, the following pairings were used:

- All of the time ➔ Expert
- Most of the time ➔ Advanced
- Sometimes ➔ Intermediate
- Not very well ➔ Some skill
- Not at all ➔ Beginner

To perform the analysis, the self-assessed and actual skill ratings were coded between 1 and 5. Five was assigned to the ratings of "All of the time" and "Expert," and 1 was assigned to "Not at all" and "Beginner." The actual skill code was then subtracted from the self-assessment code to determine an "Assessment Index," i.e., the discrepancy of the self-assessment of one's skills relative to the actual assessment of their skills. The Assessment Index range is from -4 to +4. A negative number indicates that the self-assessment rating was lower than the actual skill demonstrated. A positive number indicates that the self-assessment rating was higher than the actual skill demonstrated. An Assessment Index of zero indicates that the student accurately self-assessed their actual skill level. The further the Assessment Index value is from zero (in either a negative or a positive direction), the larger the discrepancy between a student's self-assessment and the actual assessment of their skill.

Tables 13 through 17 below were used to ascertain the percentages of students whose self-assessments were at least two skill categories, higher or lower, from the actual assessments of their computer skills. These students may be the most likely in need of additional motivation or guidance, given the large discrepancy in their perceptions version actual scores. The results of comparing the self-assessment scores to the actual skills scores are shown in Tables 13 through 17.

The results of the Assessment Index analysis of Computer Concepts showed that 19.3% of the students rated themselves at least two categories higher than their actual skill. And, 34.6% of the students accurately assessed their skill, as shown by the Assessment Index of 0.

For Excel, 32.9% of the students rated themselves at least two categories higher than their actual skill. Excel was the application that had the second highest number of students with an inflated self-perception; 27% of the students accurately assessed their skill level.

Table 13. Self-assessment versus actual skills – Concepts

Concepts		Self-assessment versus Actual Skill		
Score		Assessment Index	Count	%
Average	0.8	4	1	0.2%
Standard Deviation	0.8	3	13	2.6%
Minimum	-1.0	2	81	16.5%
Maximum	4.0	1	217	44.1%
		0	170	34.6%
		-1	10	2.0%
		-2	0	0.0%
		-3	0	0.0%
		-4	0	0.0%
		Count	492	100.0%

Table 14. Self-assessment versus actual skills — Excel

Excel		Self-assessment versus Actual Skill		
Score		Assessment Index	count	%
Average	1.0	4	4	0.8%
Standard Deviation	1.2	3	57	11.6%
Minimum	-2.0	2	101	20.5%
Maximum	4.0	1	143	29.1%
		0	133	27.0%
		-1	49	10.0%
		-2	5	1.0%
		-3	0	0.0%
		-4	0	0.0%
		Count	492	100.0%

Table 15. Self-assessment versus actual skills — Access

Access		Self-assessment versus Actual Skill		
Score		Assessment Index	count	%
Average	0.2	4	5	1.0%
Standard Deviation	1.3	3	21	4.3%
Minimum	-3.0	2	49	10.0%
Maximum	4.0	1	113	23.0%
		0	151	30.7%
		-1	123	25.0%
		-2	21	4.3%
		-3	9	1.8%
		-4	0	0.0%
		Count	492	100.0%

Table 16. Self-assessment versus actual skills — PowerPoint

PowerPoint		Self-assessment versus Actual Skill		
Score		Assessment Index	count	%
Average	0.8	4	7	1.4%
Standard Deviation	1.5	3	72	14.6%
Minimum	-3.0	2	93	18.9%
Maximum	4.0	1	91	18.5%
		0	126	25.6%
		-1	89	18.1%
		-2	13	2.6%
		-3	1	0.2%
		-4	0	0.0%
		Count	492	100.0%

Table 17. Self-assessment versus actual skills – Windows

Windows		Self-assessment versus Actual Skill		
Score		Assessment Index	count	%
Average	0.1	4	0	0.0%
Standard Deviation	0.9	3	9	1.8%
Minimum	-3.0	2	25	5.1%
Maximum	3.0	1	68	13.8%
		0	312	63.4%
		-1	66	13.4%
		-2	11	2.2%
		-3	1	0.2%
		-4	0	0.0%
		Count	492	100.0%

It was found that 15.3% of the students rated their Access capabilities at least two skill categories higher than they actually demonstrated. Interestingly, 6.1% of the students, the largest for any application, underrated their abilities in Access by two categories or more. And, 30.7% of the students accurately assessed their skill level.

The students self-perceptions were most inflated for PowerPoint; 34.9% of the students rated their capabilities at least two categories higher than their actual skill. Additionally, only 25.6% of the students, the lowest for any of the areas, accurately assessed their skill.

Students were most accurate in assessing their Windows capabilities. Only 6.9% of the students rated their capabilities two or more levels higher than their actual skills. Additionally, 63.4% had an Assessment Index of 0, indicating that they accurately assessed their skill level.

Overall Self-Assessment

In Phase I, Part 1, the students were asked several general questions about their overall proficiency with computers and specific applications. Table 18 presents the results of those questions. It appears that our students' self-assessments of their overall computing proficiency (68.2% at Expert, Advanced, or Intermediate) are heavily influenced by their email (82.1% at Expert, Advanced, or Intermediate), WWW (79.1% at Expert, Advanced, or Intermediate), and word processing (83.1% at Expert, Advanced, or Intermediate) ratings.

Overall Perceptions Versus Reality

Table 19 reflects the three dimensions of our study (the students' self-assessment of their overall proficiency; the students' more detailed self-assessment for specific basic skills; and the students' actual assessment results) for the three primary software applications we cover in our introductory course. Table 19 summarizes the percentage of students who either rated (self-assessment) or tested (actual performance) in the top three skill categories (Expert, Advanced, or Intermediate).

Table 18. Overall self-assessment ratings

Skill Assessed	Self-assessment Proficiency Rating				
	Exp.	Adv.	Int.	Some	Beg.
Overall Computing Proficiency	2.2%	20.7%	45.3%	25.0%	6.7%
E-mail Proficiency	10.6%	31.1%	40.4%	13.6%	4.3%
WWW Proficiency	6.7%	30.3%	42.1%	15.7%	5.3%
Word Processing Proficiency	5.3%	36.2%	41.7%	14%	2.8%
Spreadsheet Proficiency	.6%	6.5%	23%	29.9%	40%
Database Proficiency	.4%	2.2%	12%	22.6%	62.8%
Presentation Software Proficiency	1.4%	7.7%	14.8%	19.9%	56.1%

Table 19. Research summary

	Overall Assessment *(Phase I, Part 1)*	Detailed Assessment *(Phase I, Part 2)*	Actual Skills *(Phase II)*
Excel	30.1%	60.4%	15%
Access	14.6%	36.8%	17.9%
PowerPoint	23.9%	50.4%	21.8%

For all of the applications, the students rated their capabilities to perform the specific tasks significantly higher than they rated their overall skill levels. The actual skill performance was more closely aligned with their overall assessment for Access and PowerPoint but was 15% less for Excel. This situation presents an interesting dilemma in developing teaching approaches and designing curriculum. When students already think they know the material, they may become disengaged from the course. This presents a challenge for instructors to motivate the students, as well as to effectively explain to the students that they really do not know the concepts or skills.

FUTURE TRENDS

Certainly, one of the current issues in IT education is the need to gain a better understanding of the incoming skills of our students. Having a better understanding of what IT skills students bring to class facilitates the move from teacher-centered instruction to student-centered instruction. This movement should accommodate our student's diverse learning styles, prior experience, and knowledge. We may, for example, want to look at CD-based learning for computer application skills. Jeffries (2001) found significant differences in cognitive gains and satisfaction for nursing students using a CD-ROM compared to traditional lectures for learning oral medication administration. There are many CD-based products available for teaching basic computer skills. Further investigation into their usefulness, or the usefulness of other teaching approaches, could be beneficial.

Once we have a better understanding of the incoming skills of our students, we can begin to look at the effectiveness of the learning that takes place in our course. We have initiated an effort to measure our students' learning. At the end of the semester, students participated in a second set of self-assessment and actual-assessment exercises. This data may be useful to help us determine the extent of learning that occurred during the semester. It may also help identify the gaps that exist in our curriculum. Further, analyzing our students' self-perceptions at the end of the course will help to identify if students become more realistic and accurate in predicting their actual skill levels related to information technology. Specifically, we plan on reviewing the change between the pretest Assessment Index and the posttest Assessment Index. Additionally, we would like to investigate student performance for each of the detailed skills that comprised the major skills areas. This should help us focus the curriculum to avoid covering skills that students already know, and should allow for more time on difficult skills, or skills currently not covered due to time constraints.

We also anticipate conducting a longitudinal study of students' computer literacy and to more fully explore the factors that influence a student's self-assessment of their computing skills.

CONCLUSION

The objective of this research effort was to determine the incoming computing skills levels of business students. We found that incoming students have the most skill with Windows operating systems tasks; 94.7% of them performed at the Expert, Advanced, or Intermediate levels. There was a marked drop between this skill area and all other areas tested. No other area had greater than 21.8% (PowerPoint) of the students performing at the Expert, Advanced, or Intermediate levels. The students demonstrated the least skill in the computer concepts area; only 4.7% had an incoming skill level at the Expert, Advanced, or Intermediate levels. By discovering what level of computer literacy our students actually have, and pinpointing areas where students lack proficiency, we feel we are now in a better position to develop curriculum to address the weaknesses.

The aspect of the research that measured the difference between students' self-assessed computer skills and their actual computer skills should help us to develop an effective and efficient solution for managing the ever-evolving technology that permeates most, if not all, of the courses in the business curriculum. In this study, there was a consistent, inflated, self-perception of computer literacy across all five of the topic areas. Students were most accurate in self-assessing their Windows capabilities; only 6.9% of the students rated their skill levels at two or more levels higher than they actually demonstrated. The largest discrepancies between the self-assessments and actual tests occurred with PowerPoint and Excel, with 34.9% and 32.9%, respectively, rating themselves two or more levels higher than the skills they demonstrated.

By discovering the differences between our students' self-perceptions and actual skills, we can focus efforts on strategies for educating and motivating students whose self-perceptions are higher than their actual skills. Overall, our goal is to use the results of the actual computing skills, coupled with the self-perception data, to develop a curriculum model that provides flexibility in tailoring course content to accommodate the evolving computer literacy of students and ultimately providing a richer educational experience for our students.

REFERENCES

Association to Advance Collegiate Schools of Business (AACSB). (1991). *Achieving quality and continuous improvement through self-evaluation and peer review: Standards for Accreditation, Business Administration and Accounting.* Adopted 1991; Revised May, 2000.

Born, R. G. & Cummings, C. W. (1994). An assessment model for computer experience, skills, and attitudes of undergraduate business students. *The Journal of Computer Information Systems, 35,* 1, 41–53.

Jeffries, P. R. (2001). Computer versus lecture: A comparison of two methods of teaching oral medication administration in a nursing skills laboratory. *Journal of Nursing Education, 40,* 7, 323–329.

Mackay, J. M., & Elam, J. J. (1992). A comparative study of how experts and novices use a decision aid to solve problems in complex knowledge domains. *Information Systems Research, 3,* 2, 150–172.

Olsen, F. (2000). Campus newcomers arrive with more skill, better gear. *The Chronicle of Higher Education, 47,* 10, A39–A43.

Rockart, J. F., & Flannery, L. S. (1983). The management of end user computing. *Communications of the ACM, 26,* 10, 776–784.

Van Vliet, P., Kletke, M., and Chakraborty, G. (1994). The measurement of computer literacy: A comparison of self-appraisal and objective tests. *International Journal of Human-Computer Studies, 40,* 1, 835–857.

Chapter XXI

Using Modulization Approach to Design Instructional Systems for Computer Literacy Courses

Kuan C. Chen
Purdue University, Calumet, USA

ABSTRACT

In this chapter, the guiding principles of the modularization content arrangement that some instructors use is offered. Eight planning steps in module instructional design are summarized. A general strategy of these principles and applications in a case study is discussed in this chapter as well. A new modularization approach in instructional design, defining the course goals and arranging the course content, are two important issues for instructors. The author hopes the process of the module instructional design through essential knowledge and skills in the computer literacy course development will not only be a valuable synthesizing experience for instructors, but also the modularization approach may be preferable to students with a variety of backgrounds.

INTRODUCTION

We are in the midst of a technological revolution that is changing our way of life. The cornerstone of this revolution, the computer, is transforming the way we communicate, do business, and learn (Long & Long, 1990). In the mainframe and minicomputer era, computing was used for transaction processing and related business applications. Given their size and cost, computers were nearly always kept locked away in safe, separate computer facilities. Only computer professionals dared enter these secured premises. Computer usages and learning were limited in certain environments. Computers today are found in millions of homes and just about in every office. As a matter of fact, most office workers have a computer connected to a local area network and the Internet. Eventually, all of us will have at least one computer, and we will use it every day in our work and leisure. Thus, learning computer usages is not an expensive and special discipline. There are a number of significant changes in learning about computers today, such as learning styles and age. Many learners and users start at an early age to use computers. Some elementary schools provide computer labs for pupils to gain basic computer skills. Most high schools also provide computer application courses for students, ranging from typing classes to basic software development. Some students even start to use computers in childhood by using game software for fun. During the growing process, they learn how to use the system, how to use different inputs and outputs, how to process data to turn it into information, etc. Furthermore, some students even have the capability to write their own programs, design their own Web sites, or build their own computer systems. The students we mentioned here are "a lot of them" or "some of them." This implies that not all students have a strong background. Some may do well with hardware, some may have strong knowledge in software, or some may be comfortable with both. Then again, some may have limited knowledge in computer information systems. However, computer literacy courses, in general, are required for college students with different majors. In other words, computer literacy courses need to be taught to students with a variety of backgrounds.

Instructional design for a computer literacy course becomes a big challenge to instructors or course designers. In a computer literacy course, for example, an instructor may find that some students have not yet mastered the concepts of hardware and software; others may just be beginning to learn to use the mouse and simple word processing; still others may be building their own computer and home networking. Obviously, these different sets of students need to be taught different sets of enabling knowledge and skills. It would accomplish nothing to present data management to students who are still struggling with the concept of binary codes. And, it is not likely to be of advantage to those students who already have written their own computer programs to have to suffer through lessons that require them to learn how to save and open files. Some instructors implement the cooperative learning style to have the students with strong computer backgrounds teach those with fewer background skills. However, from the viewpoint of educational resources, resources for instructors and learners are wasted. A practical solution is to adopt a modularization approach to the course. The purpose of this chapter is to investigate the adaptability of the modularization approach to the design of instructional systems. Module instructional design (MID) is examined to determine the potential utility of this technique in the design and delivery of computer literacy instructional systems. To examine this potential utility, a demonstration is provided for how it might be used in a computer literacy course.

The purposes behind implementing modularization instruction are widely varied, and consequently, the structures and functions of each must be tailored to meet the needs of educators and students. As one wise computer programmer observed, the sooner you begin to write the computer code, the longer it will take to finish. The point here is, of course, some thoughtful planning in the early stages will provide the framework for successful implementation of the project and achievement of the goals of teachers and learners. As a first step of instruction design, course objectives and the intended audience should be clearly defined. Upon completion of this chapter, readers will be able to:

1.   Identify and describe the module instruction design planning steps.
2.   Apply the module instruction design planning steps in a computer literacy course.
3.   Articulate the connection between assessment and module instruction design.

BACKGROUND

Education has always sought to provide effective and efficient instruction, but with the entry of our society into the information age, pressure has increased for education to communicate new knowledge at higher levels and increasing rates. According to Gagne (1992), instruction deals with the deliberate arrangement of events in the learner's environment for the purpose of making learning happen effectively. Therefore, to meet the instructional challenges of the information age, educators must develop efficient and effective ways of arranging the instructional events in the learner's environment, including those events that will lead to the development of higher-order thinking skills.

Efficient instruction is dependent on a sound instructional system. An instructional system may be defined as an arrangement of resources and procedures used to promote learning (Gagne, 1992). Instructional systems have a variety of particular forms and occur in many of our institutions. Instructional System Design (ISD) is one of the instructional design approaches being used in classroom teaching or training. Other than that, there are several traditional systematic approaches to training, such as Performance-Based Training (PBT) and Criterion Referenced Instruction (CRI). These approaches have some common elements:

1.   *Competency based (job related)*: The learners are required to master a Skill, Knowledge, or Attitude (SKA). The training focuses on the job by having the learners achieve the criteria or standards necessary for proper task performance.
2.   *Sequential*: Lessons are logically and sequentially integrated.
3.   *Tracked*: A tracking system is established that allows changes and updates to the training materials to be performed efficiently.
4.   *Evaluated*: Evaluation and corrective action allows continuous improvement and maintenance of training information that reflects current status and conditions.

To an extent, ISD provides a means for sound decision making to determine the who, what, when, where, why, and how of instruction. The concept of a system approach to instruction is based on obtaining an overall view of the learning process. It is characterized by an orderly process for gathering and analyzing collective and individual performance requirements, and by the ability to respond to identified instruction needs. The application of a systems approach to instruction insures that instruction programs and the required support materials are continually developed in an effective and efficient manner to match the variety of needs in an ever rapidly changing environment.

Based on the ISD theory, a modularization approach is adopted to develop a curriculum plan for the computer literacy course. The theory, concept, and development process are demonstrated. Specifically, in this chapter, an overview of computer literacy contents, knowledge and skills, and trends is presented. A variety of curriculum developments and instructional models are discussed. Because the appropriate curriculum development approach for the pedagogical context depends on the characteristics and scope of the class and student background, special attention is given to identifying the types of situations for which each approach is most suited.

MAIN THRUST OF THE CHAPTER
Problem Statement

All universities and colleges in the United States provide an introductory course in computer information systems for computer majors or non-majors. The courses might have different titles, such as computer concepts, introduction to computer information systems, computer literacy, introduction to computing, etc. In general, this is the first course to outline computer concepts and introduce information systems development in addition to some hands-on software practices. According to Long and Long (1992), computer literacy includes the following knowledge and skills:

1.   Feel comfortable using a computer system.
2.   Be able to make the computer work for you through judicious development of or use of software.
3.   Be able to interact with a computer — that is, generate input to a computer and interpret output from a computer.
4.   Understand how computers are changing society, now and in the future.
5.   Be an intelligent consumer of computer-related products and services.

The course goal is obvious and straightforward. However, for instructors and course developers, the structure of this course content is difficult to arrange because of the big gap in students' backgrounds.

Computer literacy education has received tough criticism over the past several years. Many learners believe that college graduates have neither fundamental computer skills nor basic employability competencies. This is a "yes" and "no" question regarding the learner's background and educational resources. As stated at the outset, the diverse background makes the curriculum plan harder. No matter what kind of skills and backgrounds they have, students are put in the same class setting and follow the same instructional contents. Most of the computer literacy courses are like a big manufacturing factory. In general, the course is required, so some students are just paying tuition to get the degree they need. From the college and university standpoints, for the purpose of making the courses thorough, instructors with a variety of backgrounds are hired to teach this course. Most of the time newly hired, part-time, or retiring faculty teach this course. The idea behind the instructional philosophy is that because this is the first computer introductory course, most students will pick the information up by themselves. Because this is a required course, students would be expected to learn and prepare by themselves, without any choices. To the end, the students with strong backgrounds maintain what they have learned. However, the students with limited backgrounds can suffer and find it hard to keep to the course path.

Educational Perspectives

Joan Stark and Lisa Lattuca (1997) presented an organized and methodical framework for approaching curriculum development. Defining "curriculum development" as the process by which developers solve the complex problem of constructing a learning plan by making a series of decisions, the authors discovered that their model was equally useful in planning a single lesson, an individual course, an academic program, or an entire college curriculum.

The main points of Stark and Lattuca's curriculum development framework are that the designer first identifies the goals and learning outcomes, which then provide the criteria by which all other curricular decisions are determined. With the final destination well in mind, it becomes clear what steps must be taken to get there and how it will be known when you have arrived successfully.

Having articulated the critical goal(s) and outcomes, the designer continues the planning process by asking: "What would we accept as evidence that students have attained the desired understanding and proficiencies — before proceeding to plan teaching and learning experiences." This line of questioning early in the design process encourages faculty "to think about a unit or course in terms of the assessment evidence needed to document and validate that the desired learning has been achieved."

Module Instructional Design

In this chapter, the key components and methods of module instructional design (MID) are presented, and how to apply a MID approach to the design of instruction for the computer literacy course is shown. The concept of MID is often misunderstood as involving only the design of teaching materials or the selection of certain courses for the time concerns. However, MID is a broad concept that provides a systematic, problem-solving approach to planning and designing learning experiences.

Modulization means that separate programs are produced that work together as a "system." Two main principles of MID are that course modules should be designed so they are independent of the other modules and so each module accomplishes one clear task. The first principle is that each module should be designed and can later be modified without interfering with the performance of the other modules. The second principle strives to help students and learners easily understand what each module does. In other words, MID evaluates students' assessment reports. Based on the students' assessment reports and the kind of modules you provide, the course advisor will make suggestions as to how the modules will best be used to achieve students' goals. Instructional designers balance their knowledge and awareness of all the parts needed to make the course successful and make the course doable within time and cost constraints. Seeking efficiency, the instructional designer will make suggestions based on familiarity with teaching techniques and today's technology.

Module IDS

Based on a variety of IDS literature, eight planning steps in module instructional design are summarized. They are as follows:
1. Determining a purpose:
   a. Articulating the goals: There are course goals that describe what the students will be able to do as a result of completing the course or learning experience. The goals should provide a concise picture of the overall purpose of the course, e.g., the broad, end-result, real-world performance.

2.   Writing the learning outcomes:

a.   There are course objectives that support the course goals by providing a framework for students to organize their plans for successfully completing a course. Course objectives are the intended outcomes of the course learning experience, and they define major skills, knowledge, attitudes, or abilities needed to perform a task effectively. These objectives describe the specific tasks or exercises that the students should accomplish, and they must be stated in observable, measurable, and achievable terms.

b.   The course objectives are to be closely connected with real-world performance objectives. In other words, the skills, knowledge, attitudes, or abilities should be easily applied to future learning experiences or workplace requirements.

c.   The course objectives should specify what students will be able to do upon completion of the course or program and what would be accepted as evidence that the desired learning outcomes have been achieved.

d.   The course objectives should consider the rationale and any assumptions, learning theories, changing or emerging societal conditions, etc., that stimulate and justify curricular change, innovation, and emphases.

3.   Determining the content:

a.   Organizing the subject-matter content by consulting research, experts, learners, needs assessment results, professional requirements, advisory committee recommendations, transfer program requirements, etc.

b.   The content is complete for the module purpose — that is, all of the content the students have to learn to reach the objectives is presented.

c.   The content is appropriate for the type of knowledge or material presented in the course.

i.   Facts (or propositions) to recall: Organized outline of facts and support of facts as needed

ii.   Concepts (or categories) to identify (things, actions, relations): Definition of category, primary example, and non-examples

iii.   Principles (or relationships) to apply: Relation among variables and evidence (published or demonstrated)

iv.   Skills, whether mental or physical: Present steps, including substeps, for each major step, and demonstrate the skill

v.   Attitudes: Behavioral indicators enduring over time without coercion

d.   The content is reduced to the essentials.

i.   It is in its simplest form:
1.   Fact — primary facts
2.   Concept — short definitions
3.   Principle — short definitions
4.   Skill — groups of substeps
5.   Attitude — major indicators

ii.   The "nice to know" material has been abbreviated or made a part of optional further study.

iii.   The content has been chunked and divided into sub-objectives.

iv.   The content leads to sub-assessments or exercises that ultimately lead to the module assessments.

        1.   Module assessments should be comprised of the same type and level of assessment as the sub-assessments.

        2.   When application (or performance) assessment is required, examples and practice items must be presented and feedback provided before the application assessment is administered.

4.   Determining the sequence:
    a.   Organize the content logically, and make functional decisions about the curricular structure.
    b.   Course information should include an explanation of course organization that presents a clear and simple organization of the course objectives and required activities that accompany each objective.
    c.   A matrix should visually display the modular breakdown of the course material, required readings, activities, assessments, and due dates.
    d.   Each module should follow the sequence based on the key knowledge areas and skills requirements.

5.   Defining the learners:
    a.   Consider the learners' characteristics, such as their goals, abilities, extra-academic responsibilities, etc.
    b.   Create effective learning environments for all students by using emerging knowledge.
    c.   Identify instructional resources.
    d.   The chosen delivery method (i.e., course management system) should be tested and found reliable for system use.
    e.   Determine if college facilities, equipment, and staff are sufficient to support the delivery of the course.
    f.   Make sure sufficient funding is available to fund and maintain the delivery of the course.
    g.   Make sure that delivery of the course fits within the college system time constraints (for example, college calendar and semester structure).
    h.   Demand for course management by the college should be minimal.
    i.   Identify instructional processes.
    j.   Choose activities, strategies, and instructional modalities.
    k.   Provide the instructional model
    l.   Coordinate all modules with the instructors to define the instructional processes.
    m.   Modules should not be chosen that appear to duplicate the subject matter studied in other modules.

6.   Determining assessment and evaluation techniques:
    a.   Identify learning outcomes assessment methods (if not determined in #1).
    b.   Measure the degree to which students have achieved learning outcomes. In this stage, this can determine the students' ability to take certain modules.
    c.   Define the pre-assessment.
    d.   Determine the number of credits that may be taken as optional modules at each level.

e. Make adjustments
f. Use instructors' feedback to improve the planning process and the curricular plan.
g. Use the students' feedback to change the contents of each module.

Solutions and Recommendations — Case Study

The following case is a general MID for an Introduction to Computer Information Systems course, which the author designed for Lansing Community College in Lansing, Michigan, in 2001. All the whole course modules were prepared following the steps as stated above:

1. Determining a purpose:
    Introduction to computer information systems is the first and basic course for any IT major or non-major student. The following standards were used to determine the course learning purposes and outcomes:
    a. There is a clear overview statement describing the module content in general terms.
    b. There is a module goal that describes what the students will be able to do as a result of completing the module. The goal should provide a concise picture of the overall purpose of the module. The following are the general goals for the computer literacy course:
        i.   Students' have knowledge about computer processing related to computer technology.
        ii. Students have fundamental knowledge about networks and the Internet to suit today's working environments.
        iii. Students have the skills to use a personal computer and its software applications to carry out everyday tasks.
        iv. IT major students should know the concepts of database management, information systems development, and computer language selection.
        v.   IT major students also need to study e-commence concepts and basic Web development.
    c. There are module objectives that support the module goal by providing a framework for students to use to organize their plans for successfully completing the module. Module objectives are the intended outcomes of the module, and they define skills, knowledge, attitudes, or abilities needed to perform the module activities. These objectives describe the specific tasks or exercises that students should accomplish, and they must be stated in observable, measurable, and achievable terms.
    d. All module objectives are a subset or detailed application of the course objectives. This is to ensure there is consistency among content, objectives, practice, and assessment.
        i.   All instructional activities, including assessment, must be directly related to the course objectives.
2. Determining the content:
    The course contents were referenced in the program overview and syllabus 3.0 of the International Computer Driving License (ICDL) — Training and Certification Program in the Association for Computing Machinery. Originally, there were seven modules in

the syllabus. The course is designed for IT major and non-major students, and there are eight modules in this course:

Module 1 — Computing Process and Computer Technology
Module 2 — Network, Internet, and Email
Module 3 — Word Processing
Module 4 — Spreadsheets
Module 5 — Databases Usages
Module 6 — Graphics and Presentations
Module 7 — Database Management and Information Systems Development
Module 8 — Basic E-Commerce and Web Development

Each module also provides 50 multiple-choice questions and three hands-on projects for students to take. The test modules can be taken in any sequence. If students get a score of 90% for the test and full completion of the projects will be waived for that module. Modules 1 through 6 are required for non-major IT students. For IT majors, they have to complete all eight modules. In the class setting, we suggest that different instructors can teach each module.

3.   Determining the sequence:
   a.   There is an overview that provides the structure of the ideas in the component (both main and supportive ideas), with main ideas in the component mapped to the module objective from which they are derived.
   b.   There are clear descriptions of the component objectives:
      i.   Correspond to the assessment at the end of each component
      ii. Correspond to possible real-world application of each component objective
   c.   There is a motivational segment at the start (and throughout) of each component, communicating the benefits of learning this material, including where this content will be used (for example, on the job) and the real-world consequences of its use.
   d.   There is either a review or pretest of prerequisites so that students possess or are alerted to the knowledge or skill needed to successfully learn the presented material.
   e.   There is an agenda (or a schedule), unless the module agenda (schedule) is clearly indicated on the overall course schedule.
   f.   There are complete lists of equipment and tools and time requirements.

4.   Define the learners:
   For the selection of modules to fit for different learners, there are some protocols to issue:
   a.   There is a summary for each module, in which the main ideas are summarized.
   b.   There is an integration of information, where the relationship between the current module and course objectives is communicated.
   c.   There is a reorienting assessment that links the module objective to the student's performance or demonstration of understanding of the module material.

        i.   Assessment can be self-assessment.

        ii.   Module assessments should be similar to the capstone assessments in measuring mastery.

5.   Identify instructional resources:

    a.   The college support staff can carry out and are willing to support delivery methods used in the course.

    b.   If a development team is utilized:

        i.   The team should be able to develop for the methods as designed.

        ii.   An instructional designer will oversee structure and design before content is developed.

6.   Identifying instructional processes:

The instructional processes should be:

    a.   Easy to locate — clear navigation to locate where the information to be followed can be found.

    b.   Clear — easy to comprehend (i.e., tone and vocabulary should be consistent).

    c.   Emphasized — "need to know" ideas are emphasized, and "nice to know" are minimized.

    d.   Chunked — whole concepts should be broken down into subcomponents.

    e.   Modeled — sample work should be provided to orient students to the central aspects of the material, exercise, or assessment.

7.   Determining assessment and evaluation techniques:

The evaluation of the course is proportional to:

    a.   Course importance — the extent of the evaluation should correspond to the level of need for the course, the amount of development expense, the criticality of the course outcomes, the degree of controversy of the content, and the size of the student audience for this instruction.

    b.   Resources from the program or college.

        i.   The amount of the evaluation budget is sufficient for the proposed evaluation.

        ii.   The qualifications of evaluation staff are adequate for conducting the proposed evaluation.

        ii.   A meaningful number of reviewers and students are available to participate in the evaluation of the course.

A formative evaluation will be conducted to evaluate the course's effectiveness and to influence immediate decisions about how it might be improved.

    a.   During the first semester, the course is offered online; an evaluation of the course will be conducted to determine which areas of the course are in need of improvement:

        i.   Effectiveness — the degree to which the course results in student learning.

        ii.   Efficiency — the degree to which the course increases the worth of the degree or program and decreases (or does not increase) expenses from the viewpoints of the college and the student.

        iii. Acceptability — the degree to which the course provides increased satisfaction with the degree or course outcomes.

    b.   The first semester evaluation uses several methods to gather evidence (for example, observation, interview, questionnaire, materials analysis, and assessment results).

    c.   Members of the advisory committee or faculty are asked to review the course or portions of the course. Honest feedback is sought and accepted.

    d.   Methods for evaluation will include feedback from students.

    e.   Reviews are to be done using peer reviewers, who will report on areas in which improvement would be advantageous:
        i.   Appropriate amount of relevant, accurate, complete, up-to-date course content
        ii. Acceptable, tested methods
        iii. Reasonable amount of interaction between instructor-student and student-student
        iv. Valid and real-world oriented assessments
        v.   Technically appropriate and tested media
        vi. Preparation and adoption of textbooks and other instructional materials have input from appropriately qualified people

    f.   A summative evaluation will be conducted to decide on continued use of the course:
        i.   Is the course effective (i.e., can students demonstrate understanding and improved learning of course material)?
        ii. An end-of-the-course evaluation should demonstrate that the course actually produces the intended outcomes.

8.   The modules are acceptable to the students:

    a.   Module desired — Students are receptive to this module and have the skills and resources to use the module.

    b.   Student controlled — Within the confines of the structure and schedule established for the course, students have choice of content, pacing, and mode of learning.

    c.   Relevant — The material relates to students' goals or jobs.

    d.   Conversational — The tone and vocabulary of the course material are appropriate for students.

    e.   Unbiased — The course material avoids stereotypes and biased language.

9.   Make adjustments:
    The modules are engaging.

    a.   Aesthetically pleasing — Course material is usable, attractive, and has a consistent look and feel.

    b.   Appropriately interactive — There should be frequent opportunities for evaluation of understanding that provides orientation and feedback.
        i.   Course learning activities foster instructor–student, student–content, and, where appropriate, student–student interaction.

    c.   Instructor personalized — Instructor-provided information should enhance text-based information.

d.   Varied — Rich course content includes graphics, interaction, humor, surprise, suspense, puzzles, questions, games, aids, analogies, metaphors, and/or charts.

e.   Challenging — Students' growing level of skills are matched with increasing challenges (e.g., exercises that are just above students' comfort and skill).

CONCLUSION

The modularization approach in instructional design has been widely applied to a variety of course development. It also has been used in IT curriculum development for students and learners. In this chapter, the main purpose was to follow the module instructional design approach to a computer literacy course. This course will always have students of different computer backgrounds in the class. Some of them will have strong computer backgrounds, and will take this course because it is required. Some of them will take this course because of personal interest. From the instructor perspective, it is hard to provide general instructional materials to fit all of the students' levels. From the student standpoint, the course may be distracting and waste time and money.

Incorporating the modularization approach in the course will reduce the gap. Students can go through predesign evaluation methods to choose their own module to accomplish their educational goals. All of the students may get the same credit but go through different discipline settings and methods.

REFERENCES

Association for Computing Machinery and the International Computer Driving License Foundation. (2001). *Syllabus of International Computer Driving License — Training & Certification program in the United States.* Retrieved from the World Wide Web: http://www.acm.org/icdl-us.

Capron, H. L. (2000). *Computer; Tools for an Information Age (6th ed.).* Englewood Cliffs, NJ: Prentice Hall.

Eble, K. E. (1988). *The Craft of Teaching: A Guide to Mastering the Professor's Art* (2nd ed.). San Francisco, CA: Jossey-Bass.

Gaff, J. G., Ratcliff, J. L., & Associates (1997). *Handbook of the Undergraduate Curriculum.* San Francisco, CA: Jossey-Bass Publishers.

Gagne, R. M., Briggs, L. J., & Wager, W. W. (1992). *Principles of Instructional Design* (4th ed.). New York: Harcourt Brace Jovanovich College Publishers.

Glatthorn, A. A. (1994). *Developing a quality curriculum.* Alexandria, VA: ASCD.

Hyman, R. T. (1974). *Way of Teaching* (2nd ed.). New York: J.B. Lippincott Company.

Jensen, E. (1997). Completing the puzzle: The brain-compatable approach to learning. Del Mar: The Brain Store, Inc.

Long, L. & Long, N. (1992). *Computers* (2nd ed.). Englewood Cliffs, NJ: Prentice Hall.

Long, L & Long, N. (2002). *Computers* (9th ed.). Englewood Cliffs, NJ: Prentice Hall.

Mager, R. F. (1988). *Making Instruction Work.* Belmont: David S. Lake Publishers.

McKeachie, W. J. (1986). *Teaching Tips: A Guidebook for the Beginning College Teacher* (8th ed.). Lexington, MA: D.C. Heath.

Norton, P. (2001). *Introduction to Computers* (4th ed.). New York: McGraw-Hill.

Palloff, R. M., & Pratt, K. (1999). *Building Learning Communication in Cyberspace*. San Francisco, CA: Jossey-Bass Publishers.

Parry, T., & Gregory, G. (1998). *Designing Brain Compatible Hearning*. Arlington Heights, IL: Skylight Training and Publishing Inc.

Pratt, D. (1994). *Curriculum Planning*. New York: Harcourt Brace College Publishers.

Price, R. V. (1991). *Computer-Aided Instruction: A Guide for Authors.* Pacific Grove: Books/Cole Publishing Company.

Ratcliff, J. L. (Ed.). (1992). Assessment and curriculum reform. *New Directions in Higher Education, No. 80*. San Francisco, CA: Jossey-Bass Publishers.

Satizinger, J. W., Jackson, R. B., and Burd, S. D. (2000). *System Analysis and Design — in a Changing World*, Cambridge: Course Technology.

Shaffer, K. (2001). *Step-by-Step Curriculum Development*. Lansing, MI: Lansing Community College.

Shelly, G. B., Cashman, T. J., and Vermaat, T. J. (2002). *Discovering Computers 2002 Complete Concepts for a Digital World, Web Enhanced.* Cambridge: Course Technology.

Stark, J. S., & Lattuca, L. R. (1997). *Shaping the College Curriculum: Academic Plans in Action.* Boston, MA: Allyn and Bacon.

Wiggins, G., & McTighe, J. (1998). *Understanding by Design*. Alexandria, VA: ASCD.

Chapter XXII

Information Technologies in Educational Organizations: An Innovative Collaborative Course Development, Delivery and Evaluation

Pamela Lipe Revercomb
Syracuse University, USA

Ruth V. Small
Syracuse University, USA

ABSTRACT

In this chapter, the collaborative design, development, implementation, and evaluation of a new interdisciplinary course being offered by Syracuse University's School of Information Studies and School of Education are described. The course was offered to graduate students in response to the need to revise two master's degree programs at Syracuse University and in order to satisfy new state competency standards for certification as Educational Technologists and School Library Media Specialists. The course development process, course objectives, course content and activities, and the results of a formative and summative evaluation conducted by the researchers are included, as well as recommendations for future implementation, including distance delivery.

INTRODUCTION

This evaluation study focuses on the design, development, and implementation of an interdisciplinary course in which students gain knowledge about and discuss issues related to the selection, management, and use of information technologies for teaching and learning in a wide variety of settings (e.g., schools, colleges, businesses). The survey course, offered for the first time in Fall 2001, was based on the following assumptions:

- Technology literacy is fundamental to the education of citizens of the 21st century.

- Technology integration is fundamentally a human-oriented issue, in the sense that the point is to integrate technology in meaningful ways into the life and work of people; this is especially true with regard to using technology in teaching and learning.

- Technology can provide unique and powerful opportunities to enhance learning and teaching.

- The adoption of information technology will change the way teachers teach and students learn.

In this chapter, the collaborative course development process, course objectives, course content and activities, and the results of a formative and summative evaluation, conducted by the researchers, are described. Recommendations for future implementation, including distance delivery, are included.

BACKGROUND
Collaborative Course Development

The development of the new course began as a response to the need to revise and update two master's degree programs at Syracuse University, one in the School of Information Studies and one in the School of Education, in order to satisfy current New York State certification requirements for School Library Media Specialists and Educational Technologists in schools. These requirements emphasize collaboration among educational professionals to enhance the learning of all students, including those with disabilities and special needs, and specifically, collaborative projects that support the use of instructional and information technologies for teaching and learning.

The objectives for developing the new course were to:

- Create an innovative approach to teaching and learning about information technology use in education.

- Encourage collaborative planning and teaching in the areas of information and technology literacy.

- Provide opportunities for students to work collaboratively on school-based technology projects.
- Present first-hand learning experiences from noted practitioners and researchers.
- Teach students to use technology to plan and work cooperatively.

A project team, consisting of one advanced graduate student and one faculty member from each school, used computer-based collaborative software to support their course development. Initial research was conducted to identify similar collaborative projects and interdisciplinary course development efforts at other institutions. To develop the course content and structure, the team evaluated state certification competencies, educational standards for technology-based learning curricula, and various means of assessing current technology use and instruction.

Guidelines and suggestions for the *process* of developing a course that involves the integration of more than one discipline were found to include the development of the curriculum, course objectives and framework, delivery options, support resources, and evaluation (General Education Proposal, 1977; Course Development for a New General Education Curriculum, 1989; Lambert, 1985; Spicer, 1988). Some research indicated that interdisciplinary courses and teaching tend to be highly innovative, exploring "broad-based social issues that require multiple perspectives," and incorporating a variety of methods and concepts from the disciplines involved (Abell, 1999; Gailey & Carroll, 1993). Other researchers offered useful suggestions for avoiding the pitfalls they had encountered when first designing an interdisciplinary course (e.g., Ruwe & Leve, 2001). The National Council for Accreditation of Teacher Education (NCATE) and the International Society for Technology in Education (ISTE) recently developed standards and guidelines to be used in support of technology use and integration in professional teacher preparation programs (Vanatta, 2000).

Results of Planning

Topics to be included in the curriculum were chosen to meet the instructional and information technology needs of students from both schools and in accordance with new State certification requirements. Each class session focused on a different topic. Presentations would include guest speakers who were experts on that subject, field trips to relevant educational sites, and panel discussions. A technology survey (pre- and post-) was developed to measure the students' comfort with and knowledge and use of various educational technologies. The survey was administered at the beginning of the semester, with a retest at the end. A textbook on education change models was selected, and supplemental readings related to specific class sessions were chosen. Assignments and projects were planned, including a collaborative, site-based educational technology project (ETP), preparation of a WebQuest (defined by creator Bernie Dodge of San Diego State University as "an inquiry-oriented activity in which some or all of the information that learners interact with comes from resources on the Internet"), evaluation of a Web site using a specific evaluation instrument, creation of an electronic portfolio, and a final in-class presentation on the results of their ETPs.

It was agreed that WebCT, a Web-based learning environment, would be used for communications, assignment postings, and online discussions.

COURSE DELIVERY

Format

"Information Technology in Educational Organizations," was offered as an interdisciplinary course, designed and taught by full-time faculty from Syracuse University's School of Information Studies and School of Education. Multiple instructional methods were employed, including lectures, discussions, demonstrations, role-plays, debates, labs, field trips, and hands-on activities.

Students were introduced to a wide range of existing and emerging self-contained and distributed technologies, studying them in relation to telecommunications policies, information and instructional services to diverse groups and individuals, research and learning, and collaboration. Online technology was used for communicating, learning, and completing assignments.

Learning Objectives

By the end of the course, it was our expectation that students would be able to:

- Demonstrate an ability to select, manage, and evaluate technologies used in a learning environment.
- Demonstrate an understanding of telecommunications policies that affect the use of technology in schools.
- Describe methods of determining the appropriateness and effectiveness of implementing and using a range of self-contained and distributed technologies within a learning environment.
- Demonstrate knowledge of the impact of technology on information services and instruction.
- Synthesize information presented by a variety of researchers and practitioners in course seminars and readings.
- Successfully complete site-based technology-related team projects for clients.
- Use computer-based collaborative software as one method for team interaction.
- Understand the roles of the library media specialist and the educational technologist in the application of technology for meeting curricular, faculty, and organizational needs and requirements.
- Develop skills in collaboration with other professional staff to support instruction through services that enhance the learning and independence of diverse audiences.

Content and Topics

Course content and topics included the management of technology projects, collaborative learning technologies, assistive technologies for learners with disabilities and other diverse audiences, evaluation of technology-based learning and electronic resources, digital equity, online instruction competencies, national education databases, asynchronous and synchronous distance learning tools, ethical issues relating to technology use, building online learning communities, knowledge management tools for learning environments, federal telecommunications policies, wireless communications, information technology services and resources for instruction and learning, the impact of technology on the learning environment, technology leadership, and videoconferencing systems.

Topics were often covered in several different ways, including speaker presentations, readings, panel discussions, demonstrations, and through class role-playing and brainstorming activities. Some of the guest speakers suggested relevant readings so that students would be prepared for discussion sessions after the lectures, or so they would have questions prepared for videoconference sessions.

Technology

The instructors and guest presenters demonstrated and used a variety of technologies to teach the course. The class was held in a state-of-the-art digital classroom containing computer-based presentation technology (including CD, DVD, and Internet connections), multiple cameras for videotaping, videoconferencing, and Web casting, and a Smart Board, as well as more traditional classroom technologies (overhead/opaque/video projection system, whiteboards). The technology lab manager for the School of Information Studies demonstrated the new cameras, sensors, microphones, projectors, overhead/opaque desk projector, and the remote mouse.

Communication outside of class was conducted using WebCT. WebCT allows ongoing communication between instructors and students and among the members of student teams to facilitate announcements, class discussions, and assignments. Guest speakers and other special sessions of interest to a wider audience (e.g., the entire university, distance students in remote locations, faculty and students at other colleges) were simultaneously broadcast through the Web using Web-casting technology. This technology not only allowed remote participants to synchronously view the session but also to interact with the speaker by sending questions and comments via their computers. In addition, all Web casts were archived for future viewing by students in the class and others.

Speakers and Panel Discussions

Noted guest experts and practitioners participated through presentations (in-person, web cast, and videoconference), demonstrations, and panel discussions. Some examples of guest speakers were as follows:

- One of the developers of WELES (Web-Enhanced Learning Environment Strategies), a tool for integrating NASA resources into teaching to inspire science learning.
- An expert on "the digital divide."
- A member of the International Board of Standards for Training, Performance, and Instruction's committee developing "Competencies for Online Teaching and Training (COTT)."
- The developers of a "next-generation" online learning tool prototype, combining DVD and Web technology to deliver flexible, modular, multimedia instruction and including such features as video-based case studies, active lesson book marking, and individual note indexing and review.
- A member of the development team for a set of tools for developing effective online instruction.
- The developer of a set of widely used Web evaluation tools for education and business.
- An expert who provides innovative assistive technological needs assessments for people with disabilities.

Field Trips and Labs

A number of field trips allowed students to experience a variety of innovative uses of technology at existing technology-based learning centers and resources located in the Syracuse area. Sites included libraries, teaching centers, academic units, and government-funded national projects. For example, students visited the Information Institute of Syracuse, the collective home of several U.S. Department of Education-funded projects such as the ERIC Clearinghouse on Information & Technology, AskERIC, the Virtual Reference Desk, and the Gateway to Educational Materials (GEM) Project.

A 30-workstation lab, next to the digital classroom, was reserved for demonstrations and hands-on activities, such as developing WebQuests and evaluating school Web sites.

Assignments

The primary assignment was the Educational Technology Project (ETP), which allowed students an opportunity to apply newly learned knowledge and skills to a real situation with a real client. Students worked together collaboratively, in teams, with site-based educational practitioners, to develop and implement solutions to specific technology problems within their organizations. Some examples of projects were as follows:

- Development of a module-based instructional program for a college library's data-bases.
- Examination of a high school online learning program and determination of the causes of and potential solutions to its high dropout rate.
- Development and implementation of training for elementary teachers using newly purchased technologies (e.g., FlexCam, SmartBoard).
- Planning of a professional conference for a university-based organization for school administrators to advance technology use and practice for academic success.

Additional assignments required students to create Web-based learning tools (WebQuests), evaluate educational Web sites using an established tool (Small & Arnone's WebMAC Professionalã), and develop electronic portfolios. Students were expected to upload each of the assignments to their student space on the WebCT site. The electronic portfolio was intended as a means for students to organize and present all of their electronic assignments and to provide reflective comments on their experience and growth throughout the course.

EVALUATION

Methods

An ongoing evaluation was integral to course development and delivery. Students were made aware of the fact that the course was new and that their feedback was not only encouraged but also vital to the ongoing evaluation process. The course development team directed the design of formative and summative course evaluation. Data were collected from course developers, instructors, teaching assistants, students, and guest speakers. Field-testing using formative evaluation methods occurred at various points, as the course was being developed and implemented; feedback guided revisions as the course was in progress

(Worthen & Sanders, 1973). After completion of the first offering of the course, data were again collected from all participants (instructors, graduate assistants, speakers, panel members, and students) as part of a summative evaluation effort.

Evaluation data were collected in the following ways:

- Continuous feedback while the course was in progress, focusing on experiences with technology, course materials, assignments, class sessions, and other activities via electronic interviews, focus groups, and surveys. [Students were made aware of the fact that the course was new and that their feedback was not only encouraged but also vital to the ongoing evaluation process.]

- Development and use of a series of instruments that evaluate the effectiveness of planning efforts, quality of instruction, use of technology and other resources, learning and affective outcomes, course organization, and impact of student projects on the organizations in which they are conducted.

Mid-Semester Evaluation Results

The instruments used to collect the evaluation data were designed to determine how well the objectives of the course had been incorporated (and met) through assignments, speakers, ETPs, and other class activities. Data were collected through several instruments, including pre- and post-technology surveys, mid-semester evaluations, standard university course evaluations, electronic portfolio (self-reporting) analyses and reflections, and interviews of students, guest speakers, and course developers.

At approximately the midpoint of the course, students were presented with 12 open-ended questions as a means of collecting their thoughts, reflections, and suggestions for how the course was progressing to that point. Questions focused on the following aspects of the course:

- Assignments completed
- Relevance/applicability of topics to their future plans
- Guest speakers
- Use of WebCT
- Presentation of educational technologies
- Progress on the educational technology project (ETP)
- Class presentation formats
- Textbook and readings
- Quality of instruction
- Suggestions for improvement

Overall feedback was positive for the assignments, relevance of the topics and content, guest speakers, instructors, and teaching assistants. Seventy percent of the students felt the WebCT presented many difficulties, complaining of having experienced "much frustration" while attempting to upload assignments, being uncomfortable posting to the discussion groups, and having trouble finding things on the site. Students were split 50/50 as to whether the educational technologies were being thoroughly presented, with a unanimous request for more hands-on experience. Information on the progress of their ETPs indicated that 20% of the projects were "going well," 50% were having difficulties scheduling meetings with their team or site supervisors, 30% felt they were not experienced enough to meet the demands of the project, and 20% felt they were confused or unclear about the expectations for the projects.

Although all students agreed that the variety of speakers and formats was a good concept, 40% said they would prefer the course to be less of a survey course and have more hands-on or practical activities, complaining that they felt like they were "always an audience." Seventy percent of the students wanted more focused lectures that would link the speakers to the goals and objectives of the course, suggesting that course instructors might conduct a closing summary after each presentation to stress relevance. Eighty percent of the students felt the supplemental readings were useful and informative and that the textbook was easy to comprehend, although 30% also pointed out that they thought the textbook was "pointless." Final suggestions from 70% of the students indicated that they needed more time in class to work with their ETP teams.

Several steps were taken in response to the feedback from the mid-semester evaluation. In-class demonstrations were given to show students how they would be expected to use WebCT for uploading or otherwise contributing to class assignments. ETP teams met and discussed their progress, problems, and other issues with their projects, and these were presented for class discussion and suggestions. Discussions and group brainstorming sessions were included in many class sessions following guest speakers. The textbook was used as the basis for several online discussion groups in which students participated by relating the readings to their ongoing ETP experiences.

Final Course Evaluation

Final course evaluation data was collected from the course developers, guest speakers, and students who took the course using several different instruments. Each of the students completed the standard course evaluation and was expected to write a reflective essay on their technological progress and their experiences completing the course assignments and working with their ETP teams. Interviews were conducted with three of the four course developers and a selected number of students from each school. All guest speakers were contacted and asked to complete an email interview.

RESULTS AND RECOMMENDATIONS

Technology Survey

Each student was asked to complete a technology use survey at the beginning of the course and then again at the end. The survey asked the students to evaluate their proficiency using Internet tools, databases, word processing, spreadsheets, and file management. They were also asked to rate the frequency with which they used various applications and media and how important it was to them to improve their proficiency of use. Twenty-one of the 26 students completed the pre-course technology surveys (see Appendix A); however, most did not complete the post-course survey for a number of reasons.

The plan was to have the students complete the pre-course technology surveys at the beginning of the course. The technology survey was posted on the WebCT, where students could download it and then resubmit their responses electronically. Nagging commenced when it was observed that no students had completed the surveys by mid-semester. The irony of the situation became clear when students explained that they were not submitting the surveys because they did not know how to download or upload files in an electronic learning environment like WebCT. The process was demonstrated in class, and students began submitting the surveys. Because this took place too far along in the course to still be considered a *pre*-course survey, some students did not complete the post-technology survey for comparison at the end, or simply stated that there was too little difference to compare. This further limited the use and accuracy of the surveys, because whereas a number of students finally asked for a demonstration of uploading/downloading on WebCT specifically so they would be able to complete the survey, only one student indicated that he/she needed assistance with this type of task on the completed survey — undoubtedly because they had just learned how!

Although comparison data will probably not be useful in this particular study, the experience underscores the need to assess basic skill levels at the start of the course when using electronic learning environments such as WebCT.

Electronic Portfolio

The electronic portfolios allowed students to collect and organize the assignments and activities completed in the course in an electronic format. Students were reminded that many schools and businesses now advocate the development of electronic portfolios (for students, teachers, or other professional use as well). In addition, as educational technologists and school library media specialists, they would likely be involved in teaching students how to create these portfolios. They might also serve as systems operators for a school district or business and would have to manage or assess portfolios on that network.

The electronic portfolios were expected to contain the following things:

- A synopsis of and commentary on each of the assignments and various course activities in which they had participated (e.g., role plays, use of various technologies, field trips)
- The results of their pre- and post-technology surveys
- A reflective essay describing what they found to be the highlights and challenges presented during the course and an assessment of their personal learning growth throughout the semester

In this reflective, self-reporting format, students provided insightful analyses of their experiences and growth during the course. Most of the portfolios were presented online in the student space on WebCT. Some were also highly interactive and creative as well as informative. The following example is representative of the types of thoughts students presented in their reflective essays:

> *I have learned a great deal during this course in Information Technologies in Educational Organizations. I appreciate the integration of technology in a wide variety of settings. They served to develop confidence in my ability to transfer these skills in different situations. What helped to increase my self-efficacy were the many guest speakers and practitioners that are currently experts in the field. The wide variety of topics broadened my perspective of the continuing use of and need for technological applications in the world today and in the future. This course has developed [my] ability to synthesize technologies with educational applications in many contexts.*

As with the technology survey submissions, there were still a few students who had trouble presenting their portfolios online. Tutorials might be added to future courses to ensure proficiency in this area.

Standard Course Evaluation

Students completed the standard form used by Syracuse University School of Information Studies to evaluate the instruction received in a course. These proved most valuable in assessing the content value of the course and whether or not student expectations were met. Comments regarding qualities and characteristics of the instructors, course content, and suggestions for improvement closely paralleled those of the students interviewed by the researcher. Students suggested that instructors lead topic discussions following guest speakers and panel presentations and present more hands-on use of the educational technologies presented.

Interviews

Interview protocols (Appendix B) were developed for collecting feedback from course developers, guest speakers, and students. The course developers were interviewed in person, and the others were done via email. Data was collected from three of the four course developers, four of the six selected students from the two schools, and five of the 19 guest speakers and panelists. For several months, the researchers held onto the hope that more of the guest speakers would ultimately return their email interviews in order to provide a larger base for that part of the evaluation.

Although somewhat limited in that one cannot probe unclear responses to questions in real time, the use of email interviews was helpful for collecting data from speakers who had traveled a significant distance to make their class presentations (as well as for most of the local people). However, a low percentage (26%) of the guest speakers returned their interviews, and a better means of collecting this portion of the feedback needs to be developed.

Recommendations for the Future

In addition to the suggestions in terms of data collection and evaluation, several conclusions and recommendations have emerged that will be taken into account when presenting the course in the future.

Educational Technology Project (ETP)

The educational technology projects were integral for giving the students the experience of working collaboratively with learning technologies. Although site and project supervisors attended the first class session to present their projects and were invited to attend the final presentation from their project team, there needed to be a more formal means of collecting feedback from them while projects were in progress.

Distance Learning

Much of the course format will lend itself well to a distance mode of delivery. The use of WebCT for communication and assignment postings is already functioning; many of the guest presentations were done using Web casts or videoconferencing, with students participating or asking questions live. Panel discussions, hands-on lab work, or demonstrations and field trips could be conducted during a limited on-campus residency.

One potential difficulty with presenting this course in distance mode is the coordination of the ETPs. Students should be provided with guidelines for seeking appropriate sites and supervisors for the projects in their local communities.

Technology Proficiency

One of the key problems with the use of WebCT to upload and download assignments for this course came about because some of the students could not complete the technology surveys *online* — they simply did not know how to do that. Things were further complicated by the fact that these students were typically nonresident graduate students, most of whom worked full time, so they did not get together and help each other figure out how to work with the WebCT. They were also hesitant to admit in class that they were having trouble until well into the semester. If some type of technology survey is to be employed to assess proficiency at the beginning of the course, this should be done using a paper-based instrument and be completed during the first class session. The instructors will then have an immediate assessment of the students' technological skills and can structure appropriate computer lab sessions early in the semester.

A minimum level of technological proficiency will be essential for students taking the course in distance mode and may also be needed as a prerequisite for all students taking this course in the future. A means of assessing this proficiency relative to the use of WebCT and other electronic learning environments used for the course should be developed for this purpose. At the very least, student proficiency for working in an electronic learning environment, such as WebCT, should be assessed at the beginning of the course. Tutorials or workshops could be offered if needed so that students can attain a functional level of online interaction and competence.

Instruction

In their interviews, some students commented that the reliance on guest speakers diluted the content and may have obscured the focus of the course. Others felt the expert speakers added breadth from their experience with many facets of educational technology that might not otherwise have been incorporated into a typical lecture (one instructor) format. Instruction should be balanced between the guest speakers and panel presentations, in-class debriefings, discussions, and hands-on skills presentations.

Evaluation Data Collection

Although sufficient evaluation and feedback data were collected from the interviews of the course developers and students, only a small percentage of the guest speakers responded. These were busy professional people who probably chose not to take the time to complete an email interview several weeks after the speaking engagement. In the future, a short evaluation and feedback interview could be held with speakers *immediately* after their presentation. This would ensure that feedback was received from all presenters, and that it was collected while the experience was still fresh in their minds.

CONTINUATION OF THE PROJECT

A Vision Fund Grant for Innovative Instruction from Syracuse University provided funding for the design, development, and initial implementation of this course. The focus of this first effort was on a collaborative framework for course development.

To build on initial efforts for further elaboration of both master's curricula, the Schools of Information Studies and Education will continue to collaborate on courses and projects of mutual need and interest. Both schools strongly support this project and will contribute resources to its continuation. The final project report will include recommendations for expanded collaboration between the two schools and the development of a model based on lessons learned in order to create meaningful ways to foster interdisciplinary collaboration among academic units campus-wide.

REFERENCES

Abell, A. (1999). Interdisciplinary courses and curricula in the community colleges. *ERIC Digest,* May 1999, ED#429633.

"Course Development for a New General Education Curriculum." (1989). ERIC #ED306844.

Gailey, J. D. & Carroll, V. S. (1993). Toward a model for interdisciplinary teaching. *Journal of Education for Business, 69,* 1, September/October, 36–39. ERIC #CE525627.

"General Education Proposal, Miami-Dade Community College." (1977). ERIC #ED146957.

Lambert, L. (1985). A discussion of the evaluation of the interdisciplinary seminars program of the honors college at the State University of New York at Oswego. ERIC #ED270049.

Michen, K. S. & Cutting, A. C. (2000). eEducation: Interdisciplinary crossroads. Research paper: Connecting technology to teaching and learning. ERIC #ED444454.

Ruwe, D. & Leve, J. (2001). Interdisciplinary course design. *The Clearing House, 74,* 3, January/February, 117–118. ERIC #BED101003816.

Small, R. V. & Arnone, M. P. (2000). *WebMAC Professional.* Fayetteville, NY: Motivation Mining Company.

Spicer, W. (1988). A core program for the 90s: Changing patterns for instruction. Final Report. ERIC #ED298115.

Vanatta, R. A. (2000). Evaluation to planning: Technology integration in a school of education. *Journal of Technology and Teacher Education, 8,* 3, 231–246.

Worthen, B. R. & Sanders, J. R. (1973). *Educational Evaluation: Theory and Practice.* New York: Wadsworth Publishing Company, Inc.

APPENDIX A –
TECHNOLOGY SURVEY
PRE-COURSE RESULTS

1.   Describe your *level of proficiency* using the following types of educational informational technologies.

What is *YOUR* level of proficiency in each area?	I am not familiar or prepared to do this	I need assistance to do this	I can do this with relative ease	I can teach others to do this	Mean Ratings
RATING	1	2	3	4	
INTERNET TOOLS					
a Visiting a web site	0	0	2*	19	3.9
b Using a history list and bookmark		1	7	13	3.6
c Using a search engine			5	16	3.8
d Do an advanced web search using Boolean & Logic	4	3	5	9	2.9
e Downloading a file from the Internet		1	6	14	3.6
f Creating a web page	6	4	6	5	2.5
COMMUNICATIONS					
g Sending and receiving e-mail			1	20	4.0
h Attach & open e-mail files			3	18	3.9
i Creating mailing lists and address books	1	3	6	10	3.1
j Sending, reading, and replying to listserv and bulletin board messages	1	1	7	12	3.4
DATABASES					
k Creating a database	4	7	3	7	2.6
l Entering information into a database	1	5	8	7	3.0
m Creating a report from a database	3	10	2	6	2.5
WORD PROCESSING					
n Creating a document				21	4.0
o Editing a document			1	20	4.0
p Using spell check, grammar check and thesaurus			2	19	3.9
q Modifying text appearance			2	19	3.9
r Moving and copying text between documents			2	19	3.9
s Adding bullets and paragraph numbers			4	17	3.8
t Creating tables		2	6	13	3.5
u Displaying data as a chart	1	2	5	13	3.4
v Inserting graphics into a document		2	5	14	3.6
SPREADSHEETS					
w Creating a spreadsheet		3	7	11	3.4
x Using formulas and functions in a spreadsheet	1	5	4	11	3.2
y Editing a spreadsheet		5	4	12	3.3
z Moving and copying text between documents		2	5	14	3.6
aa Creating charts	1	6	5	9	3.0
FILE MANAGEMENT					
bb Renaming a file			3	18	3.9
cc Creating a directory			10	11	3.5
dd Creating a folder			5	16	3.8
ee Formatting disks	1	1	2	17	3.7
ff Transferring a file between two drives			6	15	3.7

Note: Numbers indicate how many students selected the answer, with N = 21 for each question.

2.   Describe your *frequency of use* for the following applications.

	How often do YOU use the following applications or media?	Everyday	Several times a week	Several times a month	Once a month	Several times a year	Once a year	Never	Mean Ratings
	RATING	7	6	5	4	3	2	1	
a	Word Processing (e.g. Word, WordPerfect)	13*	7	1					6.6
b	Spreadsheet (e.g. Excel)	2	3	9	1	3	2	1	4.5
c	Presentation (e.g. PowerPoint)		3	10	4	1	2	1	4.4
d	E-Mail	20	1						7.0
e	Internet/Web Access (e.g. Netscape, Explorer)	19	2						6.9
f	Packaged Software (e.g. Simulations, Specific Curriculum)	2	6	3	3	1	1	5	4.1
g	Software Tools for Web-Based Courses (e.g. Dialogue, Blackboard, WebCT)	6	9	4			1	1	5.7
h	Graphics Programs		3	8	4	3		3	4.1
i	Publishing (e.g. MS Publisher, PageMaker)		3	2	3	4	2	7	3.0
j	Database (e.g. Access, Filemaker)	1	1	3	4	4	7	1	3.4
k	Web (HTML) Editors	1	5	5	1	1	1	7	3.7
l	Modeling or Simulation Software				1	1	3	16	1.4
m	Multimedia Software (e.g. Director)		1		1	2	2	15	1.7
n	Project Management (e.g. MS Project, SureTrack)			2		5		14	1.9
o	Handheld Devices (e.g. graphing calculators, probes)	1	2		1	4	2	11	2.4
p	Digital Camera			3	3	6	1	8	2.6

Numbers indicate how many students selected the answer, with N = 21 for each question.

3.   Describe the importance of **improving your proficiency** in using the following applications.

	How important is improving your proficiency in this software?	Very important	Somewhat important	Slightly important	Mean Ratings
	RATING	3	2	1	
a	Word processing (e.g., Word, WordPerfect)	12*	5	4	2.4
b	Spreadsheet (e.g., Excel)	9	8	4	2.2
c	Presentation (e.g., PowerPoint)	2	5	4	1.0
d	Email	13	3	5	2.4
e	Internet/Web access (e.g., Netscape, Explorer)	14	3	4	2.5
f	Packaged software (e.g., Simulations, Specific Curriculum)	4	10	7	1.9
g	Software tools for Web-based courses (e.g., Dialogue, Blackboard, WebCT)	8	10	3	2.2
h	Graphics programs	6	12	3	2.1
i	Publishing (e.g., MS Publisher)	5	9	7	1.9
j	Database (e.g., Access, Filemaker)	7	6	8	2.0
k	Web (HTML) editors	10	6	5	2.2
l	Modeling or simulation software	4	9	8	1.8
m	Multimedia software (e.g., Director)	5	9	7	1.9
n	Project management (e.g., MS Project, SureTrack)	7	6	8	2.0
o	Handheld devices (e.g., graphing calculators, probes)	4	5	12	1.6
p	Digital camera	4	12	5	2.0

Numbers indicate how many students selected the answer, with N = 21 for each question.

APPENDIX B –
INTERVIEW PROTOCOLS

Students
Use in-person, telephone, or email interview format (approximately 15–20 minutes)
Questions:
1. What, in general, did you expect from the course when you enrolled?
   a. What specifically did you expect to learn?
   b. What were these expectations based on?
2. Now that the course is over, how did it meet your expectations?
   a. Was it better?
   b. Different?
   c. Disappointing?
   d. In what ways?
3. As the course began, how did you feel about being with students from another school?
   a. Why did you feel this way?
   b. How did your feelings change as the semester proceeded?
   c. What caused your feelings to change?
4. What was it like working collaboratively?
   a. With your ETP team?
   b. With the ETP site coordinator?
   c. In groups for in-class work?
   d. What did you gain from these collaborations? Please give examples, where possible.
5. Did the presentation and use of the wide range of educational technologies in the course meet your expectations? (Explain.)
6. This course was taught using a number of different instructional formats, such as guest speakers, lab exercises, field trips, videoconferences, and live technology demonstrations. What are your thoughts about these formats and how they were used to teach the course? Please give examples, where possible.
7. What vision have you formed (as a result of this course) for:
   a. Using educational technologies in your own future teaching and learning?
   b. Collaborating with other educators to accomplish instructional goals?

Demographics:
Male/female
IST/IDD&E
Future career plans

Presenters
Should be interviewed in person immediately following presentation, if possible.
1. What are your thoughts and reflections with reference to your presentation to this class?

2. What were the highlights of your experience with the class?
3. What did you think about your interactions with the students (questions asked, discussions, etc.)?
4. How would you describe your experience working with the technologies used for your presentation?
5. What would you change if you were to speak on this same topic to a future section of this class?

Course Developers

In-person interviews (approximately 15–20 minutes)
Questions:

1. How were you involved in the development of this course (role/demographic)?
2. Please reconsider the initial objectives (handout with **Learning Objectives**) for this course.
   a. In what ways do you think these learning objectives have been met satisfactorily?
   b. Are there any instances where we have not adequately met the objectives? If so, please explain.
3. What were your expectations for the instructional aspects of this course (professors, speakers, lab exercises), and were these expectations met satisfactorily? If so, how? If not, why not?
4. One important aspect of the course was that the students gain experience working collaboratively on educational technology projects in real-life situations. What are your thoughts on the organization and implementation of these projects for the students?
5. This course was also about the practical application of a variety of technology products and their use in an instructional/training setting.
   a. What are your thoughts about the ways in which these educational technologies were introduced to the students?
   b. Do you think the students are now able to "demonstrate an ability to design, manage, and evaluate technologies used in a learning environment?" (course objective)
   c. WebCT was used to facilitate the course through a variety of online communications formats. What are your feelings about the overall usability of WebCT for this course?
   d. Are there any technologies that were not used that you would have liked to have used or any that you would like to have you used more than you did?
   e. Do you have any suggestions for presenting these types of educational technologies to students in the future?

APPENDIX C –
STUDENT ATTRIBUTES—
MAJORS, INTERESTS, AND
EXPECTATIONS FOR THE COURSE

Program of Study	Degree	Areas of Interest	Use of IDD&E Learning Theories	Use of Ed Tech & in School, Library, or Work Settings	Web Design	Use of Technologies for Distance Learning	Implementing Technology into Curriculum
Environmental & Resource Engineering	MS	Hands-on management and instruction of subordinates	x	x	x		
IDD&E	PhD						
IDD&E	Other	Music, Education, Instructional Design	x	x			
IDD&E	MS	Teaching English as a Foreign Language (TEFL)	x	x			
IDD&E	MS	Business Training and Development	x	x			
IDD&E	MS	Continuing Education, Distance Learning, Training and Development in the Workplace, Events Management	x	x			
IDD&E	MS	Distance Learning		x		x	
IDD&E	PhD	Instructional Design	x	x			
IDD&E	PhD	Training and IDD&E, Leadership Development Programs		x	x		
IST	MLS	School Media		x			x
IDD&E	MS	Distance Learning, Designing Instruction for Teachers		x	x		
IST (Telecommunications and Network Management)	MS	PCs, People and Management, Telecommunications and Network Management		x			x
IDD&E	PhD		x	x			x
IDD&E	MS	Distance Education, Business/Corporate Evaluation	x	x			x
IST	MLS	School Media		x			
(Incomplete)							
IDD&E	MS						
IST	MLS						
IDD&E	MS						
IDD&E	MS	Information Technology, Project Management		x			x
IDD&E				x			
IDD&E	PhD	Instruction Design (Distance Learning)	x	x			
(Incomplete)							
IDD&E	Other			x		x	

Chapter XXIII

Developing Graduate Qualities

Ann Monday
University of South Australia, Australia

Sandra Barker
University of South Australia, Australia

ABSTRACT

For some time, universities have endeavored to address the shortfall in skill requirements that have been identified by prospective employers of graduates. The University of South Australia (UniSA) numbers itself among these universities and has identified a number of "graduate qualities" that are required to be developed within the curriculum. This chapter explores a case-study and role-play approach to embedding graduate qualities in an undergraduate business course that is delivered to a diverse student body studying either internally or externally, in Australia or in Hong Kong. It highlights a range of issues for successful implementation and assessment of these qualities.

INTRODUCTION

The development of graduate qualities is aimed at facilitating the transition from university to graduate employment. DETYA (2000) examined employer satisfaction with graduate skills and concluded that deficiencies perceived by graduates and employers are in the areas of creativity and flair, oral business communications and problem solving, interpersonal skills, and understanding of business practice. Steven and Fallows (1998) explored "[t]he strategic decision to embed employability skills into each level of the undergraduate curriculum ..." to ensure that "... every student is fully equipped, at graduation, with the skills necessary for the very important transition into the world of employment." UniSA has adopted the approach to embed the graduate qualities into its courses rather than teach them separately.

After consultation with business, UniSA (2000a) identified that a graduate:

1.   Operates effectively with and upon a *body of knowledge* of sufficient depth to begin professional practice
2.   Is prepared for *lifelong learning* in pursuit of personal development and excellence in professional practice
3.   Is an *effective problem solver*, capable of applying logical, critical, and creative thinking to a range of problems
4.   Can work *autonomously and collaboratively* as a professional
5.   Is committed to *ethical action and social responsibility* as a professional and citizen
6.   *Communicates effectively* in professional practice and as a member of the community
7.   Demonstrates *international perspectives* as a professional and as a citizen

UniSA (2000b) requires that all programs within the university should be structured to include a plan for the development of Graduate Qualities (GQs) throughout the duration of the program.

Taylor (1997) stated that "assessment has become a potent tool in dictating institutional and professional goals" and that universities are "being assessed and publicly compared on the basis of student results, and professions being required to introduce specific learning outcomes." UniSA (2000b) views assessment as "the key to the development of Graduate Qualities" and requires academic staff to match appropriate assessment methods to the graduate qualities.

This chapter explores a case-study and role-play approach to embedding the graduate qualities in an undergraduate business course (Data Management for Administrators) and the methods identified for successful assessment of these qualities. During the course design, careful consideration was given to how the assessment related to the development of graduate qualities.

DESIGN OF THE COURSE

The course (subject), Data Management for Administrators (DMA), was designed and introduced in 1999 in response to feedback from past and present students, local businesses,

Table 1. Allocation of course units across graduate qualities

Graduate Quality	1 Body of Knowledge	2 Lifelong Learning	3 Effective Problem Solving	4 Work Autonomously and Collaboratively	5 Ethical Action and Social Responsibility	6 Communicates Effectively	7 International Perspectives
Unit weighting	1.2	0.5	1.0	0.5	0.2	1.0	0.1

Table 2.   Course summary incorporating graduate qualities

Objective	Graduate qualities	Learning outcomes	T&L strategies	Assessment activities
Work effectively in groups	Body of knowledge Lifelong learning Effective problem solver Work autonomously and collaboratively Ethical action and social responsibility Communicate effectively International perspectives	Form, storm, norm and perform as a group: Form group Determine goals of group Determine how each member can best contribute to the group's goals. Identify problems previously encountered in group work and strategies for avoiding problems. Plan a project schedule. Establish good working practices. Operate ethically within the group and with the case organization. Accept responsibility for ones actions, and the actions of the group. Manage group project.	Lecture Case study Tutorial: socialisation using small group activities, print-based learning materials	Assignment: Reflect on individual performance and performance as member of group Examination: Critically evaluate group performance with reference to good practice.
Use information-gathering techniques to determine details of the current system and requirements for its improvement	Body of knowledge Lifelong learning Effective problem solver Work autonomously and collaboratively Ethical action and social responsibility Communicate effectively International perspectives	Examine the case information. Conduct interviews with members of the case organization to clarify the problem. Examine business documents and procedures manuals as available Determine additional information needs. Establish goals of project.	Lecture, case study, role play: tutorial, web board, email, print-based learning materials	Assignment: Identify information needs of case organization.
Apply the tools and techniques of modeling and documenting the information system	Body of knowledge Lifelong learning Effective problem solver Work autonomously and collaboratively Communicate effectively	Use ERDs and normalization to model the business rules and information needs.	Lecture, case study, role play: tutorial, web board, email, print-based learning materials	Assignment: Use data modeling techniques to determine table structures of database Examination: Explain data modeling techniques with reference to lessons learned during implementation of the database

Table 2.   Course summary incorporating graduate qualities (continued)

Objective	Graduate qualities	Learning outcomes	T&L strategies	Assessment activities
Design and document effective output, input and user interface for the system with continual reference to the objectives of the business	Body of knowledge Lifelong learning Effective problem solver Work autonomously and collaboratively Communicate effectively	Apply design theory and techniques for effective input output and interface Validate inputs Produce complete and appropriate documentation	Lecture, case study, role play: tutorial, web board, email, software help desk, print-based learning materials	Assignment: Design input, output and interface based on the requirements and table structures identified Examination: Explain input, output and interface design theory as implemented in the database produced Identify and explain validation and verification techniques used in the design of the database
Partially build a user friendly database	Body of knowledge Lifelong learning Effective problem solver Work autonomously and collaboratively Communicate effectively	Identify the potential and limitations of 4GL database software. Determine the most appropriate software features for implementation. Build a user-friendly database. Design and implement an appropriate user guide to accompany the database developed.	Lecture, case study, role play: tutorial, web board, email, software help desk, print-based learning materials	Assignment: Within a workgroup, and choosing the most appropriate software features, design and implement a small-scale database using Microsoft Access ™. Examination: Critically evaluate the implications of designing and developing a database as an end-user developer

and professional organizations during a review and re-accreditation of a Bachelor of Business (Administrative Management) degree. The course forms one of 24 courses in the degree program and is a core of this program. The student body is large and from a diverse range of backgrounds. Students can study full-time, part-time, or mixed mode, in internal (on campus) or external (off campus) modes or offshore (Hong Kong). External students are primarily from Australia, but some are scattered around the world. The course is also offered as an elective to other business students.

Barker and Monday (2000) highlighted the increased development of spreadsheet and database applications by many of the business graduates, as well as other employees. In most instances, they demonstrated little understanding of the concepts of problem solving, information gathering, analysis, design, and implementation of databases or the implications of the process used in developing the application, or the quality of the applications developed, for the organization.

DMA consists of 140 hours of study over 14 weeks. Internal students attend lectures, tutorials, and workshops. External students work from a study package and have access to tutors via the Web, email, and telephone. Overseas students attend lectures delivered by visiting UniSA staff, and workshops supported by local tutors. Access to UniSA tutors throughout the semester is via email and the Web. Access to technology is not consistent; currently, it cannot be assumed that all external students have access to the Internet and, thus, the course Web page, or to email. The course is a 4.5 unit course, and the balance of the graduate qualities (GQs) is detailed in Table 1.

Table 2 provides a summary of the course objectives, graduate qualities, learning outcomes, teaching and learning strategies, and assessment activities.

TEACHING/LEARNING STRATEGY
Case-Study Teaching

Yuan (2001) identified a significant shift to alternate methods of teaching, including problem-based learning, student-centered learning, and the use of case studies. Case studies are used to describe problems or incidents based on real-life situations (Roselle, 1996). The problems to be analyzed are usually those that have occurred in the past or are likely to be encountered by the students in their professional lives (Kreber, 2001). It is essential that case studies contain sufficient data for analysis and observation to be made, while being conducted in their natural context (Yuan, 2001). When used effectively, case studies should give the students an understanding of the problems they are likely to experience in business and ways to approach these problems.

Gross Davis (1993, cited in Kreber, 2001), in summarizing research into effective case studies, listed the features of a good case study as one that tells a story, raises issues for discussion, contains elements of conflict, lacks a definitive answer, encourages students' thought processes, requires a decision to be made, and is reasonably concise. Each case study for DMA is written within these parameters. Students are supplied with the basic procedures adopted by the organization and are required to develop a small-scale database to solve the issues raised by the business.

Role Play

In DMA, role play is used to explore the case organization. Role play, as defined by Ladousse in Cutler and Hay (2000), is "a short, low input-high output, interactive teaching and learning technique." Rather than a role being mapped out for students, students are required to engage with the parties to the role play, and their role is shaped as they learn (Cutler and Hay, 2000). They also note that this enables students to tackle "live" projects, adopt a role, and view a situation from the viewpoint of their role; requires them to present arguments and defend their viewpoints in verbal and written form; and requires them to work in teams, thus developing their group skills. This approach is particularly suited to the development of a number of graduate qualities. It provides students with an opportunity to interact with each other, and members of a "business," in a group project. It allows the students to apply theory learned to a "live" case. It provides a platform for testing a range of communication media and requires students to manage themselves and the groups they work in.

Due to the diverse nature of our student audience (internal, external, and overseas), role play for DMA is performed in a number of settings — face to face, via the Web, and by using email or telephone.

DEVELOPING THE GRADUATE QUALITIES (GQS)

Body of Knowledge (GQ1)

The use of lectures as a method of teaching in higher education has long been the primary method of imparting knowledge to students. To cater for the diverse range and location of students studying at the UniSA, the body of knowledge has to be disseminated in a number of ways and has been extended to include study packages (study guides, texts, readings) in hard copy and via electronic media. The students choose their preferred method of study.

Students are not only required to demonstrate an understanding of the concepts and theories but also to apply this knowledge to real situations.

Collaborative Work (GQ4)

Kreber (2001) cited the recommendations of Gross Davis (1993) and Knoop (1984) that case studies should be used in conjunction with group work.

Business graduates are likely to experience collaborative (group or team) work during their professional careers. The UniSA (1999d) recognizes that "effective collaboration is determined as much by the ways [students] and their colleagues work with one another as by the kind of task [they] are working on."

This collaborative project introduces the students to the dynamics of a team, the advantages and disadvantages of working together to solve a common problem, and the requirements of businesses for project management and adherence to strict timelines. Group work is currently being introduced to external students in this course, and initial responses from the students have outlined that this is an important skill that has been beneficial to most of the students involved. Results of a more comprehensive investigation into the effectiveness of this implementation will be published at a later date.

For internal students, an initial lecture introduces the students to the concept of group work, and students are encouraged in the first two weeks of tutorials to get to know each other so that groups can be formed no later than Week 3. Students at UniSA are offered a huge amount of choice in their degree program, and therefore, a large number of students will never meet more than a small number of students in their 24 courses. Thus, it is more common for students to meet a group of strangers in the first session. It is considered important, therefore, to provide an opportunity for students to get to know each other early in the semester to facilitate the forming, storming, and norming stages of a project, once groups are identified. Simple problem-solving exercises are used in tutorials to encourage students to participate. In Hong Kong, students are also introduced to the concept of group work in their initial lectures, and local tutors manage fortnightly tutorials. Students in Hong Kong are part-time students studying a prescribed program. They tend to form friendships during their induction program and meet for the same courses each semester. All students are currently allowed to choose their own groups.

Group work adds to the students' understanding of lifelong learning strategies, as students learn techniques for managing difficult situations within the group, while achieving the project goals and timelines set by the business. Within the group, students are required to use oral and written communication skills to make a contribution to solving the case-based problem. The intention of case studies is to develop the problem-solving capabilities of the students by using the body of knowledge, concepts, and skills relevant to the course (Kreber, 2001).

Once groups are established, they are required to determine the goals of the group, determine how each member can best contribute to the group's goals, identify any problems previously encountered in group work and strategies for avoiding problems, plan a project schedule, allocate tasks, establish good working practices, operate ethically within the group and with the case organization, communicate effectively with fellow group members and the organization, accept responsibility for their actions and the actions of the group, while managing the group project to successful completion. At the end of the semester, internal students are required to deliver a short presentation reflecting on their approach to the project and what they have learned as an individual and as a member of a group. Throughout the semester, students are encouraged to document their approach to help them with the preparation of their presentation. External and offshore students complete a written reflection. All students are required to extend this reflection in the examination.

Problem Solving (GQ3) and Effective Communication (GQ6)

The UniSA (1999c) identifies problem solving as "…not so much a set of skills to be applied but a way of approaching…professional practice. It involves analysis — breaking down a problem into components that can be solved — and synthesis — putting together various options for an integrated solution." The university requires students to build upon their previous experience and develop further their ability to solve problems of simple and complex natures. The use of logical reasoning skills as well as intuitive and creative skills is required to present a solution to the issues or problems raised by the case study (Kreber, 2001). Students need to spend the time reading and assessing the problems in the case study to differentiate symptoms from underlying problems (Kreber, 2001). Using simple problem-solving exercises throughout the tutorials, students are encouraged to develop their logical reasoning skills and ability to analyze problems by "thinking outside the square."

Good communication skills are highly valued by employers. UniSA (1999b) highlights that different skills are required for "negotiating with colleagues, employers or clients; for persuading or informing others; for seeking cooperation or giving direction; for giving a talk or writing a manual; for receiving instructions or hearing concerns." In developing effective communication skills, students will develop an understanding of the different forms of communication, appreciate the importance of effective communication, and be able to identify the types of communication required for different purposes and audiences (UniSA, 1999b).

Students are introduced to data modeling techniques via the lecture and tutorial. Through this process, students examine the business processes of the organization and use the techniques to document the business rules and information gathered. Students are assessed on their ability to produce complete, accurate, and appropriate documentation for all stages of the project as well as design and implement an appropriate user guide to accompany the database developed.

Students are provided with different ways to gather information — face-to-face conversations, email, Web discussions, telephone conversations (external students only), and business documents, procedures manuals, and business processes presented in the case study. Using a range of media for role play encourages the more retiring students to contribute to the process. However, not all students make a contribution to discussions, and therefore, the more conscientious students tend to be more guarded in using the public forum. In instances where students feel they have a particularly good idea, they are less likely to post this on a public discussion board, preferring to contact the case business directly.

Questions are directed to the business, not to the tutors, and responses are in line with the type, tone, relevance, and quality of the questions received. Information gathering has been assessed by the quality of the questions asked and in how well the students produce a database that meets the needs of the users. When a mark has not been attached to the quality of questions asked, a marked decline in quality of questions is seen, and in particular, a large number of irrelevant questions are received. In the early stages of the project, students cannot always see the importance of their information gathering and choose to make assumptions.

Students are also presented with conflicting views from the partners in the business and have to learn how to respond to these conflicts. This approach is in line with the Gross Davis approach cited in Kreber (2001), which suggests that a good case study contains elements of conflict to assist students in the learning process. The student response to this approach was extremely varied. The more mature students naturally rose to the challenge, having faced similar situations in their working life. However, when the partners role-played conflict, the younger students, in particular, were shocked, and unsure of how to proceed. Students commented that this was a completely new learning experience for them, as they were normally given a package of information stating the question to be answered, the approach expected, and an example of how to complete the problem set.

Once the students gathered the appropriate information, the next problem-solving task they embark on is to determine the most appropriate software features for implementation, identify the potential and limitations of 4GL database software, and finally, develop a user-friendly database. Students are assessed on the usability as well as the logical and physical design of the database.

Ethical Action (GQ5), Internationalization (GQ7), and Lifelong Learning (GQ2)

Throughout the project, students are expected to demonstrate ethical action with the business, with other students, and in their approach to their university education. Certainly, any students found guilty of copying would automatically be awarded a zero as a minimum penalty, but given this is group work, this rarely happens.

Internationalization of students is not developed well within this course. While offshore students are all students studying in their home country, this is not true of onshore students. Although we have a diverse group of students onshore, they tend to stay in their ethnic groups. It may be appropriate to allocate students to groups to address this issue. This would also simulate better, normal working life, where staff members do not generally choose who they will work with. Because of the diverse range of students and their availability, this would also necessitate students learning to manage their availability and time more carefully but is likely to lead to greater conflict within the groups.

The format of tutorial/workshop delivery for offshore students is prescribed, and students are offered fortnightly workshops. Two approaches to delivering the practical component to internal students have been trialed — scheduled workshops (1999) and help desks (2000, 2001). In both cases, the sessions were not compulsory but were available for students to ask questions relating to the self-directed learning they were programmed to have completed through the study schedule. Both onshore and offshore students regularly attended workshops without prior preparation, or alternatively, did not attend at all. Tutors spent most of their time working with a small percentage of conscientious, prepared students who tended to become frustrated by those students who expected the tutor to go through the work they had not prepared.

The introduction of compulsory workshops to internal students, at the behest of the students, has not alleviated the problems, as, although they attended, they still did not undertake the appropriate preparation. Nor did this approach encourage students to develop lifelong learning qualities. Some students are not prepared to take responsibility for their learning unless the preparation has a mark attached to it. Candy et al. (1994) identified that staff, students, and graduates agree that open-book examinations, assignments, clinical case studies, negotiated learning contracts, and learning documents were the forms of assessment that were most likely to ensure effective, ongoing learning, because students were required to analyze and articulate the learning processes with the completion of the learning task. This appears to be reflected in the students' approach to the workshops conducted throughout this course. However, it needs to be recognized that the overhead on staff time increases with these approaches.

The world in which we live is constantly changing. UNESCO considers that education should last the whole life of an individual; lead to the continual acquisition and update of knowledge, skills, and attitudes; be self-fulfilling; acknowledge all available educational influences; and be motivating for people to engage in self-directed learning (Candy et al., 1994). Graduates will be required to continually develop their professional knowledge as the demands of their working life change. The introduction of lifelong learning into undergraduate courses attempts to develop students' ability to identify and tackle new problems and to locate and use information in an effective manner. UniSA (1999a) identifies that in acquiring lifelong learning skills, students will develop information literacy, understand how to manage their learning, gain confidence as learners, and value curiosity and a critical approach.

CONCLUSION

Graduate qualities develop out of the processes employed in the teaching of the course. In essence, the teaching and learning strategies were implemented to develop a positive attitude toward the continual learning process and the ability to "think outside the square." The introduction of case studies and role playing in this course has stimulated the students to explore, to enquire, to question, to motivate, and to acquire skills that they will use in their professional lives. Providing we attach a mark to the various stages of the project, students generally deliver well. This raises an interesting question in terms of whether the students are demonstrating the graduate qualities if they only attach importance to something that gains them a mark.

Candy et al. (1994) described assessment as being a measure of how something has been learned and the use the student will be able to make of this knowledge. The methods of assessment used in this course attempt, with some success, to determine the extent to which the graduate qualities of body of knowledge, effective communication, and problem solving have been attained. If students are to be encouraged to be lifelong learners, they "must be able to judge or evaluate the adequacy, completeness or appropriateness of their own learning, so whatever assessment practices are used [they] must be comprehensible to the learners so that they can be internalized as criteria for critical self-evaluation" (Candy et al., 1994).

The course currently fails to achieve a good outcome in the area of project management. At the end of the course, students reflect on their approach and identify a number of weaknesses in managing themselves, and in particular, their time. In the follow-up course, these problems recur.

The approach adopted provides an interesting learning forum for staff and students, and provides the students with the opportunity to demonstrate effective problem solving, working collaboratively (excluding external students), effective communication, and lifelong learning, as well as the ability to operate effectively on a body of knowledge. However, it needs to be recognized that this approach has a high overhead on staff time, and given the ever-increasing numbers of students, staff members are constantly exploring new ways of achieving positive results with lower overhead.

ONGOING RESEARCH

This research forms part of a wider research program being conducted by Sandra Barker and Ann Monday into the delivery of this software-based information systems course in the Administrative Management degree program.

REFERENCES

Barker, S., & Monday, A. (2000). Business students in information systems: Wizards or apprentices? *Proceedings of the Australasian Computing Education Conference*, Melbourne, Australia, December.

Candy, P. C., Crebert, G., & O'Leary, J. (1994). *Developing Lifelong Learners Through Undergraduate Education.* Canberra: Australian Government Printing Service.

Cutler, C. & Hay, I. (2000). "Club Dread": Applying and refining an issue-based role play on environment, economy, and culture. *Journal of Geography in Higher Education, 24*, 2, 179–197.

Kreber, C. (2001). Learning experientially through case studies? A conceptual analysis. *Teaching in Higher Education, 6*, 2, 217–228.

Roselle, A. (1996). The case study method: A learning tool for practising librarians and information specialists. *Library Review, 45*, 4, 30–38.

Taylor, I. (1997). *Developing Learning in Professional Education: Partnerships for Practice.* Buckingham, UK: SRHE and Open University Press.

University of South Australia. (1999a). Graduate Quality 2 leaflet. Retrieved October 4, 2001 from the World Wide Web: http://www.unisanet.unisa.edu.au/gradquals/GQleaflet2.doc.

University of South Australia. (1999b). Graduate Quality 6 leaflet. Retrieved October 4, 2001 from the World Wide Web: http://www.unisanet.unisa.edu.au/gradquals/GQleaflet6.doc.

University of South Australia. (1999c). Graduate Quality 3 leaflet. Retrieved October 4, 2001 from the World Wide Web: http://www.unisanet.unisa.edu.au/gradquals/GQleaflet3.doc.

University of South Australia. (1999d). Graduate Quality 4 leaflet. Retrieved October 4, 2001 from the World Wide Web: http://www.unisanet.unisa.edu.au/gradquals/GQleaflet4.doc.

University of South Australia. (2000a). Graduate Qualities — Overview. *Learning Connection Teaching Guide.* Retrieved September 23, 2001 from the World Wide Web: http://www.unisanet.unisa.edu.au/learningconnection/teachg/tggqo.doc.

University of South Australia. (2000b). Graduate Qualities — A program design and development process. *Learning Connection Teaching Guide.* Retrieved October 4, 2001 from the World Wide Web: http://www.unisanet.unisa.edu.au/learningconnection/teachg/GQprogdesign.doc.

Yuan, L. L. (2001). Quality of life case studies for university teaching in sustainable development. *International Journal of Sustainability in Higher Education, 2*, 2, 127–138.

Chapter XXIV

Real Live Cases in Training Management of Information Resources During the Transition to Market Economy

Dimitar Christozov
American University in Bulgaria, Bulgaria

ABSTRACT

In this chapter, the use of real live cases, based on students' experience, in training for the Information Resources Management (IRM) course is discussed. IRM is a core-required course of a MIS MBA program. This approach is compared with one that explores cases drawn from textbooks. The objective of comparison is student's learning outcome. Two groups of students, trained under the two paradigms, were selected, and their performances, after graduation, were compared. The students play key roles in their companies. Assessment shows that in given circumstances (transition from centrally planning to market-oriented economy, small enterprises, and underdeveloped information infrastructure), the use or real live cases offered by the students allows training to be kept relevant to the business practices.

INTRODUCTION

Two models of training the course "Information Resources Management" (IRM) are compared, according to the students' learning outcomes. IRM is a core course in the MBA-MIS program of the Faculty of Economics and Business Administration at Sofia University "St. Kliment Ohridski." Initially, the course was taught by exploring cases drawn by Western textbooks. The second paradigm explores cases proposed by students, which reflect students' experience. The comparison of the two models is based on students' performance, during class discussions and during their professional careers after graduation.

The primary objective of this research is to collect feedback about how students apply the IRM principles and adjust the course content and training model to their needs.

The research also addresses the issue of using real life cases offered by students, and in which circumstances this approach serves better in meeting given learning objectives. The experience of using different types of cases is shared by Earl Chrysler (2002), but in his review, real live cases offered by students are not discussed.

BACKGROUND

The objectives of the IRM course are as follows:

- To develop understanding about the role of information in a social institution as a valuable resource, critical for successful management, which needs to be managed as well as any other resource
- To clarify that information as a resource is not limited to data, but it also includes technologies of data processing, organizing, and using information effectively in decision making
- To define information needs for decisions made on different levels in a company's hierarchy, and the basic forms of support an information system has to provide
- To shape the role of Computer-Based Information Technologies

The MIS MBA program was established in 1996. During the first three years of this period, the author used a "standard" lecture-type training model, following a Western textbook — the primary text was Kanter (1994), and some lectures were based on Bucland (1991) and Schoderbek, Schoderbek, and Kefalas (1990), and cases were drawn from other Western sources, as Beaumont and Sutherland (1992). The students learned to interpret theory and to analyze cases from the textbooks. Students with broader experience expressed concern about difficulties in applying that knowledge in Bulgarian business practice. To achieve course objectives and to build practical skills to identify and solve problems, during the last 3 years, a seminar-type model was applied, which explores students' personal backgrounds and business experiences.

In class, students presented cases drawn from their experience. The case represents a company and its managerial practice. The cases were analyzed, using brainstorming and other group analytical techniques to specify the properties of the information systems the given company needed. The specification also included recommendations for improving adminis- trative structure and business processes, as well as recommendations related to data modeling and information technologies.

The students were trained to critically analyze problems applying IRM principles, and to develop practical skills in drawing specifications for building information systems. As a secondary benefit, the students achieved broader understanding of the diversity of business practices, in the particular time slot of the transition to market economy.

The period of transition (started in 1989) to a market economy in Eastern Europe coincided with the exponential growth in the use of computer-based information technologies. The two processes are going on simultaneously and heavily impact each other.

WHY THE TRAINING MODEL NEEDS REVISION

The past 12 years were characterized by a transition to a market-oriented economy. In the countries, like Bulgaria, the collapse of a centrally planned economy was followed by an unregulated business environment, partially following market principles and partially preserving a high level of governmental regulation, monopolies, and key influence of the state's bureaucracy. In such an environment, "standard" managerial models do not work properly. That is true particularly for small businesses. The following characteristics, related to IRM, of the centrally planned economy still impact the behavior of people engaged in business activities:

- The infrastructure for collecting and distributing information was organized hierarchically, and people had restricted access to reliable sources. Official sources were suspected, partially by inertia, partially because of the conflict of interests with state's officers engaged in providing services.

- People used to rely on shared interpersonal information, instead of information provided by specialized institutions, such as the Statistical Agency, and therefore, they have not developed skills for dealing with such information sources.

- Managerial experience was obtained in a monopolistic type of enterprise, without proper competition and market-driven rewards, where the role of information was neglected.

Currently, the factors that have impact on the "success" of training IRM can be classified in two groups:
1. Environmental factors:
   - The information infrastructure in the country is extremely underdeveloped, and students had limited experience in dealing with information sources in their practice.
   - Social practices show that a successful business makes managerial decisions based more often on intuition and general knowledge, or on personally delivered internal information, and not on applying theoretical models and market research, as studied in the universities.
   - The entire business environment lacks proper regulation. The legal framework in which business operates is changing frequently and heavily depends on government, bureaucracy, and monopolies.
2. Personal factors:
   - Business background and experience were accumulated primarily in small companies with guaranteed customers in a given region or area and run in conditions of shortage on the market with absence of real competition.

- In small, family-type businesses, information is shared freely among employees, without even an attempt to organize it. This leads to:

    i.   Underestimation of the role of proper administration

    ii.   Presentation of information in a manner that is not well structured, therefore, making it not helpful in the decision-making process, and of course, making its role and importance not visible

    iii.   Lack of proper documentation, which leads to a lack of history; repeating mistakes are rarely analyzed, outcomes are not measured, and management is considered a kind of art

    iv.   Making of decisions is usually done by a single person, and that person's information-processing abilities are the bottleneck for company's development and growth

All of this creates a skeptical attitude toward the content of the course and potential practical benefits in mastering the material. Also, lack of training and research materials (theoretical models, cases, studies, etc.), relevant to the current situation in Bulgaria, interfere with the proper design of the course. It is not worthy to develop such literature, because of the limited time for which it is needed. Also, during the transition, the situation changes fast. Finally, the current students are the people who are intended to transfer the economy — they must be trained to perform successfully in the current business environment with clear understanding of the principles and benefits of the modern management.

A training model is needed, which is sensitive to current students' expertise and currently used managerial practices, and flexible enough to reflect rapid changes in the business environment.

DESCRIPTION OF THE ADOPTED MODEL

The training passes in two stages:

- Lecture-dominated stage: At this stage, there is presentation of basic IRM principles with intensive discussion of problems, benefits, and difficulties. The problem-driven approach is applied. This part takes the first one-third of the duration of the course.

- Case-study seminars: At this stage, every student has to present a snapshot of a real or virtual company, based on the student's experience. The student must be able to answer any questions related to business processes, administrative structure and managerial practice, information flows, decision-making processes, etc. Other students are invited to analyze how the IRM principles are or can be implemented in the company.

The discussion follows the following scenario:

- Discussion starts with a description of the company: sector, size, structure, activities, markets.

- Special attention is placed on the decisions being made in the company, trying to place any of them on the scales: operational — strategic and structured (algorithmic) or unstructured (involving risk and uncertainty).

- For any type of decision, information needs are specified, including sources, access, interpretation, and quality assessment, as well as persons engaged in decision making.
- Business processes and information flows are defined.
- Ways of reengineering the business model to satisfy the IRM principles, including specification of the Information Systems and Technologies useful for the given case, are defined.
- The price of implementation of the Information System, including training of personnel, is evaluated.
- The overall performance of a company if it applies these procedures, compared to existing practices, is assessed.
- Feasibility is assessed, and recommendations are defined.

DESCRIPTION OF THE PERFORMED RESEARCH

This training approach, described in the previous section, was applied for the first time in the 1999–2000 academic year. Feedback from students was positive. Some students from this class shared that they had implemented the recommendations reached in class with significant success in their companies. This encouraged me to continue with the same training model and to research alumni performance.

Two groups of students, one trained according to the initial model (trained in the period of 1996–1999), and the other (trained after 1999), working for companies with similar size and type of activities, in similar key managerial positions, were identified and approached (Table 1). This actually excludes large- or medium-sized enterprises, state's owned institutions, and branches of international companies.

Further research includes identifying and applying to both groups a set of measurable criteria, which will allow clear identification of the benefits of the two approaches and will serve to further improve the training model. The criteria reflect objectives of the IRM course. Comparison was performed according to the following criteria:

C1: Existence of proper organization of internal information, facts, suppliers and supplies, delivery, claims, etc., to allow traceability of events

C2: Existence of proper organization of collecting and evaluating relevant external information

Table 1. The two groups of companies

Type of Activities	"Initial" Model	"Real-Live Cases" Model
S1: Providing intellectual services	Consulting: assets evaluation for enterprises privatization	Consulting: Personnel Agency
S2: Providing material services	Garage	Home renovation
T: Trade	Species for meat production	Electrical supplies
P: Production	Software	Software

Table 2. Results of comparison

Criteria	"Initial" Model				"Real-Live Cases" Model			
	S1	S2	T	P	S1	S2	T	P
C1	3	0	2	1	3	2	4	5
C2	1	0	3	2	4	2	4	4
C3	3	1	4	1	5	3	5	5
C4	4	0	3	5	4	2	5	5

C3:   Existence of predefined procedures and distribution of responsibilities related to information processing and decision making (the best case is to have written procedures, but, because of the size of the company, informal or by-default knowledge was accepted as well enough)

C4:   Use of Information Technologies, computers, and the Internet

For a given company, every criterion was evaluated according to a six-level scale, where 0 meant "not at all," and 5 meant "best possible." In some cases, especially for companies in the "Real-Live Cases" group, a higher grade was given, even if implementation of a proper organization is planned but still not implemented. I graded higher the understanding about what is needed and why, instead of simply the copying of the best practice in the branch, without considering the particular needs of the company. Results are presented in Table 2.

The above table, together with personal observations on the organization and administration of these companies, shows that the students trained under the "initial" model have not initiated any particular activities toward implementation of IRM principles but follow closely the mainstream of development in the sector. They know what is needed but do not believe that it is possible to be done here and now. The other group initiated implementation of IRM principles, in one case, the recommendations reached in class discussion, willing to demonstrate the benefits of well-managed information.

CONCLUSION

Using real live cases offered by students is highly demanding to the instructor, who faces difficulties in the following:

* A lack of proper preparation in analyzing cases may occur.
* The set of cases presented in a particular class may miss important issues.
* Grading is based on the presented case and participation in the discussion, and for both, it is difficult to set quantitative measures.

But, the collected data show that in given circumstances (transitioning from a centrally planning to market-oriented economy, small enterprises, and underdeveloped information infrastructure), the use of real live cases offered by the students allows training relevant to the business practices to continue.

REFERENCES

Beaumont, S. (1992). *Information Resources Management*. Oxford: Butterworth-Heinemann Ltd.

Buckland, M. (1991). *Information and Information Systems*. New York: Praeger.

Chrysler, E. (2002). Teaching IT development using live versus case projects: A comparative analysis (pp. 942–943). *Issues and Trends of Information Technology Management in Contemporary Organizations*. Hershey, PA: Idea Group Publishing.

Kanter, J. (1992). *Managing with Information*. New York: Prentice Hall.

Schoderbek, Schoderbek, & Kefalas. (1990). *Management Systems: Conceptual Considerations*. BPI IRWIN.

Chapter XXV

Business Students as End-User Developers: Simulating "Real-Life" Situations through Case Study Approach

Sandra Barker
University of South Australia, Australia

ABSTRACT

In this chapter, the introduction of "real-life" scenarios to undergraduate business students to enhance their understanding of end-user development of databases is investigated. The problems experienced with end-user development due to incomplete information, incorrect design procedures, and inadequate software knowledge are identified. It is the hope of the author that by identifying the design issue relevant to good database production and using "real-life" case studies as insight into how businesses use and store data, the students will be more aware of good practice for their future employment.

INTRODUCTION

With the increasing number of PCs available in business and the proliferation of relatively inexpensive application (4GL) software, employers are increasingly requiring business graduates to have some knowledge of the concepts of application development (Barker & Monday, 2000; Monday, 2001). Edberg and Bowman (1996) defined user-developed applications (UDAs) as "any computer-based application for which non-IS professionals (end-users) assume primary development responsibility."

The implementation of UDAs has increased due to the perception that they offer greater user control, increase flexibility, encourage innovation, and reduce the workload of the IT department (Monday, 2001). Christoff (1991) identified that the introduction of 4GL application software represented a "fundamental change in the way data is processed" and understood that this would lead to end-users developing a greater power in the design and implementation of business applications. Hobbs and Pigott (2001) stated that the force behind end-user development was that "the users themselves are in the best position to understand the requirements of the application domain and therefore to create an application tailored to their particular needs." Consequently, it has been noted that UDAs now represent a significant proportion of information systems being utilized in business (McGill, 2000).

However, there is significant evidence that businesses are only just identifying the problems associated with UDAs. While undertaking risk analysis and evaluation, organizations often overlook the risks involved with the proliferation of UDAs (Janvrin & Morrison, 2000). These risks can include incorrect design, inadequate testing, poor maintenance (McGill, 2000), erroneous data structures, insufficient organizational policies and procedures (Christoff, 1991), and lack of familiarity with development methodologies or application software (Panko & Halverson, 1996).

It is therefore apparent that more responsibility is being placed on the end-user developer to be conversant with design methodologies; data modeling techniques; theory related to effective and user-friendly input, output, and interface design; the intricacies of application software; and documentation techniques to ensure that the application they develop is robust and useful to the organization.

The majority of research in this area has focused on the development of spreadsheet applications, as these were the most common applications developed by end users. Panko (2000) has been instrumental in the research into error rates in spreadsheet development over the past two decades. Errors in spreadsheets developed by end users were located in considerable numbers (Panko & Halverson, 1996), primarily due to the fact that "user controls do not seem to approach the level of control that professional programmers have found to be necessary in a similar application." Research shows that approximately 91% of end users have had experience with spreadsheets, while as many as 44% of these can contain at least one error (Teo & Tan, 1999; Janvrin & Morrison, 2000).

With the increase in availability of database software with 4GL (application generator) ability, it seems likely that these issues and problems will also be found in the development of small-scale databases. Edberg and Bowman (2000) recognized that "UDAs represent a considerable risk to organizations since users who create applications frequently have little or no training in development methods."

Monday (2001) stated that feedback over a number of years from local businesses and professional organizations "highlighted a growing need for business graduates with a greater understanding of the opportunities afforded by 4GLs, and a competency in understanding the business needs and developing small-scale applications for local users" which can be applied to the day-to-day business problems.

Hobby (1996) highlighted the need for end users to be given some design and implementation training, where PC users were transformed into end-user developers of databases using Microsoft Access. It was identified that building database applications using 4GL software was "something slightly different from using Word and Excel — actually learning how to design a database properly."

In this chapter, case studies used to assist business students in understanding the complexities of database development are explored, and these experiences are contrasted with those of the author in industry.

THE COURSE

The University offers a range of undergraduate business degrees, including majors in Administrative Management, Commerce, International Business, and Tourism. Students in these programs are required to take an IT literacy course that provides them with a basic introduction to standard PC application software as well as an overview of the use of information systems in organizations.

Recent graduates have sought assistance from tutors in the design and implementation of small-scale databases required in their employment. It was this feedback that led to the redesign of a course that would provide students with an active introduction to the problems experienced in the end-user development of databases.

Graduates highlighted that many of them (and others in their organizations) were required to develop database applications. Mostly, these end users demonstrated little understanding of the concepts of problem solving and information gathering, and analysis, design, and implementation issues for database applications. They did not recognize the implications of the process of application development, or the quality of the applications developed, for the organization (Barker & Monday, 2000).

The graduates raised concerns, as they were being required to build applications using Microsoft software, however, they had only been introduced to the software's applications generators or "wizards" in the computer literacy course. It was as these graduates explored the need for more advanced features of the software that they began to understand the potential and the limitations of using only the wizards or basic features of the software.

Design of the application was also raised as an issue. Although a number of the graduates became proficient in the tools of the software, they had only a limited understanding of design principles in relation to data structure, inputs including data validation, outputs, and the interface. Thus, the applications tended to fail in terms of "user friendliness" and in achieving the level of accuracy and efficiency expected in data input and output. Winter, Chudoba, and Gutek (1997) suggested that this is likely to be caused partly by the lack of attention paid to the role of IS literacy in helping the end user to be efficient and effective.

As a result of these concerns, this course was developed at a level for second-year undergraduates and is core to the Administrative Management degree program. However, with the proliferation of end-user development, students from other business degrees are recognizing the benefits of taking such a course as an elective.

This first-semester course concentrates on data management, systems development theory, small-scale database construction using Microsoft Access, and the impact of end-user development on business. The course is taught using case studies written in consultation with business or based on the industrial experience of the staff working on the program.

Kreber (2001) described case studies as "the detailed description of a particular real life situation or problem as it happened in the past or as it could happen in the professional life of the student." The use of case studies is encouraged in higher education, as it tends to involve students in a more active learning process. This can be seen to be in line with the four phases of Kolb's experiential learning theory, as students experience concrete experience, abstract conceptualization, reflective observation, and active experimentation. Here, students are more likely to "foster the skills of self-directed learning" (Kreber, 2001). Knoop (1984, cited in Kreber, 2001) introduced a problem-solving model based on Kolb's theory.

This model is distinguished by five steps:
1. Identify the problem
2. Distinguish the problem from the underlying symptoms
3. Generate alternate problem-solving strategies
4. Evaluate the alternatives, and select the best strategy
5. Develop plan of implementation of best strategy

Students' experiences apply to this model, as they must first determine any information not presented in the case study that they deem necessary to solving the problem they have been presented. This takes place with the use of a Web-based discussion board available to all students through the course Web site. The course coordinator assumes the role of the primary contact person within the business and responds accordingly to student questions, allowing some latitude for the students to think about the process they are undertaking. All students have access to the questions asked by other groups or individuals and, consequently, to the answers given by the "business."

By undertaking this process, the students identify the problem and determine a strategy for solving the problem based on the information given by the business.

Case studies used in these courses alternate between service and manufacturing business sectors, as this is where the majority of graduates finds employment. The content of the case study centers on the information needs of a small business or one department within a larger organization. Students are required to understand the corporate structure and information needs of the department as well as the organization as a whole.

Internal students work in groups as recommended by Gross Davis (1993) and Knoop (1984, both cited in Kreber, 2001). External students were introduced to group work for the first time in 2002, and initial results are promising, with a large proportion of these students attaining high grades for the assignment. Feedback from these students is currently being collated, and the results of the success of this implementation will be published in the near future. Students in Hong Kong will be subjected to group work in the coming cohort of this course.

INDUSTRY EXPERIENCE

The author has been involved with the design and implementation of small-scale databases for eight years, particularly in the mining and fitness industries. As a consultant, many problems were experienced in the completion of these projects.

Understanding the Business

Most important is company knowledge: being unfamiliar with the management structure, IT capabilities, budget restrictions, and the key personnel to be involved with the project often caused problems at the commencement of the project. This lack of knowledge involved such issues as identifying the project supervisor, available software (and appropriate version), functional PC specifications, budget flexibility (including allocation for possible hardware and software upgrades), and the question of was there more than one person with the ability to respond to queries. The other issue here was a complete understanding of the processes taking place. As a consultant, the author was not an expert in the relevant industries, and therefore, time was needed to understand the activities being conducted by the business before the systems analysis could take place. When these issues were not resolved early in the project, it caused problems throughout the information-gathering and design stages of the application.

Time Management and Information Gathering

Many clashes were experienced in the information-gathering phase due to the large number of company personnel who wished to have input into the development of the application. Many projects involved discussions with primary user(s), departmental managers, senior management, and business partners. There would regularly be more than 10 staff members involved in the project, most with differing requirements and knowledge of the current system. As a commercial consultant, it was extremely important to adhere to project deadlines, however, this was often impossible due to the personnel rosters used. For example, in the mining industry, contact staff members were regularly offsite when information was required, and delays of up to 10 days could be experienced.

No detailed project schedule was prepared by either body, and this led to frustration caused by these delays. This led the author to move to the design phase prior to sourcing all of the relevant information, causing time delays on the project, as incomplete or inaccurate information was included in the logical design and not discovered until well into the implementation phase. Most of these problems were encountered due to the large distance between the organization and the consultant (sometimes over 3000 km), leading to most of the information gathering and consultation being undertaken via telephone meetings and email discussions. Closer proximity to the organization or regular on-site meetings may have alleviated some of these problems.

Alterations to Specifications

Changing specifications is the most frustrating problem that a developer has to deal with. Due to the number of people involved from the organization, there were regular in-house arguments that needed to be resolved, and often, the resolutions were not achieved prior to implementation. The project team regularly made major changes to what exactly was to be included in the application, leading to increased development time being required by the consultant.

Software Issues

Software limitations are often the hardest constraint to overcome. The organization's project team needed a particular task performed that was physically unachievable using the software available within the company. The time taken to describe the software features available or possible alternative methods of achieving the organization's requests also tended to lead to problems in achieving the deadlines of the project.

PROBLEMS ENCOUNTERED BY STUDENTS
Time Management and Software Issues

Students are challenged by the strict time constraints of the assessment; they have 10 weeks to complete the database task. Academic staff members encourage students to spend the initial weeks advancing their knowledge of the software to be used. No formal software training sessions are held for this purpose. The study program is time-tabled such that students should attempt the training theory and examples prior to attending a practical session. It is during these sessions that the students are able to ask questions and discuss alternative features that are available in the software being used. External students are given access to a telephone help line for software-based queries. While undertaking this learning, students commenced the information-gathering phase of the system development.

Information Gathering

Even though students are given a large amount of information in the case study presented, they are required to determine any important information missing from the documentation and consult directly with the business to uncover the relevant data. It is this area in which the students experience major difficulties. Information gathering is undertaken through the use of a Web-based discussion board. The problems that they encounter include minimal understanding of the process, requests for unnecessary information, inability to reword questions if an inadequate reply is received, not asking any questions, and not referring to the Web discussion board, which therefore, leads to making incorrect assumptions.

The ability to determine which information is actually relevant to solving the problem or issues they have highlighted is another problem that students experience. Students regularly try to include all of the information from the case study and are extremely reluctant to discard inappropriate and unnecessary information.

Group Issues

A problem that appears from this discussion board approach is that the enthusiastic groups ask the relevant questions, leaving those students and groups that are less organized to use the responses to other's questions. It is here that the less organized groups lose in the learning process and are unable to take any understanding of the information-gathering phase into other courses or to their ultimate employment on graduation. Group cohesion, organization, and time management are issues identified by the students as the most essential for attaining good results in the development of the database.

Logical Design Issues and Documentation

At the same time the students are learning the features of the software, they are attempting to design the database application, and they have a tendency to launch directly into physical design and implementation. This tends to cause the most problems in the case of database construction. Students who do not use data modeling techniques to identify the entities and attributes required, together with the primary keys and table relationships, experience the greatest difficulty with producing a sound, effective, and usable application.

The lack of logical design also creates problems, as the process is not documented, and students tend to get lost in the process and not understand what it is they have created. The unfortunate loss of a file through poor backup procedures leads to much distress for these students, as they have no documentation to fall back on to recreate their physical design.

Physical Design Issues

Although much discussion through lecture and tutorial sessions focused on good design characteristics of input and output screens and user-friendly interfaces, some students still chose to implement multicolor or fashion color screens without any thought to the amount of time the user may spend looking at these screens. Occupational health and safety issues were discarded in favor of "a unique look."

Those students who communicated with the business tended to produce more user-friendly interfaces. A large number of students, however, chose to make assumptions about many of the design issues (e.g., report layout, data entry procedures, and workflow issues), and therefore, their applications lacked the features required by the business.

Testing and Implementation

Misuse of or lack of validation and GUI controls were the major weaknesses across the assignments. None of the databases proved to be totally robust and user-friendly, however, several achieved a good level of development.

Finally, students experienced problems due to the lack of testing of the application. In the production of the database, students tended to enter test data after the construction of the tables and, therefore, did not test the input screens for functionality and user-friendly design. Applications were not tested for validation techniques, meaningful error messages, usability, and effective macros. A number of the students commented that the wizards were not capable of achieving the full requirements of the users; however, the case studies were all tested prior to the delivery to ensure that the wizards were sufficient for the development of these applications.

COMPARISON OF EXPERIENCES

Understanding the Business

The case studies used in this course exposed the students to the problems faced with not knowing or understanding the business type they are assessing. The lack of knowledge of the business processes, particularly in the manufacturing industries, initially causes the students major concerns, as they not only have to understand the nature of the business but also the problem necessary to be solved. At the completion of the course, many students commented about what they have learned, not only about problem-solving issues and the use of the software application but also about the business they were assessing.

Time Management and Information Gathering

The students do not tend to experience the problems inherent in the information-gathering phase of the process, as most of the information is disseminated through the case-study documentation and the discussion board. One way that students might experience this problem would be to remove the discussion board from the available facilities, thus making each group responsible for their own information gathering. Although this would simulate the process more accurately, this is generally not considered a viable option in the teaching area of large groups of students, where the same questions would be presented numerous times.

Students are not given inaccurate information or time delays due to intraorganization conflicts; however, they are only given the information they ask for, and this can sometimes lead to the introduction of poor or incomplete information. Occasionally, due to onshore and offshore teaching commitments, students are unable to contact the business which, in part, simulates the situations experienced by the author in the inability to contact key project personnel due to roster issues. Although the students only experience delays of three to four days maximum, it impacts their time management considerably, as they tend to delay starting the assignment until close to the due date rather than managing their time as they would in industry.

Software Issues

Case studies are carefully produced to ensure that all the tasks required to be completed or implemented are achievable with the software being utilized. As this is not always the case in business, students are not exposed to these issues. The course aims to give the students some awareness of the limitations of the software (as experienced by non-IS professionals), and therefore, they tend to appreciate these limitations without actually experiencing them fully.

FUTURE PLANS

In order to improve the student experience, the next phase of this course is to identify actual businesses requiring the development of a small database, and allow the students to experience, first hand, the trials and tribulations of working with an actual business.

The continual assessment of the implementation of group work with external and offshore students will be undertaken to ensure that the experience simulates that which would be undertaken in a business setting.

CONCLUSION

Although there is still room for refinement of the case-study delivery of this course, students are rising to the challenge of dealing with "real-life" business problems. Issues relating to equity between internal and external students as well as those who do not have access to the Web-based discussion forum must be addressed to ensure that all students are achieving the learning outcomes of this course.

Some students are relying heavily on other groups or group members to lead the way, without understanding the importance of the system development phases. It is these students who present only partially completed or poorly designed applications, and as such, further research is required into better ways to deliver the case-study approach.

The aim of this course is to help students to recognize the importance of the steps required to achieve a good quality software application, even though they are non-IS professionals. It also seeks to encourage students to recognize the implications of their actions and choices for the organization and not just their immediate needs. Emphasis, thus, is not purely on building a good quality, robust software application but in presenting a more holistic view of user and organizational needs.

ONGOING RESEARCH

This research forms part of a wider research program being conducted by Sandra Barker and Ann Monday into the delivery of this software-based information systems course in the Administrative Management degree program.

REFERENCES

Barker, S. & Monday, A. (2000). Business students in information systems: Wizards or apprentices? *Proceedings of the Australasian Computing Education Conference*, Melbourne, Australia, December.

Edberg, D. T. & Bowman, B. J. (1996). User-developed applications: An empirical study of application quality and developer productivity. *Journal of Management Information Systems, 13*, 1, 167–185.

Hobbs, V. J. & Pigott, D. J. (2001). Facilitating end user database development by working with users' natural representations of data. *Proceedings of the IRMA Conference*, Toronto, Canada, May.

Hobby, J. (1996). Degrees of excellence, *Computer Weekly*, August 2, 32.

Janvrin, D. & Morrison, J. (2000). Using a structured design approach to reduce risks in end user spreadsheet development. *Information and Management, 37*, 1–12.

Kreber, C. (2001). Learning experientially through case studies? A conceptual analysis. *Teaching in Higher Education, 6*, 2, 217–228.

McGill, T. J. (2000). User developed applications: Can end users assess quality? *IRMA International Conference: IT Management in the 21st Century* (pp. 106–111). Alaska.

Monday, A. (2001). The reality of teaching large groups of local and international business students to develop end-user applications. *Proceedings of the IRMA Conference*, Toronto, Canada, May.

Panko, R. R. Survey of developers. Retrieved July 17, 2000 from the World Wide Web: http://panko.cba.hawaii.edu/ssr/tables/dvelprs.htm.

Panko, R. R. & Halverson, R. P. Jr. (1996). Spreadsheets on trial: A survey of research on spreadsheet risks. *Proceedings of the 29th Hawaii International Conference on System Sciences* (pp. 326–335). Maui, Hawaii.

Ross, J. & Ruhleder, K. (1993). Preparing IS professionals for a rapidly changing world: The challenge for IS educators. *Proceedings of the 1993 Conference on Computer Personnel Research* (pp. 379–384).

Teo, T. S. H. & Tan, M. (1999). Spreadsheet development and "what-if" analysis: Quantitative versus qualitative errors. *Accounting, Management and Information Technology, 9*, 141–160.

Winter, S. J., Chudoba, K. M., & Gutek, B. A. (1997). Misplaced resources? Factors associated with computer literacy among end-users. *Information and Management, 32*, 29–42.

Chapter XXVI

E-Business Education for Everyone: Developing and Implementing Breakthrough Strategies

(Or How Can IT Practitioners and Educators Make Computer Morons Surf and Steer on E-Business Space)

Rumel V. Atienza
De La Salle University, Philippines

ABSTRACT

Since its inception at the close of the past millennium, e-business has rapidly and continuously changed the conduct of business. However, the incoming generation of the Philippine workforce, particularly those who do not have sufficient exposure to computer technology and business, may not be able to cope, due to lack of academic preparation. Information technology practitioners and academicians can turn this threat into an opportunity by adopting a system of breakthrough practices in e-business education based on benchmarking studies in various universities in Asia and North America. The system proved to be highly effective, based on its pilot run.

INTRODUCTION

As the new millennium ushered in, the new global order of the Internet-kind unfolded and exponentially changed the way people live. One of life's facets that has been most affected by this new order is the conduct of business, where products are now sold and bought online within what is now called e-business (Turban et al., 2000).

But, developments in e-business and technology have been so mercurial, courtesy of the handful of e-business and computer demigods (Knight, 2002), that most mortals may soon find themselves inadequate or obsolete. Will such a nightmare be a reality? What can be done before it happens?

In this chapter, it is hoped that answers to these questions may be found by addressing the following research problems:

1. How academically prepared is the incoming workforce of the Philippines in facing the challenges of e-business? How prepared are they vis-à-vis their counterparts in North America?
2. What breakthrough strategies can IT practitioners and academicians implement to help them prepare?
3. How effective are these strategies?

FRAMEWORK OF RESEARCH METHODOLOGY

Graduating students from the top four universities in the Philippines were surveyed in November 2000 to assess their e-business readiness.

To have a global benchmarking, graduating students from three universities in the United States, Canada, and the Philippines were surveyed in December 2000. These universities were chosen, because they were reputed to be among the pioneers in e-business education in their state or province. Furthermore, the two North American universities were also offering e-business courses to nonbusiness and noncomputer students, while the Philippine university was contemplating offering a similar course. E-commerce curricula of other universities, at least those that are published, often cater to computer or business students (Knight & Chan, 2002; Cohen, 2002). Subjects of the study were students enrolled in degree programs in engineering, science, education, or arts, that had less curricular exposure to e-business than students enrolled in computer or business-degree programs. They were assumed to be the ones that would be most likely left in the cold in e-business education.

The e-business programs for nonbusiness and noncomputer students of the three universities were reviewed, in order to develop a system of breakthrough practices that could be adopted in the Philippines. To determine the market feasibility of this system, a second survey among Philippine students was conducted. Using the survey results, a group of students brainstormed to enhance the system that would be jointly implemented by the industry and academe. This joint implementation was deemed necessary to bridge the gap between industry and academe (Knock, 2002).

To determine its effectiveness, the system was pilot-run in a Philippine university for one trimester, starting in June 2001, and the results were evaluated in September 2001.

ANALYSIS OF RESULTS

E-Business Preparedness of the Future Philippine Workforce

Graduating students from the reputed top four universities in the Philippines (Asiaweek, 2000; CHED Bulletin, 2000) were surveyed to assess the e-business preparedness of the future Philippine workforce. From this survey (with sampling sizes of 81 to 95 per university), the following were revealed (see Tables 1 and 2):

1. On a scale of 5, student's knowledge of the e-business was at a moderate average of 3.57. This was startling, considering that the students spent relatively long times surfing the Internet. At 7.1 hours per week, it was at par with the United States' university student's average (www.student.net).

2. This lack of knowledge of e-business could be explained by the meager 8.8 hours the student spent during his entire stay in the university to study about e-business or the Internet in classes. Follow-up interviews revealed that less than 1 hour of this time was spent on discussions about e-business.

3. Students enrolled in Computers (Comp) or Business (Bus) knew e-business better than students in Arts/Education (Art/Edu) and Engineering/Science (Eng/Sci). This was mainly due to the higher average surfing time (SURF) and time spent in studying e-business (STUDY) by the former. Regression analysis proved that knowledge of e-business (KNOW) was greatly influenced by SURF and STUDY at 95% confidence level, as embodied in the regression line: $KNOW = 1.31 + 0.17 SURF + 0.10 STUDY$, with $R = 0.8126, (t = 5.1), (t = 3.9), (t = 3.7)$. Computer usage time (USE), was not significantly correlated with KNOW.

4. Most Philippine students (93%) believed that e-business would not be just a fad. All students of computer degrees agreed.

Table 1. E-business preparedness of Philippine students, by university (as of January 2001)

	Universities				
	A	B	C	D	Ave
(USE)Ave. time spent using computer for the past 6 months (hours per week):	15.1	11.2	14.6	14.79	13.9
(SURF)Ave. time spent in surfing the internet for the past 6 months (hours per week	7.8	4.6	7.4	8.57	7.1
(STUDY)Time spent in class studying about internet or e-business for the past 3 years	9.3	4.4	9.6	11.89	8.8
(KNOW) Knowledge of e-business (on scale of 5)	3.66	3.33	3.73	3.84	3.57
(NOT FAD)% of students who believe Ecommerce is not a fad	0.918	0.93	0.91	0.88	0.91

Table 2. E-business preparedness of Philippine students, by course

	Course				
	Comp	Bus	Eng/Sci	Art/Edu	Ave
USE	20.53	15.49	11.39	8.30	13.93
SURF	9.02	8.78	6.52	4.37	7.17
STUDY	14.35	9.25	8.15	3.54	8.82
KNOW	4.02	4.01	3.25	3.01	3.57
NOT FAD	1.00	0.89	0.89	0.86	0.91

Table 3. E-business readiness of students in US, Canada and RP (as of January 2001)

*Students in Arts/Education/Eng'g/Science	Country of University			
	US	CN	RP	Ave
USE	12.8	11.8	10.3	11.6
SURF	10.3	7.1	5.8	7.7
STUDY	24.4	7.3	5.1	12.3
KNOW	4.19	3.51	3.29	3.7
NOT FAD	0.95	0.93	0.88	0.9

E-Business Preparedness: Benchmarking in Three Countries

To benchmark with other countries, surveys and interviews were also conducted in two universities in the United States and Canada (sample size of 60 and 70, respectively). The results were compared with those of a Philippine (RP) university. Respondents in these surveys were limited to the graduating students of Eng/Sci and Art/Edu, because they were the ones most likely unexposed to e-business (as was partly proven by the results of the earlier survey) (Table 3).

Philippine students lagged moderately behind in USE. The gaps, however, became pronounced in SURF, STUDY, KNOW, and NOTFAD. The difference between the Philippine and U.S. universities was 12.3 hours in STUDY, almost a full point in a five-point scale in KNOW and 7% in NOTFAD.

This information proved that Philippine students in noncomputer/business courses were not as prepared as their counterparts in the United States and Canada (CN) in facing the challenges of e-business.

The Best Breakthrough Practices

The e-business curricular programs of the three universities were also reviewed to develop a system of breakthrough practices that could be adopted by academicians and practitioners in the Philippines, and hopefully, the rest of the world. The best practices were as follows:

1.   Establish an e-business institute that utilizes faculty and business professional expertise. The institute will expose its academic community to real-world applications to develop an e-business knowledge base. It will develop partnerships with corporate sponsors and government to establish and promote the university and its locale as a leading e-business center.

2.   The institute will not be affiliated with any of the faculty departments to entice students from any department to enroll in the institute.

3.   It will bestow on every graduate of the institute the title of "Fellow of the Institute." This title is expected to open doors in e-business-related careers or to be e-commerce literate. To be a fellow, the student must do the following:
     - Be enrolled in a degree program of the university
     - Complete an e-business training program

4.   The training program will include e-business courses (regular courses offered by the departments deemed e-business related), lecture series (with speakers from private and government entities), and course modules.

5.   Students not in the Fellowship program may attend the lectures for free on a first-come-first-served basis to entice them to e-business.
6.   The institute will also offer a certificate program for nonstudents (professionals, educators, out-of-school youth) for a fee to widen the patronage of e-business.

Feasibility of Adopting the System of Breakthrough Practices

The feasibility of adopting, in the Philippines, the system of breakthrough practices was initially tested through a second survey of graduating students in the top four Philippine universities (sample size of 360).

Graduating students were asked which option and number they would choose if they were given the chance to go back to the sophomore level and take for a half-term period each of the subjects listed in Table 4.

The numbers and corresponding options were as follows:
1.   Do not enroll in that particular e-business subject.
2.   Pay half the tuition fee but do not receive a certificate or earn credits.
3.   Pay the tuition fee equivalent and earn equivalent units.
4.   Pay the tuition fee and earn a certificate.
      Note: The option "Take for free" was not offered, because it was financially draining to any university.

As shown in Tables 4 and 5:
1.   The overall desire to take e-business subjects was 2.6 on a scale of 4. This meant that students liked the idea of taking e-business as a course but were not willing to pay fees just to earn a certificate. The responses were relatively kurtotic, with deviation of 1.2.
2.   Introduction to e-business and Web site development were the most desired, with a significantly higher rating than the rest, while E-Legal/E-Personnel/E-Financial Management was the least desired. (Descriptions of these subjects were provided in the questionnaire but are omitted in this paper for brevity.)
3.   By course, the overall ratings were highest for Comp and lowest for Art/Edu. Introduction to E-business was the only subject rated significantly well by the students from Eng/Sci and Art/Edu.

Table 4. E-subjects to be taken in the university if given the chance

| | Desire to Take Subject | | | | |
| | Universities | | | | |
E-Subjects	A	B	C	D	Ave
Introduction to ECommerce					2.77
EMarketing					2.63
EOperations Management					2.58
Website Development					2.82
EHardware & Security					2.54
ELegal & Epersonnel & Efinancial Management					2.43
ECommerce Strategy					2.53
Overall	2.59	2.67	2.59	2.57	2.61

Table 5. Desire to take subject, by course

E-Subjects	Course				
	Comp	Business	Eng/Sci	Art/Edu	Ave
Introduction					2.77
EMarketing					2.63
EOperations					2.58
Website					2.82
Ehardware/Security					2.54
Elegal/personnel/financial					2.43
EStrategy					2.53
Average	2.80	2.70	2.50	2.39	2.61

From Tables 6 and 7, it is shown that the top reasons for not taking specific e-business courses were failure to see relevance (25% of respondents) and lack of interest (24% of respondents). Top reasons for taking specific courses were the desire to learn something new and be well-rounded.

Table 6. Reasons for not taking a particular subject, by course

	% of Responses				
	Course				
	Comp	Busi	Eng/Sci	Art/Edu	Ave
I do not see its relevance to my degree	0.24	0.26	0.26	0.25	0.25
I do not have the aptitude for such topics	0.18	0.18	0.14	0.15	0.16
I am not very adept with computer subjects	0.12	0.15	0.11	0.14	0.13
I am not interested in topics such as those	0.27	0.18	0.24	0.25	0.24
I do not have the time	0.18	0.22	0.23	0.15	0.19
I do not think Ecommerce will last for long	0.00	0.01	0.02	0.05	0.02

Table 7. Reasons for taking a particular subject, by course

Reasons for Taking a Particular Subject	% of Responses				
	Course				
	Comp	Busi	Eng/Sci	Art/Edu	Ave
I want to get the certificate/units for whatever purpose	0.15	0.14	0.17	0.18	0.16
I want to get certificate/units for a possible career in IT	0.23	0.25	0.17	0.19	0.21
The subject is a critical success factor in my profession	0.21	0.23	0.12	0.23	0.20
I like computers and computer-related topics	0.12	0.09	0.19	0.08	0.12
I like the topics even if there is no EC component	0.03	0.04	0.10	0.12	0.07
I like to learn something new and be well-rounded	0.26	0.25	0.25	0.20	0.24

Enhancement of the System

Using the survey results, 72 students from the Philippine university, De La Salle University, brainstormed to develop the following enhancements to the system. Among hundreds of other ideas, these were judged by students as critical:

1. Evoke exigency: Students should be made aware that knowledge of e-business is a critical need in their profession and in every aspect of their lives.
    - Introduction to E-business should be included in every curriculum to enlighten the students on the benefits of e-business and knowledge of e-business. Co-curricular training should also be provided in the form of symposia, conferences, etc. Gradually, essential transactions in student life, such as enrollment and reservations, should be made online to intensify their dependence on e-business and hunger for e-business education.
    - Practitioners should stipulate in hiring that an applicant's knowledge of e-business is preferred. Gradually, stages in hiring must be carried out online to reiterate this point.
2. Develop desire: Students must be lured to e-business by addressing the usefulness and ease issues of e-business technology.
    - Following the Technology Acceptance Model and World Wide Web principle (Lederer et al., 2000) that perceived usefulness and ease will result in a desire for and usage of technology, students in all courses should be offered an e-business course that they find useful in their prospective professions, such as Web site development and introduction to e-commerce, as a main course or an elective. Then, additional topics, starting with ones that they can easily grasp relative to their courses, may be offered, such as E-marketing and E-commerce strategic management. The priority ranking in offering these courses in various fields should follow the rankings based on the second survey.
    - Incorporate e-business discussions in regular courses. Through constant expo sure to e-business, students' desire for learning and getting into it will intensify.
    - Provide online gimmicks such as campus survival tips, fashion 911, social affair monitor, and freebie goods so that students will always surf.
    - Practitioners will reinforce this desire by having promotional gimmicks online.
3. Blur the borders: Impress on the students that e-business causes blurring of geographical, functional, and temporal boundaries (Afuah & Tucci, 2001). As such, e-business education is also borderless and is not a course under a particular college, yet, is strongly supported by all.
    Industry, academe, and government must institutionalize their concerted programs to push e-business education. Exchange of resources must be seamless.
    The culmination of this effort is the establishment of the E-Business Institute described in an earlier section.
4. Reap the rewards: Once the student becomes adept in e-business, things will be able to be done more productively, and the student will be more marketable, both as a student and as a professional.

The practitioner will be able to employ highly productive personnel who will create demand, reduce cost, and deliver on time, among other benefits.

The academician will be happy and content that he was able to help at least two souls, the student and his future employer, while the institution's enrollment soars.

Testing the Waters through a Pilot Run

To test the system's effectiveness, some strategies were pilot-run in the engineering college of the Philippine university involved in benchmarking. Some strategies could not be tested because of time and resource constraints. The strategies that were pilot run, their manners of implementation, and the results are discussed below.

Strategy: 1. Evoke Exigency (a) and (b) (Please Refer to the Previous Section for Details).

Manner: In the third trimester of SY 2000–2001, posters and newspaper articles on the benefits of knowing e-commerce to the careers of noncomputer or nonbusiness students were posted on bulletin boards in the college. A one-page article on e-commerce and its benefits to one's career and day-to-day life was published on the student newspaper. Two announcements for job openings that stipulated "knowledge of e-commerce preferred" were also posted for two consecutive weeks.

The college offered "Introduction to E-Commerce" for the first time in the first trimester of SY 2001–2002 as an elective, along with two other new electives.

Thirty students enrolled were surveyed as to whether the "media blitz" of the previous trimester influenced them to enroll in the course.

Results: The two e-commerce sections were filled, with 75 enrollees on the first day of enrollment, while the two other electives had only a total of 10 students enrolling. This validated the study's finding that nonbusiness/computer students would enroll in e-commerce provided they would earn units.

Among the students surveyed as to the effectiveness of media blitz, only one-third saw at least one of the media announcements, and all of these admitted they were greatly influenced to enroll in e-business by the announcements. Of the remaining two-thirds, 75% had learned from other media sources the importance of knowing e-commerce. The other 25% were convinced by their classmates that the course would be useful to them in the future.

Strategy: 2. Develop Desire (a)

Manner: The e-commerce subject offered to the engineering students contained the following topics, enumerated with percent of time devoted to them: Web site development (50%), introduction to e-commerce (15%), e-marketing (10%), e-commerce strategic management (10%), e-hardware/security (5%), and e-legal/personnel/finance (10%).

At the end of the trimester, 30 students were surveyed as to how much they liked the subject and the different topics offered.

Results: The students liked the contents of the topics and the manner in which they were taught (4.90 and 4.75, respectively, on a scale of 5). The topic that a significant number wanted to put more time on was e-hardware and security. Although the survey did not ask why, it might be because, being engineering students, they were interested in hardware and machine aspects.

Strategy: 3. Reap the Rewards (a), (b), and (c)

Manner: The students developed Web sites for 20 professors and 10 companies who evaluated the students' works later.

Results: The faculty members and company managers liked the Web sites and rated them with averages of 4.5 and 4.75 on a scale of 5, respectively. All six managers expressed their willingness to hire the students as computer systems analysts or engineers.

CONCLUSION

The incoming members of the Philippine workforce, particularly the graduating students of noncomputer or nonbusiness courses, are not well prepared to face the challenges of e-business, more so when compared to their counterparts in North America. However, practitioners and academicians can help them overcome these predicaments by adopting breakthrough strategies. These strategies can be divided into four stages, namely, *evoke exigency, develop desire, blur the borders, and reap rewards.* These strategies that were partly implemented in a pilot run proved to be effective.

REFERENCES

Afuah, A., & Tucci, C. (2001). *Internet Business Models and Strategies.* New York: McGraw-Hill Irvin.

CHED 2000 Bulletin. Commission on Higher Education. Manila.

Cohen, E. (2002). Curriculum model of the Information Resource Management Association and the Data Administration Managers Association. In E. Cohen (ed.). *Challenges of Information Technology Education in the 21st Century.* Hershey, PA: Idea Group Publishing.

http://www.asiaweek.com. (January 31, 2001).

http://www.lasalle.edu/academ/ecommerce, (January 31, 2002).

http://www.student.net. (January 31, 2001).

Knight, L. V., & Chan, S. S. (2002). E-commerce curriculum strategies and implementation tactics: An in-depth examination of De Paul University's experience. In E. Cohen (ed.). *Challenges of Information Technology Education in the 21st Century.* Hershey, PA: Idea Group Publishing.

Kock, N., Auspitz, C., & King, B. (2002). Bridging the industry-university gap: An action research study of a Web-enabled course partnership. In E. Cohen (ed.), *Challenges of Information Technology Education in the 21st Century.* Hershey, PA: Idea Group Publishing.

Lamersdorf, W., & Merz, M. (1998). *Trends in Distributed Systems for Electronic Commerce.* Heidelberg, Germany: Springer-Verlag Berlin.

Lederer, A. et al. (2000). The technology acceptance model and the World Wide Web. *Decision Support Systems, 29,* 269–282.

McLaren, C. H., & McLaren, B. J. (2000). *E-Commerce Business on the Internet.* Cincinnati, OH: South-Western Educational Publishing.

Turban, E. et al. (2000). *Electronic Commerce: A Managerial Perspective*. Upper Saddle
River, NJ: Prentice Hall.

Chapter XXVII

Information Management in Public Sector Agencies: A Context-Sensitive Conceptual Framework of CIO Competence

Maurice W. Green
University of Washington, USA

ABSTRACT

Managerial responsibilities for information technology (IT) have, increasingly, been consolidated in the person of the "chief information officer" (CIO). Despite the increased prevalence of the CIO position, no one model has emerged that explains what can realistically be expected of the CIO in various organizational contexts. This is particularly true of the public-sector CIO. In this chapter, insight into the problems, challenges, and requisite competencies for public-sector CIOs is provided. The conceptual framework of CIO competence presented here is multidimensional and interdisciplinary in nature. In the chapter, the importance of considering the contextual setting in which CIOs operate in understanding the competencies he or she deems critical to the CIO role is illustrated. The competencies deemed critical by CIOs with differing perceptions of the role of IT, as well as those deemed critical by CIOs managing different size IT units, are contrasted. The discussion should inform academicians developing IT management curricula and practitioners engaged in CIO search and development activities.

INTRODUCTION

The need to more effectively and efficiently manage information has led organizations to focus more heavily on the values and challenges of effectively integrating information technology (IT) into their operations. The dynamism of many industries, coupled with the unbridled growth in IT innovations, dictates that organizations periodically rethink the key elements for them in effectively managing their information resources. The *appropriate* approach to managing information resources continues to evolve. Some approaches that have proved effective in the past often hold little relevance in present and future situations. Determining the appropriate role of IT has become a critical agenda item for practitioners within organizations and an intriguing area of research for academicians. A central figure in both arenas for making such a determination is the chief information officer (CIO).

Admittedly, research in this area is difficult due to the constant influx of IT innovations, as well as changes in organizational strategies and management objectives. In addition, most research related to the CIO targets private-sector corporations. There is comparatively little known about CIOs who work in public-sector agencies.

Thus, the primary goal of this chapter is to provide a deeper understanding of the critical competencies for CIOs in relation to their public-sector work environments. To this end, first, a conceptual framework of competence in the CIO position is developed. Here, CIO competence is conceptualized in terms of what CIOs need to know and what activities CIOs need to engage in. A secondary goal of this chapter is to stress the need to account for the context in which the CIO performs his or her job. To this end, the sensitivity of the conceptual framework of CIO competence in relation to two aspects of the CIO's work environment is examined. The two aspects of the CIO's work environment that are examined are IT unit size and IT vision. These two aspects of the CIO's work environment are referred to as the two contextual settings for the remainder of this chapter.

The chapter is intended to flow as follows. First, a comprehensive framework of CIO competence is presented for level-setting purposes, which will provide the basis for discussions in later sections. Second, the importance of placing competence in context is briefly discussed, along with an examination of the various facets of the conceptual framework in relation to the context of the CIO's work environment. Finally, the utility of the conceptual framework in informing the reframing of IT management pedagogy is discussed.

BACKGROUND

Over the past two decades, many organizations have come to rely on their information base as a critical asset. Though organizations, private and public, differ markedly in terms of their information environment (e.g., type of information collected, information sources, information use, information management approach, etc.), the information base is universally becoming one of the most valuable organizational resources. As Porter and Millar stated, "Dramatic reductions in the cost of obtaining, processing, and transmitting information are changing the way we do business" (Porter & Millar, 1985, p. 2). More recently, Michael Dubose Chairman, President and CEO of Aftermarket Technology Corporation, stated, "...information access and flow is absolutely critical to today's businesses" (Prince, 1999, p. 66).

Attempts to better harness the power of information for process redesign, new and enhanced product and service offerings, and overall improvements in organizational effectiveness and efficiency have increased organizations' reliance on information technology (IT). Most organizations have integrated some arrangement of IT within or throughout their operations. Whether an organization is a leader or a follower in its respective industry, IT and the information infrastructure it supports have become a critical component in the management and operations of modern organizations (McKenney et al., 1995).

There are many examples of IT innovations leading up to the Y2K era that have enabled cost reductions in information access, processing, and flow across a myriad of organizational forms. The Department of Transportation's CIO, George Molaski, stated that "IT has become an integral part of virtually all transportation systems. Successful mission performance is now heavily reliant on IT" (Hickey, 1999, p. 43). Examples of the creative application of IT for competitive and strategic initiatives continue to emerge at an increasing, and in some cases, an alarming rate. This has become a normal, rather than an exceptional, component of the business that organizations conduct.

Not surprisingly, the manner in which IT is deployed is as varied as the information environments and decision-making processes that drive its use. Unfortunately, not a single model has emerged that ensures the effective use of IT in all contexts. Despite the uncertainty of success, organizations continue to expand the scope (i.e., reach and range) of their IT applications (Keen, 1991). Though the cost of IT relative to processing power is improving dramatically, the overall corporate expenditure on IT continues to rise. This phenomenon has caused many organizations to rethink their management of information, the requisite IT, and the associated costs. Managerial responsibility for these processes is increasingly being consolidated in the person of the *chief information officer* (Dodaro, 1997; Stephens, 1995).

William Synott defined the "chief information officer" (CIO) as the "senior executive responsible for establishing corporate information policy, standards, and management control over all corporate information resources" (Synott & Gruber, 1981, p. 66). Twenty years later, organizations have run the gambit in attempting to correctly implement the position within the context of their specific environment.

It is worth mentioning that although many organizations now have a CIO role, the CIO title is not as common (Frenzel, 1992). This is especially true in the public sector. Generally, public-sector agencies still opt for such titles as "Director of Management Information Systems," "Vice President of Data Processing," "Associate Commissioner of Information Technology," among others (Penrod et al., 1990). Despite the infrequent use of the CIO title in the public sector, past research has found "remarkable consistency between the primary functions reported for CIOs in the literature and those performed by our survey respondents" (Penrod et al., 1990, p. 16). As such, in this chapter, these titles are considered synonymous with the "chief information officer" title and position.

MAIN THRUST OF THE CHAPTER

Reframing IT Management Pedagogy to Address the Need for Interdisciplinary Education and Practice

Despite the insight gained from past private- and public-sector-based CIO research, "no one model is emerging for the CIO and supportive organization" (Penrod et al., 1990, p. 9). For example, John Thomas Flynn, CIO of the State of Massachusetts since 1994 explains, "There was no model in state government for CIO when I took the position....I ended up modeling my job after the position at General Motors, which had divisional information officers report to the CIO" (Newcombe, 1999, p. 12). The lack of the CIO position within public-sector agencies, until relatively recently, may stem from chief decision makers who are uninformed as to what the CIO position is about. Flynn expounded on his situation by saying he "...had to explain to [his state's] Gov. William Weld what the [CIO] title meant" (Newcombe, 1999, p. 12).

Determining the appropriate roles of IT and the CIO has become critical to organizational success and dictates serious consideration to the development of interdisciplinary curricula for training the next generation of IT managers. Admittedly, research in this area is difficult due to the constant influx of IT innovations, as well as changes in organizational strategies and management objectives. The *appropriate* approach to managing information resources continues to evolve. Some approaches that have proved effective in the past often hold little relevance in present and future situations.

The approach here is to elucidate that which is relatively static in a domain that is increasingly dynamic. Specifically, a conceptual framework of CIO competence comprised of dimensions of the role that will likely endure over time is developed. Again, CIO competence is viewed broadly in terms of what CIOs need to know and what activities CIOs need to engage in.

In large part, the conceptual framework is based on data collected through exploratory in-depth interviews and semistructured interviews with public-sector CIOs. All interviewees worked within New York State government agencies and were the individuals foremost responsible for management of their agencies' information resources.

A noteworthy aspect of the interviews and the development of the conceptual framework is that they follow the admonishment of Graham T. Allison in his *Lessons for Research in Public Management* (Allison, 1980). The following lists one of Allison's lessons that was applied here:

The effort to develop public management as a field of knowledge should start from problems faced by practicing public managers.

Exploratory In-Depth Interviews

The exploratory in-depth interview data were examined to determine the key problems facing public-sector CIOs and to discern the requisite dimensions of the conceptual framework of CIO competence. The semistructured interview data were used to define the six dimensions of the conceptual framework of CIO competence that emerged from the exploratory interview data. The definitions are comprised of sets of attributes that the interviewees associated with each dimension. These data resulted in a six-dimensional preliminary conceptual framework of competence in the CIO role (Figure 1). To this end, the following questions were of primary interest:
1.   What are the dimensions of CIO competence?
2.   What are the defining attributes of these dimensions?

Four exploratory in-depth interviews were conducted with New York State government agency CIOs. All of the interviews were conducted in person by the same interviewer and lasted from one to one and one-half hours in duration. The purpose of the interviews was to gain a richer understanding of the public-sector domain in which NYS government agency CIOs operate and the common problems they deal with. Specifically, six major areas of the CIO's work environment were explored:

1. Organization structure
2. Client relations
3. IT unit structure
4. IT planning process
5. IT project portfolio
6. CIO profile and critical success factors

A series of questions were posed that related to each of these six areas. Responses indicated five categories of problems and challenges that these interviewees are confronted with. In the subsequent subsection, the problems and challenges are presented and discussed. Immediately following is a list of the five categories, along with select problems and challenges within each:

1. Organizational problems
   - The CIO does not report directly to the top decision maker.
   - The CIO is not perceived as a *true* member of the top management team.
2. Operational problems
   - The CIO does not actively participate in agency and program planning.
   - There is a lack of standards and protocol to control end-user development.
3. Educational problems
   - Program managers are often not IT literate.
   - Many are skeptical of the value of IT.
4. Resource problems
   - Agencies continue to manage the bottom-line to the exclusion of the top-line.
   - There are inadequate levels of central investment for IT and training.
5. Political problems
   - State elections and political appointments can radically change the agency agenda.
   - Resource allocations are based on ineffective metrics.

Organizational Issues, Controversies, and Problems
CIO Does Not Report Directly to the Top Decision Maker

Most interviewees felt that the CIO is removed from the mainstream organization, because the CIO does not report directly to the top decision maker. The following quotes provided evidence:

Figure 1. Preliminary conceptual framework of CIO competence

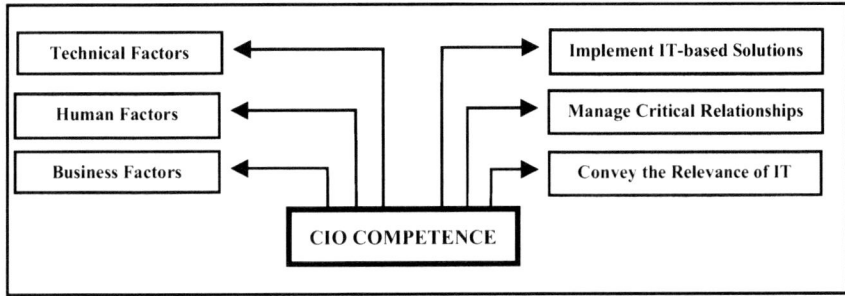

> *Where it is here (CIO position within the agency's chain of command) is not correct because of the buffer created by the current structure, which includes the associate commissioner. The head of MIS should report directly to the commissioner.*

> *I'm more convinced than ever that an organization such as ours should have a much more substantial commitment from the agency. Reporting at a higher level goes right along with that.*

When the interviewees were asked why they felt the CIO, often, does not report directly to the top decision maker, the following problem was revealed.

CIOs are Not Perceived as True Members of the Top Management Team

The culture within the represented agencies is one in which the CIO and the IT unit are perceived as serving a support role, rather than a leadership role. As such, the CIO is not a true member of the top-management team. The following quote illustrates this point:

> *The traditional boardroom members perceive CIOs as "techies," second-class members of the boardroom. Speak when spoken to. The perception is that people in leadership positions in the IT unit are not boardroom material.*

When the contributions of the CIO and the IT unit are viewed purely in a support capacity, IT is relegated to a reactive, rather than proactive posture. By the time the CIO's perspective is solicited, the strategy has often been set.

This issue was followed up on to determine why the interviewees felt that program managers do not perceive the CIO as top management material. The following problem was revealed.

CIOs Do Not Speak the Language of the Program Heads and the Top Decision Maker

In all fairness to some top-management teams, CIOs have contributed to the "second-class" status that they occupy in many boardrooms. The following quote is an indication of this sentiment:

> *With some exceptions, they [CIOs] are too technical. If I get too technical when talking to program heads, their eyes gloss over and I'm dead!*

When a CIO speaks in "technobabble," the top management teams get turned off, and in turn, turn the CIO off until they feel that the CIO can be useful. To combat this situation, CIOs must exhibit competence regarding the business issues that managers from varying program areas deal with on a day-to-day basis. It is not that the CIO's technological knowledge or, in some cases, expertise is not valued. Rather, it is the manner, perceived or actual, that the CIO leverages technical knowledge with the business of the agency. This point is made in the following quote:

> *CIOs may not be technologists per se, but they need to understand the importance of technology for the business of what they are doing.*

Underlying such an understanding dictates that the CIO remain up to date regarding the evolving *agency objectives and strategies*, as well as the technologies relevant to them. Competence in this regard is reflected in the "business factors" and "technical factors" dimension of the conceptual framework.

Once program managers gain confidence in the CIO's understanding of the business issues pertinent to the agency, they are more likely to solicit the CIO's technical expertise. Prior research conducted in the private sector found that CEOs wanted a "CIO who could conciliate and diffuse. Someone who can eventually enthuse the top management team" (Feeny, Edwards, & Simpson, 1992).

Following this track, the interviewees were asked how CIOs could leverage their technical expertise, proactively, in a manner that generates top management support for their recommendations. The following suggestions were rendered:

> *A lot has to do with how you roll out your technology plan. If top management can see the relevance of it to what they're trying to do, and you have a chance to brief them and explain as you go through the budgets and things, as to what it can really do for the institution, then you educate them in the process.*

The notion of the CIO as an educator that is expressed in the above quote is reflected in the activities comprising the "convey the relevance of IT" dimension of the conceptual framework. Another interviewee went on to say:

> *In 1993, we basically proved to ourselves and those from where we get our financial support and our budget, that the proposed projects for 1994 were in fact workable, doable, and cost-effective. We had a lot of skeptics out there.*

The idea that the CIO must overcome skepticism in order to gain support for proposed initiatives is captured in the "manage critical relationships" dimension of the conceptual framework. Another CIO added:

> *The deployment of personalities, skills, and technology, trying to bring those three things together in a way that makes sense, and in which we gain support of people along the way so that we don't force down their throats [IT] solutions that they are not comfortable with.*

These data suggest that beyond the business and technological issues, the CIO must recognize that IT initiatives will have an impact on the end-user community and necessarily the organization as a whole. Understanding the people issues relates to the "human factors" dimension in the conceptual framework. The CIO's ability to integrate a business focus with technical knowledge and an understanding of the social environment in order to engage in effective and efficient systems development initiatives is exemplified in the "implement IT-based solutions" dimension of the conceptual framework.

It appears that in order to effectively engage in the activities comprising the three activity-based dimensions (i.e., convey the relevance of IT, manage critical relationships, implement IT-based solutions), the competent CIO needs to rely on the information comprising the three knowledge-based dimensions (i.e., business factors, human factors, technical factors). Conversely, it is not just what the CIO knows that ultimately defines his or her competence. Rather, competence is also comprised of what the CIO does with what they know. Leadership expert Warren Bennis made the point well in his foreword to Burt Nanus' book *Visionary Leadership*, when he stated, "Action without vision is stumbling in the dark. Vision without action is poverty-stricken poetry" (Nanus, 1990).

Due to space constraints, examples of the remaining four problem categories are briefly presented below.

Operational Issues, Controversies, and Problems

The CIO Does Not Actively Participate in Agency and Program Planning

Respondents indicated that the IT unit is treated as a separate organization within the larger agency.

There are agencies where the technology unit is so far away from the programs that they probably don't know each other if they meet on the street, and that's a problem.

Past research in the private sector indicates that IT innovations result from top-management's perception and acceptance of the CIO as a partner in the development of the overall corporate and subunit strategies (McKenney, 1995).

The absence of the CIO in the strategy formulation process beyond IT reduces the potential reach and range of IT (Keen, 1991). Also, this can result in the fragmented implementation of IT with the long-term result being:

> *We also have many islands of computing external to this [IT unit] organization.*

Lack of Standards and Protocols to Control End-User Development

There are continuous requests for service placed upon the IT unit by groups across the agency. Limited resources have caused a substantial backlog of service requests within the IT unit. Often, individuals and groups cannot wait and opt to take matters into their own hands:

> *Most managers must cobble together information on their PCs just to find out basic things like where their budgets are. So we have a long way to go. We're not satisfied.*

Unfortunately, quick fix solutions are often pursued in the absence of standards. Thus, the CIO is placed in the unenviable position of attempting to dictate how users must satisfy their own needs:

> *It's a combination of the reality of the size of the organization, and the inability to have absolute standardization of data. We would like a much higher level of standardization. We try to persuade our clients to apply good practices. When they don't, we try to help them to survive with their own approaches and support them as much as possible.*

Educational Issues, Controversies, and Problems

Program Managers are Often Not IT Literate

Recall that CIOs must speak the language of program heads and the top decision maker. The same rationale applies here but in the other direction. CIOs must become more business literate, so too must program management become more technologically literate. The following quote is a call for such education:

> *People in the boardroom are unaware of what technology can do for them.*

The challenge for the CIO is to effectively *convey the relevance of IT* and then help program managers make sound decisions regarding the agency's information resources. The following quote provides insight into why it is important for the CIO to engage in such educational processes:

> *It's hard to say no when the CEO and senior staff say, "Wouldn't you like to do this?"*

Saying "no" becomes easier when it is accompanied by a logical explanation that is aligned with the agency's business strategy. Furthermore, business leaders will be more receptive to hear the merits of the explanation when they are technologically sophisticated enough to understand the alternatives and their implications. It then becomes incumbent upon the CIO to proactively cultivate a technologically astute business community within the agency, rather than leaving such education solely to chance encounters that will often prove unproductive.

Many are Skeptical of the Value of IT

Proposed change is an educational process. The probability of success increases when education takes place in both directions between program management and the CIO. On the one hand, management and end users must articulate their needs and goals to the CIO in comprehensive terms. On the other hand, the CIO must disseminate a vision of IT that highlights the relevance of IT to the business of the agency. This point is made clear in the following quote:

> *You need very knowledgeable business people who understand and who can convey the needs, goals, and objectives of the business. In addition, you need very good technology people who understand the technological choices. Choices like, when to reach for a standard, when to deviate from the norm, how to manage the technology, and which technology to engage in. You're going to need some very skilled people to deal with that. They need not be your CIO, but if the CIO is smart enough, he or she will have a group like that around.*

CIOs that can facilitate information sharing across groups of this sort reveal their true purpose and value, and gain the support of colleagues from both domains. It is in such an environment that CIOs can maximize their worth by acting as a partner to those within program areas, and an advocate of those within the IT unit.

Resource Issues, Controversies, and Problems

Agencies Continue to Manage the Bottom-Line to the Exclusion of the Top-Line

Organizations in the private and public sectors have a tendency to focus on managing the bottom-line (what can we afford to invest), rather than managing the top-line (what can we ill-afford *not* to invest) with regard to IT (Keen, 1991):

> *Unfortunately, in the public sector, your budget is a one-year thing. Most strategic changes take five to ten years, but you can't guarantee your budget.*

The Internet in my mind... is going to be the foundation of the National Information Infrastructure (NII). We're saying we need to carefully architect ourselves so we can deal with that open architecture of anything to anything.

The information age is one where people are empowered by their technology, and technology has to be considered an enabling capacity. It gives you an opportunity for a great deal of innovation at the individual level. Everybody is not only a consumer, but [also] a provider.

The key words from the quote above are "enabling capacity," which suggests viewing IT as a means of achieving something that could not be achieved without the technology, as opposed to IT in a support capacity.

Inadequate levels of central investment in IT and training

Procuring adequate levels of funding for investment in IT is a major challenge in government agencies, whether for strategic or support purposes. Nearly all of the interviewees stressed this point.

> We've been trying for several years to move to the IBM system exclusively. It's very hard in a state agency to get the financial backing necessary to make such a transition.

> We don't have email, five years ago we didn't have word processing, we don't have an HRM system. We just built a financial system. We're contractors and project managers and we've had virtually no project management tools.

> There needs to be more central investment of resources for problem solving and coordination, data management, and networks.

> One of the toughest things in the state of New York is that when budget times are tough, and there hasn't been a year in the last ten when they were not, the first thing to go is training and travel.

Political Issues, Controversies, and Problems

State elections and political appointments can radically change the agency agenda

Changes in state leadership, ushered in by elections and political appointments, often result in highly unpredictable and radical changes in leadership and agendas at the agency level.

One of my critical success factors is whether or not I'll keep my job after the new governor steps in. A lot of the guys and gals down the street will not, and that's not necessarily based on past performance.

We have to address the needs of various constituents internal and external to the agency that often have competing interests and objectives.

CIOs are often left chasing a moving target, as they adjust to the change in leadership. Furthermore, because some of the old guard remains intact, the CIO must deal concurrently with old habits while attempting to adapt the agency to the infusion of new ones. Managing in such an environment means that the CIO must fulfill multiple roles that can be at odds with one another.

Resource Allocations are Made Based on Ineffective Metrics

Unlike their private-sector counterparts, CIOs in the public sector are often not rewarded for saving their organizations money. Rather, they are in a sense punished by budget cuts in the next fiscal year, if they managed a surplus in the previous year. Consequently, the system encourages waste, as evidenced in the following quote:

If you run a surplus this year, next years budget will be cut by that amount. So at year-end, what's the easiest way to avoid that? Invest in hardware!

Further complicating matters:

In the public sector, the people who spend the money on you may not be the people who get the return on their investment.

The exploratory in-depth interviews provide a rich data set for better understanding the problems and challenges confronting CIOs in the public sector in particular, but insight can be gained into the CIOs position regardless of sector. The approach taken here of taking those problems and making inferences regarding the requisite CIO competencies is a logical first step toward conceptualizing competence in the role. A logical next step it seems is to explicate the specific competencies that underlie each of the six identified dimensions.

As such, a second round of interviews was conducted. The nature of those semistructured interviews and the results are discussed next.

Semistructured Interviews

The semistructured interviews represented the second lesson for research on public management from Allison's 1980 work that was followed here:

2.   It is possible to learn from experience the skills, attributes, and practices that competent managers exhibit and those that less successful managers lack.

Five NYS government agency CIOs participated in semistructured face-to-face interviews consisting of open- and closed-ended questions. Each interview lasted approximately one and one-half hours in duration. The interviews consisted of a *two-step exercise* that focused on each of the six dimensions, one at a time. The intent was to define the six dimensions of the conceptual framework by identifying the attributes (i.e., factors and activities) that the interviewees most commonly associate with each dimension.

Step 1: The interviewees were presented with a quotation from the literature. Select words or phrases within the quotation were highlighted that related directly to the dimension in question. Respondents were asked to list five factors (given a knowledge-based dimension) or five activities (given an activity-based dimension) that they deemed to be critical in relation to the highlighted text.

Step 2: The interviewees were presented with a preliminary set of factors or activities drawn from the literature and the exploratory in-depth interviews. The participants were then asked to indicate which of the factors or activities from each set was critical in relation to the highlighted text within the quotation. The number of preliminary attributes for each dimension is displayed below (see Appendix A for the lists associated with the six preliminary sets of attributes for each dimension):

- 18 business factors
- 34 technical factors
- 14 human factors
- 12 convey relevance of IT activities
- 18 manage critical relationship activities
- 13 implement IT-based solutions activities

The two-step exercise was employed so as to reduce respondent bias toward the preliminary sets. The exercise progressed on a quote-by-quote, dimension-by-dimension basis. As each dimension was examined, a new quotation was introduced until all six dimensions had been addressed.

The small sample size precludes conventional data analysis of the responses. Indeed, the objective was to gain insight using the depth rather than breadth of the data, to enable clearer definitions of the constructs under study (Feeny et al., 1992). The general rule applied here was that if four or more respondents identified a given attribute as critical, the attribute was retained. This approach refined the six preliminary sets of attributes, yielding the factors and activities presented in Table 1.

The refined sets of attributes were integrated into the preliminary conceptual framework, producing the following revised conceptual framework (Figure 2).

The Need for Contextual Grounding

The development of a conceptual framework that captures the attributes and skills desired in the CIO position warrants consideration of the organizational context in which the CIO operates. As mentioned earlier, the approach here is to elucidate that which is relatively static in a domain that is increasingly dynamic. It is the author's position that the six dimensions of the conceptual framework will remain relatively static. It is also the author's position that the underlying dimension attributes (i.e., factors and activities) deemed critical by CIOs are more apt to evolve over time, as the IT management landscape continues to evolve.

In the short term, different CIOs will deem various factors and activities more important than their colleagues. Indeed, in the long term, some of the factors and activities will likely be replaced by factors and activities more appropriate to the predictably changing and increasingly complex IT management arena.

Former Director of MIT's Center for Information Systems Research (CISR), John F. Rockart, amplifies this point, "I don't want the job of CIO. It's far too complex! It takes an incredible individual to address the technical issues, human issues, and organizational issues" (Rockart, 1996). Adding to the complexity of the CIO job is the fact that the position varies, and deservedly so, based on the organizational context in which the CIO operates. "The role of the CIO is undoubtedly changing faster than that of any other top functional manager. Yet the pace of evolution differs significantly from company to company, as well it should, because of several factors:

Table 1. Refined sets of dimension attributes

Focus on Business Factors (12)	
Agency mission	5/5
Agency goals and objectives	5/5
Agency policies	5/5
Agency resources	5/5
External constituencies	4/5
Internal constituencies	4/5
Internal IT users	4/5
Top-level managers	4/5
Middle-level managers	4/5
Low-level managers	4/5
Program decisions	4/5
Government policies and regulations	4/5
Knowledge of Technical Factors (10)	
LANs	5/5
Client/server hardware and software	5/5
Relational databases	5/5
Executive information systems	4/5
Email	4/5
Mainframes and minicomputers	4/5
Decision support systems	4/5
Object-oriented tools	4/5
CASE tools	4/5
Internet/WWW	4/5
Understanding of Human Factors (6)	
Formal reporting structures	5/5
Inter-unit power struggles	5/5
Informal reporting structures	4/5
Intra-unit power struggles	4/5
Successful people who embody values and character of the agency and its culture	4/5
Set of expectations that groups have for members	4/5
Convey the Relevance of IT Activities (7)	
Conducting pilot projects to test the potential of IT	5/5
Disseminating information about the need for IT-based change	5/5
Disseminating results of completed IT projects	5/5
Stressing the economic context of IT to senior managers	4/5
Promoting IT as an agent of agency transformation	4/5
Disseminating information about the cost-benefit of IT-based change	4/5
Disseminating information about IT initiatives and solutions at other agencies	4/5
Manage Critical Relationships Activities (10)	
Actively participate in top-management decision making	5/5
Speak the language of program managers	5/5
Stay abreast of developments (IT/non-IT) in other program areas	5/5
Educate managers regarding IT architectures	5/5
Explain to users that their feedback is critical to system benefit expansion	5/5
Educate managers and end-users regarding lead times	4/5
Provide information on a selective basis to gain support for IT-based change	4/5
Insist on good user documentation of your existing system	4/5
Insist that systems are documented as they are developed for review and control purposes	4/5
Insist that program managers sign-off on each stage of development prior to beginning subsequent stages	4/5
Implement IT-Based Solutions Activities (9)	
Create a participative IT planning process	5/5
Coordinate multiple IT projects	5/5
Employ an iterative development approach to ensure flexibility to evolving requirements	5/5
Involve those to be affected by IT-based change in systems design and implementation	5/5
Procure and organize the technological expertise necessary for systems design and implementation	5/5
Participate in IT projects	4/5
Disseminate results of completed IT projects	4/5
Encourage and employ the development of applications by end-users to reduce IT project backlog	4/5
Procure and allocate the equipment needed for systems development	4/5

Figure 2. Revised conceptual framework of CIO competence

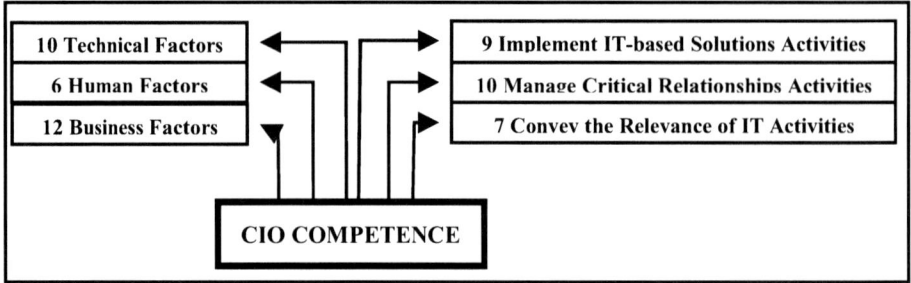

- The economy
- Industries the organization serves
- Organization size and structure
- Organizational objectives
- Political forces within the organization
- Organization's stage of IS growth
- Personal attributes and managerial skills of the incumbent CIO

Rockart also stated, "In short, the exact role of a particular CIO in a particular company at a particular point is contingent upon the above and other factors. ...Each has a direct impact on the role of the CIO" (Rockart & Bullen, 1982, p. 6).

Solutions and Recommendations: Putting the Conceptual Framework into Context

As stated in the introductory section, an important secondary goal of this chapter is to gain a deeper understanding of the critical competencies for public-sector CIOs *in relation to their work environment*. To this end, a questionnaire was administered to assess the competencies comprising the conceptual framework in relation to two aspects of the CIO's work environment: IT unit size and IT vision. These two aspects of the CIO's work environment are referred to as the two contextual settings for the remainder of this chapter. The questionnaire represents the third lesson for research on public management from Allison's 1980 work that was followed here:

3.   Careful review of private management rules of thumb that can be adapted to public management contexts will pay off.

Questionnaire

Initially, a contact list of 54 institutional representatives was acquired from the Executive Director of the New York State Forum for Information Resource Management (NYSFIRM). NYSFIRM is an agency that provides a forum for dialogue to occur between member agencies and facilitates the sharing of IT-related experiences (e.g., challenges, triumphs, etc.) among all NYSFIRM member agencies.

All 54 institutional representatives were telephoned in order to identify the name and address of the chief information officer — head of the information resource management (IRM) function — within their agency. Because the CIO title is not widely used in New York State government agencies, the highest ranking information resource manager within the agency was treated as the agency's CIO. The "chief information officer" title is broadly applied to all members of the sample, regardless of the actual title used within their given agencies. The appropriate names and addresses were obtained for 54 chief information officers (CIO) employed within New York State government agencies from the original contact list.

Respondents

Forty-one useable CIO questionnaires were returned for an overall response rate of 76%. Thirty-six of the respondents were male, and five were female. The most commonly reported titles were "director" and "assistant director." In fact, only one of the 41 respondents actually held the "CIO" title. These data are consistent with previous research surrounding IT management in the public sector (Penrod et al., 1990).

There are undoubtedly an infinite number of contextual factors that may affect the appropriate role and, hence, the critical competencies for the CIO. Two factors related to the CIO's work environment were examined and are presented here in order to identify which of the factors and activities comprising the six dimensions, different CIO groups deem critical from the six sets identified through the semistructured interview data.

Measurement of CIO Competence

Measurement of CIO competence is based on the respondents' assessment of the importance of the six dimensions of CIO competence. The first three dimensions represent three knowledge bases integral to the CIO job. The attributes that comprise the three knowledge-based dimensions are called "factors":

- Business factors dimension
- Human factors dimension
- Technical factors dimension

The last three dimensions represent three sets of activities that are vital to the CIO job. The attributes that comprise the three activity-based dimensions are called "activities":

- Convey the relevance of IT activities dimension
- Management critical relationships activities dimension
- Implement IT-based solutions activities dimension

In assessing the importance of the factors that comprise each knowledge-based dimension, respondents used a 10-point Likert-type scale to "indicate the extent to which the following 'factors' are critical for you to absolutely be cognizant of and focused on" (CA = cannot assess, 1 = not important, 10 = critical). Similarly, in assessing the importance of the activities which comprise each activity-based dimension, respondents used the 10-point Likert-type scale to "indicate the extent to which the following 'activities' are critical for you to perform" (CA = cannot assess, 1 = not important, 10 = critical).

Responses were organized into three categories: responses of 8, 9, or 10 were categorized as a "critical" rating; 5, 6, or 7 as "fairly important"; and £4 as "not important." If a respondent selected the "CA" response, his or her data for that attribute was not included in the analysis, because CA is a valid response but cannot be assigned to the any of the aforementioned three categories. If a respondent did not select the "CA" response and did not rate the attribute using the 10-point scale, that respondent was excluded from the mean calculation of that attribute for the associated CIO group.

IT Unit Size Contextual Setting

IT unit size relates to the number of staff employed by the agency's IT unit. The size of the IT unit was used to segment the respondents into two groups. Respondents were asked to self-select themselves into one group. One group is comprised of CIOs who manage an IT unit staff of less than 30 (i.e., Small IT Unit). The other group is comprised of CIOs who manage an IT unit staff of greater than or equal to 30 (i.e., Large IT Unit). One of the 41 respondents did not respond to this question. The two resulting "IT unit size" CIO groups are presented below:

- Small IT Unit Staff: <30 ($n = 19$)
- Large IT Unit Staff: ^{3}30 ($n = 21$)

Using the 10-point scale described above, a profile was developed for the large and small IT unit CIO groups (Table 2). Each profile consists of those factors and activities within the six dimensions of the competence framework that at least two-thirds (^{3}67%) of the group respondents rated critical (i.e., 8, 9, or 10). The results of the comparative analysis of the CIO competence ratings for the "Small IT Unit" and "Large IT Unit" CIO groups are presented next.

Critical Factors

As illustrated in Table 8.3e, the two groups are similar in terms of the number of factors (i.e., business, human, and technical) that they feel are critical for them to focus on. For example, across the three knowledge-based dimensions, a total of 13 factors emerged as critical for the Small IT Unit CIO group to focus on, while 14 factors were critical for the Large IT Unit CIO group. However, there are some differences across the two groups in terms of the types of critical factors and the extent to which each group feels that a given factor is critical (see percentages to the right of each critical factor listed).

Focus on Business Factors

Nine of the 12 business factors emerged as critical in the Small IT Unit CIO profile, compared to eight in the Large IT Unit CIO profile. Six of the 12 business factors emerged as critical in both of the IT unit size CIO profiles:

- Agency mission
- Agency objectives and goals
- Agency policies
- Agency resources

Table 2. CIO competencies: small IT unit versus large IT unit

SMALL IT UNIT STAFF CIOs (*n* =19)	%	LARGE IT UNIT STAFF CIOs (*n* = 21)	%
Business Factors — high-level agency characteristics (9 of 12)	**%**	**Business Factors — high-level agency characteristics (8 of 12)**	**%**
BF11: Focus on top-level managers (KG)	89	BF2: Focus on agency objectives and goals (PA)	95
BF1: Focus on agency mission (PA)	79	BF1: Focus on agency mission (PA)	86
BF12: Focus on program decisions made outside the IT unit (DO)	75	BF7: Focus on internal constituencies (KG)	86
BF7: Focus on internal constituencies (KG)	74	BF11: Focus on top-level managers (KG)	81
BF8: Focus on internal IT users (KG)	72	BF3: Focus on agency policies (PA)	76
BF10: Focus on middle-level managers (KG)	71	BF6: Focus on government policies and regulations (DO)	71
BF2: Focus on agency objectives and goals (PA)	68	BF5: Focus on external constituencies (KG)	70
BF3: Focus on agency policies (PA)	68	BF4: Focus on agency resources (DO)	67
BF4: Focus on agency resources (DO)	68		
Human Factors — socioorganizational characteristics (1 of 6)	**%**	**Human Factors — socioorganizational characteristics (2 of 6)**	**%**
HF5: Focus on successful people who embody the agency's values, character, and culture (EE)	84	HF5: Focus on successful people who embody the agency's values, character, and culture (EE)	81
		HF6: Focus on set of expectations that members of a group have for one another (EE)	70
Technical Factors — forms of IT (3 of 10)	**%**	**Technical Factors — forms of IT (4 of 10)**	**%**
TF2: Focus on LANs (CT)	79	TF2: Focus on LANs (CT)	80
TF9: Focus on electronic mail (CT)	79	TF9: Focus on electronic mail (CT)	75
TF10: Focus on World Wide Web/Internet (CT)	68	TF1: Focus on mainframes/minicomputers (LIT)	74
		TF4: Focus on relational databases (IIT)	70
Convey the Relevance of IT — supporting activities (0 of 7)	**%**	**Convey the Relevance of IT — supporting activities (4 of 7)**	**%**
		CR7: Promote IT as an agent of agency transformation (PIS)	76
		CR5: Disseminate information about the results of recently completed IT-based projects (PTS)	71
		CR2: Stress the economic value of IT to senior managers (PTS)	67
		CR4: Disseminate information about the benefits and costs of IT-based change (PTS)	67
Manage Critical Relationships — supporting activities (3 of 10)	**%**	**Manage Critical Relationships — supporting activities (4 of 10)**	**%**
MR1: Actively participate in top-management decision making (ERM)	78	MR1: Actively participate in top-management decision making (ERM)	85
MR2: Speak the language of managers from other program areas (ERM)	68	MR2: Speak the language of managers from other program areas (ERM)	85
MR10: Explain to users that their feedback is critical to expanding a system's benefits (CUI)	68	MR3: Stay abreast of developments in the program areas of other managers (ERM)	85
		MR10: Explain to users that their feedback is critical to expanding a system's benefits (CUI)	80
Implement IT-Based Solutions — supporting activities (1 of 9)	**%**	**Implement IT-Based Solutions — supporting activities (6 of 9)**	**%**
PI7: Involve those affected by IT-based change in its design and implementation (CPC)	84	PI7: Involve those affected by IT-based change in its design and implementation (CPC)	95
		PI9: Procure and organize technical expertise for development (PIR)	90
		PI1: Create a participative IT planning process (CPC)	81
		PI8: Procure and allocate the equipment (e.g., hardware/software) needed for systems development (PPR)	71
		PI4: Disseminate results of IT projects (CPC)	70
		PI5: Encourage an iterative IS development approach (DDA)	70

- Internal constituencies
- Top-level managers

The Small IT Unit CIO group indicated that focusing on the key constituent group "top-level managers" is their most critical business factor out of the nine business factors that emerged as critical for the group. Top-level managers ranked fourth out of the eight critical business factors that emerged in the Large IT Unit CIO profile.

In contrast, The Large IT Unit CIO group indicated that focusing on the principal aim "agency objectives and goals" is their most critical business factor out of the eight business factors that emerged as critical for the group. Agency objectives and goals ranks seventh out of the nine critical business factors in the Small IT Unit CIO profile.

The major difference between the critical business factors for the two profiles lies in the types of decision outcomes and key groups that they feel are critical to focus on, beyond those that they have in common. In addition to the six critical business factors common to both profiles, three others emerged as critical in the Small IT Unit CIO profile that are absent from the Large IT Unit CIO profile:

- Internal IT users
- Middle-level managers
- Program decision made outside the IT unit

These data suggest that the Small IT Unit CIO group is inclined to focus on more key groups that are internal to their agencies than is the Large IT Unit CIO group. In addition, the Small IT Unit CIO group is more inclined to focus on the outcomes of decisions that are made external to the IT unit but still internal to their agencies.

In contrast, two business factors emerged as critical in the Large IT Unit CIO profile that are absent from the Small IT Unit profile:

- External constituencies
- Government policies and regulations

These data suggest that the Large IT Unit CIO group is inclined to focus on more key groups that are external to their agencies, than is the Small IT Unit CIO group. In addition, the Large IT Unit CIO group is also more inclined to focus on the outcomes of decisions that are made external to the IT unit, and are also made external to their agencies.

The size of the IT unit that the CIO manages appears to be related to the type of high-level agency characteristics (i.e., business factors) that they feel are critical to focus on. CIOs who manage a Small IT Unit staff are more inclined to focus on business factors that have an internal orientation with respect to their agencies. Further, CIOs who manage a Large IT Unit staff are inclined to focus on business factors that have an external orientation with respect to their agencies.

Understanding of Human Factors

One of the six human factors emerged as critical in both of the IT unit size contextual setting profiles:

- Successful people who embody the agency's values, character, and culture

Both the Small IT Unit and Large IT Unit CIO groups indicated that this is the most critical human factor for them to focus on. This human factor is categorized as an employee expectation. These data indicate that it is critical for both of the IT unit size CIO groups to identify and focus on individuals that serve as role models of behavior desired in an agency employee.

In addition, the Large IT Unit CIO group indicated that focusing on the "set of expectations that members of a group have for one another" is another critical human factor of the employee expectation type. This human factor did not emerge as critical in the Small IT Unit CIO profile.

CIOs who manage Large IT Units are inclined to identify a set of expectations that relate to a group of employees, rather than relying solely on identifying a single employee who serves as a role model, when attempting to understand their agency's socio-organizational environment. Perhaps the relative size of their agencies as illustrated earlier, compared to their Small IT Unit CIO colleagues, makes identification of a single employee impractical and similar to finding a needle in a haystack. The size of the IT unit may dictate that focusing on multiple human factors is necessary to understanding the socio-organization.

Knowledge of Technical Factors

Three of the 10 technical factors emerged as critical in the Small IT Unit CIO profile, compared to four in the Large IT Unit CIO profile. Two communication technologies emerged as critical in both the Small IT Unit and Large IT Unit CIO profiles:

- LANs
- Electronic mail

These two technical factors ranked first and second, respectively, in both IT unit size CIO profiles.

In addition, the Small IT Unit CIO group indicated that the "World Wide Web/Internet" is another communication technology that is critical for them to focus on. In contrast, the Large IT Unit CIO group indicated that limited impact technologies, such as mainframes/minicomputers, as well as indirect impact technologies, such as relational databases, are additional critical technical factors for them to focus on.

These data suggest that communications technologies that enable people to work together and apart more effectively are critical for CIOs to focus on, regardless of the size of the IT unit that they manage. Further, as the IT unit size increases, the importance of technologies that have an indirect or limited impact on how people work together become more critical for the related CIOs to focus on. This is not surprising, because mainframes/minicomputers have long been far more common in large organizations than in smaller ones.

Critical Activities

The size of the IT unit that the CIO manages appears to be positively related to the number of activities felt critical to engage in. Only four activities emerged as critical for the Small IT Unit CIO to perform across the three activity-based dimensions (i.e., convey the relevance of IT, manage critical relationships, and implement IT-based solutions). In contrast, 14 activities emerged as critical in the Large IT Unit profile.

Convey the Relevance of IT Activities

None of the seven convey the relevance of IT activities emerged as critical in the Small IT Unit CIO profile. Perhaps the relative size of the agency does not make educating agency constituents as to the potential value of IT a critical activity. In contrast, four convey the relevance of IT activities emerged critical in the Large IT Unit CIO profile:

- Promote IT as an agency of agency transformation
- Disseminate information about the results of recently completed IT projects
- Stress the economic value of IT to senior managers
- Disseminate information about the benefits and costs of IT-based change

The first conveys the relevance of IT activity that emerged as critical in the Large IT Unit CIO profile, "promoting IT as an agent of agency transformation," relates to providing intangible support for IT initiatives. This is the only activity of this type that emerged as critical in the Large IT Unit CIO profile. The remaining three critical activities relate to providing tangible support for IT initiatives.

Conventional wisdom tells us that the larger the agency within which IT projects are pursued, the greater the potential costs, organizational impact, number of stakeholders, and the higher the project's profile. Such activities are probably not deemed critical for Small IT Unit CIOs, because the stakes are just not as high for them.

These data suggest that CIOs who operate within large agencies are more inclined to attempt to educate constituents by producing tangible support for IT initiatives. The willingness or reluctance of constituents to lend their support to the CIO in the future probably hinges, in part, on the Large IT Unit CIO's ability to perform such activities effectively.

Manage Critical Relationships Activities

Three of the 10 manage critical relationships activities emerged as critical in both the Small IT Unit CIO profile and the Large IT Unit CIO profile:

- Activity participate in top-management decision making
- Speak the language of managers from other program areas
- Explain to users that their feedback is critical to expanding the benefits of their systems

The first two approach the management of critical relationships through direct interaction with managers, outside the IT unit environment. The third involves solicitation of end-user feelings as to how their information systems (IS) can be made more effective, while instilling in them a sense of ownership over their IS and empowerment in how their IS evolves.

These data indicate that interactions with program management in their areas of expertise and empowering end users by encouraging their input for the enhancement of their systems are critical activities related to managing relationships, regardless of the size of the IT unit that the CIO manages.

One additional manage critical relationships activity emerged as critical in the Large IT Unit CIO profile that is absent from the Small IT Unit profile:

- Stay abreast of developments in the program areas of other managers

This finding suggests that the larger the IT unit, and presumably the agency, the more critical it is that the CIO work harder to keep up with ongoing developments in diverse locations throughout the agency.

Implement IT-Based Solutions Activities

One of the nine implement IT-based solutions activities emerged as critical in both the Small IT Unit CIO profile and the Large IT Unit CIO profile:

•   Involve those to be affected by an IT-based change in its design and implementation

Here again, regardless of the size of the IT unit being managed, the data suggest that it is critical for CIOs to empower employees by encouraging their input and active involvement in the development of their systems. In addition, it appears that activities related to the empowerment of employees may be even more critical during the implementation stage, than earlier on in the IS development process (i.e., manage critical relationships). That is, a higher percentage of both groups indicated the criticality of this sort of activity (i.e., empowering employees) during the implementation stage than was indicated for a similar activity involved in lobbying for and procuring resources for IT initiatives.

For example, 84% of the Small IT Unit CIOs and 95% of the Large IT Unit CIOs indicated that "involving those to be affected by IT-based change in its design and implementation" is critical. In contrast, only 68% of the Small IT Unit CIOs and 80% of the Large IT Unit CIOs indicated that "explaining to users that their feedback is critical to expanding the benefits of their systems" is a critical activity when managing critical relationships.

Five additional activities emerged as critical in the Large IT Unit CIO profile that are absent from the Small IT Unit CIO profile:

•   Create a participative IT planning process
•   Disseminate results of IT projects
•   Procure and organize the technical expertise for development
•   Procure and allocate the equipment needed for systems development
•   Encourage an iterative IS development approach

The first two relate to cultivating project champions by encouraging the collective participation of IT and non-IT personnel in IT project initiatives as early on as the initial planning stages. Cultivating project champions can increase support and morale for IT projects, while helping to identify potential sources of project resistance. Such outcomes can help increase the likelihood of project success.

The third critical activity relates to procuring intellectual resources, such as the technical expertise necessary for the design and implementation of the IS. The fourth critical activity involves procuring the physical resources, such as the hardware and software, necessary for IS development. The last critical activity relates to directing the IS development approach that is used throughout the IT project's development activities.

These data indicate that more activities are critical during the implementation process for Large IT Unit CIOs than Small IT Unit CIOs. This may be related to the increased potential for exposure and impact of the IS in the larger agencies as compared to smaller agencies.

IT Vision Contextual Setting

The *perception of the role of information technology* (IT) is synonymous with the concept of one's *vision* for how IT ought to be exploited within a given organizational environment. The term "vision" has been defined in several ways. Most definitions agree that vision is one's conceptualization of a *potential future state* of an entity that is widely shared with others (Collins & Porras, 1991; James, 1985; Locke, 1991; Nanus, 1992; Nanus & Bennis, 1989; Robbins & Duncan, 1988; Walton, 1989).

Developing a vision is a means of describing an idea and its potential impact. Former AT&T Executive, Archie McGill stated, "The issue is that incremental change will get you a ticket into day-to-day survival, but it won't get you a ticket for long-range survival. The only way I know to get at fundamental change is by creating new visions of the company, the organization, and its direction" (Walton, 1989, p. 53). Leadership expert Burt Nanus suggested that articulating and gaining support for a vision (i.e., selling one's vision; acting as a champion) increases the probability of successfully transforming the vision into reality (Nanus, 1992).

Escalating IT costs, increased market pressure, and the growing sophistication of end users have sparked interest among practitioners and researchers to develop a means of focusing stakeholder attention and commitment toward broadly defined, common objectives for IT. An IT vision is essentially an organization's rationale for investing in IT resources by articulating the *role of IT within the organization*, in the future (e.g., 1 to 5 years). Past research has shown the usefulness of considering the nature and impact of the organizational leaders' shared *vision* of the role of IT (Feeny et al., 1992; Armstrong, 1995). In fact, Feeny et al. (1992) found the IT vision contextual factor to be "the single most powerful discriminator" in their study of the CEO/CIO relationship.

The Feeny et al. (1992) CIO instrument, which operationalized Schein's (1989) four strategic IT visions, is used here for the IT vision contextual setting. Presumably, the four IT visions presented below relate to the *factors* CIOs consider when making decisions and the *activities* that govern their behavior:

- Transform: Agency can be fundamentally changed through the use of IT, including the terms of our relationships with suppliers and customers and the boundaries among us ($n=26$).
- Informate Up: Data and transactions allow more clear and organized management views of the state and dynamics of the agency ($n = 7$).
- Informate Down: Data and transactions provide a fuller picture at the operator level, with members of the workforce gaining insight into their activities ($n = 3$).
- Automate: Role of IT is to replace expensive, unreliable human labor, or at least transform its productivity ($n = 4$).

Respondents were asked to indicate which of the four visions "best describes your perception of the role of IT within your agency."

Due to the small sample sizes of the latter three groups (i.e., informate up, informate down, automate) these three groups were combined into one "Nontransform" group. Because the Transform group represents the only CIOs sampled who perceive the role of IT to be one in which their agency can be *fundamentally changed*, rather than merely a support capacity, this seemed to be an acceptable consolidation for the IT vision contextual setting

CIO groups. Segmenting respondents in this manner resulted in two groups for the IT vision contextual setting:

- Transform ($n = 26$)
- Nontransform ($n = 14$)

Using the 10-point scale described above, a profile was developed for both the transform and nontransform IT unit CIO groups (Table 3). Each profile consists of those factors and activities within the six dimensions of the competence framework that at least two-thirds (^{3}67%) of the group respondents rated critical (i.e., 8, 9, or 10). The results of the comparative analysis of the CIO competence ratings for the "Transform" and "Nontransform" CIO groups are presented next.

Critical Factors

As illustrated in Table 3, the two groups differ substantially in terms of the number of factors (i.e., business, human, and technical) that they feel are critical for them to focus on. For example, across the three knowledge-based dimensions, a total of 17 factors emerged as critical in the Transform CIO profile, while only seven factors emerged as critical in the Nontransform CIO profile. The two groups also differ in terms of the types of critical factors and the extent to which the group feels that a given factor is critical (see percentages to the right of each critical factor listed).

Focus on Business Factors

Four of the 12 business factors emerged as critical in both of the IT vision CIO profiles:

- Agency mission
- Agency objectives and goals
- Top-level managers
- Internal constituencies

Focusing on the principal aim "agency objectives and goals" is the most critical business factor out of the total of 10 that emerged in the Transform CIO profile. This factor ranks fourth out of the four critical business factors that emerged in the Nontransform CIO profile. In contrast, the principal aim "agency mission" is the most critical business factor out of the four that emerged in the Nontransform CIO profile. This factor ranks third out of the 10 critical business factors that emerged in the Transform CIO profile. The key group "top-level managers" is the second most critical business factor for both groups.

In addition to the four listed above, six other business factors emerged as critical in the Transform CIO profile that are absent from the Nontransform CIO profile:

- Agency policies
- External constituencies
- Program decision made outside the IT unit
- Agency resources
- Government policies and regulations
- Middle-level managers

Table 3. CIO competencies: transform IT vision versus nontransform IT vision

Table 3 CIO Competencies: Transform IT Vision Versus Nontransform IT Vision			
TRANSFORM IT VISION CIOs (*n* = 26)		**NONTRANSFORM IT VISION CIOs (14)**	
Business Factors — high-level agency characteristics (10 of 12)	**%**	**Business Factors — high-level agency characteristics (4 of 12)**	**%**
BF2: Focus on agency objectives and goals (PA)	92	BF1: Focus on agency mission (PA)	86
BF11: Focus on top-level managers (KG)	88	BF11: Focus on top-level managers (KG)	79
BF1: Focus on agency mission (PA)	85	BF7: Focus on internal constituencies (KG)	71
BF7: Focus on internal constituencies (KG)	85	BF2: Focus on agency objectives and goals (PA)	69
BF3: Focus on agency policies (PA)	81		
BF5: Focus on external constituencies (KG)	77		
BF12: Focus on program decisions made outside the IT unit (DO)	76		
BF4: Focus on agency resources (DO)	73		
BF6: Focus on government policies and regulations (DO)	73		
BF10: Focus on middle-level managers (KG)	69		
Human Factors — socioorganizational characteristics (2 of 6)	**%**	**Human Factors — socioorganizational characteristics (1 of 6)**	**%**
HF5: Focus on successful people who embody the agency's values, character, and culture (EE)	88	HF5: Focus on successful people who embody the agency's values, character, and culture (EE)	79
HF6: Focus on set of expectations that members of a group have for one another (EE)	73		
Technical Factors — forms of IT (5 of 10)	**%**	**Technical Factors — forms of IT (2 of 10)**	**%**
TF2: Focus on LANs (CT)	92	TF9: Focus on electronic mail (CT)	72
TF9: Focus on electronic mail (CT)	84	TF4: Focus on relational databases (IIT)	71
TF3: Focus on client/server hardware and software (HIT)	72		
TF10: Focus on World Wide Web/Internet (CT)	72		
TF4: Focus on relational databases (IIT)	68		
Convey the Relevance of IT — supporting activities (2 of 7)	**%**	**Convey the Relevance of IT — supporting activities (0 of 7)**	**%**
CR7: Promote IT as an agent of agency transformation (PIS)	88		
CR4: Disseminate information about the benefits and costs of IT-based change (PTS)	69		
Manage Critical Relationships — supporting activities (4 of 10)	**%**	**Manage Critical Relationships — supporting activities (0 of 10)**	**%**
MR1: Actively participate in top-management decision making (ERM)	88		
MR2: Speak the language of managers from other program areas (ERM)	84		
MR10: Explain to users that their feedback is critical to expanding a system's benefits (CUI)	84		
MR3: Stay abreast of developments in the program areas of other managers (ERM)	80		
Implement IT-Based Solutions — supporting activities (5 of 9)	**%**	**Implement IT-Based Solutions — supporting activities (2 of 9)**	**%**
PI7: Involve those affected by IT-based change in its design and implementation (CPC)	92	PI7: Involve those affected by IT-based change in its design and implementation (CPC)	86
PI1: Create a participative IT planning process (CPC)	88	PI9: Procure and organize technical expertise for development (PIR)	71
PI9: Procure and organize technical expertise for development (PIR)	84		
PI8: Procure and allocate the equipment (e.g., hardware/software) needed for systems development (PPR)	73		
PI5: Encourage an iterative IS development approach (DDA)	68		

These six business factors add a focus on decision outcomes made external to the Transform CIOs' IT unit that is neglected in the Nontransform CIO profile. Further, these data indicate that the Transform CIOs also extend their focus in the area of key constituent groups to encompass agency managers below the executive level, as well as constituents external to their agencies. In addition, the Transform CIO profile stresses a broader focus on principal aims that govern the operations within the agency.

The Transform CIO group is inclined to focus on a more complete set of principal aims, key groups, and decision outcomes external to the IT unit.

The data suggest that the CIO's vision of the role of IT within the agency is related to the scope of high-level agency characteristics (i.e., business factors) that are critical to focus on.

Understanding of Human Factors

One of the six human factors emerged as critical in both of the IT vision contextual setting profiles:

- Successful people who embody the agency's values, character, and culture

In addition, the Transform CIO group indicated that focusing on the "set of expectations that members of a group have for one another" is another critical human factor. This human factor did not emerge as critical in the Nontransform CIO profile.

Focusing on the set of expectations that group members have for one another may have emerged as critical in the Transform CIO profile because of the potential for IT initiatives to change the way people work and interact. Anticipating the potential pockets of resistance to such change could be critical to increasing the potential of IT project success.

Knowledge of Technical Factors

Two of the 10 technical factors emerged as critical in both of the IT vision CIO contextual setting profiles:

- Electronic mail
- Relational databases

In addition, the Transform CIO profile stresses three additional critical technical factors that did not emerge in the Nontransform CIO profile:

- LANs
- Client/server hardware and software
- World Wide Web/Internet

These data suggest that the Transform CIO group is more focused on enhancing the agency's communication networks by expanding the range of internal capabilities to reach external information stores.

Critical Activities

The CIO's perception of the role of IT appears to be related to the number of activities that felt to be critical to be performed. Only two activities emerged as critical in the

Nontransform CIO profile across the three activity-based dimensions (i.e., convey the relevance of IT, manage critical relationships, and implement IT-based solutions). In contrast, 11 activities emerged as critical in the Transform CIO profile.

Convey the Relevance of IT Activities

None of the seven convey the relevance of IT activities emerged as critical in the Nontransform CIO profile. On the other hand, two activities related to educating agency constituents as to the potential value of IT emerged as critical in the Transform CIO profile:

- Promote IT as an agent of agency transformation
- Disseminate information about the benefits and costs of IT-based change

These two activities are associated with providing intangible support and providing tangible support for IT initiatives, respectively.

The support role of IT that is associated with the Nontransform IT visions may explain why this CIO group does not place as much emphasis on actively educating constituents of the agency regarding the potential of IT-based initiatives. In contrast, perhaps the more innovative application of IT that is associated with the Transform IT vision explains why two such activities emerged as critical in the Transform CIO's profile.

Manage Critical Relationships Activities

None of the manage critical relationships activities emerged as critical in the Nontransform CIO profile. On the other hand, four of the 10 activities related to lobbying for the requisite resources for IT-based initiatives emerged as critical in the Transform CIO profile:

- Actively participate in top-management decision making
- Speak the language of managers from other program areas
- Stay abreast of developments in the program areas of other managers
- Explain to users that their feedback is critical to expanding the benefits of their systems

The first three relate to the management of relationships with managers outside the IT unit through direct interaction and by keeping current with developments in their program areas. The fourth relates to the management of relationships with end users by soliciting their input for use in system upgrades.

These data indicate that interactions with program management and end users are critical activities in gaining support for the innovative use of IT within agencies. Such activities do not appear critical for CIOs who view their agency's primary use of IT as being for support purposes.

Implement IT-Based Solutions Activities

Two of the nine implement IT-based solutions activities emerged as critical in both CIO profiles:

- Involve those to be affected by an IT-based change in its design and implementation
- Procure and organize the technical expertise for development

These data suggest that regardless of whether the dominant use of IT within the agency is perceived as transformational or not, CIOs feel it is critical to empower employees by encouraging their active involvement in IS development efforts. The data also suggest that it is critical for the CIO to engage in human resource development commensurate with the needs of IT initiatives.

Three additional activities emerged as critical in the Transform CIO profile that are absent in the Nontransform CIO profile:

- Create a participative IT planning process
- Procure and allocate the equipment needed for systems development
- Encourage an iterative IS development approach

The first involves identifying project champions by approaching IT project initiatives through cooperative participation. The next relates to hardware and software procurement necessary for IS development. The last critical activity that emerged in the Transform CIO profile relates to managing the IS development and implementation approach employed.

These data suggest that more activities are critical for the CIO during the implementation process for transformational IT designs than for IS that merely support existing agency operations.

FUTURE TRENDS

In this chapter, insight was provided into the landscape of public-sector IT management, by starting with an identification of common problems faced by practicing public-sector CIOs. Further, the discussion illustrates the usefulness of conceptualizing CIO competence in terms of types of knowledge that CIOs should rely on and types of activities CIOs should engage in.

There are many contextual factors not considered here that, in addition to a CIO's discretion, will decide which factors and activities (underlying each of the six dimensions) a given CIO will deem critical (Figure 3). Follow-up research on CIO competence should more deeply examine the contextual setting in which the CIO operates. In fact, the author is currently conducting a research project where the conceptual framework of CIO competence is being assessed in relation to leadership styles exhibited by CIOs in institutions of higher education. In that study, respondents are being segmented by the Carnegie Classification System utilized by higher education institutions. Whereas the underlying factors and activities that emerge critical in that study will undoubtedly vary across respondent groups, the position of the researcher is that the overarching six dimensions of the framework remain important across groups.

CONCLUSION

The conceptual framework of CIO competence presented here provides a comprehensive mechanism for framing courses and stimulating lively classroom discussions related to IT management, its challenges, and opportunities. A picture is worth a thousand words. The consideration of contextual factors as influential in dictating how CIOs perceived the critical factors and activities involved in their jobs will embellish such discussions, further stretching students' thinking.

Figure 3. The research model

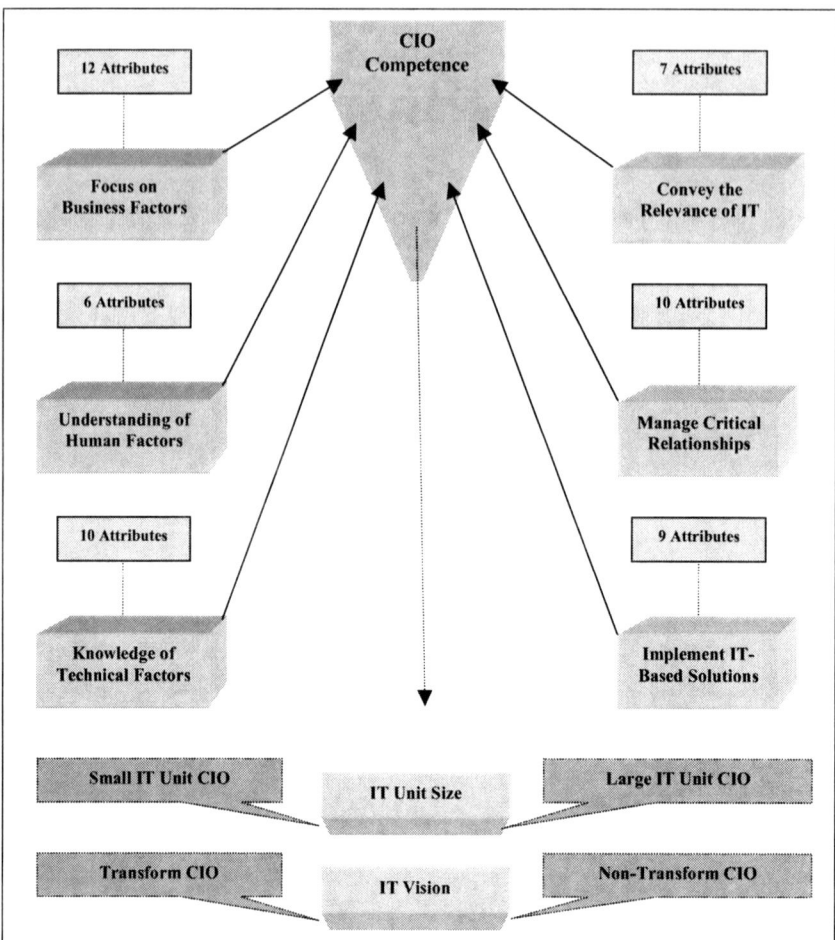

Too few organizations are fortunate enough to have as part of their workforce individuals who possess an interdisciplinary and multidimensional perspective. In private-sector firms, this sort of employee is increasingly viewed as a critical resource and valuable asset to the organization. Public-sector agencies must more actively search for and develop such individuals. The need for more individuals that possess an interdisciplinary and multidimensional perspective, across sectors, is matched only by the need for educational programs and approaches that competently and effectively satisfy this demand.

REFERENCES

Allison, G. T. (1990). Public and private management: Are they fundamentally alike in all unimportant respects? *Proceedings for the Public Management Research Confer-*

ence, November 19–20, 1979 (Washington, D.C.: Office of Personnel Management, OPM Document 127-53-1, February 1980, pp. 27–38).

Applegate, L. M. & Elam, J. J. (1992). New information systems leaders: A changing role in a changing world." *MIS Quarterly, 16,* 4, December.

Barnard, C. I. (1938). *The Functions of the Executive.* Washington, DC: Howard University Press.

Brancheau, J. & Wetherbe, (1996). Key issues in information systems management: 1994–95 SIM Delphi Results.

Brown, M. C. (1982). Administrative succession and organizational performance: The succession effect. *Administrative Science Quarterly, 29,* 245–273.

Buckholtz, T. J. (1994). Identity crisis. *CIO Magazine,* May, 15.

Center for Technology in Government. (1997). Developing and delivering government services on the World Wide Web: Recommended practices for New York State.

Chen, R. (1998). The eighth stage of information management: Information resources management (IRM) vs. knowledge management (KM), and the Chief Information Officer (CIO) vs. the Chief Knowledge Officer (CKO). *International Forum on Information and Documentation, 23,* 1 (January/March), 18–24.

Feeny, D. F., Edwards, B., & Simpson, K. (1992). Understanding the CEO/CIO relationship. *MIS Quarterly, 16,* 4, 435–448.

Grover, V. et al. (1993, Fall). The Chief Information Officer: A study of managerial roles. *Journal of Management Information Systems, 10,* 2, 107–130.

Grover, V., Teng, J. T. C., & Fiedler, K. D. (1993). Information technology enabled business process redesign: An integrated planning framework. *OMEGA International Journal of Management Science, 21,* 4, 433–447.

Hickey, K. (1999). A CIO on the job." *Traffic World, 258,* 13 (June 28), 43.

Jones, M. C., Taylor, G. S., & Spencer, B. A. (1995). The CEO/CIO relationship revisited. An empirical assessment of satisfaction with IS. *Information and Management, 29,* 3, 123–130 Sept. (37).

Keen, P. G. W. (1991). *Shaping the Future: Business Design through Information Technology.* Boston, MA: Harvard Business School Press.

Keen, P. G. W. (1992). Information technology and the management difference: A fusion map." *IBM Systems Journal, 32,* 1.

Nanus, B. (1992). *Visionary Leadership: Creating a Compelling Sense of Direction for Your Organization, 1st ed.* San Francisco, CA: Jossey-Bass.

Penrod, J. I., Dolence, M. G., & Douglas, J. V. (1990). *The Chief Information Officer in higher education.* CAUSE, The Association for the Management of Information Technology in Higher Education, Professional Paper Series #4.

Prince, C. J. (1999). Will the CIO role be obsolete?" *Chief Executive Magazine,* 146, 64–67, July/August.

Rainey, H. G., Backoff, R. W., & Levine, C. N. (1976). Comparing public and private organizations. *Public Administration Review* (March–April).

Rockart, J. F. (1996). CIO panel discussion. International Conference on Information Systems (ICIS).

Rockart, J. F., Ball, L., & Bullen, C. V. (1982). Future role of the information systems executive. *MIS Quarterly*/Special Issue.

Shafritz, J. M. & Hyde, A. C. (1992). *Classic of Public Administration, 3rd ed.*

State Education Department. (1996). Changing business at SED: The role of information technology.

State Education Department. (1997). The Governor's Task Force on Information Resource Management.

Stephens, C. S. (1995). *The Nature of Information Technology Managerial Work: The Work Life of Five Chief Information Officers*. Westport, CT: Quorum Books.

Synott, W. R. & Gruber, W. H. (1981). *Information Resource Management: Opportunities and Strategies for the 1980s*. New York: John Wiley & Sons.

APPENDIX A

- **18 Business Factors**

1.	Agency mission
2.	Agency goals
3.	Agency objectives
4.	Agency policies
5.	Agency resources
6.	External constituencies
7.	Internal constituencies
8.	Internal IT users
9.	Top-level managers
10.	Program decisions
11.	Government policies and regulations
12.	Low-level managers
13.	Middle-level managers
14.	Standards
15.	Financial decisions
16.	Industry trends
17.	External IT users
18.	Vendors

- **34 Technical Factors**

1.	Speech recognition interfaces
2.	Natural language interfaces
3.	Mouse
4.	Touch screens/Light pens
5.	EIS
6.	Voicemail
7.	Email
8.	FAX
9.	VSAT
10.	EDI
11.	High-end workstations
12.	ISDN
13.	Desktop publishing
14.	LANs
15.	Biomolecular computing
16.	Nanotechnology
17.	Data extraction and conversion software
18.	Online ext. database searching
19.	Client/server hardware
20.	Client/server software
21.	CASE
22.	CD-ROM and optical storage
23.	Relational databases
24.	4GLs/query languages

25.	Prototyping
26.	32-bit PCs
27.	Hypertext/hypermedia
28.	Expert systems/AI
29.	Mainframes and minicomputers
30.	DSS
31.	Computerized libraries
32.	PBX
33.	Calendaring and tickling software
34.	Neural networks

- **14 Human Factors**
    1. Formal reporting structures
    2. Objects/actions/events that enable the exchange of ideas
    3. Inter-unit power struggles
    4. Shared attitudes/perceptions that help one understand the agency
    5. Informal reporting structures
    6. Extraordinary individuals who personify high achievement
    7. Intra-unit power struggles
    8. Ceremonial activities
    9. People who embody agency values/character
    10. Actions that reinforce norms and values
    11. Expectations that groups have for members
    12. Past events that illustrate norms and values
    13. Fictional stories that help explain activities
    14. Verbal symbols reflecting agency culture

- **12 Convey the Relevance of IT Activities**
    1. Conducting pilot projects to test the potential of IT
    2. Disseminating information about the need for IT-based change
    3. Disseminating results of completed IT projects
    4. Stressing the economic context of IT to senior managers
    5. Promoting IT as an agent of agency transformation
    6. Disseminating information about the costs and benefits of IT-based change
    7. Disseminating information about IT initiatives and solutions at other agencies
    8. Directing IT-based seminars
    9. Regularly participating in IT-based seminars
    10. Regularly participating in field-based seminars
    11. Stressing the competitive context of IT to senior managers
    12. Stressing the organizational context of IT to senior managers

- **18 Manage Critical Relationship Activities**
    1. Actively participate in top-management decision making
    2. Speak the language of program managers
    3. Stay abreast of developments (IT/non-IT) in other program areas
    4. Educate managers regarding IT architectures
    5. Explain to users that their feedback is critical to system benefit expansion

6. Educate managers regarding lead times
7. Educate end-users regarding lead times
8. Provide information on a selective basis to gain support for IT-based change
9. Insist on good user documentation of your existing system
10. Insist that systems are documented as they are developed for review and control purposes
11. Insist that managers sign-off on each development stage prior to beginning subsequent stages
12. Educate end-user regarding IT architectures
13. Educate managers regarding IT architectures
14. Bargaining with resistant employees to change their minds about IT-based change
15. Insist that the systems design report be formally approved by the program manager affected
16. Educate end-users regarding the IT platform
17. Use power/threats to change the minds of employee who are resistant to IT-based change
18. Insists that systems design report specify exactly how to operate the system

- **13 Implement IT-Based Solutions Activities**
  1. Create a participative IT planning process
  2. Coordinate multiple IT projects
  3. Employ an iterative development approach to ensure flexibility to evolving requirements
  4. Involve those to be affected by IT-based change in systems design and implementation
  5. Procure and organize the technological expertise necessary for systems design and implementation
  6. Participate in IT projects
  7. Disseminate results of completed IT projects
  8. Encourage the development of applications by end-users to reduce IT project backlog
  9. Procure and allocate the equipment needed for systems development
  10. Encourage and employ the reuse of existing program code to expedite application development
  11. Provide training and support for employees affected by an IT-based change
  12. Develop and disseminate information policies that govern IS development and use and dictate system responsibilities
  13. Employ a rigid step-by-step SDLC methodology to ensure identification and documentation of requirements

Section III:

Information
Technology
in
Education

Chapter XXVIII

Empirical Study of Students' Perceptions of Online Courses

Judith C. Simon
The University of Memphis, USA

Lloyd D. Brooks
The University of Memphis, USA

Ronald B. Wilkes
The University of Memphis, USA

ABSTRACT

The recent proliferation of availability of online courses and programs has caused some concerns related to ensuring that the time and cost investments provide beneficial results, both to students and the institutions providing the material. Students' perceptions of these programs are likely to affect their interest in enrolling in them. Schools need an awareness of these student perceptions to determine if a need exists to modify the delivery of online programs. This study was designed to determine current perceptions of online programs by potential students, compared with the traditional on-campus environment. Findings indicate those issues that are most important to students in course delivery and their beliefs as to whether these issues are more likely to be delivered through online or through traditional on-campus courses.

INTRODUCTION

More than 14 million persons participated in online classes in the year 2000, and some predictions have suggested that e-learning will become a $2 billion industry by 2004 (Peltz,

2000). According to Weil (2001), 54% of U.S. higher education institutions are currently offering e-learning courses. Weil cited an International Data Corporation prediction that this will grow to 87% by 2004. Many universities are experiencing increasing pressures to offer college courses online, partly due to competition with other colleges and universities and offerings available through the business sector. An increasing number of traditional colleges and universities are offering online degree programs. Many AACSB-accredited Business schools provide courses and complete programs online. And, new schools have been created that exist solely in cyberspace (Peltz, 2000). Students can complete undergraduate degree programs in fields as diverse as nursing, business, engineering, and technology.

There are several possible reasons for schools offering online programs: to increase revenues and credit hour production, to better utilize limited resources, to serve an expanded geographic area or student population, to serve the existing student population differently, or some combination of all of these reasons.

Students may also take online courses for a variety of reasons: location convenience, time convenience, cost perceptions, quality perceptions, and a variety of other possible reasons.

Some online courses have been implemented so quickly that insufficient time has been available to allow in-depth assessment of the desires, interests, and concerns of their potential direct customers, i.e., students. The study described here was developed to identify students' expectations and current perceptions of online courses and programs offered by colleges and universities. The results are expected to facilitate effective planning and development of these courses in the future. This study focuses on perceptions of potential students and does not attempt to measure curriculum or performance of current students.

BACKGROUND

Convenience has been widely quoted as a primary reason for students taking online courses. Persons already in the workforce or on military bases can take courses without interrupting careers and work schedules. And, online courses are ordinarily offered on a more regular basis than traditional course offerings.

Critics of online instruction point out that a Web-based educational program has at least one disadvantage in that it does not provide a forum for physical contact and live debate between students and faculty. This viewpoint about online degrees is given by many elite universities. They claim that it is impossible to replicate a classroom environment with online courses. Harvard University professor W. Earl Sasser indicated that Harvard "will never offer" an MBA degree online, because it would distract from the residential experience (Symonds, 2001). Kumar et al. (2002, p. 140) cited "strong evidence that students perceive interaction, student-to-student and student-to-instructor, to suffer as a result of virtual education."

But, many information technology professionals argue that there is little difference between getting a degree on campus or over the Web. They point out that many traditional colleges, including the University of Chicago and Stanford University, have initiated online instructional programs. Massachusetts Institute of Technology (MIT) plans to post lecture notes and reading assignments for most of its 2000 courses on the Web for free, as part of a program called OpenCourseWare (Symmonds, 2001). And Robert Baker, a systems consultant at Emergent Information Technologies, Incorporated, in Newport Beach, California, observed that students taking online courses are not isolated and can get to know faculty and other students by using online discussion boards (Dash, 2000).

Schooley (2001) cited case studies indicating that online education leading to graduate and undergraduate degrees is developing at a fast pace, and that this approach works well for the motivated, self-disciplined learner. She further stated that online university courses are not a substitute for books but rather a way to communicate with the instructor and other classmates. The same level of textbook reading will be required as is required for traditional courses. Exams in an online instruction environment consist of "open book" exams, where the answer represents a synthesis and application of material provided in the course. Online instruction requires more interaction, cooperative projects, and online problem solving than is required in many traditional courses.

Online instruction is offered, in many instances, because it is perceived to be cost effective. PWC Consulting was awarded a $453 million, five-year contract by the U.S. Army to develop an electronic university for military personnel that allows them to study from multiple locations. Some universities offer combination programs. For example, Duke University's Fuqua School of Business offers MBA degrees that provide about 65% of the work online and about 35% of the work in residency. Duke charges up to $90,000 for the program versus $60,000 for its traditional residential MBA degree program (Symonds, 2001).

Online instruction has expanded outside the bounds of degree programs. For example, General Motors Corporation announced that it is encouraging its 88,000 salaried employees to take online courses in areas such as marketing, finance, and e-business (Schneider, 2001). According to International Data Corporation, company spending on online instruction for employees is expected to grow from $6.3 million in 2001 to more than $23 billion by 2004.

Perceived Quality of Online Classes and Degrees

One critical indicator of the success or failure of any program is the extent to which graduates are accepted in the job market. Quigley (2001) cited a *Business Week* magazine survey conducted in 2000 reporting that (based on a survey of 250 corporate recruiters) most recruiters are "somewhat skeptical of online business school graduates' skills." Many executives do not feel that online degree programs have been offered long enough to prove themselves with on-the-job performance of MBA degree graduates. Many schools do not distinguish between online degree programs and traditional degree programs.

Some educators are concerned about the rapid growth of online degree programs. Others have questioned the superiority of online instruction when compared with classroom-based instruction.

Online Student Demographics and Concerns

Many students currently taking online courses are "nontraditional." The typical student enrolled in an online course is older, with a full-time job and a degree. Some have families and are using online instruction as a way to spend more time at home. Students who complete online degree programs appear to be highly motivated. Students who are required to travel as part of their job also find online courses attractive.

Students also look for institutions that provide online instruction in an attractive format. Many public, as well as private, educational institutions have initiated online degree programs to meet student expectations. Community colleges and regional universities have moved into the online arena. Students can earn a large number of different degrees and certificates online.

The University of Phoenix Online (2002) is the largest private provider of online instruction in the country, with over 38,000 students enrolled in bachelor's, master's, and doctoral degree programs. Their Web site claims the following benefits for students enrolling in online degree programs:

- Attend class at times and places that fit their schedule.

- Complete 100% of their education via the Internet.

- Earn their degree in two or three years.

- Classes are offered one at a time, for five to six weeks, so they can focus on one subject.

- Programs are continually updated to provide skills and expertise in high demand.

- All faculty members hold a master's or doctoral degree.

- All coursework is designed to apply to their work environment.

Faculty Concerns

Online courses may be developed by curriculum specialists with little or no participation from the faculty member who will conduct the class. Much e-learning is self-directed and not led directly by faculty members. A fear is that faculty members will no longer be curriculum developers and participate in intellectual debates within their disciplines. Instead, there is a concern that "faculty will become mere shepherds herding their passive sheep through pre-prepared fields of outdated and insubstantial information." Many faculty members have a perspective that Web-based academics must be driven by the interaction between students and faculty in order "to generate debate, conversation, and participation" (Accetta, 2001).

Faculty members are also concerned that students will not get the same campus experience that is provided to students who are enrolled in traditional programs. Some schools require that students check in online for a specified number of times each week. Many programs also require some amount of on-campus time, as well as meetings via conference calls. Some programs incorporate team projects that require students being together during specified points during the course. Some programs require one or more retreats in a traditional lecture/seminar format.

Many faculty members are skeptical about the short time period required to obtain a degree at some online schools. The American InterContinental University-Online (2002) advertised that an MBA degree could be earned in as little as eight months, and that a degree in Information Technology could be earned in as little as 10 months. Additional concerns include the following:

- Students need to be prepared to engage in self-directed learning.

- Measures for quality assurance must also be included in the system to assure that cheating does not take place, that the student does the work, and that the course has rigor and quality.

- Students must understand faculty expectations and know who to contact for technological and instructional needs.

There are also concerns about technical, administrative, and pedagogical issues that arise as faculty consider moving from a traditional classroom environment into a Web-based environment. Logistical concerns relate to providing students with the same level of support (e.g., library, bookstore, advising) in both environments. Pedagogical considerations involve issues relating to management of course quality and control over the learning environment.

THE STUDY

To obtain data related to perceptions of online courses by potential students, a survey instrument was distributed to over 300 students enrolled in high school business courses. These students were assumed to be more likely to be online customers for college-level courses than students who were already near completion of a college degree. These students could represent a large potential target market in the future.

Demographics

Demographic data were collected so that responses could be compared in several ways. The majority of the study focused on students' awareness of online offerings and their current perceptions. A total of 381 students participated in this study. A large majority were upperclassmen, i.e., high school juniors and seniors, as shown in Table 1.

A majority of the participants were female, as shown in Table 2.

A high percentage of students (88.97%) indicated that they have access to a computer at home, which could have a direct effect on ability to participate in online courses. A lack of access to a computer could have affected their perceptions. A comparison of accessibility by gender showed that the difference between genders was slight, as shown in Table 3.

Table 1. Grade classifications of participants (n = 373)

Classification	Percentage of Respondents
Freshman	4.56
Sophomore	24.40
Junior	33.51
Senior	37.53

Table 2. Gender of participants (n = 376)

Gender	Percentage of Respondents
Male	41.22
Female	58.78

Table 3. Access to a computer at home by gender (n = 380)

Gender	Percentage with Access
Male	89.03
Female	88.50

Current Status Regarding Taking Online Courses

Students were asked to describe their current status regarding taking a course online and were allowed to select more than one response. As shown in Table 4, about one-fourth of the respondents indicated that they would not take an online course. Not surprisingly, few had already taken or were currently taking a course online.

The results for categories shown in Table 4 were also compared by gender, as shown in Table 5. Again, there was little difference in the results for males versus females.

Ratings of Issues' Importance

The remainder of the survey had two parts, each with a listing of issues for students to consider. Thirty-eight students failed to respond to a majority of the questions in this part of the survey and were eliminated from further calculations.

In the first section, students were asked to indicate how important each identified issue was to them in deciding whether to take a course online or in an on-campus environment. A Likert-type scale was used, with 1 representing "not at all important" and 5 representing "extremely important." A mean was calculated as a basis for determining which issues were considered important (defined as a mean of at least 4.0). A majority of the issues had means

Table 4. Current status regarding online courses (n = 378)

Status Regarding Online Courses	Percentage of Respondents
I would not take a course online.	24.87
I would consider taking a course online.	58.20
I would like to take a course online.	28.04
I plan to take a course online.	6.35
I am currently taking a course online.	0.26
I have completed a course online.	0.49

Table 5. Current status regarding online courses by gender

Status Regarding Online Courses	Percentage — Male	Percentage — Female
I would not take a course online.	24.52	24.78
I would consider taking a course online.	56.77	58.41
I would like to take a course online.	26.45	28.76
I plan to take a course online.	6.45	6.19
I am currently taking a course online.	0.65	0.00
I have completed a course online.	1.94	0.00

below 4.0, but none had a mean below 3.0. The issues with a mean of at least 4.0 are displayed in Table 6. The issue with the highest mean as to importance was "knowledge gained."

Ratings that a Characteristic is More Likely True for Online Versus On-campus

For the second section, students were asked to consider the same issues as in the previous section but to indicate the likelihood that each issue was a characteristic of an online versus on-campus course, with 1 representing "much more likely in an online course" and 5 representing "much more likely in an on-campus course." A mean was calculated to identify which issues were considered much more likely in an online course (defined as a mean of no greater than 2.0) and which were considered much more likely in an on-campus course (defined as a mean of at least 4.0). A majority of the issues had means below 4.0, but only one had a mean below 3.0. That one issue, "submitting assignments electronically," had a mean of 2.48, which did not place it in the "much more likely" category for an online course. The issues with a mean of at least 4.0 are displayed in Table 7.

A cluster plot or "scatter diagram" was developed to illustrate the results for all the variables used in the study. As shown in Figure 1, all but one of the items were clustered in the upper right corner, which represents the section for higher importance and higher likelihood that the characteristic would be in an on-campus course. As discussed above, the only item in the left side of the diagram was "submitting assignments electronically."

Table 6. Issues considered important in making course environment decisions

Issue	Mean
Knowledge gained	4.35
Skills acquired	4.29
Access to information (resource materials)	4.20
Time required to complete coursework	4.16
Costs of tuition and fees	4.13
Schedule flexibility to accommodate work responsibilities	4.13

Table 7. Issues that are much more characteristic of an on-campus course

Issue	Mean
Opportunity for live interaction and discussion among students	4.07
On-campus exams	4.05
Opportunity for live interaction and discussion between faculty and students	4.04

Figure 1. Comparison of importance with likelihood of being on-campus versus online

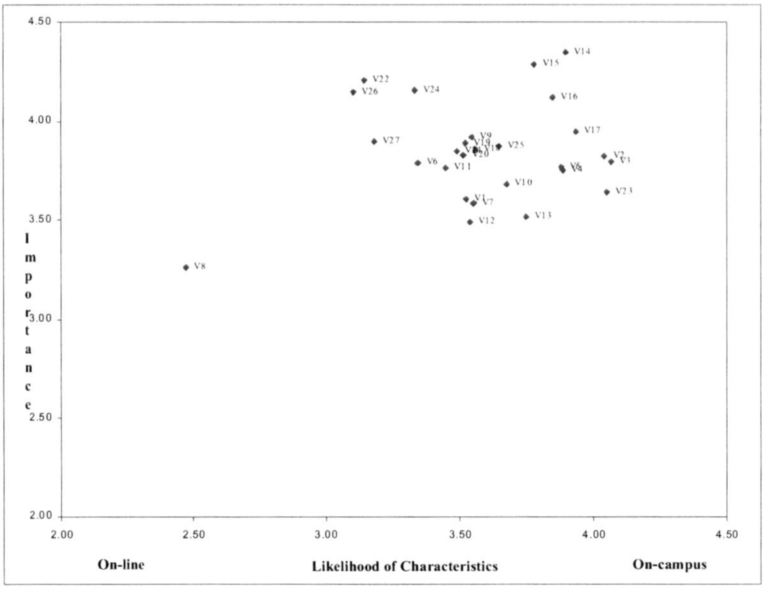

The issues identified as most important were given further review, because those issues were not given particularly strong ratings as either online or on-campus options. Table 8 repeats the issues identified as most important that were shown in Table 6 but identifies their means for the comparison of "much more likely in an online course" versus on-campus. All had means greater than 3.0, which placed them closer to the on-campus likelihood. Three of these issues considered most important had means that were rather close to 4.0, the value needed to be in the category of "much more likely in an on-campus course" than an online course. The issues are listed in the same order of importance shown in Table 6.

SUMMARY AND CONCLUSIONS

Most students who participated in this study had access to computers at home, making it easier for them to consider the possibility of online coursework. However, no significant differences were found between gender in access level or current status of interest in taking online courses.

Students identified some issues that they believed were important. They also indicated which issues they believed were more likely to be a characteristic of an online course and those that were more likely to be a characteristic of an on-campus course. None of the issues they identified as important were also identified as more likely to be a characteristic of an online course.

Perhaps these potential students may not be ready to consider the less traditional online option. For example, students rated "knowledge gained" as their most important issue in making this decision and also rated it more likely to be a characteristic of an on-campus than

Table 8. Important issues related to online versus on-campus instruction

Issue	Mean
Knowledge gained	3.90
Skills acquired	3.78
Access to information (resource materials)	3.15
Time required to complete coursework	3.33
Costs of tuition and fees	3.85
Schedule flexibility to accommodate work responsibilities	3.10

Note: Much more likely in an online course = 1; much more likely on campus = 5.

an online environment. Institutions wanting to increase the number of online students might need to look for documentation of successful results from taking courses in that manner in order to alter this perception.

Some additional advertising might be useful to institutions promoting the on-campus option, as not all students' perceptions represent actual facts. For example, students indicated that higher costs for tuition and fees were more likely a characteristic of an on-campus environment, although the costs are higher for online courses at institutions in the participants' local geographic area.

FUTURE RESEARCH CONSIDERATIONS

Students' perceptions of online programs should continue to be monitored by institutions wanting to increase their participation in these programs. If these students' responses are representative of potential students in general, institutions investing significant dollars in online programs might want to investigate further the perception that on-campus courses are providing more of the characteristics the students think are important.

REFERENCES

Accetta, R. (2001, February 26). E-learning crossfire. *INFORMATIONWEEK.com*. Retrieved June 25, 2002, from http://www.informationweek.com/826/elearning_6side.htm.

American InterContinental University-Online (n.d.). Why AIU online? Retrieved July 12, 2002, from http://aiudegreeonline.com/why.jsp.

Dash, J. (2000). IT pros give online universities high marks. *CNN.com*. Retrieved June 21, 2002, from http://www.cnn.com/2000/TECH/computing/09/15/online.college.idg/.

Kumar, A., Kumar, P., & Basu, S. C. (2002). Student perceptions of virtual education; An exploratory study. In M. Khosrow-Pour (Ed.), *Web-Based Instructional Learning* (pp. 132–141). Hershey, PA: IRM Press.

Peltz, P. (2000, November 18). Do virtual classrooms make the grade? *CNN.com*. Retrieved July 12, 2002, from http://www.cnn.com/2000/TECH/computing/11/18/index.elearning/cover.elearning/index.html.

Quigley, A. (2001, May 21). Six degrees of separation. *eLearn Magazine*. Retrieved May 30, 2002, from http://www.elearnmag.org/subpage/sub_page.cfm?article_pk=1&page_number_nb=1&title=FEATURE%20STORY.

Schneider, M. (2001, April 5). GM gives log-on learning a boost. *BusinessWeek Online*. Retrieved June 25, 2002, from http://www.businessweek.com/bwdaily/dnflash/apr2001/nf2001045_517.htm.

Schooley, C. (2001). Online universities introduce alternatives for higher education. *Planning Assumption*. GIGA Information Group.

Symonds, W. C. (2001, December 3). Giving it the old online try. *BusinessWeek Online*. Retrieved May 29, 2002, from http://www.businessweek.com:/print/magazine/content/01_49/b3760072.htm?mainwindow.

University of Phoenix Online (2002). Benefits of UOP online. Retrieved June 25, 2002, from http://online.uophx.edu.

Weil, N. (2001, June 26). University net courses help pros make the grade. *CNN.com*. Retrieved July 3, 2002, from http://www.cnn.com/2001/TECH/internet/06/26/university.net.courses.idg/index.html.

Chapter XXIX

Community Informatics–
Enabling Emancipatory
Learning

Wal Taylor
Central Queensland University, Australia

John Dekkers
Central Queensland University, Australia

Stewart Marshall
Central Queensland University Australia

ABSTRACT

In this chapter, a philosophical framework used in the development of an online course is provided. This philosophical framework is largely based on sociological theory that argues the need for a student-centered approach to learning in the modern age. The authors argue that this is an appropriate approach for the present and the future, which they consider will increasingly need to address changing learner needs and demands. A learner-centered approach can provide for self-paced learning, peer assessment, and opportunities for interactions with fellow students, work colleagues, and other peers. To date, there have been few examples of the integration of information technologies with emerging trends in distance and lifelong learning.

INTRODUCTION

In this chapter, a new philosophical stance and framework for online teaching, which emphasizes the importance of placing the student at the center of the learning process is articulated. This is achieved by directly engaging the student in "one to one," "one to many," and "many to many" forms of learning by maximizing the benefits of a relatively low-level information technology platform. The philosophical stance has its origins in social theory and addresses the emerging demands of learners to accommodate the pressing needs for flexibility in time management and location.

The future learning environment will be increasingly ubiquitous and require the full capacity of information technology operating asynchronously and at a distance to engage the needs of "lifelong" and "life wide" learners while minimalizing the extra demands of teachers and facilitators. It is also expected that students would come from increasingly wider backgrounds with different aspirations for learning and learning styles. There has also been an increasing trend that students demand alternative forms of interaction with their teachers, other students, and the educational institution's administration. Online courses have a great inherent flexibility to cater for a wider range of students' needs and demands, particularly with respect to different interaction possibilities. Unfortunately, while there have been many examples of online teaching and learning, there is a dearth of new philosophical frameworks that maximize the inherent capacities of information technologies to guide the delivery of courses.

BACKGROUND

It is well documented that the use of Information Communication Technologies (ICT) in the context of teaching and learning can increase the possible use of a greater range of teaching and learning options for on-campus and distance education modes of course presentations, through open learning, online, and resource-based learning, etc. Furthermore, in the provision of distance education, the use of learning centers, small groups, or individuals can bring new learning opportunities into local community advantage. This can assist in the development to "learning communities" by widening access in local communities to eduction and training opportunities, increasing interpretation of knowledge in a local context, and supporting existing educational systems (Longworth, 1999).

The use of ICT by regional (territorial) communities as a technology strategy or discipline is defined in this chapter as "community informatics" (CI). As indicated by Gurstein (2000), CI can link ICT at the community level with emerging opportunities in community development and lifelong learning. As such, this term brings together the concepts of ICT and that of community development based on individual growth within a framework of shared learning, sharing experience across cultural and geographic boundaries and interpreting information from within a community context to create applicable knowledge.

In conjunction with the developments in the use of ICT to improve equity of access for distance education, there has also been an increasing realization of the need for educational institutions to provide a leadership role in society for democratic process and to address issues of equity (Harkavy, 1998).

In this chapter, the role of online approaches for distance education from a theoretical stance is addressed. The dangers of unitary approaches that the use of ICT can promote are exposed, and an approach is outlined that can assist local communities in benefiting from a wider interpretation of knowledge available through online distance education.

THE ONLINE CONTEXT OF COURSE PRESENTATION

While less than a decade ago, most teaching and learning was made available through face-to-face contact and the use of print, there is now a myriad of options for teaching and student learning using media such as videoconferencing, audioconferencing, the Internet, email, CD-ROM, etc.

Despite this, online processes of education are often seen as an adjunct to current practices, with the teacher/tutor as the "expert." Nevertheless, there is also an emerging literature on ways that videoconferencing can support distance education and how online chat groups can be used to support learning (see, for example, Kelly & Shing Ha, 1998; Tsang & Fong, 1998).

A current tension within the provision of education is that a framework for the presentation of online distance education is evolving that may limit potential benefits of ICT by trying to fit the technology to traditional practice rather than using the technology to develop new approaches. For example, critical theory has contended since the 1930s that the values associated with technicism and instrumental rationality have increasingly and destructively dominated education in modernity (Agger, 1991; Held, 1980). From this perspective, there then develops an overly goal-oriented approach in organizations and individuals (Gorry & Scott-Morton, 1971; Dryzek, 1990). This goal-oriented approach can create a "tunnel vision" that may be blinding to alternative approaches (Williams & Duczynski, 2000). Foremost in these goal-seeking approaches is a unitary vision of an organization, where society is perceived as an integrated whole with the interests of the individual, the organization, and society as synonymous. (Falconer et al., 2000). The limitations of such above-mentioned pardigms become even more apparent in a multicultural environment.

In the above context, Habermas (1984) provided a foundation for scrutinizing the foregoing practices through communicative action, which balances instrumental rationality and technicism (White, 1988). Following such an approach, *discourse* would allow lecturers, tutors, and students to disclose their worldview orientations relevant to the subject matter. This communication is "progressively less distorted by socially oppressive, asymmetrical relations of power" (Alvesson & Willmott, 1992).

THE LEARNING INTERACTION

As alluded to above, a critical aspect in the development of learning communities is that people develop skills in self-directed and for-group learning. In this context, student and lecturer interaction can be described in three categories, "one to one," "one to many," and "many to many" (Romm & Taylor, 2000). The focus in "face to face" teaching and learning settings and in distance education has been on the "one to many" mode, where the lecturer/tutor shares knowledge with many students in an "expert" to a "learner" paradigm that reinforces the unitary view of rationality. This approach lends itself to a power relationship, which is at odds with the Habermasian view of communicative action (Habermas, 1984). In this situation, there is no automatic gravitation to a shared discourse, where the context of the learning from different worldviews is shared and apparent. Even in the "one to one" mode, there is often the assumption of rationality and an "expert to learner" paradigm.

The "many to many" mode is not as frequently used in the traditional distance education or the online approaches to teaching. Even when this mode is practiced, it is more than likely to be seen as a parallel process to the traditional view of *real* teaching (Romm & Taylor, 2001).

Despite the foregoing, a major and continuing influence of ICT in education has been to cause a paradigm shift from a teacher-directed model to a group-based learning model as shown in Table 1 (UNESCO, 1998).

The extent to which the above-mentioned learning environments and education models can be used for distance education students depends on a number of variables, including geographical location, student learning style, availability and access to ICT, as well as cost factors (Watkins & Biggs, 1996).

As mentioned above, online distance education courses can take many approaches and include new forms of interaction that involve learners in open discourse, providing increased contextual and emancipatory dimensions. In the provision of a distance education, new approaches can involve an open discourse approach as part of the delivery mechanism. Such an approach can also address issues of differences in understanding brought about by cultural diversity.

AN ONLINE TEACHING MODEL FOR DISTANCE EDUCATION

A number of approaches (methodologies) have been reported for the delivery of online courses in the above-mentioned literature. In this section, the benefits of an online course devised by Romm and Taylor (2000) that provides opportunities for learners in meeting a range of individual and group learning needs are described and explained. The online course is for distance education students and has been trialled for a number of courses at the postgraduate and undergraduate levels and uses "one to many," "one to one," and "many to many" forms of interaction with students.

The instructional materials for this course (irrespective of what area is being taught) include: a video that contains detailed explanations on how the course functions; a Course Outline that provides necessary student information about the course, e.g., the study schedule, assignment and exam requirements, contact persons, etc. (this document is available online as part of the course's Web site and is also available to the students on a CD-ROM or as a hard copy); a textbook; and a class email list.

Table 1. Successive education models

Model	Focus	Role of Student	Technology
Traditional	Teacher	Passive	Blackboard/TV/radio
Information	Student	Active	PC and AV
Knowledge	Group	Adaptive	PC and network and AV

Students are expected to subscribe electronically to the class email list. They are then encouraged by the lecturer to introduce themselves to the class online by informing the group about something about themselves, their interests, their current work or study areas, and their backgrounds. This helps to contextualize the backgrounds of the class members and, hence, provides a framework for discussion, interpretation, and linking across the group. This process also provides information that allows the lecturer to divide the class into weekly presentation groups. Where possible, the allocation allows people of diverse backgrounds to be brought together into vibrant but cohesive groups. The allocation to groups is completed by the second week of the semester. By this time, students are expected to establish contact with their virtual group members and start working on their assessment tasks. This time is also used to seek out incompatibilities in the groups, try to resolve any conflicts, and help people learn to work together. While reallocation across groups is available during this initial time, it is only used as a last resort when it is obvious that it is necessary in order to achieve a cohesive team effort. Any traditional cultural or ethnic differences are treated with immediate sensitivity. On Week three of the semester, the first group makes its presentation to the class online. The presentation consists of an article (which the students have to enclose, attach, or simply establish a hyperlink to) and a critique that links the article with the reading in the book for the week.

Feedback from students contributes to the mark for the presentation. The above process is repeated for 10 weeks until the end of the semester, with each week dedicated to an in-depth discussion on a different topic that is related to the reading for that week.

The major advantages of the model are as follows:

It involves the three modes of teacher–student interaction. Students have interaction with the teacher in the traditional "one to many" mode, when they interact with the course material and the lecturer in normal post and electronic interactions. Students have the immediate possibility of "one to one" interaction with the lecturer by mail, telephone, or email for points of clarification or detailed discussion. However, the bulk of the interaction is through the "many to many" mode, where students interact through their groups in the development of their presentations to the class and in commenting on other group presentations.

The process of having students interact within groups off the class email list means that the class email list does not get flooded primary discourse. It is only the group position that ends up on the class email list. However, this does not prevent individuals presenting their perspectives as a component of the group contribution, and in the end, all views are captured in the presentations. The model provides the opportunity for individuals who feel disadvantaged in the group process to interact directly with the lecturer who acts a moderator. There is also the opportunity for group members to raise the issue of nonparticipation of individual group members with the lecturer. As the interactions are all online, participation is verifiable from the electronic log.

It provides flexibility for lecturer and learner. Supplementary readings are chosen by the students to allow contextualization of the material and to increase discourse around different worldviews. Hence, it supports the concepts of Communicative Action as proposed by Habermas (1984) to address the issues of technical, instrumental, and bureaucratic rationality. Temporal effort is negotiated within groups, and this allows the pressures of modern life to be accommodated. All of these negotiations are carried out within the group, and the lecturer is only involved as a last resort. This process also addresses the criticism directed at unitary organizational approaches, which fail to recognize power, politics, and conflict. This process embeds the concepts of plurality, which recognize different worldviews. The approach also provides flexibility for the lecturer, in that the weekly assessments can be conducted online from any physical location with Internet access. The model also helps to address the increasing issue of text currency, as increasing volumes of textbook and application information is produced and becomes easily accessible. Also, the model ensures that the work for the lecturer is the same, regardless of class size.

It allows for increasing understanding across cultural groupings.   Because the students are geographically isolated within groups, meaning is negotiated every week within the context of the subject matter. This ensures that different ethnic backgrounds can be more easily accommodated in the learning process. The process of discussing meaning of applications allows the terminology to be contextualized and shared meaning to be developed within the learning subgroup, and subsequently, within the whole class group.

It accommodates regular and timely asynchronous interaction.   While asynchronicity has been a component of traditional distance learning for some time, some online approaches have, in fact, provided pressure for synchronous availability of student and lecturer. This is often out of step with modern requirements, which need to accommodate different time zones, employment status, family commitments, etc.

It mitigates issues of power and social presence.   Social presence has been found to be an inhibitor to communication, understanding, and learning. Personal salience molds interaction and filters out messages and meaning (Daft & Lengel, 1986; Culnan & Markus, 1987). Social presence also fundamentally affects how participants sense emotion, intimacy, and immediacy and depends not only on the words people speak but also on the verbal and nonverbal cues, body language, and context (Rice, 1993). Social presence is also ethnically heterogeneous. In researching online groups, Wellman et al. (1996) found that limiting social presence is a factor in removing inhibition, increasing creativeness, and strengthening weak social ties in narrowly focused groups such as learning groups. Hence, the nonvideo-based online medium is likely to increase learning outcomes across class, culture, gender, and age.

It strengthens hard and soft skills.   As discussed above, a pluralist approach is being posited as a more appropriate mechanism for learning and living in an increasingly globalizing world. Hence, there is a need for education to provide skills that suit such an environment. The model outlined here not only provides content and the ability to contextualize this across a range of situations and cultures, but it also provides training in processes that facilitate increased learning through collaboration, discourse, and different world views. Students learn important online skills, how to be citizens of an online community, and how to contribute to a virtual team, including dividing the work between the team members, resolving conflicts, developing ideas and projects, and providing positive feedback to others about their work.

RELEVANCE TO FUTURE TRENDS

This discussion has provided a philosophical framework and an example of the delivery of an online course that addresses the emerging trends in demand for subject-based and lifelong learning experiences. There will no doubt be an increasing trend for delivery of courses of the nature described in this chapter, as increasing proportions of the community will need to choose online education and training because of lifestyle needs and demands. However, an equally compelling reason for this trend is that wider community use of ICT should result in the adoption of online learning as a natural learning choice. This is because a wider spectrum of interaction opportunities with others (learners, teachers, peers, etc.) are possible along with more immediate and wider access to alternative information sources. This is in contrast to traditional forms of teaching which can restrict the context of interactions in the learning process.

CONCLUSION

This chapter began with the proposition that a wider participatory approach being advocated for service delivery in organizational management has application in distance education. An underlying theme developed throughout the chapter suggests that new ICT-based approaches can provide substantive advantage for DE, because they can substantiate advantages for courses and help liberate educational processes from the domination of unitary approaches. These unitary approaches, often justified in terms of order, quality, and management, are now being increasingly used to equip individuals, organizations, and communities with the means to deal with the increasing complexity of information availability brought about by information communication technology.

The approach outlined in the online teaching model presented above provides a mechanism for a wider engagement in, and interpretation of, the learning process through use of ICT, which reduces the negative impact of social presence, increases the use of weak ties in the learning process, and provides a degree of anonymity to increase contribution. It recognizes the reality of power relationships, politics, and conflict in the learning process and brings them into the process rather than ignoring their existence. Thus, with the approach, skills, which are becoming increasingly important in the application of knowledge and learning in a community setting, are developed. It encourages a pluralistic interpretation, which allows learning to be discussed, and it is locally contextualized across wide variations in culture and experience. As such, it provides structure and opportunity for communities to engage in learning in new ways and provides much more than a new service delivery option for DE. It is important to recognize the potential for centrality and lack of reality associated with ICT. However, a CI approach to distance education allows individuals, groups of individuals, and communities to "*live an ongoing learning experience*" and to locally apply and interpret learning from outside their immediate constructs. In this sense, the application of CI recognizes the dynamics of structuration, which occurs when nonpassive actors interact with institutional structures, and which provides the interactions for changes in structure and processes for the delivery of products and services (Giddens, 1991; Orlikowsky, 1992).

This iterative process of sharing the interpretation of information and its local application in a forum of learners, involving a range of cultural understanding, can obviously provide for better understanding and educational outcomes.

But, the learning model discussed above also provides for the following:

- Greater understanding across cultures, because geography and place do not restrict the process

- A better focus on applications from the learning
- A wider network of relationships in weak tie networks that have been demonstrated to provide increased understanding and community benefit
- A mechanism for participative change in the content and process of service delivery to keep it temporally and situationally relevant
- A means to extend learning into a community development context

From the foregoing, it is clear that the delivery of useful Community Informatics outcomes for DE requires centers and models to ensure that the community is engaged across all of its components to support lifelong learning and to develop learning communities. The experiences discussed in this chapter need to be further refined through more formal evaluation. The authors are involved with the Rockhampton-based community informatics center, the COIN (Community Informatics) Internet Academy, that has the development of evaluative models and the definition of impediments to their adoption as its major objectives.

REFERENCES

Agger, B. (1991). *A Critical Theory of Public Life: Knowledge, Discourse and Politics in an Age of Decline.* London: Palmer Press.

Alvesson, M. & Willmott, H. (1992). Critical theory and management studies: An introduction. In M. Alvesson & H. Willmott (eds.). *Critical Management Studies.* London: Sage Publications.

Culnan, M. J. & Markus, M. L. (1987). Information technologies. In F. Jablin et al. (eds.). *Handbook of Organizational Communication: An Interdisciplinary Perspective.* Newbury Park, CA: Sage.

Daft, R. & Lengel, R. (1986). Organizational information requirements in media richness and structural design. *Management Science, 32*, 5, 554–571.

Dryzek, J. S. Green reason: Communicative action for the biosphere. *Environmental Ethics, 12*(3), 195-211.

Falconer, D. J. et al. (2001). Critical approaches to information systems planning: Refining the research agenda. *Proceedings of the 33rd IEEE Computer Society Hawaii International Conference on System Sciences*, Maui, Hawaii. January.

Giddens, A. (1991). *Modernity and Self Identity.* California: Stanford University Press.

Gorry, G.A. & Scott Morton, M. S. (1971). A framework for management of information systems. *Sloan Management Review, 13*, 1, 55–70.

Gurstein, M. (2000). *Community Informatics: Enabling Communities with Information and Communications Technologies.* Hershey, PA: Idea Group Publishing.

Habermas, J. (1984). *The Theory of Communicative Action: Reason and the Rationalization of Society.* Boston, MA: Beacon Press.

Harkavy, I. (1998). School-community-university partnerships: Effectively integrating community building and education reform. Paper presented to the Conference on Connecting Community Building and Education Reform: Effective School, Community, University Partnerships, Joint Forum U.S. Department of Education, U.S. Department of Housing and Urban Development, Washington, D.C., May 12.

Held, D. (1980). *Introduction to Critical Theory.* Cambridge: Polity Press.

ICDE Conference. (2000). Papers from the ICDE Conference, Distance Education — An Open Question. Adelaide, September, 9–13.

Kelly, M. E., & Shing Ha, T. (1998). Borderless education and teaching and learning cultures: The case of Hong Kong. *Australian Universities Review, 1*, 26–33.

Longworth, N. (1999). *Making Lifelong Learning Work*. London: Kogan Page.

Orlikowski, W. (1992). The duality of technology: Rethinking the concept of technology in organizations. *Organization Science, 3*, 398–427.

Rice, R. (1993). Media appropriateness using social presence theory to compare traditional and new organizational media. *Human Communication Research, 19*, 4, 451–484.

Romm, C., & Taylor, W. (2000). Online education — Can we combine efficiency with quality? In *Proceedings Australian Conference for Information Systems (ACIS)*, Brisbane, December 6–8.

Romm, C. & Taylor, W. (2001). Teaching online is about Psychology — not technology. In M. Khosrow-Pour (ed.). *Proceedings of IRMA Conference,* Hershey, PA: Idea Group Publishing.

Tsang, P. & Fong, T. L. (1998). Learning support via the Web: How do I know it made a difference? *Proceedings of the 12th Annual Conference of the Asian Association of Open Universities*. New Delhi, 4–6 November.

UNESCO. (1998). Papers from the World Conference on Higher Education. Paris, October 5–9.

Watkins, D. & Biggs, J. (1996). *The Chinese Learner: Cultural, Psychological and Contextual Influences.* Melbourne, Australia: ACER.

Wellman, B. et al. (1996). Computer networks as social networks: Collaborative work, telework, and virtual community. *Annual Review of Sociology, 22*, 213–238.

White, S. K. (1988). *The Recent Work of Jurgen Habermas: Reason Justice and Modernity.* Cambridge: Cambridge University Press.

Williams, M. C. & Duczynski, G. (2000). Moral poverty of computing higher education. In F. Sudweeks & C. Ess (eds.). *Cultural Attitudes Toward Technology and Communication.* School of Information Technology, Murdoch University, Murdoch, WA, Australia.

Chapter XXX

An Examination of ICT Planning Maturity in Schools: A Stage Theory Perspective

Julie Mackey
Christchurch College of Education, New Zealand

Annette Mills
University of Canterbury, New Zealand

ABSTRACT

Information and communication technology (ICT) has the potential to revolutionize teaching and learning as well as school administration, yet little is known about the maturity of ICT planning in schools and the manner in which schools plan for the acquisition and use of these technologies in the educational environment. However, as school investments in ICT increase and they become more reliant on ICT, effective planning becomes more central to schools' ability to maximize their use of technology. This research examines ICT planning in schools and proposes a four-stage model of the evolution of ICT planning maturity in schools. The model emerges from case studies conducted in eight New Zealand primary schools and provides insight into the nature of ICT planning in schools and the factors that contribute to planning maturity.

INTRODUCTION

Information systems (IS) planning[1] and the degree to which that planning is clearly linked into an organization's strategic goals have been widely recognized as key factors in the successful use of information technology (IT)[2] within the organization (see, for example, Watson et al., 1997). While many organizations in our community are pursuing these objectives, little is known about the extent or effectiveness of IS planning in schools, particularly in terms of meeting the schools' strategic objectives, even though information and communication technologies (ICT)[3] are now widely used in educational settings.

Over a decade ago, Telem (1993) suggested that the use of IT as a management tool in educational contexts was a neglected area of research, particularly in terms of lack of an underlying knowledge base. Although the ensuing years have seen an increased research focus on ICT in educational management, this focus has concentrated more on evaluative analysis of the efficacy of management information systems, computerized school information systems, and specific applications of information technology (see, for example, Barta, Telem, & Gev, 1995; Fung et al., 1997) than on understanding how schools develop their ICT systems and integrate them into their management systems and practices.

ICT planning as it relates to schools can be defined as the process of identifying the information and communication technologies used to support the educational and administrative goals of schools and of deciding how these technologies will be developed and managed (Lederer & Sethi, 1988; Smits & van der Poel, 1996). According to Latham (1998), however, ICT planning of this sort is still in its infancy in schools. His analogy is apt if we assume that schools, like businesses, take time to develop their ICT strategies in a manner that is commensurate with their strategic objectives. In this chapter, we present a study designed to document the evolution of ICT planning maturity in schools, and to identify, in particular, the factors and stages that influence and characterize integration between ICT planning and educational strategy. From our results, we suggest a common evolutionary pathway for ICT planning in schools and provide a foundation on which to propose a "stages of growth" model for characterizing and evaluating ICT planning in these settings. But before describing our study and the model arising out of it, we consider it useful to give brief accounts of some of the stages of growth models present in IS literature; the ways that schools tend to use ICT to achieve their organizational objectives; and the current state of play regarding ICT usage in educational settings within New Zealand.

Stages of Growth Models

The notion that organizations evolve is encapsulated in various stages of growth models that are widely used in organizational and IS research. In IS literature, these models are based on the premise that organizations move through various stages of maturity in their use and management of IS (Nolan, 1973; Huff, Munro, & Martin, 1988; King & Teo, 1997; Teo & King, 1997). For example, King and Teo (1997) proposed a four-stage model conceptualizing the integration of information systems planning (ISP) and business planning (BP) over time, to better enable the effective support of business strategies. These four stages are as follows:

1. *Separate planning with administrative integration*: In this stage, IS planning is technically oriented and nonstrategic. Performance criteria for the IS function are likely to focus on operational efficiency and cost minimization, and existing work processes may be automated.

2. *One-way linked planning with sequential integration: In this phase, IS development* considers business goals first. The IS strategy is, therefore, likely to support the business strategy and contribute to its implementation.

3. *Two-way linked planning with reciprocal integration*: Here, IS planning not only supports but also influences business planning. Business goals and IS capabilities are jointly considered.

4. *Integrated planning with full integration between business planning and IS planning*: This stage is characterized by the joint development of IS and business strategies and realization of the critical nature of IS applications to the success of business strategy.

Although researchers debate the accuracy and completeness of these various models, they do provide organizations with useful benchmarks with which to determine their current state of maturity and planning for future growth. More specifically, Robson (1997), for example, suggested that such knowledge provides organizations with a base from which to develop appropriate IS-related strategies, management styles, control approaches, and investment levels. Schools similarly can use such models to determine their ICT planning maturity and to develop appropriate strategies for future growth.

ICT Planning in Schools

The complexity of the educational environment provides a particularly interesting context in which to study ICT planning. First, unlike businesses, schools tend to focus on the use of ICT to support learning objectives rather than business objectives, yet, like businesses, they work with limited resources and financing. Second, technology in schools is also not always well established (Latham, 1998). As such, schools provide a contemporary context in which to examine how ICT usage evolves within an organization. They also provide a venue to examine how this process is affected when many of the people within an organization have only a limited understanding of ICT development and planning, as tends to be the case in schools. Teachers and school administrators often acquire their information technology skills "on the job," yet are expected to initiate the planning and implementation of ICT within the school (Ministry of Education, 1999). Third, much of the small amount of research that has been conducted on the integration of ICT plans and educational strategic plans focuses on large tertiary institutions (see, for example, Barta et al., 1995; Fung et al., 1997; Rice & Miller, 2001), which have very different organizational structures, more complex information systems needs, and greater numbers of specialist IT staff than do elementary and secondary schools.

The need to identify how ICT planning evolves within schools and the characteristics of each stage of that evolution would seem obvious. Such research not only would help fill a gap in knowledge but also, and more importantly, would enable school administrators to better understand the factors contributing to ICT-educational strategy alignment and successful ICT integration and growth.

ICT Implementation and Associated Planning in New Zealand Schools

Within New Zealand, as overseas, the potential of ICT to enhance learning has attracted considerable interest over recent years. In 1990, a report published by the New Zealand

Ministry of Education recommended that the New Zealand Government support ICT initiatives within school communities and provide associated professional development for teachers so as to ensure that all students, at all levels and in all subjects, would benefit from information technology. Eight years on (1998), the Ministry of Education released a national strategy to support ICT use in schools. This strategy saw funding provided for at least 50% of the costs of approved capital projects associated with implementing ICT in schools. In 1999, additional funding, comprising a one-off grant of NZ$M24.716 and operational funding of NZM$10 per annum, was made available to all state and integrated[4] schools. The schools were eligible to apply for grants, provided that they prepared an ICT plan and that this plan met the criteria set by the Ministry of Education.

One of the key initiatives at this time in the endeavor to help schools plan how they would implement and manage ICT and use it to facilitate the integration of learning technologies into teaching and learning was the provision of one-day workshops titled *Principals First: First Principles.* The underlying principle of the workshops and their associated planning guide (Ministry of Education, 1999) was that learning technologies should support each school's overall learning vision. The guide held that effective integration of learning technologies into teaching and learning required schools to develop "a shared understanding of teaching and learning; a comprehensive learning technologies plan; and re-engineering of teaching and learning and of school administration processes" (pp. 1–3). For most schools, achieving these aims would be a complex undertaking, encompassing educational and administrative areas.

The most common action taken by principals following their attendance at the workshops was the preparation of a strategic ICT plan. Eighty-six percent of the primary principal attendees and 75% of the secondary principal attendees indicated that they had done this (Information Technology Action Group/ITAG, 2000, p. 39). The funding that the schools received on the basis of these plans was invested in various aspects of ICT development, including networking, hardware and software acquisitions, and staff development. However, recent reports (ITAG, 2000; Education Review Office/ERO, 2000; Knezek & Christensen, 1999) indicated that ICT planning and implementation have not progressed beyond these early stages of technology adoption, which are characterized by teachers learning how to use ICT and gaining confidence in that use, to the later stages of adoption, characterized by adapting and creatively using ICT within new educational contexts, such as strategic planning and management. It is this concern that prompted our decision to undertake our investigation of ICT planning maturity in schools with a view to developing a mechanism that would allow school staff to pause, assess the current status of ICT implementation and usage within their schools, and then, where necessary, plan ways of ensuring that these technologies would be used to the best pedagogical and administrative advantage.

HOW WE CONDUCTED THE STUDY

We used an interpretive case study approach, guided by hermeneutic principles (Butler, 1998; Klein & Myers, 1999), to examine the status of ICT planning and its integration with educational strategic planning in eight New Zealand state primary schools.[5] We considered this approach the best for providing the type of "rich" qualitative data that we deemed necessary to gain insight into each school's commitment to ICT and the extent and nature of its implementation of ICT.

The eight schools ranged in size from a small two-teacher rural school to a large 20-teacher urban school, and all were located within a 60-kilometer radius. The decile ratings[6] of the schools ranged from 3 to 10 (Table 1). We chose to conduct our study in primary schools rather than secondary schools, because we considered that the former would offer a more manageable context in which to study ICT planning. Primary schools are less complex than secondary schools in terms of structure, and their smaller size means that they are less likely to have IT managers or technical specialists. One of our concerns was that primary school principals with little or no knowledge of ICT management are expected to plan for the implementation of ICT into their schools.

The small size of the sample is acknowledged as a limitation of the study. However, some effort was made to include a mixture of rural and urban schools, and to include some schools with lower decile ratings. Furthermore, the schools included those that were regarded by their peers to be at the forefront of ICT implementation in the community, as well as those that hesitated to be part of the study because the principals considered that they were only just beginning to plan and implement ICT development in their schools.

Our data collection consisted of semistructured, face-to-face interviews with the principals of the schools and analysis of the schools' ICT plans and supporting documents, as well as excerpts from each school's strategic plan. The interviews, which were all conducted by one of us, typically lasted 40 to 60 minutes and were recorded and later transcribed for analysis. The main focus of the interview was to develop an understanding of what ICT planning meant within the school environment and to describe the process involved in this planning. The interviews also included discussion relating to the planning environment and the intended and perceived effects of the planning process.

All but one of the principals had participated in the *Principals First* planning workshops, and all were closely involved in ICT planning and school strategic planning. The interviews were conducted in a manner that enabled the principals to trace the progression of ICT planning in their schools from early planning attempts through to completion of their

Table 1. Demographic details of case study schools

School	Type	Roll	Number of Full-time Teachers	Decile Rating	Location
1	Full primary	37	2	10	Rural
2	Full primary	150	9	7	Rural
3	Contributing (Years 1–6)	550	20	10	Urban
4	Full primary	543	23	10	Urban
5	Contributing (Years 1–6)	143	7	3	Urban
6	Full primary	390	17	10	Rural
7	Full primary	307	15	6	Urban
8	Full primary	479	19	10	Urban

Note: Full primary schools cater for children from ages five through to 12 to 13, while contributing schools cater for children from ages five to 10.

respective current ICT plans. As the heads of state primary schools, the principals all had their functions governed by similar governmental regulations, responsibilities, and expectations regarding school management and operation. The principals rated themselves across the range of experience in ICT planning from those "*just beginning to get on board with ICT planning*" to those who perceived themselves as *leaders* in their adoption and implementation of ICT in schools.

Seven of the eight school principals were able to provide copies of their schools' ICT plans and supporting documents, as well as excerpts from or copies of their schools' strategic plans. We compared the information in these documents with what was said in the interviews, as well as with publicly available examples of school strategic plans, ICT plans, and Education Review Office (ERO) reports.[7]

The data analysis consisted of two main aspects. First, we formally analyzed the written ICT plans in relation to their format and content. A comparison table was used to chart format, length, time span, objectives, statement of belief, philosophy, technical detail, and links to other documentation (for example, policies). Second, we compared the information from the transcribed interviews with the written plans. This approach allowed us to critically interpret the interview responses to individual questions in relationship to the larger and more complex picture provided by the interview data in their totality and by the data from the document analysis.

DEVELOPMENT OF A FOUR-STAGE MODEL OF ICT PLANNING

Our evaluation of the schools' strategic plans and ICT plans, along with the interview findings, allowed us to identify those factors (see below) that seemed to influence ICT planning in the eight schools. This work, in turn, enabled us to discern a pattern *across* the schools, in which ICT planning appeared to evolve from an unplanned state through to some form of alignment with educational objectives set in the schools' strategic plans. This pattern provided the basis of our proposed four-stage model of ICT planning maturity. The model, which is detailed in Figure 1 and discussed later in this section, presents not only the characteristics that appear to define stages of planning maturity within schools, but also the evolutionary progression through these stages over time.

Factors Affecting ICT Planning in Schools

Progress in planning was not necessarily related to the length of time between formulation of the initial ICT plan and implementation of its provisions or to externally driven factors, such as Ministry of Education requirements. Rather, it seemed to relate more to factors unique to each school. This statement has even more relevance when we consider that the schools, as state primary schools, were all operating within similar parameters yet were demonstrably different in terms of their ICT-related competence and commitment. This was certainly evident in the extent to which the schools had endeavored to comply with Ministry of Education (MOE) ICT objectives. While most of the schools had adapted the MOE planning templates to suit their own needs, the depth and detail provided varied considerably. Some plans followed the MOE criteria exactly, and were brief and simple; others were more comprehensive and supported by policies, guidelines, and other detailed information. It

Figure 1. Four-stage model of ICT planning in schools

	STAGE 1: LITTLE OR NO PLANNING	STAGE 2: EARLY FORMAL PLANNING	STAGE 3: FOCUSED FORMAL PLANNING	STAGE 4: MATURE INTEGRATED PLANNING
Descriptor	*Planning has a technical and operational focus. Plans may be informal and not clearly documented.*	*Planning moves into a more formal phase and there is a shift in focus from the technical aspects to the educational value of ICT.*	*Planning begins to recognize the value of ICT to facilitate the school's strategic objectives and is characterized by the adoption of ICT to modify or even reengineer some of the processes within the school.*	*ICT planning is aligned with and is integral to the school's strategic planning process. The innovative or creative use and development of ICT within the school contributes significantly to the school goals.*
CATEGORIES				
CURRICULUM	Few, if any, links exist between ICT use and curriculum objectives. There is an emphasis on providing students with opportunities to use computer applications such as word processing in the classroom.	The school is beginning to focus on how ICT can be used to support teaching and learning, e.g., identifying useful Internet sites for students. Some emphasis is evident on developing students' ICT skills in different applications, such as creating electronic slide shows or using different technologies (e.g., scanning photographs); may include curriculum specific software (e.g., math games or reading programs).	There is a maturing understanding of how ICT can support and enhance teaching and learning across curriculum areas. A shift from isolated skills acquisition to a more contextual skill development is evident (e.g., students learn to use spreadsheet-graphing techniques to collate survey information). Understanding of ICT broadens to include a range of ICT, such as scanners, digital cameras, Internet, email.	ICT is an integral tool in the teaching and learning process. The use of ICT is planned but does not dominate curriculum objectives. Students use a wide range of technologies across curriculum areas as ICT becomes a tool for thinking and learning.
PROFESSIONAL DEVELOPMENT (PD)	The proportion of novice ICT users is high. PD is narrow in focus. The emphasis is on developing basic computing skills and confidence.	Staff members are at different levels of competency and confidence, still with a number of beginners. PD may be targeted to staff needs and is beginning to link skill development to possible curriculum applications.	Increasing levels of staff competency are evident across a range of technologies and software applications. Targeted PD is likely to focus on contextual skill development and curriculum application as teachers and trainers recognize the importance of linking new skills to curriculum areas.	A reasonable proportion of the staff have well-developed ICT skills and confidently use a range of technologies. PD is likely to become increasingly customized and specific. PD may have a strong curriculum focus, or may require the development of skills to support wider school objectives.
INFRASTRUCTURE DEVELOPMENT	Acquisition of technology is piecemeal. Computers are likely to be stand alone.	Infrastructure development is more structured, with an increased emphasis on compatibility, upgradability, and connectivity. The school may be considering networking and the physical arrangement of computers in pods or suites. Planning includes acquisition of complementary technologies (e.g., scanners, digital cameras.)	Planning for ICT infrastructure is formal and linked to other aspects of school planning, such as property development. The ICT infrastructure development is taking shape. Long-term plans for ICT replacements and acquisitions complement the existing infrastructure and the school vision for future ICT use.	A highly developed infrastructure is in place with established networks and adequate resourcing. The school may be exploring new and innovative technologies to enhance existing capability, e.g., wireless applications for increased mobility and flexibility, ASDL (Asymmetrical Digital Subscriber Line) for higher performance Internet links.
ADMINISTRATION	Basic office functions are computerized (e.g., correspondence, school newsletters, accounting records).	Additional administrative functions are computerized, e.g., student details database, library resource management. There is an increasing awareness of the potential of ICT to enhance communication, e.g., through the use of email and the Internet.	The school is beginning to explore additional administrative applications to enhance the efficiency and effectiveness of administrative systems (e.g., student records system, shared file directories or an intranet for staff curriculum resources). Some teachers use ICT applications for administrative purposes, e.g., curriculum planning, student reports. There is some recognition that ICT may facilitate other objectives (e.g., school Web site used to communicate with families for whom English is not a first language).	Teachers, as well as administrative staff, use electronic resources to enhance communication, resource sharing, and student record management and reporting. Improved recording and reporting systems provide analysis tools to identify and support targeted needs (e.g., "at risk" students, talented and gifted students). The school identifies and implements innovative ICT solutions (e.g., to communicate with the wider school community via interactive Web sites, list-servers, online forums).

would seem that while the criteria had set a minimum standard for ICT planning in schools, and the requirement that schools prepare ICT plans for funding, had encouraged them to begin a process of formal ICT planning, the following factors influenced where the schools went from there.

1.   **School Size**

In School 1 (refer to Table 1), the small, two-teacher rural school, the principal was, as he said, "responsible for everything," a situation that is common in schools of this size. When asked how he would rate the planning and implementation of ICT in his school compared to other schools, he replied that, "We're somewhere a little below the middle." We found this school to be the least sophisticated in terms of planning for and using ICT. In contrast, some of the larger schools had teachers with special interests and well-developed skills in ICT, or teacher-librarians with interest and skills in library information systems, or they had an established ICT curriculum team. School 3, a 20-teacher urban school, had a full-time ICT facilitator based in the school.

2.   **ICT Competence and Attitudes of Top Management**

The ICT competence of the schools' principals, coupled with their attitudes toward using ICT, appeared to be an important factor influencing ICT planning and development. For example, the principal of School 3 (Principal 3) demonstrated an active interest in ICT: "*I really enjoy using it, and if I had time to find out more, I would be right in there. I try to model it, and I'm probably one of the better users in the school.*" She expected staff to use ICT as a tool in their own planning. All staff had been given laptops and were required to use these to prepare long-term plans, and to email them to the principal. The school was also trialing an assessment package, and there was recognition that teachers needed access to computers at home (thus, laptops), because this is when they had time to enter assessment data. The laptops doubled as an extra classroom computer during the day.

The seven other principals did not match Principal 3's degree of confidence with ICT, and several indicated that they had little experience of using technologies such as email and the Internet that are reasonably well established in the wider New Zealand community. In general, these principals appeared to have little expectation of their staff to use ICT for anything other than classroom tuition.

3.   **Staff ICT Competence and Attitudes**

The level of ICT competence exhibited by the schools' staff (for example, hardware/software knowledge, operating skills, software use, and ability to use ICT in delivering the curriculum) varied within and between schools. For some schools, the different levels of competence evident among their staff made it difficult to determine an appropriate ICT-related professional development strategy. As the principal of School 8 observed, "*We have to work hard at recognizing that staff are going to be in different places. The bigger the staff, the worse it is. We have 19 staff – 19 different stages almost.*" Those schools with staff with specialist ICT knowledge/skills were able to rely on them for valuable input into the ICT planning process. However, Principal 3 believed that staff's willingness to learn about ICT was more important than actual staff expertise.

The attitudes that staff held regarding the role of ICT in the school also appeared to influence ICT planning maturity. Principal 8, for example, considered that effective use of ICT in the school depended on staff sharing a common belief in the value of ICT for schools. Principal 5, in describing how his school had first implemented ICT and then sought to develop a vision regarding its use, observed that it would have been better if the vision had been fostered before the implementation. He was particularly concerned about teachers making statements like, "*I don't feel confident with this,*" and "*Our kids don't need this.*"

4.   The Existing ICT Infrastructure

The nature of the ICT infrastructure within the schools reflected the extent and effectiveness of past planning and also appeared to influence how effective a school would be in realizing future ICT-related initiatives. Schools that had accumulated technology without any long-term plan identified issues such as the need to change operating platforms because older computers were becoming too costly to maintain or were incompatible with newer hardware and software. Principal 8 noted that when his school first began to plan seriously for ICT, it already had in place "*a collection of computers, with some Apples and some PCs of varying ages and descriptions, and they required a fair bit of bringing together to decide which way we were going to proceed.*" In contrast, schools that had planned their ICT development from the outset had acquired specific components to enhance their general capability. School 3, for example, had planned for and had in place a well-developed, single-platform infrastructure with a school-wide network and a laptop for each teacher/classroom. The ability of this school to build effectively on its infrastructure would doubtless be greater than the ability of those schools that had not planned their infrastructures.

While some of the schools had one or two staff with some technical knowledge, or a board member or parent who could provide advice, others struggled with the technical decisions to be made (for example, which server to purchase; how best to network the school). The lack of in-house technical expertise, coupled with the cost of hiring external expertise, was a problem for most schools.

5.   Alignment Between the Schools' ICT-Related Strategies and Educational Strategies

Of the schools, only the principal from School 3 had clearly articulated the role of ICT in supporting school strategic planning in respect of teaching, learning, and improving its administrative functions. The documentation from two of the other schools revealed some obvious links between their strategic plans and their ICT plans. For example, School 8 stated in its ICT plan its intention to "*utilize the computer resource . . .* [and] *to continue staff development in ICT,*" while School 7 intended to "*build an (ICT) resource area . . .* [and] *establish an IT program and plan that will ensure that children are provided with opportunities to develop their knowledge of and skills in the use of IT.*" However, for the remaining schools, we were unable to find links between the two plans.

Our analysis of the schools' strategic plans confirmed that only one or two schools saw ICT as a tool that could go beyond supporting curriculum initiatives to supporting changes and improvements within the school. For example, although the plans had common strategic objectives like, "*the promotion of the school or its activities*" and "*the need to focus on numeracy and literacy,*" ICT was infrequently identified as a tool for supporting either of these objectives. Only Schools 3 and 6 were using ICT to enhance the recording and analysis of student progress, and only School 6 had clearly articulated this use in its ICT and strategic plans.

The role that ICT can play in facilitating school administration appeared to have been overlooked in the strategic planning of all schools except School 3. While many of the seven remaining principals identified the large administrative workloads carried by themselves and the teachers, when asked how they thought ICT might be used to support such functions, their responses indicated they had not seriously considered the potential of ICT to improve administration and communications as well as resource sharing in the wider school community. Although they reported that their schools were using standard office applications for word processing, desktop publishing, and maintaining student records, these principals indicated that they were only just beginning to use email for their own communications. Although a few were using the Internet to access information from the Ministry of Education and other school-related sites, the principals had not explored the possibilities of using ICT for communication and collaboration within the school, for example, digital school calendars, planning templates, shared curriculum planning, and central storage of resources (CD-ROMs, digital images) on school networks or intranets. And, they had not considered using computerized reporting systems and email for daily absences, parent and staff communications, or interactions with staff in other schools. In short, their schools had yet to embark on the "re-engineering of teaching and learning and of school administration processes" referred to in the planning guide (Ministry of Education, 1999, pp. 1–3).

Overall, there was little evidence of explicit, formal integration between the schools' ICT plans and their formal strategic plans. Where links existed, they tended to focus on the core business of teaching and learning and, except for School 3, did not consider the potential of ICT to enhance broader areas such as administrative functions and collaboration or communication with the wider school community.

The Model

In addition to outlining the four stages of our model, Figure 1 provides a set of benchmarks that correspond to each of the stages. These benchmarks are organized across the four categories of *curriculum*, *professional development*, *infrastructure development*, and *school administration*. While the first three categories are based on funding criteria set by the Ministry of Education (ERO, 2000), the fourth category, *school administration*, emerged from our data analysis. The use of ICT to support school administration was an implied area of focus in the Ministry of Education's national ICT strategy for schools (MOE, 1998), although explicit reference was not included in the funding criteria (ERO, 2000).

From our interview and document evidence, we determined that the four stages are not discrete but are points along a continuum of planning maturity. The benchmark characteristics associated with each stage are, therefore, similarly, indicators of progress along an evolutionary pathway rather than examples of discrete categories. The following discussion illustrates the four stages (and their benchmark characteristics) and identifies some of the drivers (key factors) that enable schools to progress from one stage to the next in their planning (see Figure 2 and Panel 1). Throughout, examples are used from the case study evidence, not because they epitomize a stage with particular clarity, but because they demonstrate characteristics that are useful in explaining and describing the proposed theory for ICT planning in schools.

Stage 1: Little or No Planning

Schools at this stage of planning have established an ICT budget, but the emphasis is on equipment acquisition (technical) and operations. Stage 1 schools have technical goals, such as establishing and operating an ICT network, providing Internet access, having a computer in every classroom, and achieving a reasonable computer-to-student ratio. However, schools at this stage have not yet considered how ICT could be used to support the

Figure 2. Summary of stage drivers

STAGE 1	STAGE 2	STAGE 3	STAGE 4
LITTLE OR NO PLANNING	EARLY FORMAL PLANNING	FOCUSED FORMAL PLANNING	MATURE INTEGRATED PLANNING

- Developing a shared vision for ICT with all staff.
- Formal planning and review.
- Principal and staff willing to learn.
- Appropriate professional development.
- Some commitment to resourcing the ICT infrastructure.

- Increasing acceptance and understanding of the role of ICT to support learning.
- Top management commitment (e.g., from principal and Board of Trustees).
- Planned and effective professional development for all staff.
- Commitment to ICT resourcing for medium-term development.
- Growing knowledge, experience, and understanding of technical aspects.

- A school culture that believes in the value of ICT to enhance and support both curriculum and administrative areas.
- Strong vision and knowledgeable leadership by the principal.
- Commitment to specific and appropriate professional development.
- Innovative approach to ICT use—willing to be leaders.
- Ability to maximize support from external agencies, e.g., business partnerships, professional development contracts.

educational goals of the school. Strategic planning is, therefore, negligible or nonexistent, and there are no links between ICT planning and school strategic planning. The benchmarks for this stage include limited or no formal written plans, a piecemeal approach to hardware acquisitions without an overall plan, no educational vision for the use of ICT, a narrow view of ICT (focused mainly on the placement of computers in classrooms), and professional development focused on equipping teachers with basic computing skills that are not necessarily related to curriculum integration.

The schools that participated in this study were (at the time of the interview) beyond the stage of having only limited or no ICT plans. This was because the principals had participated in the *Principals First* workshops and had developed strategic ICT plans to secure government funding. However, some of the principals indicated that their schools had engaged in little or no ICT planning before the MOE initiatives. For example, Principal 5 stated, *"We didn't have any formal plan. We had an informal plan which basically set a platform of using Apples . . . the catalyst was the need to complete a Ministry application in order to get funding."* The funding round clearly had provided an incentive to develop formal plans: *"We had to do it to qualify for the particular funding through the Ministry. That was the first time"* (Principal 4).

One or two schools were still on the borderline between Stage 1 and 2 in some areas. For example, professional development in Schools 2 and 4 focused on acquiring skills, with few links to curriculum integration. The planning for ICT infrastructure appeared to be another area where schools were struggling to make the transition from Stage 1 to Stage 2. Principal 4 suggested that while his school was considering options for a computer suite, it was holding off on plans to network its computers. The problems associated with selecting appropriate hardware and determining the most appropriate ICT developments were also concerning Principal 2.

Stage 2: Early Formal Planning

This stage signals the beginning of formal links between ICT planning and educational strategy and indicates a shift in focus from technical aspects to the educational value of ICT. Stage 2 schools are characterized (benchmarked) by formal planning and review, the development of a shared vision for ICT, a willingness to learn and embrace new technologies, appropriate professional development, and some commitment to resourcing the ICT infrastructure. Although formal ICT planning in its early stages is evident in Stage 2 schools, explicit links between ICT plans and school strategic planning are not clearly evident.

School 1 exemplified a Stage 2 school. Small and with limited access to ICT resources, its initial (informal) ICT planning focused on acquiring computers and software for classroom use and identifying how the children would use these computers. Its first formal ICT plan for the MOE lacked depth and focused on acquiring digital technologies such as cameras and scanners, and communication technologies such as email and the Internet. The principal stated that while the school's ICT planning was well below average, there were implicit links between the school's ICT strategic plans. However, document analysis revealed that these links were confined to listing items associated with professional development of staff and curriculum delivery. There was no specification of objectives, actions, and performance criteria.

Neither the principal nor his staff had well-developed ICT skills, and all were relatively new computer users. The lack of technical knowledge and expertise within the school appeared to be a major factor affecting the school's ability to plan for ICT. For example, the

Panel one. Key factors facilitating evolution from one stage to the next

---

Stages 1 to 2 (Example: School 1)
Key factors
- Formal ICT planning and reviews
- Targeted professional development
- Willingness to learn
- Development of a shared vision among staff for ICT in schools
- Some commitment to resourcing ICT infrastructure development

Principal 1 exhibited a commitment to involving his staff, including the school secretary, in the planning process. He identified shared vision as an important aspect of writing the formal plan, and held a strong belief that ICT was a tool to be used in the learning process. He believed planning provided an important framework for development, and a reference point to check what had been accomplished. He also regarded the review process as important.

It was evident from this principal's comments on professional development that he was a willing learner. He modeled his attitude of embracing ICT to staff, and he engaged in professional development as a co-learner alongside staff. He ensured that professional development, which was beginning to focus on curriculum integration, targeted the individual needs of the teachers. He also placed some emphasis on continuing to resource ICT infrastructure development within the school and had identified potential development projects such as networking classroom computers and the library.

Stages 2 to 3 (Example: School 6)
Key factors
- Increasing acceptance and understanding of the role of ICT to support learning
- Strong management commitment to using ICT to support administrative functions
- Planned and effective professional development
- Strong commitment to resourcing ICT
- Growing knowledge, experience, and understanding of the technical aspects of ICT infrastructure planning and development.

The importance of management commitment for ICT planning maturity was clearly evident in School 6, where the principal appeared to be a driving force behind the plans to implement electronic recording and reporting systems for supporting administrative functions. This focus seemed to have been initiated by prior experience with and an awareness of the benefits of analyzing student records to identify students requiring special programs. This principal also believed that effective school administration requires the efficient use of ICT, and he had developed a sound appreciation of the potential that ICT held in schools for purposes beyond teaching and learning.

There was evidence also in this school of a strong commitment to resourcing ICT in the school, and an expectation that the ICT investment should support teaching, learning,

continued on following page

Panel one. Key factors facilitating evolution from one stage to the next (continued)

and administration in a relevant manner. The principal considered the school's well-established professional development program to be effective and that it related ICT use to curriculum objectives. The principal had also gained valuable experience in dealing with technical consultants and vendors and had the knowledge and confidence to determine whether proposed solutions were appropriate for the school.

Stages 3 to 4 (Example: School 3)
Key factors
- Strong belief in the value of ICT to support curriculum and administrative objectives
- Strong vision and leadership provided by top management
- Planned professional development
- Innovative approach to ICT use
- An ability to recognize and leverage the support of external agencies/business partnerships
- Strong commitment to ICT resourcing that is driven by targeted development policies
- Willingness to be a leader among other schools.

School 3's culture strongly valued and encouraged ICT use. Its principal had built with vision upon the previous management's commitment to ICT. She had a wide knowledge of ICT and its educational application, and encouraged innovation and creativity in the use of ICT within the school environment. She actively sought to model ICT use and encouraged staff use by creating appropriate organizational expectations, for example, requesting electronic copies of long-term plans to be emailed or stored in a shared directory. The principal also took a strong leadership role, placing value on being a part of a community of learners in ICT and fostering interest and understanding by sharing resources and ideas. Most importantly, she had a core belief in the value the ICT holds for education.

The school demonstrated a strong commitment to providing well-planned professional development opportunities for staff, including training sessions, seminars, and workshops on the use of ICT in education. The case evidence also suggested a strong commitment to ICT resourcing coupled with a careful purchasing policy as an important characteristic of planning maturity. Maximizing the support received from external service providers further enhanced the school's ability to provide appropriate resources.

---

principal found it difficult to make decisions on technical matters, such as identifying network requirements: "*I'll have to get my head around networking because there are different types.*" This lack of knowledge necessitated reliance on external expertise, but the principal found the advice received was not always what was best for the teachers and students.

The principal's comments in this regard, along with other evidence, suggest that Stage 2 schools tend to be aware of the gaps in and problems with their infrastructure. Certainly, the principal of School 1 held that the ICT plan should provide for targeted professional development, and, indeed, the school was beginning to shift its professional development focus from acquiring application skills to learning how to integrate ICT into the curriculum in a meaningful way. The school was also beginning to focus on identifying appropriate Internet sites for children, and staff members were learning how to download material for classroom use.

Stage 3: Focused Formal Planning

By this stage, schools have begun to recognize the value of ICT to enhance administrative and communication functions as well as teaching and learning. They have a more comprehensive understanding of the potential of ICT to contribute to the school's strategic objectives, and they are using ICT to modify or reengineer some of the processes within the school. Their strategic educational planning reciprocally identifies and promotes these processes.

Although many of the schools exhibited characteristics of Stage 3 ICT planning maturity, most were mixtures of Stages 2 and 3, with some categories having greater planning focus than others. For example, School 5 demonstrated a Stage 3 approach to using technology for supporting administrative efficiency and effectiveness but was very much Stage 2 in its struggle to understand how best to use ICT to enhance classroom learning. Schools 6, 7, and 8, while exhibiting some Stage 2 characteristics, leaned far more toward Stage 3 maturity. These three schools had well-developed plans for the use of ICT and its application to teaching and learning. School 8, in particular, had a well-developed network plan and initial plans for using the school Web site to reach families, in the school community, with non-English speaking backgrounds. School 7 had included ICT in its property management plan and was designing an ICT center for wider use by the community; for this school, ICT planning was an accepted part of the school planning process. The three schools were also beginning to explore how ICT could be used to support other functions, such as administration.

School 6 provided a particularly clear example of the Stage 3 characteristics of understanding how ICT can be used to support teaching, learning, and increased efficiency in school administration, and of increasing levels of staff competency across and within application areas. As such, we document it in some detail here.

This school had reasonably well-developed infrastructures and a written ICT plan dating back to 1994, although the latter had not been significantly updated until 1999. Staff development was personalized to meet the needs of individual staff and coordinated throughout the school to ensure increasing sophistication in ICT use. The principal also considered that the school had "*trained the trainer*" and was reaping the benefits of staying with the same external service provider.

School 6's utilization of ICT to improve the efficiency and effectiveness of its student records system is especially interesting. The school's reasonably transient population made the ability to produce information and reports on demand important. The principal was convinced that a computer-based student record system would meet this need. He also believed this could become a powerful tool for teachers in the classroom, allowing them to access information that would help them provide better programs of work for individual students and groups.

Other indicators of planning maturity were evident in the school's plans regarding ICT and other ICT-related needs. For example, the school wanted to ensure that new equipment could be upgraded to meet future needs, and that the purchase and implementation of equipment would be conducted in a comprehensive rather than piecemeal fashion to ensure better vendor support. The school was also taking account of its ICT needs when making property improvements. For example, it intended to install a fiber-optic cable underneath a new walkway system.

Stage 4: Mature Integrated Planning

Stage 4 indicates a stage of maturity in which planning acknowledges the integral role of ICT in supporting or enhancing the wider school objectives. ICT planning is aligned with and integral to the school's strategic planning process. The innovative or creative development of ICT within the school contributes significantly to achieving school goals.

Of the schools, School 3 was the most advanced in respect of ICT planning. For this school, ICT was an integral part of teaching, learning, and administrative support. There was a high level of ICT competence among staff, a well-developed ICT infrastructure, and a vision as to how ICT could be used in new and innovative ways to support school objectives.

The main factor that characterized this school as a Stage 4 school was its strong focus on teaching and learning, and its clear understanding of how ICT provides tools for thinking and learning. In addition, the school had developed a sound single-platform IT infrastructure with established networks, adequate hardware, and a laptop for every teacher/classroom. Moreover, it was the lead school in an ICT professional development cluster, with one of its staff providing specialist ICT support for the cluster.

School 3 also had a well-known reputation for being innovative in its use of ICT. The principal considered that, in this regard, it was probably among "*the top 10 percent in the city.*" She made an interesting comparison between her present school (rated Decile 10) and her previous school (rated Decile 3). In her view, the two schools were comparable in their planning and implementation of ICT, suggesting that decile rating may not be a highly significant factor in predicting where a school is at in terms of ICT planning maturity.

Marked enthusiasm for ICT and its potential to contribute to the learning environment in innovative and creative ways appears to be a notable characteristic of Stage 4 schools. The principal of School 3 pointed to plans to introduce software that would allow collaboration among staff within the school and across other schools, as well as with members of the wider education and school communities. This vision for collaboration and interactive participation was also evident in the principal's comments about a school Web site currently under construction. The aim of the site, she said, was to go beyond providing information, to supporting interactive communication with and by the wider school community.

School 3 also had a well-established business partnership with an educational computing company offering support in terms of professional development and purchasing opportunities. There were reciprocal benefits for the computer firm, as the school was providing a trial site for some of the firm's initiatives.

SUMMARY

Our findings confirmed that ICT planning and strategic planning in schools is not a clearly defined area, and that numerous factors, internal and external, impact on the planning process and outcomes. In spite of this complexity, it was evident that across schools, ICT planning matures from a focus on technology acquisition to a focus on the effective use and integration of technologies that are in line with the schools' strategic plans.

STUDY LIMITATIONS

Our study and the model arising out of it are governed by limitations inherent in our methodology. The first limitation concerns the interpretive nature of the study. While researcher bias cannot be eliminated in this type of research, it is acknowledged as a factor affecting data collection and analysis. Certainly, it may have inadequately represented the participants' perceptions of ICT planning and the priorities they awarded to certain facets of ICT planning. Moreover, the retrospective nature of the interviews makes it difficult to validate the accuracy of responses given, which may be impacted by problems of recall. However, because most schools did not begin to develop formal ICT plans until 1999, the relative recency of events minimized the potential for poor recall. Document analysis also provided a secondary source of information, which was useful in validating respondents' perceptions.

The second limitation lies with the use of one respondent in each school. Although a pretest (designed to test the interview format and check that the principal would be able to answer the queries and provide the documentation) showed that the principal was the best person to interview, because he or she was likely to be the person most aware of ICT planning in the school and the person most conversant with the school's strategic plans, interviewing a wider cross-section of personnel (for example, teachers, school administrators) would have enabled triangulation of the findings as well as further insight into the issues explored.

A third concern is that the research context was confined to a small number of New Zealand primary schools. While this situation supported cross-case comparisons and the identification of trends among the schools, it may have limited the wider applicability of the findings to environments that do not have similar characteristics. The skewed nature of the sample (yielding five Decile 10 schools of the eight schools that participated in the study) may also have limited interpretation, but it allowed one important observation to be made, namely, that marked differences in ICT planning and implementation among schools may not be influenced by decile rating. Nevertheless, future research should consider a wider range of schools.

CONCLUSION

Achieving effective integration of ICT within the educational process is a complex undertaking, encompassing educational and administrative areas. Although the schools that participated in this study tended to address these issues differently, the information that we collected about them allowed us to identify characteristics of planning as well as some of the factors that enable schools to move forward in their planning and implementation of ICT. The value of this research is therefore twofold. First, it supports the notion that ICT strategy planning evolves over time, thereby offering a tool for assessing and explaining the evolution of ICT planning in schools, providing direction for growth, and providing a basis for further study of ICT in schools. Second, it highlights the impact of external and internal factors on ICT planning in schools.

In similar vein to the study conducted by King and Teo (1997), our study revealed a progression from unformulated ICT plans with piecemeal implementation of hardware and software, through to the development of coherent and focused plans that emphasize the strategic goals of the school in the areas of teaching, learning, and administration. It seems that as schools develop skills in planning for ICT, they tend to identify opportunities to enhance the core business of teaching and learning through the innovative use of ICT in administrative, collaborative, and support roles.

While external influences can make a school move forward in its ICT planning (as happened in relation to the MOE requirement that schools provide ICT plans in order to qualify for ICT funding), our findings indicate that internal factors are more likely to influence the movement from one stage of planning to the next. These include the extent to which school management is committed to ICT use, staff attitudes toward and beliefs about ICT, the amount of experience that staff have in using ICT, and their knowledge about its potential for teaching, learning, and administrative support. Principals, in particular, seem to play a vital role in determining the planning maturity of their schools. It would appear that a principal with sound knowledge of and commitment to ICT can override a good number of the internal factors that can hinder ICT planning maturity in schools.

One of the most significant findings in this study was the lack of vision evident among Stages 1, 2, and 3 schools regarding the potential that ICT has to facilitate and enhance administrative, communication, and collaborative functions within the school system. Similarly, the potential for ICT to improve recording, analyzing, and reporting student progress and achievement appeared to be an underdeveloped area among the participating schools.

The development of a stage model of ICT planning maturity for schools provides a tool for analyzing current planning processes and assessing maturity vis-à-vis each of the planning categories proposed by the model. In this regard, it also offers further evidence of the usefulness of stage theory in understanding organizational development and IS strategy-business strategy alignment. The model descriptors (Figure 1) provide benchmarks for highlighting areas of deficiency, assessing future directions, and providing assurance to school leaders that as they work toward planning maturity. The stage drivers (Figure 2) go beyond the basic stage model to provide direction on aligning ICT planning with school strategic planning.

It needs to be noted, though, that these stages and their associated drivers reflect our interpretations of observations made among eight schools and assessment of publicly available documents. Although these findings represent an important contribution to understanding the evolution of ICT planning in schools, the research limitations provide opportunity for further research to confirm or refine our model's proposed stages of maturity.

ENDNOTES

[1]   Information systems planning is the term used to describe the process of determining objectives for organizational computing and identifying potential applications that should be implemented in the organization (Teo & King, 1997).

[2]   Information technology is defined as the hardware and software that allow the access, retrieval, storage, organization, manipulation, and presentation of information by electronic means (Ministry of Education, 1998).

[3]   Within the school context, IT is nowadays more commonly termed ICT, and it is the term/abbreviation that will generally be used throughout this chapter when reference is made to this context.

⁴   State schools are fully funded by the government, as are integrated schools, except for the funding of some property-related expenses.

⁵   Primary schools cater for children aged five to 12/13 years.

⁶   Decile ratings reflect the socioeconomic strata from which the school draws its population. Decile 1 schools draw their students from areas of greatest socioeconomic disadvantage, while Decile 10 schools draw their students from areas of least socio-economic disadvantage. (For further information on this matter, see http://www.ero.govt.nz/.)

⁷   The Education Review Office is the government department that reports publicly on the quality of education in all New Zealand schools and early childhood services.

REFERENCES

Barta, B., Telem, M., & Gev, Y. (1995). *Information technology in educational management*. London: Chapman & Hall.

Butler, T. (1998). Towards a hermeneutic method for interpretive research in information systems. *Journal of Information Technology, 13*, 285–300.

Education Review Office (ERO). (2000). *The implementation of information and communication technologies (ICT) in New Zealand schools*. Retrieved February 2001 from http://www.ero.govt.nz/Publications/pubs2000/implementationICT.htm.

Fung, A. C. W. et al. (eds.). (1997). *Information technology in educational management of the future*. Paper presented at the International Conference on Information Technology in Educational Management (ITEM), 22–26 July 1996, Hong Kong.

Huff, S. L., Munro, M. C., & Martin, B. H. (1988). Growth stages of end-user computing. *Communications of the ACM, 31*, 5, 542–550.

Information Technology Advisory Group. (ITAG). (2000). *ICT in schools 1999*. Retrieved February 2001 from http://www.med.govt.nz/pbt/infotech/ictschools1999/index.html.

King, W. R., & Teo, T. S. H. (1997). Integration between business planning and information systems planning: Validating a stage hypothesis. *Decision Sciences, 28*, 2, Spring, 279–308.

Klein, H. K. & Myers, M. D. (1999). A set of principles for conducting and evaluating interpretive field studies in information systems. *MIS Quarterly, 23*, 1, 67–93.

Knezek, G., & Christensen, R. (1999). Stages of adoption for technology in education. *Computers in New Zealand Schools*, November, 25–29.

Latham, A. (1998). Strategic information systems planning: A necessary evil for schools? *Journal of Applied Management Studies, 7*, 2, 267–273.

Lederer, A. L., & Sethi, V. (1988). The implementation of strategic information systems planning. *MIS Quarterly, 12*, 3, 445–461.

Ministry of Education (MOE). (1990). *Sallis report of the consultative committee: Information technology in the school curriculum*. Wellington: Ministry of Education.

Ministry of Education (MOE). (1998). *Interactive education: An information and communication technologies strategy for schools*. Retrieved February 2001 from http://www.tki.org.nz/.

Ministry of Education (MOE). (1999). *Learning technologies planning guide for schools: Using ICT to improve teaching and learning*. Wellington: Learning Media.

Nolan, R. L. (1973). Managing the computing resource: A stage hypothesis. *Communications of the ACM, 16,* 7, 399–405.

Rice, M., & Miller, M. T. (2001). Faculty involvement in planning for the use and integration of instructional and administrative technologies. *Journal of Research on Computing in Education, 33,* 3, 328–337.

Robson, W. (1997). *Strategic management and information systems.* Pitman Publishing: London.

Smits, M.T. & van der Poel, K.G. (1996). The practice of information strategy in six information intensive organizations in The Netherlands. *Journal of Strategic Information Systems, 5,* 93–110.

Telem, M. (1993). Information technology: A missing link in educational research. *Journal of Research on Computing in Education, 26,* 1, 123–143.

Teo, S. H. & King, W. R. (1997). Integration between business planning and information systems planning: An evolutionary-contingency perspective. *Journal of Management Information Systems, 14,* 1, 185–214.

Watson, R. T. et al. (1997). Key issues in information systems management: An international perspective. *Journal of Management Information Systems, 13,* 4, 91–115.

Chapter XXXI

On-Line Case Discussion: A Methodology

Henri Isaac
Paris Dauphine University, France

ABSTRACT

Over the past several years, a number of research studies have investigated the application of Internet technologies to the classroom. Most of the research focus on asynchronous technology such as newsgroups or Web sites, or on GSS. No research investigates the possibility of conducting on-line case discussion. As case discussion in the classroom is a key pedagogical method in an executive program, our research examines a methodology for on-line case discussion. In this chapter, the results of an experiment conducted in an executive MBA program to investigate the use of on-line case discussion is presented. First, other research to determine the distinguishing characteristics of case discussion is reviewed. Then, the pedagogical context for the experiment is provided, and the experimental method is described. Finally, the results of a satisfaction questionnaire completed by the participants in the experiment are presented. Suggestions for further research and experiments are also discussed.

INTRODUCTION

Over the past several years, a number of research studies have investigated the application of Internet technologies to the classroom. No research has investigated the possibility of conducting synchronous on-line case discussion, however. As case discussion in the classroom is a key pedagogical method, especially in an executive program, the research described in this chapter examines the conditions in which such a pedagogical method can be used in a virtual environment. We are interested in determining if technology-based tools can be used to create interactivity that is similar to that found in classroom case discussion. First, we review the literature. Then, we describe an experiment to investigate the use of on-line case discussion and present the results of that experiment. Finally, we discuss a study of students' satisfaction.

LITERATURE REVIEW

The case method is, by nature, a teaching method adapted to the classroom and especially to executive programs (Benbasat, Goldstein, & Mead, 1987; Erskine, Leenders, & Mauffette-Leenders, 1981; Matejka & Coss, 1981). This pedagogical method is common, and many faculty members use it to teach Information Technology or Management Information Systems. Interactivity is one of the distinguishing characteristics of this pedagogical method. Many undergraduate and graduate programs have introduced Web-based learning, which is defined as any kind of learning that makes significant use of the WWW (Goodyear, 2001). These technologies are interactive through text, voice, graphics, video, shared workspaces, or combinations of these forms. Most of the Web-based programs, however, use multimedia Web sites and newsgroups. Most of the commercial platforms have many functions, enabling asynchronous discussion and collaborative work. One of these tools is the chat function, which enables synchronous discussion. Thus, recreating a classroom case discussion is a new possibility. Most other research, however, is focused on asynchronous capabilities (Goodyear, 2001; Tyran & Shepherd, 2001). Synchronous technologies such as IRC or Instant Messenger encourage clarity of expression and formalization of knowledge. On the contrary, synchronous technologies are time consuming. It is also hard to capture real-world working practices or tacit knowledge with this type of electronic media.

Another criticism with on-line chat discussion is the lack of expressive richness. As Goodyear (2001) stated, "This is most clearly the case with text-based communications and it is often cited as a major drawback of this form of web-based learning. Some 'workarounds' include the use of 'emoticons' (such as a :<) to represent irony or joke. But it is also worth noting that 'expressive richness' can work — or fail to work — on a number of levels. Text-based messages may not have the expressive richness of a quick and lively verbal exchange. On the other hand, well-crafted text can be much more rich than the stumbling improvisations we all hear and produce in seminars."

The development of teaching programs based on electronic platforms raises the question of the effectiveness of these tools in the learning processes (Tyran & Shepherd, 2001). The experiment conducted for this research aims to test a system seeking an interactive equivalent to that of a traditional classroom case discussion, thus providing for a comparison between the classroom teaching process and the virtual teaching process (Asensio, Hodgson, & Trehan, 2000; Tyran & Shepherd, 2001).

EXPERIMENTAL METHOD

The design of the experiment respects the principles of the constitution of virtual learning communities in order to build a technical and cognitive environment that provides for dialogue within a community (Berge & Collins, 1993; Berge, 1998; Kollock, 1997).

Pedagogical Context

The Dauphine-UQAM Executive MBA program was created in 1999 by the University of Paris Dauphine and the University of Quebec at Montreal (UQAM). It is offered in various countries in Europe, including France, Lebanon, and Turkey, as well as in Canada. It is a part-time MBA program that is taught three days per month (Friday, Saturday, and Sunday) for 24 months. Thirty-eight students enrolled in the program in September 2001. In order to create a competitive advantage over other executive MBA programs in Europe, the program sponsors chose to rely extensively on information technologies in the program's courses. An intranet system was established for the courses based on WebCT tools. Training on the use of the different WebCT tools (on-line documents, newsgroup, chat, electronic black-board) was provided to all professors and students participating in the program.

In one of the courses in the program, "Information and Information Technologies," an experiment was conducted using WebCT tools to facilitate on-line case discussion.

The population participating in the experiment were the students enrolled in the Executive MBA in Fall 2001, consisting of 38 executives. A case was made available on the program's intranet at the beginning of the "Information and Information Technologies" course in September. The course, which ended in December, was divided into 10 classroom sessions (two sessions per month). The case chosen illustrated the themes of the last two sessions of the course in December. The case presents a traditional French company going into e-business. Its conceptual themes are linked to e-business and include value migration, business process reengineering, IT infrastructure, extranets, and IT project management. The case examines the problem of going digital and using electronic relations to conduct business.

Most of the students did not have experience in on-line discussion before entering the Executive MBA program. Therefore, we trained the students in on-line discussion before starting the case discussion by conducting four on-line sessions on specific subjects related to the course.

During the course, we scheduled different milestones related to the case in order to enable all students to have time to read the case, prepare it, and participate in the discussions on the intranet. As the case discussion would be difficult without questions to help students prepare their contributions, we prepared four such questions. Then we divided the case discussion into four sessions of 45 minutes each, with each session dedicated to one question. For example, the first question of the case was to establish a strategic analysis of the company based on a classical SWOT analysis.

DESIGN OF THE EXPERIMENT

To manage the case discussions, we used different electronic communication tools in WebCT to build an on-line case discussion system. These tools and their use in the experiment were as follows:

- *Calendar*: Each on-line session was scheduled using this tool. The tool generated an electronic reminder to the students each time a new session was scheduled.
- *Chat*: This tool was used for on-line case discussion. For 4 weeks prior to the classroom session on the case, we scheduled a 45 minute discussion on one question on Wednesday at 9:00 PM. Each student was supposed to log in and participate in the discussion. Because the students were executives, only about 20 students were on-

line each Wednesday. The total discussion was recorded and made available soon afterward on a dedicated newsgroup, so that missing students could read the discussion.

• *Newsgroup*: We created a dedicated newsgroup for the case discussion. The newsgroup was divided into five discussion areas, one for each question about the case, and one for the recorded on-line discussions. Students were expected to post for each question a short assignment consisting of a one-page Word™ document.

Figure 1 summarizes the experimental design.

The evaluation of participation was based on the tracking tool in WebCT and on the analysis of individual contributions to the discussion.

EVALUATION OF SYSTEM SATISFACTION

After all case discussions were finished, a questionnaire was completed by the students. The questionnaire asked for a subjective evaluation of the efficiency of the system and the satisfaction of the students with the system, by collecting opinions on specific aspects of the system using a one- to five-point Likert scale. Two open-ended questions were included that asked for the three main positive and three main negative aspects of the system in order to collect qualitative evaluations of the system. We received 29 usable questionnaires from the 38 students (76%). Responses to the relevant questions are shown in Table 1.

Participation

Several dimensions of participation were evaluated in the questionnaire, and particularly, whether the system facilitated participation in the discussion (Howell-Richardson &

Figure 1. The experimental design

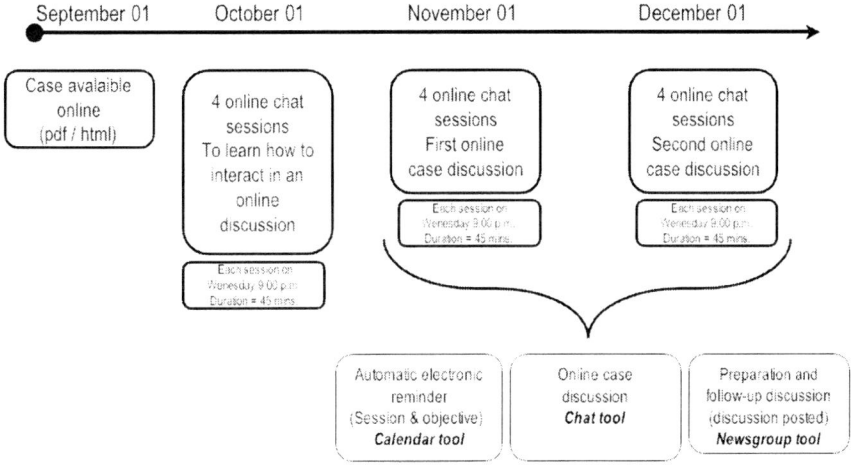

Table 1. Results of the satisfaction questionnaire

	Mean
Q4- The technical system is satisfactory.	3.96
Q5- The objective of each discussion session is known in advance.	4.36
Q6- The duration of the on-line sessions is sufficient.	4.36
Q7- During the sessions, I actively participated in discussion.	3.39
Q8- I prepared the sessions.	4.07
Q9- I used the newsgroup before and after discussions.	2.89
Q10- Overall, on-line discussions were as thorough as classical sessions.	2.75
Q11- It is easy to follow conversation during chat.	2.68
Q12- It is easy to express myself during discussions.	3.43
Q13- I express myself better during chat than during class sessions.	2.32
Q14- It is easy for me to express myself in a concise fashion during discussions.	3.50
Q15- I am capable of handling online discussion.	4.54
Q16- The division of cases into four sessions facilitated discussion.	3.89
Q17- The case discussions were longer than during a classical session.	3.68
Q18- Each question was treated in more depth than would be during classical sessions.	3.00
Q19- I can more easily express myself in these sessions than during classical sessions.	2.65
Q20- I give my own opinions more easily.	2.67
Q21- The exchanges are more direct.	3.32
Q22- The discussions focus rapidly on essentials.	2.93
Q23- There was less digression than during discussions in a classical session.	2.54
Q24- The interventions of the professor permitted more lively discussion.	4.39
Q25- The interventions of the professor refocused the discussion.	4.36
Q26- There were more exchanges between students than between students and the professor.	3.64
Q27- Overall, I appreciate on-line case discussion.	3.93
Q28- On-line case discussion is more efficient than classical sessions.	2.54
Q29- I get more from on-line discussion than from classical sessions.	2.54

Mellar, 1996; Walsh et al., 1996). We also asked if it was easy for the student to give personal opinions in the discussion. Finally, we asked students whether their participation was higher than in classroom case discussion.

The average rate of participation was 70%. Nonparticipation might be explained by the nature of the students (executive) and the scheduled time of the discussions (9:00 PM). The length of the session (45 minutes) was enough for most of the participants (Q6).

Students said that they were active in discussion (Q7). This response is consistent with what we observed during the on-line sessions and with the fact that students prepared the session (Q8). The ability to handle on-line discussion is a critical point in participation. Students felt that they had the ability to handle on-line case discussion after the training period (Q15). Students also felt comfortable with technical aspects of the discussion (Q4). However, they said it was not easy to follow the discussions (Q11). This might be explained by the fact that during this experiment, the average number of participants was about 20 students.

Handling 20 students in an on-line discussion is difficult; it is the role of the professor to encourage discussion and make sure all students participate. Participation is highly related to the intervention style of the teacher (Erskine, Leenders, & Maufette-Lendeers, 1981). Most students agreed that the professor in the course intervened appropriately during the on-line discussion (Q24). This result is consistent with former research on intervention in a virtual classroom that pointed to the fact that intervention is a key success factor (Berge, 1996; Salmon, 2000). On-line discussion is not as easy to control, however. We observed some students who logged in but just "listened" to the on-line discussion and did not participate. The number of participants is an obstacle to focused discussion, even though we divided the case discussion into four main questions.

Nature of On-line Discussion

The case discussion lasted four sessions of 45 minutes each for a total of three hours. This duration enabled more time than we usually have in a classroom. Three hours of discussion enabled the students to discuss details and to go into deep analysis of problems embedded in the case. The students felt that the discussion was more in-depth on-line and that many more aspects of the case were discussed (Q18). We also asked if the on-line interface made it easier for the student to give a personal opinion without the presence of group pressure (Booher & Seiler, 1982). Students felt that there was little change from classroom discussion in this regard (Q20). Students felt, however, that the direction of the discussion changed; they had more exchange between participants on-line than in a traditional classroom discussion (Q26), and these exchanges were more direct (Q21). We also evaluated if on-line discussion was more focused than in a classroom, where sometimes students forget the initial question. Participants did not think on-line discussion was more focused than in traditional classroom discussion (Q23). In addition, students did not think they got more from the on-line discussion than from a classroom discussion (Q29). In conclusion, students did not perceive real differences with traditional case discussion. This result is consistent with former research on differences between group discussions and groupware discussions (Tyran, 1997; Tyran & Shepherd, 2001).

Student Satisfaction

The overall satisfaction of the students was high (average 7.14 on a 1 to 10 scale). This satisfaction may be related to learning a new way of interacting rather than to the efficiency of the system. Students were asked about whether on-line case discussion is more efficient than traditional discussion and their response was neutral (Q28). This is consistent with Wheeler's (1997) research. The results of his study showed no significant differences in the performance of the learning process between traditional teaching and groupware-based teaching. Asked if they participated more on-line than in a traditional case discussion, students answered negatively (Q13). What is also noticeable is the fact that few students use the newsgroup before or after the on-line discussion (Q9). The qualitative answers provided additional confirmation of the answers to the questions in the questionnaire.

DISCUSSION AND FUTURE TRENDS

Because the experiment is based on a small number of participants, the conclusions are limited. The first interesting result in this experiment is that the design of the system enables in-depth discussion. This means that the lack of expressive richness can be surmounted by an appropriate system of case discussion. In this experiment, traditional criticisms against instant messaging did not arise. Most of the students did not complain about this point but rather about the speed of the discussion. The second interesting result is that students do not perceive significant differences between a traditional classroom case discussion and a virtual one. This should lead many Web-based programs to enable such a pedagogical method. Combining synchronous tools and asynchronous tools is likely to be the best way to create an effective Web-based learning program. In this experiment, we observed that students did not use the newsgroup dedicated to the case discussion as much as we might have expected. Instead, they were focused on the on-line discussion. We suggest that further experiments give a specific assignment to a group of students that will be posted in the dedicated newsgroup. The other students should read the assignment before going into the discussion. This approach will increase the use of the newsgroup. An increase in participation is also possible by asking a group of students to be the moderators of the discussion. The professor in this new configuration is the only moderator. With such a system, interactivity may be as great as it is in a classroom case discussion.

CONCLUSION

This experiment tested a system for on-line case discussion in an executive MBA program. The system was successful with good student participation and a good level of satisfaction by the students. In this experiment, we were concerned about whether we would get the same interactions as we get in traditional classroom case discussion. The experiment results suggest that students do not see much difference between on-line and classroom discussions. Also suggested is that students do not change their attitudes when chatting, which implies that the on-line interface is neutral for this type of executive student. What is identified as an obstacle is the number of participants. Our group was large, making it difficult for some students to express themselves and to follow the discussion. Another finding of this experiment, which is consistent with the literature (Asensio, Hodgson, & Trehan, 2000; Salmon, 2000), is the key role of the moderator in leading the participation.

REFERENCES

Asensio, M., Hodgson, V., & Trehan, K. (2000). Is there a difference: Contrasting experiences of face to face and online learning. In M. Asensio et al. (eds.). (2000). *Networked Learning*. Lancaster: Lancaster University & University of Sheffield.

Benbasat, I., Goldstein, D., & Mead, M. (1987). The case research strategy in studies of information systems. *MIS Quarterly, (11)*, 3, 369–388.

Berge, Z. (1996). The role of the online facilitator/instructor. Available online: http://star.ucc.nau.edu/~mauri/moderate/teach_on-line.html.

Berge, Z. (1998). Guiding principles in web-based instructional design. *Education Media International, (35)*, 2, 72–86.

Berge, Z. & Collins, M. (1993). Computer conferencing and online education. *The Point Electronic Journal on Virtual Culture, (1)*, 3. Available online: http://cac.psu.edu/~mauri/bergev1n3.html.

Booher, R. K. & Seiler, W. J. (1982). Speech communication anxiety: An impediment to academic achievement in the university classroom. *Journal of Classroom Interaction, (18)*, 1, 23–27.

Erskine, J. A., Leenders, M. R., & Mauffette-Leenders, L. A. (1981). Teaching with cases. Research and Publications Division, School of Business Administration, The University of Western Ontario, London, Ontario, Canada.

Goodyear, P. (2001). Effective networked learning in higher education: Notes and guidelines. CSALT, Lancaster University, Lancaster, LA1 4YL, England. Available online: http://csalt.lancs.ac.uk/jisc/advice.htm.

Howell-Richardson, C. & Mellar, H. (1996). A methodology for the analysis of patterns of participation within computer-mediated communication courses. *Instructional Science, 24*, 47–69.

Kollock, P. (1997). Design principles for online communities. *The Internet and Society: Harvard Conference Proceedings*, Cambridge, MA: O'Reilly & Associates.

Matejka, J. K. & Coss, T. J. (1981). *The Business Case Method: An Introduction*. Richmond, VA: Robert F. Dame, Inc.

Salmon, G. (2000). *E-Moderating: The Key to Teaching and Learning Online*. London: Kogan Page.

Tyran, C. K. (1997). GSS to support classroom discussion: Opportunities and pitfalls. *Proceedings of the 30th Annual Hawaii International Conference on Systems Sciences*, IEEE.

Tyran, C. K. & Shepherd, M. (2001). Collaborative technology in the classroom: A review of the GSS research and a research framework. *Information Technology and Management, 2*, 395–418.

Walsh, K. R. et al. (1996). Learning with GSS: A case study. *Proceedings of the 29th Annual Hawaii International Conference on Systems Sciences*, IEEE.

Chapter XXXII

A Comparison Between the Use of IT in Business and Education: Applications of the Internet to Tertiary Education

Stephen Burgess
Victoria University, Australia

Paul Darbyshire
Victoria University, Australia

ABSTRACT

Since the mid-1990s, there have been many claims that the Web has become the new paradigm for teaching. However, most academics do not use the Web as a replacement for teaching, but to provide extra benefits for their students. There is a strong parallel between this use of the Internet for teaching, and the use of IT in business for providing added-value products or administrative efficiencies. In this chapter, the similarities between the use of IT in business and education are discussed, and the categorization of aspects of Web use in education using standard business categories relating to savings and quality are explored. The results are obtained from a survey of academics conducted internationally using the Web, and it surveys perceptions of benefits gained from supplementing teaching with Web-based services. The results revealed similar usage levels of Administrative and

Educational Features to aid tertiary education on the Internet. The administrative uses showed slightly more benefits for the institution than for students and vice-versa for educational uses. In both types of uses, their adoption seemed to be based upon how difficult the feature was to set up as well as the added-value benefits it provided. An analysis of the correlation of the benefits identified for institution and students showed a correspondence between most of the uses, with a few interesting differences.

INTRODUCTION

For many years, information technology (IT) has been used to find ways to "add value" for customers to entice them to purchase the products and services of a business. This chapter examines the possibility of translating the benefits of "added value" to the use of the Internet by tertiary educators for subject and course delivery. Many educators use the Internet to supplement existing modes of delivery. Importantly, the Internet is providing a number of "added value" supplemental benefits for subjects and courses delivered using this new, hybrid teaching mode. There are two aspects to subject delivery to where "added-value" benefits may be applied, and that is in the *administrative tasks* associated with a subject and the *educational tasks*. In both instances, IT solutions can be employed to fully or partially process some of these tasks. Given the complex and often fluid nature of the education process, it is rare that a fully integrated solution can be found to adequately service both aspects of subject delivery. Most solutions are partial in that key components are targeted by IT solutions to assist the subject coordinator in the process. If we examine closely the underlying benefits gained in the application of IT to these tasks, there is a strong parallel to the benefits to be gained by business organizations with similar applications of IT. While the actual benefits actually sought by academics depend on the motivation for the IT solution, the perceived benefits can be classified using standard categories used to gauge similar commercial applications.

BACKGROUND

In order to investigate the benefits of using Web-based techniques to supplement traditional teaching in terms of business efficiencies, the reasons commercial organizations use IT are examined. The different aspects of subject delivery also need to be considered in order to draw a parallel with the ultimate benefits to be gained.

Information Technology: Efficiency and Added Value

There are a number of reasons for using IT in organizations today (O'Brien, 1999):

- *For the support of business operations*: This is usually to make the business operation more efficient (by making it faster, cheaper, and more accurate).
- *For the support of managerial decision making*: Support is provided by allowing more sophisticated cost–benefit analyses, providing decision support tools, and so forth.
- *For the support of strategic advantage*: This refers to the use of Porter's (1985) three generic strategies as a means of using information technology to improve competitiveness by adding value to products and services.

It has been recognized for a number of decades that the use of computers can provide cost savings and improvements in efficiencies in many organizations. Porter and Millar (1985) have generally been credited with recognizing that the capabilities of information technology can extend further to providing organizations with the opportunity to add value to their goods. Value is measured by the amount that buyers are willing to pay for a product or service. Porter and Millar (1985) identified three ways that organizations can add value to their commodities or services (known as *generic strategies for improving competitiveness*):

- Be the lowest cost producer.

- Produce a unique or differentiated good (providing value in a product or service that a competitor cannot provide or match, at least for a period of time). If an organization is the first to introduce a particular feature, it may gain a competitive advantage over its rivals for a period. Some ways in which information technology can be used to differentiate between products and services are as follows (Sandy & Burgess, 1999):

  - Quality
  - Product support
  - Time

- Provide a good that meets the requirements of a specialized market.

The next sections examine the possibility of translating the benefits of "added value" to a particular application of IT, the use of the Internet by tertiary educators to assist with subject and course delivery.

Aspects of Course and Subject Delivery

Jansen et al. (2002) suggested that online learning is useful because it can supplement existing learning environments; it provides a standardized environment for learning, and can be used as a management environment to monitor and stimulate learning. Beirne, Brecht, and Sauls (2002) examined the use of the Internet from the viewpoint of treating the student as an information client. They classify student needs into five areas: activities for careers growth (student organizations), employment opportunities, scholarship opportunities, administrative information, and subject (course) information. They examine academic department Web pages, faculty (staff) Web pages, and subject Web pages. This chapter specifically concentrates upon those activities related to the area of student need encompassing subject delivery (subject information) and subject Web pages.

Beirne, Brecht, and Sauls (2002) identified four aspects of course information: program requirements, instructor information, subject (course) scheduling, and subject information. Alternatively, Darbyshire and Wenn (2000) identified two overall aspects to course and subject delivery, the educational and administrative components. These are just separate ways of classifying similar requirements. Delivery of the educational component of a subject to students is the primary responsibility of the subject coordinator, and this task is the most visible from a student's perspective. However, the administration tasks associated with a subject form a major component of subject coordination, but these responsibilities are not immediately obvious or visible to the students.

It is essential that all aspects of subject delivery be carried out as efficiently as possible. To this end, IT, and in particular, Web-based solutions, can be applied to both aspects of subject delivery. That Web-based solutions are a suitable vehicle to use has been almost universally accepted by students, teachers, and academic administrators (Tillett, 2000). Other advantages are the ease with which information can be disseminated, its interactivity, its use as a real-time communication medium, and the ability to use text, graphics, audio, and video (Kaynama & Keesling, 2000).

There are a number of administrative tasks associated with subject coordination for which IT solutions can be applied in the application. These include (Byrnes & Lo, 1996; Darbyshire & Wenn, 2000):

- *Student enrollment*: While most universities have a student enrollment system administered at the institute level, there are often local tasks associated with enrolment, such as user account creation and compilation of mail lists, etc. Some of these tasks can be automated (Darbyshire & Wenn, 2000).
- *Assignment distribution, collection, and grading*: The written assignment remains the basic unit of assessment for the vast majority of educators, and there have been many initiatives to computerize aspects of this task. Some of these include *Submit* (Hassan, 1991), *NetFace* (Thompson, 1988), *ClassNet* (Boysen & Van Gorp, 1997), and *TRIX* (Byrnes & Lo, 1996).
- *Grades distribution and reporting*: Techniques for this range from email to password protected Web-based database lookup.
- *Informing all students of important notices*: Notice boards and sophisticated managed discussion facilities can be found in many systems. Examples include products such as *TopClass*, *Learning Space*, *Virtual-U*, *WebCT*, and *First Class* (Landon, 1998).

Many of the tasks viewed as educational can also employ IT solutions in order to gain perceived benefits. Some of these include: *Online class discussions*; *Learning*; *Course outline distribution*; *Seminar notes distribution*; *Answering student queries*. Just how many of these are actually implemented will relate to a number of factors, such as the amount of face-to-face contact between lecturers and students. However, using the Internet for many of these can address the traditional problems of students misplacing handouts and staff running out of available copies.

Discussion management systems are being integrated into many Web-based solutions. These are usually implemented as threaded discussions, which are easily implemented as a series of Web pages. Other tools can include chat rooms or listserv facilities. Answering student queries can take place in two forums, either as part of a class discussion or privately. Private discussions online are usually best handled via an email facility, or in some instances, store and forward messaging systems may replace email.

Implementing IT solutions to aid in the actual learning process is difficult. These can range from Intelligent Tutoring Systems (Ritter & Koedinger, 1995; Cheikes, 1995), to facilitated online learning (Bedore et al., 1998). However, the major use of IT solutions in the learning process is usually a simple and straightforward use of the Web to present hypertext-based structured material as a supplement to traditional learning.

Using Internet Technologies to Improve Efficiency and Add Value

With the recent explosion in Internet usage, educators have been turning to the Internet in attempts to gain benefits by the introduction of IT into the educational process. In this chapter, subject delivery at the university level is considered. The benefits sought from such activity depend on the driving motivation of the IT solution being implemented. While many may not perceive a university as a business (and it is not advocated here), it is nonetheless possible to match the current uses of the Internet in tertiary education with traditional theory related to the reasons why firms use IT. This notion has partially been promoted by Jansen et al. (2002), who have compared the notion of the relationship between the educational institution and student and compared that with organizations providing added value for customers through their products and services. They chose to examine added value from the viewpoint of Amit and Zott (2000), who suggested that IT can provide benefits by way of innovation, improving customer relations, complementary products or services, and improving efficiencies. These can be loosely mapped into Porter and Millar's three generic strategies listed earlier.

Internet technologies in education, which are used for the learning process, target the student as the main stakeholder. While the motivation may be the enhancement of the learning process to achieve a higher quality outcome, we can loosely map this to the "*support of managerial decision making*" concept identified earlier. Such technologies allow educators to obtain a far more sophisticated analysis of individual student's learning progress, and thus provide them with decision support tools on courses of action to take to influence this process.

Technology solutions that target the academic as the stakeholder (Darbyshire & Wenn, 2000; Central Point), implement improvements or efficiencies that can be mapped to the "*support of the business operation*" previously identified. Improvements or efficiencies gained from such implementations are usually in the form of automated record keeping and faster processing time, ultimately resulting in lower costs in terms of academic time, and added value to the students.

By default, the university also becomes a stakeholder in the implementation of either of the above types of technology enhancements. Benefits gained by students and staff by such uses of technology translate ultimately to lower costs for the institution or the provision of more and better quality information. The benefits of such systems can be mapped onto the "*support of strategic advantage*" concept (as Porter's low cost and differentiation strategies), previously identified as a reason for using technology in business. If these institutions are to regard themselves as a business, then the successful use of IT in subject delivery could give the university a strategic advantage over other universities, which it would regard as its business competitors. Most of the reported advantages gained from online supplementation of teaching relate to cost savings in terms of efficiency, flexibility, and convenience. These represent the traditional added-value benefits of lower cost and faster access to goods in the commercial world. Thus, we can use the measures of *Money Savings*, *Time Savings*, *Improved Quality*, and better *Product Information* as categories to measure the benefits gained from the introduction of IT to supplement teaching.

ADDED VALUE FOR EDUCATORS? A SURVEY OF IS WORLD MEMBERS

The authors were interested to investigate the extent of appreciation of the value-added benefits that the Internet can offer to tertiary educators, institutions, and their students. Do educators consider the value to students and to the institution when they set up Web pages?

A Web-based survey was conducted through the IS World discussion list to gain an initial idea of the level of appreciation that existed.

IS World is a Web-based resource that has been set up for the benefit of information systems academics and researchers around the world. The following description of the community served by the resource comes from the IS World Web site:

> *...our core population are information systems researchers and educators working in colleges and universities throughout the world. We believe that our worldwide community consists of approximately 5000 of whom many are accessible through our faculty directory. Approximately 2000 of them also monitor ISWorld, our discussion list.*
>
> *(http://www.isworld.org/isworld/mission.html, IS World, 2000)*

A general email was posted to the IS World discussion list on January 29, 2001. A request was made for tertiary educators to respond, outlining their uses of the Internet in tertiary education and how the uses "added" value for the institution and for students. The survey was targeted toward educators rather than administrators, as it was felt that they would have a greater appreciation of the added value for both the institution and students. It was not specifically aimed at IT educators, but at any tertiary educator using the Internet to assist with course and subject delivery. It is understood, however, that most respondents would be IT educators due to the list membership. The survey consisted of a matrix, where

Figure 1. Sample screen from the IS World online survey

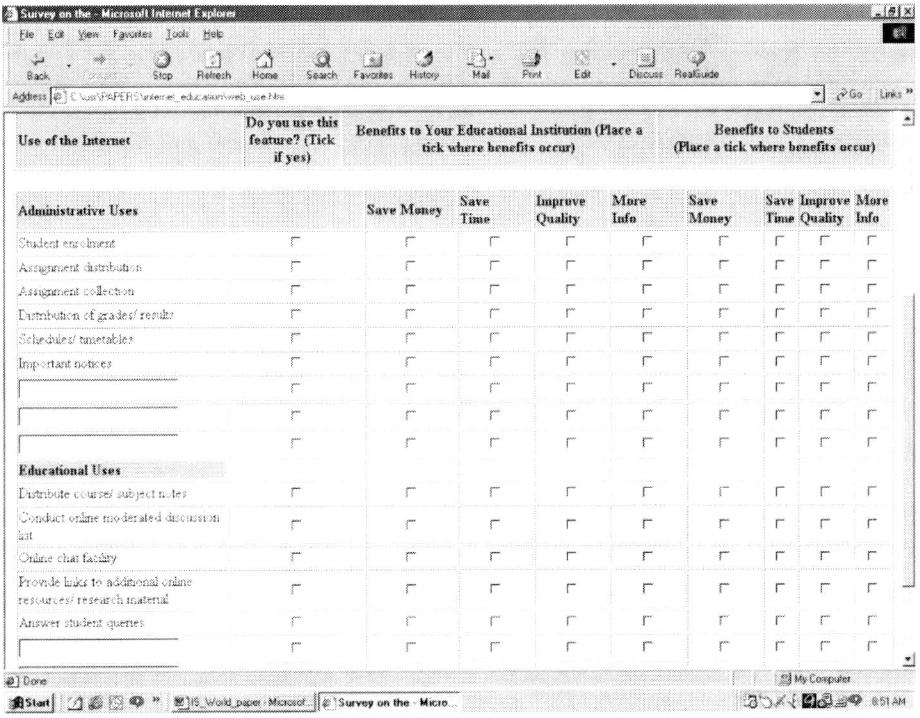

users selected various options by clicking on them. The rows of the matrix indicated six administrative and five educational uses of the Internet. The columns of the matrix allowed respondents to indicate if they used the feature, and then identify the added-value benefits the feature provided to the educational institution and to students. The added-value benefits described were: Save money; Save time; Improve quality; and (provide) More information. A sample screen from the online survey can be viewed in Figure 1. Respondents were not requested to indicate the level of usage of each feature. The items within the categories of "administrative uses" and "educational uses" were developed by the authors, based on their combined tertiary teaching experience of more than 30 years and use of the Internet to assist with course and subject delivery since the mid 1990s.

Upon filling out the survey and clicking the "Submit" button, the results were emailed to the authors. They were then cut and pasted from the email into a Microsoft Excel 2000 spreadsheet. There were 43 responses to the survey between 29 January and 4 February 2001. Most of these (33) were received within one day of the initial email. While there was not an overwhelming response from the list, the authors feel that there were enough responses to make some observations.

Results

The administrative uses of the Internet were adopted, on average, by 72% of respondents, while educational uses were adopted by 69%. Table 1 shows the results of the ISWorld survey, divided into Administrative and Educational uses. Note that figures have been shaded where 50% or more of respondents suggested a particular added-value benefit.

Table 1 shows the average level of benefits identified for all administrative uses (refer to the row labelled "Overall Administrative'). The most common benefit for administrative uses was to save time for the institution and for students. Most of the benefits were perceived as being similar for both groups, except that more than twice the respondents felt that the institution saved money through Administrative uses than felt that students saved money. The row labelled "Overall Educational" shows the average level of benefits identified for all educational uses. In contrast to administrative benefits, the more respondents indicated

Table 1. Results from IS World survey

Types of Uses	Feature Used	Institution Benefits				Student Benefits			
		Save Money	Save Time	Improve Quality	More Info	Save Money	Save Time	Improve Quality	More Info
Administrative Uses									
Student Enrolment	47%	40%	85%	45%	50%	10%	80%	40%	40%
Assignment distribution	84%	56%	92%	42%	31%	17%	64%	47%	42%
Assignment collection	51%	27%	77%	18%	5%	23%	82%	14%	9%
Distribution of Grades	72%	29%	65%	42%	29%	6%	68%	42%	42%
Schedules/Timetables	91%	49%	74%	54%	38%	23%	67%	46%	46%
Important Notices	88%	37%	82%	47%	53%	13%	71%	47%	55%
Overall Administrative	72%	41%	79%	43%	35%	16%	70%	41%	41%
Educational Uses									
Distribute course/subject notes	98%	60%	74%	50%	40%	31%	79%	60%	50%
Conduct Online Moderated Discussion List	51%	18%	32%	59%	45%	5%	41%	77%	68%
Online Chat Facility	28%	17%	42%	75%	50%	8%	58%	92%	58%
Provide links to additional resources	91%	10%	41%	46%	54%	15%	56%	64%	64%
Answer Student Queries	77%	12%	70%	52%	36%	12%	85%	58%	55%
Overall Educational	69%	26%	55%	53%	45%	17%	67%	66%	58%

educational benefits of the Internet for students than for institutions. More respondents saw their use as providing more information and improving quality more on average than the administrative uses.

Administrative Uses

This section discusses the results for the Administrative uses. Table 1 shows the level of Administrative usage of the Internet by respondents. The "information provision" usages were the most commonly used (Important notices, schedules/timetables, assignment and grade distribution). Less common were the more "interactive' options, assignment collection, and student enrollment.

Most of the benefits for each particular administrative use are fairly close for students and the institution, except for instances where the benefits save money. In most of these instances, more respondents saw the benefits flowing to the institution than to students.

Assignment collection is an interesting administrative use of the Internet. Few respondents saw benefits in relation to more information or the quality of information being provided to institutions or students. This would be expected, as the task of submitting an assignment would generally add little useful knowledge to the student or the staff member.

Around 80% of respondents that had implemented these last two features indicated that they saved time. This was the highest recognition of "time saved" benefits of all of the administrative uses.

The key here may be the level of difficulty involved in setting up the two features. It is extremely easy to set up the distribution of assignments and student grades on the Internet.

Educational Uses

This section discusses the results for the Educational uses. As with Administrative usages, the easiest features to set up were the most commonly used (Distribute Course/Subject Notes, Provide External Links). Less common were the more "interactive" options, discussion lists, and online chat groups. About three quarters of respondents used the Internet to answer student queries (probably by email). As with Administrative uses, most of the benefits are similar for students and the institution, with (again) some differences for instances where the benefits save money more for the institution than students.

However, in contrast to administrative benefits, more respondents saw the differences in the benefits of educational uses flowing to students than to institutions. In three of the uses, saving time *was not* the most common benefit identified. These were the provision of external links to additional resources, discussion lists and online chats, where improved quality of information and more information were more commonly identified.

Discussion

All respondents to the survey identified as least one type of Internet usage to assist them. Approximately seven out of ten adopted Administrative uses, and roughly the same proportion adopted Educational uses. This supports the notion identified in the literature that the technology would be accepted in the tertiary education field. The following findings support the notion that educators identify the value-added uses of the Internet in tertiary education.

The most common benefit for administrative uses was to save time for the institution and for students. Most administrative benefits were similar for both groups, except for "save money" (where more than twice the respondents felt that the institution saved money than students). The "information provision" administrative usages were the most commonly used (Important notices, schedules/timetables, assignment, and grade distribution). Less common were the more "interactive" options, assignment collection, and student enrollment. Educational uses of the Internet were seen as providing slightly more benefits for students than institutions. Their use were seen as providing more information and improving quality more on average than the administrative uses. As with Administrative usages, the easiest educational features to set up were the most commonly used (Distribute Course/Subject Notes, Provide External Links). Less common were the more "interactive" options, discussion lists, and online chat groups. About three quarters of respondents used the Internet to answer student queries (probably by email). As with Administrative uses, most of the benefits are similar for students and the institution, with (again) some differences for instances where the benefits save money more for the institution than students. More respondents saw the differences in the benefits of educational uses flowing to students than to institutions than with administrative uses. In three of the uses, saving time *was not* the most common benefit identified. These were the provision of external links to additional resources, discussion lists, and online chats, where improved quality of information and more information were more commonly identified.

COMPARISON OF BENEFITS FOR INSTITUTION AND STUDENTS

A comparison of responses for each of the areas was carried out by calculating the correlation coefficient for responses for the institution against those returned for students. The correlation coefficient was calculated using the Data Analysis Toolpak in MS Excel 2000. In this case, as the correlation coefficient approaches the value 1, it means that there is a greater likelihood that there is a positive association between the two sets of numbers (that is, benefits for institution and students). Table 2 shows these results.

Table 2. Correlation between institution and student responses

Type of Use	Correlation Coefficient (Institution Versus Student Results)
Administrative	
Student enrollment	0.95
Assignment distribution	0.43
Assignment collection	0.99
Distribution of grades	0.75
Schedules/timetables	0.57
Important notices	0.87
Educational	
Distribute course/subject notes	0.44
Conduct online moderated discussion list	0.96
Online chat facility	0.98
Provide links to additional resources	0.99
Answer student queries	0.98

For administrative uses, there was a high correlation between the benefits identified for institutions and students in the areas of student enrollment, assignment collection, and important notices. For all of these benefits, the fact that the functions saved time was the dominant factor for institution and students. Assignment distribution was seen as saving time and money, mainly for the institution.

The correlation of benefits between institution and students for educational uses was high for all uses except for the distribution of course and subject notes. These were seen to mainly save time and money for the institution, but will also save time and improve the quality of information available to students.

Future Studies

The next stage of this study is to investigate whether students perceive that they have received benefits to the same degree that the educators think they have. Another aspect of the study will be to refine the meaning of "value" into something that can be quantified, rather than results based just on opinion. For instance, if a Web-based feature saves money, how much does it save? If it saves time, how much time? If more information is provided, how much more? If the information provided is of better quality, how can this be assessed?

There are still many tertiary educators that do not use the Internet to assist with their teaching in any way. The ultimate goal of this project is to produce a set of guidelines that will lead "novice" Web educators through the mire of setting up Web sites, indicating those features that are easiest to set up to provide "instant" value for the institution and students. Then those features that take longer to set up but can provide different types of added value for both parties can be considered.

CONCLUSION

The majority of tertiary educators use the Internet to supplement existing modes of delivery. Importantly, the Internet is providing a number of "added value" supplemental benefits for subjects and courses delivered. There are two aspects to subject delivery to where added-value benefits may be applied, and that is in the *administrative tasks* associated with a subject and the *educational tasks*. Most of the reported advantages gained from online supplementation of teaching relate to cost savings in terms of efficiency, flexibility, and convenience. These represent the traditional added-value benefits of lower cost and faster access to goods in the commercial world. The measures of *Money Savings*, *Time Savings*, *Improved Quality*, and better *Product Information* can be used as categories to measure the benefits gained from the introduction of IT to supplement teaching.

A survey of 43 tertiary educators, conducted through the IS World discussion list, revealed similar usage levels of Administrative and Educational Features to aid tertiary education on the Internet. The Administrative uses showed slightly more benefits for the institution than for students and vice-versa for Educational uses. In both types of uses, their adoption seemed to be based upon how difficult the feature was to set up as well as the added-value benefits it provided. An analysis of the correlation of the benefits identified for institution and students showed a correspondence between most of the uses, with a few interesting differences.

REFERENCES

Alexander, S. (1995). Teaching and learning on the World Wide Web, *Proceedings of AusWeb'95*, [22/5/1999], http://www.scu.edu.au/sponsored/ausweb/ausweb95/papers/education2/alexander/.

Amit, R. & Zott, C. (2000). *Value Drivers of e-Commerce Business Models*, Knowledge @ Wharton, http://206.107.131.155/archive/papers/978.pdf, [2000, 30/6/2000].

Bedore, G. L., Bedore, M. R., & Bedore, G. L. Jr. (1998). *Online Education: The Future is Now*, Socrates Distance Learning Technologies Group, Academic Research and Technologies.

Beirne, T., Brecht, H. D., & Sauls, E. (2002). Using the Web to serve students as information clients. *Proceedings of Informing Sciences and IT Education Conference (CD-ROM)*. University College Cork, Cork, Ireland, June 19–21.

Boysen, P. & Van Gorp, M. J. (1997). ClassNet: Automated support of Web classes. Paper presented at the *25th ACM SIGUCCS Conference for University and College Computing Services*, Monterey, CA.

Byrnes, R. & Lo, B. (1996). *A Computer-Aided Assignment Management System: Improving the Teaching–Learning Feedback Cycle*. Retrieved February 12, 1999 from the World Wide Web: http://www.opennet.net.au/cmluga/byrnesw2.htm.

Cheikes, B. A. (1995). GIA: An agent-based architecture for intelligent tutoring systems. Paper presented at the *Proceedings of the CIKM'95 Workshop on Intelligent Information Agents*.

Darbyshire, P. (1999). Distributed Web based assignment submission and access. *Proceedings — International Resource Management Association*, IRMA '99. Hershey, PA: Idea Group Publishing.

Darbyshire, P. & Lowry, G. (2000). An overview of agent technology and its application to subject management. *Proceedings International Resource Management Association*, IRMA 2000, Alaska, USA.

Darbyshire, P. & Wenn, A. (2000). A matter of necessity: Implementing Web-based subject administration. In *Managing Web Enabled Technologies in Organizations*. Hershey, PA: Idea Group Publishing.

Earl, M. J. (1989). *Management Strategies for Information Technology*. New York: Prentice Hall.

Hassan, H. (1991). The paperless classroom. Paper presented at ASCILITE '91, University of Tasmania, Launceston, Australia.

IS World. (2001). Mission and objectives. Retrieved March 11, 2001 from the World Wide Web: http://www.isworld.org/isworld/mission.html.

Jansen, W. et al. (2002). The added value of e-learning. *Proceedings of Informing Sciences and IT Education Conference (CD-ROM)*. University College Cork, Cork, Ireland, June 19–21.

Kaynama, S. A. & Keesling, G. (2000). Development of a Web-based Internet marketing course. *Journal of Marketing Education, 22*, 2, August, 84–89.

Landon, B. (1998, 10/4/98). *On-line Educational Delivery Applications: A Web Tool for Comparative Analysis*, [Web Page]. Centre for Curriculum, Transfer and Technology, Canada. Retrieved October 10, 1998 from the World Wide Web: http://www.ctt.bc.ca/landonline/.

O'Brien, J. A. (1999). *Management Information Systems, Managing Information Technology in the Internetworked Enterprise* (4th ed.). New York: McGraw Hill.

Parker, M. M. & Benson, R. J. (1988). *Information Economics: Linking Business Performance to Information Technology*. New York: Prentice Hall.

Porter, M. E. & Millar, V. E. (1985). How information gives you competitive advantage. *Harvard Business Review, 63*, 4, July–August, 149–160.

Ritter, S. & Koedinger, K. R. (1995). Towards lightweight tutoring agents. Paper presented at the *AI-ED 95 —World Conference on Artificial Intelligence in Education*, Washington, D.C.

Sandy, G. & Burgess, S. (1999). Adding value to consumer goods via marketing channels through the use of the Internet. *CollECTeR '99: 3rd Annual CollECTeR Conference on Electronic Commerce*, Wellington, New Zealand, November.

Scott Tillett, L. (2000). Educators begin to reach out — The net cuts costs, simplifies management and could make distance learning a winner. *InternetWeek*, 835, October 30, 49–56.

Thompson, D. (1988, 14/3/98). *WebFace Overview and History*. [Web page]. Monash University. Retrieved January 2, 1999 from the World Wide Web: http://mugca.cc.monash.edu.au/~webface/history.html.

WBT Systems. (1997). Guided learning — Using the TopClass server as an effective Web-based training system, WBT Systems White Paper, http://www.wbtsystems.com.

Chapter XXXIII

Virtual Government: Online-Services within the Public Sector

Birgit J. Oberer
University of Klagenfurt, Austria

ABSTRACT

In this chapter, an overview of electronic government is given. Online electronic services, like inquiry possibilities that are made available to its interaction partners (citizens and businesses) by administration authorities, are one proof of changes in the public sector because of modern information and communication technologies. Electronic government includes all governmental measures at the levels (union, states, and local governments) for qualitative improvements in citizen's different spheres of life and for optimization of business processes within the administration. It can cause an improvement of the relationship between administration, citizens, and businesses. The author gives an overview about selected current international electronic government incentives, introduces analysis methods for these governmental strategies, and shows developed guidelines for implementing electronic government.

INTRODUCTION

Since the 1990s, economies experience changes because of information and communication technologies. These changes take place in the public sector too. The use of information and communication technologies enables the development of electronic government and causes an improvement in the relationship between administration, citizens, and business. E-government includes all administrative measures at all levels (union, states, and local governments) to improve the requirement satisfaction for citizens (qualitative improvements in many spheres of life) and businesses and to optimize the business processes within the administration (structural changes). In reaching these targets, there are used information and communication technologies (Aichholzer, 1999). Possible interaction partners in the area of Electronic Government are Government, Citizens/Customers, and Business (Muralt-Müller, 2000). In this chapter, we show current electronic government strategies of Australia, Switzerland, and the European Union (EU), especially Austria, a country that is one of the leading members within the EU in doing e-government. After stating governmental strategies, an interesting aspect would be to evaluate the different national strategies and draw up a ranking — European Union wide or worldwide. But, all members of the European Union (and all other countries) deal in different ways with information technologies and electronic government. It will not be wise to compare the national strategies and to rate them with points. Therefore, there will be drawn up critical conditions for electronic government, like demand orientation and other general conditions, followed by a short comparative view of the mentioned strategies and portals in the field of electronic government according to the relevant criterions. In the following section, guidelines for implementing electronic government incentives will be provided. An implementation concept was developed, addressed to all responsible for e-government issues within administration, including organizational, technical, and legal aspects. The guide can be seen as a metamodel for implementing e-government that has to be adjusted to specific circumstances. All general necessary phases within the implementation process will be shown. Attention is turned on the consideration of administrative targets, the evaluation of critical criteria for online services, and a classification scheme for evaluating online services.

STATE OF THE ART
Australia — A Pioneer in Electronic Government

Australia can be seen as a pioneer in electronic government. In the early 1990s, Australia already had a clear electronic government vision and began to develop its own strategies for doing e-government. Today, the administrative authorities of Australia — both at government top level and at the level of states and territories — can be seen as leading in the area of e-government. In the following, governmental initiatives for implementing e-government and e-government initiatives of selected states or territories will be shown. The Australian activities of e-government can be found in all possible areas: information, interaction, and transaction. In 1994, different strategies were published for doing e-government, followed by the formation of several governmental councils and departments. The purpose of forming several national institutions was to create conditions and to be able to take steps in enabling the administration and its customers (citizens and business) to participate in the worldwide development of information technology. In 1998, the Business Entry Point (BEP) was implemented as a portal for simplification of information procurement at the federal and national levels. The Web appearance of authorities and departments were completed with the Commonwealth Government Entry Point (FedGov), which contains all administrational services.

The states and territories made efforts as well to be able to use the information and communication technologies effectively. In this section, some national strategies in the area of electronic government will be shown. Most strategies will not be comparable, because most states set up different priorities.

Within the states, New South Wales (NSW) is one of the pioneers in the areas of e-government (in 1997, the first online-vision for interactive communication between citizens, business, and administration, was published). Connect.nsw is an Internet-based approach for the whole administration, used to flatten administration processes.

Another e-government approach has started the national administration of Canberra in the early 1990. The Austouch Citizen Information System was developed, which was based on public touchscreen-kiosk systems. It offers information about government and community services in Canberra and makes it possible for citizens to identify responsible agencies easily and make payments for the following areas: housing and land rates, business payments and commercial licences, motor vehicles, gazettes, publications and legislation, tickets, permits, bookings, and fees.

Electronic Government in the EU

In 1994, some members of the European Union began to formulate their specific strategies for the development of their national information society. Some members like the Netherlands, Finland, and Denmark started before 1994 with the announcement of reports and action plans. Other countries started much later to deal with the new information and communication technologies (Europäische Kommission, 2000). In 1996, Sweden, Germany, and Luxembourg published strategies and national programs. Most countries chose different ways to develop their own national strategies. National committees were founded for information societies (Belgium, Finland), consulting institutions (Sweden, Ireland), committees of ministers (France, Spain, Greek, Portugal), public control committees for information technologies (Ireland, Italy), and groups of experts (Austria, Spain, Denmark, Netherlands). Most stated initiatives and strategies were basis for further discussion and were not followed by concrete action plans: Greek — first white paper in 1995, second white paper in 1999, no action plan; and Italy — government agenda in 1995, reference scheme in 1997, no action plan. Other countries like France or Austria prepared concrete action plans after having published their first strategies. Austria developed its first initiative in 1994, and developed an action plan in 1997 (Ayer, 2000). In the following section, it will be shown how electronic government is realized in Austria, a country that is partly leading within the EU in doing e-government (Europäische Kommission, 1998).

E-Government Strategies in Austria

There are three different supply models for electronic government: information, communication, and transaction. In most countries, the first level, information, is realized. In some countries, you can find approaches of the second level: communication. Most of the time, this communication is limited to offering email functions for users. The third level, transaction, is not at all or not sufficiently realized in the countries of the European Union. In Austria, there are realized services at Level 1 (information) and Level 2 (communication) in a sufficient way and partly in Level 3 (transaction):

- Information provision to citizens from the administration (citizen information systems)
- Access for users to relevant data from a coordination authority (mostly for business relevant data)
- Creation of value-added products (mainly for geographic information systems)

For the first level (information), Austria offers a sufficient citizen/business information system with components for Level 2 (communication): the information system help.gv.

With this tool, the first step has been taken in the area of electronic government. This information system is a classic example of how e-government should be done. Therefore, some other countries, like Switzerland, have adopted the main ideas of help.gv for developing their own information systems (Schweizer Bundesrat, 1998). The main ideas of the help.gv concept are as follows:

- Creation of a Citizen Information System (divided into about 40 spheres of life): the user can select from these topics organized in alphabetical order.

- Creation of a Business Information System (divided into different topics of business life): Enterprises have the possibility of choosing the appropriate topic for receiving the wanted information.

- Combination of the two created information systems within one unique portal. The user can enter the help.gv portal and can choose whether to enter as a citizen for getting citizen-related information or entering for getting business-related information.

Within the scope of the citizen information part corresponding to the selected topic, you can find the appropriate forms for download (information level). But, there is still a media break in the chain of the processes of this Citizen Information System. Until now, you could download the form, fill it out, and give it to the corresponding authority, which has to register your data separately. According to governmental strategies, most mentioned media breaks should be eliminated until 2003. Having removed these media breaks, the third sort of contact, the transaction, will be realized (planned for 2005). In addition to the information procurement, you can contact administrative authorities via email options (communication level). The Business Information System is organized in the same way as the Citizen Information System. You can search information corresponding to the appropriate topic, and you can get information, download forms, and contact administrative authorities. Transactions are realized partly, too. In Austria, electronic record archives were implemented in 2000, where all prepared records are available for specific members (Aichholzer, 1998).

Electronic Government in Switzerland

According to the strategies published in the Swiss area of electronic government, there seems to be a strong dependence on the Austrian concept of help.gov. Therefore, the description of the Swiss way of dealing with electronic government will be accordingly shorter than the former sections. The main idea of electronic government is networking all governmental offers digitally (Lenk, 2000). Especially in federalistic structured countries, like Switzerland, citizens have to deal with heterogeneous cantons and local governments. In this case, a networking of all governmental offers is necessary for the functioning of electronic administration. In 1998, the Swiss government published a Strategy for the Information Society (Arbeitsgruppe e-government, 1997). One instrument for reaching the targets of the strategy is the Guichet virtuel. It is a Web portal that will allow customer-oriented and service-oriented access to the electronic administrational supply at all levels of government (administration, parliament, courts, union, cantons, and local governments). The Guichet virtuel is a *planned* Web portal; it will go online at the end of 2002. One aim of the Guichet virtuel is to improve the relationship between administration and citizens. The Guichet virtuel will not be a citizens' information system like help.gv is in Austria. Nevertheless, the main ideas of the Guichet virtuel follow the concept of the Austrian Information System. The planned Web portal will be an entry point for citizens and business in searching relevant information at the top level of government (union) or at the lower levels (cantons, local governments). A link system will be implemented, with references to already existing Web pages of the union, single cantons, or various local governments. The Guichet virtuel will be realized in three phases [information procurement (one-way communication), communication (interaction), and transaction] and structured in spheres of life like education, business, finances, health, government, security, and society.

For the successful implementation of electronic government, systems there must have some critical general conditions developed (Oberer, 2002). Principles are public access, possibility of selecting the conventional method of contact or the electronic one, prevention of abuse, creation of trust in the service's quality on the part of the users, and measurements for adjusting the administrational processes (redesign or optimization of processes). Areas for reaching a sufficient development of e-government are demand orientation of the services, organizational, legal, and technological conditions, which will be explained in this section (Europäische Kommission, 2000).

Demand Orientation

The demand for electronic governmental services has been proved empirically. The main interests of citizens as users of governmental services are simple: fast information procurement and transactions to simplify contact to governmental authorities. The use of electronic administrational services therefore should be demand and impact orientated. As criteria for the demand, empirical surveys, user-feedback possibilities, or the number of visitors or the volume of contacts to administrational authorities can be used (Europäische Kommission, 2000).

Organizational Conditions

The redesign of administrational processes and structures according to the New Public Management (NPM) approach include: reform of tasks and structures as well as modernization "within" for higher efficiency and better control of transactions. The premise is that the development of electronic government and the redesign of administrational processes and structures must agree with each other and have to be synchronized. Coordination has to take place in three areas:
- Coordination of organizational and technological redesign
- Coordination of technical organization decisions at all levels of electronic government
- Synchronization of internal (administrational) changes and external offers of services of administration

Legal Conditions

Mainly, the following legal conditions should be met:
- Formulation of an information policy
- Definition of rules for access and use of electronic services by citizens and businesses
- Regulations about security infrastructure

Technological Conditions

The use of modern information and communication technologies is important. According to these general conditions, the electronic government strategies of the above-mentioned countries could be evaluated as shown in Table 1. A lot of pros and cons exist within the area of electronic government. In Australia, there should be more nationwide coordination and synchronization. However, in Austria, the transaction level should be reached much faster, and in Switzerland, no concrete portal exists. There is no country you can say that has reached a sufficient standard for e-government applications.

Table 1.

Critical Conditions	Positive (+)	Negative (-)
Australia		
Demand orientation	Early activities in the area of electronic government Demand orientated offer of services Information-, communication-level realized, transaction level partly realized	Less empirical surveys Wide range of sometimes confusing procurement possibilities (portals) in all States and Territories No overall portal
Organizational conditions	Concrete redesign initiatives Coordination of organizational and technological redesign	Poor coordination of technical organization decisions
Legal conditions	Information policy available Regulation for access to administrational services Good security infrastructure	
Technological conditions	Effective use of information and communication technologies	
Austria		
Demand orientation	Sufficient surveys before doing e-government Highly demand-orientated Citizens Information System Information and communication levels realized, transactions planned Information System clearly arranged in two parts: citizens, business	
Organizational conditions	Partly realized organizational redesign Sufficient coordination when redesigning Concrete strategies for redesign of processes and structures	Poor coordination of technical organization decisions
Legal conditions	Most regulations are formulated by the European Union (EU) Information policy available Regulation for access to administrational services Good security infrastructure	Not enough legal adjustments in the legislation for required e-government security issues
Technological conditions	Effective use of information and communication technologies (regulations by the EU)	Partly insufficent effectivity in using information and communication technologies
Switzerland		
Demand orientation	Good surveys about citizens/users needs High degree of demand orientation	
Organizational conditions	Partly realized organizational redesign Sufficient coordination when redesigning	Web appearance of single local governments National coordination too slow
Legal conditions	Information policy available On average, good legal adjustments to e-government issues	
Technological conditions	Effective use of information and communication technologies	No concrete Web portal available (online start at the end of 2001)

IMPLEMENTATION CONCEPT

The following implementation concept has been developed as a guideline for all who are responsible for implementing electronic government and the provision of public services in the area of administration (Oberer, 2001). Organizational and legal aspects will be shown as well as technical ones. This guide can be seen as a proposal for an e-government strategy, where the concrete strategy has to be modulated regarding actual circumstances.

The main idea of the guidelines is a classification of the development process in different temporal steps with different synthesizing content (Oberer, 2001).

Provisional results of one step can be seen as the basis for the following step and as decision support for the decision maker. Nevertheless, there is no one-way information provision (single-loop). Furthermore, it will be supported that results of subsequent steps can be used for the improvement of decisions in former steps (feedback-loops). The underlying e-government process is a dynamic one with steady organizational and technical changes and adjustments. Therefore, of special interest for adjustments are changes of legal conditions for services, development of demand for a service, new platforms, and IT-security issues. The different steps of the e-government development process are as follows:

Initialization

In this firm step, an e-government team must be formed that has to become qualified for doing e-government, and the human resources union has to be integrated in this initialization process.

Strategy

The main idea of this step is according to the global administrational targets to identify and evaluate online-providable administrational services. At the end of this step, which of the evaluated services will be implemented should be stated and provided electronically.

Analysis

In the former step, identified services are analyzed in detail regarding data protection and resulting security issues. Additionally, the underlying processes are analyzed, and optimization possibilities are evaluated.

Concept

This includes a predefinition of the required information technology for the realization of the electronic services according to the current circumstances and the existing platforms. Furthermore, there have to be developed and completed existing IT security concepts.

Realization

The required technology and software has to be procured and installed and adjusted to current circumstances. Furthermore, new components have to be integrated according to existing security concepts, and the qualification process for the staff must be started.

Test

Functional tests, revision of IT-security issues, and test modes must be prepared.

Implementation

A stepwise implementation of online services with attending marketing activities must be done.

In the following section, the phases *initialization, strategy,* and *analysis* should be discussed in detail, because they are the main base for all other steps within the concept for implementing e-government strategies successfully.

Initialization

The main activities during this phase of the development process for e-government services are the brainstorming and exchange of information between all administrational members who are integrated in this development process. A team for the implementation of e-services must be formed and qualified, which will have to evaluate potential online services in Step 2 (analysis). The required actions can be divided in different single activities.

In the following section, possible activities during the period of initialization will be shown. It has to been taken into consideration that most of the mentioned steps should be done in parallel with each other for increasing a time-saving potential.

> *activity_1: Information provision to all who are involved in the development process and all administrational members who will have to do e-services.*

The leader of the process has to make the others sensitive to e-government issues. Two different sessions of such an information event should be held: the first for the top and middle management of the administration and the second for all other administrational members, to quiet fears of possible changes.

The main issues can be the definition of e-government (usage, targets, advantages for the administration), examples for online services, chances and risks of an e-government project, and an explanation of the administrational implementation concepts.

> *activity_2: Form an e-government team.*

This e-government team has to accompany the project during the whole development process and should be composed of a main team supported by other selected qualified persons who accompany the team temporarily.

> *activity_3: Start-up the e-government project.*

Provide a public announcement of the project, including a provision for required financial and personnel resources and timing of the current step within the development process.

There is a sum of qualification the main team should possess, like experience in project management, legal conditions (for administrational services in general, privacy, security issues), organizational conditions (overview about organizational area matrix), IT-security issues (encryption, signatures, security management), and information technology (workflow, client server architecture).

activity_end: At the end of each step, a checklist should be developed for evaluating all results of the above-mentioned activities.

Strategy

In this step of the development process, existing online services and services that are not able to be done electronically should be evaluated. After identification of these services, the evaluation of single services for setting priorities begins. At the end of this step, a strategy for the implementation of e-government should be developed, and guidelines for doing e-government at the concerning administration department should be published. The required actions can be divided in different single activities.

In the following section, possible activities during the period of strategy development will be shown.

activity_1: Predefinition of administrational targets that have to be weighted according to importance for the administration should be accomplished.

Typical administrational targets are as follows:
- **Rationalization**
  Avoidance of media breaks can make administrational work much more efficient, and a decrease in efforts for human resources can be created. Apart from the simplification for personnel, an improvement for the administration's customers, citizens as well as businesses and other administrational departments, can be seen.
- **Customer focus**
  The selection of suitable methods (service improvement, more transparent and faster business processes), adjusted to customers' demand, can create marginal utility for citizens, businesses, and other administrational departments.
- **Image improvement**
  Because of modern and innovative online services, an administrational department can improve administration's image by creating marginal utility for customers. The effectiveness and efficiency of the administration should be presented to the public.
- **Public–private partnership**
  When offering e-government online services together with industry, a public–private partnership can be discussed. The focus of this cooperation can be the outsourcing of specific services to the private sector or the marketing of private activities at public sites.

activity_2: Measurement criteria for online services should be defined.

These criteria can be created according to the administrational targets and priority rules that were defined during activity_1.

activity_3: Online services should be classified and evaluated.

One method for evaluating e-government incentives is to create classification schemes for these initiatives and strategies (Oberer, 2000). In a classification scheme, different

Table 2. Criteria for classification schemes

Transparent and simple assignment of e-government procedures to different classes
The classes should show the value-added utility for users of e-government (citizens and businesses)
The classes should differentiate the potential for increasing efficiency within administration authorities
The class assignment should show the degree of complexity for realization

characteristics of an e-government procedure are analyzed for assigning the procedure to different classes. Table 2 shows the criteria for suitable classification schemes (Oberer, 2000).

Targets of the classification include the evaluation of main features of procedures and the creation of comparable initiatives. There are two main views within the schemes: the user view and the IT view. Within these views, there are two main features, which can be found in every scheme:

- User-view: The online-availability of services
- IT-view: The possibility for information technology based on e-government procedures

According to the above-mentioned views of users and information technology, a two-dimensional classification scheme can be developed, which is shown in Figure 1 (Oberer, 2001).

Each rectangle represents one class, orientated by the corresponding state of the two possible views. Within the user view, the following states are possible (Oberer, 2001):

- Information: Public online access to administrational information
- General service: Public online access to administrational information with respect to special needs
- Individual service: Information provision to identified persons and legal entities
- Within the IT view, the following states are possible (Oberer, 2001):
- Media break: Information-technology-based service provision without continuous processing
- No media break: Information-technology-based service provision with continuous processing
- Automation: Complete information-technology-based service provision and processing, no human interaction necessary

The more to the right and the more upward, the less weaknesses can be found within e-government processes. The two-dimensional classification scheme does not include a concept for showing the dimension of the administration. No comment is made on how efficient for the administration the evaluated e-government incentives are. E-government incentives should improve administrational business processes as well as citizens/businesses

Figure 1. Two-dimensional classification scheme

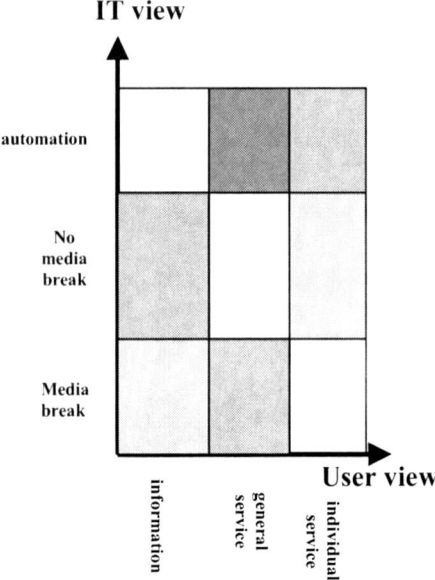

Figure 2. The portfolio considers the user, IT, and administration view

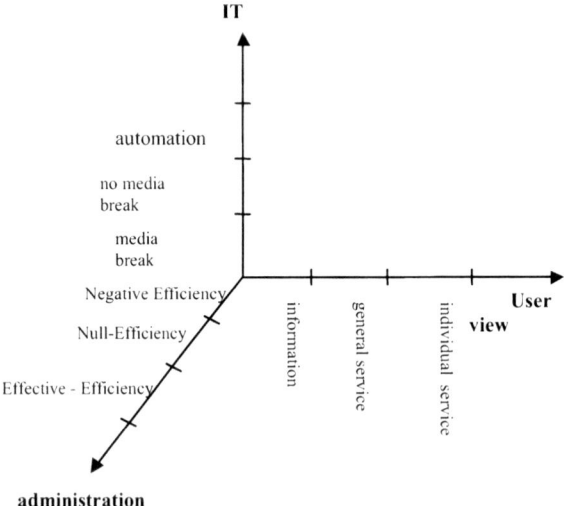

contact with the administration. The classification scheme has to be enlarged with the dimension of the administration to a three-dimensional portfolio, which is shown in the Figure 2.

The user and IT views remain unchanged (Oberer, 2001).

Within the administration view, the following states are possible:

Figure 3.

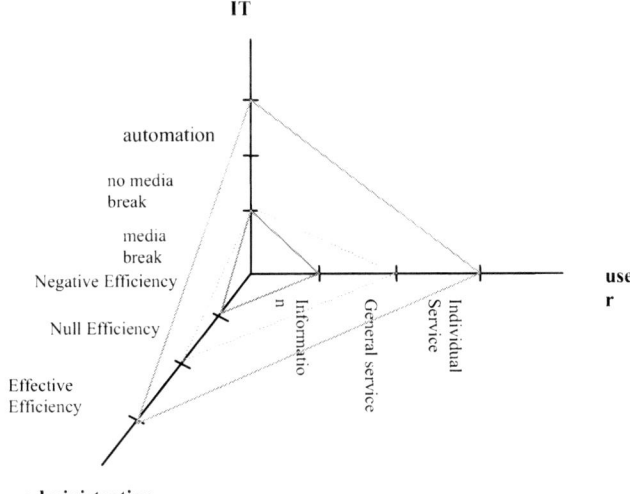

- Negative-efficiency: Large-scale administrational work because of e-government incentives
- Null-efficiency: No effect on administrational work because of e-government strategies and activities
- Effective-efficiency: Decrease in administrational work because of e-government initiatives

Figure 3 shows possible efficiency levels and state combinations for e-government approaches.

Analysis

In this step of the implementation process, a business process analysis should be done followed by a business process reengineering process with optimization of the analyzed processes (Figure 4).

activity_1: Add up all e-government processes, assign them to services, and visualize the processes.

First, all subcomponents of a process are added, and then an inquiry for all parts of the subprocesses, like sequences, responsible persons, means of labor and receiver(s) of output (copies), must be done.

activity_2: Evaluate critical processes.

Processes can be seen as critical because of their frequency, complexity, or (high) percentage of human resource interaction.

activity_3: Optimize the process.

Figure 4.

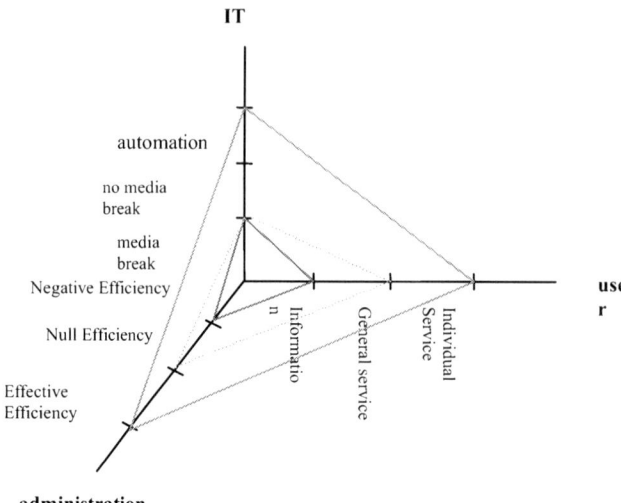

During this analysis step, weaknesses of processes and online services must be evaluated.

activity_4: Develop online services.

The target of this process step is to summarize the planned optimization activities to one planned IT project. Normally, to-do lists are used for adding the single optimization steps in a common way.

activity_5: Evaluate legal requirements (laws and regulations).

activity_6: Adjust the former defined e-government strategy according to planned reengineering operations.

Strengths and Weaknesses Analysis

In the following section, it is shown how a strengths and weaknesses analysis can be done for e-government incentives using critical conditions.

Table 3 shows a strengths and weaknesses analysis for an exemplary administrational department. On the vertical axis are mentioned the critical conditions for e-government strategies. They are demand orientation, organizational conditions, legal conditions, and technological conditions. On the abscissa, it has to be evaluated whether the department has taken measures in the different areas that can be defined as positive or negative within the development process of electronic services.

This analysis can be done for one department or more administrational units. When doing this for one unit (single-department analysis), all "positive" measures must be evaluated, and whether and how they can be improved must be considered. Furthermore, all

Table 3. Strengths and weaknesses analysis

Administrational Department		
	Positive (+)	Negative (-)
Demand orientation		
Organizational conditions		
Legal conditions		
Technological conditions		

"negative" measures must be evaluated as to whether they are done wrong or are less effective and efficient and how they can be improved.

Classification Portfolios

If the analysis is done for more than one administrational unit (multidepartment analysis), it has to be started like a single-department analysis. Additionally, the results of all administrational departments have to be compared. For doing this analysis, the classification portfolios introduced in the previous section can be used. The use of classification portfolios enables the evaluation of the utility for the user, the degree of information technology use, and the state of efficiency for the administration. Classification portfolios for single electronic government approaches (single-department analysis) can be shown, and there will be shown a comparative portfolio of all approaches (multidepartment analysis).

Figure 5 shows the classification portfolio for multidepartment electronic government approaches with the highest realized state combination (Oberer, 2002). At the IT view, the highest reached state lies above media break (there are incentives for overcoming media breaks in the near future); the tendency from the user's point of view, can be stated between "general service" and "individual service." The highest reached state at the administrational

Figure 5. Classification portfolio for multidepartment electronic government approaches

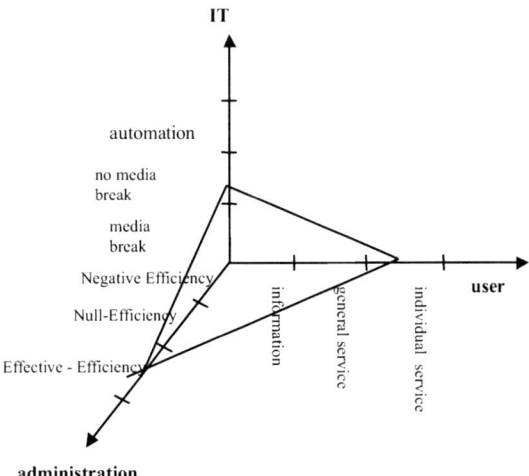

Figure 6. Comparative classification portfolio

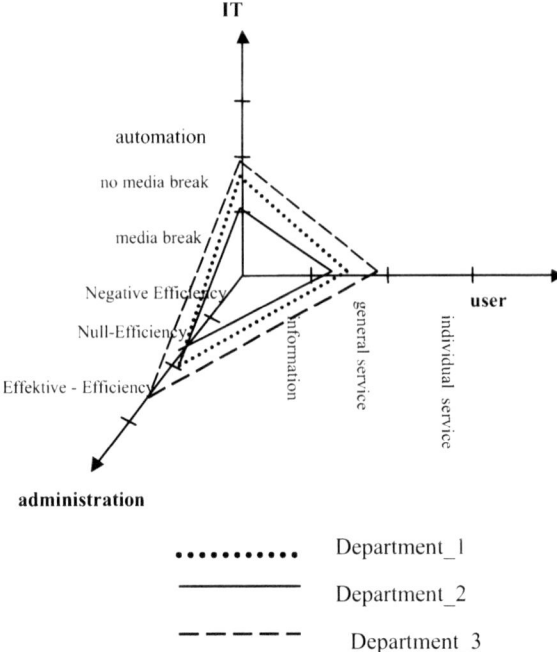

dimension lies near "effective efficiency" (nevertheless, most of the current approaches are null-efficient or negative-efficient).

Figure 6 shows a comparative classification portfolio (multidepartment analysis). The larger the triangle between the states of the three dimensions, the higher the reached states (higher efficiency, higher user utility, and technological progress), and the higher the development that can be expected (Oberer, 2002). According to this comparison of average value, Department_3 shows the highest utility (efficiency, user utility, and technological progress), followed by Department_1 Austria. On the average, Department_2 shows the lowest average utility.

CONCLUSION

Within this chapter, an overview about the state of the art in the area of electronic government was presented, including a nationwide and international comparison of e-government strategies using different analysis methods the author developed.

Guidelines for implementing e-government were introduced. The main phases within the implementation process for electronic government were shown. Attention was turned to administrational targets, the evaluation of online services, and the classification of these services. It was shown how to differentiate between single-department analyses and multidepartment ones, and concepts like strengths and weaknesses analysis and classification portfolios were introduced for doing these analyses.

REFERENCES

Aichholzer, G. & Schmutzer, R. (1999). E-Government — Elektronische Informationsdienste auf Bundesebene in Österreich. Institut für Technikfolgen-Abschätzung der österreichischen Akademie der Wissenschaften. Wien.

Arbeitsgruppe e-government der Koordinationsgruppe Informationsgesellschaft. (1997). Guichet virtuel - Der elektronische Weg zu Verwaltung, Parlament und Gericht. Bern.

Ayer, B. (2000). Bericht über die Studien zu den Guichets Virtuels in der Welt. Studien der Schweizerischen Bundeskanzlei.

Europäische Kommission. (1998). Grünbuch EU KOM. Brüssel.

Europäische Kommission. (2000). eine Informationsgesellschaft für alle. Berlin.

Muralt Müller Hanna. (2000). E-Government als neue Herausforderung. In Proceedings 1. Swiss eGovernment Symposium. Zurich. Switzerland.

Oberer. (2000). *Classification Portfolio for Electronic Government Approaches*. Klagenfurt, Austria.

Oberer. (2001). *Future Trends of Electronic Government*. Klagenfurt, Austria.

Oberer. (2002). *Guidelines for Doing E-Government*. Vienna, Austria.

About the Authors

Tanya McGill is a Senior Lecturer in the School of Information Technology at Murdoch University in Western Australia. She has an M.B.A. from the University of Western Australia and a Ph.D. from Murdoch University. Her major research interests include end user computing and information technology education. Her work has appeared in various journals including the *Journal of Research on Computing in Education, European Journal of Psychology of Education, Journal of the American Society for Information Science,* and *Journal of End User Computing.*

* * * * *

Rumel V. Atienza is an Associate Professor of Industrial Engineering at the College of Engineering, De La Salle University (Manila, Philippines). He holds a B.S. in Mathematics from the University of the Philippines, and M.B.A. and Ph.D. in Industrial Engineering (Candidate) from De La Salle University. He is also the Executive Director of the Virtual E-commerce Institute of DLSU. He is the author of *System Analysis and Design* and *System Approach to Records Management.*

Aybüke Aurum is a Senior Lecturer at the School of Information Systems, Technology and Management, University of New South Wales, Australia. She received her B.Sc. and M.Sc. in geological engineering, and M.E. and Ph.D. in computer science. She is the Deputy Director of the Center for Advanced Empirical Software Engineering Research Group (CAESER). She is also the Founder and Group Leader of the Requirements Engineering Research Group (ReqEng) at the University of New South Wales. Her research interests include the management of software development process, software inspection, requirements engineering, individual decision making process, and knowledge management.

David A. Banks is a Lecturer in the School of Accounting and Information Systems at the University of South Australia where he has been based since 1998. He has taught information systems policy and e-commerce subjects at the undergraduate level and currently teaches information systems development methodologies and collaboration and electronic commerce, both at in master's level courses. He previously worked at a UK university for 12 years teaching a variety of undergraduate and masters subjects including computer systems architecture, project management, data communications and group decision support systems. Prior to working in the education sector, he worked for 16 years with a UK telecommunications company, dealing with data networks and video systems. From 1993 to 1994, he was the Visiting Research Fellow at the Auckland Institute of Technology. His research interests are in the areas of information systems, education and technology support for group processes.

Sandra Barker is a Lecturer in the School of Accounting and Information Systems at the University of South Australia, where she has been based since 1999. She teaches internal and external students in Australia and in Hong Kong. Her current subject areas are end-user development and desktop publishing for business at the undergraduate level and end-user development at the masters level. She previously owned her own business, developing small-scale databases and designing business documents for the mining and fitness industries. She has an ongoing research interest in the area of end-user development of small-scale databases, as well as distance education, information literacy, and the implementation and development of graduate qualities.

Steve Benson is a Senior Lecturer in Management Information Systems at Edith Cowan University in Western Australia. He is a co-author of the 2002 publication, *Information Systems: A Business Approach*, and his teaching portfolio includes network management, Web commerce security, information systems and systems development. His background includes motor vehicle engineering, management and geology. He has a first class honors degree in Computer Science and a master's in Systems Design from Manchester University. He maintains a small but thriving consultancy providing specialist services to Australia and North America. His non-academic interests include motorcycling, roller blading, playing guitar and violin and training German Shepherd dogs.

Lloyd D. Brooks is a Professor of Management Information Systems in the Fogelman College of Business and Economics at the University of Memphis, USA. He received a B.S. from Middle Tennessee State University, an M.S. from the University of Tennessee, and an Ed.D. from the University of Tennessee. He has taught many business courses and specializes in database management concepts and applications. He also serves as advisor for M.B.A. and M.S. students. He has written numerous textbooks and journal articles on a variety of business topics. He also makes many presentations regarding instructional strategies and has obtained major grants from federal, state, and other organizations.

Stephen Burgess (M.Bus. RMIT, Ph.D. Monash) is a Senior Lecturer in the School of Information Systems at Victoria University, Melbourne, Australia. He has a bachelors degree in Accounting and a Graduate Diploma in Commercial Data Processing, both from Victoria University, Australia; an M.Bus (Information Technology) from RMIT, Australia, and a Ph.D. at Monash University, Australia in the area of small business to consumer interactions on the Internet. His research and teaching interests include the use of IT in small business, the strategic use of IT, B2C electronic commerce, and Management IT education. He has recently edited a book through Idea Group Publishing, *Managing Information Technology in Small Business: Challenges and Solutions*, and is track chair in the area of small business and information technology at the IRMA international conference (www.irma-international.org). Stephen is a co-founder of the new research group and IRMA Special Research Cluster on Small Business and Information Technology (www.businessandlaw.vu.edu.au/sbirit/).

David D. Carbonara is currently an Assistant Professor in the Instructional Technology Program of the School of Education at Duquesne University, USA. He teaches courses in instructional technology and information literacy to undergraduate students. On the master's level, he facilitates courses in technology and education and instructional technology management. He is part of a team that is starting a doctoral program in Instructional Technology. He was Director of Information Technology at Bethel Park School District for 21 years. He coordinated the integration of K–12 curriculum with technology applications, designed the 1800 node network, 40+ Windows NT servers, a Compaq (DEC) Alpha cluster, a 10 Mbps Internet connection, gigabit ethernet, ISDN connections, and the voicemail and email systems. He managed the State of Pennsylvania's Link-to-Learn grant and the Federal Government's erate program. As a consultant to school districts and organizations, he coordinates teams in the field of technology planning and management. He holds an earned doctorate in Science Education with a minor in educational measurement, a master's degree in middle school education, and is certificated in Secondary Mathematics, Secondary General Science and Instructional Technology Supervision.

Kuan C. Chen, Ph.D., is Assistant Professor of Information Systems and Computer Programming at Purdue University, Calumet, USA. His primary teaching responsibilities are in Web programming, e-commerce, and networking. Research interests are focused on the e-commerce client/server side programming, network design and security, instructional design for information technology training, data mining, system dynamics, information technology economics of information systems, and applications of neural networks to network design. In his consulting career, he specialized in Internet marketing planning and research, information technology project evaluation and feasibility studies, Web site planning and analysis, and networking planning and design. Dr. Chen previously was Professor of Computer Information Systems at Lansing Community College, Lansing, Michigan. Prior to arriving at Lansing Community College, Dr. Chen worked as an Information Analyst at Electronic Data Systems (EDS) in Lansing, Michigan. Dr. Chen holds two doctoral degrees in Applied Economics and Tourism Information Systems from the Michigan State University as well as an M.B.A. degree in Management Sciences from National Cheng-Kung University at Taiwan. He has published numerous articles in information technology, instructional design, and tourism and hospitality management. He is an active participant in several professional journals and serves on three paper reviewer boards. He has been a Visiting Professor at several universities: Purdue University West Lafayette, Bowling Green State University, IVY Tech State College, and Davenport University.

Dimitar Christozov has more than 20 years of experience in a cross-section of areas such as computer science, quality management, and information systems. He graduated in Mathematics in 1979 from Sofia University "St. Kliment Ohridski." His major activities with the Central Institute of Mechanical Engineering–Sofia (1979–1986) was in development of information systems to support research of machines' reliability, CAD and CAM. In 1986, he completed his doctoral thesis, "Computer aided evaluation of machines' reliability." At the Information Center for Technology Transfer "Informa" (1986—1993) Dr. Christozov was involved in establishing the national information network for technology transfer and continue his research in the areas of technologies assessment, integral quality measures, and information systems for quality management. In these areas, he was recognized as one of the leading experts in Bulgaria. Since 1993, Dr. Christozov joins the American University in Bulgaria as a Professor of Computer Science. Additionally, he was engaged in design and implementation of the IT stream of courses and MIS MBA at the Faculty of Economics and Business Administration of the Sofia University. Professor Christozov has published three separate volumes, 26 papers in refereed journals and proceedings, and more than 50 presentations at conferences, seminars, and colloquiums.

Paul Darbyshire is a Lecturer in the School of Information Systems at Victoria University, Melbourne, Australia. He lectures in Object-Oriented systems, C, Java programming, Internet Programming, and has research interests in the application of Java and Web technologies to the support of teaching, as well as the application of AI to multiagent systems. His current research is in the use of Reinforcement Learning and multiagent systems to simulate land combat as a complex adaptive system.

John Dekkers is based in the Faculty of Informatics and Communications at Central Queensland University (CQU), Rockhampton, Australia. He started his working life as a science teacher moving on to be a research wine chemist. He was lured back to academic life to complete a Ph.D. in inorganic Chemistry at the Australian National University. During his academic career, he was the foundation head Science and Mathematics Education Centre at Curtin University. The past 20 years have been spent as Professor and head of the Distance Education Centre at CQU, during which time he established an international reputation in the design and development of student support systems using ICT in developing countries. His more recent pursuits are in the area of community informatics, in which he teamed up with Wal Taylor at the COIN Internet Academy.

Georg Disterer is a full professor at the Department of Business Administration, University of Applied Sciences and Arts, Hannover/Germany. His fields of interest include Information Systems and Information Management. His working experience includes positions as management consultant and as administrative director in a professional service firm. Disterer has published many publications about information management, project management, and knowledge management (georg.disterer@wirt.fh-hannover.de).

Michael Dixon is a Senior Lecturer in Telecommunications Management at Murdoch University in Western Australia. He holds a Ph.D. from Murdoch University and an M.B.A. in Telecommunications Management from Golden Gate University of San Francisco, CA. He has been heavily involved in the development of new degrees in telecommunications management and electronic commerce and in the establishment of a Regional Cisco Networking Academy at Murdoch University. He is also a certified Cisco Certified Network Professional (CCNP), Cisco Certified Design Professional (CCDP), and Cisco Certified Academy Instructor (CCAI). His major research interests include information technology education, data communications, and neural networks.

Ashley G. Durham is a Technical Advisor at the Centers for Medicare & Medicaid Services in the Department of Health and Human Services, USA. She received her Ph.D. in Information Systems from UMBC and has an eclectic educational background in the humanities and business management. Current research interests include adaptive user interface and intelligent tutoring systems design, knowledge representation, and most recently, infant neurological development and learning behavior and theory.

Annette Easton is an Associate Professor in the Information and Decisions Systems Department of the College of Business Administration at San Diego State University, CA, USA. She serves as co-director of the Strategic Technologies and Research Center in the College. She received her Ph.D. in Management Information Systems from the University of Arizona. Her research interests include team-based information systems design, information systems education, and group support systems.

George Easton is an Associate Professor in the Information and Decisions Systems Department of the College of Business Administration at San Diego State University, USA. He serves as Co-Director of the Strategic Technologies and Research Center in the College. He received his Ph.D. in Management Information Systems from the University of Arizona. His research interests include group support systems, e-commerce, systems development, and information systems education.

Henry H. Emurian is an Associate Professor of Information Systems at UMBC, USA. His background includes degrees in clinical psychology (American University) and computer science (The Johns Hopkins University). Prior to his current position at UMBC, he worked in the Psychiatry Department at the Johns Hopkins University. His current research interests focus on technology education strategies, and he maintains an interest in stress-related effects of computer work.

Janos Fustos is a Professor at Metropolitan State College of Denver, USA. He earned his Dr. Univ. in Engineering Management from the University of Veszprém in Hungary. He previously taught at the College of Muenich in Germany and University of Veszprém in Hungary. Dr. Fustos is the author of several books on the Web and HTML. He has published in journals and proceedings on a variety of topics such as management, e-commerce, and the Internet. Dr. Füstös has also translated scholarly publications from and to Hungarian and is listed in Lexington Who's Who.

Adrian Gardiner is a Lecturer at the School of Information Systems, Technology and Management, University of New South Wales, Australia. His main research interests are in the areas of creativity support, behavioral issues in the use of OLAP, and decision support systems.

Chad Grabow has been involved with computer systems design and implementation for 30 years. His career experiences have spanned business, consulting, the military, and educator positions at the undergraduate and graduate levels. His areas of specialty include database management systems, data communications/telecommunications, and advanced information systems planning and implementation. He emphasizes the integration of local business application in the classroom to leverage practical experiences for students. He was awarded his Ph.D. from Iowa State University. He also possesses an M.S. and an M.A., as well as two baccalaureate degrees.

Maurice W. Green received his B.S. in Computer Information Systems from DeVry Institute of Technology, M.S. in Management Information Systems from Marist College, and Ph.D. in Information Science from the State University of New York at Albany. Dr. Green joined the faculty of The Information School of the University of Washington in January 1999. Dr. Green's research interests relate to the IT management process across various organizational contexts.

The foci of his research are the role and competencies of the chief information officer (CIO) in the IT management process. Professor Green teaches the following courses: Management within Information Organizations; Strategy Development and Leadership; Project Management; Systems Analysis and Design; and Diversity within the Information Field.

Meliha Handzic is a Senior Lecturer at the School of Information Systems, Technology and Management, University of New South Wales, Australia. She is the founder and the group leader of the Knowledge Management Research Group (kmRg) in the University of New South Wales. Her main research interest is knowledge management, more specifically, processes and enablers of knowledge creation, sharing, organization, and discovery. Her other interests include forecasting and decision support.

Henri Isaac, Ph.D., is Assistant Professor at Paris Dauphine University (France). He is in charge of e-learning in the Executive M.B.A. Dauphine program. He has developed many pedagogical intranets for the different M.B.A. programs of Paris Dauphine University. His research is focused on the impact of IT on management and the rise of virtual company.

Morgan M. Jennings is a Professor at Metropolitan State College of Denver, USA. She earned her Ph.D. in Educational Technology from the University of Northern Colorado. Before teaching at Metro, she spent a year at Lehigh University as a visiting professor. Jennings' research interests are engaging and immersive learning environments and alternative methods for teaching programming courses. Publication topics include learning environments, educational Web use and e-commerce curriculum.

Susan K. Lisack is an Assistant Professor in the Computer Technology Department at Purdue University, USA, where she has over 20 years of experience teaching in the areas of software development and database. Professor Lisack holds certification as an Oracle8i Certified Database Administrator, and also coordinates the departmental Cooperative Education program.

Glenn Lowry is Professor of Management Information Systems at United Arab Emirates in Al Ain. He earned the Ph.D. in information systems from Rutgers University. He served in senior academic and administrative posts at Virginia Tech, the University of Iowa, University of Technology, Sydney, the University of Tasmania, the University of Bahrain, and at Victoria University. He has also worked in industry as an account manger at Technical Aid Corporation in Washington, DC, and has consulted to NCR, Fujitsu, Sumbershire Management (Singapore), and the Victoria Government Department of Health and Human Services. He has lectured throughout the United States, Australasia, Europe, the United Kingdom, Africa, and the Middle East. With research interests in technology-led innovation and change management, cross-cultural technology acceptance, software engineering, research methods, and information systems education, Professor Lowry has authored 60+ papers and six books.

Wendy Lucas is an Assistant Professor in the Department of Computer Information Systems at Bentley College in Waltham, MA, USA. She received her B.S. in Electrical Engineering from Tufts University, her M.S. in Management from the Sloan School of Management at M.I.T., and her Ph.D. from the Electrical Engineering and Computer Science Department at Tufts

University. The topic of her dissertation was a visual approach to querying and presenting multimedia data, and her research interests include Web search interfaces, information retrieval and presentation, and information visualization.

Linda Lynam is a lifelong Missouri resident, with Accounting and M.B.A. degrees from Central Missouri State University, USA. For the last 12 years, she has taught the general education computer and the business software application courses at Central Missouri State University. A leader in computer concepts and computer applications education, her work includes creation of an online business computer applications course for university freshman. The course's projects will be published by McGraw-Hill. She has designed a general education concepts course, which is being used by all sections of the course. In 1998, she developed real-world, business-based projects for a high school summer computer camp.

Julie Mackey is a Senior Lecturer in the School of Secondary Teacher Education at the Christchurch College of Education (New Zealand). Her research and teaching interests include the integration of information and communication technology into the learning and teaching process; information and communication technology planning; and preservice teacher education.

Stewart Marshall is the foundation Dean and a Professor of the Faculty of Informatics and Communication at Central Queensland University in Australia. Although originally an Electrical Engineer with the Central Electricity Generating Board in the UK, Prof. Marshall has worked in higher education since 1973 in England, Papua New Guinea, Australia and Southern Africa. He was the foundation professor of communication at the Papua New Guinea University of Technology, the foundation professor of communication studies in the Faculty of Arts at Monash University, and the foundation coordinator of academic studies and professor of distance education at the Institute of Distance Education at the University of Swaziland in Southern Africa. His research interests are in the role of communication and information technologies in distance education, especially in developing countries. Prof. Marshall has published several books and over 70 book chapters, refereed articles and conference papers.

Charles H. Mawhinney is a Professor at Metropolitan State College of Denver, USA. He earned a Ph.D. in Business and an M.B.A. from the Katz Graduate School of Business at the University of Pittsburgh and a B.S. in Mathematics from Carnegie-Mellon University. He previously taught at Bentley College, Indiana University of Pennsylvania, and Ahmadu Bello University (Nigeria). Dr. Mawhinney has published in numerous journals, including *Information & Management, Journal of Management Information Systems, Journal of Computer Information Systems, Computer Personnel, Journal of Research on Computing in Education, CIS Educator Forum,* and *ACM-SIGCSE Bulletin.*

Annette Mills is a Senior Lecturer in Information Systems at the University of Canterbury (New Zealand). She received her Ph.D. in Information Systems from the University of Waikato (1996, New Zealand). Her research interests include user sophistication, end-user computing, technology adoption, IS education, and IT in developing countries.

Ann Monday is a Lecturer in the School of Accounting and Information Systems at the University of South Australia, where she has been based since 1997. She teaches internal and external students in Australia and in Hong Kong. Her current subject areas are decision support and end-user development at the undergraduate level and information and systems for competitive advantage at the masters level. She previously worked in the UK tertiary sector for 17 years, teaching a range of information systems subjects at undergraduate and masters levels. She has also taught in Singapore. Previous research was in the area of quality monitoring in the manufacturing sector and more recently in education, decision support, email policy, supply chain management, and enterprise systems.

Birgit J. Oberer, MBM, SenLec, SenCon, FI CO BA BI. Oberer is affiliated with the University of Klagenfurt, Department of Business Administration, Austria and University of Applied Sciences JOANNEUM, Department of Industrial Management, Austria. Her industrial experience includes serving as a Consultant in e-business, e-government, and e-commerce; serving as Consultant in business process reengineering; serving as a Consultant in simulation and optimization systems, virtual enterprises and e-business; and serving as a Consultant in advanced planning and optimizing. Her research interests include e-government/e-commerce/e-business; Business Process Modeling and Business Process Reengineering; Virtual Enterprises, Supply Chain Management, and ERP; Simulation, Planning, Scheduling, and Optimization; and Logistics and Production Management.

Parviz Partow-Navid has been at CSLA, USA, in the Department of Information Systems since 1983. He is currently Department Chair of Information Systems. He earned his M.B.A. and Ph.D. from the University of Texas at Austin in operations research and mathematical programming. His publications in the information systems area can be found in several journals: *Computers and Operations Research, Journal of Applied Business Research, Journal of Systems Management, Journal of Information Technology Management, Software Engineering,* and *Technological Horizons in Education Journal.* Dr. Partow's interests are in decision support systems, intelligent systems, e-commerce, Internet security, and distance learning.

Norman Pendegraft is Associate Professor of Management Information Systems in the College of Business and Economics at the University of Idaho, USA. His interests include the impact of IT on organizations and simulation.

Pamela Lipe Revercomb is a Doctoral Student at Syracuse University School of Information Studies, USA, where her dissertation research will focus on older adults and computer information, evaluation, and problem-solving skills. She received a B.A. in Literature from Ithaca College, a Masters in Education from the University of Pennsylvania, and a master's in Library Science from Syracuse University. Before entering the doctoral program, she worked as a teacher and school library media specialist for 13 years. As adjunct faculty, she has taught undergraduate information technology students skills for reporting and presenting information.

Judith C. Simon is a Professor and Department Chair of Management Information Systems in the Fogelman College of Business and Economics at the University of Memphis, USA. She received a B.S. from Oklahoma State University, an M.B.A. from West Texas State University, and an Ed.D. from Oklahoma State University. She has taught over 30 courses and currently focuses on courses related to computer literacy, Internet programming, and decision support systems. She has published numerous articles in academic journals and conference proceedings. She has also written numerous textbooks, including several on computer concepts and computer applications. She previously worked for a manufacturing company and keeps current on business concerns by serving as a consultant for various organizations.

Gayla Jo Slauson is an Associate Professor of Accounting and Information Technology at Mesa State College in Grand Junction, Colorado, USA. She has been teaching computer information systems courses for over 12 years. Her teaching and research interests include ethics, systems analysis and design, WWW search tools, and business software applications. She earned her M.B.A. from the University of Southern Colorado, in addition to a baccalaureate degree from MSC, and is also a C.C.P. (Certified Computing Professional).

Erick D. Slazinski is an Assistant Professor in the Computer Technology Department at Purdue University, USA, where he teaches advanced database systems. Professor Slazinski has over 12 years of industry experience.

Ludwig Slusky, Ph.D., is a Professor of Information Systems at California State University, Los Angeles, CA, USA. He was also an E-Learning Provider Practitioner in administering international distance learning program over the Internet for Russia. Dr. Slusky is the author of a book on cases for database design and the author of various papers published by Software Engineering, Information and Software Technology, Data Management, Idea Group Publishing, and papers presented at diverse conferences. Dr. Slusky's interests are in databases, e-development, e-commerce, and international distance learning.

Ruth V. Small is Professor and Director of the school media program in the School of Information Studies at Syracuse University, USA. She received her doctorate in 1986 in instructional design, development, and evaluation. Ruth's research focuses on the motivational aspects of information use; her work has earned her the 1997 Highsmith Research Award from the American Association of School Librarians and the 2001 Baber Research Award from the American Library Association. She serves on the Editorial Boards of *School Library Media Research*, *School Libraries Worldwide*, and *The Journal of Global Information Management*. In 1996, she received her School's "Professor of the Year" teaching award. Pamela Lipe Revercomb and Ruth V. Small have made several state conference presentations together on the evaluation and use of computer-based information for school library media specialists.

Anthony D. Stiller is a Lecturer in Information Systems at the University of the Sunshine Coast in Queensland, Australia, where he teaches in the field of electronic commerce in undergraduate and postgraduate courses. His research and practical experience as a consultant has led to theoretical and practical advances in e-commerce and e-business, particularly in the development of a procedural framework for small-to-medium enterprises to follow when developing their business and financial strategy. He is a regular contributor and reviewer of papers at refereed conferences, journal articles, and book chapters.

Sharon W. Tabor is an Assistant Professor in the Networking, Operations, and Information Systems Department, College of Business and Economics, at Boise State University, USA. She received her Ph.D. in Business Computer Information Systems from the University of North Texas, following an M.B.A. and B.A. in accounting and 20 years of business experience with major organizations such as American Airlines, IBM, and Control Data. Her teaching emphasis is in electronic commerce and networking and telecommunications. Dr. Tabor's research interests include electronic commerce strategy and success factors and IS education issues.

Wal Taylor is attached to the COIN Internet Academy, which is a collaborative community informatics research activity between the Faculty of Informatics and Communication at Central Queensland University, Australia, and the Rockhampton City Council. Wal has 30 years experience in community economic development in rural and regional areas at both practitioner and management levels in the public sector, on regional economic development boards, and with community development groups. He has been recognized for his work with a range of community awards and is the Rockhampton Citizen of the Year for 2001. His current research interests are in the role of information technologies in communities in regional urban settings.

Rodney Turner is a Lecturer in Information Systems at Victoria University in Melbourne, Australia. He has a master's degree in education from Monash University and information systems from RMIT. Apart from Victoria University, he has held teaching positions at RMIT and at Swinburne University. He has also worked on Australian aid projects in the Philippines and in China involving information technology. He has authored more than 20 papers. His research interests are in information systems education and technology acceptance in developing nations.

Kam Hou Vat is currently a Lecturer in the Department of Computer and Information Science, under the Faculty of Science and Technology, at the University of Macau, Macau, SAR, China. His current research interests include learner-centered design with constructivism in Software Engineering, architected applications developments for Internet software, information systems for learning organizations, information technology for knowledge synthesis, and collaborative technologies in electronic organizations. He can be reached at fstkhv@umac.mo.

Jingli Wang has been working at the Wharton School Computing since January 2001 as a Programmer Analyst. Her primary function is design, development, and maintenance of Web-based applications supporting the academic missions and administrative functions of several programs and centers at the Wharton School Computing. Before joining the Wharton School Computing, Wang worked as a Systems Engineer/Consultant at a consulting company in Maryland. She earned her Master of Science degree in Information Systems at UMBC, USA.

Ronald B. Wilkes is an Assistant Professor of Management Information Systems in the Fogelman College of Business and Economics at the University of Memphis, USA. He received a B.S.E. from the University of Tennessee–Martin, an M.B.A. from Memphis State University, and a Ph.D. in Management Information Systems from the University of Minnesota. His primary research interests are in management of the information technology resource. He has published articles in several conference proceedings. He has consulted with a variety of organizations in the public and private sectors on the management of information technology. Prior to entering academia, he was Vice President of Systems for Data Communications Corporation, Memphis, and Vice President of Development for Cylix Communications,

Memphis. He was President of the Memphis Chapter of the Society for Information Management. He served most recently as Vice-President and Chief Technology Advisor for Global Operations and Technology at CitiCorp.

Index

W

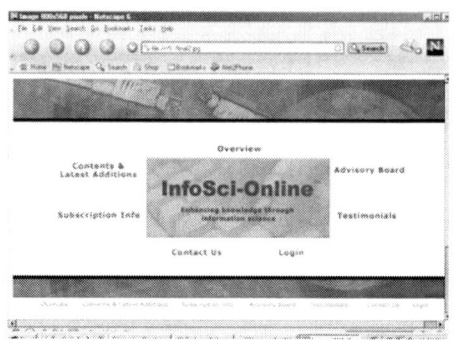

International Journal of Distance Education Technologies (JDET)

The International Source for Technological Advances in Distance Education

ISSN:	1539-3100
eISSN:	1539-3119

Subscription: Annual fee per volume (4 issues):
Individual US $85
Institutional US $185

Editors: Shi Kuo Chang
University of Pittsburgh, USA

Timothy K. Shih
Tamkang University, Taiwan

Mission

The *International Journal of Distance Education Technologies* (**JDET**) publishes original research articles of distance education four issues per year. **JDET** is a primary forum for researchers and practitioners to disseminate practical solutions to the automation of open and distance learning. The journal is targeted to academic researchers and engineers who work with distance learning programs and software systems, as well as general participants of distance education.

Coverage

Discussions of computational methods, algorithms, implemented prototype systems, and applications of open and distance learning are the focuses of this publication. Practical experiences and surveys of using distance learning systems are also welcome. Distance education technologies published in **JDET** will be divided into three categories, **Communication Technologies, Intelligent Technologies, and Educational Technologies**: new network infrastructures, real-time protocols, broadband and wireless communication tools, quality-of services issues, multimedia streaming technology, distributed systems, mobile systems, multimedia synchronization controls, intelligent tutoring, individualized distance learning, neural network or statistical approaches to behavior analysis, automatic FAQ reply methods, copyright protection and authentification mechanisms, practical and new learning models, automatic assessment methods, effective and efficient authoring systems, and other issues of distance education.

For subscription information, contact:

Idea Group Publishing
701 E Chocolate Ave., Suite 200
Hershey PA 17033-1240, USA
cust@idea-group.com
URL: www.idea-group.com

For paper submission information:

Dr. Timothy Shih
Tamkang University, Taiwan
tshih@cs.tku.edu.tw

CPSIA information can be obtained at www.ICGtesting.com
Printed in the USA
BVOW060612291011

274613BV00007B/28/P

9 781931 777537